THE **SPEAK** SOLUTION

S0-AFF-306

Print + Online

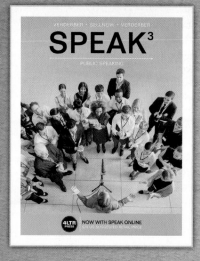

VERDERBER • SELLNOW • VERDERBER

SPEAK³

PUBLIC SPEAKING

4LTR PRESS — NOW WITH SPEAK ONLINE
$79 US SUGGESTED RETAIL PRICE

MANAGE MY COURSE — STUDENT

SPEAK3

CHAPTER 1
Foundations of Public Speaking

CHAPTER 2 — *Stagefright*
Your First Speech

SPEAK³ delivers all the key terms and core concepts for the **Public Speaking** course.

SPEAK Online provides the complete narrative from the printed text with additional interactive media and the unique functionality of **StudyBits**—all available on nearly any device!

What is a StudyBit™? Created through a deep investigation of students' challenges and workflows, the StudyBit™ functionality of **SPEAK Online** enables students of different generations and learning styles to study more effectively by allowing them to learn their way. Here's how they work:

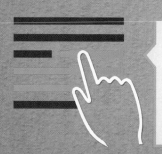

COLLECT WHAT'S IMPORTANT
Create StudyBits as you highlight text, images or take notes!

WEAK
FAIR
STRONG
UNASSIGNED

RATE AND ORGANIZE STUDYBITS
Rate your understanding and use the color-coding to quickly organize your study time and personalize your flashcards and quizzes.

StudyBit™

TRACK/MONITOR PROGRESS
Use Concept Tracker to decide how you'll spend study time and study YOUR way!

85%

PERSONALIZE QUIZZES
Filter by your StudyBits to personalize quizzes or just take chapter quizzes off-the-shelf.

○ CORRECT
○ INCORRECT
○ INCORRECT
○ INCORRECT

SPEAK3
Kathleen S. Verderber, Deanna D. Sellnow,
Rudolph F. Verderber

Vice President, General Manager, 4LTR Press:
Neil Marquardt

Product Director, 4LTR Press: Steven E. Joos

Product Manager: Laura Redden

Content/Media Developer: Patricia Hempel

Product Assistant: Lauren Dame

Marketing Manager: Sarah Seymour

Marketing Coordinator: Aya Hojadova

Content Project Manager: Darrell E. Frye

Manufacturing Planner: Ron Montgomery

Production Service: MPS Limited

Sr. Art Director: Bethany Casey

Internal Design: Lou Ann Thesing / Thesing
Design

Cover Design: Hxdbzxy/Shutterstock.com;
Vepar5/Shutterstock.com

Cover Image: Caiaimage/Martin Barraud/OJO+
/Getty images

Intellectual Property Analyst: Alex Ricciardi

Intellectual Property Project Manager: Nick
Barrows

Computer and tablet illustration:
© iStockphoto.com/furtaev

Smart Phone illustration: © iStockphoto.com
/dashadima

Last ad: Shutterstock.com/Rawpixel.com

Library of Congress Control Number: 2015960034

Student Edition ISBN: 978-1-305-65948-3

Student Edition with Online ISBN: 978-1-305-65950-6

Cengage Learning
20 Channel Center Street
Boston, MA 02210
USA

Cengage Learning is a leading provider of customized learning solutions
with employees residing in nearly 40 different countries and sales in more than
125 countries around the world. Find your local representative at
www.cengage.com.

Cengage Learning products are represented in Canada by Nelson Education, Ltd.

To learn more about Cengage Learning Solutions, visit **www.cengage.com**

Purchase any of our products at your local college store or at our preferred
online store **www.cengagebrain.com**

Printed in the United States of America
Print Number: 01   Print Year: 2016

VERDERBER/SELLNOW/VERDERBER

SPEAK³

BRIEF CONTENTS

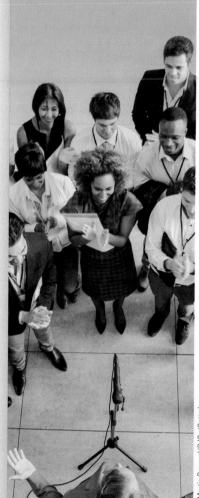

Caiaimage/Martin Barraud/OJO+/Getty Images

CONTENTS

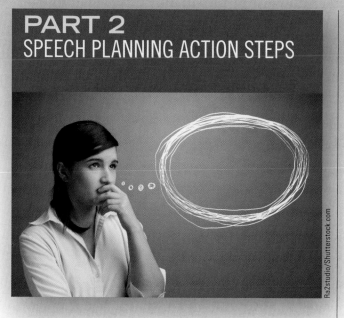

PART 2
SPEECH PLANNING ACTION STEPS

Ra2studio/Shutterstock.com

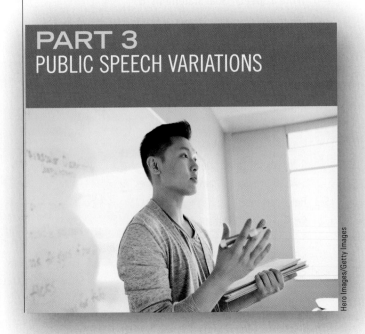

PART 3
PUBLIC SPEECH VARIATIONS

Hero Images/Getty Images

Six Action Steps Toward Effective Speeches

Action Step 1

Determine a speech goal that is appropriate to the rhetorical situation. (Chapter 4)

A. Brainstorm and create concept map for topics.
B. Analyze the rhetorical situation.
C. Develop a speech goal statement that is adapted to the rhetorical situation.

Action Step 2

Understand your audience and adapt to it. (Chapter 5)

A. Understand audience diversity.
B. Tailor your speech to address their needs, interests, and expectations.

Action Step 3

Gather and evaluate information. (Chapter 6)

A. Examine areas where you need additional information.
B. Locate, evaluate, and select a variety of information types and sources.
C. Record information.
D. Cite sources.

Action Step 4

Organize and develop ideas into a well-structured outline (the body). (Chapters 7 and 8)

A. Identify and organize two to four main points.
B. Construct a thesis statement.
C. Develop your main points, and create transitions between them.
D. Outline the speech body (including transitions).
E. Create the speech introduction.
F. Create the speech conclusion.
G. Compile the reference list.
H. Complete the formal speech outline.

Action Step 5

Choose, prepare, and use appropriate presentational aids. (Chapter 9)

A. Identify presentational aids that will clarify, emphasize, or dramatize your message.
B. Use a symbol system other than (or in addition to) words in your aids.
C. Make sure your visual aids are large enough to be seen and audio aids are loud enough to be heard.
D. Prepare and display your presentational aids professionally.
E. Plan when to use aids and integrate them during your speech.

Action Step 6

Practice oral language and delivery style. (Chapters 10 and 11)

A. Practice to develop an oral style using language that is appropriate, accurate, clear, and vivid.
B. Practice until the delivery is conversational, intelligible, and expressive.
C. Practice integrating presentational aids until you can do so smoothly and confidently.
D. Practice until you can deliver your speech extemporaneously within the time limit.

SPEAK
ONLINE

ACCESS TEXTBOOK CONTENT ONLINE— INCLUDING ON SMARTPHONES!

Includes Videos & Other Interactive Resources!

MANAGE MY COURSE ˅   STUDENT

SPEAK3

CHAPTER **1**

Foundations of Public Speaking

CHAPTER **2**

Your First Speech

4LTR
PRESS

1 Foundations of Public Speaking

LEARNING OUTCOMES

1-1 Describe the nature and purpose of public speaking as a liberal art.

1-2 Identify the ethical responsibilities of effective public speaking.

1-3 Explain how public speaking fits within the realm of communication.

1-4 Define the components of the rhetorical situation.

1-5 Examine effective speech components of content, structure, and delivery.

After finishing this chapter go to **PAGE 18** for **STUDY TOOLS.**

Sound Familiar?

Dominic just returned from a two-day training and development workshop where he learned how to use a new online purchase-order software program. Dominic's supervisor now wants him to lead a series of training sessions for the other 50 to 60 purchasing clerks at the company where he works.

Diana is heartbroken when she learns her grandmother has passed away. Although her grandmother had been sick for some time, Diana is caught off guard when her mother asks her to represent the family by delivering the eulogy at the funeral.

1-1 PUBLIC SPEAKING AS A LIBERAL ART

Do the situations above sound familiar? Which one illustrates someone who will be giving a "speech"? Actually, since the definition of **public speaking** is a sustained formal presentation by a speaker to an audience, both are examples of public speaking. Public speaking today might occur in a face-to-face professional setting as it will for Dominic, or in a non-professional setting as it will for Diana. It may even occur in an online environment such as during a webinar or video conference.

When we say public speaking is a **liberal art**, we mean that public speaking knowledge and skills are fundamental to participating effectively in a democratic society regardless of major or profession. So that's why a course devoted to public speaking is often required in a general education curriculum.[1] Public speaking is

a powerful right for engaged citizens—a right that also carries with it several important ethical responsibilities. Public speaking has been revered as a civic right in democratic civilizations dating back to ancient Greece. **Civic rights** are the essential conditions for individuals to live happy and successful lives.[2]

1-1a The Civic Right of Public Speaking

Since ancient times, liberal arts education has been at the center of study for free people in democracies. In fact, the word "liberal" means "free," and in ancient Greece it was the type of general education offered to free men (yes, back then it was restricted to men). Public speaking was central because it was the means by which free men conducted business, made public decisions, and gained and maintained power.[3] The Greek tradition of public speaking as a means to dissent, denounce, persuade, proselytize, preach, condemn, and convince gave rise in nineteenth-century London, England to Speaker's Corner. For roughly two decades, workers would gather at the park to protest against the suppression of their rights, including the right to assemble. In 1872, the British government designated a parcel of land in London's Hyde Park as a public speaking location. Although not the only location of the sort, Speakers' Corner in Hyde

Park has since become a symbol of public discourse and debate, and, although some of its speakers have been famous (Karl Marx, George Orwell), most speakers who have engaged in public speaking there are everyday individuals passionate about a variety of issues, including free speech.[4] Today effective public speakers continue to reap rewards in personal relationships, the work world, and the public sphere.[5]

Certainly, the formal study of public speaking equips us to give effective presentations; however, the process of preparing these speeches accomplishes something even more important. The study of public speaking teaches us not *what* to think but *how* to think—a central skill for a responsible citizen living in a democracy, especially the sound bite–saturated, image-managed, political environment we live in today. Essentially, we learn to think critically about what we read, see, and hear. When we choose a topic, we must consider why we are speaking and what we think is important enough to present to others. We must critically

> **public speaking** a sustained formal presentation by a speaker to an audience
>
> **liberal art** a body of general knowledge needed to effectively participate in a democratic society
>
> **civic rights** the essential conditions for individuals to live happy and successful lives

1-1b The Power of Public Speaking

Democratic civilizations throughout history have understood the importance of public speaking as a right. Like them, we know that effective public speaking is empowering in several ways. First, public speaking skills empower us to participate in democratic processes. Free speech is a hallmark of democracy. The policies a democratic government adopts are a direct result of the debates that occur across the nation: in living rooms; over pizza at the local hangout; on blogs and social networking sites; in the media; as well as in our executive, legislative, and judicial branches of government. Effective public speaking skills give us the confidence to voice our ideas on important public issues.

Second, public speaking skills empower us to communicate our ideas and opinions in ways that all audience members can understand. Most of us have had an unfortunate experience with a teacher who "talked over our heads." The teacher understood the material but was unable to express it clearly to us. When we can express our ideas clearly, we are more likely to share them. When others understand our ideas, they learn from us.

Third, public speaking skills empower us to achieve our career goals. Research shows that, for almost any job, one of the most highly sought-after skills in new hires is oral communication skills. In fact, a 2015 survey of employers conducted by the non-profit group the National Association of Colleges and Employers found that of the top ten skills employers seek in entry-level job candidates, two relate directly to public speaking—the ability to communicate verbally with people inside and outside an organization (3) and the ability to sell and influence others (10).[6] The attractiveness of public speaking skills only increases at higher levels on the career ladder. Research involving hundreds of executives has shown that communication and presentation skills are in the top five skills that companies prize most in their leaders.[7] So whether you aspire to a career in business, industry, government, the arts, or education, good communication skills are a prerequisite to your success.

1-2 ETHICAL RESPONSIBILITIES OF PUBLIC SPEAKERS

Ethics are a set of moral principles held by a society, group, or individual that differentiate right from wrong. In other words, ethics reflect what we believe we "ought to" and "ought not to" think and do. As audience members, we expect speakers to behave ethically. Likewise, as speakers, we expect audience members to behave ethically. What standards should we conform to as ethical

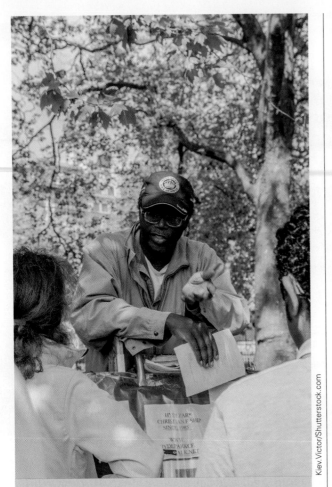

Speakers' Corner in London's Hyde Park is still used for public debate and discussion.

evaluate the credibility, validity, and reliability of the information we collect. We must thoughtfully consider how to organize our ideas and choose words that will be both clear and compelling. And we must adjust to the nonverbal reactions of our listeners to ensure they are getting the meaning we intend.

Learning to think critically as we prepare and present our own speeches also equips us to analyze the messages offered by others. We become able to critically evaluate the information and arguments of others, identify reasoning flaws, and realize unethical communication practices. Democracies thrive only in settings where citizens are capable of fulfilling their civic responsibilities to analyze, think about, and eloquently speak out about important issues. So public speaking is a liberal art— an essential skill for free, engaged citizens.

ethics moral principles that a society, group, or individual hold that differentiate right from wrong and good behavior from bad behavior

Tanewpix/Shutterstock.com

Public speaking is a **vehicle** for ideas...

though research has shown that a similar percentage (81 percent) of students believe those guilty of plagiarism should face stiff punishment.[11] As a result, many colleges and universities now use plagiarism-detection software programs regularly when grading student work. In most colleges, plagiarism can result in failing an assignment or the entire course, and it can even lead to being suspended from school. In the world beyond the classroom, plagiarism has led to lawsuits and has ruined promising careers. Here are some tips to remember so you don't plagiarize unintentionally:

- If you change a few words at the beginning, in the middle, or at the end of a material, but copy much of the rest and don't cite the source of the information, you are plagiarizing.

- If you completely paraphrase the unique ideas of another person and do not credit that person, you are plagiarizing.

- If you purchase, borrow, or use a speech or essay in part or in whole that was prepared by another and present it as original, you are plagiarizing.[12]

2. Ethical communicators act with integrity. In other words, ethical communicators "practice what they preach." The person who says, "Do what I say, not what I do," lacks integrity. In other words, a speaker who implores listeners to quit smoking and then goes outside and lights up lacks integrity. A listener who espouses the importance of civility but then interrupts and heckles speakers lacks integrity.

3. Ethical communicators behave fairly. Fair communicators attempt to act impartially and acknowledge any potential bias they might have regarding a topic. For speakers, behaving fairly means researching and accurately reporting all sides of an issue. For listeners, it means considering all of the evidence that a speaker presents, even when that evidence contradicts their beliefs.

4. Ethical communicators demonstrate respect. Behaving respectfully means showing regard for others, including their point of view, their rights, and their feelings. For example, speakers show respect for their audience by choosing language and humor that is inclusive

communicators? Five generally agreed-upon ethical standards are honesty, integrity, fairness, respect, and responsibility. Let's look at how public speakers meet each of these responsibilities.

1. Ethical communicators are honest. In other words, ethical public speakers tell the truth. An audience expects that what you tell them will not be made up, will not be your personal belief presented as fact, and will not be an exaggeration. To make sure that what you say is truthful, you will need to research your topic carefully and present all sides of controversial issues accurately.

In addition, honest speakers do not engage in **plagiarism** by presenting others' ideas as their own. Instead, they properly credit the ideas of others they use in their speech. After a delivering graduation speeches at two district high schools in Newton, Massachusetts, district Superintendent David Fleishman was fined for using—and not citing—excerpts from the commencement speech Governor Duvall Patrick had delivered at Boston University the month prior. Although Fleishman had cited historian David McCullough in his address, Fleishman neglected to include attributions for the governor's material. Even though Patrick's excerpts were a small portion of Fleishman's speech, Fleishman acknowledged that he and other public officials needed to be "as careful in their spoken remarks as they are in their written remarks—something that too often gets lost."[8]

Sadly, according to a survey conducted by the Pew Research Center in conjunction with the *Chronicle of Higher Education*, plagiarism is commonplace among college students today and has increased dramatically over the past decade.[9] Results of a survey conducted by the International Center for Academic Integrity indicate that as many as 80 percent of college students admit to plagiarism[10]—even

> **plagiarism** passing off the ideas, words, or created works of another as one's own by failing to credit the source

and inoffensive. Listeners demonstrate respect by giving their undivided attention to the speaker. In other words, it is disrespectful to send or read texts, e-mails, or Facebook posts or in any other way "multitask" during a speech.

5. **Ethical communicators are responsible.** Responsible communicators recognize the power of words. So ethical speakers advocate only for things that are in the best interest of audience members. Similarly, ethical listeners critically evaluate the positions that speakers advocate and do not blindly accept positions that are not in their best interest.

Throughout this book, we will elaborate on how these ethical communication principles should guide you as you both present and listen to speeches.

1-3 PUBLIC SPEAKING AS COMMUNICATION

communication the process of creating shared meaning

participants the individuals who assume the roles of senders and receivers during an interaction

senders participants who form and transmit messages using verbal symbols and nonverbal behaviors

receivers participants who interpret the messages sent by others

messages the verbal utterances, visual images, and nonverbal behaviors to which meaning is attributed during communication

encoding the process of putting our thoughts and feelings into words and nonverbal behaviors

decoding the process of interpreting the verbal and nonverbal messages sent by others

feedback the reactions and responses to messages that indicate to the sender whether and how a message was heard, seen, and interpreted

channels both the route traveled by a message and the means of transportation

Public speaking is a specialized type of communication. So, to become effective public speakers, we need to understand what communication is. **Communication** is the process of creating shared meaning. At its core, communication involves forming and transmitting messages to achieve mutual understanding or to incite action. To understand how the communication process works, let's look at its essential elements: participants, messages, feedback, channels, interference/noise, and contexts/settings.

1-3a Participants

Participants are the individuals who assume the roles of senders and receivers during an interaction (see Exhibit 1.1). As **senders**, participants form and transmit messages using verbal symbols (words) and nonverbal behaviors. **Receivers** interpret the messages sent by others. Although all participants serve as both senders and receivers, in public speaking contexts one participant acts primarily as sender and presents an extended message to which the other participants listen, interpret, and provide mostly nonverbal feedback. So when Dominic presents his training workshop, he will act as the sender, and his coworkers will be the receivers. And when Diana eulogizes her grandmother, she will act as the sender, and the mourners in attendance will act as the receivers.

1-3b Messages

Messages are the verbal utterances, visual images, and nonverbal behaviors used to convey thoughts and feelings. We refer to the process of creating messages as **encoding** and the process of interpreting them as **decoding**. In public speaking situations, messages are typically speeches that are prepared beforehand and presented by one participant.

1-3c Feedback

Feedback consists of the reactions and responses sent by receivers to let the sender know how the message is being interpreted. We can express feedback verbally by telling the sender what we understand or think about a message, or we may indicate our understanding and reaction through nonverbal behavior, like nodding our heads to indicate agreement, raising eyebrows to register our surprise, or cocking our head and furrowing our eyebrows to indicate that we do not understand. Nonverbal feedback can be positive and show engagement, as just described, or it can be negative, such as shaking one's head in disagreement, sighing, texting during the speech—or even dozing. One highly publicized instance of negative feedback occurred during the State of the Union address in 2015. Each year, the Supreme Court justices are expected to attend the President's State of the Union address and remain visually stoic and unresponsive throughout, but, in 2015, as President Obama was speaking, Justice Ruth Bader Ginsberg fell asleep.[13] When audiences listen to a speech, usually most of their feedback is nonverbal. So as Dominic conducts his workshop, he observes the facial expressions of his coworkers for feedback about whether his message is making sense. He also periodically stops and asks for feedback in the form of actual questions.

1-3d Channels

Channels are both the route traveled by a message and the means of transportation. We send and receive

Exhibit 1.1
Model of Communication

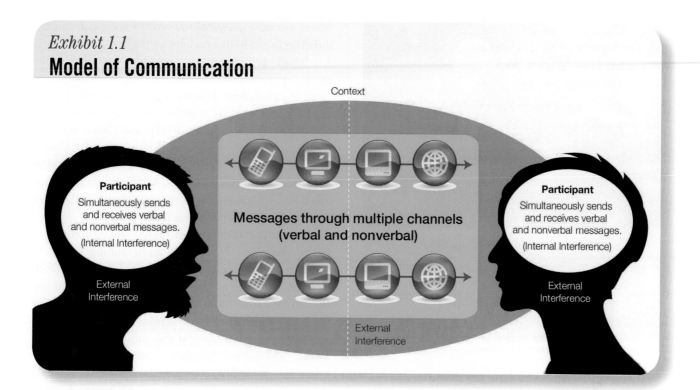

Context

Participant
Simultaneously sends and receives verbal and nonverbal messages.
(Internal Interference)

External Interference

Messages through multiple channels
(verbal and nonverbal)

Participant
Simultaneously sends and receives verbal and nonverbal messages.
(Internal Interference)

External Interference

External Interference

messages primarily through auditory (speaking and hearing) and visual (seeing) channels. Sometimes these channels are enhanced by technology. We call these technology-enhanced auditory and visual (i.e., audiovisual) channels **mediated channels**. Dominic and Diana send and receive verbal and nonverbal messages when they speak in a face-to-face setting, but this is not exactly the case for speeches delivered in technological environments. For example, during a videoconference, the speaker and the audience are not physically present in the same location. This phenomenon of simulated presence made possible through the use of digital technology is known as **virtual presence**.

1-3e Interference/Noise

Interference, also referred to as **noise**, is any stimulus that interferes with the process of achieving shared meaning. Noise can be physical or psychological. *Physical noise* is any external sight or sound that distracts us from the message. For example, when someone enters the room or someone's cell phone goes off while a speaker is talking, we might not hear the message. Similarly, when we get an e-mail or Facebook update while listening to a speaker online, we might be distracted from

> Most audience feedback is
> # nonverbal.

the message. *Psychological noise* refers to the thoughts and feelings we experience that compete with the sender's message for our attention. So when we daydream about what we have to do at work today or feel offended when a speaker uses foul language, we are being distracted by psychological noise.

1-3f Contexts

Communication context refers to the environment in which communication occurs.[14] Communication contexts differ by the number of participants and the balance of roles among them.[15] Let's briefly look at four of these.

Intrapersonal communication (i.e., self-talk) is communicating with yourself. Usually this is done by thinking through choices, strategies, and the possible

mediated channels channels enhanced by audiovisual technology

virtual presence simulated presence made possible through the use of digital technology

interference/noise any stimulus that interferes with the process of achieving shared meaning

communication context the environment in which communication occurs

intrapersonal communication communicating with yourself (i.e., self-talk)

U.S. Supreme Court Justice Stephen Breyer discreetly nudges Justice Ruth Bader Ginsburg to keep her awake as President Barack Obama delivers the State of the Union Address on January 20, 2015.

consequences of taking action. When you sit in class and consider what you'll have for dinner tonight, you are communicating intrapersonally. Much of our intrapersonal communication occurs subconsciously.[16] When we drive into the driveway "without thinking," we're communicating intrapersonally but at a subconscious level. When we give a speech and notice confused looks on listeners' faces, we might communicate intrapersonally as we recognize the need to rephrase our explanation.

Interpersonal communication is communication between two people who have an identifiable relationship with each other.[17] Talking with a friend on the sidewalk between classes, visiting on the phone with your mother, and texting or chatting online with a family member or friend are all examples of interpersonal communication. Interpersonal communication sometimes occurs in a public speech setting when, during a question-and-answer session, a speaker directs remarks to one audience member.

Small group communication typically occurs among approximately three to ten people.[18] Examples of small groups include a family, a group of friends, a group of classmates working together on a class project, and a management team in the workplace.[19] Some research suggests there are more small groups in the United States than there are people. Small group communication occurs in a public speech setting when a team is asked to work together to research, prepare, and deliver a presentation on a particular topic.

Public communication occurs among more than ten people by one primary sender to multiple receivers, and may occur face-to-face or via mediated, technology-driven channels. One form of public communication is **mass communication**, which is communication produced and transmitted via mass media to large segments of the population at the same time. Examples include newspapers, magazines, books, blogs, listservs, television programs, movies, Web sites, Facebook pages, Twitter tweets, and YouTube posts. Another form is public speaking, which is a sustained, formal, oral presentation delivered to an audience that is typically present at the time. As technology and media become increasingly accessible, however, the lines between mass communication and public speaking are blurring. For example, when the U.S. President gives a State of the Union address, some people are present in the house chamber at the U.S. Capitol, others watch on live TV or over the Internet, and still others view it later in the form of televised snippets or a Web site video (e.g., YouTube).

interpersonal communication
communication between two people

small group communication the interaction that occurs in a group of approximately three to ten people

public communication communication that occurs among more than ten people where one message is presented to the participants who function as receivers whose own messages are limited to feedback

mass communication communication produced and transmitted via media to large audiences

 AUDIENCE-CENTERED SPEAKING AND THE RHETORICAL SITUATION

The communication discipline as a formal field of study in colleges and universities is fairly young.[26] The study and practice of public speaking, however, has a long and rich history dating back more than 2,000 years to ancient Greek (e.g., Aristotle, Plato, and Isocrates) and Roman (e.g., Cicero) philosophers. They were, in fact, the ones who coined the terms *rhetoric* and *oratory* to describe the processes of preparing, presenting, and critiquing public speeches.

TECH TALK

The Loudspeaker and the Democratization of Public Speaking

In 1919, President Woodrow Wilson spoke at San Diego's Balboa Stadium to promote the establishment of the League of Nations. The speech was unique for two reasons. First, it had been nearly twenty years since a U.S. president had visited the city. (Benjamin Harrison was the last to visit in 1891.) Second, as Wilson touted the League's benefits, he spoke through two large horns that carried his voice into a microphone and out through amplified loudspeakers. No president before him had ever used such a device, and even though its inventors had used the device previously in different speaking contexts, they both attended the event and operated the system.[20]

When Edwin Jensen and Peter Pridham invented the first loudspeaker in 1911, they practically revolutionized the nature of public speaking. Within four years, they had improved upon their original prototype and

President Woodrow Wilson addressing a large crowd of 50,000 people gathered at the Balboa Stadium in San Diego in 1919. Multiplex megaphones are installed at the speaker's stand and all through the audience.

were amazed that a voice amplified through the new system could be heard a mile away. For the first time in history, a speaker could address a large audience across vast, noisy spaces with clarity and nuance.[21]

Before Wilson's historic address at Balboa Stadium, Jensen and Pridham had tested their amplification system live on several occasions. They premiered the system on December 24, 1915 in San Francisco to approximately 100,000 people who congregated at the foot of City Hall to hear Christmas music emanating from the speakers.[22] Just a week later, the inventors installed a sound system in San Francisco's Civic Auditorium to enable Governor Hiram Johnson to speak from his house a few miles away where he lay ill.[23]

Orators had spoken before large audiences long before the technological innovation of the loudspeaker and public address system; architectural expertise allowed even ancient cultures to amplify a speaker's voice across a significant distance. Electronic amplification, however, helped democratize public speaking in ways that were unthinkable prior to its invention. No longer did a person need a church rectory or well-built amphitheater (and permission to use it) to deliver a message to many people at once. Anyone who could afford some loudspeakers could make themselves heard.

Since the invention of the loudspeaker, the trajectory of communication technology has resulted in more people having greater access to communication with larger and larger audiences. Ten years before the invention of the loudspeaker, the first successfully transmitted radio signal heralded incredible potential for mass communication across large distances. Within six years of Wilson's amplified address, Philo Taylor Farnsworth transmitted the first television signal, adding a new layer of depth to mass communication.[24] The first communications satellite launched in 1963, with the invention of the Internet's predecessor occurring before the decade's end, continuing the stream of technology that led inexorably toward the global, near-instantaneous communication that is one of the primary applications of modern technology.[25]

Today, horn-style loudspeakers have been largely supplanted by the ubiquitous headset, allowing the speaker to circulate freely in front of—and even in—the audience. Moreover, satellite and Internet broadcast technology has fueled the widespread popularity of public speaking as entertainment through TED talks and YouTube videos. In fact, technology has given the average person direct access to more open ears (and eyes) than any ancient Greek could have imagined.

Fundamental to public speaking then and now is *audience*. The ancient Greek philosopher, teacher, and public speaker Aristotle is often credited with claiming, "The audience is the end and object of the speech."[27] What he meant was that the eloquence of your words is irrelevant if the words are not heard by, are not understood by, or do not affect the people to whom you are speaking. Frankly, whether conveyed in written, oral, or visual form, or some combination of them, and whether delivered in a face-to-face setting or via a mediated channel, a message is effective only if it is understood and internalized by the people being addressed. Today, we recognize that the effectiveness of any speech depends not just on understanding the audience but also on how well the message addresses the entire rhetorical situation. Let's turn now to a discussion of the rhetorical situation generally.

1-4a The Rhetorical Situation

The **rhetorical situation** is the composite of the speaker, audience, and occasion. Exhibit 1.2 illustrates the rhetorical situation in a Venn diagram. As you can see, the rhetorical situation is the place where the speaker, audience, and occasion overlap. Lloyd Bitzer, the rhetorical scholar who introduced the concept of the rhetorical situation, believed that the particular speech given by an individual to an audience on a specific occasion is also the result of some real or perceived specific need that a speech might help to address.[28] Bitzer referred to this as the **exigence**.[29] This term can be defined as "something that a situation demands or makes urgently necessary and that puts pressure on the people involved."[30]

On April 19, 2015, Baltimore, Maryland resident Freddie Gray, a 25-year-old African-American man, died from severe spinal injuries while in police custody. The death of Freddie Gray prompted both peaceful protests and violent riots in the city of Baltimore, while sparking national debates and protests concerning police–civilian relations, especially when involving youth and minority groups.

The riots in Baltimore served as a catalyst for social change and public discourse, creating an exigence, or an instance that demands verbal and written responses. When Freddie Gray died, the incident altered how daily life operated in Baltimore and created a sense of chaos, compelling public figures and citizens to verbally respond.

With a reputation for being media-friendly and having worked on building police–community relations for months, Baltimore Mayor Stephanie Rawlings-Blake should have been well prepared to meet the demands of the rhetorical situation prompted by the riots. Yet, surprisingly, she found herself struggling to express herself publicly in ways that

rhetorical situation the composite of the occasion, speaker, and the audience that influences the speech that is given

exigence some real or perceived need that a speech might help address

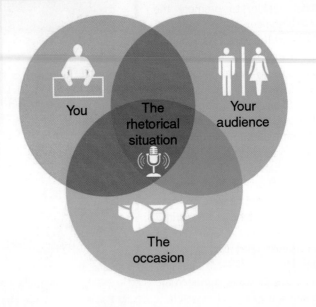

Exhibit 1.2
The Rhetorical Public Speaking Situation

You

The rhetorical situation

Your audience

The occasion

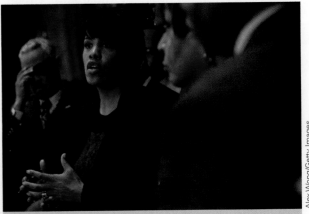

Baltimore Mayor Stephanie Rawlings-Blake spoke at a news conference following the death of Freddie Gray.

Alex Wong/Getty Images

eased tensions and calmed the city.[31] She was lambasted for remarks she made at a press conference that seemed to suggest that her administration was condoning destruction by rioters.[32] Instead of calming tensions, the lack of clarity in her remark inflamed other speakers, officials, citizens, and journalists, requiring her to make clarifying statements in subsequent public speeches and conferences.[33]

By contrast, when Baltimore City State Attorney, Marilyn Mosby, gave a formal speech at a press conference in which she announced the indictment of the police officers involved in Mr. Gray's death, she had a strong message and a confident delivery. Running over twenty minutes long, Ms. Mosby's speech was formal and informational and also included moments in which she passionately expressed her convictions and made personal connections with the audience.[34]

In addition to city officials, the police commissioner, the governor of Maryland, and even the president spoke out in response to the exigence created by the riots. President Obama made an address to the nation thanking those who participated in peaceful protests and condemning those who chose looting or arson to make a statement.[35]

An exigence can also allow for people who do not usually choose to participate in public discourse to speak out. After a community meeting with church leaders, gang members contacted the local media asking for time to tell their story as it related to the violent riots that were taking place.[36] To promote peace, the Baltimore Symphony Orchestra (BSO) gave a free outside concert attended by more than 1,000 people. The orchestra's principal oboist spoke to the media on behalf of the event, as did the BSO's music director, Marin Alsop, who passionately declared to the audience, "We will always be here for you."[37]

1-4b Speaker

The **speaker** is the source or originator of the speech. As the speaker, what you discuss, and how you express those ideas, will depend on your interests, beliefs, background, and public speaking skills. You will choose topics that you care about, know something about, and want to inform or persuade others about. Dominic, for example, will be training his coworkers to use the new purchase order requisition and tracking program based on personal knowledge he gained earlier. Diana will share stories about her grandmother, someone she knew well and loved dearly, in ways that will likely lead her audience to feel warmly about her grandmother, too.

1-4c Audience

The **audience** is the specific group of people to whom your speech is directed. **Audience analysis** is the process of learning about the diverse characteristics of audience members, and **audience adaptation** is the process of tailoring your message to address exigence in terms of the unique interests, needs, and expectations of the audience. For example, organizers of benefit concerts today recognize that many audience members are tech-savvy, so they appeal for donations online and via text messages in addition to toll-free phone lines.

1-4d Occasion

The **occasion** encompasses the expected purpose for the speech and the setting (i.e., location) where it will be given. Only a few weeks after signing with the College of Mount Saint Joseph, student and basketball player Lauren Hill was diagnosed with diffuse intrinsic pontine glioma (DIPG), a rare type of incurable pediatric brain cancer. Undaunted, Lauren held onto her dream of playing collegiate basketball and used her situation to raise awareness for DIPG. With only a few months to live, Lauren fulfilled her dream by starting her team's 2014 game against Hiram College. Before the tip off, Dr. Tony Aretz, the president of Mount St. Joseph, marked the occasion with an inspiring pregame speech delivered to the audience of 10,000 attendees, including professional athletes from the WNBA and the NFL, who filled the Cintas Center arena in Cincinnati. He said, "Lauren's dream to play basketball in a Mount uniform will come true this afternoon. But more important to Lauren is that now you all know what DIPG is. Ten thousand of you are here to share in her day. Today, we play for 22."[38]

The occasion for a speech is not always momentous, as in the case of Dr. Aretz's pregame speech, but it most always involves a synergy between the purpose of the speech and the setting in which it is delivered.

When the congregation assembles at a church, synagogue, or mosque, they expect to hear a message about religious texts or principles. When physicians attend professional meetings, they expect to hear scientific

speaker the source or originator of the speech

audience the specific group of people to whom your speech is directed

audience analysis the process of learning about the diverse characteristics of audience members and then, based on these characteristics, to predict how audience members are apt to listen to, understand, and be motivated to act on your speech

audience adaptation the process of tailoring your message to address exigence in terms of their unique interests, needs, and expectations

occasion the expected purpose for a speech and the setting, or location, in which the speech is given

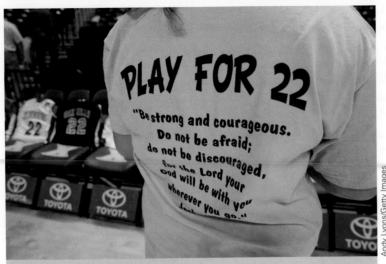

Andy Lyons/Getty Images

Dr. Tony Aretz' inspiring speech evoked a phrase heard around the world: "Play for 22."

restaurant to an audience of twenty. Dominic's approach will be different, for example, when he addresses all 60 of his coworkers during the overview session than when he meets with smaller groups of 10 to 15 in breakout sessions throughout the day. In addition, since the overview speech will be recorded and posted on the company Web site, he will also need to address that *virtual audience* while he speaks. One way he can do so is to address the camera as if it is another "person" in the group.

So while effective speeches are tailored to address audience exigence, they do so in ways that adhere to the overlapping elements and constraints of the entire rhetorical situation. Now let's consider how effective public speakers do this via the primary principles of effective speeches: content, structure, and delivery.

presentations about new treatments. Imagine what would happen if the local rabbi were to present his sermon to the physicians and the physician were to present her findings at the synagogue service! The setting is also an important aspect of the occasion. The speech you prepare to give in a large auditorium for an audience of more than one thousand is likely to be different than the speech you would prepare to give in a

ethos everything you say and do to convey competence and good character

 1-5 # EFFECTIVE SPEECH COMPONENTS

When we give a speech, our goal is to create and achieve shared meaning with our audience members. As shown in Exhibit 1.3, we accomplish this through the rhetorical appeals of ethos, pathos, and logos.[39] **Ethos** includes

Exhibit 1.3
Components of an Effective Speech

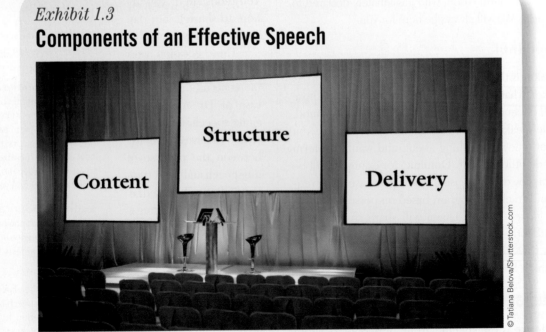

Content Structure Delivery

© Tatiana Belova/Shutterstock.com

everything we say and do to convey competence and good character. Dressing appropriately, being poised as we speak, citing credible sources, and speaking within the time parameters allotted, for instance, convey ethos. **Pathos** consists of everything we say and do to appeal to emotions, which can range from negative emotions such as fear or dread to positive emotions such as adventure or joy. **Logos** includes everything we say and do to appeal to logic and sound reasoning. Essentially, effective speeches use ethos, pathos, and logos in content, structure, and delivery.

> Effective speakers are conversational, intelligible, poised, and expressive in their **delivery**.

1-5a Content

Content is the information and ideas you present. It includes the speech purpose and main points, as well as the evidence, supporting material, and reasoning used to develop each main idea. Evidence consists of all the facts, examples, and data that help clarify or explain your main ideas. Evidence can come from your own experiences as well as from research materials you collect. Effective evidence has sufficient breadth and depth. *Breadth* refers to the amount and types of evidence you use. *Depth* is the level of detail you provide from each piece of evidence. Evidence is effective when it is logically linked to the main idea it supports.

Peter Kramer/NBC/NBCU Photo Bank via Getty Images

Comedian Drew Lynch has received acclaim for his comedic routine, which acknowledges the permanent stutter he suffered following a sports injury. According to the Stuttering Foundation of America, more than 3 million Americans suffer from this speech disability.

The ideas you choose to present depend on what is appropriate for your audience and the occasion, and you adapt your content so that it includes **listener-relevance links**, which are statements informing listeners of how and why they should be interested in or care about an idea. Doing so makes the exigence of your ideas transparent. Diana's purpose is to praise her grandmother's attributes. She decides to focus on two main values her grandmother both preached and practiced: a positive attitude and perseverance. She plans to begin each main point with a listener-relevance statement about the universal nature of her grandmother's values. She then intends to develop each main point with several brief examples to provide breadth and one more detailed story to add depth.

1-5b Structure

Structure is the framework that organizes the speech content. Clear structure helps listeners follow your ideas as they listen.[40] Effective structure consists of both macrostructure and microstructure elements. **Macrostructure** is the overall organizational framework used to present your speech content. Effective macrostructure consists of four elements: the introduction, body, conclusion, and transitions. You may not realize it, but you have already studied macrostructure—you use it when you write formal papers for school. Now you will learn how to adapt what you have already learned to formal, oral messages.

Careful attention to macrostructure is even more important when you craft a speech than when you write an essay. A reader can easily reread a poorly written essay to try to understand the author's intent, but an audience does not usually have the opportunity to listen to a speech again, unless it is being recorded and posted to an accessible Web site. So the introduction should be structured to build audience interest in your topic and preview your main points (tell them

pathos everything you say and do to appeal to emotions

logos everything you say and do to appeal to logic and sound reasoning

content the information and ideas presented in the speech

listener-relevance links statements informing listeners of how and why they should be interested in or care about an idea

structure the framework that organizes the speech content

macrostructure the overall organizational framework you use to present your speech content

Tribute Speech
Evaluation Checklist

You can use this checklist to critique a speech you hear in class. (You can also use it to critique your own speech.)

Content

1. Were all main points addressed per the assignment? _____

2. Were two to three pieces of evidence provided for each main point (breadth)? _____

3. Was one extended piece of evidence provided for each main point (depth)? _____

4. Were listener-relevance links provided for each main point? _____

5. Did the speech fall within the time constraints of the assignment? _____

Structure

1. Did the speech provide all the basic elements of an effective speech: introduction, body, conclusion, and transitions? _____ (*macrostructure*)

2. Did the introduction catch the audience's interest? _____ identify the speech topic/goal? _____ preview the main points? _____

3. Were transitions provided between each main point? _____

4. Did the conclusion remind the audience of the main points? _____ motivate the audience to remember the main ideas of the speech? _____

5. Did the speaker use words that were appropriate and inclusive? _____ accurate and clear? _____ vivid and expressive? _____ (*microstructure*)

Delivery

1. Was the speaker intelligible in terms of volume? _____ rate? _____ pronunciation? _____ enunciation? _____

2. Was the speaker conversational? _____

3. Did the speaker look up from his or her notes most of the time and make eye contact with the audience? _____

4. Did the speaker appear professional, poised, and confident? _____

5. Was the speaker expressive in term of changes in rate and volume? _____ strategic pauses? _____ appropriate facial expressions? _____ appropriate gestures? _____

Based on these criteria, evaluate the speech (check one):

☐ **excellent**   ☐ **good**   ☐ **satisfactory**   ☐ **fair**   ☐ **poor**

what you are going to tell them). The speech body contains the main ideas and supporting material used to develop each one (tell them). The conclusion reminds the audience of your main ideas and motivates them to remember what you have said (tell them what you told them). Speech macrostructure also includes **transitions**—statements that verbally summarize one main point and introduce the next one.

Whereas macrostructure is the overall framework for your speech, **microstructure** is the specific language and style you use within your sentences. Effective speeches are understandable and memorable when speakers use appropriate, accurate, clear, and vivid language, and when they use rhetorical style devices such as alliteration, onomatopoeia, personification, similes, metaphors, and analogies.

1-5c Delivery

Delivery, how you use your voice and body to convey your message, can dramatically affect the audience's ability to understand, remember, and possibly act on your message.[41] Effective speakers are conversational, intelligible, poised, and expressive in their delivery. Being *conversational* means sounding as though you are having a spontaneous conversation with your audience, rather than simply reading to them or performing in front of them. A conversational style is the hallmark of TED talks. (TED stands for technology, entertainment, and design.) Although it appears spontaneous, that conversational style is the result of hours of practice. Musician Amanda Palmer is noted for giving a popular TED talk on the art of asking, and, although a performer by trade, Palmer says she, "slaved over that talk" and practiced constantly. She even went so far as to approach someone at a bar and ask him, "Can I tell you a story?"—all so she could practice her delivery.[42]

Intelligible speakers use a rate, volume, and pitch that is easily understood. If you are speaking in a second language, have a pronounced accent, or have a speech impediment, you might find that speaking somewhat slower improves your intelligibility. *Poised* speakers stand

How you use your voice and body to convey your message can dramatically affect the audience's ability to understand, remember, and possibly act on your message.

confidently without fidgeting, swaying, or using any other potentially distracting bodily action. Being poised also means making eye contact with your audience members in face-to-face settings, or with the camera when delivering ideas via media, rather than focusing solely on your notes. Being *expressive* means changing your pitch, volume, rate, and so forth to emphasize the emotional intent of your ideas. Generally, you want to sound a bit more dramatic than you would in casual conversation. For example, you might speak more quickly or loudly to underscore your emotional convictions or to stress key words or phrases, or you might pause strategically to call attention to important ideas. Being expressive also means using appropriate facial expressions to reflect your conviction about the topic and gestures to reinforce important points.

transitions statements that verbally summarize one main point in a speech and introduce the next one

microstructure the specific language and style you use within the sentences of your speech

delivery how you use your voice and body to present your message

SAMPLE OUTLINE FOR SPEECH OF TRIBUTE
Grandma Frances: My Hero

This chapter concludes with an outline of Diana's speech of tribute to her grandmother with commentary. As you read, consider how you might address the rhetorical situation effectively as you develop the content and structure, as well as practice the delivery of, your speeches.

Speech Outline
Grandma Frances: My Hero

General Goal:
To pay tribute to or honor someone

Introduction

I. [Diana shows a visual aid image of several well-known superheroes from popular culture.] What makes someone a hero? Do you have any? Who are they and why do you consider them heroes?

Attention getter

II. A simple definition of a hero is someone who is admired for his or her noble qualities. So a hero doesn't have to be someone famous. Based on this definition, I bet most of us in this room can identify at least one hero, one person we admire and look up to. When I think of my heroes, one important person always comes to mind: my Grandma Frances. (Show visual aid photograph of Grandma Frances.)

Listener relevance and credibility

III. In the next few minutes, let's talk about my Grandma Frances as a hero who taught me by her example how to maintain a positive attitude and to persevere through good times and bad.

Thesis statement with main point preview

Body

I. I consider Grandma Frances a hero because she modeled a positive attitude in all situations.

First main point

A. We all want to be happy and healthy. Did you know that study after study shows a direct link between a positive attitude and improved mental and physical health? Who wouldn't want that?

Supporting material (listener relevance)

B. When it came to having a positive attitude, Grandma Frances was a "rock star." You couldn't get to her.

Supporting material

1. One story that really shows how grandma would "turn lemons into lemonade" with a smile on her face the whole time occurred one summer when I was about nine years old and my parents, two brothers, and I joined grandma and grandpa on a week-long fishing expedition in Canada. (Show visual of our family just before leaving for the trip.)

2. As we packed for the trip, grandpa announced that we wouldn't need to pack food because we were going to eat what we caught and really live off the land (or in this case, off the water I suppose). Although I don't know whether grandpa knew it at the time, grandma packed a few things just to be safe. With that, we headed out on our family fishing adventure from our comfortable homes in central Minnesota to the rugged countryside of Saskatchewan, Canada.

3. As luck would have it, we couldn't catch a fish to save our souls. We tried fishing early in the morning, throughout the day, and into the evening. We hired guides who took us to "secret spots" where they claimed we would be sure to catch fish. We had pretty much exhausted the food supplies Grandma Frances had packed, having just finished the last package of hot dogs. We wondered what we would eat for the next four days as grandma was saving the water we had used to boil the franks. My mom asked Grandma Frances what she was doing with the water, and grandma responded, "Well, we might need to make wiener water soup." So you see, when I talk about grandma as an eternal optimist, I don't necessarily think about making lemonade from lemons, but I surely do think about making soup out of leftover wiener water.

4. After doing the dishes, Grandma Frances said she was going to try her luck fishing right off the dock. No one from our group had tried fishing from the dock because we were told that nobody caught anything that way. Well, all I can say is they didn't know my Grandma Frances! When the fish started biting for grandma, the whole family joined her, catching our limit right off the dock.

In fact, we caught so many fish for the next three days that we ate fish for every meal and still came home from our adventure with coolers full. (Show picture of our family holding a stringer of fish standing on the dock).

Transition

Not only do I consider grandma a hero for teaching me to have a positive attitude but also for teaching me to persevere.

II. Grandma Frances was always doing things that demonstrated her will to persevere, and she encouraged me to do so as well.	**Second main point**
A. Throughout our lives, most of us have been inundated with messages about the importance of believing in ourselves and persevering—whether from children's stories like "The Little Engine that Could," songs like "I will Survive," movies like "Rocky," or even symbols like Nike's "Just Do It" logo (show a visual of the Nike symbol). In fact, perseverance could even be considered a cultural norm about how we ought to live.	**Supporting material (listener relevance)**
B. One way Grandma Frances taught me the value of perseverance was through modeling when people could have discouraged her. When people made fun of her for using unusual words as a way to improve her vocabulary, she didn't let it get to her. She just kept on doing it. For example, she would do the crossword puzzle in the newspaper every day and then use at least two words she learned doing it in conversation that day. I remember one time she used an unfamiliar word and her friends responded by teasing her with a made up word: "polly-go." But Grandma Frances just smiled and kept on doing puzzles and using new words every day.	**Supporting material**
C. Another way Grandma Frances taught the value of perseverance was by encouraging me when others discouraged me. One example that stands out happened when I was in grade school. As many of you know, I come from a family of singers, and one time my brothers and I were singing. I guess I didn't hit all the right notes, and I recall a family member telling me that my brothers were really good singers, but I didn't seem to have the "gene." Grandma simply replied, "She just has a smaller range right now. It will get larger as she gets older." I never forgot what Grandma Frances said. I kept singing and practicing and, luckily for my music professors in college and the kids I work with in the choirs I direct now, my range did expand. I sometimes wonder about what I would be doing today if I had listened to the discouragers rather than Grandma Frances.	**Supporting material**

Conclusion

I. We all have heroes we admire for their noble qualities. Grandma Frances, who taught me the value of a positive attitude and perseverance, was my hero.	**Thesis restatement and main point review**
II. [Diana shows visual aid again of superheroes from popular culture.] Grandma Frances may not be able to fly through the air like Superman, scale buildings like Spider-Man, or even wield a Lasso of Truth like Wonder Woman, but she will always be a superhero to me.	**Main point review and clincher**

Quick Quiz (answers in Solutions Appendix)

T F 1. Public speaking can occur in an informal setting.

T F 2. The meaning of what a speaker is saying is almost always easy to interpret.

T F 3. During communication, noise can occur due to physical reasons or psychological reasons.

T F 4. Interpersonal communication is another term for self-talk.

T F 5. The participants in a communication process are known as senders and receivers.

6. Newspapers and magazines are examples of:

   a. mass communication
   b. small group communication
   c. interpersonal communication
   d. intrapersonal communication
   e. targeted communication

7. During a lecture on police training, an audience member raises his hand and asks the speaker to clarify the last point that he made. This is an example of:

   a. encoding
   b. decoding
   c. noise
   d. channels
   e. feedback

8. All of the following are principles that ethical speakers should follow EXCEPT:

   a. Ethical communicators are honest.
   b. Ethical communicators are responsible.
   c. Ethical communicators have integrity.
   d. Ethical communicators keep their speeches short.
   e. Ethical communicators are fair.

9. The source or originator of a speech is the:

   a. audience
   b. speaker
   c. teacher
   d. professor
   e. research

10. All of the following are basic elements of the communication process EXCEPT:

   a. messages
   b. channels
   c. poise
   d. noise
   e. feedback

Chapter Takeaways

List three key takeaways from this chapter:

-
-
-

SPEAK
ONLINE
STUDY YOUR WAY
WITH STUDYBITS!

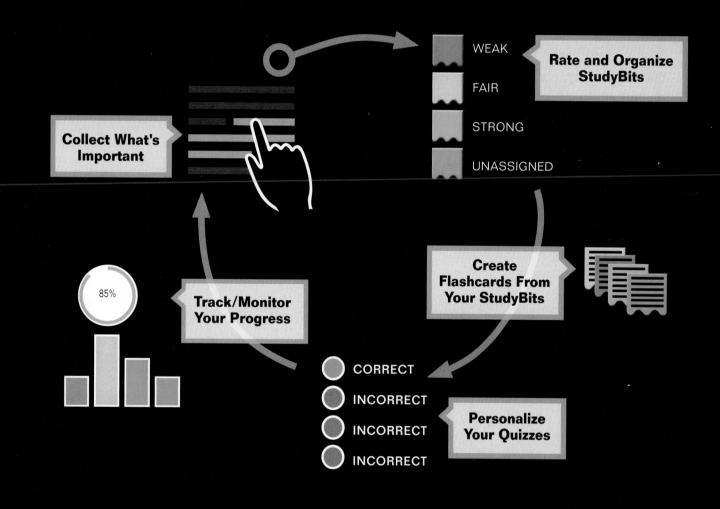

2 Your First Speech

LEARNING OUTCOMES

2-1 Describe the nature of public speaking apprehension.

2-2 Practice several public speaking apprehension management methods and techniques.

2-3 Identify the six steps in an effective speech action plan and use them to prepare and present a speech of self-introduction.

After finishing this chapter go to **PAGE 36** for **STUDY TOOLS.**

Sound Familiar?

Keith has recently been hired as an engineering intern at a Fortune 500 consumer-products company. He was only slightly nervous on his first day until his manager explained that all the interns would be giving short speeches at the end of the week to introduce themselves to the team. Furthermore, per company custom, Keith would have to create a photograph collage about himself to project on screen as he delivered his quick speech. His manager assured him that the speeches were short and the audience friendly. Still, Keith broke out in a sweat, and his heart began to race—just at the thought of speaking. "How am I ever going to do this?" he thought. "I am too shy to stand up in front of preschoolers, let alone professionals!"

2-1 UNDERSTANDING THE NATURE OF PUBLIC SPEAKING APPREHENSION

You might be thinking, "Poor, Keith. If he's that nervous, his manager should really let him send an introductory email." Or you might relate to Keith. You might even be thinking that people like you and Keith who suffer from severe public speaking apprehension—or stage fright—should not be put through such turmoil.

What you might not know, however, is that as many as 76 percent of experienced public speakers claim to feel fearful before presenting a speech.[1] For example, did you know that award-winning actors Meryl Streep, Kim Basinger, and Harrison Ford, Prince Harry of the British royal family,[2] billionaire investor Warren Buffet,[3] former professional football player Ricky Williams, preacher Joel Osteen,[4] and entrepreneur Sir Richard

Branson[5] all experience fear about speaking in front of others? In spite of their fear, all are effective public speakers today because they employ strategies for managing their nervousness—strategies we will discuss in this chapter.

Public speaking apprehension is the level of fear a person experiences when anticipating or actually speaking to an audience. In a survey conducted by Chapman University, 61.9 percent of Americans responded that they were somewhat to very afraid of public speaking, with roughly 9 percent responding that they were very afraid.[6] In fact, public speaking ranked as the top fear, narrowly edging out the fear of heights and beating bugs, snakes, drowning, needles, and flying by roughly 6 to 10 points.[7] Even people with high levels of apprehension can be effective and confident public speakers. In fact, having some public speaking apprehension makes one a better public speaker than having none at all. Why? Because those feelings we label as fear are really a sign of the adrenaline boost that will help us perform at our best. Just as an adrenaline boost helps us perform better as athletes, musicians, and actors, it also helps us deliver better public speeches when we manage it effectively.[8] So, if you are lackadaisical about giving a speech, you probably will not do a good job.[9] Because at least some tension is constructive, the goal is not to eliminate nervousness but to learn how to manage it.[10]

Now that we understand that some public speaking apprehension is normal and can actually help you do a better job, let's identify some symptoms you may experience and the causes for speaking apprehension. Then we'll describe several techniques you can use to manage public speaking apprehension in ways that will make you a more effective public speaker.

2-1a Symptoms

The symptoms of public speaking apprehension vary among individuals and range from mild to debilitating. Symptoms can be cognitive, physical, or emotional. *Cognitive symptoms* include negative self-talk, which is also the most common cause of public speaking apprehension.[11] For example, a highly apprehensive person might do what Keith did in the "Sound Familiar?" section and dwell on thoughts such as "I'm going to make a fool of myself" or "I just know that I'll blow it." *Physical symptoms* may be stomach upset, flushed skin,

public speaking apprehension the level of fear a person experiences when anticipating or actually speaking to an audience

Exhibit 2.1
Phases of Public Speaking Apprehension

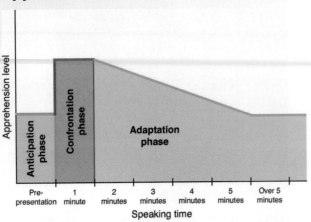

(Graph: Apprehension level vs. Speaking time showing Anticipation phase, Confrontation phase, and Adaptation phase across Pre-presentation, 1 minute, 2 minutes, 3 minutes, 4 minutes, 5 minutes, Over 5 minutes)

sweating, shaking, lightheadedness, rapid or pounding heartbeats, stuttering, and vocalized pauses ("like," "you know," "ah," "um"). *Emotional symptoms* include feeling anxious, worried, or upset.

Luckily, public speaking apprehension gradually decreases for most of us as we speak. Researchers have identified three phases we proceed through: anticipation, confrontation, and adaptation.[12] Exhibit 2.1 depicts this cycle visually.

The **anticipation phase** is the anxiety we experience before giving the speech, both while preparing it and waiting to speak. The **confrontation phase** is the surge of anxiety we feel as we begin delivering the speech. This begins to fall about a minute or so into the speech. The **adaptation phase** is the period during which our anxiety level gradually decreases. It

anticipation phase the anxiety you experience prior to giving the speech, including the nervousness you feel while preparing and waiting to speak

confrontation phase the surge of anxiety you feel as you begin delivering your speech

adaptation phase the period during which your anxiety level gradually decreases

self-talk intrapersonal communication regarding success or failure in a particular situation

typically begins about one minute into the presentation and tends to level off after about five minutes.[13] So, it's normal to be nervous before you speak; in fact, when managed effectively, nervousness can result in a better speech than having no nervousness at all.

There are many ways to measure your level of public speaking apprehension. Exhibit 2.2 presents a short self-assessment survey you can complete to gauge your level of apprehension.

2-1b Causes

Public speaking apprehension is most commonly caused by negative self-talk.[14] **Self-talk** is defined as intrapersonal communication regarding perceived success or failure in a particular situation. Negative self-talk increases anxiety. Negative self-talk generally focuses on a fear of being stared at, a fear of the unknown, a fear of failure, or a fear of becoming fearful. Where do these negative thoughts come from? Research suggests three common roots: biologically based temperament, previous experience, and level of skills.

Biologically Based Temperament

For a few of us, public speaking apprehension stems from our biologically based temperament. According to this theory, people who are extroverted tend to experience lower levels of public speaking apprehension than people who are introverted. Similarly, people who are generally anxious or shy tend to experience higher anxiety than people who are not.[15] Does this mean that naturally introverted, anxious, and shy people are doomed to be ineffective public speakers? Of course not. Many people—including celebrities and public speaking professors—are introverted and yet enjoy a great deal of public speaking success.

Previous Experience

Our level of apprehension may also result from our past experiences with

> Apprehension is commonly experienced by first-time speakers. Fortunately for many of us, it gradually decreases as we speak.

wavebreakmedia/Shutterstock.com

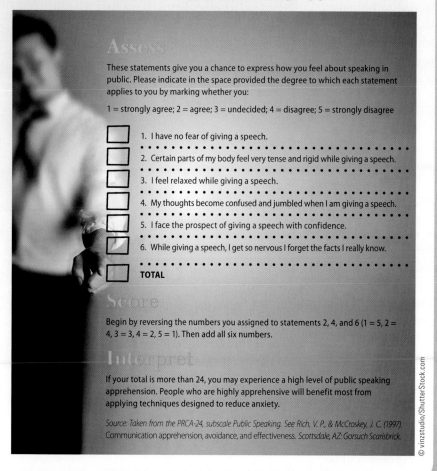

Exhibit 2.2
Self-Assessment of Public Speaking Apprehension

Assess

These statements give you a chance to express how you feel about speaking in public. Please indicate in the space provided the degree to which each statement applies to you by marking whether you:

1 = strongly agree; 2 = agree; 3 = undecided; 4 = disagree; 5 = strongly disagree

1. I have no fear of giving a speech.
2. Certain parts of my body feel very tense and rigid while giving a speech.
3. I feel relaxed while giving a speech.
4. My thoughts become confused and jumbled when I am giving a speech.
5. I face the prospect of giving a speech with confidence.
6. While giving a speech, I get so nervous I forget the facts I really know.

TOTAL

Score

Begin by reversing the numbers you assigned to statements 2, 4, and 6 (1 = 5, 2 = 4, 3 = 3, 4 = 2, 5 = 1). Then add all six numbers.

Interpret

If your total is more than 24, you may experience a high level of public speaking apprehension. People who are highly apprehensive will benefit most from applying techniques designed to reduce anxiety.

Source: Taken from the PRCA-24, subscale Public Speaking. See Rich, V. P., & McCroskey, J. C. (1997). Communication apprehension, avoidance, and effectiveness. Scottsdale, AZ: Gorsuch Scarisbrick.

© vinzstudio/ShutterStock.com

public speaking. In other words, some of us actually learned to fear public speaking! Research tells us that most public speaking apprehension stems from such socialization.[16] We are socialized in two main ways: through modeling and reinforcement. **Modeling** is learning by observing and then imitating those you admire or are close to.[17] **Reinforcement** is learning from personal experiences so that past responses to our behavior shape expectations about how our future behavior will be received.[18]

Consider your past. How did modeling affect your current communication behavior? What was oral communication like growing up in your home

modeling learning by observing and then imitating those you admire or are close to

reinforcement learning from personal experiences so that past responses to our behavior shape expectations about how our future behavior will be received

TECH TALK

Social Media Diminishes Speaking Apprehension—Which Isn't Always a Good Thing

The Internet and social media have given a voice to just about anyone looking to share their opinion. Although most people fear speaking before an audience in public, an afternoon spent on YouTube confirms that many people don't experience the same level of apprehension when addressing an audience over social media—even when the potential audience is many times larger than a public speaking class or school auditorium.

As mentioned in the opening of the chapter, the effects of public speaking apprehension are actually part of the adrenaline boost that comes before performing a potentially demanding feat. That rush is generally absent when you post a status update to Twitter or Tumblr or upload a Vine or YouTube video. Without the rush, we are calmer and less anxious about speaking, and that can make us bolder in our speech.

Bolder can quickly become daring or inappropriate, however. For example, most people would never consider getting drunk or using vulgarity on stage during a demonstration speech, but that is exactly the premise of a YouTube series of cooking demonstration videos. Without a live audience, it can be easy to forget that there is an audience at all and adopt a "no one is looking" attitude. When preparing to create a speech for delivery through social media, remember that tension can be constructive and help you perform better, which will be important when the audience for your video speech turns out to be thousands of people.

and in your community? Did family or community members talk openly with each other a great deal, or were they quiet and reserved? Did any of your family members do much public speaking? What were their experiences? If your family tended to be quiet and reserved and avoided speaking in public or showed fear about it, your own preferences and fears may stem from modeling. Emmy-winning actress, writer, and comedian Tina Fey was once asked what it was like around her dinner table growing up. She remarked that "the whole family played to each other," her "mom's a dry wit," and her dad "has a good sense of silliness." Their modeling not only rubbed off on her as a comedian but also helped her eventually overcome being a "shy, nerdy" teenager.[19]

How others have reinforced our public speaking efforts also influences how apprehensive we feel about it. We have all had many "public speaking" experiences, from reading aloud or giving presentations in class, to accepting an award at a banquet. If the responses to your speaking in the past were generally positive, you probably learned to feel confident about your ability. If, on the other hand, the responses were negative, you probably learned to feel fearful of public speaking. If your elementary school teacher humiliated you when you read aloud, or if friends laughed at your acceptance speech, you will probably be more apprehensive about speaking in public than if you had been praised for your efforts. But negative past experiences do not have to influence your future. There are many strategies you can use to manage apprehension and become an effective public speaker. We will discuss some of these strategies in the next section.

Level of Skills

An important source of public speaking apprehension comes from having underdeveloped speaking skills. This "skill deficit" theory suggests that most of us become apprehensive because we don't know how to (or choose not to) plan or prepare effectively for our public presentations. As you become skilled at using the six-step speech-planning and preparation process we introduce in this chapter, you will gain confidence and become a more skilled—and effective—public speaker.

2-1c Effects

In addition to having identifiable symptoms and causes, public speaking apprehension also produces some recognizable effects. According to executive speaking coach Anett Grant, the fear we have on the inside produces three common behaviors on the outside: using

Comic actress Tina Fey admits to having been a shy, nerdy teenager.

distracting expressions, babbling, and mechanical speech.[20]

Facial expressions are an important part of communication, and when those expressions reflect our inner fears, they can present a distraction for our listeners. Grimaces, tight-lipped smiles, furrowed brows, and perpetually surprised looks detract from your message. Often, we are totally unaware of the range of various distracting expressions we make. In addition to practicing in front of a mirror, asking a trusted friend or mentor to help you identify distracting expressions you make while speaking can be the first step toward eliminating them.

Another common result of the anxiety related to speaking apprehension is babbling. It is as if our mouths start speaking as a way to distract our minds from the level of anxiety we are feeling. The free flow of speech characteristic of babbling is often overly detailed, hard to follow, and generally incoherent. The audience has trouble understanding the message or the goal of the speech.

Finally, apprehension can result in mechanical speech patterns. Instead of using a delivery style and structure appropriate to public speaking, we revert to speaking in a style more appropriate for writing. The speech comes off as stiff and jerky and seems more like reading than speaking.

Using the methods described in this chapter for managing public speaking apprehension can help mitigate the behavioral effects of speech anxiety.

2-2 MANAGING PUBLIC SPEAKING APPREHENSION

Because public speaking apprehension has multiple causes, we describe a few general methods, several specific techniques, and a six-step speech-planning and preparation process that will help you manage anxiety and boost your confidence about public speaking.

2-2a General Methods

There are five common methods for reducing public speaking apprehension:

1. Communication orientation motivation (COM) methods are designed to reduce anxiety by adopting a "communication" rather than a "performance" orientation.[21] According to communication researcher Michael Motley, speakers with a **performance orientation** view public speaking as demanding special delivery techniques that will impress audiences "aesthetically"[22] and audience members as hypercritical judges who will not overlook even minor mistakes. When we approach public speaking with a performance orientation, our self-talk tends to focus on our fear of failing, which increases our anxiety. On the other hand, speakers with a **communication orientation** view public speaking as an opportunity to engage in conversation with a number of people about an important topic. We focus on getting our message across rather than on how the people in our audience are judging us as a performer. Sir Richard Branson, billionaire entrepreneur and founder of Virgin Group, which includes subsidiaries in music, travel, and more, has adopted the communication orientation. He approaches public speaking as if he is having a chat with people in his living room rather than to an audience of hundreds or thousands of people. He has found the technique to be really successful, saying, "And in fact when I do public speaking, I don't do formal speeches where I read from cues or reading from notes. I just sit on the stage and have a chat and it seems to work well."[23]

2. Visualization is a general method for reducing apprehension that

RTimages/Shutterstock.com

Monkey Business Images/Shutterstock.com

communication orientation motivation (COM) methods techniques designed to reduce anxiety by helping the speaker adopt a "communication" rather than a "performance" orientation toward the speech

performance orientation viewing public speaking as a situation demanding special delivery techniques to impress an audience aesthetically or viewing audience members as hypercritical judges who will not forgive even minor mistakes

communication orientation viewing a speech as just an opportunity to talk with a number of people about an important topic

visualization a method that reduces apprehension by helping speakers develop a mental picture of themselves giving a masterful speech

involves picturing ourselves giving a masterful speech. Like COM techniques, visualization helps us overcome cognitive and emotional symptoms of apprehension arising from a fear of failure. Joe Ayres and Theodore S. Hopf, two scholars who have conducted extensive research on visualization, found that if people can visualize themselves going through an entire speech-preparation and speech-making process effectively, they will have a much better chance of succeeding when they actually give their speeches.[24]

By visualizing the process of speech making, not only do people seem to lower their general apprehension, but they also report fewer negative thoughts when they actually speak.[25] So, you want to use visualization activities to manage apprehension as you prepare your speeches. (Access **Visualizing Your Success at SPEAK3 Online**; this activity will guide you through a visualization in which you will imagine that you successfully accomplish the complete speech-preparation and presentation process.)

3. Relaxation exercises include breathing techniques and progressive muscle relaxation exercises. For these exercises to be effective, you must learn how to do them and practice them regularly so they eventually become habitual. Then you will be able to use them to calm yourself in the moments before you speak.

Let's take a closer look at breathing techniques. We were all born breathing correctly, using the muscles in our abdomen to draw air into and push air out of our lungs. But when we become anxious, the muscles in our abdomens tense, and so we take shallower breaths, often raising our shoulders to get air into our lungs and dropping them to expel the air. Shallow breathing contributes to anxiety, depression, and fatigue.[26] Think of your lungs as balloons that fill up with air. Have you ever seen someone making balloon animals? If so, you probably noticed that, when the artist wanted part of the balloon to remain uninflated, he or she squeezed that area off with the hand. Shallow breathing is like filling only the top half of the balloon because, when your abdominal muscles tighten, you stop air from filling the bottom half of your lungs. Fortunately, we can retrain ourselves to breathe from the abdomen and thereby reduce our anxiety.

We can also train our bodies to relax by practicing progressive muscle relaxation exercises. Essentially, you systematically tense certain muscle groups for about ten seconds and then relax them for another ten seconds while focusing on what the relaxed state feels like.[27] Once you teach your body to relax on command, you can call it to do so before beginning to give your speech, again allowing the adrenaline rush to work for you. Exhibit 2.3 offers some suggestions for relaxation techniques.

4. Systematic desensitization is a method that reduces apprehension by gradually visualizing yourself in and then performing increasingly more frightening events while remaining in a relaxed state.[29] Essentially, once you are in a relaxed state, you imagine yourself in successively more stressful speech-planning and speech-making situations—for example, researching a speech topic in the library, practicing the speech out loud in front of a roommate, and delivering the final speech to your audience. Once you can maintain a relaxed state while visualizing yourself in each event, you try performing each event while maintaining the learned state of calmness. The ultimate goal of systematic desensitization is to transfer the calm feelings we attain while visualizing to

relaxation exercises
breathing techniques and progressive muscle relaxation exercises that help reduce anxiety

systematic desensitization
a method that reduces apprehension by gradually visualizing oneself in and performing increasingly more frightening events while remaining in a relaxed state

---

Exhibit 2.3
Relaxation Techniques

Abdominal Breathing

Lie on the floor and place your hand on your abdomen. Consciously focus on filling your abdomen with air when you inhale by watching your hand rise. Then, as you release the air, watch your hand lower again.

Sighing

By sighing right before it is your turn to speak, you can release tension and lower your anxiety level, allowing the inevitable rush of adrenaline to work for you, not against you.[28]

Progressive Muscle Relaxation Exercises

Consciously tense and relax each of these muscle groups twice and then move onto the next group: hands, arms, shoulders, neck, lips, tongue, mouth, eyes and forehead, abdomen, back, midsection, thighs, stomach, calves, feet, and toes.

the actual speaking event. Calmness on command—it works. Research tells us that more than 80 percent of those who try this method reduce their level of anxiety.[30]

5. Cognitive restructuring is a process designed to help you change your intrapersonal communication about public speaking. The goal is to replace anxiety-arousing negative self-talk with anxiety-reducing positive self-talk. The process consists of four steps.

I. Identify your fears. Write down all the fears that come to mind when you know you must give a speech.

II. Analyze how rational these fears are. Most fears about public speaking are, in fact, irrational because public speaking is not life threatening.

III. Develop positive coping statements to replace each negative self-talk statement. Exhibit 2.4 is an example of how Keith used this process to help manage his anxiety. There is no one list of coping statements that will work for everyone, but you can develop your own list of positive coping statements to replace negative self-talk. Psychologist Richard Heimberg of the State University of New York at Albany asks his clients to consider just how many listeners in an audience of 100 would even notice or care if the clients did what they're afraid of doing when giving a speech. Ultimately, he concludes with the question, "Can you cope with the one or two people who [notice or criticize or] get upset?"[31]

IV Incorporate your positive coping statements into your life so that they're second nature. You can do this by writing your statements down and reading them aloud to yourself each day, as well as before you give a speech. The more you repeat your coping statements to yourself, silently and aloud, the more natural they will become and the more unnatural your negative thoughts will seem.

6. Self-distancing self-talk is a general method for minimizing the effect public speaking anxiety has on your performance. When you engage in self-talk, how do you refer to yourself? Do you use the first-person pronoun "I" or do you use the second person pronoun "you" or maybe even refer to yourself in the third person? It turns out that how you refer to yourself during self-talk has a significant impact on your public speaking performance.[32]

Researchers have found that people who use I-statements (*self-immersive language*) when processing their anxious thoughts and feelings before giving a speech perform worse compared to people who talk to themselves in the second or third person (*self-distancing language*). When we use

cognitive restructuring the systematic process of replacing anxiety-arousing negative self-talk with anxiety-reducing positive self-talk

self-distancing self-talk a general method for minimizing the effect of public speaking anxiety on performance by talking to oneself in the second or third person

Exhibit 2.4
Negative Self-Talk versus Positive Coping Statements

Negative Self-Talk	Positive Coping Statements
I'm afraid I'll stumble over my words and look foolish.	Even if I stumble, I will have succeeded as long as I get my message across.
I'm afraid everyone will be able to tell that I'm nervous.	They probably won't be able to tell I'm nervous, but as long as I focus on getting my message across, that's what matters.
I'm afraid my voice will crack.	Even if my voice cracks, as long as I keep going and focus on getting my message across, I'll succeed at what matters most.
I'm afraid I'll sound boring.	I won't sound boring if I focus on how important this message is to me and to my audience. I don't have to do somersaults to keep the audience's attention because my topic is relevant to them.

pixfly/Shutterstock.com

self-immersive language, we tend to perceive stress as threatening. By contrast, using self-distancing language shifts our perspective to see stress as a challenge (not a threat).[33]

Interestingly, you can experience a positive impact from using self-distancing self-talk for even a short period of time. Using it right before giving a speech will help you give a better speech performance. Moreover, you'll have fewer negative feelings about the performance and be less exhausted afterward.[34]

Professor Ethan Kross tested this out in a research study asking people to engage in self-talk for only five minutes before giving an impromptu speech. Kross says, "People who used 'I' had a mental monologue that sounded like, 'Oh, my god, how am I going to do this? I can't prepare a speech in five minutes without notes. It takes days for me to prepare a speech!'[35] The people who used 'you' were more likely to give themselves support with language like 'Ethan, you can do this.'"[36]

All six of these methods for reducing public speaking apprehension have successfully helped people reduce their anxiety. If you think you'll experience public speaking apprehension in this course, which of these techniques do you think might help you? Have you already tried some of them in other situations? If they helped, do you think you could apply them to reduce your anxiety about giving a speech? For most people, using several of them yields the best results.[37]

For an activity that will help you develop positive coping statements to replace negative self-talk, go to **Restructure Your Expectations at SPEAK3 Online**.

2-2b Specific Techniques

In addition to these six general methods, we recommend several specific techniques to employ in the days before you deliver your speech and on the day you actually give it.

1. Allow sufficient time to prepare. As soon as you know the day you are to give your speech and the expectations for it, identify the topic and begin to prepare. Ideally, you should spend at least a week to ten days researching, organizing, and practicing your speech.

2. Use presentational aids. Recall that one of the major fears that increase public speaking anxiety is the fear of being stared at. Although it is human nature to enjoy being recognized for things we've done well, it is not human nature to be the constant center of attention for a prolonged amount of time.[38] When we give a public speech, all eyes are focused constantly on us, and we can feel conspicuous. Using presentational aids allows us to direct the audience's attention toward something else at carefully placed points during the speech, which can diminish the sense of being constantly stared at and the anxiety that can accompany it.

3. Practice your speech aloud. When you practice your speech aloud, you get comfortable hearing yourself talk about your topic. You identify sections of the speech where your ideas may not flow and where you need to do additional preparation. By the third or fourth time you have practiced aloud, you will notice your delivery becoming easier, and you will gain confidence in your ability to present your ideas to others.

Many successful speakers not only practice aloud alone but also practice in front of trusted friends who serve as a "practice" audience and give the speaker feedback. If possible, practice your speech in the room where you'll ultimately deliver it. Hearing your voice in the room where you'll speak reduces anxiety that can arise as a result of the fear of the unknown because you now know what it will feel like to present your speech in that room. Finally, on the night before your speech, review your speech plan immediately before you go to sleep. That way, as you sleep, your mind will continue to prepare.[39]

4. Dress up. We tend to feel more confident when we know we look good. By dressing up a bit for our speech, we reduce anxiety about being stared at because we feel good about how we look. Also, dressing up enhances credibility (ethos) because doing so sends a message that we care about the audience, the occasion, and the message.

5. Choose an appropriate time to speak. If you have a choice about whether you will give your speech first, last, or somewhere in between, pick the time that works best for you. Some speakers become more nervous when they sit and listen to others, so they are better off speaking early in the class period. Others find that listening to their peers calms them, so they are better off speaking later in

We tend to feel more confident when we know we look good.

the class period. If given a chance, choose to speak at the time that is optimal for you.

6. **Use positive self-talk.** Immediately prior to getting up to speak, coach yourself with a short "pregame pep talk." Remind yourself about the importance of what you have to say. Remember all the hard work you have done to be prepared and recall how good you are when you are at your best. Remind yourself that nervousness is normal and useful. Tell yourself that you are confident and ready. And remember that *what* you say to yourself is just as important as *how* you address yourself. Use self-distancing self-talk to address yourself as "you" or by your first name. Doing so will bolster your confidence and help you perform better.

7. **Face the audience with confidence.** When it is time, walk purposefully to the front. Plant yourself firmly yet comfortably and take a second or two to look at the audience. Take a deep breath (you might even silently count to five while reviewing the first lines of your speech in your head) and begin your well-rehearsed introduction.

8. **Focus on sharing your message.** Although you may feel nervous, your audience rarely "sees" it. Continue to focus on sharing your ideas with the audience rather than focusing on your nerves.

2-3 DEVELOPING AN EFFECTIVE SPEECH PLAN

Whether you are a marketing account manager presenting an advertising campaign idea to clients, a coach trying to motivate your team for its game with your arch rival, or a student giving a speech in class, you can manage anxiety, demonstrate confidence, and be more effective when you develop and follow an effective **speech plan**—a strategy for achieving your speech goal.

In this section and throughout the book, we will work through a six-step process for planning and preparing speeches grounded in the works of major speech scholars across the ages. Ancient Roman philosophers actually clarified five general rules for effective public speeches more than 2,000 years ago. These rules, known as the **canons of rhetoric**, still hold true today.[40] These five canons are *invention* (an effective speech has convincing content), *arrangement* (an effective speech is clearly organized), *style* (an effective speech uses appropriate language), *delivery* (an effective speaker delivers the speech with confidence, fluency,

and strategic retention aids), and *memory* (an effective speaker rehearses the speech and creates prompts to remember the speech during delivery).

While classical approaches to speech planning were speaker-focused, scholars now recognize that effective speeches are audience-centered and address the rhetorical situation.[41] The speechmaking skills we propose, therefore, are both rooted in ancient wisdom and informed by contemporary research. The six Speech Action Plan steps are:

1. Determine a speech goal that is appropriate to the rhetorical situation.

2. Understand your audience and adapt to it.

3. Gather and evaluate information.

4. Organize ideas into a well-structured outline.

5. Choose, prepare, and use appropriate presentational aids.

6. Practice oral language and delivery style.

These steps are also illustrated in Exhibit 2.5. Let's briefly preview what you will learn in each step.

2-3a Step 1: Select a Specific Speech Goal That Is Appropriate to the Rhetorical Situation

Your **speech goal** is a specific statement of what you want your audience to know, believe, or do. To arrive at an appropriate speech goal, you need to consider yourself as the speaker, the audience, and the occasion. Doing so will encourage your audience to pay attention because they will perceive your speech as relevant to them.

Begin by selecting a topic that you know something about, that interests you, and is important to you. Although you might occasionally speak on a topic that is unfamiliar to you, you will usually speak on topics that meet these tests.

Next you need to think about your audience so you can address the topic in ways that will be relevant to their needs, interests, and desires. Who are they? What do they need to know about your topic? What do they already know? To answer these questions, you need to make a preliminary audience analysis based on their gender, culture,

> **speech plan** a strategy for achieving your speech goal
>
> **canons of rhetoric** five general rules for effective public speeches
>
> **speech goal** a specific statement of what you want your audience to know, believe, or do

average age, education level, occupation, income level, and group affiliation. Then you can assess the kinds of material and information they are likely to be motivated to listen to.

You also need to consider the occasion. What is the size of the audience? When will the speech be given? Where will the speech be given? Are there any peculiarities of the room? What is the time limit for the speech? What are the particular expectations for the speech?

Once you determine a topic based on your interest and expertise, the audience, and the occasion, you are ready to phrase your speech goal. Every speech has a general and a specific goal. For most classroom speeches, the general goal is usually either to inform, where your goal is shared understanding, or to persuade, where your goal is to convince your audience to believe something or persuade them to take action. We will discuss several other general goals, which Aristotle called *ceremonial speeches* (e.g., to introduce, to entertain, and to celebrate), in later chapters.[42]

Your specific speech goal articulates exactly what you want your audience to understand, believe, or do. For instance, Glen, a bioengineering major, might phrase his persuasive speech goal as, "I want to convince my audience of the value of genetic engineering." Keith was glad his supervisor told everyone to focus on the same three main points for this speech. He phrased his specific speech goal as, "I want my audience to understand a bit about my personal background, what I am majoring in, and what I plan to do when I graduate."

For any speech, it is important to consider the audience's initial level of interest in your goal, their ability to understand the content of the speech, and their attitude toward you and your topic. If you believe your audience has very little interest in your topic, you will need to adapt by explaining how and why the topic is important or relevant to them. Not only will you need to adapt your speech by piquing audience interest, but if you believe that your audience doesn't know much about your topic, you will want to provide the basic information they need to understand your speech.

Finally, you will need to adapt to your audience's initial attitude toward your topic.

2-3c Step 3: Gather and Evaluate Information

In addition to drawing on material from your own knowledge and experiences, you can draw on the expertise of others by reading printed materials, conducting interviews and surveys, and searching online. You should gather and evaluate verbal, visual, and audiovisual material that you might draw on to develop your speech outline or your presentational aids. You will need to evaluate the information and sources and select only the items you deem to be truthful and credible. For instance, as a student of bioengineering, Glen is able to explain the process of genetic engineering because he has studied it in his classes. His

2-3b Step 2: Understand Your Audience and Adapt to It

Once you have a clear and specific speech goal based on the speaker, audience, and occasion, you begin the task of understanding your audience more fully and how to adapt your speech to it. Recall from Chapter 1 that audience adaptation is the process of tailoring your speech's information to the needs, interests, and expectations of your listeners. You will want to do so continually throughout the speech-planning and practicing process.

The specific goal of your speech will depend on your audience.

Rawpixel/Shutterstock.com

personal knowledge also helps him evaluate and select additional information and sources he locates doing research on his topic.

2-3d Step 4: Organize Ideas into a Well-Structured Outline

Begin organizing your speech by identifying the two to four major ideas you want your audience to remember. Then turn each major idea into a complete sentence. These sentences will become the main points for the body of your speech. Next you combine your speech goal with each major idea into a succinct thesis statement that describes specifically what you want your audience to understand, believe, or do when you have finished speaking. This process provides the overarching framework, or macrostructure, of your speech.

Africa Studio/Shutterstock.com

Main points must be arranged in an organizational framework that helps the audience understand and remember them. Two of the most basic organizational frameworks are chronological and topical. **Chronological** means following an order that moves from first to last. You can see by looking at Keith's thesis statement with main point preview that his speech will be organized chronologically. **Topical** means following an order of interest. For instance, Gina, who decides to inform her audience about the three proven methods for removing harmful toxins from the body, may begin with the simplest one—keeping hydrated—and ending with the most difficult one—eating more natural whole foods.

Having identified and ordered the main points, you are ready to outline the speech body. You do so by adding information as subpoints to support each of your two to four main points. At least one subpoint used to elaborate on each main point should provide listener relevance by articulating why or how the information relates to the audience's needs, interests, or desires.

After you have outlined the speech body, you will outline your introduction and conclusion. Your introduction should get attention, establish listener relevance and speaker credibility, and lead into the body of the speech. Your conclusion should provide closure by reminding the audience of your main points and speech goal in a positively memorable way.

2-3e Step 5: Choose, Prepare, and Use Appropriate Presentational Aids

We live in what many have dubbed the "digital age." As a result of the plethora of technological sources available to us—computers, laptops, iPads, iPods, smartphones, etc.— today we need to present public speeches via multimodal messages (visual, oral, written) and channels (face-to-face, print, technology-enhanced). Whereas presentational aids were once considered optional embellishments, today most audiences expect them. So, even for a very short speech, you may decide to use a presentational aid to clarify, emphasize, or dramatize your goal and main points. You might use computer technology to help you convey various ideas through models, charts, graphs, pictures, audios, videos, or audiovisuals. Note in your outline precisely where you will use them and practice using them when you rehearse your speech.

2-3f Step 6: Practice Oral Language and Delivery Style

In your practice sessions, you need to choose the wording of main points and supporting materials carefully. If you have not practiced various ways of phrasing your key ideas, you run the risk of missing a major opportunity for communicating your ideas effectively. In practice sessions, work on the appropriateness, accuracy, clarity, and vividness of your wording. Recall that these language choices make up the microstructure of your speech.

Although a speech is composed of words, how effective you will be is also largely a matter of how well you use your voice and body to deliver your speech. You will want to present the speech intelligibly (i.e., in a way that others will understand it), conversationally, and expressively. You will also want to use good posture and eye contact (look at

chronological following an order that moves from first to last

topical following an order of interest

members of the audience while you are speaking) to appear confident and comfortable, as well as use facial expressions and gestures that emphasize emotional intentions and clarify structure.

Very few people can present speeches effectively without considerable practice. Practicing out loud gives you confidence that you can talk conversationally and expressively to accomplish your speech goal within the time limit. Don't try to memorize the speech, which is likely to increase anxiety because you may fear forgetting what you planned to say. Instead, practice delivering your speech extemporaneously based on speaking notes consisting of key words and phrases that remind you of structure, main points, and delivery cues.

Exhibit 2.5 summarizes the six action steps of an effective speech plan in outline form. These steps will be explained in more detail in later chapters of this book. As you read, you will see specific speech-preparation activities that are related to each action step. By completing all of these activities, you will gain confidence in your ability to be effective when you give your speech.

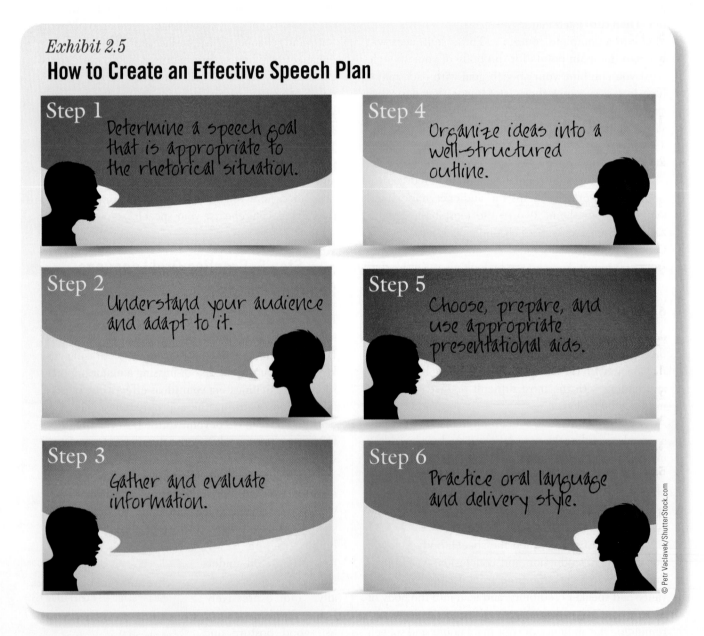

Exhibit 2.5

How to Create an Effective Speech Plan

Step 1 Determine a speech goal that is appropriate to the rhetorical situation.

Step 2 Understand your audience and adapt to it.

Step 3 Gather and evaluate information.

Step 4 Organize ideas into a well-structured outline.

Step 5 Choose, prepare, and use appropriate presentational aids.

Step 6 Practice oral language and delivery style.

© Petr Vaclavek/ShutterStock.com

Self-Introduction Speech
Evaluation Checklist

You can use this checklist to critique a speech of self-introduction that you hear in class. (You can also use it to critique your own speech.) As you listen to the speaker, consider what makes a speech effective. Then answer the following questions.

Content

1. Were all main points addressed per the assignment? _____

2. Were two or three pieces of evidence used to develop each main point (breadth)? _____

3. Was one extended piece of evidence used to add depth? _____

4. Were listener-relevance links provided for each main point? _____

5. Did presentational aids enhance clarity, embellish key ideas, or dramatize an important point? _____

6. Did the speech fall within the time constraints of the assignment? _____

Structure

1. Did the speech provide all the basic elements of an effective speech: introduction, body, conclusion, and transitions? _____ (macrostructure)

2. Did the introduction catch the audience's interest? _____ identify the speech topic/goal? _____ preview the main points? _____

3. Were transitions provided between each main point? _____

4. Did the conclusion remind the audience of the main points? _____ motivate the audience to remember the main ideas of the speech? _____

5. Did the speaker use words that were appropriate and inclusive? _____ accurate and clear? _____ vivid and expressive? _____ (microstructure) _____

6. Were the presentational aids constructed and displayed effectively? _____

Delivery

1. Was the speaker intelligible in terms of volume? _____ rate? _____ pronunciation? _____ enunciation? _____

2. Was the speaker conversational? _____

3. Did the speaker look up from his or her notes most of the time and make eye contact with the audience? _____

4. Did the speaker appear professional, poised, and confident? _____

5. Was the speaker expressive in terms of changes in rate and volume? _____ strategic pauses? _____ appropriate facial expressions? _____ appropriate gestures? _____

6. Did the speaker integrate presentational aids gracefully? _____

Based on these criteria, evaluate the speech (check one):

☐ **excellent**   ☐ **good**   ☐ **satisfactory**   ☐ **fair**   ☐ **poor**

I Choose Robots

What follows is an outline of Keith's speech of self-introduction. As you read, consider how you might address the rhetorical situation effectively as you develop a speech of self-introduction for your own audience. How will you develop your content including presentational aids, organize your ideas, and practice your delivery?

Use the speech evaluation checklist that follows this outline to evaluate Keith's content (breadth, depth, listener relevance, choice of presentational aids), structure (macrostructure, microstructure, construction of presentational aids), and delivery (voice, body, integration of presentational aids).

Speech Outline

I Choose Robots

General Goal:
To introduce oneself

Introduction

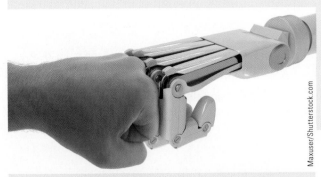

Maxuser/Shutterstock.com

I. Robots. For this speech I got to thinking, how would my friends and family describe me in one sentence? Keith loves Robots.

Attention getter

II. When you come from a family of imaginative thinkers, you might think it would be easy to follow in their footsteps. For instance, my dad collects hot air balloons and rides them in various parts of the world. My mother is a professor of archeology, and has spent her career studying the Incas of Peru. But before I became interested in robot technology, unlike other kids my age who loved music or playing soccer, I never had a passion.

Listener relevance and credibility

III. When I was 15, after watching a documentary on robot engineering, I became fascinated by the idea of building one of my own. Shortly after, I assembled my first robot in the 9th grade: a chicken that could peck with wheels for talons. From then on I was hooked. Now, as a student of Robotic Engineering at Georgia Institute of Technology, I am thrilled to be your new Industrial Robotics and Engineering Intern.

Body

I. Robotics is more than the attempt to build objects that mimic life; robotics improve life.

First main point

A. Last summer, as the Engineering Intern for the Metropolitan Transportation Authority in New York City, I learned firsthand how engineering can change people's lives.

Subpoint (listener relevance)

1. Up until that point, I had never used technology to build something that directly affected a large group of people.

2. Our team created more efficient and safer mechanisms for subway car transportation.

3. When I learned that 5.6 million people use the New York City subway system in one week, I realized then that engineering had led me to something much larger than myself.

B. When Albert Einstein discovered his Special Theory of Relativity, he called it the "happiest moment of my life." **Subpoint**

1. I think we can agree most people don't pay attention to who is designing their subway car; they just ride it.

2. When I started to see how science could affect the world, and remain relatively unknown to others, it didn't make me upset, but the opposite.

3. I felt like a secret agent, seeking out problems and hunting down solutions, all unbeknownst to the everyday civilian.

Transition

Now that you know a little more about me, what makes me tick, and what brought me to this company, I'd like to share my goals for this summer as the Industrial Robotics and Engineering Intern.

II. I love engineering because it gives me the power to alter the systems of infrastructure that shape our world. Isn't it exciting to be able to improve a stranger's life? **Second main point**

A. That's why I find consumers and products to be so interesting.

B. In my internship position this summer I plan to accomplish three things at our company:

1. Help streamline assembly line efficiency.

2. Find new uses for robotics in product manufacturing. **Subpoints (listener relevance)**

3. Build models for future technologies and programs.

C. I'm additionally interested in researching how other companies achieve similar results, and how we can use Industrial Robotics to make our product the most energy efficient, and produce them in the fastest time possible.

Transition

As I move forward in my career after college, I hope to design cost-efficient robot systems that create incentives for businesses to invest in green technology.

III.

A. Green technology is a field with many theoretical and practical challenges. One of the biggest problems I see in developing green energy technology is making it cost effective for consumers and fiscally advantageous for investors.

B. In order to make environmentally friendly technology, most investors will need the promise of a fiscal gain in order to make it happen. **Subpoints (listener relevance)**

1. That is why for my senior thesis, I am currently designing mockups for a solar powered robot with a sustained battery life that can manually adjust its own solar panels to catch the most light.

2. One of the disadvantages of solar power energy is that devices using solar energy can only operate when conditions are sunny. Next year at college, I plan on creating a model that can hold its charge for long periods of time without sun.

C. By designing a solar powered robot with sustained battery life, I hope to achieve four main things: **Subpoint**

1. Work toward achieving eventual cost benefits when using green technology.

2. Develop interest on campus surrounding green technology.

3. Attract the attention of companies that are seeking to develop their own green technology.

4. Eventually build a solar robot model that can be modified and used by anyone from car manufacturers to agricultural companies.

Conclusion

I. The field of robot engineering is incredibly wide reaching and vast. Georgia Tech is currently sending its robot Icefin to probe for undocumented sea life not only beneath Antarctica's Ross Ice Shelf, but inside the oceans of Jupiter's moon, Europa, as well.

II. As a Georgia Tech student, I'm eager to bring my knowledge of industrial robot technology to the company, and work with new and exciting concepts.

Thesis restatement with main point review

III. In my favorite robot movie, *The Iron Giant*, the gentle giant says: "You are who you choose to be." I believe by choosing to create innovative robot technology, we can design new production methods, achieve higher manufacturing standards, make better products for consumers, and improve the world for all of us who share it.

Clincher

References

Chappell, Bill (2015, May 01). Tesla CEO Elon Musk Unveils Home Battery; Is $3,000 Cheap Enough? National Public Radio. Retrieved online from http://www.npr.org/sections/thetwo-way/2015/05/01/403529202/tesla-ceo-elon-musk-unveils-home-battery-is-3-000-cheap-enough.

Cardwell, Diane (2015, April 18). Solar Power Battle Puts Hawaii at Forefront of Worldwide Changes. New York Times. Retrieved online from http://www.nytimes.com/2015/04/19/business/energy-environment/solar-power-battle-puts-hawaii-at-forefront-of-worldwide-changes.html?smprod=nytcore-iphone&smid=nytcore-iphone-share&_r=2.

Israel, Brett (2015, April 2). New robotic vehicle provides a never-before-seen look under Antarctica. Research Horizons. Retrieved online from http://www.rh.gatech.edu/news/393131/new-robotic-vehicle-provides-never-seen-look-under-antarctica.

Modern Materials Handling Staff (2015, May 25). Industrial robotics market to reach $44.48 billion by 2020. Modern Materials Handling. Retrieved online from http://www.mmh.com/article/industrial_robotics_market_to_reach_44.48_billion_by_2020.

Woody, Todd (2012, October 31). How Robots Are Making Solar Power Cheaper. Forbes. Retrieved online from http://www.forbes.com/sites/toddwoody/2012/10/31/how-robots-are-making-solar-power-cheaper/.

Wudka, Jose (1998, September 24). In context: What Albert Einstein said when he discovered his Special Theory of Relativity. University of California, Riverside. Retrieved online from http://physics.ucr.edu/~wudka/Physics7/Notes_www/node85.html.

In context: example of a recognized robotics event. Retrieved online from http://www.msichicago.org/whats-here/events/national-robotics-week/.

In context: how many people ride the New York City subway in a week. MTA. Retrieved online from http://web.mta.info/nyct/facts/ffsubway.htm.

STUDY TOOLS 2

LOCATED IN TEXTBOOK

☐ Tear-out Chapter Review cards at the end of the book

☐ Review with the Quick Quiz below

LOCATED ON SPEAK3 ONLINE AT CENGAGEBRAIN.COM

☐ Review Key Term flashcards and create your own cards

☐ Track your knowledge and understanding of key concepts in speech communication

☐ Complete practice and graded quizzes to prepare for tests

☐ Complete interactive content within SPEAK3 Online

☐ View the chapter highlight boxes for SPEAK3 Online

Quick Quiz (answers in Solutions Appendix)

T F 1. Speaking apprehension may actually make you a better speaker.

T F 2. During the adaptation phase, a speaker's level of anxiety begins to decrease.

T F 3. One way to reduce public speaking apprehension is to develop a mental picture of giving a great speech.

T F 4. For most people, speaking apprehension results from previous negative experiences in public speaking.

T F 5. Public speaking apprehension occurs only in the moments before giving a speech.

6. Which of the following is not a specific technique for managing apprehension?

a. practicing the speech aloud
b. using relaxation exercises
c. writing a very short speech
d. allowing sufficient preparation time
e. using presentation aids

7. The symptoms of public speaking apprehension can be cognitive, physical, or:

a. existential
b. emotional
c. tactile
d. intellectual
e. spiritual

8. The process of tailoring a speech's information to the needs, interests, and expectations of the audience is called:

a. audience analysis
b. audience interpretation
c. audience adaptation
d. audience scanning
e. audience examination

9. The first step of effective speech planning is:

a. practicing oral language and delivery style
b. gathering and evaluating information to use
c. understanding your audience and adapting to it
d. selecting a speech goal that is appropriate to the rhetorical situation
e. choosing, preparing, and using appropriate presentational aids

10. The three phases that most speakers proceed through in dealing with apprehension are:

a. confrontation, adaptation, transformation
b. anticipation, education, illustration
c. causation, confrontation, conciliation
d. solicitation, conduction, mentalization
e. anticipation, confrontation, adaptation

Chapter Takeaways

List three key takeaways from this chapter:

-

-

-

3 Listening and Responding

After finishing this chapter go to **PAGE 50** for **STUDY TOOLS.**

LEARNING OUTCOMES

3-1 Explain what listening is and why it's important to study in a public speaking course.

3-2 Describe why effective listening is so challenging.

3-3 Employ specific strategies to improve your listening skills.

3-4 Practice providing constructive speech critiques.

Sound Familiar?

Bart storms into the kitchen and bursts out, "Beth, do you have my car keys? I can't find them, and I have to go—now!"

Every time Beth tries to answer, Bart interrupts her. He's getting increasingly exasperated, but he won't stop long enough to listen. Finally, Beth takes his hands, looks him in the eye, and says firmly, "Bart, listen. I went out this morning, so I left the keys in the car for you."

"Gee whiz, Beth, why didn't you tell me?"

Does this conversation sound familiar? Do you ever find yourself jumping to conclusions like Bart, especially when you're under pressure? We shouldn't underestimate the importance of listening; it can provide clarification, help us understand and remember material, improve our personal and professional relationships, and increase our ability to evaluate information effectively.[1] In fact, survey after survey reports that listening is one of the most important skills employers seek in job candidates.[2] What is somewhat troubling, however, is the fact that fewer than 2 percent of us have had any formal listening training.[3] So the skills you learn and apply from this chapter will set you apart in ways that will benefit you both personally and professionally.

We begin with a discussion of what listening is and some challenges we must overcome to listen effectively. Then we offer several specific strategies to improve listening skills related to each of the steps in the active listening process. Finally, we provide guidelines to follow as you prepare effective and ethical constructive speech critiques.

3-1 WHAT IS LISTENING?

Recall that communication is the process of creating shared meaning. So to be effective, *speakers* must present messages clearly and compellingly AND *listeners* must accurately interpret what is said.

People sometimes make the mistake of thinking that hearing and listening are the same thing, but they're not. **Hearing** is a physiological process and listening is a cognitive one. According to the International Listening Association, "**Listening** is the process of receiving, attending to, constructing meaning from, and responding to spoken or nonverbal messages."[4] Listening is important because 50 percent or more of the time we spend communicating involves listening.[5] Yet, even when we try to listen carefully, most of us remember on average only about 45 percent of what we hear the hour after hearing it and only about 30 percent two days later.[6]

As we've already mentioned, effective listening is a key to success in most occupations. Listening skills have long been recognized as an important skill in the corporate environment[7]; in a recent survey of CEO performance evaluations, only 23.2 percent of respondents said that listening skills were one of their CEO's biggest strengths.[8] Moreover, nearly 21 percent of respondents cited a lack of listening skills as their CEO's biggest weakness.[9] Listening skills (or lack thereof) are often at the root of company success or failure. When

hearing the physiological process that occurs when the brain detects sound waves

listening the process of receiving, attending to, constructing meaning from, and responding to spoken or nonverbal messages

How would you describe this type of listening?

want to really understand and critically evaluate the worth of a message, we engage in *critical listening*. Because we need to hear, understand, evaluate, and assign worth to the message, as well as remember and recall it, critical listening requires more psychological processing than the other types of listening.[11]

3-2 LISTENING CHALLENGES

To become effective listeners in any situation, we first need to overcome four key challenges. These challenges are rooted in our listening apprehension, our biases, our preferred listening style, and our approach to processing what we hear.

3-2a Apprehension

Listening apprehension is the anxiety we feel about listening. Listening apprehension may increase when we are worried about misinterpreting the message or when we are concerned about how the message may affect us psychologically.[12] For example, if you're in an important meeting or job training session, you may worry about trying to absorb all the important technical information needed to do your job well. Or you might feel anxiety when the material you need to absorb is difficult or confusing. Likewise, your anxiety may increase when you feel ill, tired, or stressed about something else going on in your life at the time. Listening apprehension makes it difficult to focus on the message.

3-2b Bias

All people bring their own biases to a communication event, and those biases influence how well we listen. Biases can interfere with effective listening. For example, if you have strong opinions about public education in your community, you may find yourself mentally arguing with a speaker who expresses ideas that conflict with your opinions.

In addition to the philosophical biases we carry into a listening situation, other implicit biases can prevent us from being good listeners. For example, when you call a customer service line, consider how your reactions differ if you are connected to a representative whose native language is English compared to a representative who is a nonnative English speaker. Research has long shown that people of all ages and ethnicities exhibit some degree of visual implicit association bias,[13] and recently the same has been shown for speech interactions as well. Listeners commonly experience greater challenges understanding and listening to foreign-accented speech, and those challenges influence a listener's perceptions about speakers with accents.[14]

employees fail to listen effectively to instructions, they usually make mistakes. Mistakes cost the organization time and money. And when supervisors don't listen effectively to employees when they share their creative ideas and solutions or concerns about potential problems, again, the result may be lost time and money. A supervisor's lack of effective listening behaviors can also cause their employees to feel emotionally exhausted and influence whether they intend to quit or stay with the company.[10] Of course, when employees do not listen and respond to customers, they are bound to fail. So it simply makes sense to improve listening skills.

We choose to listen for various reasons depending on the situation. For example, when we listen to music for enjoyment and to speakers because we like their style, we engage in *appreciative listening*. When we listen to infer what more a speaker might mean beyond the actual words being spoken, we engage in *discriminative listening*. For instance, when a doctor is explaining test results, we might also try to discern whether the results are troubling or routine. When our goal is to understand, remember, and recall information—for example, material a professor shares during a classroom lecture—we engage in *comprehensive listening*. When we listen to provide emotional support, we engage in *empathic listening*. Finally, when we

listening apprehension the anxiety we feel about listening

© Daniel_Dash/ShutterStock.com

3-2c Style

Listening style is our favored and usually unconscious approach to listening.[15] Each of us favors one of four listening styles, and only a few people can switch effectively between styles based on the situation.[16]

Content-oriented listeners focus on and evaluate the facts and evidence. Content-oriented listeners appreciate details and enjoy processing complex messages that may include a good deal of technical information. Content-oriented listeners are likely to ask questions to get even more information.

People-oriented listeners focus on the feelings their conversational partners may have about what they are saying. For example, people-oriented listeners tend to notice whether their partners are pleased or upset and will encourage them to continue based on nonverbal cues like head nods, eye contact, and smiles.

Action-oriented listeners focus on the ultimate point the speaker is trying to make. Action-oriented listeners tend to get frustrated when ideas are disorganized and when people ramble. Action-oriented listeners also often anticipate what the speaker is going to say and may even finish the speaker's sentence for them.

Finally, **time-oriented listeners** prefer brief and hurried conversations and often use nonverbal and verbal cues to signal that their partner needs to be more concise. Time-oriented listeners may tell others exactly how much time they have to listen; interrupt when they feel time pressures; regularly check the time on their smartphones, watches, or clocks; and may even nod their heads rapidly to encourage others to pick up the pace.

Each of these styles has advantages and disadvantages. Content-oriented listeners are likely to understand and remember details but miss the overall point of the message and be unaware of the speaker's feelings. People-oriented listeners are likely to understand how the speaker feels, empathize, and offer comfort and support. However, they might become so focused on the speaker's feelings that they miss important details or fail to evaluate the facts offered as evidence. Action-oriented listeners may notice inconsistencies but, because they tend to anticipate what will be said rather than hearing the speaker out, may miss important details. Finally, time-oriented listeners are prone only to partially listen

Time-oriented listeners often use verbal and non-verbal cues to signal that a conversation needs to be more precise.

to messages while also thinking about their time constraints; thus, they might miss important details and be insensitive to their partner's emotional needs. In our opening scenario, Bart fell victim to the consequences of being too action-oriented and time-oriented when listening to Beth. With these challenges in mind, let's turn now to some specific techniques we can employ to improve our active listening skills in both face-to-face and virtual settings.

3-2d Processing Approach

Research suggests that people tend to listen in two ways—passively or actively—based on the rhetorical situation. In other words, we listen more carefully when the topic seems important (exigence) to us (audience), we trust and respect the sender, and during times when we are not constrained by other distractions or obligations (occasion). **Passive listening** is the habitual and unconscious process of receiving messages. When we listen passively, we are on automatic pilot. We may attend only to certain parts of a message and assume the rest. We tend to listen passively when we aren't really interested or when we are trying to multitask. By contrast, **active listening** is the deliberate and conscious process of attending to, understanding, remembering, evaluating, and responding to messages. Active listening requires practice. The rest of this chapter focuses on helping you become a better active listener.

listening style our favored and usually unconscious approach to listening

content-oriented listeners listeners who focus on and evaluate the facts and evidence

people-oriented listeners listeners who focus on the feelings their conversational partners may have about what they are saying

action-oriented listeners listeners who focus on the ultimate point the speaker is trying to make

time-oriented listeners listeners who prefer brief and hurried conversations and often use nonverbal and verbal cues to signal that their partner needs to be more concise

passive listening the habitual and unconscious process of receiving messages

active listening the deliberate and conscious process of attending to, understanding, remembering, evaluating, and responding to messages

3-3 ACTIVE LISTENING IMPROVEMENT STRATEGIES

Effective active listening is a complex psychological process made up of five steps. In this section, we offer techniques to improve listening related to each step (see Exhibit 3.1).

3-3a Attending

Effective active listening begins with attending. **Attending** is the process of intentionally perceiving and focusing on a message.[17] Poor listeners have difficulty exercising control over what they attend to, often letting their mind drift to thoughts totally unrelated to the topic. One reason for this is because people typically speak at a rate of about 120 to 150 words per minute, but our brains can process between 400 and 800 words per minute.[18] This means we usually assume we know what a speaker is going to say before he or she finishes saying it. So our minds have lots of time to wander from the message. In our opening vignette, for example, Bart seemed to have trouble attending to Beth, in part, because he thought he knew what she was going to say before she said it.

attending the process of intentionally perceiving and focusing on a message

Not only does the gap between speaking rate and processing create opportunities for inattention, but research suggests that the average attention span for adults today is 20 minutes or less.[19] Some reports even claim that, thanks to the Internet, satellite TV, DVR, and smartphone technology, our attention spans have become considerably shorter.[20] Consider your own experiences listening to speeches, class lectures, and other extended presentations. Do you ever find yourself daydreaming, texting, checking email or Facebook, or even adding pins to your Pinterest boards? Do you find yourself multitasking in similar ways when participating in a teleconference, webinar, or other online presentation?

The first step to becoming an effective active listener, then, is to train ourselves to focus on or *attend* to what people are saying regardless of potential distractions. Let's consider four techniques for doing so.

1. Get physically ready to listen. Good listeners create a physical environment that reduces potential distractions and adopt a listening posture. For example, you might turn off background music, your cell phone, and your computer so you won't be tempted to turn your attention to them when you are trying to listen. You can also adopt a listening posture by sitting upright in your chair, leaning slightly forward, and looking directly at the speaker or screen.[21]

Exhibit 3.1
Effective and Ineffective Listening Behaviors

	Effective Listening Behavior	Ineffective Listening Behavior
Attending to the Speech	Physically and mentally focusing on what is being said, even when information doesn't seem relevant Adjusting listening behavior to the specific requirements of the situation	Seeming to listen but looking out the window and letting your mind wander Listening the same way regardless of the type of material being presented
Understanding/ Remembering Speech Information	Determining organization by identifying goals, main points, and supporting information Asking yourself questions to help you identify key aspects of the speech Silently paraphrasing to solidify understanding Seeking out subtle meanings based on nonverbal cues Taking good notes	Listening to individual bits of information without regard for structure Seldom or never reconsidering what was said Seldom or never paraphrasing Ignoring nonverbal cues Relying on memory alone
Evaluating and Responding	Assessing quality of content, structure, and delivery	Relying on gut reactions

Smartphones are just one source of electronic distraction in our world. When listening to a speaker, having the device in an inaccessible place may help you focus as a listener.

consciously considering how we might benefit from learning the information to improve some aspect of our life.

3-3b Understanding

Understanding is accurately interpreting a message. Sometimes we may not fully understand a speaker's message because the speaker uses words that are not in our vocabulary or discusses complex technical concepts that are new to us. Other times, we might miss the emotional intent of the message. Let's discuss four strategies that can improve listening to understand.

2. Resist mental distractions. Work consciously to block out wandering thoughts while listening to a speech or webcast that might come from a visual distraction (e.g., someone entering the room), an auditory distraction (e.g., people chatting), or a physical distraction (e.g., headache, growling stomach). In today's culture, smartphones and tablets are a routine, if not perpetual, source of distraction—even when the device is set to silent, its presence alone can tempt our minds to wander away from the speaker. A successful technique for resisting such distractions is to remove them.[22] For example, put your phone or tablet in an inconvenient or inaccessible location or give it to a friend for the duration of a speech.

3. Hear the speaker out. Far too often, we stop listening because we disagree with something a speaker says, we assume we know what the speaker is going to say, or we become offended by an example or word used. We must train ourselves not to interrupt or even mentally argue with a speaker and stay focused throughout the message. When Beth realized Bart was not hearing her out, she helped him regain focus by taking his hands in hers and looking him in the eye.

4. Find personal relevance. Sometimes speakers articulate relevance for us, as when a professor says, "Pay attention because this will be on the test." But we can also discover relevance for ourselves by

1. Identify the goal and main points. Sometimes peoples' thoughts are well organized and easy to follow. Other times, however, we must work hard to decode the speaker's goal, main points, and some of the key details.

For instance, during a PTA meeting, a teacher gives a short presentation on the problem of bullying. Her goal is to explain what can be done in school to deter this behavior. In her speech, she presents two main ideas: what teachers can do and what students who are harassed can do. She gives examples, statistics, and specific recommendations to develop each of the points she makes. When she is finished, audience members who have listened carefully can remember her goal and state steps that both teachers and harassed students can take, even though they may not remember the specific examples and statistics that she used to develop each point. To be an effective listener, ask yourself, "What does the speaker want me to know or do?" (goal); then ask, "What are each of the main points?"; and finally ask, "What details explain or support each of the main points?"

2. Ask questions. A **question** is a statement designed to clarify information or get additional details. Although ethical listeners demonstrate respect by waiting until

understanding accurately interpreting a message

question a statement designed to clarify information or get additional details

the speaker is finished to ask questions, you can make notes of any questions you have as you listen. Some of these questions may eventually be answered as the speaker moves through the presentation. However, others may not. Then, you can pose these remaining questions during the question-and-answer period following the presentation, privately approach the speaker after the presentation, or use the questions to do additional research about the topic yourself later.

3. Paraphrase silently. Paraphrasing is putting a message into your own words. It is not simply repeating what is said. After listening, try to summarize your understanding. So, after the speaker explains the criteria for selecting the best cell phone plan, you might say to yourself, "In other words, the key to deciding whether an unlimited plan is cost effective depends on how many minutes I'm likely to spend talking and texting on the phone each month."

4. Observe nonverbal cues. We interpret messages more accurately when we observe the nonverbal behaviors that accompany the words. Good speakers use their tone of voice, facial expressions, and gestures to emphasize important points and clarify structure. You can improve your listening skills by noticing where and how the speaker is attempting to emphasize or clarify points and then keying in on those comments. Had Bart observed Beth's nonverbal cues, he could have saved himself unnecessary emotional frustration about finding his keys and getting to school in time for class.

3-3c Remembering

Remembering is being able to retain and recall information later. In other words, it is the process of moving information from short-term to long-term memory. We may find remembering difficult, for instance, because we filter out information that doesn't fit our listening style, our listening anxiety prevents us from recalling what we have heard, we engage in passive listeing, we practice selective listening and remember only what supports our position, and we fall victim to the primacy-recency effect of remembering only what is said at the beginning and end of a message. Let's consider three techniques to improve memory.

1. Repeat the information. Repetition—saying something mentally two,

Repetition helps store information in your long-term memory.

Brian A Jackson/Shutterstock.com

three, or four times—helps store information in long-term memory.[23] So if a speaker makes an important point or offers a key statistic, repeat it in your head two or three times to help make it "stick."

2. Construct mnemonics. A mnemonic device associates a special word or very short statement with new and longer information. One of the most common mnemonic techniques is to form a word with the first letters of a list of items you are trying to remember. For example, most beginning music students learn the mnemonic "*every good boy does fine*" for the notes on the lines of the treble clef (E, G, B, D, F) and the word *face* (F, A, C, E) for the notes on the spaces of the treble. So you might try to construct a mnemonic to help remember the two to four main points in a speech.

3. Take notes. Note taking is a powerful method for improving your memory of what you have heard in a speech. Not only does note taking provide a written record that you can go back to, but by taking notes you also take a more active role in the listening process.[24]

What constitutes good notes varies by situation. For a short speech, good notes may consist of a statement of the goal, a brief list of main points, and a few of the most significant details. Or they might be a short summary of the entire concept (a type of paraphrase). For lengthy presentations, good notes will also include more detailed statements of supporting material, as

paraphrasing putting a message into your own words

mnemonic device a memory technique in which you associate a special word or very short statement with new and longer information

TECH TALK

Tech Talk—Does Technology Make It Easier or Harder to Listen?

For some of us, listening is no easy feat. Give us an empty room with a single speaker, and we'll still find a way to get lost in the ether of thought. The best listeners take good notes frequently to stay focused and ensure they comprehend the message being presented.

Computers, smartphones, and other mobile devices offer many useful tools to aide in note taking, from apps such as Evernote and OneNote that lend organization and structure to any stray thought, to recording software that can capture an entire spoken lecture and convert it into text. But is this technology improving our ability to listen and retain information, or simply adding to the noise?

While typing on a computer might enable faster, more accurate note taking, it doesn't help us actually encode that information very well. Research shows that multitasking taxes the brain and increases stress levels, diminishing productivity.[25] Unlike a pen and notebook, computers are full of distractions, from pop-up notifications to a seemingly harmless game of solitaire to the entire Internet. Only about 10 percent of the population possesses a brain suited for multitasking.[26]

Furthermore, a 2014 study from Princeton University and the University of California showed that taking notes longhand improves retention more than typing notes on a laptop—even when the laptop is used solely for note taking. Writing by hand takes longer and often requires the note taker to reframe the message in their own words, leading to better processing and learning overall.[27]

The same issue arises when recording with a smartphone. While you might capture the speaker's message word for word, your brain has more opportunity to idly wander. In an ideal scenario, however, you could write notes *while* recording, returning later to the transcript and comparing it with the notes for maximum retention.

As a listener, the best role for your technology is an auxiliary one. Keep your eyes and ears focused on the speaker, taking notes by hand when necessary. A smartphone recording can give you an opportunity to revisit the speaker's message, and note-taking software can help organize and clean up handwritten notes after the message has been delivered.

Taking notes longhand is shown to improve retention more than typing them on a laptop or other electronic device.

well as questions that arise while listening. And keep in mind that taking notes is not the same as taking dictation. Your goal is not to transcribe the speech but to capture its important points. Review the basics of effective listening and note taking by going to your SPEAK3 Online and reviewing: **Effective Listening and Note Taking.**

3-3d Evaluating

Evaluating is critically analyzing a message to determine its truthfulness, utility, and trustworthiness. Critical analysis is especially important when being persuaded to believe, support, or act on what was said. If you don't critically analyze messages, you risk being misinformed or, worse, going along with ideas that violate your values.

To evaluate messages effectively as you listen, try to separate facts from inferences. **Facts** are statements whose accuracy can be verified as true. If a statement is offered as a fact, analyze it thoughtfully to determine if it is true. **Inferences** are assertions based on the facts presented. When a speaker makes an inference, you need to determine whether the inference is valid. You can ask: (1) What are the facts that support this inference? (2) Is this information really central to the inference? (3) Is there other information that would contradict this inference? Separating facts from inferences helps us realize

> **evaluating** critically analyzing a message to determine its truthfulness, utility, and trustworthiness
>
> **facts** statements whose accuracy can be verified as true
>
> **inferences** assertions based on the facts presented

Preventing Listener Burnout

Listening takes effort and, like all pursuits that require energy, it's important to be mindful of the risks of burnout. Traci Ruble is a therapist who gets paid to listen, yet at home she had fallen into what she calls bad "listening hygiene." Listening burnout in her professional life was preventing her from listening to her family members. To overcome burnout and be a better listener, she recommends practicing these simple steps.

- Ask yourself if you want to listen. If the answer is no, identify the obstacle and postpone the conversation.

- Before listening, take a few deep breaths to help you slow down and be present in the moment.

- Remove distractions, especially digital ones, and give the person your full attention.

- Look the person in the eye and resist your own urges to talk. The person in the listening role should not be driving the conversation.[28]

the difference between a verifiable observation and an opinion related to that observation. Separating facts from inferences is important because inferences may be false, even if they are based on verifiable facts.

Also critical to evaluating the facts is knowing the source of those facts. Consider the reliability of the source of the information you are being presented. Today's media landscape includes many partial and impartial sources, and being able to differentiate between the two is a critical skill. During question and answer periods, ask speakers who do not cite their sources where they found their data and statistics. Adopting a critical perspective about where information and data come from will help you as a listener—and as a speech writer and speaker.

3-3e Responding

Responding is providing feedback. When Beth wasn't getting through to Bart, she added nonverbal cues to help him focus on what she was saying. Responding during a speech also usually occurs through nonverbal behaviors (e.g., smiling, head-nodding, brow-furrowing).

> **responding** providing feedback to the speaker; can be verbal or nonverbal
>
> **constructive critique** an evaluative response that identifies what was effective and what could be improved in a message

Sometimes, however, you need to prepare a formal written evaluation, or critique, of a presentation by a classmate, colleague, or employee. Typically, a critique is based on your critical analysis of how well the speech and speaker performed on specific key criteria. In the next section, we focus on techniques for responding effectively and ethically in constructive speech critiques.

3-4 CONSTRUCTIVE CRITIQUES

A **constructive critique** is an evaluative response that identifies what was effective and what could be improved in a message. Constructive critiques consist of statements that evaluate all elements of a speech.

3-4a Constructive Critique Statements

Constructive critique statements follow four guidelines.

1. Constructive critique statements are specific. Comments like "great job" or "slow down" are too vague to truly help a speaker improve. Instead, describe specific things the speaker did to make you conclude that the speech was great (or not so great). For example, you might tell the speaker that she used transitions in a way that helped you follow her train of thought or point out specific places where you would have liked her to present the material at a slower pace or show a supporting visual.

2. Constructive critique statements begin with observations about what was effective or done well. Begin with positive observations so that you reinforce what the speaker did well. When we are reinforced for what we have done, we are more likely to continue doing it. By the same token, there is room for improvement in any speech. Because the goal of a critique is to help the speaker improve, describe the specific problems you observe in the speech and then offer suggestions for overcoming them.

3. Constructive critique statements explain how and why the observed behavior affected the speech. For example, if you suggest that the speaker slow down while previewing the speech's main points, your statement will be more helpful if you also explain that the speaker's rate did not allow the audience time to remember the points.

4. Constructive critique statements are phrased as personal perceptions. You can ensure this by using "I" rather than "you" language. For example, instead of using "you" language to say, "You need to slow down," use "I" language: "During the preview of main points, I had trouble listening because they were presented faster than I could understand and remember them." In the "Sound Familiar?" section, Beth used "I" statements when trying to get Bart to comprehend her critique. Think about how much different the tone of her message would have been if she had said:

"Bart you're not listening to me. If you would ever listen to me you would understand that your keys are in your car. I left them there because I know you're in a hurry to get to class" rather than what she did say:

"Bart, listen. I've been trying to tell you—I went out to get milk this morning and knew you would be leaving soon, so I left the keys in the car for you."

3-4b Constructive Critique Elements

Constructive critiques consist of statements about a speech's content, structure, and delivery.

1. Content critique statements focus on the speech's goal, main points, and supporting material used to develop them. For example, you might comment on how effectively the speaker used reasoning to tie a piece of evidence to the main point it supports. Or you might comment on the breadth and depth of the information used to develop each main idea. You might observe how relevant, recent, or credible the speaker's evidence seemed to be. Or you might talk about how effective content offered in a presentational aid was or could have been. Exhibit 3.2 illustrates ineffective and effective constructive critique statements regarding content.

2. Structure critique statements focus on the speech's macrostructure (overall framework) and microstructure (language and style). You might provide feedback on elements of the introduction (e.g., attention grabber, listener relevance, speaker credibility, thesis statement with main point preview), body (e.g., organizational pattern, transitions), or conclusion

Make your critiques constructive so people will listen to them.

Exhibit 3.2
Types of Comments about Content

Ineffective
- Interesting stories.
- Too short.

Effective
- **I liked the story about your trip to the carnival.** The many details you provide made it sound really fun.
- **I would have liked to hear another example for each main point.** This would have helped me better understand why the carnival was so significant to you.

Exhibit 3.3
Types of Comments about Structure

Ineffective
- Nice transitions.
- Boring introduction.

Effective
- **Your transitions reminded me of the main point.**
- **Because you finished one main point and introduced the upcoming main point in your transition,** I found it easy to follow your ideas.
- **I would have tuned in to the speech more quickly** if you had begun with a great story about the carnival to capture my attention before starting your thesis.

Exhibit 3.4
Types of Comments about Delivery

Ineffective
- Great gestures!
- Slow down.

Effective
- **I really liked how you gestured while you stated your transitions.** It made it even clearer to me that we were moving to the next main point.
- **When you previewed your main points, you were speaking so quickly that I didn't catch them.** For me, it would be helpful if you had spoken more slowly so I could have processed the main points. That way, I would have followed along better throughout the speech.

(e.g., thesis restatement with main point review, clincher, call to action). You might also offer statements about the speaker's language and style choices (e.g., appropriate, inclusive, accurate, clear, vivid, expressive). And you might offer statements about the construction of presentational aids (e.g., size, color, labels, layout, design). Exhibit 3.3 offers some examples of ineffective and effective constructive critique statements regarding structure.

3. Delivery critique statements focus on the speaker's use of voice and body. In commenting on voice, you might consider intelligibility (e.g., understandable rate, volume, pronunciation, enunciation), conversational style (e.g., fluent, spontaneous), and emotional expression (e.g., changes in rate, pitch, or volume; strategic pauses; stresses on key words). In commenting on body, you might consider attire, poise, posture, eye contact, facial expressions, gestures, and movement. You can consider if the speaker's mannerisms distracted you from the message or enhanced it. You can also comment on how well the speaker used voice and body to integrate presentational aids (e.g., conceal, reveal, reference). Exhibit 3.4 provides a couple of examples of ineffective and effective constructive critique comments regarding delivery.

Certainly, you can help other speakers improve by offering constructive critiques. But you can also help yourself by completing a self-critique after each speech you give using the same approach you use to critique others. This self-critique approach is actually a form of cognitive restructuring that can help reduce your anxiety because it forces you to temper negative self-talk with positive self-talk immediately after your speech. Exhibit 3.5 presents a list of general criteria for preparing a constructive critique.

Exhibit 3.5
General Criteria for a Constructive Critique

Content

- Does the speaker establish common ground and adapt the content to the audience's interests, knowledge, and attitudes?
- Does the speaker seem to have expertise in the subject areas?
- Does the speaker have high-quality sources for the information given in the speech?
- Does the speaker reveal the sources of the information?
- Are the sources relevant? recent? varied? distributed throughout the speech?
- Does the information presented explain or support each of the main points?
- Are presentational aids appropriate and well used?
- Is each main point supported with breadth? depth? listener relevance?

Structure

- Does the introduction of the speech get attention, establish listener relevance and credibility, and lead into the topic?
- Has the speaker stated a clear goal for the speech?
- Are the main points of the speech clearly stated, parallel, and meaningful?
- Do transitions lead smoothly from one point to another?
- Does the information presented explain or support each of the main points?
- Does the speaker use language that is appropriate, accurate, clear, and vivid?
- Does the speaker use a compelling style?
- Does the conclusion summarize the main points and end with a clincher?

Delivery

- Does the speaker sound intelligible? conversational? expressive?
- Is the presentation fluent?
- Does the speaker look at the audience?
- Does the speaker use appropriate facial expressions?
- Were the pronunciation and articulation acceptable?
- Does the speaker have good posture?
- Does the speaker have sufficient poise?

Constructive Critique
Evaluation Checklist

Use the following checklist to ensure you make constructive critiques of others' speeches.

_____ **1.** Did you offer specific statements?

_____ **2.** Did you begin with statements about what the speaker did well?

_____ **3.** Did you offer statements for improvement?

_____ **4.** Did you provide an explanation (why) for each statement?

_____ **5.** Did you use "I" language to phrase each statement as a personal perception?

_____ **6.** Did you offer statements about content?

_____ **7.** Did you offer statements about structure?

_____ **8.** Did you offer statements about delivery?

_____ **9.** Did you offer statements about presentational aids?

Additional tools and resources are found at SPEAK 3 Online at **www.cengagebrain.com**.

STUDY TOOLS 3

LOCATED IN TEXTBOOK

☐ Tear-out Chapter Review cards at the end of the book

☐ Review with the Quick Quiz below

LOCATED ON SPEAK3 ONLINE AT CENGAGEBRAIN.COM

☐ Review Key Term flashcards and create your own cards

☐ Track your knowledge and understanding of key concepts in speech communication

☐ Complete practice and graded quizzes to prepare for tests

☐ Complete interactive content within SPEAK3 Online

☐ View the chapter highlight boxes for SPEAK3 Online

Quick Quiz (answers in Solutions Appendix)

T   F   1. One way to be an effective listener is to resist mental distractions.

T   F   2. The goal of appreciative listening is to understand and remember what has been said.

T   F   3. Note taking is not a good technique to use during a public speech.

T   F   4. Someone who is good at hearing is definitely good at listening.

T   F   5. Most executives in North America believe that listening is important for the corporate environment.

6. During a public lecture on French history, Edward is listening with the goal of evaluating how accurate the lecture is. He is using:

a. appreciative listening
b. critical listening
c. empathic listening
d. discriminative listening
e. comprehensive listening

7. While listening to the senator's speech, Jackie pays particular attention to how the senator is using his hands and arms. She is using:

a. appreciative listening
b. critical listening
c. empathic listening
d. discriminative listening
e. comprehensive listening

8. All of the following are techniques that can be used to improve understanding and memory EXCEPT:

a. observe nonverbal cues
b. determine the speaker's organization
c. silently paraphrase key information
d. take good notes
e. identify the benefits of attending to the speaker's words

9. According to research data, about _____ percent of people have had formal training in listening.

a. 2
b. 10
c. 25
d. 50
e. 90

10. The process of paying attention to what the speaker is saying, regardless of interferences, is called:

a. attending
b. listening
c. focusing
d. realizing
e. inventing

Chapter Takeaways

List three key takeaways from this chapter:

-

-

-

4 Determining an Appropriate Speech Goal

LEARNING OUTCOMES

4-1 Identify potential speech topics.

4-2 Analyze audience demographic and subject-related data.

4-3 Use audience data ethically.

4-4 Analyze the occasion for your speech.

4-5 Select a speech topic appropriate to the rhetorical situation.

4-6 Write a specific speech goal statement tailored to the rhetorical situation.

After finishing this chapter go to **PAGE 68** for **STUDY TOOLS.**

Sound Familiar?

As Kameron and Kayla left the classroom together, Kayla asked him, "What is your speech going to be about?"

"I have no idea," Kameron said. He hesitated, then added, "Not true—I do have an idea, but probably not a good one because of our audience."

Kameron lowered his voice and continued, "I was kind of thinking of speaking about supporting gay marriage. But I'm not sure our class is the right audience for it. What do you think?"

"Well, it's definitely topical, but I don't know what our classmates would think," Kayla said. "Maybe think about other topics that more of our classmates can relate to."

Whenever we are invited to give a speech, whether in the classroom or some other setting, the first thing we must do is decide upon a speech topic and goal. For many of us, this can feel pretty daunting. But it doesn't have to be. In this chapter, we'll walk you through an efficient process for determining a specific speech goal that is appropriate to the rhetorical situation.

Recall from Chapter 1, and as is reiterated in Exhibit 4.1, the elements of the rhetorical situation include you (and your knowledge and intentions), the audience (and their knowledge and expectations), and the occasion (the setting, purpose, and constraints). Because the audience is a crucial component of the

ra2studio/Shutterstock.com

Exhibit 4.1
The Rhetorical Public Speaking Situation

The rhetorical situation

rhetorical situation, effective speech goals are based on audience analysis, the process of learning about the diverse characteristics of audience members, and audience adaptation, the process of tailoring your message to address their unique needs, interests, and expectations. This step in the speechmaking process is rooted in what communication scholars refer to as *uncertainty reduction theory*.[1] Although effective speakers adapt to their audience throughout the speechmaking process, they begin at the point of determining a specific speech goal.

SPEECH ACTION STEPS

1. **Determine a speech goal that is appropriate to the rhetorical situation.**
2. **Understand your audience and adapt to it.**
3. **Gather and evaluate information.**
4. **Organize ideas into a well-structured outline.**
5. **Choose, prepare, and use appropriate presentational aids.**
6. **Practice oral language and delivery style.**

1

ACTION STEP

Determine a speech goal that is appropriate to the rhetorical situation

A. Brainstorm and create concept map for topics.

B. Analyze the rhetorical situation.

C. Develop a speech goal statement that is adapted to the rhetorical situation.

ROBYN BECK/Getty Images

Speeches are most compelling when they address the rhetorical situation. When Patricia Arquette accepted her Best Supporting Actress Academy Award in 2015, she used the occasion to make a strong plea: "It's our time to have wage equality once and for all, and equal rights for women in the United States of America.²"

To determine a specific speech goal adapted to the rhetorical situation, begin by identifying lots of subjects and topics that interest you. Then, based on your analysis of both the audience and the occasion, narrow your topic list down to include only those that (a) interest you and you know something about, (b) can be adapted to address the needs, interests, and expectations of the audience, and (c) are appropriate for the occasion.

4-1 IDENTIFY POTENTIAL SPEECH TOPICS

Good speech topics come from subjects we have some knowledge about and interest in. What is the difference between a subject and a topic? A **subject** is a broad area of knowledge, such as contemporary cinema, renewable energy, computer technology, or the Middle East. A **topic** is a narrower aspect of a subject. So, if your broad area of expertise is contemporary cinema, you might feel qualified to speak on a variety of narrower topics such as how the Academy Awards nomination process works; the relationships among movie producers, directors, and distributors; or how technology is changing movie production and distribution. Let's look more closely at how you can identify subjects that interest you and then potential topics you might explore for an upcoming speech.

subject a broad area of expertise, such as movies, renewable energy, computer technology, or the Middle East

topic a narrower aspect of a subject

brainstorming an uncritical, nonevaluative process of generating associated ideas

4-1a Subjects

You can identify subjects by listing those that (1) are important to you and (2) you know something about. Subjects may be related to careers that interest you, your major area of study,

special skills or competencies you have or admire, your hobbies and interests, as well as social, economic, or political issues that interest you. So, if your major is marketing, your hobbies are skateboarding and snowboarding, and issues that concern you include illiteracy, substance abuse, and obesity, then these are *subjects* from which you can identify potential speech topics.

At this point, you might be thinking, "What if my audience isn't interested in the subjects and topics that interest me?" In reality, topics in any subject area can be made interesting when they are adapted to address the needs and expectations of the audience.

Exhibit 4.2 contains subject lists that Kayla helped Kameron come up with for the speech contest. They chose to organize the subjects by using three broad headings: (1) career interests, (2) hobbies, and (3) issues of concern.

4-1b Brainstorming and Concept Mapping

A topic is a specific aspect of a subject, so from one subject you can identify many topics related to that subject. Two methods for doing so are brainstorming and concept mapping. **Brainstorming** is an uncritical, nonevaluative process of generating associated ideas. When you brainstorm, you list as many ideas as you can without

Exhibit 4.2

Kameron's Subject Lists

Career Interests
- Web site designer
- Teacher
- Computer programmer
- Event planner

Hobbies
- **Bouldering**
- **Bird watching**
- **Disc golf**
- **Video games**

Issues of Concern
- **Climate change**
- **Human rights**
- **Civil rights**
- **Fracking**

Let's consider what types of demographic and subject-related audience data you might collect, data-gathering methods you might use, and specific things to consider for using audience data ethically in your speeches.

4-2a Demographic Audience Data

Helpful demographic information includes, for example, each person's approximate age, education level, sex, occupation, socioeconomic status, race, ethnicity, religion, geographic uniqueness, and first language. Exhibit 4.4 presents a list of questions that may help you uncover important demographic information.

4-2b Subject-Related Audience Data

In addition to demographic data, you will also want to collect subject-related audience disposition data. More specifically, you ought to consider their level of knowledge, initial level of interest in, and attitude toward your potential topics. You might also ponder how credible listeners might perceive you to be about each of your potential topics. Once you know this information, you can use a process of elimination to choose a topic and goal that will offer some new information, insight, or perspective on a topic for that particular audience. Let's take a closer look at each of these aspects of subject-related audience disposition data.

Audience Knowledge

What can you expect your average audience member to already know about your subject? What topics are likely to provide new information for most of them? How can you adjust the perspective you take on the topic to go beyond what most of them probably already know? Because we live in a digital age where most people have instant access to general information on nearly any topic by doing a quick Google search on our laptops, iPads, and smartphones, determining this piece of subject-related audience data is crucial when selecting a speech topic. When you choose a topic that most audience members already know about or can learn about quickly on their own via an Internet search, you will bore them if you are not really creative. On the other hand, if you choose a topic for which your audience has insufficient background knowledge, you will need to provide the background or risk confusing them. For instance, if your subject is music, you can expect that an audience of traditional-age college students will know the general history of rock 'n' roll, including

evaluating them. If the subject for Kameron's speech was civil rights, he could brainstorm to come up with a list of potential topics, such as the role of women suffragists in gaining the right to vote, the rise and fall of Jim Crow laws in the American South, the pro-life/pro-choice debate, gun control, and same-sex marriage.

Concept mapping is a visual means of exploring connections between a subject and related ideas.[3] To generate connections, you might ask yourself questions about your subject, focusing on who, what, where, when, and how. In Exhibit 4.3, you can see an example of what Kameron's concept map looked like for the gun control topic. Notice how concept mapping allowed him to think more deeply about a general topic idea.

Speech Planning Action Step 1, Activity 1A will help you develop a list of topic ideas to use for your speeches in this course. See the Student Response box immediately following the activity for a sample of how one student completed this exercise.

4-2 ANALYZE THE AUDIENCE

Because addressing the specific needs and expectations of your intended audience is integral to the rhetorical situation, you need to examine who they are by collecting both demographic and subject-related data. This information will help you select and tailor your topic and goal to meet the needs, interests, and expectations of your audience.

> **concept mapping** a visual means of exploring connections between a subject and related ideas

Exhibit 4.3

TOPIC: Immigration

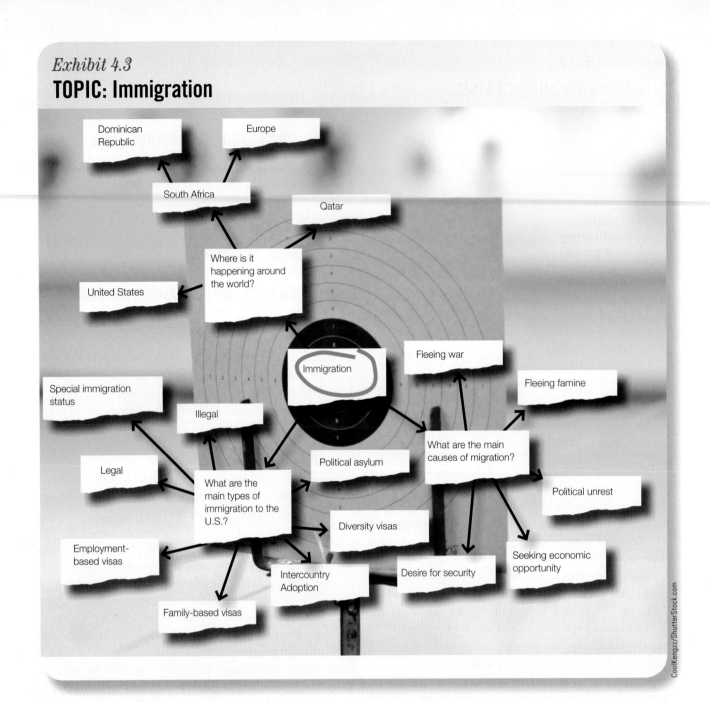

Dominican Republic

Europe

South Africa

Qatar

Where is it happening around the world?

United States

Immigration

Fleeing war

Fleeing famine

Special immigration status

Illegal

Political asylum

What are the main causes of migration?

Legal

What are the main types of immigration to the U.S.?

Political unrest

Diversity visas

Employment-based visas

Intercountry Adoption

Desire for security

Seeking economic opportunity

Family-based visas

CoolKengzz/ShutterStock.com

the major performers. So the topic "A Brief History of Rock 'n' Roll" might bore them because you aren't offering new information or insight or perspective. However, a speech on the contributions of girl bands to the development of rock 'n' roll might draw on the audience's background knowledge but offer new information to most audience members.

Audience Interest

How likely are audience members to be interested in your topic? You can actually make educated guesses about this piece of subject-related data based on the demographic data you collect. For instance, suppose you would like to

speak on the subject of cancer drugs. If your audience is made up of health-care professionals, they might well be interested in the topic, but also might already know a good deal about it. You would need to make sure to delve deeper into the topic to ensure interest. On the other hand, if your audience is a beginning public speaking class made up mostly of 18- and 19-year-old students, then unless they have had personal experience with cancer, they may not naturally be interested in the topic. So you can either choose another topic or make an extra effort to determine why 18- and 19-year-olds ought to know about cancer drugs and articulate this relevance throughout the speech.

Exhibit 4.4
Demographic Audience Analysis Questions

Age: What is the age range of the audience? Its average age?

Education: What percentage has a high school, college, or postgraduate education?

Sex: What percentage is male? female?

Socioeconomics: What percentage comes from high-, middle-, or low-income families?

Occupation: Is a majority from a single occupational group or industry? Or diverse occupational groups?

Race: Is audience mostly of the same race, or is there a mixture?

Ethnicity: What ethnic groups are in the audience? Is a majority from the same cultural background?

Religion: What religious traditions are followed by audience members?

Geographic uniqueness: Are audience members from the same country, state, city, or neighborhood?

Language: What are the most common first languages spoken? What language (if any) is common to all?

Audience Attitude

What might your audience's initial disposition be toward your topic? This is especially important when you are trying to influence their beliefs or move them to take action. You can determine your audience's attitudes toward your topic directly by surveying them, which we will discuss in the next section. If you cannot survey the audience directly, you might try to see if published opinion polls related to your subject are available. Then you can estimate your audience members' attitudes by studying these opinion polls and extrapolating their results to your audience.

Once you have an idea about your audience's initial attitude toward the topic, you can tailor your specific goal in ways that will allow you to influence rather than alienate them. For example, one reason the immigration debate tends to be so heated stems from different attitudes based on personal experiences. People whose family recently immigrated to the country or who live close to borders that experience large influxes of migrants would likely come to the speaking situation with a different initial attitude than people who live in regions with a small immigrant population or whose families have been in the country for generations.

Audience Perception

Will your audience recognize you as a subject matter expert? Will you need to establish your credibility as you speak? **Credibility** is the audience's perception of you as knowledgeable about the topic, trustworthy (honest, dependable, and ethical), and personable (friendly, sincere, and genuinely committed to the topic, occasion, and audience). Consider, for example, transnational celebrity activism. Although superstars from George Clooney to

Angelina Jolie to Madonna to Bono might easily be perceived as credible when speaking about their careers as actors or singers, they might need to take additional measures to ensure that audiences perceive them as credible when speaking about issues related to global politics.

Tailoring your speech to your audience based on both demographic and subject-related data is crucial not only to determine an appropriate topic and goal but throughout the speech preparation and delivery process. Thus, we devote the next chapter to a deeper discussion about how to do so.

4-2c Data-Gathering Methods

You can employ a number of different methods to gather audience data. We focus on four of them here.

1. Conduct a survey. Although it is not always possible, the most direct way to collect audience data is to survey the audience. A **survey** is a direct examination of people to gather information about their ideas and opinions. Some surveys are done as interviews, others as written questionnaires. Four common items used in surveys are two-sided, multiple-response, scaled, and open-ended.

- **Two-sided items** force respondents to choose between two answers, such as yes/no, for/against, or pro/con. Suppose you wanted to understand your audience members' attitudes toward violence in

credibility the perception that you are knowledgeable, trustworthy, and personable

survey a direct examination of people to gather information about their ideas and opinions

two-sided items survey items that force respondents to choose between two answers, such as yes/no, for/against, or pro/con

ACTION STEP ACTIVITY

Identify Potential Speech Topics

The goal of this activity is to help you identify potential speech topics.

1. **Develop a subject list.**
   a. **Divide a sheet of paper into three columns. Label column 1 "Major and career interests," label column 2 "Hobbies and activities," and label column 3 "Issues of concern."**
   b. **Working on one column at a time, identify subjects of interest to you. Try to identify at least three subjects in each column.**
   c. **Place a check mark next to the one subject in each list that you would most enjoy speaking about.**
   d. **Keep the lists for future use in choosing a topic for an assigned speech.**

2. **For each subject you have checked, brainstorm a list of topics that relate to that subject.**

3. **Look at the topics you have brainstormed. In which do you have the most interest and expertise? Place a check mark beside one or two of these.**

4. **Then, for each item on the brainstorm list that you have checked, develop a concept map to identify smaller topic areas and related ideas that might be developed into future speeches.**

Student Response: Identify Potential Speech Topics

Step 1: Subject List

Major and Career Interests	Hobbies and Activities	Issues of Concern
Teaching	Singing	School violence
√ Childcare	Volunteering	Breast cancer research
Chef	Rock climbing	Cyberbullying
Coaching	Swimming	Childhood obesity

Step 2: Brainstorm List for "Childcare"

Parental care

Family care

Nannies

In-home group care

Parent cooperatives

Day care

Step 3: Concept Map for "Day Care"

Using Brainstorming and Concept Mapping to Identify Speech Topics

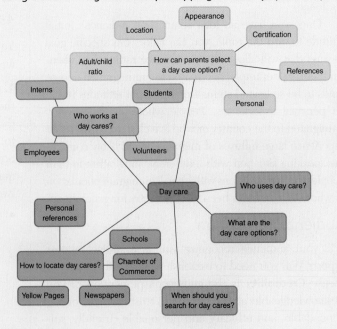

Rawpixel/Shutterstock.com

video games. You might phrase several questions with two-sided answers, such as:

Do you believe video games contain too much violence?

☐ Yes ☐ No

Do you play video games (e.g., Bioshock, Grand Theft Auto, Halo, Call of Duty)?

☐ Yes ☐ No

Respondents can answer two-sided items quickly, and they are easy to sort during analysis. Two-sided items, however, don't account for nuanced responses, so they must be carefully worded.

- **Multiple-response items** give respondents several alternatives from which to choose; they are especially useful for gathering demographic data. For example:

What is the highest level of education you have completed?

☐ Some high school ☐ High school diploma ☐ Some college

☐ Associate's degree ☐ Bachelor's degree ☐ Master's degree

☐ Doctorate degree ☐ Post-doctorate ☐ Other

Multiple-response items can also be used to assess the extent of knowledge audience members have about a topic. For example:

Indicate what you know about the water supply by placing an X next to each topic you already know about.

☐ How aqueducts work

☐ How water is purified

☐ The difference in water consumption among cities, industry, and agriculture

☐ Where California's water comes from

- **Scaled items** measure the direction or intensity of respondents' feelings or attitudes toward something. For example:

Indicate the extent to which you agree or disagree with the following statement:

Adult video games contain too much violence.

☐ Strongly agree ☐ Agree ☐ Neutral

☐ Disagree ☐ Strongly disagree

Scaled items can also be used to assess audience interest. For example:

Please place a check next to the response that best describes your interest in learning about each of the following.

How water is purified:

☐ Very interested ☐ Somewhat interested

☐ Uninterested

How aqueducts work

☐ Very interested ☐ Somewhat interested

☐ Uninterested

How water is distributed among the United States

☐ Very interested ☐ Somewhat interested

☐ Uninterested

- **Open-ended items** encourage respondents to elaborate on their opinions without forcing them to answer in a predetermined way. These items yield rich information, but the wide variety of responses can be difficult to analyze. For example, to determine what you would need to do to establish your credibility on the subject of video game violence, you might ask:

multiple-response items survey items that give the respondents several alternative answers from which to choose

scaled items survey items that measure the direction and/or intensity of audience members' feelings or attitudes toward something

open-ended items survey items that encourage respondents to elaborate on their opinions without forcing them to answer in a predetermined way

How can you tell if someone is an expert on video game violence?

2. **Observe informally.** If you are familiar with members of your audience (as you are with members of your classroom audience), you can learn a lot through informal observation. For instance, after being in class for even a couple of sessions, you should be able to estimate the approximate age or age range and the ratio of men to women. Because you are all in college, you know the educational level. As you listen to your classmates talk, you will learn more about their interest in, knowledge of, and attitudes about many issues.

3. **Question a representative.** Sometimes you can find out about your audience by questioning a representative. When you are invited to speak to a group you are unfamiliar with, ask your contact person for demographic and subject-related audience data. You should specifically ask for data that will help you narrow the focus of your topic and goal, as well as tailor the speech itself to address your listeners' needs, interests, and expectations.

4. **Make educated guesses.** If you can't get information any other way, you can make educated guesses based on indirect data such as the general makeup of the people who live in a specific community, belong to a certain or

similar organization, or are likely to attend an event of this nature. Suppose, for example, a nonprofit group you support asks you to give a speech on volunteer opportunities they offer. You are to give the speech to high school guidance counselors who oversee community service projects for students. You can infer a number of things about audience members. First, all will be college-educated high school counselors in your community. There will be both women and men. They will be interested in your topic, but their knowledge about specific opportunities at the nonprofit you will discuss will vary.

Exhibit 4.5 is a form you can use to summarize the demographic and subject-related audience data you collect. Now that you understand audience analysis, you can complete Speech Planning Action Step 1, Activity 1B. See the Student Response box immediately following the activity for a sample of how one student completed this exercise.

4-3 ETHICAL USE OF AUDIENCE DATA

Once you have collected audience data, you can use it to tailor your speech to their interests, needs, and expectations. To demonstrate respect for everyone, you will want to avoid making inappropriate or inaccurate assumptions based on demographic or subject-related

TECH TALK

Tech Talk—Digital Polling Made Easy with Google Forms

Even if you don't have time to organize a focus group before your next public speaking assignment or have access to professional polling services such as Gallup, you can still use polling to help you learn more about your audience's demographics, interests, and knowledge, so you can tailor your message. Google Forms offers a free and easily distributable way for anyone to issue a poll and gather information from an audience.

Polls generated with Google Forms can be shared with participants through email, a link, or embedded on a website, enabling quick turnaround for responses. The polls can be left open to the public or restricted to a particular group. Additionally, Google Forms can process 2 million cells of data—and generate automatic summaries of response statistics.[5]

Google Forms may not provide audience information at the same level of depth as a professionally conducted survey or focus group, but it has proven to be useful in applications as varied as a middle school's social-emotional needs assessment to a detailed examination of hockey team loyalty across New Jersey by one of the state's leading news sites.[6] If you need to gather information from your audience on short notice, chances are Google Forms is a fine tool for the job.

Exhibit 4.5

Audience Analysis Summary Form

My subject is _____

Data were collected:

_____ by survey _____ by questioning the person who invited me

_____ by direct observation _____ by educated guessing

Demographic Data

1. The average audience member's education level is _____ high school _____ college _____ postgraduate.

2. The ages range from _____ to _____ . The average age is about _____ .

3. The audience is approximately _____ percent male and _____ percent female.

4. My estimate of the average income level of the audience is _____ high _____ moderate _____ low.

5. Most audience members are of _____ the same occupation/major (which is _____)
   _____ different occupations/majors.

6. Most audience members are of _____ the same race (which is _____)
   _____ a mixture of races.

7. Most audience members are of _____ the same religion (which is _____)
   _____ a mixture of religions.

8. Most audience members are of _____ the same nationality (which is _____)
   _____ a mixture of nationalities.

9. Most audience members are from _____ the same state _____ the same city _____ the same neighborhood
   _____ different areas.

10. Most audience members speak _____ English as their first language _____ English as a second language (ESL).

Subject-Specific Data

1. The average audience member's knowledge of the subject is likely to be _____ extensive
   _____ moderate _____ limited because _____
   _____ .

2. The average audience member's interest in this subject is likely to be _____ high _____ moderate
   _____ low because _____ .

3. The average audience member's attitude toward my subject is likely to be _____ positive
   _____ neutral _____ negative because _____
   _____ .

4. My initial credibility with the audience is likely to be _____ high _____ medium _____ low because
   _____ .

Conclusion

Based on these data _____
_____ ,

which relate to my speech topic in the following ways:
_____
_____ ,

I will tailor my speech in the following ways: _____
_____
_____

ACTION STEP ACTIVITY

Analyzing Your Audience

1. **Decide on a method for gathering audience data.**
2. **Collect the data.**
3. **Copy or duplicate the Audience Analysis Summary Form (Exhibit 4.5).**
4. **Use the information you collected to complete the form.**
5. **Write two short paragraphs to describe what these audience demographics and subject-related data might suggest about listeners' knowledge, interests, attitudes, and expectations toward your topic.**
6. **Refer to this audience analysis information to address audience relevance throughout the speech-planning process.**

To download a copy of the Audience Analysis Summary Form, go to SPEAK 3 Online at www.cengagebrain.com to access the chapter resources.

Student Response: Analyzing Your Audience

Audience Analysis Summary Form

Demographic Data

1. **The average audience member's education level is ___ high school _X_ college ___ postgraduate.**
2. **The ages range from _19_ to _24_ The average age is _about 20_ .**
3. **The audience is approximately _65_ percent male and _35_ percent female.**
4. **My estimate of the average income level of the audience is ___ upper _X_ middle ___ lower.**
5. **Most audience members are of _X_ similar occupations/majors ___ different occupations/majors.**
6. **The audience consists primarily of ___ the same race _X_ a mixture of races.**
7. **Most audience members are of ___ the same religion _X_ a mixture of religions (because I can't really tell).**
8. **The audience consists primarily of _X_ the same nationality (which is _American_) ___ a mixture of nationalities.**
9. **Most audience members are from _X_ the same state ___ the same city ___ the same neighborhood ___ different areas.**
10. **Most audience members speak _X_ English as their first language ___ English as a second language (ESL).**

Summary description of key audience characteristics: _From these data, I conclude that most audience members are similar to one another and to me. We are all college students. Most of us are around 20 years old, which suggests that we have a common generational view, as well as possess an understanding of technological advancements that have made it easier to catch human trafficking online, like tracing emails and messages sent on the Internet. There are more men than women in the class, and, although we are primarily Americans, we represent a diverse mix of races. I can't really tell if we are similar or different in terms of religious affiliation. I would have to probe more specifically for that information if it seems pertinent for my ultimate topic and speech goal. Although most audience members speak English as their first language, there are also two international students who do not speak English as their first language. I will want to avoid marginalizing them by using visual aids to help them comprehend important information throughout the speech._

Subject-Specific Data

1. **The average audience member's knowledge of the subject is likely to be ___ extensive ___ moderate _X_ limited because** _the audience is mostly comprised of communication students, not political science or social justice students._
2. **The average audience member's interest in this subject is likely to be ___ high _X_ moderate ___ low because** _although it is a topic of public importance, students do not possess a direct connection with the topic to make it applicable to their own life._
3. **The average audience member's attitude toward my subject is likely to be ___ positive _X_ neutral ___ negative because** _if the audience is uninformed about the subject, they may not understand the severity of the problem._
4. **My initial credibility with the audience is likely to be ___ high ___ medium _X_ low because** _this is our first speech and they don't know that I am a social justice major, or that my mother works for Homeland Security specifically protecting victims of human trafficking._

_Summary__: The majority of my audience is uninformed about human trafficking and most likely only has a moderate interest in the subject. My speech must cover why human trafficking is relevant to everyone in the audience and convince even those who feel they are not connected to the subject matter that the issue is important. Because my audience doesn't know about my mother's experiences protecting human trafficking victims, nor do they have prior knowledge that I am a social justice major, it is safe to assume my audience will not initially perceive me to be a reliable speaker. Because of this, I will need to prove my knowledge of the subject by using quality sources, verbally citing them, and sharing my personal connection to the subject matter throughout my speech._

information you have collected. Two potential pitfalls to keep away from are marginalizing and stereotyping.

Marginalizing is the practice of ignoring the values, needs, and interests of some audience members, leaving them feeling excluded from the speaking situation. For example, if you discover that most of your audience members have played video games, you will want to avoid marginalizing the few members who have never done so. So you might quickly describe the goal and show a brief demonstration of a popular video game in the introduction of your speech on violence in video games.

Stereotyping is assuming all members of a group have similar knowledge, behaviors, or beliefs simply because they belong to that group. If, for example, you find out that the average age of your audience is 65, you might stereotype by assuming that most of them know nothing about video games when, in fact, many have either played them or observed family members doing so. To avoid stereotyping based on demographic data, you also need to collect subject-related data from listeners.

You can also reduce your chances of marginalizing or stereotyping by recognizing and acknowledging the diversity represented in your audience. **Audience diversity** is the range of demographic and subject-related differences represented in an audience. So while the average age of your audience may be 65, there may also be some in the audience who are much younger. Similarly, although most audience members may be familiar with video games, a few may know very little about them.

4-4 ANALYZE THE OCCASION

The occasion of a speech is made up of the speech's expected purpose and setting (location). Answers to several key questions about the occasion should guide you when selecting your topic and throughout the speech-making process.

1. What is the intended purpose (exigence) of the speech? In other words, why does the audience think this speech is being given? At a religious service, for example, the congregation expects the sermon to have a religious theme. At a national sales meeting, the field representatives expect to hear about new products. For your classroom speeches, a major expectation is that your speech will meet the assignment criteria.

Leigh Prather/Shutterstock.com

...respect your audience by honoring time limits.

2. What is the expected length? Time limits for classroom speeches are usually quite short, so you should choose a topic that is narrow enough to be accomplished in the time allotted. "Three Major Causes of the Declining Honey Bee Population" could probably be presented in five minutes, but "A History of Human Impact on the Environment" could not. Time-limit expectations are not unique to classroom speeches. Adhering to audience time-limit expectations demonstrates respect. For example, consider a time when you paid a hefty ticket price to attend a live concert or other public event. If the main event was shorter than you expected it to be, you probably felt cheated. Or consider when a teacher kept you in class longer than the allotted time. You may have become frustrated because it seemed the instructor failed to respect the other commitments (e.g., other classes, jobs) you juggled along with that particular course. Speakers who speak for more or less time than has been allotted can seriously interfere with event programming and lose the respect of both their hosts and their audiences.

3. Where will the speech be given? Rooms vary in size, lighting, and seating arrangements. Some are single level, some have stages or platforms, and some have tiered seating. The space affects the speech. For example, in a long, narrow room, you may need to speak loudly to be heard in the back row. If you are speaking in an auditorium to a large group of people, you will need to speak loudly and perhaps use a microphone. You will also need to use large gestures and presentational aids that can be seen and heard easily in all parts of the room. The brightness of the room and the availability of room darkening shades may impact what kinds of visual aids you can use. So you will want to know and consider the layout of the room as you plan your speech. If possible, visit the room in advance either physically or virtually via online photo galleries or virtual tours posted on the venue's Web site. The more you know about the location where you will be giving your speech, the better able you will be to tailor it to be most effective in that setting.

marginalizing ignoring the values, needs, and interests of certain audience members, leaving them feeling excluded from the speaking situation

stereotyping assuming all members of a group have similar knowledge, behaviors, or beliefs simply because they belong to the group

audience diversity the range of demographic and subject-related differences represented in an audience

4. When will the speech be given? A speech given early in the morning requires a different approach from one given right after lunch or in the evening. If a speech is scheduled after a meal, for instance, the audience may be lethargic, mellow, or even on the verge of sleep. So you may want to plan to insert more material designed to gain and regain audience interest throughout. Similarly, where you are placed on the schedule of events should influence your speech planning. For example, if you are first, you may need to "warm up" the audience and be prepared to deal with the distraction of latecomers entering the room while you are speaking. If you speak later in the program, you may need to integrate attention-catching material to keep the interest of a weary audience.

5. What equipment is necessary and available? Would you like to use a microphone, lectern, flip chart, smartboard, computer, or LCD projector to display visuals or audiovisuals? If so, does the room have an adequate means for displaying visuals and projecting audio? Do you plan to use the Internet and, if so, is the room wired for Internet or Wi-Fi? It is your responsibility to check with your host to make sure the equipment can be made available or to make alternative arrangements. Regardless of the arrangements made, however, experienced speakers anticipate potential problems and always prepare a backup plan. So if you plan to show a computerized slide show, you might also prepare handouts of key slides in case the equipment fails.

Speech Planning Action Step 1, Activity 1C will help you understand the occasion so that you take into consideration your purpose, audience expectations, and location as you choose your topic and develop your speech. See the Student Response box immediately following the activity for a sample of how one student completed this exercise.

1C ACTION STEP ACTIVITY

Analyzing the Occasion

The goal of this activity is to help you understand your speech occasion. Fill in answers to the following questions:

1. What is the intended purpose (exigence) for the speech? _____

2. What is the expected length? _____

3. Where will the speech be given? _____

4. When will the speech be given? _____

5. What equipment is necessary and available? _____

Write a short paragraph mentioning which aspects of the occasion are most important to consider as you prepare your speech and why.

Access Action Step 1, Activity 1C at SPEAK 3 Online at www.cengagebrain.com. to complete this activity online.

Kameron's Student Response: Analyzing the Occasion

1. **What is the intended purpose (exigence) for the speech?** *A persuasive speech*

2. **What is the expected length?** *4–6 minutes*

3. **Where will the speech be given?** *Memorial Auditorium to about 100 people (including students, teachers, administrators, communication experts, and community members)*

4. **When will the speech be given?** *I am the first of 8 speakers to compete at 9:30 a.m. on Monday morning.*

5. **What equipment is necessary and available?** *LCD projector, computer, and screen*

Time is certainly important: *Four to six minutes is not very long. I plan to time my speech when I practice to make sure I stay within the expected time limits.*

4-5 SELECT A TOPIC

As you review your topic list, compare each to your audience profile. Are any topics too simple or too difficult for this audience's knowledge base? If so, eliminate those topics. Are some topics likely to bore the audience and you can't think of any way to pique their interest with new insight or a new perspective on them? Eliminate those as well. How might the audience's age range, ethnicity, and other demographic features mesh with each topic? By asking these and similar questions, you will be able to identify topics that are appropriate for the audience.

Next consider the occasion. Are some topics inappropriate for the intended purpose? Are some too broad to cover adequately in the time allotted? Would any require equipment that cannot be made available where you will be speaking? Answers to these kinds of questions will help you identify topics appropriate to the occasion.

Speech Planning Action Step 1, Activity 1D will help you select your topic. See the Student Response box immediately following the activity for a sample of how one student completed this exercise.

1D

ACTION STEP ACTIVITY

Selecting a Topic

Use your responses to Action Step Activities 1A, 1B, and 1C to complete this activity.

1. Look over the concept map you prepared in Activity 1A. List each of the specific topics that you generated:

   _____   _____   _____
   _____   _____   _____

2. Using the information you compiled in Activity 1B (audience analysis), compare each topic to your audience profile. Eliminate topics that seem less appropriate for this specific audience. List each of the remaining topics:

   _____   _____   _____

3. Compare each of the remaining topics to the information you compiled in Activity 1C (analysis of the occasion). Eliminate topics that seem less appropriate. List each of the remaining topics:

   _____   _____   _____

4. The remaining topics are appropriate to the rhetorical situation (you, the audience, and the occasion). So, select the topic from this list that you are most excited about sharing with others. My topic will be: _____

You can complete this activity at SPEAK 3 Online at www.cengagebrain.com.

Student Response: Selecting a Topic

1. Look over the concept map you prepared in Activity 1A. List each of the specific topics that you generated:

   Low-cost ways to travel   _Study abroad programs_
   Youth hostels   _Working on cruise ships_
   Organizing alternative spring break group trips   _Elderhostel_

2. Using the information you compiled in Activity 1B (audience analysis), compare each topic to your audience profile. Eliminate topics that seem less appropriate for this specific audience. List each of the remaining topics:

   Low-cost ways to travel   _Study abroad programs_
   Youth hostels   _Organizing alternative spring break group trips_

3. Compare each of the remaining topics to the information you compiled in Activity 1C (analysis of the occasion). Eliminate topics that seem less appropriate. List each of the remaining topics:

   Study abroad programs   _Youth hostels_
   Organizing alternative spring break group trips

4. The remaining topics are appropriate to the rhetorical situation (you, the audience, and the occasion). So, select the topic from this list that you are most excited about sharing with others. My topic will be:
   My topic will be organizing alternative spring break group trips.

4-6 WRITE A SPEECH GOAL STATEMENT

Once you have chosen your topic, you are ready to identify and write the general goal of your speech and then to write your specific goal statement tailored to the audience and occasion.

4-6a Understanding General and Specific Speech Goals

The **general goal** is the overall intent of the speech. Most speeches intend to entertain, to inform, or to persuade, even though each type of speech may include elements of

general goal the overall intent of the speech

other types. Consider the following examples. Jimmy Kimmel's opening monologue on *Jimmy Kimmel Live* is generally intended to entertain, even though it may include persuasive elements. Likewise, presidential campaign speeches are generally intended to persuade, even though they also include informative material. The general goal is usually dictated by the occasion. (In classroom speeches, the instructor usually specifies it.)

Whereas the general goal is typically determined by the occasion, the **specific goal** (or specific purpose) is a single statement that identifies the exact response a speaker wants from the audience. For an informative speech about "Vanishing Honeybees," for example, you might state the specific goal as, "I would like the audience to understand the four reasons honeybees are vanishing." If your general goal is to persuade, however, you might state the specific goal as, "I intend to convince the audience to donate money to *Honeybee Advocacy International*." In the first example, the goal is informative: The speaker wants the audience to understand the reasons. In the second example, the goal is persuasive: The speaker wants to persuade the audience to donate money.

4-6b Phrasing a Specific Speech Goal

A specific speech goal statement must be carefully crafted because it lays the foundation for organizing your speech. The following guidelines can help you write an effective specific speech goal statement.

1. Write a first draft of your speech goal in one complete sentence. Remember Kameron from our opening vignette? He ultimately decided on the topic of same-sex marriage for his speech. He wrote his first speech goal draft this way:

I want my audience to agree that same-sex marriage should be allowed.

Kameron's draft is a complete sentence, and it specifies the response he wants from the audience: *to agree* that same-sex couples should be allowed to marry. Thus, he is planning to give a persuasive speech.

specific goal a single statement that identifies the exact response a speaker wants from the audience

2. Make sure the goal statement contains only one idea. Suppose Kameron had first written:

I would like the audience to agree that same-sex marriage should be allowed and that parents and teachers should talk to children about these issues without shame.

This statement would need to be revised because it includes two distinct ideas: allowing same-sex marriage and talking to children about it without shame. Either one could be a worthy goal—but not both in one short speech. Kameron needs to choose one of these ideas. If your goal statement includes the word *and*, you probably have more than one idea and need to narrow your focus.

3. Revise the statement until it clearly articulates the general goal. If your general goal is to inform, you might use phrases such as "to understand," "to recognize," "to distinguish," or "to identify." If the general goal is to persuade, you might use phrases such as "to believe," "to accept," "to change," or "to do." If Kameron wanted to inform his audience, his specific goal might be worded:

I want my audience to understand the issues surrounding same-sex marriage.

This general goal, *to understand*, suggests that Kameron would lay out the various perspectives about same-sex marriage and stop short of advocating one position over the others.

4. Revise your statement until it articulates the precise focus of your speech tailored to the audience. Kameron's draft "I want my audience to agree that same-sex marriage should be allowed" is still fairly vague. Exactly what about same-sex marriage is it that Kameron wants his audience to believe? Here is where you need to consider your audience analysis and adapt your specific goal in ways that address listeners' needs, interests, and expectations. What is it about the topic that your particular audience should know and why?

Kameron reasons that his audience members are citizens in a nation that values and respects human rights for all, so he revises his specific speech goal this way:

I want my audience to agree that anyone in a committed relationship based on mutual love and respect should have the right to marry.

Before we close this chapter, we want to tell you a bit more about Kameron from the opening vignette and his speech. Although Kayla is not a real person, Kameron is a real student named Kameron Slade from Queens, New York. Kameron actually won a speech competition in 2012 for a speech in which he advocated for same-sex marriage. His performance earned him the right to compete in a much larger speech contest.

ACTION STEP ACTIVITY

Writing a Specific Goal

Type of speech: _____

1. Write a first draft of your specific speech goal using a complete sentence that specifies the type of response you want from the audience.

2. If the statement contains more than one idea, select one and rewrite the statement.

3. Revise the statement until it clearly articulates the general goal.

4. Revise the statement until it articulates the precise focus of your speech tailored to your intended audience.

Write the final draft of the specific speech goal:

_____
_____
_____
_____
_____
_____
_____
_____
_____
_____
_____
_____

You can complete this activity online with Speech Builder Express, a speech outlining and development tool that will help you complete the action steps in this book to develop your speech. You can access Speech Builder Express at SPEAK 3 Online at www.cengagebrain.com.

Student Response: Writing a Specific Goal

Type of speech: *informative*

1. Write a first draft of your specific speech goal using a complete sentence that specifies the type of response you want from the audience.
   I want the audience to understand how a fire is lit without a match.

2. If the statement contains more than one idea, select one and rewrite the statement.
   I want my audience to recognize the basic steps necessary in lighting a fire without a match.

3. Revise the statement until it clearly articulates the general goal.
   I want to teach the audience how to light a fire without a match.

4. Revise the statement until it articulates the precise focus of your speech tailored to your intended audience. Write the final draft of the specific goal:
   I want to teach my audience to recognize the three basic steps involved in lighting a fire without a match.

Kameron Slade delivered his speech to the New York City Council. Is this rhetorical situation different than Kameron's classroom?

When he was told he would not be allowed to compete unless he changed his topic, a public outcry went viral. He did ultimately get to deliver his speech and even went on to give it to the New York City Council.[7] But why did the contest organizers want to censor the topic? They did not believe Kameron had the needed subject-related credibility for such a speech because Kameron was only 10 years old.

A good specific speech goal statement will guide you as you research your speech. Once you have completed your research, you will revise your specific speech goal into a thesis statement, which will be the foundation on which you will organize the speech. Exhibit 4.6 gives several additional examples of general and specific informative and persuasive goals.

Speech Planning Action Step 1, Activity 1E will help you develop a well-written specific goal statement for your speech. See the Student Response box immediately following the activity for a sample of how one student completed this exercise.

Exhibit 4.6
General and Specific Goals

Informative Goals

- **General goal:** To inform the audience about e-books
- **Specific goal:** I want the audience to understand the differences between the Kindle and the Sony/iPad approaches to electronic books.
- **General goal:** To inform the audience about forms of mystery stories
- **Specific goal:** I want the audience to be able to identify the three basic forms of mystery stories.

Persuasive Goals

- **General goal:** To persuade the audience that saving for retirement is important
- **Specific goal:** I want the audience to begin a personal ROTH IRA funded this year with at least 2 percent of their income.
- **General goal:** To persuade the audience to get involved with the food bank
- **Specific goal:** I want to persuade the audience to volunteer to work on the campus food drive for our local food bank.

STUDY TOOLS 4

LOCATED IN TEXTBOOK

- ☐ Tear-out Chapter Review cards at the end of the book
- ☐ Review with the Quick Quiz below

LOCATED ON SPEAK3 ONLINE AT CENGAGEBRAIN.COM

- ☐ Review Key Term flashcards and create your own cards
- ☐ Track your knowledge and understanding of key concepts in speech communication
- ☐ Complete practice and graded quizzes to prepare for tests
- ☐ Complete interactive content within SPEAK3 Online
- ☐ View the chapter highlight boxes for SPEAK3 Online

Quick Quiz (answers in Solutions Appendix)

T F 1. Marginalizing is the action of assuming that all members of the audience have similar knowledge, behaviors, or beliefs because they belong to the same group.

T F 2. While audience analysis focuses on a study of the intended audience, audience adaptation is the process of tailoring the speech's information to the needs of the audience.

T F 3. Information about members' age, education, gender, and income comprise demographics.

T F 4. A key step for determining a specific speech goal is to understand the speech occasion.

T F 5. Brainstorming is an evaluative, critical process.

6. A(n) _____ is a broad area of expertise.

   a. topic
   b. area
   c. motif
   d. theme
   e. subject

7. A question such as "Do you think social network sites are a waste of time?" is an example of a(n):

   a. multiple-response item
   b. two-sided item
   c. scaled item
   d. response item
   e. open-ended item

8. A speaker who is perceived to be very knowledgeable and personable has a lot of:

   a. personality
   b. ethics
   c. motivation
   d. credibility
   e. intensity

9. When analyzing the occasion of a speech, you should ask all of the following EXCEPT:

   a. What is the appropriate length of the speech?
   b. How large will the audience be?
   c. How much am I being paid for the speech?
   d. What are the special expectations for the speech?
   e. Where will the speech be given?

10. An effective way to minimize stereotyping is to:

   a. collect data audience related to your subject
   b. make the audience homogenous
   c. ask the audience to assume the same things
   d. tell the audience that they are all equal
   e. ignore special needs in the audience

Chapter Takeaways

List three key takeaways from this chapter:

-
-
-

5 Adapting to Audiences

LEARNING OUTCOMES

5-1 Address initial audience disposition toward your topic.

5-2 Highlight common ground with your audience.

5-3 Articulate the relevance of your speech to your audience.

5-4 Establish your credibility as knowledgeable, trustworthy, and personable.

5-5 Employ strategies to enhance comprehension and retention.

5-6 Overcome potential language and cultural differences.

5-7 Create your own audience adaptation plan.

After finishing this chapter go to **PAGE 82** for **STUDY TOOLS.**

BraunS/Getty Images

Sound Familiar?

Having grown up in California, Megan knew firsthand the difficulties of living with water shortages. She wanted her classmates to better understand the issues surrounding responsible water usage, but gaining and maintaining the interest of classmates who live in states with abundant water supplies would be challenging.

J.J.'s audience analysis confirmed his assumption: most of his classmates realized they shouldn't talk or text while driving. Yet their survey responses revealed that 90 percent of them did so anyway! Convincing them to stop engaging in this dangerous behavior would be a challenge.

In the previous chapter, we talked about how to conduct an audience analysis and then use it to narrow your topic and determine your speech goal. Effective speakers don't stop there. Effective speakers use audience adaptation—the process of tailoring the speech to the needs, interests, and expectations of the audience—to inform everything from researching the topic to organizing the main points to developing them with supporting material to making language choices and practicing delivery. In this chapter, we offer guidelines for doing so by acknowledging initial audience disposition, establishing common ground, demonstrating relevance, gaining credibility, enhancing information comprehension and retention, and overcoming potential language and cultural differences.

5-1 INITIAL AUDIENCE DISPOSITION

Initial audience disposition is the knowledge and opinions your audience has about your topic before they hear you speak. Recall that this information helped you narrow the topic and determine your speech goal. You should also consider initial audience disposition when determining your main points, selecting supporting material, and making language choices. For example, if you were giving a speech on refinishing wood furniture, you may face an audience whose initial attitude is that refinishing furniture is complicated and boring. On the other hand, you may face an audience of young homeowners who love DIY Network and are really looking forward to your talk. Although the process you describe in both situations will be the same, your approach to explaining the steps will differ somewhat. If your audience thinks refinishing furniture is boring and complicated, you will need

 2

ACTION STEP

Understand your audience and adapt to it

A. Understand audience diversity.

B. Tailor your speech to address their needs, interests, and expectations.

to pique their interest and convince them that the process is really simpler than they initially thought. And if you know your audience enjoys watching DIY Network, you can play upon these interests by making reference to some popular DIY Network shows.

> **initial audience disposition**
> the knowledge of and opinions about your topic that your listeners have before they hear you speak

Ellen DeGeneres understands that her U.S. audience tunes into her show for warm-hearted laughter and fun. The appeal of her format is now being tested with a new audience, as the first daily U.S. talk show broadcast in China.[1]

5-2 COMMON GROUND

People are unique, with different knowledge, attitudes, philosophies, experiences, and ways of perceiving the world. So it is easy for audience members to assume they have nothing in common with you or with the other audience members. As a speaker, your goal is to identify and highlight **common ground**, a sense of shared background, knowledge, attitudes, experiences, and philosophies. You can build common ground by using personal pronouns, asking rhetorical questions, and drawing on common experiences.

common ground the background, knowledge, attitudes, experiences, and philosophies audience members and the speaker share

personal pronouns "we," "us," and "our"—pronouns that directly link the speaker to members of the audience

rhetorical questions questions phrased to stimulate a mental response rather than an actual spoken response from the audience

5-2a Use Personal Pronouns

One way to establish common ground is to use **personal pronouns**—"we," "us," and "our." For example, in her speech about hurricanes, Megan used personal pronouns to establish common ground in this way:

Let's discuss how much water we use every day.

By using "let's discuss" rather than "I'll explain," Megan created a sense of common ground that she and her audience would work together to form a common understanding about water usage.

5-2b Ask Rhetorical Questions

A second way to establish common ground is to pose **rhetorical questions**—questions phrased to stimulate a mental response rather than an actual spoken response from the audience. Rhetorical questions are often used in speech introductions but can also be used effectively in transitions and other parts of the speech. For instance, notice how this transition, phrased as a rhetorical question, creates common ground:

When watching a particularly violent TV program, have you ever asked yourself, "Did they really need to be this graphic to make the point?"

Used in this way, rhetorical questions highlight similar attitudes among the speaker and audience members and pique interest about the content that is to come.

5-2c Draw from Common Experiences

Another way to establish common ground is by sharing personal stories and examples illustrating things you and your audience have in common. In her speech about water usage, Megan tried to establish common ground in her introduction in this way:

Close your eyes and imagine a hot summer day. Picture yourself at an amusement park or doing chores outside or biking along a sunny trail. As the day wears on, you get hot, thirsty, and dirty. No matter how enjoyable the day, at the end—or even in the middle—all you want to do is chug a tall glass of ice water, snack on some juicy berries, and get cleaned up. But what if you couldn't? What if

there was only enough water either to flush the toilets for the evening or to shower? Worse, what if you opened the tap and nothing came out? Although this might sound far-fetched, water security is a real and pressing issue in my home state of California and the drought it is experiencing actually presents a severe economic, environmental, and agricultural threat to the entire United States.

Although Megan realized that very few if any of her classmates had probably ever experienced a severe drought, she drew upon a common experience she knew they could all relate to: how important water is in our daily lives.

5-3 RELEVANCE

Another important way to tailor your speech to your audience is by demonstrating **relevance**—adapting information in ways that help audience members realize its importance to them. Listeners pay attention to and are interested in ideas that affect them personally in some way ("What does this have to do with me?") and lose interest when they don't see how a speech relates to them. You can demonstrate relevance by emphasizing timeliness, proximity, and personal impact of the ideas you share throughout your speech.

5-3a Emphasize Timeliness

Information has **timeliness** when it is useful now or in the near future. For example, in a speech about the hazards of using a cell phone while driving, J. J. demonstrated relevance via timeliness with this introduction:

Most of us in this room, as many as 90 percent of us in fact, are a danger to society. Why? It's because we talk or text on our cell phones while driving. Recent reports released in 2012 from the National Safety Council reveal that cell phone distracted driving is the most common cause of accidents today—even more common than driving under the influence (DUI). Did you know that when you talk on the phone when you're driving—even if you do so on a hands-free set—you're four times more likely to get into a serious crash than if you're not doing so? This issue is far from harmless and is certainly one each of us should take seriously.

By referencing recent statistics not only about texting but also about talking on the phone while driving, J. J. demonstrates relevance that the topic of his speech is timely. Megan did so by talking about recent orders

To keep a topic relevant, emphasize its proximity to your audience.

Marquisphoto/Shutterstock.com

issued by the state government of California telling farmers to stop drawing water to irrigate their crops.

To see an example of how timeliness can affect a message—President Ronald Reagan's 1986 speech on the *Challenger* space shuttle disaster—go to **Demonstrating Timeliness** in SPEAK3 Online.

5-3b Emphasize Proximity

Listeners are more likely to be interested in information that has **proximity**, a relationship to their personal "space." Psychologically, we pay more attention to information related to our "territory"—to us, our family, our neighborhood, or our city, state, or country.

> **relevance** adapting the information in a speech so that audience members view it as important to them
>
> **timeliness** showing how information is useful now or in the near future
>
> **proximity** the relevance of information to personal life space

To Increase Interest, Take a Page from the Newspaper Industry

When writing a news story for a newspaper, magazine, or Web site, reporters don't always have the luxury of knowing exactly who comprises their audience. Reporters writing general news pieces must be especially mindful that their work may be read by a wide and disparate audience. To make a piece appeal to the widest possible audience, reporters often hone in on the newsworthy aspects of the story. Newsworthiness is a measure of the information contained within a story about recent events or happenings.[2]

The concept of newsworthiness can be beneficial as you develop a speaking topic. Showcasing newsworthy aspects of your speech can help you maintain audience interest. A story's newsworthiness is based in part on timeliness, proximity, and impact. There are three additional factors of newsworthiness you can consider as you develop a speech:[3]

1. **Prominence:** Certain topics draw the public eye more than others and are thus regarded as more prominent. Working with a prominent topic will likely command more attention from your audience, as a greater number of people will have been exposed to your subject matter. For example, a celebrity with cancer is a more prominent topic than an ordinary citizen with the disease.
2. **Novelty:** This is a measure of how unique or downright weird a topic is. While a dog biting a man may not make the news (or a good topic for a speech), a man biting a dog is novel and far more interesting.
3. **Conflict:** All good narratives feature some sort of conflict, whether internal or external. Strife, war, and social unrest, while unfortunate aspects of daily life, make for newsworthy stories and relatable topics.

Not all speech topics are necessarily newsworthy—and that's okay. But if you can find a way to capitalize on a topic's newsworthiness, your speech will likely be more interesting and relatable to a larger and more diverse audience.

OCTOBER 10, 2015

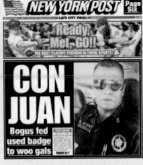

OCTOBER 9, 2015

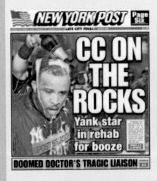

OCTOBER 6, 2015

OCTOBER 5, 2015

You have probably heard speakers say, "Let me bring this close to home for you . . ." and then make their point by using a local example. As you do research, look for statistics and examples that emphasize proximity for your audience. For example, J. J. used the latest cell phone distracted driving accident statistics in his state and a story reported in the local paper of a young mother who was killed as a result of cell phone distracted driving.

5-3c Emphasize Personal Impact

When you emphasize a serious physical, economic, or psychological impact of your topic, audience members are interested in what you have to say. Consider, for example, how you perk up when your instructor says "you might want to jot this down because it will be on the test." That's an example of emphasizing personal impact because remembering it will help you earn a better grade. Megan emphasized personal impact by citing statistics about how much water is needed to produce the popular fresh foods her audience said were their favorites—avocados, strawberries, and grapes. J.J. emphasized personal impact by showing how much higher everyone's auto insurance is today as a result of cell phone distracted traffic accidents.

5-4 SPEAKER CREDIBILITY

Credibility is the audience's perception of a speaker as trustworthy and knowledgeable about the topic. The impact of credibility on speaker success has been a fundamental concept in public speaking since Aristotle described it as *ethos* more than 2,000 years ago. Having been understood as a key concept for so long, it is no wonder that several theories exist about how speakers develop credibility.

Some people are widely known as experts on a particular topic. When these people give a speech, they don't have to do much to establish their credibility. For example, when Dr. Elizabeth Blackburn gives a speech about cancer research, her credibility on the topic is established by her position as a professor of biology and physiology at the University of California, San Francisco, her reputation as one of the most influential researchers in the field of cancer science, and the fact that she won the Nobel Prize for Physiology and Medicine.[4]

By contrast, when Jack Andraka gives a speech on a new testing mechanism to diagnose pancreatic cancer, he must work to establish his credibility. That's because, even though Jack is affiliated with the Johns Hopkins University and won the Gordon E. Moore award at the Intel Science and Engineering Fair, Jack is a teenager.[5] When he speaks on his discovery, Jack works to establish credibility with his audience.

Like Jack, most of us need to adapt our remarks to help establish credibility with our audience. We can do so by articulating our knowledge and expertise, conveying trustworthiness, and displaying personableness.

5-4a Articulate Knowledge and Expertise

Audience members' assessment of your **knowledge and expertise** depends on how well you convince them that you are qualified to speak on this topic. You can do so directly and indirectly.

You can articulate your expertise directly by disclosing your personal experiences with the topic, including formal education, special study, demonstrated skill, and your "track record." For example, in his cell phone distracted driving speech, J. J. explained:

I became interested in the issue of cell phone distracted driving after being involved personally in an accident caused by a driver who was talking on the phone. Since then, I've done a great deal of research on the subject and am involved in a grassroots organization devoted to passing legislation to ban driving while phoning or texting in our state.

Megan articulated knowledge and expertise by sharing information about the types of water conservation activities her family had been practicing every day for years. When you can articulate personal experience with your topic, your audience will perceive you as knowledgeable about the material.

Similarly, when ideas are developed through specific statistics and high-quality examples, audience members are more likely to view a speaker as knowledgeable. J.J. did so by citing the most recent statistics released by the National Safety Council, and Megan did so by citing reports she found at the U.S. Drought Monitor Web site and statistics published by the National Oceanic and Atmospheric Administration (NOAA).

Audience members also assess knowledge and expertise through indirect means. Audiences have an almost instinctive sense of when a speaker is "winging it." Most audiences will perceive speakers who do not appear to have command of the material as less knowledgeable and speakers who are confident, fluent, and easy to follow as more knowledgeable.

5-4b Convey Trustworthiness

Trustworthiness is the extent to which the audience believes what you say is accurate, true, and in their best interests. People assess trustworthiness by judging the speaker's character and motives.

As you prepare, consider how you will demonstrate good character—that you are honest, industrious, dependable, and ethical. For example, when you credit the source of your information as you speak, you demonstrate good character. You are confirming that you did not make up the information (honesty) and that you are not plagiarizing (ethics).

> **credibility** the perception that you are knowledgeable, trustworthy, and personable
>
> **knowledge and expertise** how well you convince your audience that you are qualified to speak on the topic
>
> **trustworthiness** the extent to which the audience can believe that what you say is accurate, true, and in their best interests

Being personable involves making a good impression, projecting a pleasing personality, and being friendly.

How trustworthy you seem also depends on how the audience views your motives. If people believe that what you are saying is self-serving rather than in their best interests, they will be suspicious and view you as less trustworthy. Early in your speech, show how audience members will benefit from what you are saying. For example, in his speech on toxic waste, Brandon described how one community's ignorance of toxic waste disposal allowed a toxic waste dump to be located in their community, which led to serious health issues. He then shared his motive by saying, "My hope is that this speech will give you the information you need to thoughtfully participate in decisions like these that may face your community."

5-4c Display Personableness

Personableness is the extent to which one projects a pleasing personality. Quite simply, we have more confidence in people we like. We quickly decide how much we like a new person based on our first impressions. This fact is actually based on a communication concept known as *impression formation and management*, which is rooted in the theory of symbolic interactionism.[6] These first impressions are based on what we infer about people from what we see, such as how they dress, how physically attractive we find them, how well they speak, whether they smile and appear friendly, and even how they carry themselves. Although first

personableness the extent to which you project an agreeable or pleasing personality

learning style a person's preferred way of receiving information

impressions are not always correct, we still use them. That's why a successful business professional might wear an oversize graphic T-shirt, baggy shorts, and a backward ball cap when hanging out with friends; put on khakis and a polo shirt to go to the office; and dress in a formal blue suit to make a major presentation at a professional conference. He or she adjusts appearance to convey appropriate personableness in different settings.

Besides dressing appropriately, you can increase the chances that the audience will like you by smiling at individual audience members before beginning your remarks and by looking at individuals as you speak, acknowledging them with a quick nod. You can also demonstrate personableness by using appropriate humor. By appropriate humor, we mean humor that demonstrates respect for diverse listeners by not potentially offending a particular group (e.g., sexist, ageist, racist) or the values held by them.

 5-5 ## INFORMATION COMPREHENSION AND RETENTION

You also need to adapt your speech to ensure comprehension and retention throughout it. Five ways to do so are (1) appealing to diverse learning styles, (2) using transitions, (3) choosing specific and familiar language, (4) using vivid language and examples, and (f) comparing unfamiliar ideas with familiar ones.

5-5a Appeal to Diverse Learning Styles

A **learning style** is a person's preferred way of receiving information. Because we differ in our preferred learning styles, you should present your ideas in ways that make it easy for all audience members to understand and remember what you are saying. Models for understanding learning styles have been developed by many scholars.[7] One prominent model, called Kolb's cycle of learning, conceptualizes learning preferences along four dimensions: feeling, thinking, watching, and doing.[8] Kolb's model is actually rooted in John Dewey's experiential learning theory.[9] Exhibit 5.1 illustrates the watching, doing, feeling, and thinking dimensions of the learning cycle.

Some people prefer to learn by "watching" and easily understand and remember things they see and relate to well-designed visual aids and vivid examples they can

Exhibit 5.1
Kolb's Cycle of Learning

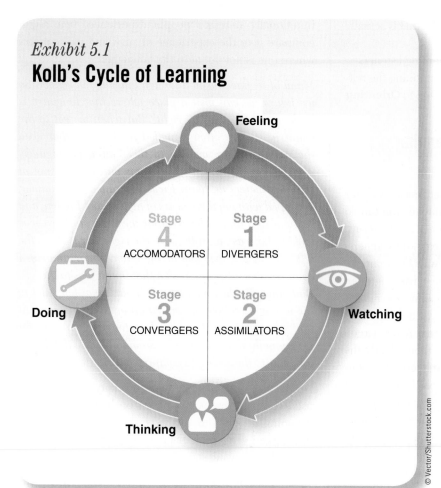

© Vector/Shutterstock.com

picture in their minds. Others prefer to learn by doing. For these people, hands-on activities aid their comprehension and memory. People who prefer to learn by doing relate well when speakers provide real-life applications and clearly state how the speech topic is relevant to their personal or professional lives.

Some people learn best when their feelings are engaged. These people learn well from stories and other supporting material that appeal to their emotions or senses. Other people learn well by thinking about factual material and connect well when ideas are supported with detailed definitions, explanations, facts, and statistics.

Although each of us has a preferred learning style, research also reveals that all people learn most effectively when ideas are presented in ways that "round" the entire cycle of learning.[10] So as you develop your speech, adapt to diverse learning styles by presenting information in ways that appeal to each of the four dimensions (watching, feeling, doing, and thinking).

For example, suppose you are trying to make the point that understanding simple directions can be a problem for functionally illiterate people. You could do so by saying:

For instance, a person who is functionally illiterate might not be able to read or understand a label that says, "Take three times a day after eating."

Now look at how much richer this explanation becomes when it is developed in ways that appeal to different learning styles:

Many Americans are functionally illiterate. In fact, about 35 million people, or 20 percent of the adult population, have serious difficulties with common reading tasks (thinking). That means that one of every five people cannot read well enough to understand how to bake a frozen pizza, how to assemble a child's bicycle from printed instructions, or which bus to catch from the signs at the stop (feeling). Many functionally illiterate people don't read well enough to follow the directions on this bottle [show an enlarged image of the label on a medicine bottle that reads, "Take three times a day after eating"] (watching). Not only that, they wouldn't know they need to "press down while turning" to remove this cap [demonstrate removing the cap from the pill bottle] (doing). So the directions on a prescription bottle like this [show visual aid of enlarged prescription bottle with directions written in garbled nonsense words] are basically meaningless.

5-5b Use Transitions

When listeners have trouble following a speaker's organization, they have difficulty understanding the message. So you should use transitions to help your audience follow along. A **transition** is a sentence or two that summarizes one main point and introduces the next one. Suppose your goal is to explain the three phases of clinical trial a cancer drug must pass through to earn FDA approval. After explaining the goals of the first phase, you might use a transition like this: "So the goal of the first phase is to see whether a drug that is safe in animals is also safe in humans. Phase I trials are not designed to

> **transition** a sentence or two that summarizes one main point and introduces the next one

determine whether or not the drug works; that is actually the goal in Phase II trials."

To see an excellent example of orienting listeners—former President Bill Clinton's speech outlining the reasons for NATO involvement in Kosovo—go to **Orienting Listeners** in Speak3 Online.

5-5c Choose Specific and Familiar Language

Words have many meanings, so you want to make sure your listeners understand the meaning you intend. You can do so by using specific language and choosing familiar terms. Specific words clear up the confusion caused by general words by narrowing the focus in some way. For example, saying "a feisty little year-old Yorkshire terrier" is more specific than "a dog." Narrowing the meaning encourages your listeners to picture the same thing you are.

You should also use familiar words. Avoid jargon and slang terms unless (1) you define them clearly the first time you use them and (2) they are central to your speech goal. For instance, in a speech on the four major problems faced by functionally illiterate people in the workplace, your audience will need to understand what you mean by "functionally illiterate." You should offer your definition early in the speech: "By 'functionally illiterate,' I mean people who have trouble accomplishing simple reading and writing tasks."

5-5d Use Vivid Language and Examples

Vivid examples help audience members understand and remember abstract, complex, and novel material. One vivid example can help us understand a complicated concept. As you prepare, find or create real or hypothetical examples and illustrations to help your audience understand new and complex information. For example, in the functionally illiterate definition, the description "people who have trouble accomplishing simple reading and writing tasks" can be made more vivid by adding: "For instance, a functionally illiterate person could not read and understand the directions on a prescription label that states, 'Take three times a day with a glass of water. Do not take on an empty stomach.'"

5-5e Compare Unfamiliar Ideas with Familiar Ones

An easy way to adapt material to your audience is to compare new ideas with ideas the audience already understands. As you prepare, identify places where you can use comparisons. In the speech on functional illiteracy, if you want the audience of literates to sense what functionally illiterate people experience, you might compare it to the experience of surviving in a country where one is not fluent in the language:

Many of us have taken a foreign language in school. So we figure we can visit a place where that language is spoken and "get along," right? But when we get to the country, we are often appalled to discover that even the road signs are written in this "foreign" language. And we can't quite make the signs out, at least not at sixty kilometers an hour. I was in France last summer, equipped with my three years of high school French, and I saw a sign that indicated that the train station I was looking for was "à droit"—"to the right," or is it "to the left"? I knew it was one or the other. Unfortunately, I couldn't remember and took a shot that it was to the left. Bad move. By the time I figured it out, I was ten miles in the wrong direction and ended up missing my train. At that moment, I could imagine how tough life must be for functionally illiterate people. So many "little details" of life require the ability to comprehend written messages.

Devon, a student at the University of California, used comparisons in his speech on how the Japanese economy affects U.S. markets. To help his audience understand geographic data about Japan, he could just quote the following statistics:[11]

Japan is small and densely populated. The nation's 127 million people live in a land area of 138,500 square miles, giving them a population density of 917 persons per square mile.

Instead, he used a comparison to enhance understanding:

Japan is a small, densely populated nation. Its population of 127 million is nearly half that of the United States. Yet the Japanese are crowded into a land area of only 138,500 square miles—roughly the same size as California. Just think of the implications of having nearly half the population of the United States living here in California, where 38 million people—about one-fifth of that total—now live. In fact, Japan packs 917 persons into every square mile of land, whereas in the United States we average about 91 persons per square mile. Overall, then, Japan is about 10 times as crowded as the United States.

Even though most of his listeners probably don't know the total land area of the United States, they do know that the United States covers a great deal of territory. Likewise, his California audience would have a sense of the size of their home state compared with the rest of the nation. Devon researched statistics on the United States and California to make these comparisons. If Devon were speaking to an audience in another state, he could tailor his ideas by using information about that state instead of California.

5-6 LANGUAGE AND CULTURAL DIFFERENCES

Western European speaking traditions inform the approach to public speaking we discuss in this book. However, public speaking is a social act that varies across cultures. So when you address an audience consisting of people from ethnic and language groups different from your own, you should make two adaptations: try to be understandable when speaking in a second language and show respect by choosing culturally appropriate supporting material.

5-6a Work to Be Understood When Speaking in Your Second Language

When speaking to an audience in a language that is not your native language, audience members may have difficulty understanding you because you may speak with an accent, mispronounce words, choose inappropriate words, or misuse idioms. You can help your audience understand you by speaking more

iStockphoto/Thinkstock

Help your audience associate the unfamiliar . . . with the familiar.

slowly and articulating as clearly as you can. By slowing your speaking rate, you give yourself additional time to pronounce difficult sounds and choose words whose meanings you know. You can also use visual aids to reinforce key terms and concepts as you move through your speech. Doing so assures listeners that they've understood you correctly.

One of the best ways to improve is to practice in front of friends who are native speakers. Ask them to take note of words and phrases that you mispronounce or misuse. Then they can work with you to correct your pronunciation or to help you choose better words to express your ideas. Also keep in mind that the more you practice speaking the language, the more comfortable you will become with it.

5-6b Choose Culturally Appropriate Supporting Material

When speaking to audiences who are vastly different from you, it will take work to find out about their culture and experiences so you can adapt your ideas and information to them. This may mean conducting additional research to find relevant supporting material. Or it may require you to elaborate on ideas that might be self-explanatory in your own culture. For example, suppose that Maria, a Mexican-American exchange student, were giving a narrative/personal experience speech for her speech class at Yeshiva University in Israel on the *quinceañera* party she had when she turned fifteen. Because students in Israel probably don't have any experience with the Mexican coming-of-age tradition of *quinceañera* parties, they may have trouble understanding the significance of this event unless Maria uses her knowledge of the bar mitzvah and bat mitzvah coming-of-age ritual Jewish celebrations as comparisons.

5-7 FORMING A SPECIFIC AUDIENCE ADAPTATION PLAN

You now understand the challenges speakers face in developing and maintaining audience interest and understanding, and you have read about the adaptation techniques that can help you overcome these challenges. At this point, you can develop your own adaptation plan by answering the following questions:

ACTION STEP ACTIVITY

Recognizing Opportunities for Audience Adaptation

To identify opportunities for audience adaptation, state your potential topic and then answer the following questions.

Potential topic: _____

1. What is my audience's initial disposition toward my speech topic likely to be?
2. What common ground do audience members share with one another and with me?
3. How relevant will the audience find this material?
4. How can I demonstrate that the material is timely, proximate, and has personal impact for this audience?
5. What can I do to enhance my credibility?
6. How can I make it easier for audience members to comprehend and remember the information?
7. What language or cultural differences do audience members have with one another and with me?

Access this activity—Action Step 2, Activity 2—and view another student sample of this activity at SPEAK 3 Online at www.cengagebrain.com.

Student Response: Recognizing Opportunities for Audience Adaptation

Potential topic: *The effects of the California drought*

1. **What is my audience's initial disposition toward my speech topic likely to be?**
   Initially, audience members will most likely be only moderately interested in the California drought. I hope to make audience interest spike by demonstrating that the California drought is more than an inconvenience for local residents, but a severe economic, environmental, and agricultural threat affecting the entire United States.

2. **What common ground do audience members share with one another and with me?**
   My audience and I share U.S. residency, which is very important for this issue, because California farmers, who use 80 percent of California's water, supply our nation with a third of all vegetables and two thirds of all fruits and nuts consumed in the country. Our shared stake in our country's food supply highlights the common ground between my topic and my classmates' interests. I can also use personal pronouns and rhetorical questions to further my audience's sense of the topic's relevancy. My audience will have minimal background knowledge about the California drought, so I must explain all of the foreign concepts that I will introduce.

3. **How relevant will the audience find this material?**
   Initially, audience members with little connection to the state of California and/or environmental issues are unlikely to consider the California drought as a personally relevant issue.

4. **How can I demonstrate that the material is timely, proximate, and has personal impact for this audience?**
   I will make the material timely by explaining that water insecurity will inevitably increase water bills and food prices, make certain foods unavailable, harm farmer's businesses, use irreplaceable fresh groundwater, and lead to a serious agricultural problem in the United States. I will also use videos and photos and will point to other recent examples of water scarcity, like the Aral Sea, which after being tapped for irrigation purposes, is now completely dry.

5. **What can I do to enhance my credibility?**
   To assure my audience of my credibility, I will use quality research sources and verbally cite them during my speech. In my introduction, I will discuss my experiences studying desalination techniques when I interned abroad in Israel, as well talk about my first-hand experiences with living in a California drought.

6. **How can I make it easier for audience members to comprehend and remember the information?**
   I will round the cycle of learning by showing time lapse videos of water reserves drying up in California (watching), sharing my concerns about the drought and water insecurity (feeling), giving clear facts and statistics showing how the California drought not only affects California citizens, but all citizens in the United States. (thinking), and finally outlining how to prevent water insecurity and minimize our water footprint (doing).

(Continued)

7. What language or cultural differences do audience members have with one another and with me?

I will be speaking in my first language, but because my audience will have minimal knowledge surrounding the topic, I will explain all technical terms and foreign concepts. I will refrain from using informal slang words which might be unfamiliar to my audience, and speak at a slower rate than usual, paying special attention to articulation. Because some of my class-mates are international students, I will perform additional research to see if droughts and water scarcity are issues in their home countries. If I do find examples, I will include them in my speech.

Sources

Buchanan, L., Keller L. J., Park, H. (2015, May 21). Your contribution to the California drought.The New York Times.Retrieved online from: http://www.nytimes.com/interactive/2015/05/21/us/your-contribution-to-the-california-drought.html?_r=1.

Clark Howard, B (2014, October 2). Aral Sea's eastern basin is dry for first time in 600 years. National Geographic.Retrieved online from: http://news.nationalgeographic.com/news/2014/10/141001-aral-sea-shrinking-drought-water-environment/.

Dimick, D. (2014, August 21). If you think the water crisis can't get worse, wait until the aquifers are drained. National Geographic. Retrieved online from: http://news.nationalgeographic.com/news/2014/08/140819-groundwater-california-drought-aquifers-hidden-crisis/.

Harris, E. (2015, June14). Israel bringing its years of desalination experience to California.NPR.Retrieved online from: http://www.npr.org/sections/parallels/2015/06/14/413981435/israel-bringing-its-years-of-desalination-experience-to-california

1. What is my audience's initial disposition toward my topic? What can I do to enhance audience interest?

2. What common ground do audience members share with one another and with me? How and where can I use personal pronouns, rhetorical questions, and common experiences to enhance the perception of common ground?

3. How relevant will the audience find this material? How can I demonstrate that the material is timely, proximate, and has personal impact for audience members?

4. What can I do to enhance my credibility? How did I develop my expertise on this topic, and how can I share that with the audience? How can I demonstrate my trustworthiness as I speak? What will I do to help the audience perceive me as personable?

5. How can I make it easier for audience members to comprehend and remember the information? What types of material can I use to appeal to different learning style preferences? What key terms will I need to define? What new concepts might I develop with vivid language and examples? What new ideas might I want to compare to ones the audience is already familiar with?

Adapt your ideas to your audience's cultural experiences.

6.   What language or cultural differences do audience members have with one another and with me? If I will be speaking in a second language, how will I increase the likelihood that the audience will understand me? What cultural differences do I need to be sensitive to, and what culturally appropriate material might I search for and use?

Speech Planning Action Step 2, Activity 2 will help you identify opportunities for audience adaptation as you develop your speeches. See the Student Response box immediately following the activity for a sample of how one student completed this exercise.

STUDY TOOLS

LOCATED IN TEXTBOOK

☐ Tear-out Chapter Review cards at the end of the book

☐ Review with the Quick Quiz below

LOCATED ON SPEAK3 ONLINE AT CENGAGEBRAIN.COM

☐ Review Key Term flashcards and create your own cards

☐ Track your knowledge and understanding of key concepts in speech communication

☐ Complete practice and graded quizzes to prepare for tests

☐ Complete interactive content within SPEAK3 Online

☐ View the chapter highlight boxes for SPEAK3 Online

Quick Quiz (answers in Solutions Appendix)

T   F   1. As a speaker, it is important to understand the knowledge and opinions that the audience has about a topic before they hear you speak.

T   F   2. One way to increase the relevance of information is to make it timely.

T   F   3. Rhetorical questions are supposed to have only one answer.

T   F   4. In general, adapting to the audience's attitude is important only for persuasive speeches.

T   F   5. A great way to establish expertise on a subject is to demonstrate your track record on it.

6. In her speech on income taxes that she is giving to a local school board, Courtney shows her audience that a decrease in taxes will harm school funding. She is:
   a. establishing relevance
   b. demonstrating proximity
   c. demonstrating timeliness
   d. adapting to the audience
   e. demonstrating ethics

7. A learning style is the way a person prefers to receive:
   a. criticism
   b. praise
   c. information
   d. encouragement
   e. feedback

8. When an audience finds that a speech is relevant, it means that they consider the information in the speech:
   a. timely
   b. witty
   c. depressing
   d. important
   e. contrasting

9. To summarize a main point and move on to the next main point, you should use:
   a. transitions
   b. links
   c. connections
   d. bridges
   e. spans

10. The knowledge, attitudes, and beliefs shared between the audience and speaker is known as:
    a. similarity
    b. commonality
    c. foundation
    d. bridge
    e. common ground

Chapter Takeaways

List three key takeaways from this chapter:

-

-

-

6 Topic Development

LEARNING OUTCOMES

6-1 Locate and evaluate information sources about your topic.

6-2 Select relevant information about your topic.

6-3 Record information accurately.

6-4 Cite sources appropriately.

After finishing
this chapter go to
PAGE 102 for
STUDY TOOLS.

Sound Familiar?

Justin was concerned. He was scheduled to give his speech in a week, but he hadn't even begun to conduct any research. A couple of months ago, he had read a magazine article about vanishing honeybees while in the doctor's office waiting room and decided that it would be an interesting topic for his informative speech. Although he couldn't remember the name of the magazine, he pulled out his laptop and googled "vanishing honeybees." To his surprise, he got 110,000 hits. He wondered how in the world he would go about sorting through all this information and all these sources to determine which ones would be best for his speech.

Justin's experience is not unusual. Most of us have formed opinions about a variety of subjects based on our personal experiences, interactions with others, and things we've read or watched online or on television. But when it comes to presenting our ideas in a public forum, we need to do research to find evidence to support them. **Evidence** is essentially any information that clarifies, explains, or otherwise adds depth or breadth to a topic. What is particularly challenging in the digital age we live in today is not an inability to find the information we're looking for, but sorting through the array of information at our fingertips to evaluate and select the best information for our speeches. In this chapter, we explain how to locate and evaluate a variety of information types and sources, identify and select the best information, and then cite the sources of that information appropriately in your speech.

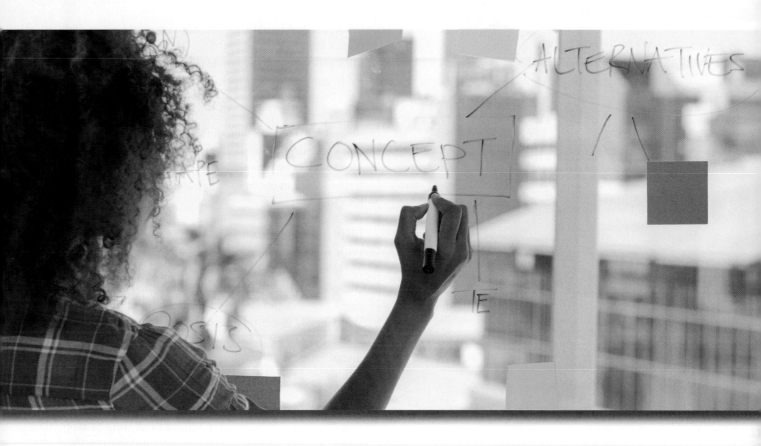

6-1 LOCATE AND EVALUATE INFORMATION SOURCES

How can you quickly find the best information related to your specific speech goal? You can start by assessing your own knowledge and experience. Then you can move to **secondary research**, which is the process of locating information discovered by other people. This includes doing Internet and library searches for relevant books, articles, general references, and Web sites. Information (a.k.a. evidence) can come in written, visual, audio, and audiovisual forms. Justin, for example, discovered an interview with actress Ellen Page done by Bill Maher posted on YouTube, an informative video posted on the USDA's Web site, and a chart showing the progression of this crisis over the past decade posted by the National Agriculture Statistics Service. If the information you find from secondary sources doesn't answer all your questions, you may need to conduct **primary research**, which is the process of collecting data about your topic directly from the real world.

3 ACTION STEP

Gather and evaluate information

A. **Examine areas where you need additional information.**

B. **Locate, evaluate, and select a variety of information types and sources.**

C. **Record information.**

D. **Cite sources.**

6-1a Personal Knowledge and Experiences

One form of evidence can be personal knowledge and experiences. For instance, saxophone

evidence any information that clarifies, explains, or otherwise adds depth or breadth to a topic

secondary research the process of locating information that has been discovered by other people

primary research the process of conducting your own study to acquire the information you need

© iStockphoto.com/Blend_Images

Draw on your skills, knowledge, and experiences when giving speeches.

players know how to select and care for a reed, entrepreneurs know the key features of a good business plan, and dieticians know a good deal about healthy diets. So Diane, a skilled long-distance runner, can draw from her own knowledge and experience to develop her speech on "How to Train for a Marathon." If you have personal knowledge and experience about the topic, however, you should also share your **credentials**—your experience or education that qualifies you to speak with authority on a specific subject. For Diane, establishing her credentials means briefly mentioning her training and expertise as a long-distance runner before she launches into her speech about training for a marathon.

6-1b Secondary Research

Most of us usually begin to develop a topic by searching online for sources and information. For example, we can search Web sites, blogs, YouTube, and discussion boards, as well as online libraries and databases. Some sources are available digitally either free or for a fee. Some might require a visit to a library to pick up hard copies or

credentials your experience or education that qualifies you to speak with authority on a specific subject

hits links to all sorts of Web pages, images, videos, articles and other sources that include material about the keywords entered into a search engine

through interlibrary loan. We can also ask librarians for help online via "ask the librarian" links or in person at a library. Because most of us do research online these days, we begin this section with a discussion of some guidelines for doing so effectively, efficiently, and ethically. We focus specifically on using search engines, encyclopedias such as Wikipedia, commercial and nonprofit organization Web sites, personal and corporate blogs, and online social networks. Then we talk about different types of sources you can use both online and in local libraries and how to evaluate them.

Internet Sources

With today's technology, we have instant access to a plethora of information about any topic. The challenge comes in sifting through all this information and evaluating it to select the best evidence to support our claims. We typically begin online searches by typing keywords into a general search engine such as Google or Bing, metasearch engines such as Dogpile or MetaCrawler, or online library databases such as EBSCOhost, Google Scholar, or LexisNexis. Links to many different library databases can be found on any library's Web site. These searches reveal **hits**, which are links to all sorts of Web pages, images, videos, articles, and other sources that include material about the keywords. In our opening vignette, recall that Justin typed the words "vanishing honeybees" into Google and got 110,000 hits.

Many times one of the hits will be to an online encyclopedia entry in Wikipedia. These entries can be a good starting point for learning general information and for locating additional references about a given topic. Justin read the Wikipedia entry that came up from his "vanishing honeybees" search and learned that the official name for the phenomenon is colony collapse disorder. He also perused the Reference List and Further Reading list accompanying the Wikipedia entry, where he found articles published by the *New York Times*, *Science News*, and the *Proceedings of the National Academies of Science* among others. And he discovered several helpful Web sites listed under External Links from organizations such as the United States Department of Agriculture (USDA) and the National Honey Board. There is nothing wrong with starting the research process by reading a Wikipedia entry. In fact, doing so can be quite helpful, but Wikipedia should never be cited as an actual source. It's a great place to familiarize yourself with a topic, but it's unreliable for sourcing.

Other hits may include commercial Web sites, which are created and maintained by for-profit organizations. Commercial Web site URLs typically end in .com. Commercial Web sites can be helpful for locating information about a company such as the National Honey Board, for finding current or popular culture material, and for finding presentational aids. Justin found a short audiovisual clip to use in his speech about the vanishing honeybee phenomenon.

Nonprofit organization Web sites can be distinguished from commercial sites because their URLs will usually end in .org. Nonprofit organizations are dedicated to issues or causes and can often provide examples of emotional appeal. For example, Justin found some startling statistics about the $15 billion in crops the United States would lose without the bees needed to pollinate the plants.

Blogs are Web sites that provide personal viewpoints of their author. They can be created and maintained by an individual or an organization. They might be focused on a particular subject and include images, audios, and audiovisuals. Because they are often biased toward the opinion of the blogger, information on blogs may need to be verified with other sources. However, blogs can be a good source for finding public opinion examples and to humanize the topic. The most efficient way to find blogs is to use a blog search engine such as Google Blog Search or Blogarama. Justin found some interesting opinions on *Dady Cherie's News Junkie Post* blog. Because blogs can be written by anyone, you will need to determine whether the author is credible by locating his or her credentials. If you cannot determine answers—as was the case for Justin—you should not use the information in your speech.

Online social networks are Web sites where communities of people interact with one another over the Internet. Some popular examples include Facebook, LinkedIn, Twitter, and Instagram. As with blog posts, postings on these sites can be used to find supporting material to humanize a topic, appeal to emotions, and serve as presentational aids.

Other Types of Sources

You can also find pertinent information in sources that can be found online or in a local library. These include encyclopedias, books, articles in academic journals and magazines, news media, statistical sources, biographies, quotation books and Web sites, and government documents.

1. Encyclopedias. Encyclopedia entries (including Wikipedia, which we discussed earlier) can serve as a good starting point by providing an overview about your topic. But because encyclopedias provide only overviews, they should never be the only source you rely on. General encyclopedias contain short articles about a wide variety of subjects. In addition, specialized encyclopedias focus on areas such as art, history, religion, philosophy, and science (e.g., *African American Encyclopedia, Latino Encyclopedia, Asian American Encyclopedia, Encyclopedia of Computer Science, Encyclopedia of Women, Encyclopedia of Women in American Politics*). As we have already mentioned, Wikipedia is a popular research tool that is also controversial because there is no way to confirm the credibility of the people posting information in its entries. Nevertheless, reference lists and notes sections can point you in the direction of good sources you can use to develop your speech.

2. Books. If your topic has been around for a while, books have likely been written about it. Although books are excellent sources of in-depth information about a topic, keep in mind that most of the information in a book is probably at least two years old by the time it is published. So books are not a good resource if your topic is very recent or if you're looking for the latest information. You can also use the library call number for one book to physically locate other books on the same subject. For example, when Diane went to the shelves to locate a book called *Improving Sports Performance in Middle and Long-Distance Running*, she discovered a number of related books located in the same area, including one she would also use in her speech titled *Advanced Sports Nutrition* by Dr. Dan Benardot.

3. Articles. Articles, which may contain more current or highly specialized information on your topic than a book would, are published in **periodicals**—magazines and journals published at regular intervals. The information in periodical articles is often more current than that published in books because many periodicals are published weekly, biweekly, or monthly. So a periodical article is likely to be a better source for a topic that's currently "in the news." Most libraries subscribe to electronic databases that index periodicals, and many can be found via a general online search. Justin's general search using Google, for example, revealed articles in online periodicals by *Time, Newsweek,* and *Science News*.

4. News Media. News media articles can provide facts about and interpretations of both contemporary and historical issues. They can also provide information about local issues and perspectives.

---

blogs Web sites that provide personal viewpoints of their author

online social networks Web sites where communities of people interact with one another over the Internet

periodicals magazines and journals published at regular intervals

Researching for the Star Role

Researching is critical for developing effective public speeches. The same is true of actors who play famous figures who deliver speeches in the context of the film. Even before David Oyelowo, right, was cast to play Dr. Martin Luther King, Jr. in the Academy Award-winning film *Selma*, he was preparing for the role. He read books, watched documentaries, and devoured anything he could get his hands on about the civil rights leader. King's actual speeches were not licensed for the film, so Oyelowo had to imagine how King would have delivered the series of fictional speeches that comprised 15 to 20 percent of the film. Oyelowo's goal throughout was to bring to his performance the quality of transcendence that Dr. King exemplified in historical situations. And although Oyelowo did not receive an Oscar for his performance, he will get another chance, as Steven Spielberg has asked him to reprise his role as Dr. King. This time, however, Oyelowo will deliver King's actual speeches.[1]

JStone/Shutterstock.com

Keep in mind, however, that most authors of news media articles are journalists who are not experts themselves on the topics they write about. So it is best not to rely solely on news media articles for your speech. Today, most traditional news media publications are available online (e.g., *New York Times*, *Wall Street Journal*), which makes them very accessible. Two electronic newspaper indexes that are most useful if they are available to you are the National Newspaper Index, which indexes five major newspapers—the *New York Times*, *Wall Street Journal*, *Christian Science Monitor*, *Washington Post*, and *Los Angeles Times*—and Newsbank, which provides not only the indexes but also the text of articles from thousands of newspapers, as well as business journals, newswires, broadcast transcripts, and more. You might also find good information in online-only news sources such as the Huffington Post and the Drudge Report. Keep in mind, however, that online news sources are frequently biased in one direction or another, putting their credibility in question.

5. Statistical sources. Statistical sources present numerical information on a wide variety of subjects. When you need facts about demography, continents, heads of state, weather, or similar subjects, access one of the many single-volume sources, such as *The Statistical Abstract of the United States* or *The World Factbook*, that report such data. Justin, for example, consulted the *National Agriculture Statistics Service* to gather statistics about the declining honeybee population in the United States.

6. Biographies. When you need an account of a person's life, from thumbnail sketches to reasonably complete essays, you can consult a biographical reference source. Some examples include *Who's Who in America* and *International Who's Who*, *Contemporary Black Biography*, *Dictionary of Hispanic Biography*, *Native American Women*, *Who's Who of American Women*, and *Who's Who among Asian Americans*. You can easily find these sources at a local library or bookstore, as well as online at outlets such as Amazon.com. Many famous people also have some of their biographical information posted on Web sites. For her speech about running, Diane found biographical information about Paula Radcliffe by reading several Web sites about the famous female marathoner.

7. Quotation books and Web sites. A good quotation can be especially provocative as well as informative, and there are times you want to use a quotation from a respected person. *Bartlett's Familiar Quotations* is a popular source of quotes from both historical and contemporary figures. Some others include *The International Thesaurus of Quotations*; *Harper Book of American Quotations*; *My Soul Looks Back, 'Less I Forget: A Collection of Quotations by People of Color*; *The New Quotable Woman*; and *The Oxford Dictionary of Quotations*. Some popular quotation Web sites include The Quotations Page and Quoteland.com. You might also find good quotations on social networking sites such as Twitter and Facebook.

8. Government documents. If your topic is related to public policy, government documents may provide useful information. The *Federal Register* publishes daily regulations and legal notices issued by the U.S. executive branch and all federal agencies. It is divided into sections, such as rules and regulations and Sunshine Act meetings. Of special interest are announcements of hearings and investigations, committee meetings, and agency decisions and rulings. The *Monthly Catalog of United States Government Publications* covers publications of all branches of the federal government.

Skim Sources

Because your search of sources is likely to uncover far more information than you can use, you will want to skim sources to determine whether or not to read them in full. **Skimming** is a method of rapidly going through a work to determine what is covered and how.

As you skim an article, think about whether the source really presents information on the area of the topic you are exploring and whether it contains any documented statistics, examples, meaningful visuals, or quotable opinions. You can start by reading the **abstract**—a short paragraph summarizing the research findings. As you skim a book, read the table of contents carefully, look at the index, and review the headings and visuals in pertinent chapters, asking

beboy/Shutterstock.com

the same questions as you would for a magazine article. A few minutes spent skimming will save you hours of research time.

Evaluate Sources

The validity, accuracy, and reliability of sources vary. **Valid sources** report factual information that can be counted on to be true. Tabloid and gossip magazines and newspapers are generally considered less valid sources than mainline news publications that use "fact-checkers" before publishing articles. **Accurate sources** attempt to present unbiased information and often include a balanced discussion of controversial topics. For example, the Congressional Record presents an accurate account of what each member of U.S. Congress said on the House or Senate floor. A newspaper account of a member's speech, however, may report only part of what was said and may even distort the remark by taking it out of context. **Reliable sources** are those that have a history of presenting valid and accurate information. Four criteria

can help you evaluate the validity, accuracy, and reliability of sources.

1. Authority. The first test of a source is the expertise of its author and/or the reputation of the publishing or sponsoring organization. When an author is listed, you can check the author's credentials through biographical references or by seeing if the author has a home page listing professional qualifications. You can use the electronic periodical indexes or check the Library of Congress to see what else the author has published in the field.

On the Internet, you will find information that is anonymous or credited to someone whose background is not clear. In these cases, your ability to trust the information depends on evaluating the qualifications of the sponsoring organization. URLs ending in ".gov" (governmental), ".edu" (educational), and ".org" (organizational) are noncommercial sites with institutional publishers. The URL ".com" indicates that the sponsor is a for-profit organization. If you do not know whether you can trust the sources, then do not use the information.

2. Objectivity. Although all authors have a **stance**—an attitude, perspective, or viewpoint on a topic—be wary of information that seems excessively slanted. Documents that have been published by business, government, or public interest groups should be carefully scrutinized for obvious biases or good public relations fronts. To evaluate stance in articles and books, read the preface or identify the thesis statement. These often reveal the author's point of view. When evaluating a Web site, look for its purpose. Most home pages contain a purpose or mission statement (sometimes in a link called "About"). Armed with this information, you

skimming a method of rapidly going through a work to determine what is covered and how

abstract a short paragraph summarizing the research findings

valid sources information sources that report factual information that can be counted on to be true

accurate sources information sources that attempt to present unbiased information and often include a balanced discussion of controversial topics

reliable sources information sources that have a history of presenting valid and accurate information

stance an attitude, perspective, or viewpoint on a topic

are in a better position to evaluate stance and recognize excessive source bias regarding the topic.

3. **Currency.** In general, more recent information is preferred unless, for example, you are documenting a historical event). So, unless you're doing a speech on a historical event, be sure to consult the latest information you can find. One of the reasons for using Web-based sources is that they often provide more up-to-date information than printed sources,[2] but that isn't always the case. To determine how current the information is, you need to find out when the book was published, the article was written, the study was conducted, or the article was placed on the Web or revised. Web page dates are usually listed at the end of the article. If no dates are listed, you have no way of judging how current the information is.

4. **Relevance.** During your research, you will likely come across a great deal of interesting information. Whether that information is appropriate for your speech is another matter. Relevant information is directly related to your topic and supports your main points, making your speech easier to follow and understand. Irrelevant information will only confuse listeners, so you should avoid using it no matter how interesting it is.

Go to **SPEAK3 Online** for additional criteria you can use to evaluate your sources.

6-1c Primary Research

When there is little secondary research available on your topic or on a main idea you want to develop in your speech, or when you wonder whether what you are reading about is true in a particular setting, consider doing primary research, which is conducting your own study in the real world. But keep in mind that primary research is much more labor intensive and time consuming than secondary research, and in the professional world, much more costly. You can conduct fieldwork observations, surveys, interviews, original artifact or document examinations, or experiments.

fieldwork observations (ethnography) a form of primary research based on fieldwork observations

interview a planned, structured conversation where one person asks questions and another answers them

interview protocol the list of questions you plan to ask

Fieldwork Observations

You might choose to learn about a group of people and their practices by conducting **fieldwork observations**, which is a method also known as **ethnography**. Essentially, you carefully observe people or groups of people while immersed in their community. You can conduct fieldwork as a *participant observer* by engaging in interactions and activities with the people you are studying, or as a *non-participant observer* by observing but not engaging with them. If, for instance, you are planning to talk about how social service agencies help homeless people find shelter and job training, or the process involved in adopting a pet, you can learn more by visiting or even volunteering for a period of time at a homeless shelter or humane society. By focusing on specific behaviors and taking notes on your observations and interpretations of them, you will have a record of specific information to use in your speech.

Surveys

Recall that a *survey* is a canvassing of people to get information about their ideas and opinions. Surveys may be conducted in person, over the phone, via the Internet, or in paper-and-pencil documents. At times, your secondary research will reveal publications that summarize findings from surveys, which have been conducted by other people or organizations. At other times, you may want to conduct your own survey. For example, you might prepare a brief survey using SurveyMonkey or Qualitrics and post a link to it on Facebook or Twitter.

Interviews

Like media reporters, you may get some of your best information from an **interview**—a highly structured conversation where one person asks questions and another answers them. You might conduct your interview in person, over the telephone, or online using software such as Skype or Adobe Connect. To be effective, you'll want to select the best person to interview, prepare a solid **interview protocol** (the list of questions you plan to ask), and adhere to several ethical guidelines when conducting and then processing the actual interview.

Selecting the best person. Somewhere on campus or in the larger community are people who have expertise in the topic area of your speech. Usually a bit of research and a few e-mails or telephone calls will lead you to a good person to talk with about your topic. For instance, for a speech on "how to get a music recording contract," you might begin by asking a professor in the music department for the name of a music production agency in the area. Or you could find one by searching online. Once you find a Web site, you can usually locate an "About Us" or "Contact Us" link, which will offer names, titles, e-mail addresses, and phone numbers. You should be able to find someone appropriate for your purpose from this list. Once you have identified a potential interviewee, you should contact the person to make an appointment. You can do so either by e-mail or telephone. Be forthright in your reasons for scheduling the interview. Whether your interview is for a class speech or for a different audience, say so. You should also tell the person how long you expect the interview to take and suggest several dates and time ranges so the person can select the date and time that works best for him or her. If you make the appointment more than a few days in advance, you should contact the person again the day before the interview to confirm the date, time, and location (in person or Internet address information) of the interview.

Before your interview, make sure you have researched the topic, especially anything the interviewee has written about it. Likewise, do your research to understand the expert's credentials. Interviewees are more likely to talk with you if you appear informed, and being informed will ensure that you ask better questions. You don't want to waste the interviewee's time by asking questions you could find elsewhere.

Preparing the interview protocol. The heart of an effective interview is the interview protocol, which is a list of good questions you plan to ask. How many questions you ask depends on how much time you will have for the interview. Begin by listing the topics you want to cover. Exhibit 6.1 presents a list of topics for an interview with a music producer when the goal is to learn about how to find and sign new talent. Then prepare a couple of **rapport-building questions**, which are nonthreatening questions designed to put the interviewee at ease and demonstrate your respect. For his speech on vanishing honeybees and colony collapse disorder (CCD), Justin began his interview with "How did you get interested in doing research on CCD?"

Just as the topics in a well-developed speech are structured in an outline with main points, subpoints, and supporting material, a good interview protocol is structured into primary and secondary questions. **Primary questions** are introductory questions about each major interview topic. **Secondary questions** are follow-up questions

designed to probe the answers given to primary questions. Some follow-up questions probe by simply encouraging the interviewee to continue ("And then?" "Is there more?"). Others probe into a specific detail the interviewee mentioned or failed to mention. For the music producer interview, for example, you might probe with: "You didn't mention genre. What role might that play in your decision to offer a contract?" And finally, some probe into feelings: "How did it feel when her first album went platinum?"

Open questions are broad-based queries that ask the interviewee to provide perspective, ideas, information, or opinions ("Why do you think the vanishing honeybee crisis is happening so quickly and dramatically today?" "What are some kinds of behaviors you have seen bees exhibit when afflicted with this disease?" "What would you recommend people like me who aren't scientists or beekeepers do to help?" "What research studies are you working on next?"). Open questions enable the interviewer to find out about the person's perspectives, values, and goals, but they do take time to answer.[3]

Closed questions are narrowly focused and require very brief (one- or two-word) answers. Some require a simple yes or no ("Do you believe we can stop the CCD crisis?"); others need only a short response ("What do you believe to be the most significant cause of CCD?"). By asking closed questions, interviewers can control the interview and obtain specific information quickly. But the answers to closed questions cannot reveal the nuances behind responses, nor are they likely to capture the complexities surrounding the topic.[4]

Open and closed questions may also be neutral or leading. **Neutral questions** do not direct a person's answers. "What can you tell me about your work with Habitat for Humanity?" and "What criteria do you use in deciding whether or not to offer an artist a contract?" are neutral questions. By contrast, **leading questions** guide respondents toward providing certain types of information and imply that the interviewer prefers or expects one answer over another. "What do

rapport-building questions non-threatening questions designed to put the interviewee at ease

primary questions introductory questions about each major interview topic

secondary questions follow-up questions designed to probe the answers given to primary questions

open questions broad-based questions that ask the interviewee to provide perspective, ideas, information, or opinions

closed questions narrowly focused questions that require only very brief answers

neutral questions questions phrased in ways that do not direct a person's answers

leading questions questions phrased in a way that suggests the interviewer has a preferred answer

Exhibit 6.1
Sample Interview Questions

Rapport-Building Opener

How did you get interested in becoming a music producer?

Major Topic Questions

Primary Question #1: How do you find artists to consider for contract?

Secondary Question: Is this different from the methods used by other producers?

Secondary Question: Do artists ever come to you in other ways?

Primary Question #2: Once an artist has been brought to your attention, what course of action follows?

Secondary Question: Do you ever just see an artist or band and immediately sign them?

Secondary Question: What's the longest period of time you "auditioned" an artist or band before signing them?

Primary Question #3: What criteria do you use in deciding to offer a contract?

Secondary Question: How important are the artist's age, sex, or ethnicity?

Primary Question #4: Can you tell me the story of how you came to sign one of your most successful artists?

Secondary Question: What do you think made the artist so successful?

Primary Question #5: Can you tell me the story of an artist you signed who was not successful?

Secondary Question: Why do you think this artist failed?

Secondary Question: Do you think it was a mistake to sign this artist?

© dwphotos/ShutterStock.com

you like about working for Habitat for Humanity?" and "Having a 'commercial sound' is an important criteria, isn't it?" are leading questions.

Conducting the interview. To guide you in the process of conducting effective and ethical interviews, we offer this list of best practices.

- **Dress professionally.** Doing so sends a message to the interviewee that you *respect* the time the person is giving and take the interview seriously.

- **Be prompt.** You also demonstrate *respect* by showing up prepared to begin at the time you have

agreed to. If you are conducting the interview in person, remember to allow enough time for potential traffic or parking problems.

- **Be courteous.** Begin by introducing yourself and thanking the person for taking the time to talk to you. Remember, though, that while interviewees may enjoy talking about the subject and be flattered by your interest, they most likely have nothing to gain from the interview. So you should let them know you are grateful for their time. Most of all, *respect* what the interviewee says regardless of what you may think of the answers.

- **Ask permission to record the interview.** If the interviewee says "no," *respect* his or her wishes and take careful notes instead.

- **Listen carefully.** At key places in the interview, repeat what the interviewee has said in your own words to be sure you really understand. This will ensure your subject that you will report the answers *truthfully* and *fairly* during your speech.

- **Keep the interview moving.** You do not want to rush the person, but you do want to behave *responsibly* by getting your questions answered during the allotted time.

- **Monitor your nonverbal reactions.** Demonstrate *integrity* by maintaining good eye contact. Nod to show understanding, and smile occasionally to maintain a friendly persona. How you look and act is likely to determine whether the person will warm up to you and give you an informative interview.

- **Get permission to quote.** Be sure to get permission for exact quotes. Doing so demonstrates that you *respect* the interviewee and want to report his or her ideas *honestly* and *fairly*. Doing so also communicates that you have *integrity* and strive to act *responsibly*. You might even offer to let the person see a copy of the formal outline before you give the speech. That way, he or she can double-check the accuracy of direct quotations.

- **Confirm credentials.** Before you leave, be sure to confirm your interviewee's professional title and the company or organization he or she represents. Doing so is acting *responsibly* because you'll need these details when explaining why you chose to interview this person.

- **End on time.** As with arriving promptly, ending the interview when you said you would demonstrates *respect* for the interviewee and his or her valuable time and that you act *responsibly* and with *integrity*.

- **Thank the interviewee.** Always close the interview by thanking the interviewee. This closure leads to positive rapport should you need to follow up with them later. It also demonstrates that you *respect* his or her valuable time. You may even follow up with a short thank-you note after you leave.

Processing the interview. Because your interview notes were probably taken in an outline or bullet-point form, the longer you wait to translate them the more difficult doing so will be. Sit down with your notes as soon as possible after the interview to make more extensive notes of the information you may want to use in your

Each episode of the television show "Mythbusters" is actually made up of a series of simple experiments. Adam Savage and Jamie Hyneman, co-hosts, prepare for an episode.

speech. If you recorded the interview, take some time to **transcribe** the responses by translating them word for word into written form. If at any point you are not sure whether you have accurately transcribed what the person said, take a minute to telephone or e-mail him or her to double-check.

Although it is typically a best practice to conduct your interviews in person, that is not always possible. When time or distance make a face-to-face interview impossible, people will instead conduct an interview over the telephone, via e-mail, or using videoconferencing software such as Skype or Google Chat.

Original Artifact or Document Examinations

Sometimes the information you need has not been published. Rather, it may exist in an original unpublished source,

transcribe to translate interview responses word for word into written form

such as an ancient manuscript, a diary, personal correspondence, or company files. Or you may need to view an object to get the information you need, such as a geographic feature, a building, a monument, or an artifact in a museum. Many original artifacts and documents or illustrations of them can also be found online.

Experiments

You can design a study to test a **hypothesis**, which is an educated guess about a cause-and-effect relationship between two or more things. Then you can report the results of your experiment in your speech. Keep in mind that conducting experiments well can take time, and you must understand the principles of the scientific process to be able to trust results of a formal experiment. However, sometimes you can do an informal experiment to test the results of a study you learn about elsewhere.

Speech Planning Action Step 3, Activity 3A will help you evaluate and compile a list of potential sources for your speeches in this course. See the Student Response box immediately following the activity for a sample of how one student completed this exercise.

6-2 SELECT RELEVANT INFORMATION

Once you have collected a variety of sources, you need to identify different types of information to use as evidence in your speech. You might select factual statements, expert opinions, and elaborations conveyed in written, aural, and/or visual forms.

6-2a Factual Statements

Factual statements are those that can be verified. "A recent study confirmed that preschoolers watch an average of twenty-eight hours of television a week" and "The microprocessor, which was invented by Ted Hoff at Intel in 1971, made the creation of personal computers possible" are both statements of fact that can be verified. The chart Justin found illustrating the decreasing honeybee population in the United States and the recorded

hypothesis an educated guess about a cause-and-effect relationship between two or more things
factual statements information that can be verified
statistics numerical facts

excerpt Marney played from Taylor Swift's platinum album are also examples of factual evidence that can be verified.

One way to verify factual information is to check it against other sources on the same subject. Never use any information that is not carefully documented unless you have corroborating sources. Factual statements may come in the form of statistics, examples, and definitions.

Statistics

Statistics are numerical facts. Statistical statements, such as "Only five of every ten local citizens voted in the last election" or "The national unemployment rate for May 2015 was 5.5 percent," can provide impressive support for a point, but when statistics are poorly used in a speech, they may be boring and, in some instances, downright deceiving. Here are some ethical guidelines for using statistics.

1. **Use only statistics you can verify to be reliable and valid.** Taking statistics from only the most reliable sources and double-checking any startling statistics with another source will guard against the use of faulty statistics.

2. **Use only recent statistics so your audience will not be misled.**

3. **Use statistics comparatively.** You can show growth, decline, gain, or loss by comparing two numbers. For example, according to the Bureau of Labor Statistics, the national unemployment rate for May 2015 was 5.5 percent. This statistic is more meaningful when you also mention that this figure has held about steady for three months or when you compare it with 9.6 percent in May 2010 or 4.4 percent in May 2007.

4. **Use statistics sparingly.** A few pertinent numbers are far more effective than a battery of statistics.

5. **Display statistics visually.** Your audience is more likely to understand statistics when you illustrate them on a chart, graph, or some other visual aid.

6. **Remember that statistics are biased.** Mark Twain once said there are three kinds of lies: "lies, damned lies, and statistics."[5] Not all statistics are lies, of course, but consider the source of the statistics you'd like to use, what that source may have been trying to prove with these data, and how that situation might have influenced the way the data were collected and interpreted. In other words, evaluate the source thoughtfully for validity, accuracy, and reliability.

ACTION STEP ACTIVITY

Gathering and Evaluating Information Sources

The goal of this activity is to help you compile a list of potential sources for your speech.

1. Brainstorm a list of keywords related to your speech goal.
2. Identify gaps in your current knowledge about the topic.
3. Use a search engine like Google or Bing to identify potential information sources.
4. Use a library database (either at the library or online) to identify additional potential information sources.
5. Skim the sources to decide which are likely to be the most useful.
6. Evaluate each source for validity, accuracy, and reliability.
7. Determine what (if any) primary research you might conduct to fill remaining gaps.

Student Response: Gathering and Evaluating Information Sources

Speech goal: *I would like the audience to understand why honeybees are vanishing.*

1. **Brainstorm a list of keywords related to your speech goal.** *honeybees, bumblebees, beekeepers, colony collapse disorder*
2. **Identify gaps in your current knowledge about the topic.** *Because I'm a biology major and have done an eight-week internship in the field, I am familiar with the kinds of works I'll need to seek out in order to fill any gaps in my knowledge.*
3. **Use a search engine like Google or Bing to identify potential information sources.** *I searched using Google and found a Wikipedia entry I used as a starting point to locate other Web sites, a YouTube video by the USDA, an interview with a beekeeper, and an interview by Bill Maher with Ellen Page I could use in my speech.*
4. **Use a library database (either at the library or online) to identify additional potential information sources.** *Journal of Bee Biology, Science, Biology Quarterly, Entomol*
5. **Skim the sources to decide which are likely to be the most useful.**
6. **Evaluate each source for validity, accuracy, and reliability.**
7. **Determine what (if any) primary research you might conduct to fill remaining gaps.** *I will interview my adviser, who has been studying the vanishing bees since 2006.*

Examples

Examples are specific instances that illustrate or explain a general factual statement. One or two short examples such as the following ones provide concrete details that help make a generalization meaningful.

One way a company increases its power is to acquire another company. When Delta bought out Northwest Airlines it became the world's largest airline company.

3-D printing is exploding in popularity. In fact, sales of 3-D printers are expected to jump to $13.4 billion by 2018, up from just $1.6 billion last year.

Examples can be real like these, or hypothetical. **Hypothetical examples** are specific illustrations based on reflections about future events. They develop the idea "What if . . . ?" In the following excerpt, John A. Ahladas presents some hypothetical examples of what it will be like in the year 2039 if global warming continues.

In New York, workers are building levees to hold back the rising tidal

> **examples** specific instances that illustrate or explain a general factual statement
>
> **hypothetical examples** specific illustrations based on reflections about future events

waters of the Hudson River, now lined with palm trees. In Louisiana, 100,000 acres of wetland are steadily being claimed by the sea. In Kansas, farmers learn to live with drought as a way of life and struggle to eke out an existence in the increasingly dry and dusty heartland. . . . And reports arrive from Siberia of bumper crops of corn and wheat from a longer and warmer growing season.[6]

Because hypothetical examples are not themselves factual, you must be very careful to check that the facts on which they are based are accurate. Three principles should guide your use of examples. First, use at least one example to support every generalization. A generalization without an example (or other piece of evidence to support it) can be judged by the audience as nothing more than your opinion. Second, the examples should be clear and specific enough to create a picture the audience can understand. Consider the following generalization and supporting example.

Generalization: *Electronics is one of the few areas in which products are significantly cheaper today than they were in the 1980s.*

Supporting example: *In the mid-1980s, Motorola sold cell phones for $5,000 each; now a person can buy a cell phone for under $50.*

With this single example, the listener has a vivid picture of the tremendous difference in about a thirty-year period. You can often achieve this first guideline best by sharing it in the form of a presentational aid. For example, you could show an enlarged advertisement for a Motorola cell phone in the 1980s along with a recent one.

Third, the examples you use should be representative. If cell phones were the *only* electronics product whose prices had dropped so much over that same period, this vivid example would be misleading and unethical. Any misuse of data is unethical, especially if the user knows better. To extend our thinking about illustrating examples, you might show several advertisements for different electronic devices from the 1980s and today.

Definitions

A **definition** is a statement that clarifies the meaning of a word or phrase. Definitions serve to clarify in three ways. First, definitions clarify the meaning of terminology that is specialized, technical, or otherwise likely to be unfamiliar to your audience. For example, when Dan talked about bioluminescence, he clarified the meaning of the word *bioluminescence* with the following definition: "According to *Encyclopaedia Britannica Online*, bioluminescence is the emission of visible light by living organisms like fireflies." Although dictionaries and encyclopedias contain definitions, your speech topic might require you to find definitions through prominent researchers or professional practitioners. For example, in a speech about eating disorders, you might go to the Web site of the American Dietetic Association for your definition of the term *eating disorders*.

Second, definitions clarify words and terms that have more than one meaning. For example, because *child abuse* is a term that encompasses a broad range of behaviors, you might choose to define it in a way that acknowledges which behaviors you intend to focus on in your speech.

Third, particularly with controversial subjects, definitions clarify your stance on the subject. For example, in a speech about domestic violence against women, former U.S. Secretary of Health and Human Services Donna Shalala defined such violence as "terrorism in the home."[7]

6-2b Expert Opinions

Expert opinions are interpretations and judgments made by an authority in a particular subject area. They can help explain what facts mean or put them in perspective. "Watching twenty-eight hours of television a week is far too much for young children" and "Having a firewire port on your computer is absolutely necessary" are opinions. Whether they are expert opinions or not depends on who made the statements. An **expert** is a person recognized as having mastered a specific subject, usually through long-term study. When you use the opinions of experts in your speech, remember to cite their credentials. During a speech in Amsterdam, the Netherland's chief of defense Peter van Uhm stated that the murder rate in Europe has dropped by a factor of 30 since the Middle Ages. He then introduced his topic of how armies are important for creating less violent, more peaceful societies and cited the following expert.

In his latest book, Harvard professor Steven Pinker... concludes that one of the main drivers behind less

definition a statement that clarifies the meaning of a word or phrase

expert opinions interpretations and judgments made by authorities in a particular subject area

expert a person recognized as having mastered a specific subject, usually through long-term study

violent societies is the spread of the constitutional state and the introduction on a large scale of the state monopoly on legitimized use of violence.[8]

6-2c Elaborations

Both factual statements and expert opinions can be elaborated on through anecdotes and narratives, comparisons and contrasts, or quotations.

Anecdotes and Narratives

Anecdotes are brief, often amusing stories; **narratives** are accounts, personal experiences, tales, or lengthier stories. Because holding audience interest is important and because audience attention is likely to be captured by a story, anecdotes and

> **anecdotes** brief, often amusing stories
> **narratives** accounts, personal experiences, tales, or lengthier stories

narratives are worth looking for or creating. The key to using them is to be sure the point of the story directly addresses the point you are making in your speech. Good stories may be humorous, sentimental, suspenseful, or dramatic. Speakers often find anecdotes and brief narratives on social media sites such as YouTube.

In the following speech excerpt, John Howard makes a point about failure to follow guidelines.

The knight was returning to the castle after a long, hard day. His face was bruised and badly swollen. His armor was dented. The plume on his helmet was broken, and his steed was limping. He was a sad sight.

The lord of the castle ran out and asked, "What hath befallen you, Sir Timothy?"

"Oh, Sire," he said, "I have been laboring all day in your service, bloodying and pillaging your enemies to the West."

"You've been doing what?" gasped the astonished nobleman. "I haven't any enemies to the West!"

"Oh!" said Timothy. "Well, I think you do now."

There is a moral to this little story. Enthusiasm is not enough. You need to have a sense of direction.[9]

Comparisons and Contrasts

One of the best ways to give meaning to new ideas is through comparison and contrast. **Comparisons** illuminate a point by showing similarities, whereas **contrasts** highlight differences. Although comparisons and contrasts may be literal, like comparing and contrasting the murder rates in different countries or during different eras, they may also be figurative.

Figurative comparison: In short, living without health insurance is as much of a risk as having uncontrolled diabetes or driving without a safety belt.[10]

comparison illuminating a point by showing similarities

contrast illuminating a point by highlighting differences

plagiarism the unethical act of representing another person's work as your own

Figurative contrast: If this morning you had bacon and eggs for breakfast, I think it illustrates the difference. The eggs represented "participa- tion" on the part of the chicken. The bacon represented "total commitment" on the part of the pig!*[11]

Quotations

At times, information you find will be so well stated that you want to quote it directly in your speech. Because audiences want to listen to your ideas and arguments, they do not want to hear a string of long quotations. Nevertheless, a well-selected quotation may be perfect in one or two key places.

Quotations can both explain and enliven. Look for quotations that make a point in a particularly clear or vivid way. For example, in his speech "Enduring Values for a Secular Age," Hans Becherer, executive officer at Deere & Company, used this Henry Ford quote to show the importance of enthusiasm to progress:

Enthusiasm is at the heart of all progress. With it, there is accomplishment. Without it, there are only alibis.[12]

Frequently, historical or literary quotations can reinforce a point vividly. Cynthia Opheim, chair of the Department of Political Science at Southwest Texas State University, in her speech "Making Democracy Work," used this quote from Mark Twain on the frustration of witnessing legislative decision making:

There are two things you should never watch being made: sausage and legislation.[13]

When you use a direct quotation, you need to verbally acknowledge the person it came from. Using any quotation or close paraphrase without crediting its source is **plagiarism**, the unethical act of representing another person's work as your own.

6-2d Diverse Cultural Perspectives

When identifying factual statements, expert opinions, and elaborations to develop your speech, be sure to include a variety of cultural perspectives. For example, when Carrie was preparing her speech on proficiency testing in grade schools, she purposefully searched for articles written by noted Hispanic, Asian, and African American, as well as European American, authors. In addition, she interviewed two local school superintendents—one from an urban district and another from a

Brynjar Gunnarsson/Shutterstock.com

suburban district. Doing so boosted Carrie's confidence that her speech would accurately reflect diverse perspectives on the issue of proficiency testing.

 6-3 ## RECORD INFORMATION

As you find information to use as evidence in your speech, you need to record it accurately and keep a careful account of your sources so you can cite them appropriately during your speech. How should you keep track of these sources and information? One way to do so is to compile an annotated bibliography of the sources you believe are relevant and prepare a hand-written or electronic research card for each piece of information you might use in the speech.

6-3a Annotated Bibliography

An **annotated bibliography** is a preliminary record of the relevant sources you find pertaining to your topic. It includes a short summary of the information in that source and how it might be used to support your speech. Your annotated bibliography can be used to create your research cards as well as your speech reference list later. A good annotated bibliography includes:

- A complete bibliographic citation for each source, using an appropriate style guide such as APA or MLA;

- Two or three sentences summarizing the information in the source;

- Two or three sentences explaining how the information might support your speech; and

- Any direct quotations you might want to include verbatim in your speech.

6-3b Research Cards

Although not necessary, some speakers find research cards useful for arranging the information they might cite during the speech. **Research cards** are individual 3 × 5- or 4 × 6-inch index cards or electronic facsimiles that identify (a) one piece of information relevant to your speech, (b) a keyword or theme the information represents, and (c) the bibliographic source that identifies where you found it. Then you can easily find, arrange, and rearrange individual pieces of information according to keyword or theme while you prepare your speech. Exhibit 6.2 shows a sample research card.

Exhibit 6.2
A Sample Research Card

Topic: Recycling

Key Term/Main Idea: Salvage Glut

Recycling in the U.S. is reaching a crisis due to falling demand for salvaged material both domestically and abroad. Declining demand has pushed the prices for the recycled materials down to the point where recyclers risk not being able to cover processing costs. When that happens, scrap dealers will no longer accept cans and cardboard for recycling.

Hagerty, J. R. and Tita, B. U.S. awash in glut of scrap materials. Wall Street Journal, B1.

iStockphoto/Thinkstock

The number of sources and pieces of information you will need depends in part on the type of speech you are giving and your own expertise. For example, a five-minute speech on the causes and effects of Ebola would probably require three or more research cards from different sources under each heading. Selecting and using a variety of information types from several different sources helps you develop an original approach to your topic, a broader research base, and multiple perspectives on it. Speech Planning Action Step 3, Activity 3B, will help you prepare research cards for the sources you compiled in Activity 3A. See the Student Response box immediately following the activity for a sample of how one student completed this exercise.

6-4 ## CITE SOURCES

In your speeches, as in any communication in which you use information beyond your own personal knowledge and experience, you need to acknowledge the sources. Specifically mentioning your sources not only helps the audience evaluate the content but also adds to your credibility. Frankly, failure to cite sources constitutes plagiarism. Just as you would provide internal references or footnotes in a

annotated bibliography a preliminary record of the relevant sources you find pertaining to your topic

research cards individual index cards that identify information speakers might cite during a speech

ACTION STEP ACTIVITY

Record Relevant Information on Research Cards

The goal of this activity is to review the source material that you identified in Action Step Activity 3A and to record specific information you might use on research cards.

1. Carefully read all sources and information you have identified and evaluated as appropriate for your speech.

2. As you review an information item you think might be useful in your speech, record it on a research card or on the appropriate electronic research card.

Student Response: Record Relevant Information on Research Cards

Speech goal: *I would like the audience to understand the national significance of the California drought, and the irreplaceable nature of ground water, in order to ultimately persuade them to be in favor of national water conservation.*

Card 1
Topic: *The problem*

Heading: *Scope*

The U.S. agricultural industry depends on California farmers, who account for 80 percent of all water usage in the state. It takes roughly 300 gallons of water to grow the amount of California-grown food purchased each week by the average U.S. citizen. That adds up to 15,600 gallons per year per person.

Buchanan, L., Keller L. J., Park, H. (2015, May 21). Your contribution to the California drought. The New York Times. Retrieved online from: http://www.nytimes.com/interactive/2015/05/21/us/your-contribution-to-the-california-drought.html?_r=1.

Card 2
Topic: *The problem*

Heading: *Severity*

Our nation's water consumption is simply unsustainable. As grocery stores across the country stock up on every kind meat, berry, or variety of veggie you can imagine, agriculture is forced to use precious groundwater to keep up with demand for food. Once depleted, groundwater takes thousands to millions of years to replenish.

Dimick, D. (2014, August 21). If you think the water crisis can't get worse, wait until the aquifers are drained. National Geographic. Retrieved online from: http://news.nationalgeographic.com/news/2014/08/140819-groundwater-california-drought-aquifers-hidden-crisis/.

Card 3
Topic: *Consequences*

Heading: *Future repercussions*

Freshwater depletion due to farming has already happened in other parts of the world. The Aral Sea, which was once the fourth largest freshwater lake on the planet, is now dry due to crop irrigation. The lake, which is thousands of years old, was destroyed in only half a decade.

Clark Howard, B. (2014, October 2). Aral Sea's eastern basin is dry for first time in 600 years. National Geographic. Retrieved online from: http://news.nationalgeographic.com/news/2014/10/141001-aral-sea-shrinking-drought-water-environment/.

Card 4
Topic: *Solving the problem*

Heading: *Future solutions*

Desalination technology is an important component of any solution, but water conservation should always be the most important first step. Without prioritizing water conservation, we will be left high and dry—for real.

Harris, E. (2015, June14). Israel bringing its years of desalination experience to California. NPR. Retrieved online from: http://www.npr.org/sections/parallels/2015/06/14/413981435/israel-bringing-its-years-of-desalination-experience-to-california.

written document, so must you provide oral footnotes during your speech. **Oral footnotes** are references to an original source, made at the point in the speech where information from that source is presented. The key to preparing oral footnotes is to include enough information for listeners to access the sources themselves and to offer enough credentials to enhance the credibility of the information you are citing. You need to cite oral footnotes for any information including, for example, visuals, audio-visuals, and interviews. Justin provided this oral foot-note for his interview with the honeybee expert: "I had the privilege of interviewing one of the nation's leading colony collapse disorder scholars, Dr. Susan Stromme. She explained that the radiation emitted from cell phones is one cause of death for the bees." Exhibit 6.3 gives several examples of appropriate speech source citations.

Speech Planning Action Step 3, Activity 3C, will help you prepare oral citations for the sources you recorded in Activity 3B. See the Student Response box immediately following the activity for a sample of how one student completed this exercise.

oral footnote reference to an original source, made at the point in the speech where information from that source is presented

Exhibit 6.3

Appropriate Speech Source Citations

Where	What	How
Books	Cite the title of the book and the name of its author. You may cite the book's publication date or the author's credentials if doing so boosts credibility.	*Sam Quinones, journalist and former* Los Angeles Times *reporter, stated in his book* Dreamland: The True Tale of America's Opiate Epidemic . . . *But to get a complete picture, we have to look at the statistics. According to the 2015 Statistical Abstract, the level of production for the European economic community rose from . . .*
Journal or Magazine Articles	Cite the name of the publication in which you found the article. You may cite the article's author and title if doing adds credibility.	*According to an article about the Federal Reserve in last week's* Bloomberg Businessweek . . . *In the latest Gallup poll cited in the June 2015 issue of* The Atlantic . . . *Chris Mullin, professor of entomology at Pennsylvania State University, wrote an article about pesticides and honeybees published in 2015 in the* Journal of Agricultural and Food Chemistry *that . . .*
Newspapers	Cite the name of the newspaper and date of the article. You may cite the article's author and his or her credentials if it adds credibility.	*According to a May 25, 2015, article in the* Washington Post . . .
Interviews	Cite the name and credentials of the person interviewed and the date the interview took place. If you cite the interview more than once, you need only cite the interviewee's name in subsequent oral footnotes.	*In an interview with the* Wall Street Journal *on October 13, 2014, JCPenney CEO Marvin Ellison said . . .* *In my telephone interview on September 29 with Dr. Susan Nissen, physican for physical medicine in Kansas City, Kansas, I learned that . . .*

Exhibit 6.3
Appropriate Speech Source Citations (*Continued*)

Where	What	How
Internet Sources	Cite the Web site's author, his or her credentials, and the date of the site's most recent revision. If there is no author, cite the credentials of the Web site's sponsoring organization. Do not cite the URL as part of your oral footnote.	*According to a January 2016 posting on the official Web site of the American Heart Association . . .*
Television Programs	Cite the name of the program and the date of the original broadcast. You may also cite the name of the reporter for the news program if it boosts credibility.	*According to a documentary film titled Good Soil and broadcast on PBS in the summer of 2015, . . .*
Public Speeches	Cite the name and credentials of the speaker, as well as the occasion and date of the speech.	*In a speech about the importance of corporate governance in emerging markets delivered at the 2011 Conference on Corporate Governance and Transparency in Buenos Aires, Argentina, Ronald Berenbeim, the principal researcher at The Conference Board, stated . . .*

3C

ACTION STEP ACTIVITY

Citing Sources

On the back of each research card, write a short phrase you can use as an oral footnote during your speech.

Student Response: Citing Sources

According to journalist Dennis Dimick, of National Geographic Magazine, the Soviet Union used the Aral Sea's lake water to create 20,000 miles of canals, 45 dams, and over 80 reservoirs, to irrigate cotton and wheat crops.

STUDY TOOLS **6**

LOCATED IN TEXTBOOK

☐ Tear-out Chapter Review cards at the end of the book

☐ Review with the Quick Quiz below

LOCATED ON SPEAK3 ONLINE AT CENGAGEBRAIN.COM

☐ Review Key Term flashcards and create your own cards

☐ Track your knowledge and understanding of key concepts in speech communication

☐ Complete practice and graded quizzes to prepare for tests

☐ Complete interactive content within SPEAK3 Online

☐ View the chapter highlight boxes for SPEAK3 Online

Quick Quiz (answers in Solutions Appendix)

T F 1. A biography about a historical figure is not an appropriate source of secondary information.

T F 2. According to the text, the heart of an effective interview is a list of good questions.

T F 3. Primary research involves looking for information that others have discovered.

T F 4. Because statistics are a great way to present information, a speaker should use as many as possible.

T F 5. In addition to research that others have done, your personal experience can be a good source of information for a speech.

---

6. All of the following are examples of primary sources EXCEPT:
   a. surveys
   b. fieldwork
   c. interviews
   d. a Web site of famous quotations
   e. experiments

7. The list of questions you plan to ask during an interview is known as the:
   a. interview assessment
   b. interview cards
   c. interview inquiries
   d. interview basics
   e. interview protocol

8. Information that clarifies, explains, or adds depth or breadth to a topic is called:
   a. data
   b. evidence
   c. research
   d. findings
   e. scanning

9. Encyclopedias, newspapers, and scholarly journals are all examples of:
   a. tertiary sources
   b. primary sources
   c. secondary sources
   d. redundant sources
   e. expert sources

10. The four criteria that should be used when evaluating sources are authority, relevance, objectivity, and:
    a. currency
    b. importance
    c. popularity
    d. veracity
    e. origins

Chapter Takeaways

List three key takeaways from this chapter:

-

-

-

7 Organizing the Speech Body

LEARNING OUTCOMES

7-1 Organize your speech body into two to four main points using an appropriate main point pattern.

7-2 Construct a clear thesis statement.

7-3 Develop each main point with subpoints and supporting material.

7-4 Create effective transitions.

7-5 Outline the speech body.

After finishing this chapter go to **PAGE 117** for **STUDY TOOLS.**

Sound Familiar?

Isabel and Alyssa are taking a public speaking course online over the summer. That way they can still make progress toward graduation while living at home, where they both have great summer jobs. Most of the class is conducted asynchronously; however, every Monday afternoon from 1:00-3:00 p.m., all students are required to "attend class virtually" using Adobe Connect. That's when students deliver their formal speeches. Matt just finished delivering his speech when Alyssa got a text from Isabel:

"Matt's speech was awesome! So many powerful stories!"
Alyssa replied: "Great stories but hard to follow. What were his main points?"
Isabel responded, "Hmmm… Not sure. I hope mine will be easier to follow."
"Mine too," Alyssa exclaimed. "Uh oh. Late for work. CU."

Isabel and Alyssa's experience is not that unusual. Even well-known speakers sometimes give speeches that are hard to follow. Yet when your speech is well organized, you are far more likely to achieve your goal.

A well-organized speech has three identifiable parts: an introduction, a body, and a conclusion. In this chapter and the next, we explain the fourth speech plan action step: Organize your ideas into a well-structured outline. This chapter focuses on the speech body; the next chapter will examine introductions and conclusions. Here we describe how to (A) identify main points and arrange them using an appropriate main point pattern; (B) use them to construct a clear thesis statement;

(C) develop each main point with appropriate supporting material (evidence and reasoning) and create transitions that move the speech smoothly from one main point to the next; and (D) outline the speech body.

7-1 ORGANIZE MAIN POINTS

Organizing, the process of arranging your speech material, is guided by what you learned from your audience analysis. Begin by identifying two to four main points that will help you achieve your speech goal. In fact, the difference between an effective five-minute speech and an effective twenty-five-minute speech with the same speech goal is not the number of main points, but the extent to which each one is developed with supporting material.

7-1a Identify Main Point Ideas

For some goals, identifying main point ideas is easy. For example, if your goal is to demonstrate how to create a Web site, your main ideas will likely be the steps involved in developing a very basic one. Most times, however, determining main point ideas is more complex. How can you identify the main ideas when they

4

ACTION STEP

Organize Ideas into a Well-Structured Outline (the Body)

A. Identify and organize two to four main points.

B. Construct a thesis statement.

C. Develop your main points, and create transitions between them.

D. Outline the speech body (including transitions).

aren't so obvious? First, begin by listing the ideas you believe relate to your specific goal. You will probably find it easy to list as many as nine or more. Second, eliminate ideas that you believe this audience

organizing the process of arranging your speech material

already understands. Third, eliminate any ideas that might be too complicated or too broad for this audience to comprehend in the time allotted. Fourth, check to see if some of the ideas can be grouped together under a broader theme. Finally, from the ideas that remain, choose two to four that will help you accomplish your specific speech goal.

Let's look at how Isabel used these steps to identify the main point ideas for her speech to inform her classmates about gender inequality in the film industry. To begin, Isabel listed ideas she discovered while doing her research.

- What is gender inequality?

- What is the history of gender inequality in the U.S.?

- How can gender inequality be measured?

- Nationally, do U.S. citizens believe in gender equality?

- Is there gender equality in the film industry?

- What equipment do you need to make a movie?

- How are movies distributed?

- Do women write as many movies as men?

- Do women direct as many movies as men?

- Do actresses have as many speaking roles as men?

- What are the demographics of executives at major film studios?

- Do women directors receive as much for their budgets as male directors?

- What are the demographics of audiences who attend the movies?

- Is there a difference between how many people will attend a movie with a female protagonist versus a male protagonist?

- Do male directors make more money at the box office?

- Do female directors make as many blockbusters as male directors?

- How are women changing the film industry?

- What are the myths about women directors, writers, and actresses?

- What is the reality of these myths?

- Do myths hinder women in the film industry?

- Is gender equality in the film industry improving as time progresses?

- Is gender inequality worse in the film industry than other industries?

Second, Isabel eliminated the idea "what is gender inequality" because she knew her audience already

understood this. Third, Isabel decided the points concerning the national history of gender inequality, how to distribute a movie, and the equipment needed to make a movie were too broad to cover adequately in the time allotted for the speech and were not directly related to her goal. Fourth, Isabel noticed that several ideas seemed to be related. The percentage of female directors and female-directed blockbusters, the myths about female directors, and the amount earned by female directors at the box office seemed to go together. The percentage of movies that are written by women, how many speaking roles are written for women, and how gender equality in the film industry compared to other industries also seemed to be related. Myths about women directors, writers, and actresses and how they stack up to reality could be grouped together as well. Finally, Isabel decided that her main point ideas would be (1) understanding who chiefly runs and profits from the film industry, (2) identifying the prejudices that limit women's careers in Hollywood, and (3) disproving the myth that films starring women and directed by women do poorly at the box office. Exhibit 7.1 illustrates what Isabel's list looked like after she finished her analysis and synthesis.

Speech Planning Action Step 4, Activity 4A, will help you identify main point ideas to use for your speeches in this course. See the Student Response box immediately following the activity for a sample of how one student completed this exercise.

Remember that the number of main point ideas does not determine speech length, but rather, how thoroughly you develop each of them. The same two to four main point ideas can be developed into a speech that will last for three to five minutes, five to seven minutes, eight to ten minutes, or even into a fifty-minute major presentation.

7-1b Word Main Points

Once you have identified your two to four main point ideas, you can begin to shape each one into a clear main point. Write out a complete sentence for each main area you have identified. Let's look at how Isabel did this.

Recall that Isabel's main point ideas are understanding who chiefly runs and profits from the film industry, identifying the prejudices that limit women's careers in Hollywood, and disproving the myth that films starring women and directed by women do poorly at the box office.

Suppose she wrote her first draft of main points as follows:

I. People who profit most from the film industry

II. Sexism in the work environment

III. Myths about women at the box office

Exhibit 7.1
Results of Isabel's Analysis and Synthesis

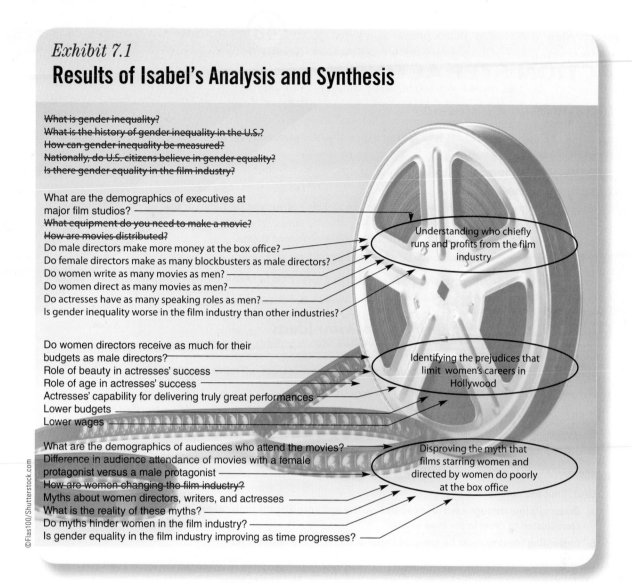

~~What is gender inequality?~~
~~What is the history of gender inequality in the U.S.?~~
~~How can gender inequality be measured?~~
~~Nationally, do U.S. citizens believe in gender equality?~~
~~Is there gender equality in the film industry?~~

What are the demographics of executives at major film studios?
~~What equipment do you need to make a movie?~~
~~How are movies distributed?~~
Do male directors make more money at the box office?
Do female directors make as many blockbusters as male directors?
Do women write as many movies as men?
Do women direct as many movies as men?
Do actresses have as many speaking roles as men?
Is gender inequality worse in the film industry than other industries?

Do women directors receive as much for their budgets as male directors?
Role of beauty in actresses' success
Role of age in actresses' success
Actresses' capability for delivering truly great performances
Lower budgets
Lower wages

What are the demographics of audiences who attend the movies?
Difference in audience attendance of movies with a female protagonist versus a male protagonist
~~How are women changing the film industry?~~
Myths about women directors, writers, and actresses
What is the reality of these myths?
Do myths hinder women in the film industry?
Is gender equality in the film industry improving as time progresses?

Understanding who chiefly runs and profits from the film industry

Identifying the prejudices that limit women's careers in Hollywood

Disproving the myth that films starring women and directed by women do poorly at the box office

©Flas100/Shutterstock.com

Some people refer to this first version of wording main points as a **preparation outline**. It provides a draft of main points but doesn't specify clearly how each main point is related to the speech goal. To begin making these relationships clear, Isabel next needs to create complete sentences for each. So she might clarify her main points like this:

I. Who profits most from the film industry?

II. Sexism significantly limits women in Hollywood.

III. There is a prominent myth that women at the box office make less money.

Study these statements. Do they seem a bit vague? Sometimes, the first draft of a main point doesn't quite capture what we want to say. So we need to rework our points to make them clearer. Let's consider Isabel's draft statements more carefully. Her three main points

are complete sentences. To assure herself that she has achieved the best wording for her main points, Isabel next applies two test questions to them.

1. Is the relationship between each main point statement and the goal statement clearly specified?
Isabel's first main point statement doesn't indicate who profits most from the film industry. So she improved this statement by saying:

A male majority dominates nearly every division of the film industry.

Similarly, she improved the second main point statement by saying:

Prejudices in Hollywood significantly limit career opportunities for women.

> **preparation outline** a first-draft speech outline that identifies main points but does not specify clearly how each is related to the speech goal

ACTION STEP ACTIVITY

Identify Main Point Ideas

Recall from Action Step Activity 1E how to draft a speech goal. Determine your general and specific speech goals, then complete the activities below.

1. List all the ideas you found that relate to your speech.

2. Next, limit the number by:

   a. Drawing a line through each idea you believe the audience already understands or that seems too broad or complicated to cover in the time allotted.

   b. Combining ideas that can be grouped together under a common theme.

3. From the remaining ideas, choose the two to four that will best accomplish your speech goal.

You can complete this activity online with Speech Builder Express. Go to SPEAK 3 Online at www.cengagebrain.com to access Action Step Activity 4A.

Student Response: Identify Main Point Ideas

General goal: *I want to inform my audience.*

Specific goal: *I want my audience to understand the basics of seasonal affective disorder (SAD).*

1. List all the ideas you found that relate to your speech.

What is SAD?	Symptoms	Causes of SAD	Historical background
Discoverer	Types of depression	Vitamin deficiencies	Locations and prevalence
Diagnoses	Medical treatments	Organic treatments	Therapeutic treatments
The role of sunshine	Light therapy	Myths	Realities

2. Next, limit the number by:

   a. Drawing a line through each idea you believe the audience already understands or that seems too broad or complicated to cover in the time allotted.

   b. Combining ideas that can be grouped together under a common theme.

3. From the remaining ideas, choose the two to four that will best accomplish your speech goal.

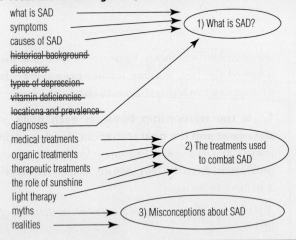

Main point ideas:

Causes

Symptoms

Misconceptions

Treatments

---

parallel wording that follows the same structural pattern, often using the same introductory words

And she revised the third main point to state:

Despite myths, films starring women and

directed by women are not at a disadvantage at the box office.

2. Are the main points parallel in structure? Main points are **parallel** to one another when their wording follows the same structural pattern, often using the same introductory words. Parallel structure is not a requirement, but it can help the audience recognize main points when you deliver your speech. So Isabel made one more small adjustment to her outline:

I. First, a male majority dominates nearly every division of the film industry.

II. Second, prejudices in Hollywood significantly limit career opportunities for women.

III. Third, despite myths, films starring women and directed by women are not at a disadvantage at the box office.

Parallelism can be achieved in many ways. Isabel used numbering: "first . . . second . . . third." Another way is to start each sentence with an active verb. Suppose Adam wants his audience to understand the steps involved in writing an effective job application cover letter. Below is Adam's first draft of the main points:

I. Format the heading elements correctly.

II. The body of the letter should be three paragraphs long.

III. When concluding, use "sincerely" or "regards."

IV. Then you need to proofread the letter carefully.

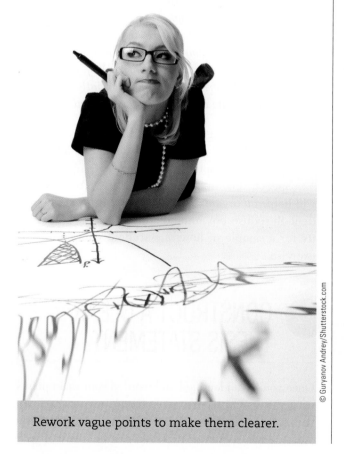

Rework vague points to make them clearer.

Adam revised his main points to make them parallel by using active verbs (italicized):

I. *Format* the heading elements correctly.

II. *Organize* the body into three paragraphs.

III. *Conclude* the letter with "sincerely" or "regards."

IV. *Proofread* the letter carefully.

7-1c Select a Main Point Pattern

A speech can be organized in many different ways. Remember your objective is to help the audience make sense of the material. Although speeches may follow many different organizational patterns, four fundamental types are time (a.k.a. sequential or chronological) order, narrative order, topical order, and logical reasons order.

1. Time order, sometimes called *sequential order* or *chronological order*, arranges main points in chronological sequence or by steps in a process. You can use time order to explain how to do something, how to make something, how something works, or how something happened. Adam's speech on the *steps* in writing a job application and cover letter is an example of time order. Here is another example.

General goal: *I want to inform my audience.*

Specific goal: *I want the audience to understand the four steps involved in developing a personal network.*

Main Points:

I. *First, analyze your current networking potential.*

II. *Second, position yourself in places for opportunity.*

III. *Third, advertise yourself.*

IV. *Fourth, follow up on contacts.*

2. Narrative order conveys ideas through a story or series of stories. Narrative order is rooted in narrative theory, which suggests that one important way people communicate is through storytelling. We use stories to teach and to learn, to entertain, and make sense of the world around us.[1] Although a narrative may be presented in chronological order, it may also use a series of flashbacks or flash forwards to increase dramatic effect. Each main point may be an event in a single story, or each main point may be a different story that

time order organizing the main points of the speech in a chronological sequence or by steps in a process

narrative order organizing the main points of the speech as a story or series of stories

© Guryanov Andrey/Shutterstock.com

illustrates the thesis. Lana shared her story about having anorexia by using three stories as main points.

General goal: *I want to inform my audience.*

Specific goal: *I want my audience to understand how anorexia nervosa affects the lives of its victims and their loved ones.*

Main points:

I. *First, let's talk about the story of a typical day as a recovering anorexic.*

II. *Next, let's focus on a historical account about how I became anorexic.*

III. *Finally, let's discuss an inspirational story about two people who basically saved my life.*

3. Topical order arranges the main points using some logical relationship among them. Main points might progress from general to specific, least important to most important, most to least familiar, and so forth. Isabel used topical order from least to most important for achieving her speech goal. Here is another example:

General goal: *I want to inform my audience.*

Specific goal: *I want the audience to understand three proven methods for ridding our bodies of harmful toxins.*

Main Points:

I. *One proven method for ridding our bodies of harmful toxins is keeping well hydrated.*

II. *A second proven method for ridding our bodies of harmful toxins is reducing our intake of animal products.*

III. *A third proven method for ridding our bodies of harmful toxins is eating more natural whole foods.*

4. Logical reasons order organizes the main points according to reasons for accepting the thesis as desirable or true. Logical reasons order is often used when your general goal is to persuade.

Chronological order applies to more than time. When "The Naked Chef" Jamie Oliver hosts a cooking demonstration, he also uses chronological order.

Mr Pics/Shutterstock.com

General goal: *I want to persuade my audience.*

Specific goal: *I want the audience to donate money to the United Way.*

Main points:

I. *When you donate to the United Way, your one donation covers many charities.*

II. *When you donate to the United Way, you can stipulate which charities you wish to support.*

III. *When you donate to the United Way, you know that a high percentage of your donation will go directly to the charities you've selected.*

These four organizational patterns are the most basic ones. We will introduce you to several additional patterns in later chapters.

Speech Planning Action Step 4, Activity 4B, will help you organize your main points. See the Student Response box immediately following the activity for a sample of how one student completed this exercise.

7-2 CONSTRUCT A CLEAR THESIS STATEMENT

Once you have identified and worded your main points using an appropriate organizational pattern, you are ready to construct your thesis statement. A **thesis statement** is a one- or two-sentence summary of your

---

topical order organizing the main points of the speech using some logical relationship among them

logical reasons order organizing the main points of a persuasive speech by the reasons that support the speech goal

thesis statement a one- or two-sentence summary of the speech that incorporates the general and specific goals and previews the main points

ACTION STEP ACTIVITY

Organize Main Points

The goal of this activity is to help you organize your main points.

1. **Write your general and specific speech goal statements.**

2. **Write down the two to four main point ideas you identified in Activity 4A.**

3. **Write one sentence that summarizes what you want your audience to know about each idea.**

4. **Review the main points as a group.**

    a. **Is the relationship between each main point statement and the goal statement clearly specified? If not, revise.**

    b. **Are the main points parallel in structure? If not, consider why and revise.**

5. **Identify the organizational pattern you used.**

Student Response: Organize Main Points

1. **Write your general and specific speech goal statements.**
   General goal: *I want to inform my audience.*
   Specific goal: *I want my audience to understand the basics of seasonal affective disorder (SAD).*

2. **Write down the two to four main point ideas you identified in Activity 4A.**
   Causes and symptoms
   Misconceptions
   Treatments

3. **Write one sentence that summarizes what you want your audience to know about each idea.**
   I. *Seasonal affective disorder (SAD) is a fairly common mood disorder.*
   II. *Having the "winter blues" does not mean you have SAD.*
   III. *Talk therapy and light therapy are two kinds of treatment options.*

4. **Review the main points as a group.**

   a. **Is the relationship between each main point statement and the goal statement clearly specified? If not, revise.**

   No. The goal of the speech is to help the audience understand the basics of <u>SAD.</u> The following revision puts emphasis in the right place.

      Revision:
      I. *Seasonal affective disorder (SAD) is triggered by changes in the season affecting a person's brain chemistry and circadian rhythm.*
      II. *A misconception is that having SAD is the same as having the "winter blues."*
      III. *People with SAD have various options for treatment.*

   b. **Are the main points parallel in structure? If not, consider why and revise.**

      Revision:
      I. *People with seasonal affective disorder (SAD) are affected by changes in the season.*
      II. *People with seasonal affective disorder (SAD) have more than the "winter blues."*
      III. *People with seasonal affective disorder (SAD) have various options for treatment.*

5. **Identify the organizational pattern you used.**
   Topical

Exhibit 7.2
Sample Speech Goals and Thesis Statements

General goal: I want to inform my audience.

Specific goal: I want my audience to understand how to improve their grades in college.

Thesis statement: Three proven techniques for improving test scores in college are to attend classes regularly, develop a positive attitude, and study efficiently.

General goal: I want to inform my audience.

Specific goal: I want the audience to understand the benefits of volunteering.

Thesis statement: Some important benefits of volunteering include helping underprivileged populations, supporting nonprofit organizations, and improving your own self-esteem.

General goal: I want to persuade my audience.

Specific goal: I want my audience to believe that parents should limit the time their children spend viewing television.

Thesis statement: Parents should limit the time their children spend viewing television because heavy television viewing desensitizes children to violence and increases violent tendencies in children.

---

speech that incorporates your general and specific goals and previews the main points of the speech. A thesis statement provides a blueprint of the speech body organization. Exhibit 7.2 provides several examples of specific speech goals and thesis statements.

Speech Planning Action Step 4, Activity 4C, will help you construct a thesis statement. See the Student Response box immediately following the activity for a sample of how one student completed this exercise.

7-3 DEVELOP MAIN POINTS

Once you have identified the main points and used them to form your thesis statement, you need to develop each one with subpoints and supporting material. **Subpoints** are statements that elaborate on a main point. A main point may have two, three, or more subpoints depending on its complexity. Each subpoint is developed further with **supporting material**—evidence you gathered through secondary and primary research along with the logical

subpoints statements that elaborate on a main point

supporting material evidence you gathered through secondary and primary research along with the logical reasoning you use to link it to the main point it supports

transitions words, phrases, or sentences that show the relationship between two ideas

reasoning you use to link it to the main point it supports. You can identify subpoints by sorting through the research you compiled in your annotated bibliography and/or on research cards to find evidence (e.g., definitions, examples, facts, statistics, stories) that supports each of your main points. Once you have listed the items of information that make the point, look for relationships between and among ideas. As you analyze, you can draw lines connecting items of information that fit together logically and cross out information that seems irrelevant. Finally, one subpoint under each main point should be a listener-relevance link, a statement alerting listeners to why the main point is important to them.

Subpoints should also be written in full sentences. It also helps to include internal references for items of information you found in secondary sources. Doing so will remind you to cite them during the speech, which will enhance listeners' perception of you as credible and help you avoid plagiarism. As with main points, subpoints should be revised until they are clearly stated.

7-4 CREATE TRANSITIONS

Transitions are words, phrases, or sentences that show the relationship between two ideas. Transitions act like tour guides leading the audience from point to point

TECH TALK

Speeches in the Age of Microblogging

In today's age of microblogging, 140-character limits, and listicles, it might seem that there is no time to develop the main points of your speech and convey them in anything less than 45 minutes. It can, however, be done—and done successfully.

Just look at the TED (Technology, Entertainment, and Design) Conference, a series of presentations from some of the world's biggest and brightest thinkers. Started in 1984, "TED talks," as they're known, have been viewed more than 2 million times per day since 2006 when the conference made them free to view online.[2]

No TED talk is more than 18 minutes long—a duration that is backed by science.[3] Many of the speakers invited to present at TED are used to speaking

TED curator Chris Anderson speaking in Vancouver in 2014.

lecture-style, up to 45 minutes or more, yet research shows that the average person can only offer undivided attention for between 10 and 18 minutes, and thereafter in spurts of three to four minutes.[4]

TED curator Chris Anderson told author Carmine Gallo the reasoning behind the conference's 18-minute speaking limit: "It [18 minutes] is long enough to be serious and short enough to hold people's attention. It turns out that this length also works incredibly well online. It's the length of a coffee break." In other words, 18 minutes is the perfect length for a speech to go viral.[5]

The format proved its worth well before the advent of TED. In 1961, President John F. Kennedy brought America into the space race with a mere 15 minute speech. Dr. Martin Luther King, Jr. shared his dream of racial equality in just 17 minutes. The Gettysburg Address, one of Abraham Lincoln's most well-known speeches, contained only 246 words and lasted a matter of minutes.[6]

Longer speeches can seem impressive, and, if delivered well, might convey a sense of expertise, but in many cases they're simply unnecessary. The power of brevity is by no means a modern phenomenon, as numerous other orators have shown throughout history. So take it from TED: There's no topic you can't tackle in 18 minutes or less.

But 140 characters could be a little limiting.

Bridge your ideas with solid transitions.

throughout the speech. Good transitions are certainly important in writing; however, they are crucial for formal public speeches. If listeners get lost or think they've missed something, they can't go back and check as they can when reading. Transitions come in the form of section transitions and signposts.

Section transitions are complete sentences that show the relationship between major parts of the speech. They typically

section transitions complete sentences that show the relationship between major parts of a speech

ACTION STEP ACTIVITY

Construct a Thesis Statement

The goal of this activity is to develop a well-worded thesis statement for your speech.

1. Write the general and specific goals you identified in Activity 4A.

2. List the main point ideas you identified in Activity 4A.

3. Now write one or two complete sentences that combine your general and specific goals with your main point ideas.

Student Response: Construct a Thesis Statement

1. **Write the general and specific goals you identified in Activity 4A.**
   General goal: I want to inform my audience.
   Specific goal: I want my audience to understand the basics of seasonal affective disorder (SAD).

2. **List the main point ideas you identified in Activity 4A.**
   Causes and symptoms

   Misconceptions

   Treatments

3. **Now write one or two complete sentences that combine your general and specific goals with your main point ideas.**
   Seasonal affective disorder, also known as SAD, is a fairly common mood disorder people experience regularly in winter, summer, spring, or autumn. To better understand the nature of this form of depression, let's look at its causes and symptoms, some misconceptions, and several treatment methods.

summarize what has just been said in one main point and preview the one coming up next, acting as a bridge. Essentially, section transitions are the glue that holds the macrostructure of your speech together.

For example, suppose Adam has just finished the introduction of his speech on creating a cover letter and is now ready to launch into his main points. Before stating his first main point, he might say, "Creating a good cover letter is a process that has four steps. Now let's consider the first one." When his listeners hear this transition, they are signaled to mentally prepare to listen to and remember the first main point. When he finishes his first main point, he may say: "Now that we understand what is involved in creating the heading elements, we can move on to discuss what to include in the body of the letter."

Section transitions are important for two reasons. First, they help the audience follow the organization of ideas in the speech. Second, they help audience members remember information.

Signposts are words or phrases that connect pieces of supporting material to the main point or subpoint they address. Whereas section transitions are complete sentences, signposts are usually one-word references. Sometimes signposts highlight numerical order: "first," "second," "third," or "fourth." Sometimes they help the audience focus on a key idea: "foremost," "most important," or "above all." They can also be used to signify an explanation: "to illustrate," "for example," "in other words," "essentially," or "to clarify." Signposts can also signal that an important idea, or even the speech itself, is coming to an end: "in short," "finally," "in conclusion," or "to

signposts words or phrases that connect pieces of supporting material to the main point or subpoint they address

Exhibit 7.3

General Form for a Speech Outline

I. Main point one
- **A.** Subpoint A for main point one
  - **1.** Sub-subpoint one
    - **a.** Elaboration material (if needed)
    - **b.** Elaboration material (if needed)
  - **2.** Sub-subpoint two
    - **a.** Elaboration material (if needed)
    - **b.** Elaboration material (if needed)
- **B.** Subpoint B for main point one
  - **1.** Sub-subpoint one
    - **a.** Elaboration material (if needed)
    - **b.** Elaboration material (if needed)
  - **2.** Sub-subpoint two
    - **a.** Elaboration material (if needed)
    - **b.** Elaboration material (if needed)

II. Main point two
- **A.** Subpoint A for main point two
  - **1.** Sub-subpoint one
    - **a.** Elaboration material (if needed)
    - **b.** Elaboration material (if needed)
  - **2.** Sub-subpoint two
    - **a.** Elaboration material (if needed)
    - **b.** Elaboration material (if needed)
- **B.** Subpoint B for main point two
  - **1.** Sub-subpoint one
    - **a.** Elaboration material (if needed)
    - **b.** Elaboration material (if needed)
  - **2.** Sub-subpoint two
    - **a.** Elaboration material (if needed)
    - **b.** Elaboration material (if needed)

III. Main point three
- **A.** Subpoint A for main point three
  - **1.** Sub-subpoint one
    - **a.** Elaboration material (if needed)
    - **b.** Elaboration material (if needed)
  - **2.** Sub-subpoint two
    - **a.** Elaboration material (if needed)
    - **b.** Elaboration material (if needed)

summarize." Just as section transitions serve as the glue that holds your macrostructure together, signposts serve as the glue that holds your subpoints and supporting material together within each main point.

7-5 OUTLINE THE SPEECH BODY

Once you have developed each main point with supporting material and formed transition statements to link them, you are ready to begin putting a formal speech outline together. A **formal speech outline** is a sentence representation of the hierarchical and sequential relationships among ideas in the speech. In other words, it is a diagram of your speech material. For most speeches, you will use main points (Roman numerals: I, II, III, etc.), subpoints (capital letters: A, B, C, etc.), and sometimes sub-subpoints (Arabic numerals: 1, 2, 3, etc.). Exhibit 7.3 shows a diagram of this general form for formal speech outlines.

Speech Planning Action Step 4, Activity 4D, will help you complete the outline for the body of your speech. See the Student Response box immediately following the activity for a sample of how one student completed this exercise.

formal speech outline a sentence representation of the hierarchical and sequential relationships among the ideas presented in the speech

4d

ACTION STEP ACTIVITY

Outline the Speech Body

The goal of this exercise is to help you get started on the formal speech outline for the body of your speech. Using complete sentences, write the following:

1. The general and specific speech goals you identified in Activity 4A.

2. The thesis statement you developed in Activity 4C.

3. A transition to the first main point.

4. The first main point you developed in Activity 4B.

5. The subpoints and supporting material for your first main point.

6. A transition from your first to second main point.

7. The other main points, subpoints, support, section transitions, and signposts. Use the format shown in the Student Response to Activity 4D below.

Student Response: Outline the Speech Body

Here is the start of Isabel's speech body outline. The first main point and the first transition are shown to give you an idea of how to proceed.

General goal: *I want to inform my audience.*

Specific Speech Goal: *I would like to inform my audience about gender inequality in the American film industry.*

I. The film industry is not a diverse business. Even though the entertainment industry as a whole is extremely varied and also lucrative, the movie segment is comparatively small and run by a smaller, homogenous group of people who paradoxically reap the majority of the profits.

Listener Relevance Link: Over two-thirds of the U.S. and Canadian populations, ages 2 and up, or 229.7 million people, attended the movies at least once in 2014. That means more than 66% of our audience went to the movies last year. (MPAA, 2014)

    A. In the United States, the film industry is an important driver of the economy.

1. The U.S. film industry accounts for 1.9 million jobs and generates $47 billion dollars of income annually. (Fried, 2015)

2. By the end of 2015, the U.S. entertainment industry is predicted to be a $589 billion industry, and the global entertainment market worth a staggering $2 trillion (USD). (Statistica, 2015)

    B. But, as Darnell Hunt, author of the Hollywood Diversity Report, points out, "Hollywood is not progressing at the same rate as America is diversifying." (Hunt, 2015)

        1. Hunt's report, which studied data collected in 2013, found that in major and mini-major film studios, 100% of CEOs were male, and 94% were white. Not included in the study was Stacey Snider, former CEO of DreamWorks Studios (regarded as too small for the study); she was hired to lead 20th Century Fox after the study was completed. These surprisingly high percentages are not exclusive to the CEO role. A male majority dominates nearly every division of the film industry. (Siegemund-Broka, 2015)

        2. The Center for the Study of Women and Television and Film at San Diego State University revealed that of the top 100 grossing films in 2014, only 1.9% were directed by a woman and only 7.4% written by a woman. And the overall number of female directors in 2014 has dropped 2% since 1998. (Lauzen, 2014)

        3. The researchers also found that 91% of movie critics who write for film and entertainment publications, such as *Entertainment Weekly*, are male. Similarly, men make up 90% of the movie reviewers contributing to trade publications, such as *Variety*. (Lauzen, 2013)

(Continued)

  a. The fact that such a small percentage of film critics are women means that men are almost singularly responsible for the canon of contemporary film criticism. This creates an industry that can be incredibly disapproving of women.

  b. Take critic Rex Reed. When he reviewed actress Melissa McCarthy's comedic role in the film *Tammy*, he wrote, "the star makes no attempt to beautify herself onscreen," and for this, "She isn't … a real female clown." (Reed, 2014)

  c. The principle difference between how McCarthy and successful male comedians are received is that McCarthy alone is defined by her gender.

Transition: Now that we understand more about the gender gap in the Hollywood film industry, let's continue to examine how prejudices are working to limit women's career opportunities in Hollywood.

…

Isabel continues in the same manner for her other main points.

STUDY TOOLS 7

LOCATED IN TEXTBOOK

☐ Tear-out Chapter Review cards at the end of the book

☐ Review with the Quick Quiz below

LOCATED ON SPEAK3 ONLINE AT CENGAGEBRAIN.COM

☐ Review Key Term flashcards and create your own cards

☐ Track your knowledge and understanding of key concepts in speech communication

☐ Complete practice and graded quizzes to prepare for tests

☐ Complete interactive content within SPEAK3 Online

☐ View the chapter highlight boxes for SPEAK3 Online

Quick Quiz (answers in Solutions Appendix)

T F 1. The length of a speech is determined primarily by the number of main points.

T F 2. A speaker using narrative order would arrange the main points of a speech through a story or series of stories.

T F 3. The ideal number of central ideas of a speech is two to four.

T F 4. Section transitions help the audience follow the organization of ideas in a speech.

T F 5. In a speech outline, the main points and subpoints should be written as complete sentences.

---

6. The words, phrases, or sentences that show the connection between ideas are known as:

a. subpoints

b. relevance links

c. transitions

d. connectors

e. conjunctions

7. A one- or two-sentence summary of your speech that previews the main point is a:

a. thematic statement

b. thesis statement.

c. central statement

d. point statement

e. motif statement

8. All of the following are ways to organize the main points of a speech EXCEPT:

a. time order

b. logical reasons order

c. narrative order

d. topical order

e. intensity order

9. A speech outline is arranged by sequence and:

a. theme

b. concern

c. interest

d. geography

e. hierarchy

10. The _____ serves as a basis for the transition from the introduction to the body of the speech.

a. thesis statement

b. conclusion

c. main point

d. subpoint

e. listener-relevance link

Chapter Takeaways

List three key takeaways from this chapter:

-

-

-

SPEAK
ONLINE
PREPARE FOR TESTS ON THE STUDYBOARD!

○ CORRECT

● INCORRECT

● INCORRECT

● INCORRECT

Personalize Quizzes from Your StudyBits

Take Practice Quizzes by Chapter

CHAPTER QUIZZES

▶ Chapter 1

Chapter 2

Chapter 3

Chapter 4

4LTR PRESS

Access SPEAK ONLINE at www.cengagebrain.com

8 The Introduction and Conclusion

After finishing this chapter go to **PAGE 138** for **STUDY TOOLS.**

LEARNING OUTCOMES

8-1 Explain why solid introductions and conclusions are so important to effective public speaking.

8-2 Create an effective speech introduction.

8-3 Create an effective speech conclusion.

8-4 Complete your outline and reference list.

Sound Familiar?

Isabel asked John to listen to her rehearse her speech. As she stood in front of the room where she was practicing, she began, "I'd like to share with you the basic facts of gender inequality in Hollywood, and how women directors, screenwriters, and actors have significantly fewer opportunities than their male coworkers."

"Wait," John said. "That's your introduction?"

"Yes," Isabel replied. "I've got a lot of information to share and don't have a lot of time to say it. So, I don't want to waste any more time than necessary on my introduction."

Isabel's response might sound reasonable at first. But what Isabel fails to realize is that not everyone in the audience may be ready to listen to her speech about gender inequality in Hollywood. People might think the topic is boring, irrelevant to them, or for some other reason not worth their time. They might also wonder what makes Isabel a credible speaker on the subject. How well you start the speech may determine whether people even listen to it, and how well you finish your speech can play a major role in determining whether they will remember what you've said.

One reason the introduction and conclusion are so important is based on what psychologists call the **primacy-recency effect**: We are more likely to remember the first and last items conveyed orally in a series than the items in between.[1] This means listeners are more likely to remember the beginning and ending of your speech than what you say in the body. Another reason stems from the need for listeners to quickly grasp your goal and main points in order to follow along, as well as remember them after you've finished.

In the previous chapter, we described the tasks involved in organizing the speech body. In this chapter, we focus on creating an introduction that both gets attention and leads into the body of the speech; creating a conclusion that both summarizes main points and motivates listeners to remember; writing a title; and completing a reference list.

ACTION STEP

Organize Ideas into a Well-Structured Outline

E. Create the speech introduction.

F. Create the speech conclusion.

G. Compile the reference list.

H. Complete the formal speech outline.

8-1 THE INTRODUCTION

Once you have developed the speech body, you can decide how to introduce it. Because the introduction is so important to your success, you will want to develop two or three different introductions and then select the one that seems best for the audience you will be addressing. An introduction is generally about 10 percent of the length of the entire speech, so for a five-minute speech (approximately 750 words), an introduction of about thirty seconds (approximately 60 to 85 words) is appropriate.

An effective introduction achieves four primary goals: to get attention, convey listener relevance, establish speaker credibility, and identify the thesis statement (speech goal and main point preview). In our opening scenario, Isabel didn't really achieve any of these goals. Rather, she simply identified and defined the topic and then moved right into her first main point.

8-1a Get Attention

An audience's physical presence does not guarantee that people will actually listen to your speech. Your first goal, then, is to create an opening that will win your listeners' attention by arousing their curiosity and motivating them to want to know more about your topic. Some rhetorical strategies for doing so include startling statements, questions, stories, jokes, personal references, quotations, action, and suspense. You can determine which attention-getting device to use by

primacy-recency effect the tendency to remember the first and last items conveyed orally in a series rather than the items in between

considering which emotional tone is appropriate for your topic. A humorous attention getter will signal a lighthearted tone; a serious one signals a more thoughtful or somber tone. For instance, a speaker who starts with a funny story will put the audience in a light-hearted mood. If that speaker then says, "Now let's turn to the subject of abortion" (or nuclear war or drug abuse), the audience will be confused by the speaker's initial words, which signaled a far different type of subject.

1. A **startling statement** is an expression or example that grabs your listeners' attention by shocking them in some way. Chris used this startling statement to get his listeners' attention for his speech about how automobile emissions contribute to global warming:

Look around. Each one of you is sitting next to a killer. That's right. You are sitting next to a cold-blooded killer. Before you think about jumping up and running out of this room, let me explain. Everyone who drives an automobile is a killer of the environment. Every time you turn the key to your ignition, you are helping to destroy our precious surroundings.

2. Questions are requests for information that encourage your audience to think about something related to your topic. Questions can be *rhetorical* or *direct*. A rhetorical question doesn't require an overt response. Notice how this student began his speech on counterfeiting with these three short rhetorical questions:

What would you do with this $20 bill if I gave it to you? Take your friend to a movie? Treat yourself to a pizza and drinks? Well, if you did either of these things, you could get in big trouble—this bill is counterfeit!

Unlike a rhetorical question, a **direct question** demands an overt response from the audience. It might be a "yea" or "nay" or a show of hands. For example, here's

how author and motivational speaker Harvey Mackay started his commencement address at the University of Southern California:

Let me start by asking all of you in the audience this question: How many people talk to themselves? Please raise your hands. I count approximately 50 percent.

To the other 50 percent who didn't raise your hands, I can just hear you now, saying to yourself: "Who me? I don't talk to myself!"

Well I think all of you will be talking to yourself about the day's events on your way home this evening. This is an unforgettable moment among many fine hours you will have in your career and life.[2]

Direct questions can be helpful in getting audience attention because they require a physical response. However, getting listeners to actually comply with your request can also pose a challenge.

3. A **story** is an account of something that has happened (actual) or could happen (hypothetical). Most people enjoy a well-told story, so it makes a good attention getter. For example, Jonathan T.M. Reckford, CEO of Habitat for Humanity, started a speech on myths about affordable housing by recounting a story of an experience he had touring Asia after the tsunami:

Shortly after I joined Habitat for Humanity in 2005, I visited the tsunami-devastated countries of Asia. During that trip, I encountered a developmentally disabled gentleman named Somwang Chiochan. He lived in a community of Moken, or sea gypsies, in southwest Thailand.

Historically, the larger society has shunned the Moken people, and, because of his disability, the Moken people further discriminated against Mr. Chiochan. Before the tsunami, he had no role in the fishing village. He lived on a two-square-meter lot in a structure worse than many doghouses.

Even before the storm, his future looked pretty bleak.[3]

Mr. Reckford continued his story by describing how the village elders embarked on the plan to build a three-story residence after the tsunami. One drawback of stories is that they are often lengthy and can take more time to tell than is appropriate for the length

startling statement an expression or example that grabs your listeners' attention by shocking them in some way

questions requests for information that encourage your audience to think about something related to your topic

direct question a question that demands an overt response from the audience, usually by a show of hands

story an account of something that has happened (actual) or could happen (hypothetical)

© iStockphoto.com/macida

of your speech. Use a story only if it is short or if you can abbreviate it so that it is just right for your speech length.

4. A **joke** is an anecdote or a piece of wordplay designed to make people laugh. A joke can be used to get audience attention when it meets the *three R's test*: It must be realistic, relevant, and repeatable.[4] In other words, it can't be too far-fetched, unrelated to the speech purpose, or potentially offensive to some listeners. In his speech about being a person of integrity, for example, Joel Osteen offered this joke to get attention:

> *A kindergarten teacher asked one of her students what she was drawing a picture of. The little girl said, "I'm drawing a picture of God." The teacher replied, "Oh honey, nobody knows what God looks like." Without missing a beat, the little girl replied, "They will in a minute ..."[5]*

When jokes work, they adhere to the three R's test. If you decide to use one, be sure to consider how you will handle the situation if nobody laughs.

5. A **personal reference** is a brief account about something that happened to you or a hypothetical situation that listeners can imagine themselves in. In addition to getting attention, a personal reference can be especially effective at engaging listeners as active participants. A personal reference like this one on exercise is suitable for a speech of any length:

> *Were you panting when you got to the top of those four flights of stairs this morning? I'll bet there were a few of you who vowed you'd never take a class on the top floor of this building again. But did you ever stop to think that maybe the problem isn't that this class is on the top floor? It just might be that you are not getting enough exercise.*

6. A **quotation** is a comment made by and attributed to someone other than the speaker. A particularly vivid or thought-provoking quotation can make an excellent attention getter as long as it relates to your topic. Although it is common to quote famous people, a good quotation from *any* source can create interest in your topic.

> A vivid or thought-provoking quotation can make an excellent attention getter as long as it relates to your **topic.**

Thanks to the Internet and search engines like Google and Bing, finding compelling and relevant quotations is easier today than it was in the past.

7. An **action** is an attention-getting act designed to highlight and arouse interest in your topic. You can perform an action yourself, just as Juan did when he split a stack of boards with his hand to get attention for his speech on karate. Or you can ask volunteers from the audience to perform the action. For example, Cindria used three audience members to participate in breaking a piñata to create interest in her speech on the history of the piñata. If you choose to use audience members, however, consider soliciting participants ahead of time to avoid the possibility of having no volunteers when you ask during your speech. Finally, you can ask your entire audience to perform some action related to your speech topic. If you'd like to ask your whole audience to perform an action, realistically assess whether what you are asking is something your audience is likely to comply with.

8. To **create suspense**, word your attention getter so that what is described generates uncertainty or mystery and excites the audience. When you get the audience to ask, "What is she leading up to?" you have created suspense. A suspenseful opening is especially valuable when your audience is not particularly interested in hearing about your topic. Consider this suspenseful statement:

> *It costs the United States more than $116 billion per year. It has cost the loss of more jobs than a recession. It accounts for nearly 100,000 deaths a year. I'm not talking about cocaine abuse—the problem is alcoholism. Today I want to show you how we can avoid this inhumane killer by abstaining from it.*

Notice that by introducing the problem, alcoholism, at the end of the statement, the speaker

joke an anecdote or a piece of wordplay designed to be funny and make people laugh

personal reference a brief story about something that happened to you or a hypothetical situation that listeners can imagine themselves in

quotation a comment made by and attributed to someone other than the speaker

action an attention-getting act designed to highlight and arouse interest in your topic or purpose

creating suspense wording an attention getter so that what is described generates initial uncertainty or mystery and excites the audience

encourages the audience to try to anticipate the answer. And because the audience may well be thinking that the problem is narcotics, the revelation that it is alcoholism is likely to be that much more effective.

8-1b Establish Relevance

Even if you successfully get the attention of your listeners, to keep their attention you will need to motivate them to listen to your speech. You can do this by creating a clear listener-relevance link: a statement of how and why your speech relates to or might affect your audience. Doing this in the introduction and again for each main point helps your audience realize its exigence.[6] Sometimes your attention-getting statement will serve this function, but if it doesn't, you will need to provide a personal connection between your topic and your audience. When creating a listener-relevance link, answer these questions: Why should my listeners care about what I'm saying? In what way(s) might they benefit from hearing about it? How might my speech relate to my listeners' needs or desires for health, wealth, well-being, self-esteem, success, and so forth?

8-1c Establish Credibility

If someone hasn't formally introduced you, audience members are going to wonder who you are and why they should pay attention to what you say. So, another goal of the introduction is to begin to build your credibility. Recall from Chapter 1 that the theoretical grounding for this goal actually dates back to the ancient Greek philosophy of Aristotle in his treatise *The Rhetoric*.[7] Aristotle asserted that listeners would be motivated to both listen to and believe a speaker based on their perception of his or her *ethos* (competence, good character, and goodwill), *pathos* (appeals to emotions), and *logos* (perception of truth through evidence and reasoning). To be successful, you need to begin to establish ethos during your introductory remarks. This initial ethos responds to the questions listeners may be thinking, such as: Why should I trust you? What makes you an authority on the subject? Why should I believe you? Do you seem sincere? Do you seem like a likeable person? Do your words and actions demonstrate respect for me and this occasion? Remember, though, that your goal is to highlight how you are a credible speaker on this topic, not that you are *the* or even a *final* authority on the subject. Carmen Mariano, principal of Archbishop Williams High School in Braintree, Massachusetts, established credibility and goodwill in a "welcome back, students" speech this way:

Ladies and gentlemen, you will hear one word many times this morning. That word is welcome. Please know how much we mean that word. Please know how much I mean that word.

Why will we mean that word so much?

Because without you, this is just a building on 80 Independence Avenue. And with you, this is Archbishop Williams High School. That's right. When you walked through those doors this morning, you made this building a school again.

So welcome back.

And welcome to your school.[8]

8-1d State the Thesis

Because audiences want to know what your speech is going to be about, it's important to state your thesis. After Miguel gained the audience's attention and established relevance and credibility he said, "In the next five minutes, I'd like to explain to you that romantic love is composed of three elements: passion, intimacy, and commitment."

Stating your main points in the introduction is necessary unless you have some special reason for not revealing the details of the thesis. For instance, after getting the attention of his audience, Miguel might say, "In the next five minutes, I'd like to explain the three aspects of romantic love," a statement that specifies the number of main points but leaves the details for a preview statement that immediately precedes the main points. Ashton Kutcher opened his speech accepting the 2013 Teen Choice Ultimate Choice Award by stating his thesis this way:

In Hollywood and the industry, there are a lot of insider secrets to keeping your career going and a lot of insider secrets to making things tick. . . . My name is not even really Ashton—Ashton is my middle name. My first name is Chris. And it always has been. It got changed when I was 19 and I became an actor. But there were some really amazing things I learned when I was Chris, and I wanted to share those things with you guys because it's helped me be here today. It's really three things.[9]

marekuliasz/Shutterstock.com

MEDIA MOMENT

Inspiration from the Inverted Pyramid

You might not know by its name, but if you've ever read a news article, you have likely encountered the inverted pyramid.

Alternatively loved and loathed by journalists across all forms of media, the inverted pyramid is widely used to structure news reporting. The format is simple enough: The most newsworthy information goes at the top, with facts trailing downward throughout the article in order of importance.[10]

The inverted pyramid has existed for more than a century, and most historians agree that it was developed to capitalize upon the invention of the telegraph by allowing wire operators to get the most important information first. That lead generally includes the so-called Five W's of who, what, where, when, and why. In fact, some historians propose that one of the first inverted pyramid leads was reported by wire on a fateful night in April 1865: "The President [*who*] was shot [*what*] in a theater [*where*] tonight [*when*] and perhaps mortally wounded [*why*]."[11]

Although useful for reporting, the inverted pyramid and its Five W's should not be used for speechwriting, because the structure encourages listeners to tune out the speaker after they get the facts up front. Likewise, the structure makes it hard to tell a story because newsworthiness trumps sequence.[12] Nonetheless, the format does provide some useful insights for public speaking.

As you initially organize your speech, thinking of it in the context of the inverted pyramid can help you summarize your entire point into a single paragraph. Furthermore, this

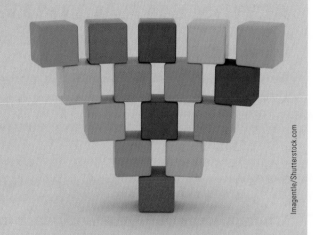

Imagentle/Shutterstock.com

type of thinking can help you filter out the least relevant supporting details, which is especially useful when you're under a tight time limit.[13]

For some speeches, it might be helpful to apply the inverted pyramid within each section of the speech body. This can create a sort of ebb and flow within your speech, with the most powerful or informative details being presented at the start of each section, followed by your supporting points. Unless your speech is long, this format should be interesting and easy for the audience to follow.

The inverted pyramid isn't the best way to tell a story—and it's certainly not ideal for organizing an entire speech—but it does offer a useful way to consider how you present your information.

 ## 8-2 SELECTING THE BEST INTRODUCTION

Because the introduction is critical in establishing a relationship with your audience and identifying your topic and goal, it's worth investing the time to compare different openings. Try working on two or three different introductions; then, pick the one you believe will work best for your specific audience and speech goal.

Your speech introduction should meet all four goals and be long enough to encourage listeners to hear you out, but not so long that it leaves too little time to develop the substance of your speech. Of course, the shorter the speech, the shorter the introduction.

Speech Planning Action Step 4, Activity 4E, will help you develop three choices for your speech introduction.

See the Student Response box immediately following the activity for a sample of how one student completed this exercise.

 ## 8-3 THE CONCLUSION

Shakespeare once said, "All's well that ends well." Effective conclusions heighten the impact of a good speech by summarizing the main ideas and leaving the audience with a vivid impression. Even though the conclusion is a relatively short part of the speech—seldom more than 5 percent (thirty-five to forty-five words for a five-minute speech)—your conclusion should be carefully planned.

The conclusion of a speech has two major goals. The first is to summarize the speech goal and main points. The second is to provide a sense of closure by driving home

ACTION STEP ACTIVITY

Creating Speech Introductions

The goal of this activity is to create several speech introductions from which to choose.

1. For the speech body you outlined earlier, write three different introductions—using different rhetorical devices (startling statement, a question, a story, a personal reference, a joke, a quotation, action, or suspense) to get attention—that you believe meet the primary goals of effective introductions and would be appropriate for your speech goal and audience.

2. Of the three introductions you drafted, which do you believe is the best? Why?

3. Write that introduction in outline form, indicating in parentheses where you are meeting each goal.

Student Response: Creating Speech Introductions

1. Write three different introductions—using different rhetorical devices (startling statement, a question, a story, a personal reference, a joke, a quotation, action, or suspense) to get attention—that you believe meet the goals of effective introductions and would be appropriate for the following speech goal and audience.

   Specific goal: *I would like the audience to understand the three ways to tell if a diamond is real.*

   (1) *We are at an age where buying diamonds might be on our minds. I would like to tell you how you can know for sure if your diamond is real.*

   (2) *Have you ever wondered if you would know if a diamond that the jeweler is trying to sell you is real? Nobody wants to be duped into spending a lot of money on a fake. As a Biology major, I have actually studied how to determine whether a diamond is real, and I would like to share three things you can look for to do so.*

   (3) *Calcite, quartz, cubic zirconia, diamond. How can you tell these minerals apart? They are all colorless and can sometimes look alike. But let me tell you three ways that you can tell if you are holding a real diamond.*

2. Of the three introductions you drafted, which do you believe is the best? Why?

   I believe the second one is the best, because the rhetorical question and listener-relevance link are likely to motivate the audience to listen, I share why they can believe me, and the thesis statement contains a main point preview.

3. Write that introduction in outline form, indicating in parentheses where you are meeting each goal.
   I. *Have you ever wondered if you would know if a diamond that the jeweler is trying to sell you is real? (attention getter)*
   II. *Nobody wants to be duped into spending a lot of money on a fake. (listener relevance)*
   III. *As a Biology major, I have actually studied how to determine whether a diamond is real, and I would like to share three things you can look for to do so. (speaker credibility and thesis statement with main point preview).*

---

the importance of your message in a memorable way. As with your speech introduction, you should prepare two or three conclusions and then choose the one you believe will be most effective for the audience and occasion.

8-3a Summarize Goal and Main Points

An effective speech conclusion includes an abbreviated restatement of your goal and main points. A summary for an informative speech on how to improve your grades might be, "So I hope you now understand [*informative goal*] that three techniques to improve your grades are to attend classes regularly, develop a positive attitude toward the course, and study systematically [*main points*]." A short summary for a persuasive speech on why you should exercise might be, "So you should exercise for at least 30 minutes each day [*persuasive goal*] to improve your appearance, as well as your physical and mental health [*main points*]."

8-3b Clinch

Although a good summary helps the audience remember your main points, a good clincher leaves the audience with a vivid impression. A **clincher** is a short statement that provides a sense of closure by driving home the importance of your speech in a memorable way. If you can, try to devise a clincher that refers back to the introductory comments in some way. Two effective strategies for clinching are using vivid imagery and appealing to action.

Vivid Imagery

To develop vivid imagery, you can use any of the devices we have discussed for getting attention (startling statement, question, story, joke, personal reference, quotation, action, or suspense). For example, in Tiffany's speech about being a vegetarian, she referred back to the personal reference she had made in her introduction about a vegetarian Thanksgiving meal:

So now you know why I made the choice to become a vegetarian and how this choice affects my life today. As a vegetarian, I've discovered a world of food I never knew existed. Believe me, I am salivating just thinking about the meal I have planned for this Thanksgiving: fennel and blood orange salad; followed by baked polenta layered with tomato, fontina, and Gorgonzola cheeses; an acorn squash tart, marinated tofu; and with what else but pumpkin pie for dessert!

Sounds good, doesn't it? Clinchers that foster vivid imagery are appropriate for both informative and persuasive speeches because they leave listeners with a vibrant picture imprinted in their minds.

Appeal to Action

The appeal to action is a common clincher for persuasive speeches. The **appeal to action** describes the behavior you want your listeners to follow after they have heard your arguments. Notice how Matthew Cossolotto, president and founder of Study Abroad Alumni International, concludes his speech on global awareness and responsibility with a strong appeal to action:

So, yes, you should have this re-entry program. Yes, you should network and explore international career opportunities. That's all good.

But I also encourage you to Globalize Your Locality. I urge you to Think Global. . . Act Global. . . Be Global.

This is an urgent call to action . . . for you and other study abroad alumni . . . to help us reduce the global awareness deficit.

You can do so by becoming involved with SAAI . . . and other organizations such as the National Council for International Visitors, Sister Cities, or Rotary International.

You can speak to local schools and community organizations about your study abroad experience and the need for more global awareness.

When you studied abroad, I'm sure you were told many times that you would be serving as unofficial ambassadors of the United States . . . your campus . . . and even your community back home.

Now that you're home again, I hope you'll become ambassadors for the value of the study abroad experience and for the need for greater international awareness.

In wrapping up . . . I'd like to leave you with this image . . . just picture in your mind's eye that iconic photograph of planet earth. I'm sure you've seen it. Taken over four decades ago . . . in December 1968 . . . on the Apollo 8 mission to the moon.

The photograph— dubbed Earthrise—shows our small, blue planet rising above a desolate lunar landscape. This photo was a true watershed in human history . . . marking the first time earthlings . . . fellow global citizens . . . had traveled outside earth's orbit and looked back on our lonely planet.

The widespread publication of Earthrise had a lot to do with launching the worldwide environmental movement. It's no accident that the first Earth Day—on April 22, 1970—took place so soon after the publication of this remarkable photograph.

We're all privileged to inhabit this same planet—truly an island in space. And voices to the contrary notwithstanding . . . whether we want to admit it or not . . . we are all, undeniably and by definition, citizens of the world.

The only question is: will we accept the responsibilities of global citizenship?

Your future . . . and perhaps the survival of the planet . . . just may depend on how many of us answer yes to that question.[14]

> **clincher** a one- or two-sentence statement in a conclusion that provides a sense of closure by driving home the importance of your speech in a memorable way
>
> **appeal to action** a statement in a conclusion that describes the behavior you want your listeners to follow after they have heard your arguments

8-3c Selecting the Best Conclusion

As with the introduction, create two or three conclusions and then choose the best one for the audience and occasion. For her short speech on women in filmmaking, Isabel created the following three variations of summaries for consideration. Which do you like best?

#1: The bottom line is that gender and age discrimination are illegal, but we still allow prejudices to dictate how women are treated in the film business. Female representation in the movies doesn't match up with our society, and it's essential that the industry catch up with modern times. Women in film need better representation now. It is possible to close the gender gap in the film industry. Let's start supporting women filmmakers, and change who gets to write the script for gender in the movies.

#2: It's time the film industry steps out of the past and into the present. No longer can we tolerate illegal discrimination as merely "just part of show business." As audience members, we have the power to create real change. Without us, the movie industry wouldn't exist. By supporting women writers, directors, and actresses, we show studios there is in fact a demand for their work. Together, we can re-write the script for gender in the movies.

#3: They say the show must go on, but how long will we allow this type of discrimination to continue? The bottom line is that the movie industry should not be above the law. While organizations like the American Civil Liberties Union plan investigations, we as the audience must act now. By supporting women writers, directors, and actresses, we show studios there is in fact a demand to see their work. Let's close the gender gap in the film industry, and re-write the script for gender in the movies.

For speeches that are no longer than five minutes, a one- to three-sentence conclusion is often appropriate. Ashton Kutcher concluded his four-minute speech very succinctly by saying, "Build your life— don't live one, build one. Find your opportunities. And always be sexy. I love you guys." (Note that, during his speech, Kutcher defined "sexy" as begin smart, thoughtful, and generous).[15]

Action Step Activity 4F will help you develop choices for your speech

formal outline A full sentence outline of your speech that includes internal references and a reference list.

Ashton Kutcher's acceptance speech at the 2013 Teen Choice Awards opened with an introduction that captured his audience's attention immediately.

Kevin Winter/Getty Images

conclusion. See the Student Response box immediately following the activity for a sample of how one student completed this exercise.

8-4 THE COMPLETE FORMAL OUTLINE WITH REFERENCE LIST

After drafting your introduction and conclusion, you have essentially drafted an outline of your speech. To complete the **formal outline**, you need to compile a list of the sources you draw from in the speech, create a title (if required), and then review your outline to make sure that it conforms to a logical structure.

8-4a Listing Sources

Regardless of the type or length of the speech, you need to prepare a list of the sources you use in it. This list will enable you to direct audience members to the specific

ACTION STEP ACTIVITY

Creating Speech Conclusions

The goal of this activity is to help you create several speech conclusions from which to choose.

1. For the speech body you outlined earlier, write three different conclusions that review important points you want the audience to remember, and include a clincher that provides closure by leaving the audience with a vivid impression.
2. Which do you believe is the best? Why?
3. Write that conclusion in outline form.

Student Response: Creating Speech Conclusions

1. Using the same speech from 4e, write three different conclusions that review important points you want the audience to remember, and include a clincher that provides closure by leaving the audience with a vivid impression.

   Specific goal: _I would like the audience to understand the three ways to tell if a diamond is real._

   (1) _So, the next time you buy or receive a diamond, you will know how to do the acid, streak, and hardness tests to make sure the diamond is real._

   (2) _Before making your final diamond selection, make sure it can pass the acid test, streak test, and hardness test. Remember, you want to make sure you're buying a real diamond and not a fake!_

   (3) _Now we all know how to tell if a diamond is real. So, folks, if you discover that the gem you're considering effervesces in acid, has a streak that is not clear, or can be scratched, you will know that it is a fake. As a result, none of us will fall victim to being duped by a crook!_

2. Which do you believe is the best? Why?

   The third one because it restates the characteristics and leaves a vivid impression.

3. Write that conclusion in outline form.

   I. _Now we all know how to tell if a diamond is real. (Goal restatement)_

   II. _If it effervesces, streaks, or scratches, it is a fake. (main point review)_

   III. _As a result, none of us will be duped by a crook! (clincher)_

---

source of any information you used and will allow you to quickly find the information at a later date. You also want to use internal references throughout the formal speech outline to help you remember what to cite and where during your speech. Doing so will ultimately enhance your credibility and help you avoid unintentional plagiarism.

Many formal bibliographical styles can be used to compile your source list (for example, MLA, APA, Chicago, CBE). Exhibit 8.1 gives examples of

> All citations should be complete—and **specific.**

citations according to the Modern Language Association (MLA) and American Psychological Association (APA) style guides. The "correct" form differs by professional or academic discipline. Check to see if your instructor has a preference about which style you use in class.

Action Step Activity 4G will help you compile a list of sources used in your speech. See the Student Response box immediately following the activity for a sample of how one student completed this exercise.

Exhibit 8.1

Examples of the MLA and APA Citation Forms

	MLA Style	APA Style
Print		
Book	Quinones, *Sam. Dreamland: The True Tale of America's Opiate Epidemic.* New York, NY: Bloomsbury Press, 2015.	Quinones, S. (2015). *Dreamland: The true tale of America's opiate epidemic.* New York, NY: Bloomsbury Press.
Academic journal	Durmelat, Sylvie. "Introduction: Colonial Culinary Encounters and Imperial Leftovers." *French Cultural Studies* 26.2 (2015): 115–129.	Durmelat, S. (2015). Introduction: Colonial culinary encounters and imperial leftovers. *French Cultural Studies*, 26(2), 115–129.
Magazine	Kelly, Andy. "Isle Be Back: Pillars of Eternity Is a Grand RPG in a Classic Form." *PC Gamer* July 2015: 58–62.	Kelly, A. (2015, July). Isle be back: Pillars of Eternity is a grand RPG in a classic form. *PC Gamer*, 267, 58–62.
Digital		
Web Site	"Build a Chicken Coop." Tractorsupply.com. n.d. Web. 25 June 2015.	Tractor Supply. (n.d.). Build a chicken coop. Retrieved from http://www.tractorsupply.com/know-how_Chicken-Coops_build-a-chicken-coop
Blog Post	Verducci, Tom. "Why Having an Election Night Will Solve All-Star Game Voting Problem." *Sports Illustrated MLB Blog.* Si.com/mlb, 23 June 2015. Web. 25 June 2015.	Verducci, T. (2015, June 23). Why having an election night will solve all-star game voting problem [Web blog post]. Retrieved from http://www.si.com/mlb/2015/06/23/all-star-game-voting-kansas-city-royals
Multimedia		
Movie	*Iris.* Dir. Albert Maysles. Prods. Laura Coxson, Rebekah Maysles, Jennifer Ash Ruddick. Magnolia Pictures, 2015.	Coxson, L., Maysles, R., and Ash Ruddick, J. (Producers) & Maysles, A. (Director). (2015). *Iris* [Motion picture]. United States: Magnolia Pictures.
Online Video	Maharishi University. "Jim Carrey's Commencement Address at the 2014 MUM Graduation." YouTube. 2014. Web. 25 June 2015.	Maharishi University. (2014, May 24). Jim Carrey's commencement address at the 2014 MUM graduation [Video file]. Retrieved from https://www.youtube.com/watch?v=V80-gPkpH6M.

8-4b Writing a Title

In most speech situations outside the classroom, it helps to have a title for your speech that lets the audience know what to expect. A title is probably necessary when you will be formally introduced, when the speech is publicized, or when the speech will be published. A good title helps to attract an audience and build interest in what you will say. Titles should be brief, descriptive of the content, and, if possible, creative. Most speakers don't settle on a title until the rest of the speech preparation is complete.

Three kinds of titles can be created: a simple statement of subject, a question, or a creative title.

1. **Simple statement of subject.** This straightforward title captures the subject of the speech in a few words.

Courage to Grow

The Dignity of Work

America's Destiny

2. **Question.** To spark greater interest, you can create a title by phrasing your speech goal as a question. A

ACTION STEP ACTIVITY

Compiling a List of Sources

The goal of this activity is to record a list of sources for your speech.

1. Review your annotated bibliography and/or research cards, as well as formal speech outline. Identify each source from which you drew information for your speech.
2. Note on your outline where you'll reference the source during your speech.
3. List the sources used in your speech by copying the bibliographical information recorded on the annotated bibliography and/or research card.
4. Using the style guide required for your class, record the bibliographic citation for each source in an alphabetical list.

Student Response: Compiling a List of Sources

1. Review your annotated bibliography and/or research cards, as well as formal speech outline. Identify each source from which you drew information for your speech.
2. Note on your outline where you'll reference the source during your speech.
3. List the sources used in your speech by copying the bibliographical information recorded on the annotated bibliography and/or research card.
4. Using the style guide required for your class, record the bibliographic citation for each source in an alphabetical list.

Sources

Dixon, Dougal. *The Practical Geologist*. New York: Simon & Schuster, 1992.

Farver, John. *Personal interview*. 23 June 2004.

Klein, Cornelius. *Manual of Mineralogy*. 2nd ed. New York: John Wiley & Sons, 1993.

Montgomery, Carla W. *Fundamentals of Geology*. 3rd ed. Dubuque, IA: Wm. C. Brown, 1997.

prospective listener may then be motivated to attend the speech to find out the answer.

Do We Need a Department of Play?

What Is the Impact of Computers on Our Behavior?

Are We Living in a Moral Stone Age?

Formal outlines help you organize your thoughts—and your speech—by ensuring that your main points and subpoints are logically connected.

3. Creative title. A more creative approach is to combine a familiar saying or metaphor with the simple statement of subject.

Teaching Old Dogs New Tricks: The Need for Adult Computer Literacy

Promises to Keep: Broadcasting and the Public Interest

Freeze or Freedom: On the Limits of Morals and Worth of Politics

The simple statement of the subject gives a clear idea of the topic but is not especially eye- or ear-catching. Questions and creative titles capture interest but may not give a clear idea of content. Creative titles often require subtitles.

8-4c Reviewing the Outline

Now that you have created all parts of the outline, it is time to put them together in complete formal outline form and review them to make sure the outline is well organized and well worded. Use this checklist to guide you.

1. Have I used a standard set of symbols to indicate structure? Main points are indicated by Roman numerals, major subpoints by capital letters, sub-subpoints by Arabic numerals, and further subdivisions by lowercase letters.

2. Have I written main points and major subpoints as complete sentences? Complete sentences help you to see (1) whether each main point actually develops your speech goal and (2) whether the wording makes your intended point.

3. Do main points and main subpoints each contain a single idea? This guideline ensures that the development of each part of the speech will be relevant to the point. Thus, rather than:

> *Organically produced food is good for the environment and for animals.*

divide the sentence so each part is stated separately:

> I. *Organically produced food is good for the environment.*
> II. *Organically produced food is good for animals.*

4. Does each major subpoint relate to or support its major point? This principle, called *subordination*, ensures that you don't wander off point and confuse your audience. For example:

> I. *Proper equipment is necessary for successful play.*
> A. *Good gym shoes are needed for maneuverability.*
> B. *Padded gloves help protect your hands.*
> C. *A lively ball provides sufficient bounce.*
> D. *And a good attitude doesn't hurt either.*

Notice that the main point deals with equipment. A, B, and C (shoes, gloves, and ball) all relate to the main point. But D, attitude, is not equipment and should appear somewhere else, if at all.

5. Are all subpoint elaborations indicated? Recall that subpoint elaborations help develop the speech. Because you don't know how long it might take to discuss these elaborations, you should include more than you are likely to use. During rehearsals, you may discuss each in a different way.

Now that we have considered the various parts of an outline, let us put them together for a final look. The sample complete formal outline at the end of the chapter illustrates the principles in practice.

Action Step Activity 4H will help you write and review a complete-sentence outline of your speech. For this activity, refer to Isabel's complete outline on the following page as the student response.

ACTION STEP ACTIVITY

Completing the Formal Speech Outline

Write and review a complete-sentence outline of your speech using material you've developed so far with the Action Steps in Chapters 4 through 8. You can view a student sample of this activity beginning on the following page.

Sample Complete Formal Outline

Who Writes the Script for Gender in the Movies?

General Goal:

I want to inform my audience.

Specific Speech Goal:

I would like to inform my audience about gender inequality in the American film industry.

Thesis Statement:

I want to inform my audience about rampant gender inequality in the American filmmaking industry and debunk cultural misperceptions that women have equal access to work on screen and backstage.

Introduction

I. Think of the last film you saw at the box office and raise your hand if you know whether the director was a man or a woman. Now, look under your seats. How many of you have a red ticket? Please stand up. You represent 93 percent of our audience; you also represent the percentage of films directed by men in 2014. Please sit down. If you have a green ticket under your seat, please stand. You represent the remaining 7 percent of films with at least one female director. **[Attention getter]**

    A. Even though we like to think of ourselves as a post-modern society in which issues of gender inequality have been completely eradicated, there are many areas where gender inequality is still extremely pronounced.

        1. In October 2014, journalist Genevieve Wood wrote for *USA Today*, "American women today enjoy unprecedented levels of opportunity," attesting that female politicians are "stuck in a time warp, channeling the problems and political causes of the '60s" (Wood, 2014).

        2. In fact, a poll conducted in March 2015, revealed that when 1,067 adults nationwide were asked if they believed in gender equality, 85 percent said yes, with only 3 percent reporting no (Vox, 2015).

    B. Today I'd like to examine how those statements add up when we look at the American film industry.

II. I am a self-described film nerd. I'm a film major and aspiring director. I've shadowed on multiple sets, and I've interned at film festivals for the past three years. This year, I've assisted professors in their study of employment diversity in the film industry. Troubled by what we discovered, I became passionate about doing my own research of the subject. **[Establishing speaker credibility]**

III. I want to share with you the basic facts of gender inequality in Hollywood, and how women directors, screenwriters, and actors have significantly fewer opportunities than their male coworkers. **[Thesis statement]**

Body

I. The film industry is not a diverse business. Even though the entertainment industry as a whole is extremely varied and also lucrative, the movie segment is comparatively small and run by a smaller, homogenous group of people who paradoxically reap the majority of the profits.

Over two-thirds of the U.S. and Canadian population, ages 2 and up, or 229.7 million people, attended the movies at least once in 2014. That means more than 66 percent of our audience went to the movies last year (MPAA, 2014). **[Listener relevance link]**

    A. In the United States alone, the film industry is an important driver of the economy.

        1. The U.S. film industry accounts for 1.9 million jobs and generates $47 billion dollars of income annually (Fried, 2015).

        2. By the end of 2015, the U.S. entertainment industry is predicted to be a $589 billion industry, and the global entertainment market worth a staggering $2 trillion (USD) (Statistica, 2015).

B. But, as pointed out by Darnell Hunt, author of the Hollywood Diversity Report, "Hollywood is not progressing at the same rate as America is diversifying" (Hunt, 2015).

   1. Hunt's report, which studied data collected in 2013, found that CEOs of major and mini-major film studios were 100 percent male and 94 percent white. Not included in the study was Stacey Snider, former CEO of DreamWorks Studios (regarded as too small for the study); she was hired to lead 20th Century Fox after the study was completed. These surprisingly high percentages are not exclusive to the CEO role. A male majority dominates nearly every division of the film industry (Siegemund-Broka, 2015).

   2. The Center for the Study of Women and Television and Film at San Diego State University revealed that, of the top 100 grossing films in 2014, only 1.9 percent were directed by a woman and only 7.4 percent were written by a woman. And the overall number of female directors in 2014 has dropped 2 percent since 1998 (Lauzen, 2014).

   3. The researchers also found that 91 percent of movie critics who write for film and entertainment publications, such as *Entertainment Weekly*, are male. Similarly, men make up 90 percent of the movie reviewers contributing to trade publications, such as *Variety* (Lauzen, 2013).

      a. The fact that such a small percentage of film critics are women means that men are almost singularly responsible for the canon of contemporary film criticism. This creates an industry that can be incredibly disapproving of women.

      b. Take critic Rex Reed. When he reviewed actress Melissa McCarthy's comedic role in the film *Tammy*, he wrote, "the star makes no attempt to beautify herself onscreen," and for this, "She isn't … a real female clown" (Reed, 2014).

      c. The principle difference between how McCarthy and successful male comedians are received is that McCarthy alone is defined by her gender.

Transition

You might be asking yourself if it matters that men dominate reviewer columns and director's chairs. Aren't actresses today offered more strong female leads than ever before?

Transition

II. Not quite. Prejudices in Hollywood significantly limit career opportunities for women. Actresses are offered fewer leading roles and general roles, have shortened careers due to ageism, and are paid less than their male costars.

Of the top 100 grossing movies in 2014, only 30 percent of speaking characters were women (Lauzen, 2015). If the people in this room were the cast of a Hollywood production, that's a lot of women to be left without a voice.

Listener relevance link

A. Movies with leading women remain a tiny fraction of what we see in theaters.

   1. In 2014, the percentage of females with protagonist roles in the top 100 grossing films was lower than it was in 2002 (Lauzen, 2015).

   2. In 2014, women acted in only 12 percent of protagonist roles (Lauzen, 2015).

   3. In fact, in movies which were written and directed only by men, women made up merely 4 percent of protagonist roles (Lauzen, 2015).

B. What do these numbers say about the culture of our film industry?

   1. When the 2015 blockbuster film, *Mad Max: Fury Road* premiered, groups of men's rights activists were irate. The movie's namesake, Mad Max, was not the true star of the film. Instead, the character who starts a rebellion to a post-apocalyptic hierarchy was Furiosa, played by actress Charlize Theron (Kamen, 2015).

2. *Wired* UK's headline read, "Mad Max: Fury Road hilariously angers 'Men's Rights Activists'," but misogyny and the representation of women are not laughing matters (Kamen, 2015).

C. Although Furiosa is one great character, depictions of strong females are still strikingly absent in the movies.

   1. In the 100 top-grossing films of 2014, women comprised only 29 percent of major characters (Lauzen, 2014.

   2. Writer, director, producer, and actor Paige Morrow Kimball says, "It's about supply and demand. Since there are fewer great roles for women, there are more female actors vying for those few great roles" (Morrow Kimbal, 2014).

D. What roles are available to women are overwhelmingly for younger women, creating a condition of ageism in the film industry.

   1. Perceived appropriate age thresholds are low for female actors.

      a. For example, actress Maggie Gyllenhaal, a Golden Globe winner and Oscar nominee, was told that, at age 37, she was too old to play the love interest of a 55-year-old man (Waxman, 2015).

   2. Yet women in film are frequently cast with love interests who double their own age.

      a. For instance, when Scarlett Johansson starred in *Lost in Translation*, she was only 18 years old, yet she was cast opposite Bill Murray, then age 52 (Buchanan, 2015).

      b. When Emma Stone played in *Gangster Squad*, she was 24 years old but cast as the love interest for 54-year-old Sean Penn's character (Buchanan, 2015).

      c. The next year, in *Magic in the Moonlight*, Stone was 25 years old and still cast opposite a 53-year-old Colin Firth (Buchanan, 2015).

   3. Even in looking at a single genre of film, it becomes clear that the lifespan of a female actor's career is much shorter than her male counterparts.

E. Not only are the number of roles and the career spans lower for female actors than their male counterparts, so is their compensation.

   1. Jennifer Lawrence won an Oscar for her performance in *Silver Linings Playbook*. She was also nominated for Oscars for her performances in *Winter's Bone* and *American Hustle*. Her co-star in *American Hustle*, Amy Adams, has received five Oscar nominations, including for *American Hustle*. On that film, however, both women were paid less than their director David O. Russell, and less than their male co-stars Bradley Cooper, Christian Bale, and Jeremy Renner (Weisman, 2014).

   2. In fact, according to a report by Forbes using data from 2013, male actors made 2.5 times as much as female actors. That means that the best-compensated female film actors made 40 cents for every dollar made by the best-compensated male film actors (Woodruff, 2015).

   3. And when *The Journal of Management Inquiry* analyzed female and male actors' wages over the past 40 years, they found that women make the most money at age 34, while men's pay continues to climb until they reach age 51 (Morrow Kimball, 2014).

Transition

It might seem that the reduced opportunities and lower compensation of women in Hollywood reflect lower box office revenues for their films. Let's examine the differences in box office performance of movies with women in the leading roles or behind the camera as compared to those with men in front of and behind the camera.   **Transition**

III. As it turns out, box office results are not affected by gender. Despite myths, it's not the gender of the leading actors that influences the box office results. The success of films starring women and directed by women are actually affected by budgets and publicity campaigns.

A. If you are a female director, statistics show that, most likely, your budget will be smaller than if the same movie were directed by a man.

For those of you who held a green ticket at the beginning of this speech, that means that your budget will be significantly lower than your classmates who held red tickets.

Listener relevance link

1. Dr. Martha M. Lauzen of the Center for the Study of Women in Television and Film found that films featuring male protagonists had an average budget of nearly $78 million. Films with female protagonists or strong female ensemble casts had an average budget of $45 million (Lauzen, 2008).

2. Similarly, films with strong female protagonists opened on fewer screens than films that featured male protagonists and had slightly shorter runs. That is, they stayed in theaters for fewer weeks, which can also affect overall box office revenues.

B. Although gender does not determine how many people show up to the movies, expensive publicity campaigns do.

1. Traditionally, the publicity budget for a movie totals 70 percent of the production budget (Shankar, n.d.).

2. Experts who advise filmmakers put that number even higher, estimating that studio films generally spend roughly equal amounts on production and marketing (Garon, 2008).

3. Therefore, if movies with female protagonists have significantly smaller production budgets, they will have lower publicity budgets. And because marketing drives business, it might *seem* that movies with female protagonists are not as popular at the box office.

C. That perception created by marketing is not reality, however.

1. Lauzen's research found that, when the budget is held constant, films with females in the leading role (or roles) perform just as well at the box office as films with men in the leading role (or roles) (Lauzen, 2008).

D. Women in the industry—and also fans—have spoken out against this misconception in an effort to drown out the discriminatory yet powerful male voices in Hollywood.

1. When Cate Blanchett won the 2014 Academy Award for Best Actress, she made this speech, "female films with women at the center" are decidedly not "niche experiences. … Audiences want to see them and, in fact, they earn money" (Selby, 2014).

2. Yet leaked emails have shown that many powerful men in Hollywood do not necessarily agree with Blanchett, like Oscar-winning screenwriter and producer Aaron Sorkin and Marvel CEO Ike Perlmutter.

   a. In an email, Adam Sorkin wrote, "The guy who wins the Oscar for Best Actor has a much higher bar to clear than the woman who wins Best Actress. … Cate [Blanchett] gave a terrific performance in *Blue Jasmine* but nothing close to the degree of difficulty for any of the five Best Actor nominees" (Boot, 2014).

   b. And when an email from Marvel's CEO Ike Perlmutter was leaked, both women and men were upset to find Perlmutter had written a list of what he called, "female movies," describing the superhero films *Elektra*, *Cat Woman*, and *Supergirl*, as "very, very bad," and "disasters" (Beger, 2015).

   c. Perlmutter, who appears to be only focused on movies which have been disappointments, fails to recognize successful films centered around women, like *The Hunger Games*, starring Jennifer Lawrence, which, when combining all three movies, has already made nearly $170 billion.

   d. The demand for female superheroes is in truth quite strong, but misconceptions that women do not bring in box office dollars remain stronger.

3. But this doesn't stop fans from demanding what they want. Devotees of Marvel superhero Black Widow have started flash mob campaigns to see Black Widow star in her very own movie, using the #WeWantBlackWidow to build support (Child, 2015).

Transition

The first step toward seeing more women in front of and behind the camera is to recognize there is a problem in Hollywood. We also need to realize our contribution in creating it and the role we can play in remedying it.

Conclusion

I.	No longer can we tolerate tacit gender and age discrimination as merely "just part of show business."	Restatement of thesis
II.	As audience members, we have the power to create real change. Without us, the movie industry wouldn't exist. The best way we can support women filmmakers is to go out and see their movies. Additionally, the American Civil Liberties Union is pushing for an investigation of the entire industry. Women actors are fighting for the cause as well, like Meryl Streep, who is sponsoring a writing lab for women screenwriters ages 40 and up.	Main point review
III.	By supporting women writers, directors, and actresses, we show studios there is in fact a demand for their work. Together, we can re-write the script for gender in the movies.	Clincher

References

Berger, L (2015, May 4). Marvel CEO doesn't believe in female superheroes. Indiewire.com. Retrieved from http://blogs.indiewire.com/womenandhollywood/marvel-ceo-doesnt-believe-in-female-superheroes-20150504?utm_source=dlvr.it&utm_medium=twitter.

Boot, W. (2014, December 15). Aaron Sorkin thinks male film roles have bigger "degree of difficulty" than female ones. *The Daily Beast*. Retrieved from http://www.thedailybeast.com/articles/2014/12/15/exclusive-sony-emails-reveal-why-aaron-sorkin-thinks-hollywood-has-a-women-problem.html.

Buchanan, K. (2015, June 2). Emma Stone, Jennifer Lawrence, and Scarlett Johansson have an older-man problem. *Slate*. Retrieved online from: http://www.slate.com/blogs/browbeat/2015/06/02/emma_stone_jennifer_lawrence_and_scarlett_johansson_have_an_older_man_problem.html.

Buckley, C. A.C.L.U., citing bias against women, wants inquiry into Hollywood's hiring practices. *New York Times* 13 May 2015: C1.

Child, B. (2015, June 8). Avenge her: Fans demand Black Widow movie with flashmob campaign. *The Guardian*. Retrieved from http://www.theguardian.com/film/2015/jun/08/black-widow-flashmob-campaign-marvel-scarlett-johansson.

Fried, N. (2015, May 19). U.S. film and TV production drives economic growth in every corner of America. Motion Picture Association of America. Retrieved from http://www.mpaa.org/u-s-film-and-tv-production-drives-economic-growth-in-every-corner-of-america/#.VXnwzpS9mE5.

Garon, J. (2008, July). An overview of the film budget. Filmmaker IQ [Web blog post]. Retrieved from http://filmmakeriq.com/2008/07/an-overview-of-the-film-budget/.

Hunt, D. and Ramón, A. (2015). Hollywood diversity report: Flipping the script. Ralph J. Bunche Center for African American Studies at UCLA. Retrieved from http://www.bunchecenter.ucla.edu/wp-content/uploads/2015/02/2015-Hollywood-Diversity-Report-2-25-15.pdf.

In context: How many people annually attend the movies in the U.S. and in Canada. Retrieved from http://www.mpaa.org/wp-content/uploads/2015/03/MPAA-Theatrical-Market-Statistics-2014.pdf.

In context: The overall box office gross of all three *The Hunger Games* films. Retrieved from http://www.boxofficemojo.com/franchises/chart/?id=hungergames.htm.

In context: The overall net worth of the film industry in the U.S. Retrieved from http://www.statista.com/statistics/237769/value-of-the-us-entertainment-and-media-market/.

In context: The overall net worth of the film industry worldwide. Retrieved from http://www.statista.com/statistics/237749/value-of-the-global-entertainment-and-media-market/.

In context: Vox survey indicating how many people believe in gender equality. (2015, March). Perry Undem Research Communication. Retrieved from https://cdn2.vox-cdn.com/uploads/chorus_asset/file/3570070/Vox_Poll_Toplines__2_.0.pdf.

Kamen, M. (2015, May 13). Mad Max: Fury Road hilariously angers "men's rights activists." *Wired UK*. Retrieved from http://www.wired.co.uk/news/archive/2015-05-13/mad-max-fury-road-mras-anger.

Lauzen, M. M. (2008). Women @ the box office: A study of the top 100 worldwide grossing films. Center for the Study of Women in Television and Film, San Diego State University. Retrieved from http://womenintvfilm.sdsu.edu/files/Women%20@%20Box%20Office.pdf.

Lauzen, M. M. (2013). Gender @ the movies: Online film critics and criticism. Center for the Study of Women in Television and Film, San Diego State University Retrieved from http://womenintvfilm.sdsu.edu/files/2013_Gender_at_the_Movies_Exec_Summ.pdf.

Lauzen, M. M. (2015). It's a man's (celluloid) world: On-screen representations of female characters in the top 100. Center for the Study of Women in Television and Film, San Diego State University. Retrieved from http://womenintvfilm.sdsu.edu/files/2014_Its_a_Mans_World_Report.pdf.

Lauzen, M. M. (2015). The celluloid ceiling: Behind-the-scenes employment of women on the top 250 films of 2014. Center for the Study of Women in Television and Film, San Diego State University. Retrieved from http://womenintvfilm.sdsu.edu/files/2014_Celluloid_Ceiling_Report.pdf.

McClintock, P. (2014, July 31). $100 million and rising: Hollywood struggles with soaring marketing costs. *The Hollywood Reporter*. Retrieved from http://www.hollywoodreporter.com/news/200-million-rising-hollywood-struggles-721818.

Morrow Kimball, P. (2014, February 2). How to fix Hollywood's gender age wage gap. *The Huffington Post*. Retrieved from http://www.huffingtonpost.com/paige-morrow-kimball/how-to-fix-hollywoods-gen_b_4761782.html.

Reed, R. (2014, July 3). Melissa McCarthy gives 'Tammy' her all, but it's nowhere near enough. *The New York Observer*. Retrieved from http://observer.com/2014/07/melissa-mccarthy-gives-tammy-her-all-but-its-nowhere-near-enough/.

Selby, J. (2014, May 3). Cate Blanchett's Best Actress Oscar 2014 acceptance speech. *The Independent*. Retrieved from http://www.independent.co.uk/arts-entertainment/films/news/oscars-2014-cate-blanchetts-best-actress-acceptance-speech-in-full-9164895.html.

Shankar, A. (N.d.) How has movie marketing and distribution evolved over time [Web blog post]? Retrieved from http://www.forbes.com/sites/quora/2014/02/11/how-has-movie-marketing-and-distribution-evolved-over-time/.

Siegemund-Broka, A. (2015, February 2). Diverse casts deliver higher ratings, bigger box office: Study (Exclusive). *The Hollywood Reporter*. Retrieved from http://www.hollywoodreporter.com/news/diverse-casts-deliver-higher-ratings-777428.

Waxman, S. (2015, May 20). Maggie Gyllenhaal on Hollywood ageism: I was told 37 is "too old" for a 55-year-old love interest. *The Wrap*. Retrieved from http://www.thewrap.com/maggie-gyllenhaal-on-hollywood-ageism-i-was-told-37-is-too-old-for-a-55-year-old-love-interest/.

Weisman, A. (14 December, 2014). Leaked: Jennifer Lawrence got American hustled in Sony deal. *Business Insider*. Retrieved from http://www.businessinsider.com/jennifer-lawrence-paid-less-than-male-co-stars-2014-12#ixzz3dKugtzcH.

Wood, G. (2014, October 3). The "war on women" is political posturing that doesn't reflect our current reality. *USA Today*. Retrieved from http://www.usatoday.com/story/opinion/2014/10/03/millennial-women-education-wage-equality-column/16644149/.

Woodruff, B. (2015, February 23). The gender wage gap is especially terrible in Hollywood [Web blog post]. *Slate*. Retrieved from http://www.slate.com/blogs/xx_factor/2015/02/23/gender_wage_gap_in_hollywood_it_s_very_very_wide.html.

STUDY TOOLS 8

LOCATED IN TEXTBOOK

☐ Tear-out Chapter Review cards at the end of the book

☐ Review with the Quick Quiz below

LOCATED ON SPEAK3 ONLINE AT CENGAGEBRAIN.COM

☐ Review Key Term flashcards and create your own cards

☐ Track your knowledge and understanding of key concepts in speech communication

☐ Complete practice and graded quizzes to prepare for tests

☐ Complete interactive content within SPEAK3 Online

☐ View the chapter highlight boxes for SPEAK3 Online

Quick Quiz (answers in Solutions Appendix)

T F 1. A good introduction will help the audience quickly grasp the goal and main points of a speech.

T F 2. A good speech introduction should only identify and define the topic quickly.

T F 3. Even though an audience is physically present at a speech, it doesn't mean they are paying attention.

T F 4. According to the primacy-recency effect, we are more likely to remember the first thing we hear rather than the last.

T F 5. The best way to create an introduction is to come up with a single idea and then stick to it.

---

6. While a good introduction previews the main points of the speech, a good conclusion _____ them.

   a. summarizes
   b. repeats
   c. contravenes
   d. reinforces
   e. tells

7. The term _____ refers to appeals to emotions.

   a. ethos
   b. chronos
   c. pathos
   d. logos
   e. kairos

8. An effective way to get the audience's attention is to:

   a. tell a story
   b. make a startling statement
   c. tell a joke
   d. ask a question
   e. All of the above.

9. A speaker can achieve a sense of closure in a conclusion by using a(n):

   a. joke
   b. adumbration
   c. wrap-up
   d. clincher
   e. preview

10. Which of the following is not one of the goals of an effective introduction?

    a. Get audience attention
    b. Demonstrate the speaker's sense of humor
    c. Establish speaker credibility
    d. Identify the thesis statement
    e. Establish listener relevance

Chapter Takeaways

List three key takeaways from this chapter:

-

-

-

9 Presentational Aids

LEARNING OUTCOMES

9-1 Identify the benefits of using presentational aids in your speech.

9-2 Describe different types of presentational aids.

9-3 Choose appropriate presentational aids for your speech.

9-4 Prepare effective presentational aids.

9-5 Display presentational aids effectively for your speech.

9-6 Plan when and how to use presentational aids during your speech.

After finishing this chapter go to **PAGE 151** for **STUDY TOOLS.**

Sound Familiar?

Scott and Carrie are returning from an Ignite Seattle event during which radio host Jason Rantz has just given a five-minute PowerPoint-aided presentation called "Fact Check Everything."[1] Ignite is a worldwide speaking movement in which speakers give five-minute presentations, aided by twenty PowerPoint slides.

"Wow! Jason's speech was really thought provoking. I'm amazed at how much my perspective on the media changed from such a short talk!" says Carrie.

"Yeah," replies Scott. "I expected death by PowerPoint, but Jason's slides helped me visualize what he was saying. They really reinforced the important points he was making."

Carrie adds, "Who knew it actually is possible to make a great PowerPoint presentation!"

Unlike the "death by PowerPoint" speeches that Scott alluded to (and that we've all had to suffer through), the speeches given at Ignite events are adapted to the way people take in information today—people for whom interacting on several different social networking sites, talking or texting on mobile phones, watching TV, and eating dinner are simultaneous activities. We live in an era when the written, oral, visual, and digital modes of communicating are merging. Whether it is a TV news program, your professor's lecture, or a motivational speech, audiences have come to expect messages to be enhanced with presentational aids. This means that as you prepare your speech, you will need to decide which

presentational aids will enhance your verbal message and motivate your audience to both pay attention and remember it. In fact, as we mentioned in Chapter 6, presentational aids have become so important that they are essentially a form of supporting material you should be looking for as you conduct research to develop your topic. Ultimately, you might use them to get attention in the introduction, to support a main point in the body, or to clinch in the conclusion.

A **presentational aid** is any visual, audio, audiovisual, or other sensory material used to enhance a message. **Visual aids** enhance a speech by allowing audience members to see what the speaker is describing or explaining. Examples of visual aids include actual objects, models, photographs, drawings and diagrams, maps, charts, and graphs. **Audio aids** enhance the speaker's verbal message with sound. Examples include musical clips from CDs and iTunes; recorded clips from conversations, interviews, and famous speeches; or recordings of nature sounds like bird calls and whale sounds. **Audiovisual aids** enhance the speech using a combination of sight and sound. Examples of audiovisual aids include clips from movies and television, YouTube videos and podcasts, as well as other events or observations captured on video. Other sensory aids include materials that enhance verbal messages by appealing to smell, touch, or taste. For example, a verbal description of a perfume's fragrance

presentational aid any visual, audio, audiovisual, or other sensory material used in a speech

visual aid a presentational aid that enhances a speech by allowing the audience to see what the speaker is describing or explaining

audio aid a presentational aid that enhances the speaker's verbal message with additional sound

audiovisual aid a presentational aid that enhances the speech using a combination of sight and sound

can be clarified by allowing audience members to smell it, and the flavor of a particular entrée can be clarified by allowing audience members to taste it.

9-1 BENEFITS OF PRESENTATIONAL AIDS

Research documents several benefits of using presentational aids. First, they clarify and dramatize your verbal message. Second, they help audiences remember your message.[2] Third, they allow you to address the diverse learning style preferences of your audience.[3] Fourth, they increase persuasive appeal. In fact, some research suggests that speakers who use presentational aids are almost twice as likely to persuade listeners than those who do not.[4] Finally, using presentational aids may help you to feel more competent and confident.[5]

Today, presentational aids are usually developed into computerized slide shows using presentation software such as PowerPoint, Media Pro, Adobe Presenter, Prezi, or Photodex, and are projected onto a large screen via a computer and LCD projector. These programs allow you to embed audio and audiovisual links from local files and the Internet, which makes it fairly simple to create effective multimedia presentations. Whether you are creating multimedia presentational aids or developing simpler ones, your purpose for using them is the same: to enhance

actual object an inanimate or animate sample of the idea you are communicating

your message without overpowering it. Speakers who violate this principle end up with what Scott called "death by PowerPoint" in the chapter opener. In this chapter, we describe various types presentational aids, criteria to consider when choosing and preparing them, and how to display and use them during your speech.

9-2 TYPES OF PRESENTATIONAL AIDS

Presentational aids range from those that are readily available from existing sources you found while conducting your research to those that are custom produced for your specific speech. As we just discussed, presentational aids include visual, audio, audiovisual, or other sensory aids.

9-2a Visual Aids

Visual aids enhance the verbal message by allowing audiences to see what you are describing or explaining. They include actual objects and models, photographs, drawings and diagrams, maps, charts, and graphs.

Actual Objects

Actual objects are inanimate or animate physical samples of the idea you are communicating. Inanimate objects make good visual aids if they are (1) large enough to be seen by all audience members, (2) small enough to transport to the site of the speech, (3) simple enough to understand visually, and (4) safe. A set of golf clubs or a Muslim prayer rug would be appropriate in size for audiences of 20 to 30. An iPhone or Galaxy might be acceptable if the speech goal is simply to show what a smartphone looks like, but it might be too small if you want to demonstrate how to use any of its specialized functions.

On occasion, *you* can be an effective visual aid. For instance, you can demonstrate the motions involved in swinging a golf club or use your attire to illustrate the native dress of a particular country. Sometimes it can be appropriate to use another person as a visual aid, such as when Jenny used a friend to demonstrate the Heimlich maneuver. Animals can also be effective visual aids. For example, Josh used his AKC Obedience Champion dog to demonstrate the basics of dog training. But keep in mind that animals placed in unfamiliar settings can become difficult to control and can then distract from your message.

Models

When an actual object is too large or too small for the room where you'll be speaking, too complex to understand visually, or potentially unsafe or uncontrollable, a model

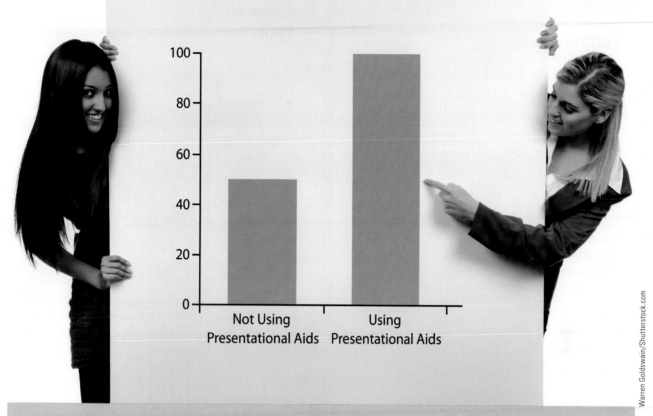

Speakers who use presentational aids are almost twice as likely to persuade listeners than those who do not.

of it can be an effective visual aid. A **model** is a three-dimensional scaled-down or scaled-up version of an actual object that may be simplified to aid understanding. In a speech on the physics of bridge construction, a scale model of a suspension bridge would be an effective visual aid.

Photographs

If an exact reproduction of material is needed, photographs can be excellent visual aids. In a speech on smart weapons, for example, before and after photos of target sites would be effective in helping the audience understand the pinpoint accuracy of these weapons. When choosing photographs, be sure that the image is large enough for the audience to see, that the object of interest in the photo is clearly identified, and, when possible, that the object of interest is in the foreground. For example, if you are giving a speech about your grandmother, and you show a photo of her with her college graduating class, you might circle her image so she's easily seen.

Simple Drawings and Diagrams

Simple drawings and **diagrams** (a type of drawing that shows how the whole relates to its parts) can be effective because you can choose how much detail to include. To

make sure they look professional, you can prepare diagrams using a basic computer software drawing program or find them already prepared in a book, an article, or on the Internet. If you do this, however, be sure to credit the source during your speech to enhance your credibility and avoid plagiarism. Andria's diagram of the human body and its pressure points, for example, visually clarified her message (see Exhibit 9.1).

Maps

Maps allow you to orient audiences to landmarks (mountains, rivers, and lakes), states, cities, land routes, weather systems, and so on. As with drawings and diagrams, include only the details that are relevant to your purpose. Exhibit 9.2 shows a map that focuses on weather systems.

Charts

A **chart** is a graphic representation that distills a lot of information into an easily interpreted visual

model a three-dimensional scaled-down or scaled-up version of an actual object

diagram a type of drawing that shows how the whole relates to its parts

chart a graphic representation that distills a lot of information into an easily interpreted visual format

Exhibit 9.1
Diagram

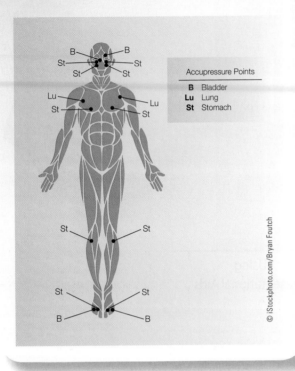

Accupressure Points

B Bladder
Lu Lung
St Stomach

© iStockphoto.com/Bryan Foutch

Exhibit 9.2
Map

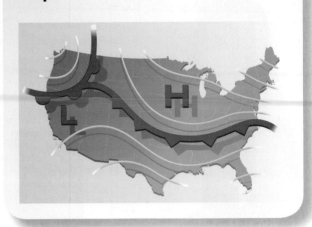

format. Flowcharts, organizational charts, and pie charts are the most common types. A **flowchart** uses symbols and connecting lines to diagram a sequence of steps through a complicated process. Tim used a flowchart to help listeners move through the sequence of steps to assess their weight (see Exhibit 9.3). An **organizational chart** shows the structure of an organization in terms of rank and chain of command. The chart in Exhibit 9.4 illustrates the organization of a student union board. A **pie chart** shows the relationships among parts of a single unit. Ideally, pie charts have two to five "slices," or wedges—more than eight wedges clutter a pie chart. If your chart includes too many wedges, use another kind of chart, or

consolidate several of the less important wedges into the category of "other," as Tim did to show the percentage of total calories that should come from the various components of food (see Exhibit 9.5).

Graphs

A **graph** presents numerical information in visual form. A **bar graph** uses vertical or horizontal bars to show relationships between two or more variables. For instance, Jacqueline used a bar graph to compare the amounts of caffeine found in one serving each of chocolate, coffee, tea, and cola (see Exhibit 9.6). A **line graph** indicates changes in one or more variables over time. In a speech

flowchart a chart that diagrams a sequence of steps through a complicated process

organizational chart a chart that shows the structure of an organization in terms of rank and chain of command

pie chart a chart that shows the relationships among parts of a single unit

graph a diagram that presents numerical information in visual form

bar graph a graph that uses vertical or horizontal bars to show relationships between or among two or more variables

line graph a graph that indicates changes in one or more variables over time

Exhibit 9.3
Flowchart

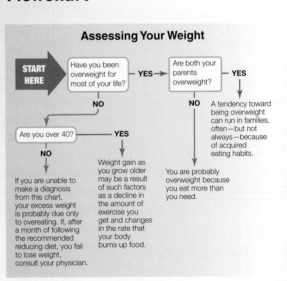

Assessing Your Weight

START HERE

Have you been overweight for most of your life? — YES →

Are both your parents overweight? — YES →

NO

NO

A tendency toward being overweight can run in families, often—but not always—because of acquired eating habits.

Are you over 40? — YES →

NO

If you are unable to make a diagnosis from this chart, your excess weight is probably due only to overeating. If, after a month of following the recommended reducing diet, you fail to lose weight, consult your physician.

Weight gain as you grow older may be a result of such factors as a decline in the amount of exercise you get and changes in the rate that your body burns up food.

You are probably overweight because you eat more than you need.

Exhibit 9.4

Organizational Chart

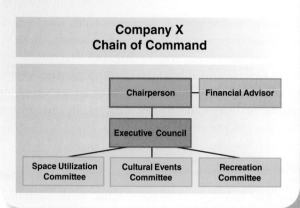

Company X Chain of Command

Exhibit 9.5

Pie Chart

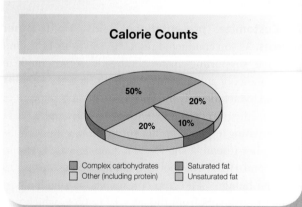

Calorie Counts

- ■ Complex carbohydrates
- □ Other (including protein)
- ■ Saturated fat
- ■ Unsaturated fat

Exhibit 9.6

Bar Graph

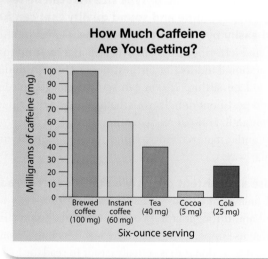

How Much Caffeine Are You Getting?

Exhibit 9.7

Line Graph

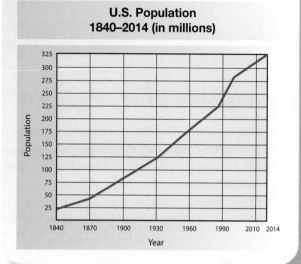

U.S. Population 1840–2014 (in millions)

about the U.S. population, for example, the line graph in Exhibit 9.7 illustrates how it has increased, in millions, from 1840 to 2014.

9-2b Audio Aids

Audio aids enhance a verbal message through sound. They are especially useful when it is difficult, if not impossible, to describe a sound in words. For example, in David's speech about the three types of trumpet mutes and how they alter the trumpet's sound, he played his trumpet so listeners could hear what he meant. If you can't or don't want to make your own sounds, you can use recorded excerpts from sources such as famous speeches, radio programs, interviews, and recordings of music or environmental sounds. For example, Susan chose to begin her speech on the future of the NASA space program with a recording of Neil Armstrong's first words as he stepped on the surface of the moon: "That's one small step for a man, one giant leap for mankind." Before using audio material, make sure you have enough time to present it (it should make up no more than about 5 percent of your speaking time) and that you have access to a quality sound system.

9-2c Audiovisual Aids

Audiovisual aids enhance a verbal message using a combination of sight and sound. For example, you can use short clips from films and videos that are relatively easy to access on Internet sites such as YouTube. Audiovisual aids are also easy to import as hyperlinks into computerized slide shows. During his speech about the use of robots in automobile production, Chad, who worked as a technician at the local Ford plant, showed a 20-second video clip of a car being painted in a robotic paint booth. As with audio clips, audiovisual aids should take no more than 5 percent of your speaking time.

9-2d Other Sensory Aids

Depending on your topic, other sensory aids that appeal to smell, touch, or taste may effectively enhance your speech. For example, a speech about making perfume might benefit from allowing your audience to smell scented swatches as you describe the ingredients used to make the scents. In a speech about Braille, Javier handed out copies of his outline written in Braille for audience members to touch. And in his speech about name-brand and generic foods, Greg actually had his audience members do a taste test of two products.

9-3 CHOOSING PRESENTATIONAL AIDS

With so many different types of presentational aids, you have to decide which ones will best illustrate the content you want to highlight. In our opening scenario, Carrie and Scott were motivated to pay attention to and remember Jason's Ignite speech in part because he took the time to carefully choose presentational aids that would best illustrate his points. Some simple guidelines can help you make good choices. Choose aids that:

- illustrate the most important ideas to understand and remember.

- clarify complex ideas that are difficult to explain verbally.

- are appropriate for the size of the audience.

- make dull information and details more interesting.

- you feel comfortable using and transporting to the speech site.

- enhance rather than overwhelm the verbal message.

- you have the time and money to prepare.

- demonstrate cultural sensitivity that will not offend members of your audience.

9-4 PREPARING PRESENTATIONAL AIDS

However simple your presentational aids may be, you still need to produce them carefully. You may need to find or create charts, graphs, diagrams, maps, or drawings. You may need to search for and prepare photographs. You may choose to look for audio, video, or audiovisual clips and then convert them to a format that you can use at your speech site. The goal is to prepare professional-looking presentational aids that will enhance your ethos (perceived competence, credibility, and character) in addition to clarifying your message and making it more memorable. To do so, follow these guidelines.

1. **Limit the reading required of the audience.** The audience should be listening to you, not reading the presentational aid. So use keywords and short phrases rather than complete sentences.

2. **Customize presentational aids from other sources.** As you conducted research, you probably found potential supporting material already represented in visual, audio, or audiovisual form. In these cases, simplify your aid to include only the information that is relevant to your specific purpose and audience. For example, Jia Li was preparing a speech on alcohol abuse by young adults. During her research, she found a graph called "Current, Binge, and Heavy Alcohol Use among Persons Aged 12 or Older by Age." The graph presented information pertaining to drinkers from the ages 12 to 65+, which was much more information than Jia Li needed. So she simplified it for her presentation and used only the information for young adults.

3. **Use a photo, print, or type size that can be seen easily and a volume and sound quality that can be heard easily by your entire audience.** Check photo, chart, and lettering size by moving as far away from the presentational aid as the farthest person in your audience will be sitting. If you can see the image, lettering, and pertinent details from that distance, your aid is large enough. If not, create another and check it again. Check audio materials for volume and sound quality in a similar way.

4. **Use a consistent print style that is easy to read.** Avoid fancy print styles and stick to one print style on the aid and throughout the computerized slide show. In addition, use uppercase and lowercase letters rather than ALL CAPS, as doing so is actually easier to read.

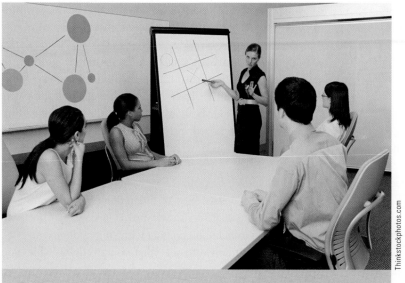

Don't play games with your audience—prepare your visuals in advance.

Thinkstockphotos.com

5. Make sure information is laid out in a way that is aesthetically pleasing. Leave sufficient white space around the whole visual, which will make it easy for audience members to identify each component. Also, use typefaces and indenting to visually represent relationships between ideas.

6. Use graphic illustrations in visuals. To truly enhance a verbal message, a presentational aid should consist of symbols other than or more than just words.[6] Visual symbols can increase retention by appealing to diverse learning styles.[7] Even something as simple as a relevant piece of clip art can make the verbal message more memorable. Of course, clip art can be overdone, so be careful not to overpower your message with unnecessary pictures or animations.

7. Use color strategically. Although black and white can work well for your visual aids, consider using color strategically to emphasize points. Here are some suggestions for using color wisely:

- Use the same background color for all your presentational aids and theme for all of the slides on your computerized slide show.

- Use the same color to show similarities between ideas, and use opposite colors (on a color wheel) to show differences.

- Use bright colors, such as red, to highlight important information. Be sure to avoid using red and green together, however, because audience members who are color-blind may not be able to distinguish between them.

- Use dark colors for lettering on a white background and light colors for lettering on black or deep blue backgrounds.

- Use no more than two or three colors on any presentational aid that is not a photograph or video clip.

- Pretend you are your audience. Sit as far away as they will be sitting, and evaluate the colors you have chosen for their readability and appeal.

Let's see if we can put all of these principles to work. Exhibit 9.8 contains a lot of important information, but notice how unpleasant it is to the eye. As you can see, this visual aid ignores all the principles we've discussed. However, with some thoughtful simplification, this speaker could produce the visual aid shown in Exhibit 9.9, which sharpens the focus by emphasizing the keywords (reduce, reuse, recycle), highlighting the major details, and adding clip art for a professional touch.

9-5 DISPLAYING PRESENTATIONAL AIDS

Once you have decided on the specific presentational aids for your speech, you need to choose a method for displaying them. As with choosing and preparing

Exhibit 9.8
A Cluttered Visual Aid

I WANT YOU TO REMEMBER THE THREE Rs OF RECYCLING

- *REDUCE* the amount of waste people produce, like overpacking or using material that won't recycle.
- *REUSE* by relying on cloth towels rather than paper towels, earthenware dishes rather than paper or plastic plates, and glass bottles rather than aluminum cans.
- *RECYCLE* by collecting recyclable products, sorting them correctly, and getting them to the appropriate recycling agency.

Exhibit 9.9
A Simple and Effective Visual Aid

The Three Rs of Recycling

Reduce the amount of waste you produce.

Reuse products instead of throwing them away.

Recycle products marked with the symbol at left.

© iStockphoto.com/Christopher Steer

aids, your goal is to display them using a method that is professional-looking and -sounding to enhance your ethos as well as your verbal message. Speakers can choose from the following methods for displaying presentational aids.

9-5a Posters

The easiest method for displaying simple drawings, charts, maps, photos, and graphs is on a poster. Because poster boards tend to be fairly small, use them only with smaller audiences (thirty people or fewer). Many professional conference presentations use poster boards to explain complex research projects.

9-5b Whiteboards or Chalkboards

Because a whiteboard or chalkboard is a staple in every college classroom, many novice (and ill-prepared) speakers rely on this method for displaying their visual aids. Unfortunately, a whiteboard or chalkboard is easy to misuse and to overuse. Moreover, they are not suitable for depicting complex material. Writing on a whiteboard or chalkboard is appropriate only for very short items of information that can be written in

flipchart a large pad of paper mounted on an easel

a few seconds. Nevertheless, being able to use a whiteboard or chalkboard effectively should be a part of any speaker's repertoire.

Whiteboards or chalkboards should be written on prior to speaking or during a break in speaking. Otherwise, the visual is likely to be either illegible or partly obscured by your body as you write. Or you may end up talking to the board instead of to the audience. Should you need to draw or write on the board while you are talking, you should practice doing so in advance. If you are right-handed, stand to the right of what you are drawing. Try to face at least part of the audience while you work. Although it may seem awkward at first, your effort will allow you to maintain contact with your audience and will allow the audience to see what you are doing while you are doing it.

9-5c Flipcharts

A **flipchart**, a large pad of paper mounted on an easel, can be an effective method for presenting visual aids. Flipcharts (and easels) are available in many sizes. For a presentation to four or five people, a small tabletop version works well; for a larger audience, a larger pad (30-by-40 inches) is needed.

As with whiteboards and chalkboards, you should prepare flipcharts prior to giving your speech. In some situations, you may write down some information

Rawpixel/Shutterstock.com

Projected visuals can offer solid support for speeches; they should be kept simple and clear, easy to read and understand.

Using Social Media as a Presentational Aid

Maintaining audience attention can be a challenge for today's public speakers. It's safe to assume that most people in the audience are carrying a wealth of distraction in their pockets, including devices abuzz with social media feeds.

Instead of viewing social media as a distraction *from* your presentation, consider incorporating it *into* your presentation as both a presentational aid and means of interacting with the audience.

Twitter's clean layout and tagging system make it especially suitable for live presentation. A good first step is to designate—and publicize—a hashtag for your speech. This will give the audience a common avenue to discuss your presentation and reach out to you. If you're speaking as part of a conference, a hashtag might already exist for the event.[8]

Onstage, encourage your audience to tweet observations and commentary regarding your speech using the unique hashtag. Monitor audience interest with an occasional glance at your laptop or tablet. If the majority of tweets indicate boredom or confusion, you can adjust your presentation accordingly.[9]

With a projector, you can use that same Twitter feed as a visual aid. The audience can watch in real time as their reactions appear on the screen. It might be useful to have an offstage "curator" with access to your account, so any blatantly offensive or irrelevant comments can be quickly hidden.

If part of your presentation involves question and answer, streamline the process through Twitter. Having audience members post their questions saves time that would otherwise be spent forming a queue or fumbling for a mic. That leaves time for more questions. Consider designating a separate hashtag for Q&A, so you can quickly locate questions amid other discussion about your presentation.[10]

By sharing your social media handle and encouraging use of the platform during your speech, you also enable your message to reach audiences well beyond the venue in which you're presenting.[11]

It's not always easy to keep 100 percent of the audience's attention 100 percent of the time. But with the right strategy, you can ensure that at least some of those luminous screens are glowing brightly for you and your message.

Avlsoft/Shutterstock.com

---

before the speech begins and add information while speaking. Also, be sure to leave a blank page between each visual on the pad to serve as both a transition page and a cover sheet. Because you want your audience to focus on visual material only when it is being discussed, you can flip to the empty page while you are talking about material not covered by visuals on the flipchart. Flipcharts can be comfortably used with smaller audiences (fewer than 100 people) but are not appropriate for larger settings.

9-5d Handouts

At times, it may be useful for each member of the audience to have a personal copy of the visual aid. In these situations, you can prepare a **handout** (material printed on sheets of paper). The benefit of using handouts is that all people in the audience can have a copy to refer to and take with them after the speech. The drawback is that distributing handouts can distract listeners' attention from you as you are speaking.

Before you decide to use handouts, carefully consider why they would be better than some other method. Handouts are effective for information you want listeners to refer to after the speech, such as a set of steps to follow later, useful telephone numbers and addresses, or mathematical formulas.

If you do decide to use handouts, distribute them at the end of the speech. If you want to refer to information on the handout during the speech, create another visual aid that you can reveal only when discussing it for use during your speech.

> **handout** material printed on sheets of paper and distributed to the audience

9-5e Document Cameras

Another simple way to display drawings, charts, photos, and graphs is with a document camera, such as an Elmo. If you choose this method, be sure to transfer drawings, charts, photos, and graphs from original sources onto sheets of 8-by-11-inch paper so you can display them smoothly and professionally.

9-5f Computers, CD/DVD Players, and LCD Projectors

Most people today prefer to present audio and audiovisual recordings, as well as computerized slideshows, using a computer and an LCD projector. However, you should always prepare back-up aids to use if equipment fails. Also, to ensure that audience members focus their attention on you when you're not talking about one of your slides or clips, insert blank screens between slides, press the "B" key on your computer, or use the "mute" key on your projector remote to display blank screens. As Scott and Carrie realized after watching Jason's Ignite speech in the opening vignette, computerized slideshows do not have to result in a "death by PowerPoint" experience when they are prepared, displayed, and used effectively.

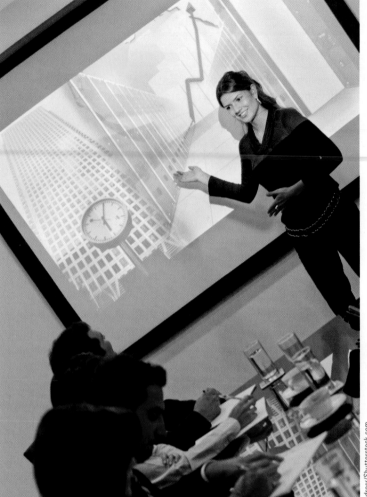

Andresr/Shutterstock.com

9-6 USING PRESENTATIONAL AIDS

Many speakers think that once they have chosen and prepared good presentational aids, they will have no trouble using them during the speech. However, effective speakers also practice using them in advance. Although we will spend more time explaining how to use presentational aids in Chapter 11 (Delivery), we introduce several guidelines for using them here, as well.

1. Plan carefully when to use each presentational aid and make a note of it on your formal outline and in your speaking notes.

2. Position presentational aids and equipment so all audience members can see and/or hear them before beginning the speech.

3. Show or play presentational aids only when talking about them so they do not distract audience members from your message.

4. Pass objects and handouts around *after* rather than during the speech so they do not distract audience members from your message.

5. Talk about the visual aid while showing it, and the audio or audiovisual aid just before and just after playing it.

6. Make eye contact with the audience while talking about the presentational aid.

Speech Planning Action Step 5, Activity 5A will help you choose, prepare, and use presentational aids. See the Student Response box immediately following the activity for a sample of how one student completed this exercise.

ACTION STEP ACTIVITY

Identifying Presentational Aids That Will Clarify, Emphasize, or Dramatize Your Message

The goal of this activity is to identify where a presentational aid would increase audience interest, understanding, and retention, and what type of presentational aid to prepare to do so.

1. Identify the key ideas in your speech for which you believe a presentational aid would increase audience interest, facilitate understanding, or increase retention.
2. For each idea you identified, list the type of presentational aid you think would be most appropriate and effective.
3. For each aid you identified, decide how you will design it.
4. For each aid you identified, decide on the method you will use to display it and how you will reference it during the speech.

Student Response: Identifying Presentational Aids That Will Clarify, Emphasize, or Dramatize Your Message

Speech goal: *I would like my audience to learn to identify common poisonous plants that grow in our area.*

1. **Identify the key ideas in your speech for which you believe a presentational aid would increase audience interest, facilitate understanding, or increase retention.**

   Leaf shape, size, and color; habitat; signs of contact

2. **For each idea you identified, list the type of presentational aid you think would be most appropriate and effective.**

   I will use two color photographs of each type of plant. The first will show the entire plant; the second will be a close-up of the leaves. I will also use photos to show the habitat in which each plant is usually found. Finally, I will use photographs to show the reactions that occur as a result of contact with the plants. I will have actual plant samples available for closer inspection after my speech.

3. **For each aid you identified, decide how you will design it.**

   I will use my digital camera to take photographs of each plant and the habitats in which I found them. These will be transferred to my computer, and then I will create a computerized slide show using PowerPoint. I will locate images of reactions to each plant online, download them, and add them to the computerized slide show. I will also collect samples of each type of plant and bring them with me to the speech.

4. **For each aid you identified, decide on the method you will use to display it and how you will reference it during the speech.**

   I will bring a memory stick with the PowerPoint presentation on it with me and use the computer and LCD projector that are available at the speaking site. I will also have backup overheads of all my photos and slides. I will reference it using a pointer because I will be speaking to an audience of at least fifty people.

STUDY TOOLS 9

LOCATED IN TEXTBOOK

☐ Tear-out Chapter Review cards at the end of the book
☐ Review with the Quick Quiz below

LOCATED ON SPEAK3 ONLINE AT CENGAGEBRAIN.COM

☐ Review Key Term flashcards and create your own cards
☐ Track your knowledge and understanding of key concepts in speech communication
☐ Complete practice and graded quizzes to prepare for tests
☐ Complete interactive content within SPEAK3 Online
☐ View the chapter highlight boxes for SPEAK3 Online

Quick Quiz (answers in Solutions Appendix)

T F 1. It is effective to show a visual aid even when you are not speaking about it.

T F 2. Presentational aids should appeal primarily to the sense of vision or hearing.

T F 3. Good presentational aids should be easy to carry.

T F 4. A presentational aid and a visual aid are identical.

T F 5. Sometimes, the speaker can use himself or herself as a presentational aid.

6. All of the following are steps you should take to prepare effective presentational aids EXCEPT:
   a. use a photo that can be easily seen by the entire audience
   b. have the audience read a lot of text
   c. use a consistent print style
   d. add pictures or symbols to add interest
   e. use color strategically

7. Aids that enhance a speech by using a combination of sight and sound are called:
   a. audiovisual aids
   b. visual aids
   c. audio aids
   d. other-sensory aids
   e. animate objects

8. If you want an audience to refer to information after a speech, you should use:
   a. flipcharts
   b. document cameras
   c. posters
   d. handouts
   e. chalkboards

9. A(n) _____ uses symbols and lines to diagram a sequence of steps.
   a. line graph
   b. pie chart
   c. flowchart
   d. organizational chart
   e. bar graph

10. Which of the following is not an advantage of using presentational aids?
   a. They enable the speaker to adapt to the audience's knowledge.
   b. They help speakers feel more competent.
   c. They allow speakers to increase the persuasive appeal of the speech.
   d. They help the audience remember information presented in the speech.
   e. They appeal primarily to one learning style.

Chapter Takeaways

List three key takeaways from this chapter:

-

-

-

SPEAK
ONLINE
REVIEW FLASHCARDS
ANYTIME, ANYWHERE!

Create Flashcards from Your StudyBits

Review Key Term Flashcards Already Loaded on the StudyBoard

4LTR
PRESS

10 Language and Oral Style

After finishing this chapter go to **PAGE 167** for **STUDY TOOLS.**

LEARNING OUTCOMES

10-1 Explain how oral style differs from written style.

10-2 Use appropriate words for the audience and occasion.

10-3 Choose the most accurate words to convey your ideas.

10-4 Use clear language.

10-5 Select vivid words that appeal to the senses and draw on rhetorical devices.

Sound Familiar?

Nathan was preparing a formal speech outline for an informative speech about the autoimmune disease known as lupus that he was going to give in public speaking class. He asked Josh for feedback.

"It sounds great for your human anatomy and physiology class," Josh said, "But it seems awfully technical for public speaking class. It might go over people's heads."

Discouraged, Nathan responded, "Good point. Back to the drawing board with a different topic."

"Actually," said Josh, "You don't really need to start over. Just adjust your language for a more general audience. Like this..."

With your outline in hand and presentational aids prepared, you are ready to move to the next step in the preparation process. In other words, you turn your focus from the macrostructure (the overall framework for organizing your speech content) to the microstructure (the specific language and style choices used to verbalize your ideas to a particular audience). In the chapter opening, Josh realizes that Nathan's speech can be adapted to his public speech class audience by choosing appropriate, accurate, clear, and vivid language.

In written communication, effective style evolves through a repetitious process of reading and revising. In a speech, effective style develops through a repetitious process of practicing aloud and revising. In this chapter, you will learn to develop language and style that is instantly intelligible to the *ear* so listeners interpret your messages as you intend.

Let's begin by clarifying how oral style differs from written style, as well as how the formal oral style used

in public speeches differs from the informal oral style we use in casual conversations with family and friends. Then we'll offer some specific strategies you can employ to ensure that your language is appropriate, accurate, clear, and vivid.

10-1 ORAL STYLE

Oral style refers to how we convey messages through the spoken word. An effective oral style differs quite a bit from written style, though when giving a speech your oral style is still more formal than everyday talk. In fact, the degree of formality required to be an effective public speaker is based on the rhetorical situation. In other words, your goal is to adapt your language to the purpose, the audience, and the occasion. For example, although your language when speaking to a small audience of colleagues at a business meeting will be more formal than when conversing with a friend at dinner, it will not be as formal as when speaking to an audience of 100 or more at a professional conference or workshop. Still, even in a formal public speaking situation, you must *establish a relationship* with your listeners. Although your oral style is slightly more formal than in everyday conversation, it

ACTION STEP

Practice Oral Language and Delivery Style

A. Practice to develop an oral style using language that is appropriate, accurate, clear, and vivid.

should still reflect a personal tone that encourages listeners to perceive you to be *having a conversation with them*. As shown in Exhibit 10.1, four primary characteristics distinguish an effective oral style from an effective written style.

1. An effective oral style tends toward short sentences and familiar language. Because listeners expect to grasp the main ideas in your speech while they listen, work to ensure your words are ones that your audience is likely to understand without having to look up definitions. Likewise, opt for short, simple sentences rather than complex ones

> **oral style** the manner in which one conveys messages through the spoken word

Exhibit 10.1
Primary Characteristics of Oral Style

Effective oral style features:

1. short sentences and familiar language
2. plural personal pronouns
3. descriptive words and phrases
4. clear macrostructural elements

© Daniilantiq/Shutterstock.com

that would require additional time for audience members to decipher. We certainly live in a digital age where live public speeches can be recorded and even posted online to be heard multiple times. Even when watching a recorded public speech, however, listeners should not be required to press "pause" to look up word meanings or "reverse" to replay complex sentences. So adapting oral style to your audience means using short sentences and familiar language.

2. An effective oral style features plural personal pronouns. Using personal pronouns such as "we," "us," and "our" creates a sense of relationship with the audience; it demonstrates respect for the audience as participants in the rhetorical situation. Remember your goal is to create a perception of conversing *with* your audience rather than presenting *to* or *in front of* them. Personal pronouns encourage that perception.

3. An effective oral style features descriptive words and phrases that appeal to the ear in ways that sustain listener interest and promote retention. By using colorful adjectives and adverbs that appeal to the senses, and rhetorical figures of speech (discussed later in this chapter), you will capture the interest of your audience and motivate them to stay focused throughout the speech.

4. An effective oral style incorporates clear macrostructural elements (e.g., main point preview, section transitions, and signposts as

speaking appropriately
using language that adapts to the needs, interests, knowledge, and attitudes of the listener and avoiding language that alienates audience members

verbal immediacy when the language you use reduces the psychological distance between you and your audience

discussed in Chapters 7 and 8). Unless your speech is being recorded and posted for additional viewing, listeners will have only one opportunity to hear it. Consequently, you need to intentionally articulate a preview of your main ideas, so listeners can place them firmly in their minds at the outset. Similarly, you need to provide clear section transitions that verbally signal when you are moving from one major idea to the next, and signposts such as "first," "second," "third," and "fourth" to help listeners follow your train of thought as the speech progresses.

Now that you have a sense of the nature of oral style as it differs from written style, let's turn our attention to some specific language choices you might make as you practice and revise your speech.

10-2 SPEAKING APPROPRIATELY

Speaking appropriately means using language that adapts to the needs, interests, knowledge, and attitudes of your listeners and avoiding language that might alienate anyone. In the communication field, we use the term **verbal immediacy** to describe language used to reduce

Helga Esteb/Shutterstock.com

Citing Nick Cannon, host of America's Got Talent, as a sufferer, added relevance to a speech about lupus.

the psychological distance between you and your audience.[1] In other words, speaking appropriately means making language choices that enhance a sense of connection between you and your audience members. In this section, we discuss specific strategies for making appropriate language choices.

10-2a Relevance

Your first challenge is to help the audience see the relevance of your topic to them. Listeners pay attention to and are motivated to listen to ideas that have a personal impact (when they can answer the question, "What does this have to do with me?"). Recall from Chapter 5 that you can help the audience perceive your topic and purpose as relevant by highlighting its timeliness, proximity, and personal impact for them. Listeners are more likely to be interested in information they perceive as timely. So whenever possible, use present tense as you explain your ideas. They see your topic as relevant when they understand how they can use it *now* or in the near future, when they see that it occurs where they live (not just in some far away place), and when they realize its potential physical, economic, or psychological impact on them personally. Josh suggested that Nathan pique listener interest in this way by pointing out that the host of *America's Got Talent*, Nick Cannon, was diagnosed with lupus nephritis. Doing so added relevance, since Cannon got his start at the cable-access channel in the town where Josh and Nathan are now attending school.

10-2b Plural Personal Pronouns

As we've already mentioned, using plural personal pronouns like "we," "our," and "us" rather than "you" or "they" also conveys a sense of connection with your listeners. When used appropriately, "we" language fosters a sense of having a conversation *with* your audience rather than speaking or presenting *in front of* them. As a result, your audience will be more open to listening

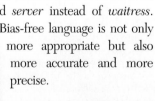

John Roman Images/Shutterstock.com

to you, believing what you say, and remembering your ideas.[2] You can easily replace "I" and "you" language with "we" language in the macrostructural elements of your speech. In your thesis statement, you can say, for example, "let's discuss . . ." rather than "I will inform you . . .," and in your section transitions, you can say "Now that we all have a clearer understanding of . . ." rather than "Now that I've explained . . ." and so on. For Nathan's speech, Josh suggested he introduce his thesis and preview using "we" language this way: "In the next few minutes, let's explore the symptoms, diagnosis, and treatment of lupus nephritis, an autoimmune disease in which the body mistakes its own tissues for foreign invaders and begins attacking them."

10-2c Linguistic Sensitivity

To demonstrate linguistic sensitivity, choose words that are respectful of others and avoid potentially offensive language. You can enhance verbal immediacy in this way by avoiding generic language, nonparallelism, potentially offensive humor, as well as profanity and vulgarity.[3]

Generic Language

Generic language uses words that apply only to one sex, race, or other group as though they represent everyone. In the past, English speakers used the masculine pronoun *he* to stand for all humans regardless of sex. This example of generic language excludes 50 percent of most audiences. The best way to avoid generic language is to use plurals: "When we shop, we should have a clear idea of what we want to buy."[4]

A second problem of generic language results from the traditional use of *man*.[5] Consider the term *manmade*. What this really means is "made by human beings," but its underlying tone is that a *male* human being made the item. Bias-free alternatives do exist—for instance, *police officer* instead of *policeman*, *synthetic* instead of *manmade*, *humankind* instead of *mankind*, *flight attendant* instead of *stewardess*, and *server* instead of *waitress*. Bias-free language is not only more appropriate but also more accurate and more precise.

> **generic language** language that uses words that apply only to one sex, race, or other group as though they represent everyone

Nonparallelism

Nonparallelism denotes when terms are changed because of the sex, race, or other group characteristics of the individual. Two common forms of nonparallelism are marking and irrelevant association.

Marking is the *addition* of sex, race, age, or other group designations to a description. For instance, a doctor is a person with a medical degree who is licensed to practice medicine. Notice the difference between the following two sentences:

Jones is a good doctor.

Jones is a good black doctor.

In the second sentence, use of the marker "black" is offensive. It has nothing to do with doctoring. Marking is inappropriate because it trivializes the person's role by introducing an irrelevant characteristic.[6] The speaker may be intending to praise Jones, but listeners may interpret the sentence as saying that Jones is a good doctor for a black person (or a woman or an old person) but not that Jones is as good as a good white doctor (or a male doctor or a young doctor).

A second form of nonparallelism is **irrelevant association**, which is when we emphasize one person's relationship to another when that relationship is irrelevant to our point. For example, introducing a speaker as "Gladys Thompson, whose husband is CEO of Acme Inc., is the chairperson for this year's United Way campaign" is inappropriate. Mentioning her husband's status implies that Gladys Thompson is chairperson because of her *husband's* accomplishments, not her own.

Offensive Humor

Dirty jokes and racist, sexist, or other "-ist" remarks may not be intended to be offensive, but if some listeners are offended, you will have lost verbal immediacy. To be most effective with your formal public speeches, avoid humorous comments or jokes that may be offensive to some listeners. As a general rule, when in doubt, leave it out.

Vulgarity and profanity are pervasive in the industry, but comedians such as Jim Gaffigan have decided to avoid it because it is out of place. In an interview with *Paste* magazine, Gaffigan noted, "What, am I supposed to throw in an f-bomb when I'm talking about bacon?"[7]

Today, "casual swearing"—profanity injected into regular conversation—is commonplace in some language communities, including college campuses.[8] As a result, some of us have become desensitized to such terms as shocking or offensive. However, when giving a public speech, we need to remember that some people in our audience may still be offended by swearing. People who casually pepper their speech with profanity and vulgar expressions are often perceived as abrasive and lacking in character, maturity, intelligence, manners, and emotional control.[9]

10-2d Cultural Diversity

Language rules and expectations vary from culture to culture. One major theory used to explain such similarities and differences is individualism versus collectivism.[10] In general, people from individualistic

---

nonparallelism denotes when terms are changed because of the sex, race, or other group characteristics of the individual

marking the addition of sex, race, age, or other group designations to a description

irrelevant association emphasizing one person's relationship to another when that relationship is irrelevant to the point

Profanity and Vulgarity

Appropriate language avoids profanity and vulgar expressions. Fifty years ago, a child was punished for saying "hell" or "damn," and adults used profanity and vulgarity only in rare situations to express strong emotions.

cultures, including North America and much of Western Europe, tend to use low-context communication, in which information is (1) embedded mainly in the messages transmitted and (2) presented directly. Conversely, people from collectivistic cultures, including much of the Middle East and Asia, tend to use high-context communication, in which people (1) expect others to know how they're thinking and feeling and (2) present some messages indirectly to avoid embarrassing the other person. Thus, speakers from low-context cultures tend to operate on the principle of saying what they mean and getting to the point. Their approach may be characterized by such expressions as "Say what you mean" and "Don't beat around the bush."[11] In contrast, speakers from high-context cultures are likely to use language that is intentionally indirect and listeners are expected to understand the message not only based on the words but also from the context in which they are uttered.

What does this mean for public speakers? When you address an audience consisting of people from ethnic and language groups different from your own, make extra effort to ensure that you are being understood. When the first language spoken by audience members is different from yours, they may not able to understand what you are saying because you may speak with an accent, mispronounce words, choose inappropriate words, and misuse idioms.

Speaking in a second language can sometimes make us feel self-conscious. But most audience members are more tolerant of mistakes made by a second-language speaker than they are of those made by a native speaker. Nevertheless, when you are speaking in a second language, you can help your audience by speaking more slowly and articulating as clearly as you can. By slowing your speaking rate, you give yourself additional time to pronounce difficult sounds and choose words whose meanings you know, as well as give your audience members additional time to adjust their ears to more easily process what you are saying. It can also be a good idea to use visual aids to reinforce key terms and concepts as you move through the speech. Doing so assures listeners that they've understood you correctly.

One of the best ways to improve when you are giving a speech in a second language is to practice in front of friends who are native speakers. Ask them to take note of words and phrases that you mispronounce or misuse. Then they can work with you to correct the pronunciation or to choose other words that better express your idea. Also, keep in mind that the more you practice speaking the language, the more comfortable you will become with it.

10-3 SPEAKING ACCURATELY

Using **accurate language** means using words that convey your meaning precisely. On the surface, speaking accurately seems simple enough. In fact, however, speaking accurately is not that simple. Here are three reasons why.

1. **Language is arbitrary.** The words we use to represent things are arbitrary symbols. That is to say, there is not necessarily any literal connection between a word and the thing it represents. For a word to have meaning, it must be recognized by both or all parties as standing for a particular object, idea, or feeling.[12] In communication studies, we often simply say the *word* is not the *thing*. In their influential book, *The Meaning of Meaning: A Study of the Influence of Language upon Thought and the Science of Symbolism*, I. A. Richards and C. K. Ogden clarify this idea using the semantic triangle.[13] As depicted in Exhibit 10.2, a "referent" is the *thing* or object we refer to with a word, which is the "symbol" we use to refer to it. Our audience then attaches meaning to that symbol, which is what Richards and Ogden label the "thought of referent." The word spelled D-O-G is nothing more than three letters used together unless all parties agree that it stands for a certain four-legged animal. To clarify, think about the fact that different groups use different words symbols for the same phenomenon. In Spanish, for instance, *el perro* stands for the same thing as *dog*

accurate language
language that conveys your meaning precisely

Exhibit 10.2
The Semantic Triangle

Thought of referent

Symbol   Referent

© Bananafish/Shutterstock.com

in English. And the storage compartment of an automobile is called a "trunk" in the United States and a "boot" in England.

2. Language is abstract. Not only is language arbitrary, but it is also abstract. In the United States, for example, the word "pet" is commonly understood to be an animal kept for companionship. Still, if Rema refers simply to her "pet," Margi may think of a dog, cat, snake, bird, or hamster. Even if Rema specifically mentions her dog, Margi still might think of dogs of various breeds, sizes, colors, and temperaments.

Because language is abstract, two people might interpret the same word quite differently. For example, when James tells Chrissie that he liked going to the movie with her, Chrissie might interpret "liked" as enjoying the movie or spending time with her.

3. Language changes over time.
New words are constantly being invented and existing words abandoned or assigned new meanings. Just think, for example, of the words that have been invented to represent new technologies, such as *texting, Googling, cyberbullying, tweeting, retweeting, webinar, app, emoticon,* and *emoji.* Some of the new words most recently added to English dictionaries include *vanity sizing* (the deliberate undersizing of clothes), *twirt* (flirt on Twitter), *mankle* (the male ankle), and *cougar* (an older woman in a romantic relationship with a younger man). Did you know that the *Oxford English Dictionary* now also includes *OMG, LOL,* and *<3* as actual words?

Some words become obsolete because the thing they represent becomes obsolete. For example, today we use *photocopiers* and *computers* to make multiple copies of print documents rather than *mimeographs* (low-cost printing presses) and *stencils.* We record audio and video data using *smartphones* rather than using *tape recorders, cassette tapes,* and *videotapes.* And we take notes on *iPads* and *laptops* rather than on paper

SeDmi/Shutterstock.com

that we organize in a *Trapper Keeper* (a loose-leaf 3-ring binder used by school children in the United States during the 1980s).

Sometimes meanings of existing words change. For example, in the United States, the word *gay* once meant *happy* and only that. Today its more common usage references one's sexual orientation. In some communities, *bad* might mean *not good,* in others it might mean *naughty,* and in others it might mean *really great* (e.g., "That movie was really bad."). Language can also change as a result of melding aspects of multiple languages. *Tex-Mex* and *Spanglish,* for instance, both blend English and Spanish, and we don't think twice about the fact that children go to *kindergarten,* a word absorbed by the United States from German immigrants.

Using accurate language is crucial to effective speaking because it helps you be **intelligible**, or clearly understood. If listeners don't understand you or what you mean, your attempt to communicate is doomed. To help ensure that the language you use in speeches is accurate, let's take a look at three concepts that affect how words are interpreted: denotation, connotation, and dialect.

10-3a **Denotation**

A word's **denotation** is its direct, explicit dictionary definition. So, denotatively, when Melissa said her dog died, she meant that her domesticated canine no longer demonstrates physical life. Nathan (from the opening vignette) offered the dictionary definition of lupus as an inflammatory disease caused when the immune system attacks its own tissues. Keep in mind that in some situations the denotative meaning of a word may not be clear. Why? One reason is that dictionary definitions reflect current and past practices in the language community. Another reason is that dictionaries often offer more than one definition for a given word. And dictionaries use words to define words. The end result is that words are defined differently in various dictionaries and may include multiple meanings that also may change over time.

Moreover, meaning may vary depending on the **context**—the position of a word in a sentence and its relationship to the words around it. For example, the dictionary definition of *right* includes both (1) correct (adjective) and (2) a more or ethical principle (noun). The situation in which a word is spoken may also clarify

intelligible capable of being understood

denotation the explicit meaning a language community formally gives a word; a word's "dictionary meaning"

context the position of a word in a sentence and its relationship to other words around it

Depending up on the context, the word "surfing" can denote very different ideas.

its denotative meaning. For example, if you're at the beach and you say you are "surfing," you probably mean you're riding the waves. But if you're sitting at your desk in front of your computer, you probably mean you're searching the Internet for information.

10-3b Connotation

A word's **connotation** is the positive, neutral, or negative feelings or evaluations we associate with it. For example, consider how your impression of Dave would differ if someone said he was "cheap" versus "frugal." The denotative meaning of both words indicates someone who doesn't like to spend a lot of money, but for most of us "frugal" has a more positive connotation than "cheap" does. Thus, our perception of a word's connotation may be even more important than its denotation in how we interpret the meaning of the word. Connotations can be neutral, positive, or negative and can be quite different for different people. For example, the word "cop" can conjure up very different connotations for different people based on previous experiences.

Ogden and Richards were among the first scholars to consider the misunderstandings that result from the failure of communicators to realize that their subjective reactions to words are a product of their life experiences.[14] For instance, when Melissa told Trish that her dog died, Trish's understanding of the message depends on the extent to which her feelings about pets and death—her connotations of the words—correspond to the feelings Melissa has about pets and death. Whereas Melissa (who sees dogs as truly indispensable friends) may be intending to communicate her overwhelming grief, Trish (who doesn't

particularly care for pets in general or dogs in particular) may miss the emotional meaning of Melissa's statement.

Connotations give emotional power to words, so much so that people will even fight and die for them. Consider the connotative meanings people assign to words like *freedom* and *honor* and *justice*. For this reason, connotations can increase the emotional appeal of your message. As you consider language options, be sure to consider audience disposition toward them and steer clear of words that might arouse unintended connotations.

10-3c Dialect

Dialect is a unique form of a more general language spoken by a specific cultural or co-cultural group.[15] These smaller groups that speak a common dialect are called **speech communities**. They can also affect listener understanding. Dialects evolve over time, and the manner in which they differ from the "standard" of the language may be influenced by other languages spoken in the region or by the ethnic group. For instance, in her book *Chicano English in Context*, Carmen Fought details how the English spoken by some Hispanic people in the Los Angeles area differs from Standard English.[16] Regional differences are also reflected in the words used to represent common things. For example, in some places a car's turn

> **connotation** the positive, neutral, or negative feelings or evaluations we associate with a word
>
> **dialect** a unique form of a more general language spoken by a specific cultural or co-cultural group
>
> **speech communities** smaller groups that speak a common dialect

signal is called a "blinker," a seesaw is a "teeter-totter," and a soft drink is a "pop" or a "coke." Some dialects also incorporate what is considered non-standard grammar, such as "he don't," "I says," "this here book," and "beings as how he was sick." If your audience doesn't share the dialect you normally speak, using it during your speeches can interfere with intelligibility. Not only that, it can also affect your ethos (the audience's perception of your competence and credibility). Because most audiences are diverse, the best way to ensure being understood by all and conveying positive ethos is to use **Standard English** (which is taught in American schools and detailed in grammar handbooks like *Hodges Harbrace Handbook*, 18th ed.[17]).

10-4 SPEAKING CLEARLY

Speaking clearly results from explaining potentially ambiguous language. Compare the clarity of the following two descriptions of the same incident:

Some nut almost ran into me awhile ago.

Last Saturday afternoon, a grey-haired man in a banged-up Honda Civic ran through the red light at Calhoun and Clifton and came within inches of hitting my car while I was waiting to turn left.

Speaking clearly decreases ambiguity and audience confusion when we speak. Let's look at four strategies for improving clarity: use specific language, choose familiar terms, provide details and examples, and limit vocalized pauses.

10-4a Use Specific Language

Specific language clarifies meaning by using precise words that narrow what is understood from a general category to a particular item or group within that category. For instance, if in her speech Nevah refers to a "blue-collar worker," you might picture any number of occupations that fall within this broad category. If, instead, she refers to a "construction worker," the number of possible images you can picture is reduced. Now you select your image from the subcategory of construction worker, and your meaning is likely to be closer to the one she intended. If she is even more specific, she may say "bulldozer operator." Now you are even clearer on the specific occupation.

Choosing specific language is easier when you have a large working vocabulary. As a speaker, the larger your vocabulary, the more choices you have from which to select the word you want. As a listener, the larger your vocabulary, the more likely you are to understand the words used by others.

One way to increase your vocabulary is to study one of the many vocabulary-building books, such as *Word Smart: How to Build a More Educated Vocabulary*, Fifth Edition or Sadlier-Oxford's series of *Vocabulary Workshop* books.[18]

A second way to increase your vocabulary is to take note of unfamiliar words you read or that people use in conversations and look them up. For instance, suppose you read or hear, "I was inundated with phone calls today!" If you wrote down *inundated* and looked it up in a dictionary later, you would find that it means "overwhelmed" or "flooded." If you then say to yourself, "She was inundated—overwhelmed or flooded—with phone calls today," you are likely to remember that meaning and apply it the next time you hear the word.

A third way to increase your vocabulary is to use a thesaurus to identify synonyms that may be more specific options. Most computer programs like Microsoft Word offer a thesaurus under the "Tools" option, or there are various options online. But be careful—avoid unfamiliar words that may make you sound intelligent but could reduce your intelligibility. For example, *somnolent* is an interesting word, but most people don't know that it is a synonym for *sleepy*.

Note, however, that having a larger vocabulary won't help your speaking unless you use it as you practice. Suppose you were practicing a speech on registering for classes and said, "Preregistration is awful." If this word isn't quite right, you can quickly brainstorm better words, such as *frustrating, demeaning, cumbersome*, and *annoying*. Then, as you continue to practice, you might say, "Preregistration is a cumbersome process."

Some speakers think that to be effective they must impress their audience with their extensive vocabularies. As a result, instead of looking for specific and precise words, they use words that appear pompous, affected, or stilted to the listener. Speaking precisely and specifically does not mean speaking obscurely. The following story illustrates the problem with pretentious words:

A plumber wrote to a government agency, saying that he found that hydrochloric acid quickly opened drainpipes but that he wasn't sure whether it was a good thing to

Standard English the form of English taught in American schools and detailed in grammar handbooks

specific language language that uses precise words to narrow what is understood from a general category to a particular item or group within that category

use. A scientist at the agency replied, "The efficacy of hydrochloric acid is indisputable, but the corrosive residue is incompatible with metallic permanence."

The plumber wrote back thanking him for the assurance that hydrochloric acid was all right. Disturbed by this turn of affairs, the scientist showed the letter to his boss, another scientist, who then wrote to the plumber: "We cannot assume responsibility for the production of toxic and noxious residue with hydrochloric acid and suggest you use an alternative procedure."

The plumber wrote back that he agreed. Hydrochloric acid worked fine. Greatly disturbed by this misunderstanding, the scientists took their problem to the top boss. She wrote to the plumber: "Don't use hydrochloric acid. It eats the hell out of pipes."

So, use a more difficult word *only* when you believe that it is the very best word for a specific context. Let's suppose you wanted to use a more precise or specific word for *building*. Using the guideline of familiarity, you might select *house*, *apartment*, *high-rise*, or *skyscraper*, but you would avoid *edifice*. Each of the other choices is more precise or more specific, but *edifice* is neither more precise nor more specific, and in addition to being less well understood, it will be perceived as affected or stilted.

10-4b Choose Familiar Terms

Using familiar terms is just as important as using specific words. Avoid jargon, slang, abbreviations, and acronyms unless (1) you define them clearly the first time they are used and (2) using them is central to your speech goal.

Jargon is the unique technical terminology of a trade or profession that is not generally understood by outsiders. Nearly every field has developed its own jargon. In an interesting series on trade lingo, NPR's Melissa Block profiled the unique terminology used by various professions. She found that marine biologists talk about *grubbing* (going underground to get a bird out of a burrow)[19]; radiologists might use the term *Aunt Minnie* to describe what they are seeing on a brain scan (if the doctor is absolutely certain of the diagnosis for the scan, it's an Aunt Minnie)[20]; and comedy writers can be overheard using *Nakamura* (a running gag that fails repeatedly) and *laying pipe* (telling the audience something the characters in a show already know)[21].

Why do groups of people, and, in this case, professions, use jargon? Bill Prady, the co-creator and executive producer of *The Big Bang Theory* television show describes jargon as verbal shorthand used to get an idea across quickly.[22] If you are preparing a speech on a technical or particular topic, you may be using jargon in your speech without realizing it.

We might forget that people who are not in our same line of work or who do not have the same hobbies may not understand the jargon that seems such a part of our daily communication. For instance, when Jenny starts talking with her computer-illiterate friend Sarah about "social MUDs based on fictional universes," Sarah is likely to be totally lost. If, however, Jenny recognizes Sarah's lack of familiarity with cyberlanguage, she can make her message clear by discussing the concepts in words her friend understands. In short, limit your use of jargon in speeches to general audiences and always define jargon in simple terms the first time you use it. Josh suggested that Nathan not only say that an erythrocyte sedimentation rate is one of several tests used to diagnose lupus nephritis, but also say what it is. So, Nathan added a sentence to say that the erythrocyte sedimentation rate test determines the rate at which red blood cells settle to the bottom of a test tube. A faster than normal rate indicates the presence of systemic disease, such as lupus.

Slang refers to informal, nonstandard vocabulary and nonstandard definitions assigned to words by a social group or subculture. For example, today the word *wicked*, which has a standard definition denoting something wrong or immoral, can mean quite the opposite in some social groups and subcultures.[23] You should generally avoid slang in your public speeches not only because you risk being misunderstood but also because slang doesn't sound professional and can hurt your credibility (ethos). Slang is so pervasive that there are entire dictionaries devoted to the specialized vocabulary of different communities.

Overusing and misusing abbreviations and acronyms can also hinder clarity. Even if you think the abbreviation or acronym is common, to ensure intelligibility always define it the first time you use it in the

jargon unique technical terminology of a trade or profession that is not generally understood by outsiders

slang informal, nonstandard vocabulary and nonstandard definitions assigned to words by a social group or subculture

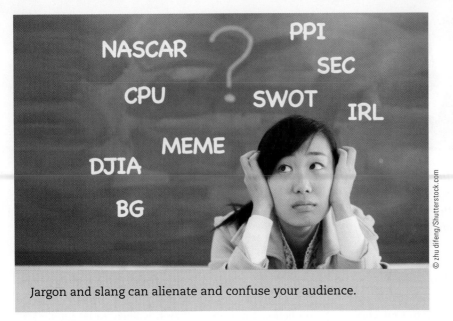

Jargon and slang can alienate and confuse your audience.

© zhu difeng/Shutterstock.com

speech. For example, in a speech about NASCAR, refer to it initially by the organization's full name and then provide the acronym: "National Association for Stock Car Auto Racing, or NASCAR." Providing the full and abbreviated forms of the name will ensure clarity for all listeners. If you are assuming right now that everyone knows what NASCAR is, it might benefit you to know one of your authors had to look it up to include it in this book!

10-4c Provide Details and Examples

Sometimes, the word we use may not have a precise synonym. In these situations, clarity can be achieved by adding details or examples. Saying "He lives in a really big house" can be clarified by adding details: "He lives in a fourteen-room Tudor mansion on a six-acre estate."

10-4d Limit Vocalized Pauses

Vocalized pauses are unnecessary words interjected into sentences to fill moments of silence. Words commonly used for this purpose are "like," "you know," "really," and "basically," as well as "um" and "uh." Terry Gross famously uses vocalized pauses in her interviews with interesting political, cultural, and scientific figures as a way to produce a more conversational style. For example, she complained about her own petite size in an interview with comedian Mindy Kaling, who quickly accused Gross of

> **vocalized pauses** unnecessary words interjected into sentences to fill moments of silence
>
> **vivid language** language that is full of life—vigorous, bright, and intense

"humblebragging." Gross replied, laughing, "No, what I am, is like, really short. And when you see, like, jackets with the shoulders drooping off of you and pants that are just, like, way too, like tight in one place and loose in another place, it's not a good thing."[29]

Although Gross's pausing style creates verbal punctuation that complements her engaging interview style, you can see how the number of times she uses "like" can start to interfere with the point she is trying to make.

We sometimes refer to vocalized pauses as "verbal garbage" because they do not serve a meaningful purpose and actually distract listeners from the message. Worse, if used profusely, vocalized pauses can damage your credibility. For example, when running for senator of New York, Caroline Kennedy inserted dozens of vocalized pauses in media interviews and other public speaking occasions. Journalists examining transcripts of the interviews between 80 and 200 uses of "you know" during several short speeches—along with many uses of "um."[30] Her inability to speak fluidly revealed her inexperience and fundamental shyness, and Kennedy quit the senate race only six weeks after entering it.[31]

Voice coach Jocelyn Rasmussen describes these verbal tics as evidence of a speaker's inexperience or doubt and that speakers are largely unaware that they use them.[32] Although a few vocalized pauses typically don't hinder clarity, practicing your speech aloud will help you eliminate them.

10-5 SPEAKING VIVIDLY

Speaking vividly is one effective way to gain and maintain audience interest and help them remember what you say. **Vivid language** is full of life—vigorous, bright, and intense. For example, a mediocre baseball announcer might say, "Jackson made a great catch," but a better commentator's vivid account might be, "Jackson leaped and made a spectacular one-handed catch just as he crashed into the center field wall." The words *leaped*, *spectacular*, *one-handed catch*, and *crashed* paint an intense verbal picture of the action. You can make your ideas come to life by using sensory language and by using rhetorical figures and structures of speech.

10-5a Use Sensory Language

Sensory language appeals to the senses of seeing, hearing, tasting, smelling, and feeling. Vivid sensory language begins with vivid thought. You are much more likely to express yourself vividly if you can physically or psychologically sense the meanings you are trying to convey. If you feel the "bite of the wind" or "the sting of freezing rain," if you hear and smell "the thick, juicy sirloin steaks sizzling on the grill," you will be able to describe these sensations. Does the cake merely "taste good" or do your taste buds "quiver with the sweet double-chocolate icing and velvety feel of the rich, moist cake"?

© ElenaGaak/Shutterstock.com

To develop vivid sensory language, begin by considering how you can re-create what something, someone, or some place *looks like*. Consider, too, how you can help listeners imagine how something *sounds*. How can you use language to convey the way something *feels* (textures, shapes, temperatures)? How can language re-create a sense of how something *tastes* or *smells*? To achieve this in your speech, use colorful descriptors. They make your ideas more concrete and can arouse emotions. They invite listeners to imagine details. Here's an example about downhill skiing:

- *Sight:* As you climb the hill, the bright winter sunshine glistening on the snow is blinding.

- *Touch and feel:* Just before you take off, you gently slip your goggles over your eyes. They are bitterly cold and sting your nose for a moment.

- *Taste:* You start the descent and, as you gradually pick up speed, the taste of air and ice and snow in your mouth invigorates you.

- *Sound:* An odd silence fills the air. You hear nothing but the swish of your skis against the snow beneath your feet. At last, you arrive at the bottom of the slope. Reality hits as you hear the hustle and bustle of other skiers and instructors directing them to their next session.

- *Smell and feel:* You enter the warming house. As your fingers thaw in the warm air, the aroma from the wood stove in the corner comforts you as you drift off to sleep.

By using colorful descriptors that appeal to the senses, you arouse and maintain listener interest and make your ideas more memorable.

10-5b Use Rhetorical Figures and Structures of Speech

Rhetorical figures of speech make striking comparisons between things that are not obviously alike to help listeners visualize or internalize what you are saying. **Rhetorical structures of speech** combine ideas in a particular way. Any of these devices can serve to make your speech more memorable as long as they aren't overused. Let's look at some examples.

A **simile** is a direct comparison of dissimilar things using the word *like* or *as*. Clichés such as "He walks like a duck" and "She's as busy as a bee" are similes. If you've seen the movie *Forrest Gump*, you might recall Forrest's use of similes: "Life is like a box of chocolates. You never know what you're going to get" and "Stupid is as stupid does." An elementary school teacher used a simile by saying that being back at school after a long absence "was like trying to hold 35 corks under water at the same time."[33] Similes can be effective because they make ideas more vivid in listeners' minds. But they should be used sparingly or they lose their appeal. Clichés should be avoided because their predictability reduces their effectiveness.

A **metaphor** is an implied comparison between two unlike things, expressed without using *like* or *as*. Instead of saying that one thing is *like* another, a metaphor says that one thing *is* another. Thus, a problem car is a "lemon" and a leaky roof is a "sieve." Metaphors can be effective because they make an abstract concept more concrete, strengthen an important point, or heighten emotions. Notice how one speaker used a metaphor effectively to conclude a speech: "It is imperative that we weave our fabric of the future with durable thread."[34]

---

sensory language language that appeals to the senses of seeing, hearing, tasting, smelling, and feeling

rhetorical figures of speech phrases that make striking comparisons between things that are not obviously alike

rhetorical structures of speech phrases that combine ideas in a particular way

simile a direct comparison of dissimilar things using *like* or *as*

metaphor an implied comparison between two unlike things without using *like* or *as*

How Easy Is Your Speech to Understand?

A simple technique for improving the clarity of your message is by writing a speech with readability in mind. Readability is the degree to which a reader can understand your words.

Currently, there are two major formulas used to determine readability: the Flesch Reading Ease Score, which grades content between 1–100, and the Gunning-Fog Index, operating on a scale of 1−14+. The formulas were developed in the 1950s by Rudolph Flesch and Robert Gunning, respectively. The two researchers noticed that most newspaper articles were written at the 12th grade reading level, while the average American adult read at the 8th or 9th grade level.[24]

Sales numbers provided the evidence to support their theories—magazines with lower reading levels outsold those with higher reading levels by a factor of over 10 to 1.[25] Simply put, more people were capable of appreciating the pulp rags written at a 6th-grade level, so they sold more copies.

Both Flesch and Gunning developed two different formulas that performed similar functions. Gunning's Fog Index calculates reading grade level by multiplying the sum of a sample passage's average sentence length and percentage of "hard" words by 0.4.[26] Flesch, who was a supporter of the Plain English Movement, developed the Reading Ease formula.[27] Scores between 90 and 100 should be comprehendible to the average 5th grader, while scores from 0 to 30 indicate college-level reading. By the measure of Flesch's formula, the best texts use shorter sentences and words.[28]

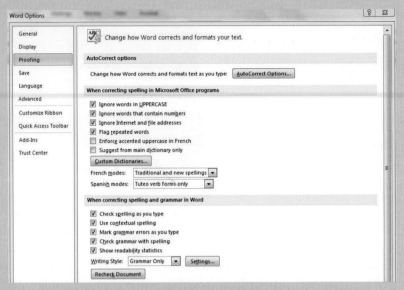

Flesch's Reading Ease scale is a built-in function of Microsoft Word, so you can check the readability of your speech text before delivering it. Under the Options tab, select "Proofing." Make sure box "Show readability statistics" is checked. Then, every time you run the spell-check function, a final box will show you the reading level and ease of your material.

Text with high levels of readability is easier for wider audiences to comprehend, whether by reading or listening. Shorter sentences and more recognizable words make it simpler for a listener to jump back into your speech if their mind wanders or "checks out." Furthermore, giving a speech written with high readability will decrease your chances of flubbing a line or word—which could help you save face more than a handful of ten-dollar words.

An **analogy** is an extended metaphor. Sometimes you can develop a story from a metaphor that makes a concept more vivid. If you were to describe a family member as the "black sheep in the barnyard," that's a metaphor. If you went on to talk about the other members of the family as different animals on the farm and the roles ascribed to them, you would be extending the metaphor into an analogy. Analogies can be effective for holding your speech together in a creative and vivid way. Analogies are particularly useful to highlight the similarities between a complex or unfamiliar concept with one that is familiar.

Alliteration is the repetition of consonant sounds at the beginning of words that are near one another. Tongue twisters such as "She sells seashells by the seashore" use alliteration. In her speech about the history of jelly beans, Sharla used alliteration when she said, "And today there are more than fifty fabulous fruity flavors from which to choose." Used sparingly, alliteration can catch listeners' attention and make the speech memorable. But overuse can hurt the message because listeners might focus on the technique rather than the speech content.

Assonance is the repetition of vowel sounds in a phrase or phrases. "How now brown cow" is a

analogy an extended metaphor

alliteration repetition of consonant sounds at the beginning of words that are near one another

assonance repetition of vowel sounds in a phrase or phrases

A memorial plaque in place of the Berlin Wall contains a fragment of the text of U.S. President Ronald Reagan's 1987 speech: "Mr. Gorbachev, open this gate! ... Tear down this wall!"

common example. Sometimes, the words rhyme, but they don't have to. As with alliteration, assonance can make your speech more memorable as long as it's not overused.

Onomatopoeia is the use of words that sound like the things they stand for, such as "buzz," "hiss," "crack," and "plop." In the speech about skiing, the "swish" of the skis is an example of onomatopoeia.

Personification is attributing human qualities to a concept or an inanimate object. When Madison talked about her truck, "Big Red," as her trusted friend and companion, she used personification. Likewise, when Rick talked about flowers dancing on the front lawn, he used personification.

Repetition is restating words, phrases, or sentences for emphasis. Ronald Reagan's address at the Brandenburg Gate in Berlin is a classic example:

In the 1950's, Khrushchev predicted: "We will bury you." But in the West today, we see a free world that has achieved a level of prosperity and well-being unprecedented in all human history. In the Communist world, we see failure, technological backwardness, declining standards of health, even want of the most basic kind—too little food. Even today, the Soviet Union still cannot feed itself. After these four decades, then, there stands before the entire world one great and inescapable conclusion:

Freedom leads to prosperity.

Freedom replaces the ancient hatreds among the nations with comity and peace.

Freedom is the victor.

…

There is one sign the Soviets can make that would be unmistakable, that would advance dramatically the cause of freedom and peace. General Secretary Gorbachev, if you seek peace, if you seek prosperity for the Soviet Union and Eastern Europe, if you seek liberalization: Come here to this gate! Mr. Gorbachev, open this gate! Mr. Gorbachev, tear down this wall![35]

Antithesis is combining contrasting ideas in the same sentence, as when John F. Kennedy said, "Ask not what your country can do for you. Ask what you can do for your country." Likewise, astronaut Neil Armstrong used antithesis when he first stepped on the moon: "That's one small step for a man, one giant leap for mankind." Speeches that offer antithesis in the concluding remarks are often very memorable.

onomatopoeia words that sound like the things they stand for

personification attributing human qualities to a concept or an inanimate object

repetition restating words, phrases, or sentences for emphasis

antithesis combining contrasting ideas in the same sentence

STUDY TOOLS 10

LOCATED IN TEXTBOOK

☐ Tear-out Chapter Review cards at the end of the book

☐ Review with the Quick Quiz below

LOCATED ON SPEAK3 ONLINE AT CENGAGEBRAIN.COM

☐ Review Key Term flashcards and create your own cards

☐ Track your knowledge and understanding of key concepts in speech communication

☐ Complete practice and graded quizzes to prepare for tests

☐ Complete interactive content within SPEAK3 Online

☐ View the chapter highlight boxes for SPEAK3 Online

Quick Quiz (answers in Solutions Appendix)

T F 1. In some situations, it is not appropriate to speak with a personal tone.

T F 2. As long as you don't intend to be offensive, the audience will not be offended by jokes you include in the speech.

T F 3. Language is symbolic because it is used to represent things, ideas, and events.

T F 4. Effective style is not something that can be developed—either you have it or you don't.

T F 5. The use of transitions and signposts is important to an effective oral style.

6. During a speech, Louis uses the word "policeman" to refer to all law enforcement officers. This is an example of:

   a. "we" language
   b. bias-free language
   c. keynote language
   d. nonparallel language
   e. generic language

7. The definition of a word given in the dictionary is the word's:

   a. semantic field
   b. denotation
   c. ambiguity
   d. nuance
   e. connotation

8. Which of the following is an example of a vocalized pause?

   a. "for instance"
   b. "secondly"
   c. "moreover"
   d. "uh"
   e. "Let's take a moment to reconsider the last point."

9. An effective oral style:

   a. tends toward short sentences and familiar language
   b. uses "you" and "they"
   c. involves using big, technical terms
   d. delivers content quickly and rapidly
   e. does not depend on the volume of the speaker's voice

10. Language that involves words and phrases that are unique and technical and not generally understood by those outside a particular group is called:

   a. jargon
   b. slang
   c. hate speech
   d. symbolic language
   e. marked language

Chapter Takeaways

List three key takeaways from this chapter:

-

-

-

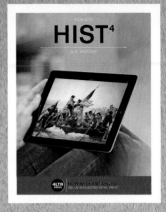

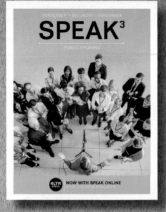

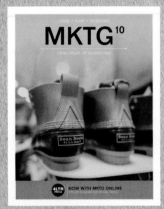

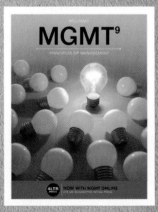

11 Delivery

LEARNING OUTCOMES

11-1 Describe the characteristics of effective delivery.

11-2 Use your voice effectively as you deliver your speech.

11-3 Use your body effectively as you deliver your speech.

11-4 Understand the different speech delivery methods.

11-5 Engage in effective speech rehearsals.

11-6 Adapt delivery appropriately while presenting your speech.

11-7 Adapt your speech and delivery for virtual audiences.

After finishing this chapter go to **PAGE 195** for **STUDY TOOLS.**

Sound Familiar?

After watching a recording of her first speech practice, Alyssa said, "That was horrible! I bored myself—and my speech is only 5 1/2 minutes long!"

Her friend Katie responded, "Don't be so hard on yourself. Your speech is good. The topic is interesting and relevant, you cite great evidence, it's well organized, and you use compelling language. You just need to make it sound conversational and dynamic. Add some delivery cues to your speaking notes, so you remember when and how to use your voice and make gestures. Then practice a few more times until you sound and look spontaneous."

"Ok," Alyssa replied. "After watching that rehearsal, I'll try anything…"

What both Alyssa and Katie recognize is that the difference between a good speech and a great speech is often how well it is delivered. In fact, research suggests that listeners are influenced more by delivery than by the content of speeches.[1] A speaker's delivery alone cannot compensate for a poorly researched, organized, or developed speech, but a well-delivered speech can rise above the ordinary and really capture an audience.

In this chapter, we begin by talking about the characteristics of effective delivery. We then describe the elements of effective delivery: use of voice and use of body. Next, we discuss three speech delivery methods and the settings in which each is most appropriate. Finally, we suggest a process for rehearsing your speech and ways to adapt to your audience while giving it in face-to-face settings and for virtual audiences.

11-1 CHARACTERISTICS OF EFFECTIVE DELIVERY

Think about the best speaker you have ever heard. What made this person stand out in your mind? In all likelihood, how the speaker delivered the speech had a lot to do with it. **Delivery** is how a message is communicated nonverbally through your voice and body. **Nonverbal communication** includes all speech elements other than

the actual words themselves.[2] These elements include your use of voice (e.g., pitch, volume, rate, quality, articulation, pronunciation, and pauses) and use of body (e.g., facial expressions, eye

delivery how a message is communicated orally and visually through the use of voice and body

nonverbal communication all speech elements other than the words themselves

contact, gestures, body language, and even appearance). Effective delivery is both conversational and animated.

11-1a Conversational

You have probably heard ineffective speakers whose delivery was overly dramatic and affected or stiff and mechanical. In contrast, effective delivery is **conversational**, meaning your audience perceives you as *talking with* them and *not performing in front of* or *reading to* them. The hallmark of a conversational style is spontaneity. **Spontaneity** is the ability to sound natural—as though you are really thinking about the ideas and getting them across to the audience—no matter how many times you've practiced.

The secret to developing a conversational style is to learn the *ideas* of your speech rather than trying to memorize every *word*. As you study your outline, you absorb these ideas, and as you rehearse out loud, you can focus on conveying them in a conversational way.

11-1b Animated

Have you ever been bored by a professor reading a well-structured lecture while mostly looking at the lecture notes rather than at the students and making few gestures besides turning the pages of those notes? Even a well-written speech given by an expert can bore an audience unless its delivery is **animated**, that is, lively and dynamic.

How can you be conversational and animated at the same time? The secret is to focus on conveying the passion you feel about your topic through your voice and body. When we are passionate about sharing something with someone, almost all of us become more animated in our delivery. Your goal is to duplicate this level of liveliness when delivering your speeches.

conversational style delivery that seems spontaneous, relaxed, and informal and allows the speaker to talk *with*, not *at*, an audience

spontaneity a naturalness of speech where what is said sounds as if the speaker is really thinking about the ideas *and* the audience as he or she speaks

animated delivery delivery that is lively, energetic, enthusiastic, and dynamic

voice the sound you produce using your vocal organs

pitch the highness or lowness of the sounds you produce

volume how loudly or softly you speak

rate the speed at which you talk

quality the tone, timbre, or sound of your voice

intelligible capable of being understood

The next two sections focus on how to use your voice and body to achieve effective conversational and animated delivery.

11-2 USE OF VOICE

Your **voice** is the sound you produce using your vocal organs (including your larynx, tongue, teeth, lips, etc.). How your voice sounds depends on its pitch, volume, rate, and quality. **Pitch** is the highness or lowness of the sounds you produce. **Volume** is how loudly or softly you speak. **Rate** is the speed at which you talk. **Quality** is the timbre that distinguishes your voice from others. Your goal in public speaking is to vary your pitch, volume, rate, and quality to achieve a conversational and animated style that is both intelligible and expressive.

11-2a Intelligibility

To be **intelligible** means to be understandable. All of us have experienced situations when we couldn't understand what was being said because the speaker was talking too softly or too quickly. If you practice your speech using appropriate vocal pitch, volume, rate, and vocal quality, you can improve the likelihood that you will be intelligible to your audience.

Most of us speak at a pitch that is appropriate for us and intelligible to listeners. However, some people naturally have voices that are higher or lower in register or become accustomed to talking in tones that are above or below their natural pitch. Speaking at an appropriate pitch is particularly important if your audience includes people who have

Ariwasabi/Shutterstock.com

When we are passionate about sharing something, we become more animated. The goal is to duplicate this energy when delivering a speech.

hearing loss because they may find it difficult to hear a pitch that is too high or too low. Intelligibility is also affected by how much a speaker fluctuates his or her pitch. In normal conversation, pitch fluctuates frequently, and perhaps even a bit more during a speech. Pitch that doesn't fluctuate often hinders intelligibility. For example, in English, a sentence that is meant to be a question is vocalized with rising pitch. If pitch doesn't rise at the end of a question, listeners may interpret the sentence as a statement instead.

Appropriate volume is the key to intelligibility. You must speak loudly enough, with or without a microphone, to be heard easily by audience members seated in the back of the room but not so loudly as to bring discomfort to listeners seated near the front. Similarly, when recording a speech to post online, you want to be heard easily but not sound as though you are shouting. You can also vary your volume to emphasize important information. For example, you may speak louder as you introduce each of your main points or when imploring listeners to take action.

The rate at which you speak can also influence intelligibility. Speaking too slowly gives your listeners time to let their minds wander after they've processed an idea. Speaking too quickly, especially when sharing complex ideas and arguments, may not give your listeners enough time to process the information completely. Because nervousness may cause you to speak more quickly than normal, you should monitor your speaking rate and intentionally slow down if necessary.

In addition to vocal characteristics, articulation, pronunciation, and accent problems can affect how intelligible your message is. **Articulation** is using the tongue, palate, teeth, jaw movement, and lips to shape vocalized sounds that combine to produce a word. Many of us suffer from minor articulation and **pronunciation** problems such as adding a sound where none appears ("athalete" for *athlete* or "warsh" for *wash*), leaving out a sound where one occurs ("libary" for *library*), transposing sounds ("revalent" for *relevant*), and distorting sounds ("truf" for *truth*). Exhibit 11.1 lists many common words that people are likely to mispronounce or misarticulate.

Accent is the inflection, tone, and speech habits typical of native speakers of a language. When you misarticulate or speak with a heavy accent during a conversation, your listeners can ask you to repeat yourself until they understand you. But in a speech setting, audience members are unlikely to interrupt to ask you to repeat something.

Accent can be a major concern for second language speakers or speakers from various regions of a country. Everyone speaks with some kind of accent, because

Exhibit 11.1
Commonly Mispronounced Words

Word	Incorrect	Correct
arctic	ar'-tic	arc'-tic
athlete	ath'-a-lete	ath'-lete
family	fam'-ly	fam'-a-ly
February	Feb'-yu-ary	Feb'-ru-ary
get	git	get
hundred	hun'-derd	hun'-dred
larynx	lar'-nix	ler'-inks
library	ly'-ber-y	ly'-brer-y
nuclear	nu'-kyu-ler	nu'-klee-er
particular	par-tik'-ler	par-tik'-yu-ler
picture	pitch'-er	pic'-ture
recognize	rek'-a-nize	rek'-ig-nize
relevant	rev'-e-lant	rel'-e-vant
theater	thee-ay'-ter	thee'-a-ter
truth	truf	truth
with	wit or wid	with

"accent" means any tone or inflection that differs from the way others speak. To clarify, natives of a particular city or region in the United States will speak with inflections and tones that they believe are "normal" spoken English—for instance, people from the Northeast who drop the *r* sound (saying "cah" for *car*) or people from the South who elongate their vowels and "drawl," or people from the upper Midwest who elongate certain vowels (e.g., "Min-ne-SOOO-ta"). But when they visit a different city or region, they are perceived as having an accent. If your accent is "thick" or very different from that of most of your audience, practice pronouncing key words so that you are easily understood, speak slowly to allow your audience members more time to process your message, and consider using visual aids to reinforce key terms, concepts, and important points. Alyssa from our opening scenario grew up in Arkansas before moving to Lexington to attend college at the University of Kentucky. Although her accent was similar to most

articulation using the tongue, palate, teeth, jaw movement, and lips to shape vocalized sounds that combine to produce a word

pronunciation the form and accent of various syllables of a word

accent the inflection, tone, and speech habits typical of native speakers of a language

of her classmates, she decided to ask Katie to listen to her speech and point out any words she might want to articulate differently or reinforce on visual aids.

11-2b Vocal Expression

Vocal expression is achieved by changing your pitch, volume, and rate; stressing certain words; and using pauses strategically. Doing so clarifies the emotional intent of your message and helps animate your delivery. Generally, speeding up your rate, raising your pitch, or increasing your volume reinforces emotions such as joy, enthusiasm, excitement, anticipation, and a sense of urgency or fear. Slowing down your rate, lowering your pitch, or decreasing your volume can communicate resolution, peacefulness, remorse, disgust, or sadness.

A total lack of vocal expressiveness produces a **monotone**—a voice in which the pitch, volume, and rate remain constant, with no word, idea, or sentence differing significantly in sound from any other. Although few people speak in a true monotone, many severely limit themselves by using only two or three pitch levels and a relatively unchanging volume and rate. An actual or near monotone not only lulls an audience to sleep but, more important, diminishes the chances of audience understanding. For instance, if the sentence "Congress should pass laws limiting the sale of pornography" is presented in a monotone, listeners will be uncertain whether the speaker is concerned with *who* should take action, *what* Congress *should do*, or *what* the laws should be. A common and easily identifiable type of vocal expression is **up-talk**, which is the tendency to end every sentence with a rising intonation. Using up-talk makes statements sound like a series of questions, and that pattern can compromise your credibility as a speaker.[3] Different from up-talk in quality but just as problematic for your credibility is **vocal fry**. This creaky vocal effect is produced by slowly fluttering the vocal cords, resulting in a popping or creaking sound at the bottom of the vocal register.[4] For example, Zooey Deschanel often speaks with a vocal fry.

In a study conducted at the University of Miami and Duke University,

Kim Kardashian is one of a number of young celebrities who utilize vocal fry.

researchers presented participants with two voice samples of the statement "Thank you for considering me for this opportunity." One sample contained the voice of a person using a normal vocal pattern, and the other used vocal fry. Participants were asked which sample belonged to the more educated, competent, trustworthy, and appealing job candidate. For each trait, participants preferred the normal vocalization. In fact, 86 percent of the female listeners and 83 percent of the male listeners said they would hire the person with the normal vocal expression over the person using vocal fry.[5] Minimizing up-talk and vocal fry will increase your credibility as a speaker.

Creating vocally expressive messages is a complex process. For example, Nick introduced his speech on legalizing marijuana as a painkiller this way:

Millions of Americans suffer needlessly each year. These people endure unbearable pain needlessly because, although our government is capable of helping them, it chooses to ignore their pain. Our government has no compassion, no empathy, no regard for human feeling. I'm here today to convince you to support my efforts toward legalizing marijuana as a painkiller for terminally ill patients.

vocal expression variety you create in your voice through changing pitch, volume, and rate, as well as stressing certain words and using pauses

monotone a voice in which the pitch, volume, and rate remain constant, with no word, idea, or sentence differing significantly in sound from any other

up-talk the tendency to end every sentence with a rising intonation

vocal fry a creaky vocal effect produced by slowly fluttering the vocal cords, resulting in a popping or creaking sound at the bottom of the vocal register

To reinforce the emotional elements of anger, disgust, and seriousness, Nick gradually slowed his rate, decreased his volume, and lowered his pitch as he emphasized, "Our government has no compassion, no empathy, no regard for human feeling."

He also used **stress**, an emphasis placed on certain words by speaking them more loudly than the rest of the sentence, to shape his meaning. Read the following sentence from Nick's speech:

Millions of Americans suffer needlessly each year.

What did Nick intend the focus of that sentence to be? Without hearing it spoken, it is difficult to say because its focus would change depending on which word Nick chose to stress. Read the sentence aloud several times. Each time, stress a different word, and listen to how your stress changes the meaning. If you stress *millions*, the emphasis is on the number of people affected. When you stress *Americans*, the fact that the problem is on a national scale is emphasized. When you stress *suffer*, notice how much more you feel the pain. When you stress *needlessly*, you can sense Nick's frustration with how unnecessary the suffering is. And when you stress *each year*, the ongoing nature of the unnecessary suffering becomes the focus. Thus, the words you stress in a sentence affect your meaning.

Pauses, moments of silence strategically placed to enhance meaning, can also mark important ideas. If you use one or more sentences in your speech to express an important idea, pause before each sentence to signal that something important is coming up, or pause afterward to allow the ideas to sink in. Pausing one or more times within a sentence can add further impact. Nick included several short pauses within and a long pause after his line, "Our government has no compassion *(pause)*, no empathy *(pause)*, no regard for human feeling" *(longer pause)*.

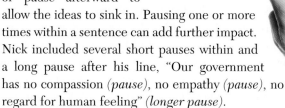
triocean/Shutterstock.com

Perhaps the most important pause you can make in your delivery is before you even begin speaking. Simon Simek is an ethnographer, and, at almost 23 million views, his speech on how great leaders inspire action is the third most popular TED talk of all time. He finds that talking right away can communicate insecurity, so he recommends walking to the stage, taking a deep breath, and pausing before starting the speech. "I know it sounds long and tedious and it feels excruciatingly awkward when you do it," Sinek says, "but it shows the audience you're totally confident and in charge of the situation."[6]

11-3 USE OF BODY

Because your audience can see as well as hear you, how you use your body also contributes to how conversational and animated your audience perceives you to be. Body language elements that affect delivery are appearance, posture, poise, eye contact, facial expressions, gestures, and movement.

11-3a Appearance

Some speakers think that what they wear doesn't or shouldn't affect the success of their speech. But your **appearance**, the way you look to others, does matter. Studies show that a neatly groomed and professional appearance sends important messages about a speaker's commitment to the topic and occasion, as well as the speaker's credibility (ethos).[7] Your appearance should complement your message, not detract from it. Three guidelines can help you decide how to dress for your speech.

1. **Consider the audience and occasion.** Dress a bit more formally than you expect members of your audience to dress. If you dress too formally, your audience is likely to perceive you as untrustworthy and insincere,[8] and if you dress too casually, the audience may view you as uncommitted to your topic or disrespectful of them or the occasion.[9]

2. **Consider your topic and purpose.** In general, the more serious your topic, the more formally you should dress. For example, if your topic is AIDS and you are trying to persuade your audience to be tested for HIV, you will want to look like someone who is an authority by dressing the part. But if your topic is spinning and you are trying to convince your audience they would enjoy taking a class at the new campus recreation center, you might dress more casually or even in sportswear.

3. **Avoid extremes.** Your attire shouldn't detract from your speech. Avoid gaudy jewelry, over- or undersized clothing, or sexually suggestive attire. Remember, you want your audience to focus on your message, so your appearance should be neutral, not distracting.

Alyssa would be delivering her speech to an audience of about 15 students who would be

stress emphasis placed on certain words by speaking them more loudly than the rest of the sentence

pauses moments of silence strategically placed to enhance meaning

appearance the way you look to others

present in the classroom and another 10–15 students who would watch online. Since most would probably be wearing anything from pajamas or sweatpants to jeans and T-shirts, she decided to dress a bit more formally in khaki pants and a navy blouse.

11-3b Posture

Posture is how you hold your body. When giving a speech, an upright stance and squared shoulders communicate a sense of confidence. Speakers who slouch may be perceived as lacking self-confidence and not caring about the topic, audience, and occasion.

11-3c Poise

Poise is a graceful and controlled use of the body that gives the impression that you are self-assured, calm, and dignified. Mannerisms that convey nervousness, such as swaying from side to side, drumming fingers on the lectern, taking off or putting on glasses, jiggling pocket change, smacking the tongue, or scratching the nose, hand, or arm should be noted during practice sessions and avoided during the speech.

11-3d Eye Contact

When giving a speech, effective **eye contact** involves looking at people in all parts of the room throughout the speech. As long as you are looking at someone (those in front of you, in the left rear of the room, in the right center of the room, etc.) and not at your notes or the ceiling, floor, or window, everyone in the audience will perceive you as having good eye contact with them. Generally, you should look at your audience at least 90 percent of the time, glancing at your notes only when you need a quick reference point. Maintaining eye contact is important for several reasons.

1. Maintaining eye contact helps audiences concentrate on the speech. If you do not look at audience members while you talk, they are unlikely to maintain eye contact with you. This break in mutual eye contact often decreases concentration on the message.

2. Maintaining eye contact bolsters ethos. Just as you are likely to be skeptical of people who do not look you in the

PathDoc./Shutterstock.com

In the U.S., speakers who fail to maintain eye contact with audiences are perceived as ill at ease and possibly insincere.

eye as they converse, audiences also will be skeptical of speakers who do not look at them. In the United States, eye contact is perceived as a sign of sincerity. Speakers who fail to maintain eye contact with audiences are perceived almost always as ill at ease and often as insincere or dishonest.[10] In some cultures across the world and some subcultures within the United States, however, direct eye contact may be perceived as disrespectful. For example, in the Japanese culture, using an averted gaze is generally considered a sign of deference and is considered more respectful than making direct eye contact. Similarly, research suggests that, in East Asian cultures, a person making direct eye contact is seen as less approachable and more unpleasant.[11] Knowing your audience becomes extremely important as you determine what kind of eye contact is most appropriate.

3. Maintaining eye contact helps you gauge audience reaction to your ideas. Because communication is two-way, audience members communicate with you while you are speaking to them. In conversation, the audience's response is likely to be both verbal and nonverbal. In public speaking, the audience's response is likely to be only through nonverbal cues. Bored audience members may yawn, look out the window, slouch in their chairs, and even sleep. Confused audience

posture the position or bearing of the body

poise the graceful and controlled use of the body that gives the impression of self-assurance, calm, and dignity

eye contact looking directly at the people to whom you are speaking

members may look puzzled by furrowing their brows or shaking their heads. Audience members who understand or agree with something you say may smile or nod their heads. By monitoring your audience's behavior, you can adjust by becoming more animated, offering additional examples, or moving more quickly through a point.

When speaking to large audiences of 100 or more people, you must create a *sense* of looking listeners in the eye even though you actually cannot. This process is called **audience contact**. You can create audience contact by mentally dividing your audience into small groups scattered around the room. Then, at random, talk for four to six seconds with each group. Perhaps start with a Z pattern, as shown in Exhibit 11.2. ❶ Talk with the group in the back left for a few seconds, then ❷ glance at people in the far right for a few seconds, and then ❸ move to a group in the middle, ❹ a group in the front left, and then ❺ a group in the front right, and so forth. Then perhaps reverse the order, starting in the back right. Eventually, you will find yourself going in a random pattern in which you look at all groups over a period of a few minutes. Such a pattern also helps you avoid spending a disproportionate amount of your time talking with those in front of you or in the center of the room.

11-3e Facial Expressions

Facial expressions are the eye and mouth movements that convey emotions. When you talk with friends, your facial expressions are naturally animated. Audiences expect your expressions to be similarly animated when giving a speech. Effective facial expressions convey **nonverbal immediacy** by communicating that you are personable and likeable. Speakers who do not vary their facial expressions during their speech and instead wear deadpan expressions, perpetual grins, or permanent scowls tend to be perceived as boring, insincere, or stern. Audiences respond positively to natural facial expressions that appear to spontaneously reflect what you're saying and how you feel about it. To assess whether you are using effective facial expressions, practice delivering your speech to

Exhibit 11.2
Maintaining Audience Contact

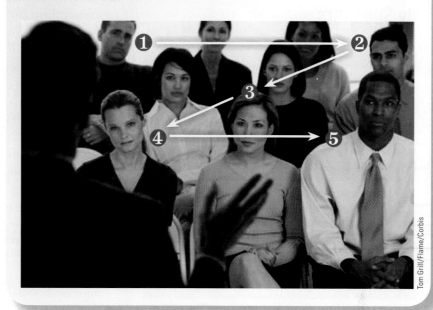

Tom Grill/Flame/Corbis

yourself in front of a mirror or record your rehearsal and evaluate your facial expressions as you watch it.

11-3f Gestures

Gestures are the movements of your hands, arms, and fingers. Effective gestures emphasize important points and ideas, refer to presentational aids, or clarify structure. For example, as Aaron began to speak about the advantages of smartphone apps, he said, "on one hand" and lifted his right hand face up. When he got to the disadvantages, he lifted his left hand face up as he said, "on the other hand." Some of the most common gestures used by speakers are shown in Exhibit 11.3.

Some people who are nervous when giving a speech clasp their hands behind their backs, bury them in their pockets, or grip the lectern. Unable to pry their hands free gracefully, they wiggle their elbows or appear stiff, which can distract audience members from the message. As with facial expressions, effective gestures must appear spontaneous and natural even though they are carefully planned and practiced. When you

audience contact creating a sense of looking listeners in the eye when speaking to large audiences

facial expression eye and mouth movements that convey emotions

nonverbal immediacy facial expressions that communicate that you are personable and likeable

gestures the movements of your hands, arms, and fingers

Exhibit 11.3
Common Hand Gestures Used by Speakers

The Supine Hand

- The supine hand with palm upward to express good humor, frankness, and generalization.

The Prone Hand

- The prone hand with palm downward to show superposition or the resting of one thing upon another.

The Vertical Hand

- The vertical hand with palm outward to indicate warding off, putting from, or a disagreeable thought.

The Clenched Hand

- The clenched hand to reinforce anger or defiance or to emphasize an important point.

The Index Finger

- The index finger to specialize or reinforce the first in a sequence of events.

only in **motivated movement**, movement with a specific purpose such as emphasizing an important idea, referencing a presentational aid, or clarifying macrostructure. For example, you might take a few steps to one side of the stage or the other each time you begin a new main point. Or, to emphasize a particular point, you might move closer to the audience. To create a feeling of intimacy before you tell a personal story, you might walk out from behind a lectern and sit down on a chair placed at the edge of the stage. To use motivated movement effectively, you need to practice when and how you will move until you can do so in a way that appears spontaneous and natural while remaining "open" to the audience (not turning your back to them).

Avoid unmotivated movement such as bobbing, weaving, shifting from foot to foot, or pacing from one side of the room to the other, because unplanned movements distract the audience from your message. Because many unplanned movements result from nervousness, you can minimize them by paying mindful attention to your body as you speak. At the beginning of your speech, consciously stand up straight on both feet. Whenever you find yourself fidgeting, readjust and position your body with your weight equally distributed on both feet.

During speech practice sessions, try various methods to monitor or alter your bodily action. Videotape provides an excellent means of monitoring your use of body to determine whether it is enhancing the message or distracting from it. You may also want to practice in front of a mirror to see how you look to others when you speak. (Although some speakers swear by this method, others find it a traumatic experience.) Another good method is to get a willing listener to critique your use of body and help you improve. Once you have identified the behavior you want to change, tell your helper what to look for. For instance, you might say, "Raise your hand every time I begin to rock back and forth." By getting specific feedback when the behavior occurs, you can make immediate adjustments.

11-4 DELIVERY METHODS

Speeches vary in the amount of content preparation and the amount of practice you do ahead of time. The three most common delivery methods are impromptu, scripted, and extemporaneous.

11-4a Impromptu Speeches

An **impromptu speech** is one that is delivered with only seconds or minutes of advance notice for preparation and is usually presented without referring to notes of any

practice and then deliver your speech, leave your hands free so that they will be available to gesture as you normally do.

11-3g Movement

movement changing the position or location of the entire body

motivated movement movement with a specific purpose

Movement refers to changing your body position. During your speech, it is important to engage

Lady Gaga Delivers

What can a musical performance teach about delivering a public speech? According to communications expert Stacey Shipman, quite a bit. After watching Lady Gaga's *Sound of Music* tribute performance at the 2015 Oscars, Shipman identified four lessons than can be applied to delivering a speech.[12]

1. **Bring heart and soul to practice and preparation.** Lady Gaga worked with her vocal coach every day for six months to ensure a confident performance.[13] By increasing your commitment to practice before giving a speech, your delivery will be more confident and your audience will sense that you are " all in."

2. **Deliver the unexpected.** Who would have guessed that Lady Gaga would appear in an elegant, full-length, white evening gown? The unexpected is the core of a memorable experience. Think about the unique perspectives you can bring to your audience to give them a memorable experience.

3. **Go big.** In her performance, Lady Gaga felt big. She took up space. As you prepare to deliver your speech, think of ways that you can use your full range of voice, passion, and motion to bring the audience into your presentation.

4. **Move with purpose.** Lady Gaga moved with purpose and control across the stage. Uncontrolled movements and frenetic gestures are distracting, so as you deliver your speech, use purposeful movements to keep your audience focused.

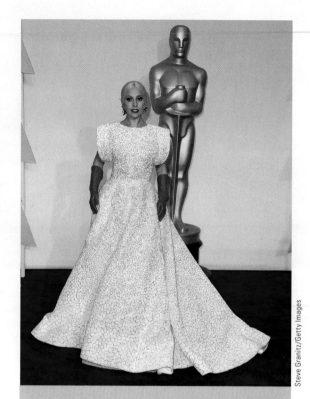

Steve Granitz/Getty Images

Speech lessons from Lady Gaga? Ryan Avery, an international speaker, says that he learned a lot about effective public speaking from pop superstar Lady Gaga. In his blog, averytoday.com, he writes that she had a strong opening, getting the crowd excited in the first 30 seconds, as well as a great closing, leaving people hugging and crying. Her beginning left people hungry for more, and her closing energized people.

kind. You may have already given an impromptu speech in class, so you know the kind of pressures and problems this type of speaking creates.

Because impromptu speakers must quickly gather their thoughts just before and while they speak, carefully organizing and developing ideas can be challenging. As a result, they may leave out important information or confuse audience members. Delivery can suffer as speakers use "ah," "um," "like," and "you know" to buy time as they scramble to collect their thoughts. That's why the more opportunities you have to use the impromptu method, the better you'll become at doing so.

Some of the most common situations you may find yourself in that will require you to speak using the impromptu method are during employment and performance review interviews, at business meetings, in class,

at social ceremonies, and to the media. In each situation, having practiced organizing ideas quickly and conveying them intelligibly and expressively will bolster your ethos and help you succeed in your professional and personal life.

You can improve your impromptu performances by practicing "mock" impromptu speeches. For example, if you are taking a class where the professor often calls on students to answer questions, you can prepare by anticipating the questions that might be asked and by practicing giving your answers out loud. Over time, you will become more adept at quickly organizing your ideas and "thinking on your feet."

impromptu speech a speech that is delivered with only seconds or minutes of advance notice for preparation and is usually presented without referring to notes of any kind

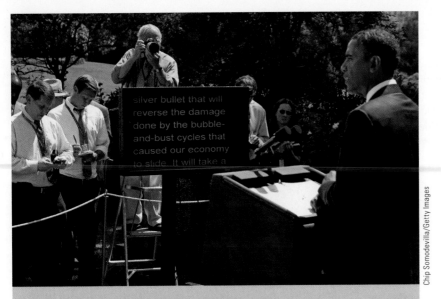

Given the high stakes involved in political discourse, it is important for political leaders to deliver precise and accurate messages. Teleprompters can help public figures ensure that they stay on point as well as manage the time allotted for the speech.

Because of the time and skill required to effectively prepare and deliver a scripted speech, they are usually reserved for important occasions that have important consequences. Political speeches, keynote addresses at conventions, commencement addresses, and CEO remarks at annual stockholder meetings are examples of occasions when a scripted speech might be appropriate and worth the extra effort.

11-4c Extemporaneous Speeches

Most speeches, whether in the workplace, in the community, or in class, are delivered extemporaneously. An **extemporaneous speech** is researched and planned ahead of time, but the exact wording is not scripted and will vary somewhat from presentation to presentation. When speaking extemporaneously, you refer to speaking notes reminding you of key ideas, structure, and delivery cues as you speak. Some speakers today use their computerized slideshows as speaking notes. If you choose to do so, however, be careful not to include too many words on any given slide, which will ultimately distract listeners from focusing on you as you speak.

Extemporaneous speeches are the easiest to give effectively. Unlike impromptu speeches, when speaking extemporaneously you are able to prepare your thoughts ahead of time and to have notes to prompt you. Unlike scripted speeches, extemporaneous speeches do not require as lengthy a preparation and practice process to be effective. In the next section, we describe how to rehearse successfully for an extemporaneous speech.

11-4b Scripted Speeches

At the other extreme, a **scripted speech** is one that is prepared by creating a complete written manuscript and delivered by reading from or memorizing a written copy. Obviously, effective scripted speeches take a great deal of time because both an outline and a word-for-word transcript must be prepared, practiced, and then delivered in a way that sounds both conversational and animated. When you memorize a scripted speech, you face the increased anxiety of forgetting your lines. When you read a scripted speech from a manuscript or teleprompter, you must become adept at looking at the script with your peripheral vision so that you don't appear to be reading and you must still sound conversational and animated. While politicians, talk show hosts, and television news anchors are usually good at achieving conversational style while reading from printed manuscripts and teleprompters, most speakers sound like they are reading and find it difficult to sound spontaneous and conversational.

scripted speech
a speech that is prepared by creating a complete written manuscript and delivered by reading a written copy or from memory

extemporaneous speech a speech that is researched and planned ahead of time, but the exact wording is not scripted and will vary from presentation to presentation

rehearsing practicing the presentation of your speech aloud

speaking notes
a keyword or phrase outline of your speech, plus hard-to-remember information such as quotations and statistics, as well as delivery cues designed to trigger memory

11-5 REHEARSAL

Rehearsing is the process of practicing your speech aloud. Inexperienced speakers often wrongly believe they are ready to present the speech once they have finished their outline. A speech that is not practiced out loud is likely to be far less effective than it would have been had you given yourself sufficient time to revise, evaluate, and mull over all aspects of the speech.[14] Exhibit 11.4 provides a useful timetable for preparing and practicing your speech. In the sections that follow, we describe how

Exhibit 11.4
Timetable for Preparing a Speech

1/18	Select topic, begin research
1/19	Continue research
1/20	Outline body of speech
1/21	Work on introduction and conclusion
1/22	Finish outline; find additional material if needed; have all presentation aids completed
1/23	First rehearsal session
1/24	Second rehearsal session
1/25	Give speech

to rehearse effectively by preparing speaking notes, handling presentational aids, and recording, analyzing, and refining delivery.

11-5a Speaking Notes

Prior to your first rehearsal session, prepare a draft of your speaking notes. **Speaking notes** are a keyword outline of your speech including hard-to-remember information and delivery cues. The best notes contain the fewest words possible written in lettering large enough to be seen instantly at a distance.

To develop your notes, begin by reducing your speech outline to an abbreviated outline of keywords and phrases. Then, if there are details you must cite exactly—such as a specific example, quotation, or set of statistics—add these in the appropriate places. You might also use separate "Quotation Cards" for direct quotations, which is what Alyssa did (see Exhibit 11.5). Next, indicate exactly where you plan to share presentational aids. Finally, incorporate delivery cues indicating where you want to use your voice and body to enhance intelligibility or expressiveness. For example, indicate where you want to pause, gesture, or make a motivated movement. Capitalize or underline words you want to stress. Use slash marks (///) to remind yourself to pause. Use an upward-pointing arrow to remind yourself to increase rate or volume.

For a three- to five-minute speech, you will need no more than three 3- by 5-inch note cards to record your speaking notes. For longer speeches, you might need one card for the introduction, one for each main point, and one for the conclusion. If your speech contains a particularly important and long quotation or a complicated set of statistics, you can record this information in detail on a separate card. Exhibit 11.5 shows some of Alyssa's speaking notes for her complete outline, which is shown at the end of this chapter. When you use a computerized slideshow, you can also use the "notes" feature for your speaking notes.

Use your notes during practice sessions just as you will when you actually give the speech. If you will use a lectern, set the notes on the speaker's stand or, alternatively, hold them in one hand and refer to them only when needed. How important is it to construct good speaking notes? Speakers often find that the act of making a note card is so effective in helping cement ideas in the mind that during practice, or later during the speech itself, they rarely use the notes at all.

11-5b Presentational Aids

Some speakers think that once they have prepared good presentational aids, they will have no trouble using them in the speech. However, many speeches with good aids have become a shambles because the aids were not well handled. You can avoid problems by following these guidelines.

1. **Carefully plan when to use the presentational aids.** Indicate in your speaking notes/outline exactly when you will reveal and conceal each presentational aid. Practice introducing and using your aids until you can do so comfortably and smoothly.

2. **Consider audience needs carefully.** As you practice, eliminate any presentational aid that does not contribute directly to the audience's attention to, understanding of, or retention of the key ideas in your speech.

3. **Position presentational aids and equipment before beginning your speech.** Make sure your aids and equipment are where you want them and that everything is ready and in working order. Test electronic equipment to make sure everything from visual displays to sound to hyperlinks work and are cued correctly.

4. **Share a presentational aid only when talking about it.** Because presentational aids will draw audience attention, practice sharing them only when you are talking about them and then concealing them when they are no longer the focus of attention. Because a single presentational aid may contain several bits of information, practice exposing only the portion you are currently discussing. On computerized slideshows, you can do so by using the "custom animation" feature to allow only one item to appear at a time, by striking the "B" key for a black screen when you aren't directly referencing the aid, and by inserting blank slides where your ideas are not being supplemented by something on the slideshow.

Exhibit 11.5
Sample Note Cards

NOTE CARD 1: Introduction
PLANT FEET . . . DIRECT EYE CONTACT . . . POISE/ETHOS! ☺

I. Famous Indian peace activist Mahatma Gandhi: "We must become the change we seek in the world."

   Tall order . . . We can make a difference right here in Lexington, KY

II. Think for a moment . . . child/homework, neighbor/leaves, stranger/ groceries . . . It's easy for college students like us to get involved.

III. I volunteer at LRM and reaped benefits (Slide 1)

IV. Benefits volunteering . . .

   a. get acquainted

   b. responsibility & privilege

   c. résumé-building skills

BLANK SLIDE, WALK RIGHT, EYE C.: Let's begin by explaining the ways volunteering can help us connect to our local community.

NOTE CARD 2: Body
I. GREAT WAY to become acquainted ☺ ☺

   LR: Comforts of home . . . unfamiliar city . . . volunteering . . . easy and quick way . . .

   Natalie Cunningham-May 2nd CQ. CARD #1)

   Social issues and conditions

   Acc to the Norris Center for Student Involvement at Northwestern University . . .

   My experience at LRM (SLIDES 2 & 3)

BLANK SLIDE, WALK LEFT, EYE C.: Not only is volunteering important . . . familiar and social issues . . . FRANKLY . . . dem society . . .

II. Civic responsibility AND privilege . . . . LR: We benefit college . . . give back.

   More Americans are taking this responsibility seriously. 2012 US Bureau of Labor Statistics: 64.3 million volunteers Sept 2010–Sept 2011. (SLIDES 4 & 5)

   Also a privilege . . . make a difference . . . feel good . . . self-actualization (SLIDE #6)

Quotation Card

#1: "My first group of students needed rides to all the various volunteer sites b/c they had no idea where things were in the city. It was really easy for the students who lived on campus to remain ignorant of their city, but while volunteering they become acquainted with Lexington and the important issues going on here."

#2: "Employers rely on credentials to certify that a young person will become a valuable employee. Credentials that document the experiences and employability skills, knowledge, and attitude."

#3: "I learned that there was a lot more that went into preparing food for the homeless than I ever thought possible. It was neat to be a part of that process."

Make sure all of your audience can see your presentational aids.

5. Display presentational aids so that everyone in the audience can see and hear them. It's frustrating not to be able to see or hear an aid. If possible, practice in the space where you will give your speech so you can adjust equipment accordingly. If you cannot practice in the space ahead of time, then arrive early enough on the day of the presentation to practice quickly with the equipment you will use.

6. Reference the presentational aid during the speech. Because you already know what you want your audience to see in a visual aid, tell your audience what to look for, explain the various elements in it, and interpret figures, symbols, and percentages. For an audio or audiovisual aid, point out what you want your audience to listen for before you play the excerpt. When showing a visual or audiovisual aid, use the "turn-touch-talk" technique.

- When you display the visual, walk to the screen—that's where everyone will look anyway. Slightly turn to the visual and touch it—that is, point to it with an arm gesture or a pointer. Then, with your back to the screen and your body still facing the audience at a slight 45-degree angle, talk to your audience about it.

- When you finish making your comments about the visual, return to the lectern or your speaking position and conceal the aid.

7. Talk to your audience, not to the presentational aid. Although you will want to acknowledge the presentational aid by looking at it occasionally, it is important to maintain eye contact with your audience as much as possible. As you practice, resist the urge to stare at or read from your presentational aid.

8. Resist the temptation to pass objects through the audience. People look at, read, handle, and think about whatever they hold in their hands. While they are so occupied, they are not likely to be listening to you. If you have handouts or objects, distribute them after the speech rather than during it.

11-5c Practice Rounds

As with any other activity, effective speech delivery requires practice. Each practice round should consist of (a) practicing aloud, (b) analyzing and making adjustments, and (c) practicing aloud again. The more you practice, the better your speech will be. During each practice round, evaluate your language choices, as well as your use of voice, body, and presentational aids. You should do as many practice rounds as needed to deliver a speech that is conversational and animated. For most speakers, we suggest a minimum of four practice rounds.

First Practice

1. Record (audio and video) your practice session so you can analyze it and make improvements. You may also want to have a friend sit in on your practice and offer suggestions afterward.

2. Read through your complete sentence outline once or twice to refresh your memory. Then put the outline out of sight and practice your speech using your speaking notes.

3. Make the practice as similar to the speech situation as possible, including using the presentational aids you've prepared. Stand up and face your imaginary audience. Pretend the chairs, lamps, books, and other objects in the room are people.

4. Write down the time that you begin or set a digital timer on your smartphone or computer.

5. Begin speaking. Regardless of what happens, keep going until you have presented your entire speech. If you

Having been lambasted for delivering a lousy acceptance speech at the Golden Globes, Anne Hathaway committed to being better prepared for the Academy Awards. She practiced an Oscar acceptance speech many, many times with the goal of being perceived as more likeable. When she won an Oscar for her best-supporting actress role in *Les Misérables*, she was prepared, and her delivery hit the mark.[15]

goof, make a repair and keep going as if you were actually delivering the speech to an audience.

6. Write down the time you finish or stop the timer. Compute the length.

Analysis

Watch and listen to your recorded performance while reviewing your complete outline. How did it go? Did you leave out any key ideas? Did you talk too long on any one point and not long enough on another? Did you clarify each of your points? Did you adapt to your anticipated audience? Were your notes effective? How well did you do with your presentational aids? If a friend sat in, ask him or her for input as well. Make any necessary changes before your second practice.

Second Practice

Immediately repeat the six steps listed for the first practice. By practicing a second time right after your analysis,

you are more likely to make the kind of adjustments that begin to improve the speech.

Additional Practice Rounds

After you have completed one full practice round, put the speech away for a while. Although you should practice the speech at least a couple more times, you will not benefit from cramming all the practices into one long rehearsal time. You may find that a final practice right before you go to bed will be very helpful; while you are sleeping, your subconscious will continue to work on the speech. As a result, you are likely to find significant improvement in delivery when you practice again the next day.

11-6 ADAPTING WHILE DELIVERING THE SPEECH

Even when you've practiced your speech to the point that you know it inside and out, you must be prepared to adapt to your audience and possibly change course a bit as you give your speech. Remember that your primary goal is to generate shared understanding, so pay attention to the audience's feedback as you speak and adjust accordingly. Here are six tips to guide you.

1. Be aware of and respond to audience feedback. As you make eye contact with members of your audience, notice how they react to what you say. For instance, if you see quizzical looks on the faces of several listeners, you may need to explain a particular point in a different way. On the other hand, if you see listeners nodding impatiently, you don't need to belabor your point and can move on. If many audience members look bored, try to rekindle their interest by conveying more enthusiasm in your voice and body.

2. Be prepared to use alternative developmental material. Your ability to adjust to your audience's needs depends on how much additional alternative information you have to share. If you have prepared only one example, you wouldn't be ready if your audience is confused and needs another. If you have prepared only one definition for a term, you may be unable to rephrase it if needed. As you prepare, try to anticipate where your audience may be confused or already knowledgeable and practice adding or dropping examples and other details.

3. Correct yourself when you misspeak. Every speaker makes mistakes. They stumble over words, mispronounce terms, forget information, and mishandle

ACTION STEP ACTIVITY

Practice Oral Language and Delivery Style

The goal of this activity is to rehearse your speech by practicing it, analyzing and refining it, and then practicing it again.

1. After you have prepared your speaking notes, find a place where you can be alone (or with a friend) to practice your speech. Follow the six points of the first practice.

2. Watch and listen to the recording. Review your outline as you do so and then complete a speech evaluation checklist to see how well you delivered your speech. (You can find the Speech Evaluation Checklist: General Criteria in Chapter 1, a more detailed checklist in this chapter, and checklists for informative and persuasive speeches in later chapters.)

List three specific changes you will make in your next practice.

One: _____

Two: _____

Three: _____

3. Go through the six practice steps again. Then assess: Did you achieve the goals you set for the second practice?

Reevaluate the speech using the checklist and do additional practice rounds until you are satisfied with your presentation.

---

presentational aids. So expect that you will make a few mistakes. It's normal. If you stumble over a phrase or mispronounce a word, correct yourself and move on. Don't make a big deal of it by laughing, rolling your eyes, or in other ways drawing unnecessary attention to it. If you suddenly remember that you forgot to provide some information, consider how important it is for your audience to have that information. If what you forgot to say will make it difficult for your audience to understand a point that comes later, figure out how and when to provide the information later in your speech. Usually, however, information we forgot to share is not critical to the audience's understanding and it's better to leave it out and move on.

4. Adapt to unexpected events. Maintain your composure if something unexpected happens, such as a cell phone ringing or someone entering the room while you're speaking. Simply pause until the disruption ceases and then move on. If the disruption causes you to lose your train of thought or has distracted the audience, take a deep breath, look at your speaking notes, and continue your speech at a point slightly before the interruption occurred. This will allow both you and your audience to refocus on your speech. You might acknowledge that you are backtracking by saying something like, "Let's back up a bit and remember where we were—."

5. Adapt to unexpected audience reactions. Sometimes, you'll encounter listeners who disagree strongly with your message. They might show their disagreement by being inattentive, heckling you, or rolling their eyes when you try to make eye contact with them. If these behaviors are limited to one or two members of your audience, ignore them and focus on the rest of your listeners. If, however, the majority of your audience is hostile to what you are saying, try to anticipate and address their concerns. You might begin by acknowledging their feedback and then trying to persuade them to suspend their judgment while they listen. For example, you could say something like, "I can see that most of you don't agree with my first point. But let me ask you to put aside your initial reaction and think along with me on this next point. Even if we end up disagreeing, at least you will understand my position."

6. Handle questions respectfully. It is rare for audience members to interrupt speakers with questions during a speech. But if you are interrupted, be prepared to respond respectfully. If the question is directly related to understanding the point you are making, answer it immediately. If not, acknowledge the question, indicate that you will answer it later, and then remember to do so. In most professional settings, you will be expected to answer questions when you've finished your speech. Some people will ask you to clarify information. Some will ask you for an opinion or to draw conclusions beyond what you have said.

Whenever you answer a question, be honest about what you know and don't know. If an audience member asks a question you don't know the answer to, admit it by saying something like, "That's an excellent question. I'm not sure of the answer, but I would be happy to follow up on it later if you're interested." Then move on to the next question. If someone asks you to state an opinion about a matter you haven't thought much about, it's okay to say, "You know, I don't think I have given that enough thought to have a valid opinion."

Be sure to monitor how much time you have to answer questions. When the time is nearly up, mention that you'll entertain one more question so as to warn listeners that the question-and-answer period is almost over. You might also suggest that you'll be happy to talk more with individuals one on one later—this provides your more reserved listeners an opportunity to follow up with you.

11-7 ADAPTING YOUR SPEECH FOR VIRTUAL AUDIENCES

When Plato, Aristotle, and Cicero engaged in public speaking thousands of years ago, the communication event occurred in real time with both the speaker and the audience physically present. Thanks to technology, however, public speeches today may be delivered in both face-to-face and virtual environments. In the opening scenario, for example, Alyssa and Katie would be delivering their speeches in a classroom with some audience members present while simultaneously streaming to several classmates who would be watching online via their computers. Their speeches would also be uploaded to the class Web site so they could watch, critique, and prepare reflective written assessments of themselves later.

Technology makes it possible to speak publicly to multiple audiences across the country and around the world. For example, Alyssa planned to post her speech to YouTube and link to it from her Facebook and Twitter accounts for extra credit. In

doing so, she hoped to reach many more college students with her volunteerism and civic engagement speech than just those sitting in the classroom. The bottom line is this: Although public speaking certainly still occurs in traditional face-to-face settings, it is no longer limited by place and time—far from it!

President Franklin Delano Roosevelt (FDR) is credited as being one of the first public figures to capitalize on the benefits of electronic media to break through the *place* limitation to reach a wider audience. Throughout his presidency in the 1930s and 1940s, FDR delivered so-called *fireside chats*, regular radio addresses about issues facing the country.[16] These speeches could be heard by anyone who chose to tune in. U.S. presidents have been offering regular addresses ever since! In fact, today President Obama posts weekly messages on YouTube and the White House Web site.[17]

Perhaps one of the most significant examples of technology overcoming the limitation of *time* comes from Martin Luther King, Jr. Over 200,000 people attended the March on Washington for Jobs and Freedom rally on August 28, 1963, to hear Dr. King's famous "I Have a Dream" speech live and in person. But more than 50 years later, we can join the 200,000 who made up that first audience to hear him deliver his powerful oration by clicking on any number of Web sites where it is archived. In fact, a quick Google search for the speech yields more than 37,400,000 hits.

To reach multiple audiences successfully, we must consider not just those who are informed about the topic, but also those who may not be informed, may

Always assume your speech is being recorded and shared.

Faraways/Shutterstock.com

be apathetic, and may even be hostile toward it. Those who have analyzed Dr. King's speech, for instance, claim he was successful in part because he used a preaching style characteristic of African-American faith communities while also transcending it to reach broader audiences. To clarify, he began by addressing the grievances of black Americans and then transitioned to focus more broadly on the bedrock of American values. Linking civil rights to the American Dream appealed not only to the audience present on the Washington Mall, but also to the millions of uncommitted Americans who watched the speech on TV.[18] In doing so, it has transcended time. Today, his speech continues to resonate as representing core American values and the American Dream.

With the proliferation of Internet accessibility comes both additional opportunities and challenges. For example, because speeches today may be easily uploaded to Web sites like YouTube with or without our permission and then quickly go viral, we also must always be cognizant of possible audiences we never intended to target. Failing to do so could result in devastating consequences. In 2015, for instance, U.S. Representative Loretta Sanchez discovered this only three days into running for the U.S. Senate seat being vacated by retiring California Senator Barbara Boxer. In remarks she made to an audience of delegates at the California Democratic convention, Sanchez described her surprise at meeting an Indian American supporter for the first time by saying, "I am going to his office, thinking that I am going to meet with a...." Then, she paused to pat her hand over her mouth while making a whooping gesture before continuing, "Right?... Because he said 'Indian American.'" Sanchez was caught on cellphone videos making the war-cry gesture, and the videos were soon posted to the Web sites of several local, regional, and national news outlets, from the Los Angeles NBC affiliate to the New York Daily News to CNN.[19]

TECH TALK

Quick Tips for Public Speaking in Cyberspace

Using tools such as Skype or Google Hangouts, it's possible to deliver a speech or presentation to an audience halfway across the world. While public speaking in cyberspace is conducted with many of the same guidelines as its real-world counterpart, the separation of speaker and audience can present some unique challenges.

A good rule of thumb for online presentations is to use more visuals than you might normally prepare for an in-person speech. Especially in cases where the audience cannot see you (a webinar, for example), additional visual cues will help focus their attention and keep them engaged.

Before the presentation, shut off your phone and any alarms, and consider keeping any pets in another room. Although a cameo from your dog or cat might be endearing, it will almost certainly distract from the point—and could throw you *and* the audience off track.

If your audience will be able to see you, wear clothing with a neutral or soft color to avoid "ghosting" or "bleeding," which may occur with bright colors. During the presentation, look into the camera and try to avoid fidgeting.

When speaking to an audience across the Web, audio can also be an issue. In person, a speaker will likely either rely on his or her own enunciation or a professional PA and microphone. Over the web, however, you may be stuck using a built-in computer mic. Wearing headphones during the presentation can prevent the mic from picking up any audience responses and creating an otherworldly echo.

Vocal delivery is particularly important when presenting online. Low-quality computer mics can amplify the effects of poor diction, so do your best to speak

Photographee.eu/Shutterstock.com

clearly. Furthermore, try to use short pauses rather than long, dramatic ones that might prompt the audience to think the sound has cut out.

To keep your cyber audience focused, plan to engage them more frequently than you would in person. Asking a direct question every 5 to 10 minutes can keep your audience alert (and less likely to multitask). It can also help you gauge their interest level if you are unable to see their reactions.

Depending on your comfort level and familiarity with the technology, giving a presentation online might seem more or less intimidating than an in-person speech, but it doesn't have to be an alien experience. Exude confidence while treating the audience with the same respect you would in a crowded auditorium, and you should have no problem speaking in the digital world.[20]

Speech Delivery
Evaluation Checklist

Check items that were accomplished effectively.

Content

_____ **1.** Was the goal of the speech clear?

_____ **2.** Did the speaker offer breadth and depth to support each main point?

_____ **3.** Did the speaker use high-quality information and sources?

_____ **4.** Did the speaker use a variety of kinds of developmental material?

_____ **5.** Were presentational aids appropriate?

_____ **6.** Did the speaker establish common ground and adapt the content to the audience with listener-relevance links?

Macrostructure

_____ **1.** Did the introduction gain attention, establish credibility and listener relevance, as well as state the goal of the speech and preview the main points?

_____ **2.** Were the main points clear, parallel, and meaningful complete sentences?

_____ **3.** Did section transitions lead smoothly from one point to another?

_____ **4.** Did the conclusion tie the speech together by summarizing the main goal and points and offering a clincher?

Microstructure

_____ **1.** Was the language appropriate?   _____ **3.** Was the language clear?

_____ **2.** Was the language accurate?   _____ **4.** Was the language vivid?

Delivery

_____ **1.** Did the speaker appear and sound conversational?

_____ **2.** Did the speaker appear and sound animated?

_____ **3.** Was the speaker intelligible?

_____ **4.** Was the speaker vocally expressive?

_____ **5.** Was the speaker's appearance and attire appropriate?

_____ **6.** Did the speaker use effective eye/audience contact throughout the speech?

_____ **7.** Did the speaker use appropriate facial expressions?

_____ **8.** Did the speaker have good posture that communicated poise and confidence?

_____ **9.** Were the speaker's gestures and movement appropriate?

_____ **10.** Did the speaker conceal and reveal the presentational aids effectively?

_____ **11.** Did the speaker reference the presentational aids effectively while discussing them?

Based on these criteria, evaluate the speech (check one):

■ **excellent**   ■ **good**   ■ **satisfactory**   ■ **fair**   ■ **poor**

Obviously, we ought to consider how we might adapt our delivery for virtual audiences. Although we are only beginning to discover the ways in which we should do so, here are a few guidelines to consider when adapting your speeches for virtual audiences.

1. Adapt your speech to address multiple audiences. Assume that any speech you give may be recorded and made available to those who are not in your immediate audience. Always consider how you might adapt not only your delivery, but also your content and structure, to accurately and respectfully address uninformed, apathetic, and oppositional audiences who may view your speech virtually.

2. Adapt your speech to account for unintended audiences. Similarly, don't say anything to one specific audience that you would not want broadcasted to a wider audience. With just a few clicks of a smartphone or iPad, an audience member can record a video and post it online. So make sure your speech content, humorous anecdotes, use of voice, and use of body are accurate and respectful.

3. Choose presentational aids carefully. Make sure the visuals and audiovisuals you use can be easily viewed and heard in an online format. Also, be sure to explain them so that those who only have audio access or who view them on a small smartphone screen can understand the information on them.

4. Become proficient with technology. Technological proficiency is no longer considered a value-added skill; it is expected of professionals today. Regularly consult with communication technology experts at your university or place of business to learn how to use and how to stay up-to-date on available technologies. Because technology continues to expand at astonishing rates, you can expect to need regular, ongoing training to keep pace with it.

5. Employ the fundamentals of effective public speaking. Although it might seem to go without saying, be sure to adhere to the strategies of effective public speaking even when delivering your speech online. The steps we have discussed regarding topic selection and development, organization, language, and delivery remain fundamental to effective speechmaking for face-to-face and virtual audiences. Treat the camera as a person. As you do so, use your voice and body in ways that are intelligible, conversational, animated, and poised just as you would if the camera were someone in the room with you.

Sample Informative Speech with Presentational Aids:

College Student Volunteering and Civic Engagement

This speech is by Alyssa Grace Millner, University of Kentucky [20]

This section presents a sample informative speech with presentational aids, given by a student and including an adaptation plan, an outline, and a transcript.

1. Read the speech adaptation plan, outline, and transcript of a speech given by Alyssa Grace Millner.

2. Identify some of the strengths of Alyssa's speech by preparing an evaluation checklist and an analysis. Then compare your answers with those of the authors.

Adaptation Plan

1. **Key aspects of audience:** The majority of listeners know what volunteering is in a general sense, but they probably don't know the ways it can benefit them as college students.

2. **Establishing and maintaining common ground:** I'll use personal pronouns throughout the speech, as well as specific examples about volunteering from volunteers right here in Lexington.

3. **Building and maintaining interest:** I'll insert listener-relevance links in the introduction and for each main point that point out how volunteering is directly related to improving the lives of college students in some way.

4. **Building credibility:** I will point out right away that I volunteer and that I've done a good deal of research on it. I'll insert examples of my own experiences throughout the speech, as well as cite credible research to support my claims.

5. **Audience attitudes:** Some may be indifferent, but according to the research I've found, most will probably be open to the idea of volunteering. They might not know how easy it can be to get started, though.

6. **Adapting to audiences from different cultures and language communities:** Although most of my classmates are U.S. citizens, there are a couple of international students in the class. So when I talk about volunteering being a civic responsibility, I'll make sure to talk about how all of us are reaping the benefits of a U.S. education; that's why we are all responsible for giving back in some way. I'll talk about it as an ethical responsibility.

7. **Use presentational aids:** I will show photographs of people engaged in volunteer work throughout the speech. I think this will make my ideas very concrete for the audience and will enhance pathos (emotional appeal). I'll also show some graphs about homelessness in Lexington and the percentage of college students who believe in volunteering. I think these will bolster my ethos as the audience will see I've done research. Finally, I'll show my résumé with elements highlighted that I've been able to include because I've volunteered. I think this will drive home my point about the future benefits for college students who volunteer while still in school.

Informative Speech Outline
College Student Volunteering and Civic Engagement

General Goal:
To inform my audience.

Specific Goal:
I want my audience to realize the benefits of volunteering in Lexington while we are still students at the University of Kentucky.

Introduction

I. The famous Indian peace activist and spiritual leader Mahatma Gandhi is known for saying "We must become the change we seek in the world." That sounds at first like an awfully tall order, but today I'd like to show you how each of us can do just that and make a difference right here in Lexington, Kentucky.

Attention getter

II. Think for a moment of a time in your life when you did something kind for someone else. Maybe you helped a child do homework, or a neighbor rake leaves, or even a stranger get groceries from the store to

Listener-relevance link

the car. Do you remember how that made you feel? Well, that feeling can be a normal part of your week when you choose to be a volunteer. And for college students like us, it's easy to get involved as volunteers in our local community.

III. Personally, I volunteer at the Lexington Rescue Mission and have reaped many benefits by doing so. (*Show slide 1: picture of me volunteering at the Mission.*) I've also done extensive research on volunteering and civic engagement.

Speaker credibility

IV. So, let's spend the next few minutes discussing the benefits volunteering can have for us as college students by focusing on how volunteering helps us get acquainted with the local community, why civic engagement is the responsibility of every one of us, and what volunteering can do to teach us new skills and build our résumés.

Thesis statement with main point preview

Transition

Let's begin by explaining the ways volunteering can connect each of us to our local community.

Body

I. Volunteering is a great way to become acquainted with a community beyond the university campus.

Most college students move away from the comforts of home to a new and unfamiliar city. Not knowing what there is to do or even how to get around can be overwhelming and isolating. Volunteering is an easy way to quickly become familiar with and begin to feel a part of this new city in addition to the campus community.

Listener-relevance link

    A. Volunteering allows you to learn your way around town.

        1. In an interview I had with Natalie Cunningham, the volunteer coordinator of the Lexington Rescue Mission, she said, "I've been working with students for several years now. While every group is different, one lingering trend is each group's unawareness of their city. It is easy for the students who live on campus to stay in their 'on-campus bubble.' Volunteering allows students to become acquainted with Lexington and the important issues facing their new home." (personal communication, January 2, 2013).

        2. It seems like a silly thing, but knowing your way around town starts to make any city feel like home. Volunteering gets you out into the local area and helps you begin to get acquainted with new people and places.

    B. Volunteering can also open your eyes to local social issues and conditions.

        1. Many nonprofit organizations and volunteer-centered groups strive to raise awareness of important social issues by getting willing volunteers involved in the local community and issues impacting the area, things like hunger and homelessness (Norris Center, 2013).

        2. The second time I showed up to volunteer at the Lexington Rescue Mission, I served food to the homeless. (*Show slide 2: group of volunteers in the kitchen.*)

           a. I served soup and hung out with other volunteers and local homeless people. One of the "veteran" volunteers explained to me that Lexington has approximately 3,000 homeless people. (*Show slide 3: homelessness statistics in Lexington.*)

           b. I was shocked to learn that we had such a large number of men, women, and children without a regular place to sleep. I wouldn't have known about this problem or the organizations working to end homelessness if I hadn't been a volunteer.

Transition

Not only is volunteering important because it helps us become familiar with a town and its social issues; frankly, as members of a democratic society, volunteering is our civic responsibility.

II. Giving back to the community through volunteer work is our civic responsibility and a privilege. Each of us in this room—whether as U.S. citizens or international students—are reaping the benefits of earning college degrees in this democratic society. With that benefit comes the responsibility and privilege of giving back. **Listener-relevance link**

A. Volunteering is our civic responsibility.

1. Wilson and Musick (1997) explain that, without active participation in the local community, civil society becomes deprived.

2. Many Americans take this responsibility seriously. In fact, the U.S. Bureau of Labor Statistics (2012) reports, "About 64.3 million people volunteered through or for an organization at least once between September 2010 and September 2011." I agree that it's important to volunteer. Giving back by volunteering helps a community in so many ways. (*Show slides 4 and 5: volunteers sorting clothes at the mission and then volunteers playing cards with people served at the shelter.*)

B. Volunteering is also a privilege. Making a difference by volunteering ends up making us feel better about ourselves and our role in the world around us.

1. In fact, college students aged 16 to 24 represent the largest growth in percentages of volunteers across the country (Corporation for National and Community Service, 2006). (*Show slide 6: bar graph of growth.*)

2. A study of first-year college students done by the Higher Education Research Institute published in January 2009 revealed that 69.7 percent of students believe it is *essential or very important* to volunteer in order to help people in need (Pryor et al., 2009).

Transition

Certainly, the privilege of giving back as volunteers is our civic responsibility and helps our local community, but we can also reap valuable résumé-building life skills by volunteering.

III. Volunteering helps teach us new skills. **Listener-relevance link**

These new skills and talents can actually make us more marketable for better jobs once we graduate.

A. Being a consistent volunteer at a nonprofit organization while attending college can strengthen your résumé.

1. "Employers rely on credentials to certify that a young person will become a valuable employee. Credentials that document the experiences and employability skills, knowledge, and attitude" (Charner, 1988, p. 30).

2. Laura Hatfield, director of the Center for Community Outreach at the University of Kentucky, points out that volunteers can include leadership, teamwork, and listening skills on their résumé because they can document the experiences where they had to use them effectively in the real world.

3. Andrea Stockelman, another volunteer at the Lexington Rescue Mission, explained some of the new skills she picked up with volunteering. She said, "I learned that there was a lot more that went into preparing food for the homeless than I ever thought possible. It was neat to be a part of that process" (personal communication, April 28, 2010). (*Show slide 7: photo of Andrea preparing food.*)

B. Volunteering at the Lexington Rescue Mission taught me new skills that bolstered my résumé. (*Show slide 8 résumé with skills highlighted.*)

1. I learned to coordinate the schedules of other volunteers.

2. I also practiced important people skills such as teamwork, empathy, conflict management, and listening.

Conclusion

I. Today we've discussed why volunteering is beneficial to college students by focusing on how volunteering can connect us quickly and easily to our local community, why it's both our responsibility and a privilege to do so, and how volunteering will benefit us after we graduate.

Thesis restatement with main point summary

II. So, I'm hoping the next time you recall a time you really enjoyed making a difference by helping someone, that memory won't come from the distant past. Instead, I hope you'll be thinking about how you are being the change you seek in the world by volunteering right here in Lexington right now.

Clincher

References

Charner, I. (1988). Employability credentials: A key to successful youth transition to work. *Journal of Career Development, 15*(1), 30–40.

Corporation for National and Community Service. (2006). *College students helping America*. Washington, DC: Author.

Norris Center. (2013, January 2). *Center for student involvement: Volunteer opportunities*. Northwestern University. Retrieved from http://www.norris.northwestern.edu/csi/community/volunteer-opportunities/

Pryor, J. H., Hurtado, S., DeAngelo, L., Sharkness, J., Romero, L., Korn, W. S., & Tran, S. (2009). *The American freshman: National norms for fall 2008*. Los Angeles, CA: Higher Education Research Institute.

United States Bureau of Labor Statistics. (2012, February 22). *Economic news release: Volunteering in the United States, 2011*. Retrieved from http://www.bls.gov/news.release/volun.nr0.htm

Wilson, J., & Musick, M. A. (1997). Work and volunteering: The long arm of the job. *Social Forces, 76*(1), 251–272.

Speech and Analysis

Speech

The famous Indian peace activist and spiritual leader Mahatma Gandhi is known for saying "We must become the change we seek in the world." That sounds at first like an awfully tall order, but today I'd like to show you how each of us can do just that and make a difference right here in Lexington, Kentucky. Think for a moment of a time in your life when you did something kind for someone else. Maybe you helped a child do homework, or a neighbor rake leaves, or even a stranger get groceries from the store to the car. Do you remember how that made you feel? Well, that feeling can be a normal part of your week when you choose to be a volunteer. And for college students like us, it's easy to get involved as volunteers in our local community. Personally, I volunteer at the Lexington Rescue Mission and have reaped many benefits by doing so. (*Show slide 1: picture of me volunteering at the Mission.*) I've also done extensive research on volunteering and civic engagement. So, let's spend the next few minutes discussing the benefits volunteering can have for us as college students by focusing on how volunteering helps us get acquainted with the local community, why civic engagement is the responsibility of every citizen, and what volunteering can do to teach us new skills and build our résumés. Let's begin by explaining the ways volunteering can connect each of us to our local community.

Volunteering is a great way to become acquainted with a community beyond the university campus. Most college students move away from the comforts of home to a new and unfamiliar city. Not knowing what there is to do or even how to get around can be overwhelming and isolating. Volunteering is an easy way to quickly become familiar with and begin to feel a part of this new city in addition to the campus community.

Analysis

Notice how Alyssa uses a famous quotation to get the attention of her audience in a way that also piques interest about the topic.

Here, Alyssa establishes listener relevance by pointing out that helping others makes us feel good and volunteering can be easy.

Alyssa mentions that she volunteers, which bolsters ethos and establishes her credibility to speak on the topic.

Notice how Alyssa's thesis with main point preview gives us a sense of the organizational framework for her ideas.

Again, as Alyssa introduces the first main point, she gets us to tune in because we all know how overwhelming and isolating we can feel when we move to a new place.

Volunteering allows you to learn your way around town. In an interview I had with Natalie Cunningham, the volunteer coordinator of the Lexington Rescue Mission, she said, "I've been working with students for several years now. While every group is different, one lingering trend is each group's unawareness of their city. It is easy for the students who live on campus to stay in their 'on-campus bubble.' Volunteering allows students to become acquainted with Lexington and the important issues facing their new home." It seems like a silly thing, but knowing your way around town starts to make any city feel like home. Volunteering gets you out into the local area and helps you begin to get acquainted with new people and places.

Volunteering can also open your eyes to local social issues and conditions. According to the Norris Center, many nonprofit organizations and volunteer-centered groups strive to raise awareness of important social issues by getting willing volunteers involved in the local community and issues impacting the area, things like hunger and homelessness. The second time I showed up to volunteer at the Lexington Rescue Mission, I served food to the homeless. (*Show slide 2: group of volunteers in the kitchen.*) I served soup and hung out with other volunteers and local homeless people. One of the "veteran" volunteers explained to me that Lexington has approximately 3,000 homeless people. (*Show slide 3: homelessness statistics in Lexington.*) I was shocked to learn that we had such a large number of men, women, and children without a regular place to sleep. I wouldn't have known about this problem or the organizations working to end homelessness if I hadn't been a volunteer. Not only is volunteering important because it helps us become familiar with a town and its social issues; frankly, as members of a democratic society, volunteering is our civic responsibility.

Giving back to the community through volunteer work is our civic responsibility and a privilege. Each of us in this room—whether as U.S. citizens or international students—are reaping the benefits of earning college degrees in this democratic society. With that benefit comes the responsibility and privilege of giving back. Volunteering is our civic responsibility. Wilson and Musick explain that, without active participation in the local community, civil society becomes deprived. Many Americans take this responsibility seriously. In fact, the U.S. Bureau of Labor Statistics reports "About 64.3 million people volunteered through or for an organization at least once between September 2010 and September 2011." I agree that it's important to volunteer. Giving back by volunteering helps the community in so many ways. (*Show slides 4 and 5: volunteers sorting clothes at the mission and then volunteers playing cards with people served at the shelter.*)

Volunteering is also a privilege. Making a difference by volunteering ends up making us feel better about ourselves and our role in the world around us. In fact, research conducted by the Corporation for National and Community Service from 2002 to 2005 shows that college students age 16 to 24 represent the fastest-growing demographic of volunteers in this country. (*Show slide 6: bar graph showing growth.*) Not only that, a study done by the Higher Education Research Institute published in January of 2009 shows that a whopping 69.7 percent of first-year college students believe it is essential or very important to volunteer to help people in need. Certainly, the privilege of giving back as volunteers is our civic responsibility and helps our local community, but we can also reap valuable résumé-building life skills by volunteering.

Volunteering helps teach us new skills. These new skills and talents can actually make us more marketable for better jobs once we graduate. Being a consistent

Quoting the volunteer coordinator is a great piece of developmental material that encourages us to trust that Alyssa's message is trustworthy. (Note that interviews are not included in the reference section but are cited in the text of the outline.)

Alyssa intersperses actual photos of her and others volunteering throughout the speech. Doing so enhances her verbal message but doesn't replace it. The photos also provide pathos, making her ideas more emotionally compelling.

Here and throughout the speech, notice how Alyssa uses effective section transitions to verbally tie the point she is wrapping up with an introduction of the point to come. This makes her speech flow smoothly so listeners can follow her train of thought and bolsters her ethos because she sounds prepared. Alyssa's careful audience analysis reveals itself here as she reminds her audience that even those who are not American citizens are benefiting as students in our educational system and, thus, have a responsibility to give back in some way.

Alyssa's choice to include national statistics of college student volunteers bolsters her credibility and provides listener relevance by reinforcing that college students are doing this, want to do this, and feel good about doing this kind of work.

volunteer at a nonprofit organization while attending college can strengthen your résumé. According to Charmer, in the *Journal of Career Development*, "Employers rely on credentials to certify that a young person will become a valuable employee. Credentials that document the experiences and employability skills, knowledge, and attitude." Laura Hatfield, director of the Center for Community Outreach at the University of Kentucky, points out that volunteers can include leadership, teamwork, and listening skills on their résumés because they can document the experiences where they had to use them effectively in the real world. Andrea Stockelman, another volunteer at the Lexington Rescue Mission, explained some of the new skills she picked up with volunteering. She said, "I learned that there was a lot more that went into preparing food for the homeless than I ever thought possible. It was neat to be a part of that process." (*Show slide 7: photo of Andrea preparing food.*)

Volunteering at the Lexington Rescue Mission taught me new skills that bolstered my résumé. (*Show slide 8: résumé with skills highlighted.*) I learned to coordinate the schedules of other volunteers. I also practiced important people skills such as teamwork, empathy, conflict management, and listening.

Today we've discussed why volunteering is beneficial to college students by focusing on how volunteering can connect us quickly and easily to our local community, why it's both our responsibility and a privilege to do so, and how volunteering will benefit us after we graduate. So, I'm hoping the next time you recall a time you really enjoyed making a difference by helping someone, that memory won't come from the distant past. Instead, I hope you'll be thinking about how you are being the change you seek in the world by volunteering right here in Lexington right now.

Students want to know how to market themselves to get good jobs. So this main point will help maintain listener interest at a point when minds might tend to wander.

By including a quotation from another volunteer, we don't have to take Alyssa's word alone.

This very clear thesis restatement with main point summary signals a sense of closure.

Notice how Alyssa ties back to her opening quotation in her clincher. This provides a sense of wrapping up without saying thank you that helps listeners feel like the speech is complete in a memorable way.

STUDY TOOLS 11

LOCATED IN TEXTBOOK

☐ Tear-out Chapter Review cards at the end of the book

☐ Review with the Quick Quiz below

LOCATED ON SPEAK3 ONLINE AT CENGAGEBRAIN.COM

☐ Review Key Term flashcards and create your own cards

☐ Track your knowledge and understanding of key concepts in speech communication

☐ Complete practice and graded quizzes to prepare for tests

☐ Complete interactive content within SPEAK3 Online

☐ View the chapter highlight boxes for SPEAK3 Online

Quick Quiz (answers in Solutions Appendix)

T F 1. It is relatively simple and easy to create a vocally expressive message.

T F 2. The more serious your speech topic, the more formally you should dress.

T F 3. Nonverbal communication includes how the speaker uses the voice and the body.

T F 4. During a speech, maintaining eye contact helps you gauge the audience's reaction to your ideas.

T F 5. It is difficult to sound both conversational and animated at the same time.

6. All of the following are characteristics of the voice EXCEPT:
   a. pitch
   b. quality
   c. rate
   d. animation
   e. volume

7. A(n) _____ speech is one that is delivered with only a few minutes advance notice.
   a. scripted
   b. impromptu
   c. spontaneous
   d. extemporaneous
   e. rehearsed

8. _____ refers to how a message is communicated orally and visually.
   a. Tone
   b. Delivery
   c. Articulation
   d. Poise
   e. Stance

9. During his speech, Vince can emphasize certain words by using:
   a. accent
   b. dialect
   c. stress
   d. markers
   e. correct pronunciation

10. A speaker using a conversational style will, in general, sound:
    a. spontaneous
    b. tense
    c. nonchalant
    d. apathetic
    e. careless

Chapter Takeaways

List three key takeaways from this chapter:

-

-

-

YOUR
FEEDBACK
MATTERS.

www.cengage.com/4ltrpress

4LTR
PRESS

12 Informative Speaking

LEARNING OUTCOMES

12-1 Explain the characteristics of informative speeches.

12-2 Describe the major methods of informing.

12-3 Prepare an informative process speech.

12-4 Prepare an informative expository speech.

After finishing this chapter go to **PAGE 227** for **STUDY TOOLS.**

Hero Images/Getty Images

Sound Familiar?

As Logan finished his informative speech, the class burst into spontaneous applause. Anna turned to her friend Ryan and whispered, "Wow, when Logan said his speech was going to be on online social networks I thought it would be boring. Was I ever wrong."

"I know, right?" Ryan responded. "I guess Professor Gaffney was right. You really CAN make a familiar topic interesting if you can share new and relevant insight about it."

"Yeah," Anna continued. "I'm going to take another look at my speech tonight to make sure I'm sharing new and relevant insight about online identity theft."

After listening to Logan, Anna and Ryan discovered firsthand what makes informative speeches effective. Effective informative speeches don't just share information. They share information that is both new and relevant for a particular audience. Not only that, Ryan and Anna also learned that even familiar topics can be intellectually stimulating when speakers share new and relevant insight about them. In this chapter, we'll share some guidelines to help you develop effective informative speeches.

12-1 CHARACTERISTICS OF EFFECTIVE INFORMATIVE SPEAKING

An **informative speech** is one whose goal is to explain or describe facts, truths, and principles in a way that stimulates interest, facilitates understanding, and increases the likelihood of remembering. In short, informative speeches are designed to educate audiences. Thus, most classroom lectures are basically informative speeches (although they may range from excellent to poor in quality). Informative speeches answer questions about a topic, such as those beginning with *who, when, what, where, why, how to,* and *how does*. For example, your informative speech might describe who popular singer-songwriter Lorde is, define Scientology, compare and contrast the similarities and differences between Pinterest and Instagram, narrate the story of golf professional Rory McIlroy's rise to fame, or demonstrate how to create and post a video on a Web site like YouTube. Informative speaking differs from other speech forms (such as speaking to persuade, to entertain, or to celebrate) in that your goal is simply to achieve mutual understanding about an object, person, place, process, event, idea, concept, or issue.

We face some unique challenges to gain and sustain listener attention when giving informative speeches. We can address them successfully by attending to five key characteristics of effective informative speeches.

12-1a Intellectually Stimulating

Your audience will perceive information to be **intellectually stimulating** when it is new to them and when it is explained in a way that piques their curiosity and interest. By *new*, we mean information that most of your audience is unfamiliar with or fresh insights into a topic with which they are already familiar.

If your audience is unfamiliar with your topic, you should consider how you might tap their natural curiosity. Imagine you are an anthropology major who is interested in prehistoric humans, not an interest shared by most members of your audience. You know that in 1991, a 5,300-year-old man—Otzi, as he has become known—was found surprisingly well preserved

> **informative speech** a speech whose goal is to explain or describe facts, truths, and principles in a way that stimulates interest, facilitates understanding, and increases the likelihood of remembering
>
> **intellectually stimulating** information that is new to audience members and is explained in a way that piques their curiosity

in an ice field in the mountains between Austria and Italy. Even though the discovery was big news at the time, it is unlikely that your audience knows much about it. You can draw on their natural curiosity, however, as you present "Unraveling the Mystery of the Iceman," where you describe scientists' efforts to understand who Otzi was and what happened to him.[1]

If your audience is familiar with your topic, you will need to identify new insights about it. Begin by asking yourself: What do listeners probably not know about my topic? Then, consider depth and breadth as you answer the question. *Depth* involves going into more detail than people's general knowledge of the topic. If you've ever watched programs on the Food Channel, that's what they do. Most people know basic recipes, but these programs show new ways to cook the same foods. Logan provided new insights by sharing details about the history of online social networks; something his audience of young users probably never thought about before. *Breadth* involves looking at how your topic relates to associated topics. Trace considered breadth when he informed listeners about Type 1 diabetes. He discussed not only the physical and emotional effects on a person with diabetes but also the emotional and relational effects on the person's family and friends, as well as the financial effects on society.

12-1b Relevant

A general rule to remember when preparing your informative speeches is this: Don't assume your listeners will recognize how the information you share is relevant to them. Remember to incorporate listener-relevance links throughout the speech. As you prepare each main point, ask and answer the question: How would knowing this information make my listeners happier, healthier, wealthier, wiser, and so forth? In other words, answer the question: Why should they care?

creative information that produces original, innovative ideas

productive thinking to contemplate something from a variety of perspectives

12-1c Creative

Your audience will perceive your information to be **creative** when it yields innovative ideas. You may not ordinarily consider yourself to be creative, but that may be because you have never recognized or fully developed your own innovative ideas. Contrary to what you may think, creativity is not a gift that some have and some don't; rather, it is the result of hard work. Creativity comes from doing good research, taking time, and practicing productive thinking.

Creative informative speeches begin with good research. The more you learn about a topic, the more material you will have to work with to develop creatively. Speakers who present information creatively do so because they have given themselves lots of supporting material to work with.

For the creative process to work, you have to give yourself time to think. Rarely do creative ideas come when we are in a time crunch. Instead, they are likely to come when we least expect it—when we're driving our car, preparing for bed, or daydreaming. We need time to mull over ideas. If you complete a draft of your outline several days before you speak, you will have time to consider how to present your ideas creatively.

For the creative process to work, you also have to think productively. **Productive thinking** occurs when we contemplate something from a variety of perspectives. Then, with numerous ideas to choose from, we can select those that are best suited to our particular audience. In the article "Thinking Like a Genius," author Michael Michalko describes several strategies you can use to become a productive thinker. They include:[2]

1. **Rethink a topic, issue, or problem from many perspectives.** Albert Einstein actually came up with the theory of relativity this way. As you brainstorm, try to think about a possible topic as it might be perceived by many different cultural and co-cultural groups. Then, as you conduct research, try to find sources that represent a variety of perspectives, as well.

2. **Make your thoughts visible by sketching drawings, diagrams, and graphs.** Galileo revolutionized science by doing this. Try concept mapping as you generate topics and approaches to them.

3. **Set regular goals to actually *produce something*.** The great NHL hockey player Wayne Gretzsky put it this way: "You miss every shot you don't take." So take some shots! Thomas Edison actually set a goal to produce an invention every ten days. J. S. Bach produced one cantata per week. And T. S. Eliot's many drafts of *The Waste*

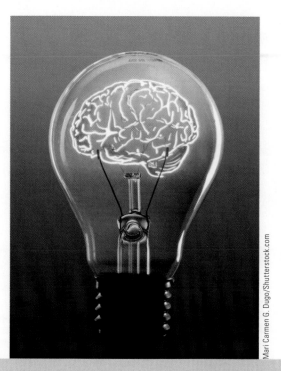

Productive thinking involves contemplating something from multiple perspectives. In this process, you'll generate many useful ideas.

Land eventually became a masterpiece. Don't let writer's block keep you from drafting an initial outline. You need to start somewhere. Getting ideas out of your head and onto paper or a computer screen gives you something to work with and revise. After all, you can't edit air.

4. Combine and recombine ideas, images, and thoughts in different ways. The Austrian monk, Gregor Mendel, combined mathematics and biology to develop the laws of heredity, which still ground the modern science of genetics today. Jennifer's list of possible speech topics included gardening (something she loved to do) and rising college tuition costs. She put the two ideas together and came up with the idea of doing an informative speech about how to use gardening (services, produce, and products) to raise money to help pay for college.

12-1d Memorable

If your speech is really informative, your audience will hear a lot of new information but will need help remembering what is most important. Emphasizing your specific goal, main points, and key facts are good starting points. Exhibit 12.1 illustrates several memory-enhancing techniques you might also use.

Exhibit 12.1
Techniques for Making Informative Speech Material Memorable

Technique	Use	Example
Presentational aids	To provide the opportunity for the audience to retain a visual as well as an audio memory of important or difficult material.	A diagram of the process of making ethanol.
Repetition	To give the audience a second or third chance to retain important information by repeating or paraphrasing it.	"The first dimension of romantic love is passion; that is, it can't really be romantic love if there is no sexual attraction."
Transitions	To increase the likelihood that the audience will retain the relationships among the information being presented, including which information is primary and which is supporting.	"So the three characteristics of romantic love are passion, intimacy, and commitment. Now let's look at each of the five ways you can keep love alive. The first is through small talk."
Humor and other emotional anecdotes	To create an emotional memory link to important ideas.	"True love is like a pair of socks: you've got to have two, and they've got to match. So you and your partner need to be mutually committed and compatible."
Mnemonics and acronyms	To provide an easily remembered memory prompt or shortcut to increase the likelihood that a list is retained.	"You can remember the four criteria for evaluating a diamond as the four Cs: carat, clarity, cut, and color."

12-1e Diverse Learning Styles

Because audience members differ in how they prefer to learn, you will be most effective when you address diverse learning styles. You can appeal to people who prefer to learn through the feeling dimension by providing concrete, vivid images, examples, stories, and testimonials. You can address the watching dimension by using visual aids and by using appropriate facial expressions and gestures. You can address the thinking dimension through clear macrostructure as well as definitions, explanations, and statistics. Finally, you can address the doing dimension by providing your listeners with an opportunity to do something during the speech or afterward. Rounding the cycle ensures that you address the diverse learning styles of your audience and make the speech understandable, meaningful, and memorable for all. Logan rounded the learning cycle with personal stories to address feeling, PowerPoint slides to address watching, clear definitions and statistics to address thinking, and by asking audience members to write down their own examples of social media sites they participate on to address doing.

12-2 METHODS OF INFORMING

Several methods exist for developing informative speech content. As Exhibit 12.2 shows, we can inform by describing, defining, comparing and contrasting, narrating, and demonstrating. Let's look at each of these methods more closely.

12-2a Description

Description is a method of informing used to create an accurate, vivid, verbal picture of an object, geographic feature, setting, event, person, or image. This method usually answers an overarching "who," "what," or "where" question. If the thing to be described is simple and familiar (like a light bulb or a river), the description may not need to be detailed. But if the thing to be described is complex and unfamiliar (like a sextant or holograph), the description will need to be more exhaustive. Descriptions are, of course, easier if you have a presentational aid, but vivid verbal descriptions can also create informative mental pictures. To describe something effectively, you can explain its size, shape, weight, color, composition, age, condition, and spatial organization.

description a method of informing used to create an accurate, vivid, verbal picture of an object, geographic feature, setting, or image

---

Exhibit 12.2
Five Methods of Informing

Description
Definition
Comparison and Contrast
Narration
Demonstration

© Petr Vaclavek/Shutterstock.com

You can describe size subjectively as large or small and objectively by noting specific numerical measurements. For example, you can describe New York City subjectively as the largest city in the United States or more objectively as home to more than 8 million people with more than 27,000 people per square mile.

You can describe shape by reference to common geometric forms such as round, triangular, oblong, spherical, conical, cylindrical, or rectangular, or by reference to common objects such as a book or a milk carton. For example, the lower peninsula of Michigan is often described as a left-handed mitten. Shape is made more vivid by using adjectives such as smooth or jagged.

You can describe weight subjectively as heavy or light and objectively by pounds and ounces or kilograms, grams, and milligrams. As with size, you can clarify weight with comparisons. So you can describe a Humvee (Hummer) objectively as weighing about 7,600 pounds, or subjectively as about the same as three Honda Civics.

You can describe color by coupling a basic color (such as black, white, red, or yellow) with a familiar object. For instance, instead of describing something as puce or ocher, you might describe the object as "eggplant purple" or "lime green."

You can describe the composition of something by indicating what it is made of. So you can describe a building as being made of brick, concrete, or wood. At times, you might describe something as what it looks like rather than what it is. For example, you might say something looks metallic even though it is actually made of plastic rather than metal.

You can also describe something by age and by condition. Together, descriptions of age and condition can give the audience cues about the worth of what is being described. For example, describing a coin as old but in mint condition indicates that the coin may be worth far more than its face value. Similarly, describing a city as ancient and well-kept produces different mental pictures than does describing a city as old and war torn.

Finally, you can describe spatial organization going from top to bottom, left to right, outer to inner, and so forth. A description of the Sistine Chapel might go from the floor to the ceiling; a description of a painting might proceed from foreground to background; and a description of a NASCAR automobile might go from the body to the engine to the interior.

12-2b Definition

Definition is a method of informing that explains the meaning of something. There are four ways to define something.

First, you can define a word or idea by classifying it and differentiating it from similar words or ideas. For example, in a speech on veganism, you might use information from the Vegan Society's Web site (http://www.vegansociety.com) to define a vegan: "A vegan is a vegetarian who is seeking a lifestyle free from animal products for the benefit of people, animals, and the environment. Vegans eat a plant-based diet free from all animal products, including milk, eggs, and honey. Vegans also don't wear leather, wool, or silk and avoid other animal-based products."

Second, you can define a word by explaining its derivation or history. For instance, the word *vegan* is made from the beginning and end of the word VEGetarIAN and was coined in the United Kingdom in 1944 when the Vegan Society was founded.[3] Offering this etymology will help your audience remember the meaning of *vegan*.

Third, you can define a word by explaining its use or function. For example, in vegan recipes, you can use tofu or tempeh to replace meat and almond or soy milk to replace cow's milk.

The fourth and perhaps the quickest way to define something is by using a familiar synonym or antonym. A **synonym** is a word that has the same or a similar meaning; an **antonym** is a word that is directly opposite in meaning. So, you could define a *vegan* by comparing it to the word *vegetarian*, which is a synonym with a similar although not identical meaning, or to the word *carnivore*, which is an antonym.

12-2c Comparison and Contrast

Comparison and contrast is a method of informing that focuses on how something is similar to and different from other things. For example, in a speech on veganism, you might tell your audience how vegans are similar to and different from other types of vegetarians. You can point out that like vegetarians, vegans don't eat meat. In contrast, semi-vegetarians eat fish or poultry. Like lacto-vegetarians, vegans don't eat eggs, but unlike this group and lacto-ovo-vegetarians, vegans don't use dairy products. So of all vegetarians, vegans have the most restrictive diet. Because comparisons and contrasts can be figurative or literal, you can use metaphors and analogies as well as making direct comparisons.

12-2d Narration

Narration is a method of informing that recounts an autobiographical or biographical event, myth, or other story. Narratives usually have four parts. First, the narration orients the listener by describing when and where the event took place and by introducing important characters. Second, the narration explains the sequence of events that led to a complication or problem, including details that enhance the development. Third, the narration discusses how the complication or problem affected key characters. Finally, the narration recounts how the complication or problem was solved. The

definition a method of informing that explains something by identifying its meaning

synonym a word that has the same or a similar meaning

antonym a word that is directly opposite in meaning

comparison and contrast a method of informing that focuses on how something is similar to and different from other things

narration a method of informing that explains something by recounting events

characteristics of a good narration include a strong story line; use of descriptive language and details that enhance the plot, people, setting, and events; effective use of dialogue; pacing that builds suspense; and a strong voice.[4]

Narrations can be presented in a first-, second-, or third-person voice. When you use first person, you report what you have personally experienced or observed, using the pronouns "I," "me," and "my" as you recount the events. Your narration will be effective if your audience can identify and empathize with you and the events you describe. "Let me tell you about the first time I tried to water-ski" might be the opening for a narrative story told in first person. When you use second person, you place your audience "at the scene" by using the pronouns "you" and "your." Second-person narration can be effective because it asks the audience to recall an event as though they are "actors" in the story. You might say, for example, "Imagine that you have just gotten off the plane in Hong Kong. You look at the signs but can't read a thing. Which way is the terminal?" When you use third person, you describe what has happened, is happening, or will happen to other people by using pronouns like "he," "her," and "they." For example, you might say "When the students arrived in Venice for their study-abroad experience, the first thing they saw was . . ." Third-person narration is effective when your audience can identify with key characters and their experiences.

12-2e Demonstration

Demonstration is a method of informing that shows how something is done, displays the stages of a process, or depicts how something works. Demonstrations range from very simple with a few easy-to-follow steps (such as how to iron a shirt) to very complex (such as demonstrating how a nuclear reactor works). Regardless of whether the topic is simple or complex, effective demonstrations require expertise, a hierarchy of steps, and vivid language and presentational aids.

In a demonstration, your experience with what you are demonstrating is critical. Expertise gives you the necessary background to supplement bare-bones instructions with personally lived experience. During a demonstration, you speak from that experience as you guide your audience through the steps. Why are TV cooking shows so popular? Because the chef doesn't just read the recipe and do what it says. Rather, while performing each step, the chef shares tips that aren't mentioned in any cookbook. It is the chef's

> **demonstration** a method of informing that shows how something is done, displays the stages of a process, or depicts how something works

Lorenzo Bevilaqua/ABC/Getty Images

Host of ABC's *The Chew*, Clinton Kelly is no stranger to process demonstration. He spent 10 years as the co-host of *What Not to Wear*, another show that explained processes to the audience in a simple and accessible way.

experience that allows him or her to say that one egg will work or how to tell if the cake is really done.

In a demonstration, you organize the steps from first to last to help your audience remember the sequence accurately. If there are many steps, grouping them will also help audiences remember. For example, suppose you want to demonstrate the steps in using a touch-screen voting machine. If, rather than presenting fourteen separate points, you group them under four headings—(1) get ready to vote; (2) vote; (3) review your choices; (4) cast your ballot—chances are much higher that the audience will be able to remember most if not all the items in each of the four groups.

Most demonstrations involve actually showing the audience the process or parts of the process. That's in part why TV shows like *The Chew* and *Flip This House* are so popular. If what you are explaining is relatively simple, you can demonstrate the entire process from start to finish. However, if the process is lengthy or complex, you may choose to pre-prepare material for some of the steps. Although you will show all stages in the process, you will not need to take the time for every single step as the audience watches. For example, many of the ingredients used by TV chefs are already cut up and measured into little bowls.

Effective demonstrations require practice. Remember that, under the pressure of speaking to an audience, even the simplest task can become difficult. (Have you ever tried to thread a needle with 25 people watching you?) As you practice, you will want to consider the size of your audience and the configuration of the room. Be sure that everyone in your audience will be able to see what you are doing.

12-3 INFORMATIVE PROCESS SPEECHES

Two of the most common patterns for organizing the macrostructure of informative speeches are process patterns and expository patterns. In this section, we focus specifically on process speeches. In the section that follows, we'll talk about expository speeches.

The goal of a **process speech** is to demonstrate how something is done, is made, or works. Effective process speeches require you to carefully delineate the steps and the order in which they occur. The steps typically become the main points and explanations of each step become the subpoints. Most process speeches rely heavily on the demonstration method of informing.

For example, Allie is a floral designer and has been asked by her former art teacher to speak on the basics of floral arrangement to a high school art class. The teacher allotted five minutes for Allie's presentation. Allie recognized that she could not demonstrate an entire floral display of any size in just five minutes. So she opted to physically demonstrate only parts of the process and bring additional arrangements in various stages of completion. For example, the first step is to choose the right vase and frog (flower holder). So she brought in vases and frogs of various sizes and shapes to show as she explained how to

choose one based on the types of flowers used and the desired visual effect. The second step is to prepare the basic triangle of blooms. Allie began to demonstrate how to place the flowers she had brought to form one triangle. Rather than trying to get everything perfect in the few seconds she had, however, she also brought out several other partially finished arrangements that were behind a draped table. These showed other carefully completed triangles that used other types of flowers. The third step is placing additional flowers and greenery to complete an arrangement and achieve various artistic effects. Again, Allie actually demonstrated how to place several blooms, and then, as she described them, she brought out several completed arrangements that illustrated various artistic effects. Even though Allie did not physically perform every part of each step, her visual presentation was an excellent demonstration of floral arranging.

Although some process speeches require you to demonstrate, others are not suited to demonstrations. For these, you can use visual or audiovisual aids to help the audience "see" the steps in the process. In a speech on remodeling a kitchen, it would not be practical to demonstrate the process; however, you could greatly enhance the verbal description by showing pictures before, during, and after the remodeling. Exhibit 12.3 provides some topic examples for process speeches.

> **process speech** a speech that explains and shows how something is done, is made, or works

INSAGO/Shutterstock.com

Make sure everyone in your intended audience can see what you are demonstrating.

Exhibit 12.3
Process Speech Topics
How to Do It
- Select running shoes
- Apply for a loan
- Install a toilet water saving device
- Bouldering

How to Make It
- Compost bin
- Rope knots
- Lefse
- Fishing flies

How It Works
- 3-D movies
- Stem cell reproduction
- Solar energy
- Digital synchronization

Process Speech
Evaluation Checklist

You can use this form to critique a process speech.

General Criteria

_____ **1.** Was the specific goal clear?

_____ **2.** Was the introduction effective in creating interest, as well as introducing the thesis and main points?

_____ **3.** Was the macrostructure easy to follow?

_____ **4.** Was the language appropriate, accurate, clear, and vivid?

_____ **5.** Were the main points developed with appropriate breadth, depth, and supporting material?

_____ **6.** Was the conclusion effective in summarizing the thesis and main points, as well as clinching?

_____ **7.** Was the speaker's use of voice conversational, intelligible, and expressive?

_____ **8.** Did the speaker's use of body (e.g., appearance, posture, poise, eye contact, facial expressions, gestures, and movement) appear poised, spontaneous, appropriate, and effective?

Specific Criteria

_____ **1.** Was the specific goal appropriate for a process speech (how to do it, how to make it, how it works)?

_____ **2.** Did the speaker show personal expertise with the process?

_____ **3.** Did the speaker emphasize the process steps?

_____ **4.** If the speaker demonstrated a process or parts of a process, was the demonstration fluid and skillful?

_____ **5.** Were presentational aids constructed effectively to help explain the process?

_____ **6.** Were presentational aids used effectively to help explain the process and easily seen by all audience members?

Based on these criteria, evaluate the speech (check one):

■ **excellent**   ■ **good**   ■ **satisfactory**   ■ **fair**   ■ **poor**

Explain:

Sample Process Speech:

Internet Identity Theft: Self-Protection Steps

Adapted from a speech by Anna Rankin[5]

This section presents a sample informative speech given by a student, including an adaptation plan, an outline, and a transcript.

1. Read the speech adaptation plan, outline, and transcript of a speech by Anna Rankin.

2. Access a video clip of sample process speeches through the Chapter 12 resources of *SPEAK 3* Online at www.cengagebrain.com.

3. Identify some of the strengths of Anna's speech by completing an evaluation checklist and preparing a one- to two-page critique identifying what she did well and what she could improve on regarding content, structure, delivery, and presentational aids.

Adaptation Plan

1. **Key aspects of audience.** Most people in my audience are probably aware of identity theft but probably don't know all the steps they can take to protect themselves from becoming victims of it.

2. **Establishing and maintaining common ground.** I will begin my speech by using a hypothetical example placing them as victims of Internet identity theft. Throughout the speech, I will refer to the audience's previous knowledge and experience.

3. **Building and maintaining interest.** I will try to gain interest in the introduction by relating the problem of Internet identity theft to college students. Throughout the speech, I will use common analogies and metaphors to explain the self-protection steps. Finally, I will use a well-designed PowerPoint presentation to capture and maintain attention.

4. **Audience knowledge and sophistication.** Because most of the class is probably not familiar with the actual self-protection steps regarding Internet identity theft, I will focus specifically on them throughout my speech.

5. **Building credibility.** Early in the speech, I will tell the audience how I got interested in Internet identity theft and the research I did to learn about it as a pre-law student.

6. **Audience attitudes.** I will try to address audience apathy by using interesting examples and compelling stories they can easily relate to.

7. **Adapting to audiences from different cultures and language communities.** I will use visual and audiovisual aids in my PowerPoint presentation to help those listeners from different cultures understand what I'm talking about even though English is not their native language.

8. **Using presentational aids to enhance understanding and memory.** Throughout the speech, I will use color-coded PowerPoint slides with headers to reinforce the steps being discussed.

Informative Speech Outline
Internet Identity Theft: Self-Protection Steps

General Goal:
To inform

Specific Goal:
I want my audience to understand the steps to protect themselves from online identity theft.

Introduction

I. Imagine this: You are filing your income tax return after starting your first real job since graduating from college. After completing the tedious online forms, you hit the "calculate" button. You are ecstatic when the online filing system says you are due a return of a whopping $2,800! Then, imagine hitting "file" to submit *your tax return and you get the error message "Your tax return has already been processed."* Someone has stolen your identity and pocketed your return.

Attention getter

II. If you think this cannot happen to you, think again! The FTC reported that, in 2014, complaints of tax-related identity theft went up by 2,300 percent (2015). Identity thieves can use Social Security numbers to receive your tax refund, or even apply for a job under your name (FTC, 2013)!

Listener-relevance link

III. Through my research, I discovered that in 2014, $16 billion was stolen from 12.7 million American identity theft victims (Javelin, 2015). And in June of 2015, one of the biggest breaches in U.S. history occurred when Chinese hackers gained access to personal data regarding 18 million U.S. government workers (Perez, 2015). Identity theft can even occur if someone digs through your trash and finds important personal data, so you should always shred documents like ATM receipts, expired warranties, and credit card bills (FTC, 2015). However, since many people use online banking, deposit checks through their smartphones, and participate in business transactions online, Internet identity theft has become far more prevalent (U.S. Department of Justice, n.d.). Internet identity theft poses a serious threat. An identity thief who accesses your information online can empty your bank account, rack up charges on your credit card, use your health insurance, or even use your identity if they're arrested (FTC, 2015).

Speaker credibility and listener relevance

IV. Today, let's discuss several simple steps we can all take to prevent Internet identity theft (*Slide 1: Three Steps to Prevent Identity Theft*). These three steps are designed to help prevent phishing, hacking, and pharming.

Thesis statement with main point preview

Body

I. The first step in preventing online identity theft is to protect yourself from phishing (*Slide 2: E-mail Phishing [Photo]*).

  A. Most likely, everyone in this room receives hundreds of e-mail messages every week. Whether it is an update from our college professor or coupons from our favorite retail stores, we are bombarded with e-mails that we do not hesitate to open or reply to.

  B. Phishing is a process through which identity thieves persuade Internet users to provide personal information by posing as legitimate organizations (NCPC, 2013).

   1. Identity thieves might send you an e-mail that appears to be from a legitimate organization.

   2. In it, they will ask you to provide personal information such as your bank account numbers, Social Security number, or personal passwords.

  C. One way to prevent phishing is by never providing personal information online without verifying the legitimacy of the sender.

   1. Beware of suspicious tech-support messages. These can potentially contain malware, which is software that allows lawbreakers remote access to your computer and its data.

2. Additionally, never give passwords over the phone. If a business calls and claims you need to give them your password in order for them to help you—this is a tip off that someone is trying to illegally access your information (FTC, 2015).

D. Another way to avoid becoming a victim of identity theft through phishing is never to click on links in e-mails from unknown sources (NCPC, 2013).

1. Clicking on these links can automatically install software on your computer that re-routes your personal information to the identity thief's personal data collection Web site.

2. Once the thief or thieves have this information, they can basically "become you" all over the Internet.

Transition

Now that we all know what we can do to keep our identity safe through good e-mail practices, let's consider how we can prevent identity theft by using the Internet wisely.

II. The second step we can take to protect ourselves from identity theft is to prevent hacking (*Slide 3: Computer Hacking [Photo]*).

A. Take a moment to think about all the personal and financial information you have stored on your electronic devices. If someone were to gain open access to your computer, or even to your smartphone for that matter, he or she would be able to steal your identity in a few clicks. **Listener-relevance link**

B. Hacking refers to a process through which an identity thief gains access to your personal computer to view documents, files, and personal information (NCPC, 2013).

C. Here are a few simple steps that can protect you from becoming a victim of hacking.

1. First, use different passwords for separate accounts and websites.

a. Update your passwords frequently—at least once every year.

b. When you open a link from an email, phishing scams will often ask you for your password. Do not give your password to unauthorized sites (Department of Communications (Au), 2014).

c. Keep your passwords 100% private.

2. The second step to protecting your identity from hacking is to avoid sharing too much information on social networking sites.

a. Be mindful about using geo tags on apps such as Instagram. Doing so creates a map for anyone to access places you have been, and places you are likely to go, which in the wrong hands, is dangerous.

b. Additionally, just because an app asks for information, doesn't mean you have to give it. Don't give apps on your phone information they don't need—like date of birth or your Social Security number (Taylor, 2015). If an identity thief finds out enough about your personal life, he or she can easily answer those "challenge" questions you use to keep your accounts and devices protected.

c. Finally, realize that you may not be intentionally "sharing" anything. When you use public Wi-Fi hotspots, your information is accessible to any else on the network savvy enough to find it. Join public Wi-Fi only if you know it is protected. Some experts recommend traveling with your own Wi-Fi hot spot, which makes it harder for hackers to find you.

3. The third and final step to protect you from identity theft through hacking is to be smart when throwing away your old computers and cell phones.

a. Never simply throw out your old personal devices. Not only is it so bad for the environment that many municipalities, such as New York City (*The Huffington Post*, 2014), consider it illegal, but old devices contain valuable personal data which can be used against you.

    b. It is always recommended to wipe a computer's hard drive clean of its data. However, there are many programs which can easily restore the data which was supposedly deleted. You can purchase advanced deletion programs, or send your computer to recognized companies like Electronic Recyclers International, where they not only recycle your old computer, but have sophisticated methods of deleting stored information (Fitzpatrick, 2014) (FTC, Shredding, 2015).

    c. However, the best way to truly protect yourself from identity fraud is to physically destroy the hard drive from a computer, or the SIM card from a cell phone (CNBC, 2015).

Transition

So now that we know how to protect our e-mail accounts from phishing and our computers from hacking, let's focus on what we need to do to protect ourselves from the most advanced method of online identity theft.

III. The third step in protecting ourselves from identity theft is to prevent pharming (*Slide 4: Pharming Web Site Dangers [Photo]*).

    A. Virtually every day, we engage in online transactions. We may log on to our online banking to make sure we have enough money for dinner with friends, we may purchase a gift for someone using Amazon.com, or we may pay tuition using the online payment system.

    B. Pharming, one of the toughest methods of online identity theft to detect, occurs when an Internet user clicks on or types in a link that sends them to a fake site. For example, if you went to type in your bank's website, and were off by a single letter, this could send you to an imposter Web site.

        1. The FBI says to be on the lookout for disparities between spellings and domain names, which are the ending of a web address, like .com, .edu, or .org (FBI, n.d).

        2. For example, imagine you receive a speeding ticket. You type in YourState.com, and are redirected to a fake website, because the real website is YourState.gov.

    C. Although pharming is the most difficult method of identity theft to detect, there are a few steps we can take to protect ourselves when making online transactions.

        1. First, look for a security symbol, or the "lock" icon on your Internet browser's status bar. This lock indicates that the Web site you are on is safe (*Slide 5: Internet Browser Safety Features*).

        2. Next, verify that the Web site is secure by inspecting the URL. A safe Web site URL will begin with https:// instead of http://

        3. Finally, look for SSL certificates. This is an easy way of knowing if the site you are visiting is authentic. This is also a sign that the site is encrypted—or protected. Never enter highly classified bank or personal information into a website that doesn't start with https:// or have a SSL certificate (GCF).

Conclusion

I. As you can see, the Internet is literally a gold mine for identity thieves when our personal information is not protected.   **Thesis restatement**

II. Fortunately, we can take steps to protect ourselves from phishing, hacking, and pharming (*Slide 9: [same as slide 1]*).   **Main point summary**

III. According to a 2015 article in *Business Insider*, young people are most vulnerable to online attacks because we are the least prepared for it. Although identity theft of individuals aged 20 to 29 makes up 18 percent of all reported cases of identity theft, when Javelin Research asked college students about their opinions on the matter, a whopping 64 percent reported that they were "not very concerned." I hope this information has inspired you to take the necessary precautions to protect yourself, and put a padlock on our gold mines so these criminals can't access them in the first place!   **Clincher**

References

Javelin Strategy & Research. (2015, March 2). $16 billion stolen from 12.7 million identity fraud victims in 2014, *Javelin*. Retrieved online through: https://www.javelinstrategy.com/news/1556/92/16-Billion-Stolen-from-12-7-Million-Identity-Fraud-Victims-in-2014-According-to-Javelin-Strategy-Research/d,pressRoomDetail

Esch, M. (December 23, 2014). Trashing electronics becomes illegal in New York. *The Huffington Post*. Retrieved online from: http://www.huffingtonpost.com/2014/12/23/new-york-electronics-recycling-law_n_6372176.html

Farzan, A. (June 9, 2015). College students are not as worried as they should be about the threat of identity theft. *Business Insider*. Retrieved online from: http://www.businessinsider.com/students-identity-theft-2015-6#ixzz3e5MLnj3U

Federal Trade Commission. (2015). Identity theft. Retrieved online from http://www.consumer.ftc.gov/articles/0271-warning-signs-identity-theft

Federal Trade Commission (2015, April). Shredding infographic. Retrieved online from: http://www.consumer.ftc.gov/articles/0527-shredding-infographic

Federal Trade Commission. (2015, May). Warning signs of identity theft. Retrieved online from http://www.consumer.ftc.gov/articles/0271-warning-signs-identity-theft

Fitzpatrick, A. (December 31, 2014). Why you should never throw away your old tech. *Time*. Retrieved online from: http://time.com/3650412/recycle-phones-e-waste

Internet Safety (N.d). *GCF*. Retrieved online from: http://www.gcflearnfree.org/internetsafety/6/print.

Internet Social Networking Risks (N.d). FBI. Retrieved from https://www.fbi.gov/about-us/investigate/counterintelligence/internet-social-networking-risks

National Crime Prevention Council. (2013). Evolving with technology: A comprehensive introduction to cyber-crime with links to resources. Retrieved online from http://www.ncpc.org/topics/fraud-and-identity-theft/evolving-with-technology

Perez, E. and LoBianco, T. (June 24, 2015). U.S. government hacking number sparks unusual drama at Senate briefing. *CNN*. Retrieved online from:http://www.cnn.com/2015/06/24/politics/opm-hacking-senate-briefing/.

Retrieved online from: https://www.fbi.gov/about-us/investigate/counterintelligence/internet-social-networking-risks.

Set and use strong passwords (Nov 27, 2014). Australian Government Department of Communications. Retrieved online from: https://www.communications.gov.au/what-we-do/internet/stay-smart-online/computers/set-and-use-strong-passwords

Tax ID Theft Tops FTC Complaints in 2014; IRS imposter complaints up more than 2,300 percent (January 26, 2015). *FTC*. Retrieved online through: https://www.ftc.gov/news-events/press-releases/2015/01/tax-id-theft-tops-ftc-complaints-2014-irs-imposter-complaints

Tax-Related Identity Theft (November 2013). FTC. Retrieved online from: http://www.consumer.ftc.gov/articles/0008-tax-related-identity-theft

Taylor, H. (2015, June 22). Ten low-tech ways to protect your privacy online. CNBC. Retrieved online from: http://www.cnbc.com/id/102777671

Tech Support Scams (January 2014). FTC. Retreived online from: http://www.consumer.ftc.gov/articles/0346-tech-support-scams

Speech and Analysis

Speech

Imagine this: You are filing your income tax return after starting your first real job after college. After completing the tedious online forms, you hit the "calculate" button. You are ecstatic when the online filing system says you are due a return of a whopping $2,800! Then, imagine hitting "file" to submit your tax return and you get the error message *"Your tax return has already been processed."* Someone has stolen your identity and pocketed your return.

If you think this cannot happen to you, think again! In 2014, the Federal Trade Commission reported that complaints of tax-related identity theft went up by 2,300% over the previous year. Identity thieves can use your Social Security number to receive your tax refund, or even apply for a job under your name! Through my

Analysis

Notice how Anna uses a hypothetical example to draw her audience into her speech with this attention getter. Not only that, she also offers listener relevance by using a dollar amount that most college students would find enticing.

This paragraph is chock full of listener relevant statements supported with evidence from reputable sources, which serve to establish Anna's credibility very well.

research, I discovered that in 2014, $16 billion was stolen from 12.7 million American identity theft victims. And in June of 2015, major news outlets reported that one of the biggest breaches in U.S. history occurred when Chinese hackers gained access to personal data regarding 18 million U.S. government workers. Identity theft can even occur if someone digs through your trash and finds important personal data, so you should always shred documents like ATM receipts, expired warranties, and credit card bills. However, since many people use online banking, deposit checks through their smartphones, and participate in business transactions online, Internet identity theft has become far more prevalent. According to the Federal Trade Commission, an identity thief who accesses your information online can empty your bank account, rack up charges on your credit card, use your health insurance, or even use your identity if they're arrested (giving *you* a rap sheet!).

Today, let's discuss several simple steps we can all take to prevent Internet identity theft (*Slide 1: Three Steps to Prevent Identity Theft*). These three steps are designed to help prevent phishing, hacking, and pharming.

> *Anna very succinctly offers her thesis and main point preview using personal pronouns and "we" language that foster a sense of immediacy with her audience.*

The first step in preventing online identity theft is to protect ourselves from phishing (*Slide 2: E-mail Phishing [Photo]*). Most likely, everyone in this room receives hundreds of e-mail messages every week. Whether it is an update from our college professor or coupons from our favorite retail stores, we are bombarded with e-mails that we do not hesitate to open or reply to.

> *As Anna presents her first main point, she also incorporates a listener relevance link that piques audience member interest.*

According to the National Crime Protection Council, phishing is a process through which identity thieves persuade Internet users to provide personal information by posing as legitimate organizations. Identity thieves might send you an e-mail that appears to be from a legitimate organization. In it, they will ask you to provide personal information such as your bank account numbers, Social Security number, or personal passwords.

> *Anna appeals to the thinking dimension of the learning cycle here with a clear definition and explanation of what phishing is.*

One way to prevent phishing is by never providing personal information online without verifying the legitimacy of the sender. Beware of suspicious tech-support messages. These can potentially contain malware, which is software that allows lawbreakers remote access to your computer and its data. And never give passwords over the phone. The Federal Trade Commission warns that, if a business calls and claims you need to give them your password in order for them to help you, that's a tip-off that someone is trying to illegally access your information.

> *Here Anna appeals to the doing dimension of the learning cycle by offering specific things listeners can DO to protect themselves from online identity theft.*

Another way to avoid becoming a victim of identity theft through phishing is never to click on links in e-mails from unknown sources. Clicking on these links can automatically install software on your computer that re-routes your personal information to the identity thief's personal data collection Web site. Once the thief or thieves have this information, they can basically "become you" all over the Internet.

> *Although this is another great action step, Anna could have improved it by offering a narrative from someone who experienced this or referencing the 2013 feature film focused on this topic.*

Now that we all know what we can do to keep our identity safe through good e-mail practices, let's consider how we can prevent identity theft by surfing the Internet wisely.

> *Anna does a great job here of tying the two points together using "we" language that fosters immediacy.*

The second step we can take to protect ourselves from identity theft is to prevent hacking (*Slide 3: Computer Hacking [Photo]*).

Take a moment to think about all the personal and financial information you have stored on your electronic devices. If someone were to gain open access to your computer, or even to your smartphone for that matter, he or she would be able to steal your identity in a few clicks, swipes, or taps.

> *Here again Anna does a great job establishing personal relevance for her second main point.*

Hacking refers to a process through which an identity thief gains access to our personal computers to view documents, files, and personal information. Fortunately, the Federal Trade Commission and the National Crime Protection Council outline several things we can do to protect ourselves from becoming a victim of hacking. The first step is to use different passwords for different accounts and Web sites. Using the same password over and over makes it easier for a hacker to gain access to all of our accounts. For that same reason, passwords should be updated yearly. No matter how frequently we update our passwords, phishing scams will often try to get us to share them. The Australian Government Department of Communication offers some sound advice for everyone with a computer: Do not share passwords with unauthorized sites. The best practice is to keep all of our passwords 100 percent private.

One of the best ways to protect ourselves from identity theft through hacking is to avoid sharing too much information about ourselves on social media sites. Whether we're on Instagram, Four-Square, or Facebook, we need to resist the urge to enable geo tags. Checking in somewhere or enabling the tags creates a map of our habits. Imagine what could happen if the patterns of where you go, when, and with whom fell into the hands of a criminal! And just because an app asks us for information about ourselves does not mean that we have to give it. Think about it: if an identity thief finds out enough about your personal life, she will be well positioned to answer all of the "challenge" questions that websites have to authenticate your identity. And it is just as important to think about *where* we are accessing information. We could be sharing our personal data without realizing it. Remember that public computers can be hacked for data, so we must be mindful which of our accounts we access at the library, for example. Public Wi-Fi hotspots pose the same risks as using public computers, so only join a hotspot if you know it's protected. An even better strategy is to travel with a personal hotspot, which makes it harder for hackers to find you—and your data.

Another way to protect our devices from hackers looking to steal our identity is to wipe clean any of our electronic devices before selling them or disposing of them. Old devices contain huge amounts of our personal data which could be used to steal our identity. Before disposing of a computer, phone, or tablet, permanently remove any personal information, for example saved passwords, photos, Web search histories, and contacts. When recycling a device, research a company, such as Electronic Recyclers International, which has sophisticated ways of shredding (that means, completely eliminating) all of the stored information on the device. The one definite way to protect ourselves from identity fraud from an old device is to physically destroy the hard drive or SIM card.

So now that we know how to protect our e-mail accounts from phishing and our computers from hacking, let's focus on what we need to do to protect ourselves from the most advanced method of online identity theft.

The third step in protecting ourselves from identity theft is to prevent pharming (*Slide 4: Pharming Web Site Dangers [Photo]*).

Virtually every day, we engage in online transactions. We may log on to our online banking to make sure we have enough money for dinner with friends, we may purchase a gift for someone using Amazon.com, or we may pay our tuition using the online pay-ment system.

Pharming, according to the National Crime Protection Council, is one of the toughest methods of online identity theft to detect. It is essentially a process through which criminals hack established Web sites, such as Amazon.com, and re-route the Web site to a "poser" Web site that looks very similar and allows them to gather our personal information during a transaction. Although pharming is the most difficult method of identity theft to detect, there are a few steps we can take to protect ourselves when making online transactions. First, we can look for the "lock" icon on the Internet browser's status bar. This lock indicates that the Web site we are on is safe (*Slide 6: Internet Browser Safety Features*). And we can verify that the Web site is secure by inspecting the URL. A safe Web site URL will begin with https:// instead of

▶ Again, this is interesting and helpful information with a lot of tips that create listener relevance. It could be even more compelling with a narrative account from someone who experienced it.

▶ Notice how Anna again provides a transition that verbally ties the two main points together creating a fluent sense of forward motion into her next main point.

▶ Here Anna provides great examples that should help her classmates see the relevance of what she is discussing and, thus, motivate them to stay tuned in.

▶ Here and throughout the speech Anna provides excellent information. What is missing, however, are personal quotations, stories, and testimonials that would appeal to the feeling dimension of the learning cycle.

http://. Finally, we can purchase encryption software that makes sure any information we send over the Internet is jumbled and unreadable to others.

As you can see, the Internet is literally a gold mine for identity thieves when our personal information is not protected. Fortunately, we can take steps to protect ourselves from phishing, hacking, and pharming (*Slide 5: [same as slide 1]*). According to a 2015 article in *Business Insider*, young people are most vulnerable to online attacks because we are the least prepared for it. Although identity theft of individuals aged 20 to 29 makes up 18 percent of all reported cases of identity theft, when Javelin Research asked college students about their opinions on the matter, a whopping 64 percent reported that they were "not very concerned." I hope this information has inspired you to take the necessary precautions to protect yourself, and put a padlock on our gold mines so these criminals can't access them in the first place!

▶ *Anna makes her conclusion more memorable by using the analogy of a "gold mine" to refer to our identities and referring to identity thieves as "criminals."*

▶ *Clincher*

INFORMATIVE EXPOSITORY SPEECHES

The goal of an **expository speech** is to provide carefully researched in-depth knowledge about a complex topic. For example, "understanding the gun control debate," "the origins and classification of nursery rhymes," "the sociobiological theory of child abuse," and "viewing hip-hop music as poetry" are all topics on which you could give an interesting expository speech. Lengthy expository speeches are known as lectures.

All expository speeches require speakers to draw from an extensive research base, choose an organizational pattern best suited to the topic and goal, and use a variety of informative methods (e.g., descriptions, definitions, comparisons and contrasts, narrations, short demonstrations) to sustain the audience's attention and help them understand the material presented.

Expository speeches include those that explain a political, economic, social, religious, or ethical issue; events or forces of history; a theory, principle, or law; or a creative work.

12-4a Exposition of Political, Economic, Social, Religious, or Ethical Issues

In an expository speech, you have the opportunity to help the audience understand the background or context of an issue, including the forces that gave rise to the issue and continue to affect it. You may also present the various positions held about the issue and the reasoning behind these positions. Finally, you may discuss various ways that have been presented for resolving the issue.

The general goal of your speech is to inform, not to persuade. So you will want to present all sides of controversial issues without advocating which side is better. You will also want to make sure the sources you are drawing from are respected experts and are objective in what they report. Finally, you will want to present complex issues in a straightforward manner that helps your audience to understand while not oversimplifying knotty issues. For example, while researching a speech on fracking—the controversial method for extracting natural gas deposits—you need to be careful to consult articles and experts on all sides of the issue and fairly represent and incorporate these views in your speech. If time is limited, you might discuss all sides of just one or two of these issues, but you should also at least mention the others as well. Exhibit 12.4 provides examples of topic ideas for an expository speech about a political, economic, social, religious, or ethical issue.

12-4b Exposition of Historical Events and Forces

It has been said that those who don't understand history may be destined to repeat it. So an expositional speech about historical events or forces can be fascinating for its own sake, but it can also be relevant for what is happening today. Unfortunately, some people think history is boring. So if your speech is about a historical event, you have a special obligation to seek out stories and narratives that can enliven your presentation. You should analyze the events you describe and the impact they had

expository speech an informative presentation that provides carefully researched in-depth knowledge about a complex topic

MEDIA MOMENT

Beware of Spreading Misinformation

The Internet may be a great place to track down information on nearly any topic, but it's also the source of poorly sourced research, opinion masquerading as truth, and marketing in the guise of fact.

In 2012, one man brought attention to this by purposefully duping a host of reporters across several major media outlets. Ryan Holiday, a digital marketing strategist and self-described "media manipulator," turned to the free-to-use media query service Help a Reporter Out (HARO) to conduct his marketing experiment.[6]

HARO seeks to connect journalists and content creators with expert sources. A reporter sends out a query on HARO, and any relevant source interested in the story can comment via email. Holiday signed himself up as a source and spent months answering every query he could find, regardless of his knowledge on the topic.[7]

With the help of reporters from established news outlets such as Reuters, ABC News, *The New York Times*, and MSNBC, among others, Holiday found himself quoted as an insomniac, embarrassed office employee, boat aficionado, and vinyl record collector. Holiday, of course, was none of these things, but his lies were thorough and his position as Marketing Director at American Apparel seemed to lend him some credibility. Though he acted as a false source on dozens of news stories, he only received one fact-checking email![8]

In an article he wrote for *Forbes* magazine, Holiday blames this reckless ignorance of source validity on the increasing rapidity of the media cycle. Publishers, reporters, editors, and media outlet owners face growing incentives to put out more and more content to generate greater clicks under shrinking deadlines. Additionally, Holiday says it's not just marketers and press agents who are manipulating the facts for unsuspecting reporters—the writers themselves are putting out material without fact-checking, all for the sake of increasing volume.[9]

kenton/Shutterstock.com

The Internet might be the easiest place for this process to occur, but it is not the only form of media guilty of spreading misinformation, willingly or otherwise. The Center for Media and Democracy's PR Watch identified 77 television stations in the U.S. that aired video press releases from companies such as General Motors and Pfizer as originally reported news stories. In nearly every one of these instances, the stations presented the companies' message without independently gathered footage or journalistic research.[10]

The problem, Holiday says, is that modern media consumers expect to receive their news for free. Because income is based on ads and clicks rather than subscriptions, content creators have no incentive to retain long-term readers (or viewers).[11] Instead, they seek to generate as much buzz as possible through sensational stories and eye-catching headlines.

It's not hard to avoid contributing to this cycle of misinformation. As you're researching information for your speech, do a service to yourself and your audience: Google your sources (and Google your sources sources), check for credibility, and, when in doubt, cross-reference your facts.

---

at the time they occurred, as well as the meaning they have for us today. For example, although many of us are familiar with the historical fact that the United States developed the atomic bomb during World War II, an expository speech on the Manhattan Project (as it was known) that dramatized the race to produce the bomb and told the stories of the main players would add to our understanding of the inner workings of "secret" government-funded research projects. It might also place modern arms races and the fear of nuclear proliferation into historical context. Exhibit 12.5 offers some topic idea examples for an expository speech about historical events and forces.

12-4c Exposition of a Theory, Principle, or Law

The way we live is affected by natural and human laws and principles and explained by various theories. Yet there are many theories, principles, and laws that we do not completely understand—or, at least, we don't understand how they affect us. An expository speech can inform us by explaining these important phenomena. The main challenge is to find material that explains the theory, law, or principle in language that is understandable to the audience. You will want to search for or create examples and illustrations that

Exhibit 12.4

Expository Topics: Politics, Economics, Society, Religion, Ethics

Politics

- Affirmative action
- Health care reform
- Climate change
- School vouchers
- Gun control
- Term limits

Economics

- Immigration
- Fracking
- Farm subsidies
- Abolishment of Federal Reserve
- Unemployment

Social Issues

- Gay marriage
- Celebrity culture
- Media bias
- Digital remixing

Religion

- Prayer in school
- Ordination of women
- Banning of Muslim burqa from public places
- The role of missionaries

Ethical Issues

- Genetic engineering
- Stem cell research
- Animal testing
- Fast fashion

Exhibit 12.5

Expository Topics: Historical Events and Forces

Historical Events

- Gandhi and his movement
- Irish immigration
- The Spanish flu epidemic
- Conquering Mt. Everest
- The Vietnam War
- Assassination of Martin Luther King Jr
- The Crusades
- The Balfour Declaration

Historical Forces

- Women's suffrage
- Building the Great Pyramids
- The colonization of Africa
- The Papacy
- The Ming Dynasty
- The Industrial Revolution
- Genocide

When a behavior is reinforced continuously, each time people perform the behavior they get the reward, but when the behavior is reinforced intermittently, the reward is not always given when the behavior is displayed. Behavior that is learned by continuous reinforcement disappears quickly when the reward is no longer provided, but behavior that is learned by intermittent reinforcement continues for long periods of time, even when not reinforced. You can see

fullempty/Shutterstock.com

demystify complicated concepts and terminology. Effective examples and comparing unfamiliar ideas with those that the audience already knows are techniques that can help you with this kind of speech. For example, in a speech on the psychological principles of operant conditioning, a speaker could help the audience understand the difference between continuous reinforcement and intermittent reinforcement with the following explanation:

examples of how behavior was conditioned in everyday encounters. For example, take the behavior of putting a coin in the slot of a machine. If the machine is a vending machine, you expect to be rewarded every time you "play." And if the machine doesn't eject the item, you might wonder if the machine is out of order and "play" just one more coin, or you might bang on the machine. In any case, you are unlikely to put in more than one more coin. But suppose the machine is a slot machine or a machine that dispenses instant winner lottery tickets. Now how many coins will you "play" before you stop and conclude that the machine is "out of order"? Why the difference? Because you have been conditioned to a vending machine on a continuous schedule, but a slot machine or automatic lottery ticket dispenser "teaches" you on an intermittent schedule.

Exhibit 12.6 provides some examples of topic ideas for an expository speech about a theory, principle, or law.

Exhibit 12.6
Expository Topics: Theory, Principle, Law

Theory

- Natural selection
- Number theory
- Psychoanalytic theory
- Social cognitive theory
- Intelligent design
- Feminist theory
- Maslow's hierarchy of needs
- Color theory: complements and contrasts

Principle

- Peter principle
- Pareto principle

Law

- Diminishing returns
- Gravity
- Boyle's law
- Moore's law

12-4d Exposition of a Creative Work

Courses in art, theater, music, literature, and film appreciation give students tools by which to recognize the style, historical period, and quality of a particular piece or group of pieces. Yet most of us know very little about how to understand a creative work, so presentations designed to explain creative works such as poems, novels, songs, or even famous speeches can be very instructive for audience members.

When developing a speech that explains a creative work, you will want to find information on the work and the artist who created it. You will also want to find sources that help you understand the period in which this work was created and learn about the criteria that critics use to evaluate works of this type. So, for example, if you wanted to give an expository speech on Frederick Douglass's Fourth of July oration of 1852 in Rochester, New York, you might need to orient your audience by first reminding them of who Douglass was. Then, you would want to explain the traditional expectation that was set for Fourth of July speakers at this point in history. After this, you might want to summarize the speech and perhaps share a few memorable quotations. Finally, you would want to discuss how speech critics view the speech and why the speech is considered "great." Exhibit 12.7 provides some examples of topics for an expository speech about a creative work.

Exhibit 12.7
Expository Topics: Creative Work

Creative Work

- Hip-hop music
- The films of Alfred Hitchcock
- Impressionist painting
- Lady Gaga's "Paparazzi"
- Salsa dancing
- Kabuki theatre
- Inaugural addresses
- Iconography
- MLK JR. National Memorial
- Catcher in the Rye: A coming-of-age novel
- The Hunger Games trilogy
- Van Gogh's Starry Night
- Spike Lee's Mo' Better Blues

Expository Speech
Evaluation Checklist

You can use this form to critique an expository speech that you hear in class. As you listen, outline the speech and identify which expository speech type it is. Then answer the following questions.

Type of Expository Speech

_____ Exposition of political, economic, social, religious, or ethical issues

_____ Exposition of historical events or forces

_____ Exposition of a theory, principle, or law

_____ Exposition of a creative work

General Criteria

_____ **1.** Was the specific goal clear?

_____ **2.** Was the introduction effective in creating interest, as well as introducing the thesis and main points?

_____ **3.** Was the macrostructure easy to follow?

_____ **4.** Was the language appropriate, accurate, clear, and vivid?

_____ **5.** Were the main points developed with appropriate breadth, depth, and supporting material?

_____ **6.** Was the conclusion effective in summarizing the thesis and main points, as well as clinching?

_____ **7.** Was the speaker's use of voice conversational, intelligible, and expressive?

_____ **8.** Did the speaker's use of body (e.g., appearance, posture, poise, eye contact, facial expressions, gestures, and movement) appear poised, spontaneous, appropriate, and effective?

Specific Criteria

_____ **1.** Was the specific speech goal to provide well-researched information on a complex topic?

_____ **2.** Did the speaker effectively use a variety of informative methods?

_____ **3.** Did the speaker emphasize the main ideas and important supporting material?

_____ **4.** Did the speaker use a variety of supporting material?

_____ **5.** Did the speaker present in-depth, high-quality, appropriately cited information?

Based on these criteria, evaluate the speech (check one):

☐ **excellent** ☐ **good** ☐ **satisfactory** ☐ **fair** ☐ **poor**

Explain:

Sample Expository Speech:
Social Media and Society

Adapted from a speech by Logan Hurley, University of Kentucky[12]

This section presents a sample expository speech adaptation plan, outline, and transcript by Logan Hurley.

1. Read the speech adaptation plan, outline, and transcript of a speech by Logan Hurley.

2. Access a video clip of Logan's speech through the Chapter 12 resources on *SPEAK 3* Online at www.cengagebrain.com.

3. Use SPEAK 3 Online at www.cengagebrain.com to identify some of the strengths of Logan's speech by completing an evaluation checklist.

4. Prepare a one- to two-page critique identifying what Logan did well and what he could improve on regarding content, structure, delivery, and presentational aids.

Adaptation Plan

1. **Key aspects of audience.** Because most of my classmates are not only aware of social media but also active users, I will focus instead on it as a social force impacting both politics and news reporting.

2. **Establishing and maintaining common ground.** I will use inclusive pronouns and relate all aspects of social media I discuss as they impact me and my audience.

3. **Building and maintaining interest.** I will build interest by pointing out that social media is getting more and more popular not only as a way to stay connected with friends but also by altering the way we engage in politics and in news reporting.

4. **Audience knowledge and sophistication.** The audience is made up of my classmates and all are 18 to 20 years old. Because they grew up using social media, I don't need to explain how the sites function. However, I will need to clarify what exactly I'm talking about when I say social media, because of assumptions and foreknowledge that the class will carry in with them.

5. **Building credibility.** I will cite credible sources and portray a thorough understanding of my sources in the speech.

6. **Audience attitudes.** I expect my audience to have some reservations in accepting that they do not fully understand the consequences of the social network world they are so accustomed to, but they should also be willing to accept the power of social media to affect change because they have grown up seeing its impact in their own lives.

7. **Adapt to audiences from different cultures and language communities.** The class consists of entirely English speakers. To adjust to those from different backgrounds, I will cite examples as large in scope as possible to encompass the impact of social media upon events that different culture-background students have likely heard of.

8. **Use presentational aids to enhance audience understanding and memory.** I will use PowerPoint slides of familiar images that are easily associated with the content I discuss.

Expository Speech Outline
Online Social Media and Society

General Goal:
To inform

Speech Goal:
In this speech, I will explain the impact of social media on our world by describing its rapid historical growth as a social force and its impact on both political processes and news reporting.

Introduction

I.	A man dies—cheery way to start out, right?—and ends up sitting there in front of heaven's pearly gates. St Peter asks, "What have you done with your life?" The man responds indignantly with, "You mean you haven't been reading my tweets!?"

Attention getter

II.	All joking aside, I imagine most of us in this room use social media, whether it be Facebook, Twitter, LinkedIn, or even—dare I say it—Myspace—remember that one?—for nostalgia. (*Slide 1: Scattered logos of significant or previously significant social media Web sites. Facebook, Twitter, Snapchat, Instagram, etc.*) To illustrate my point, go ahead and take out your smartphone, notebook, or laptop and log on to any one of them. This is a race: When you're "on," raise your hand (*time them*). Every hand went up in less than five seconds! But how many of us really understand the significant impact this modern online social network phenomenon is having our society? If we're being honest, I sincerely doubt that many of us have thought about it. We know not to post raunchy stuff on Facebook or Twitter before going to an important job interview and not to "friend" professional supervisors if we don't want them to see what we talk about online, but how much more?

Listener-relevance link

III.	After realizing I knew next to nothing about these complex social networks I use everyday, I decided to explore what the experts have to say about the nature of online social networks and how they are shaping communication practices and society today.

Speaker credibility

IV.	So today, I'd like to share what I've discovered about the history and rapid growth of our modern online social networks and how they are impacting both politics and news reporting.

Thesis statement with main point preview

Body

I.	To really understand how online social networks, that is, Web sites that allow users to easily create content and interact with one another about that content, affect our lives and the world we live in today, we first need to understand a bit about their convoluted but significant history (Curtis, 2013).

Listener-relevance

    A. Historically speaking, online social media is rather young, dating back only about 20 years to 1994 when Beverly Hills Internet created a Web-hosting service called GeoCities.com.

        1. For the first time, users could create customizable Web pages organized by interests with feedback sections and other features unavailable to non-corporate Web site creators at the time (Curtis, 2013).

        2. According to a 2009 *LA Times* article, it wasn't in the sleek and attractive style we expect today (Milian, 2009). (*Slide 2: Example GeoCities site with its unorganized content*)

        3. Although it was rather unattractive, it was still the first of its kind in being a way for users to create their own content and respond to that of others (Curtis, 2013).

    B. Three short years later, blogging took off. People began creating personas for themselves and engaging in regular, frequent dialog through blog posts, responses to posts, and of course, responses to the responses of blog posts (Curtis, 2013).

1. AOL Instant Messenger changed what users wanted from the Internet as a communication tool (*Slide 3: AIM, MSN Messenger icons*).

2. **Listener-relevance link** We all remember our middle school days of being mystified at the thought of instantly sending and receiving messages from our friends, right? Well, this was the start of that. And what's more, this was the start of a demand for instant gratification when it came to online social interaction with friends, according to Oliver Gray in a *20 Something Magazine* article posted in March 2013 (Gray, 2013).

C. In 2002 and 2003, two sites that would become outrageously popular began. Although neither is a most frequented site today, Friendster and Myspace took the Internet by storm.

1. Users of Friendster, which was invented in 2002, catapulted to 3 million in just three short months, which was a fantastic feat.

2. By 2004, however, just one year after it was created in 2003, Myspace overtook Friendster in terms of the number of accounts created.

3. That same year, 2004, marks the point when a similar site was created by a group of students at Harvard. Dubbed the college version of Friendster, it didn't receive much attention at the time, but you may have heard of it: (*Slide 4: Cartoon of Facebook icon on top of Myspace and Friendster icons*) Facebook (Curtis, 2013).

4. It's pretty incredible to think that Facebook is not even a decade old and, according to an article in the *Wall Street Journal*, boasts of having more than a billion members worldwide (Fowler, 2012).

D. Another dramatic shift occurred in 2005 when YouTube was founded.

1. Aspiring musicians found an outlet to post musical recordings.

2. Parents began posting home videos of their kids.

3. Corporations began posting recordings to promote their products.

4. People began posting hilarious creative videos that previously could only be seen on programs such as *America's Funniest Home Videos* (Curtis, 2013).

E. Today, online social networks such as Facebook, YouTube, and Twitter are taken-for-granted communication outlets for most Americans, especially digital natives like those of us here in the room today.

Transition and listener-relevance If you are like I was before I did my research, you might be thinking "so what's the big deal? Online social networks are here to stay." But, let me tell you now how they have changed and will continue to change our cultural norms; norms ranging from how we make friends, find romantic partners, and pay our taxes to how we choose our president.

II. Online social networks have changed the way a generation examines politics. (*Slide 6: Arrangement of President Obama, Hillary Clinton, Ted Cruz, Marco Rubio, other noteworthy politicians*) **Listener-relevance link**

A. Social media has fundamentally transformed the campaign trail.

1. Dwight D. Eisenhower is known for introducing the first political TV ads when he ran for president in 1952.

2. The Museum of Broadcast Communications states that this invention gave him the winning edge: personality (Lee Kaid, n.d).

3. Today, candidates find great success when using social media for this same reason. If a politician posts a photo with her family—or makes fun of herself on social media—she no longer seems like a figurehead but a real person.

4. *The Wall Street Journal* writes, "Twitter and other social-media outlets have become an extension of [candidate's] efforts to build a national following, and in many cases a way to mix personality with policy" (2015).

B. Because social media reaches such a vast audience, and with unparalleled speed, it dwarfs all campaigning mechanisms that came before it.

    1. According to Pew Research, 74 percent of adults, or voters, use social media (2014).

    2. Gender, education, and income do not play significant factors in who chooses to use social networks. This is critical for politicians. In seconds, one post on Instagram or Facebook can reach huge portions of multiple voting demographics.

        a. In 2014, 89 percent of young people reportedly use social networking sites, whereas 49 percent of adults ages 65 and up are active users.

        b. Although older people generally use social media less than younger people, 49 percent is still a substantial amount of voters.

C. Technology evolves rapidly. Today, social media is no longer a new and untapped tool—but a top priority for all campaign managers.

    1. To show how quickly social media has evolved, *The Washington Post* reports that in 2008, when Obama tweeted that he won the election, his post only received 157 retweets (Schwartz, 2015).

    2. In 2008, the app Instagram, which now has more users than Twitter, hadn't even been invented.

    3. Jump forward to the 2012 election. After the 2012 election, 800,000 retweeted Obama's announcement that he had won. In addition, the president posted a photo on his Instagram account the next day. (I know, by today's standards, waiting a day to post a photo is incredibly slow.) That post received 301,000 likes (Schwartz, 2015).

    4. That may seem like a large number, but it's actually rather small. To get perspective on how small that number is, consider this: When pop icon Taylor Swift posted a candid photo of herself laughing on the beach, she racked up 1,741,928 likes. And that is not the highest possible number of likes for Miss Swift, who has 35.1 million followers. That's just average (Instagram, 2015).

    5. Instagram now has 300 million users each month, and will surely become increasingly influential in the 2016 elections (Schwartz, 2015).

D. Social media is used for governing.

    1. According to the American political journalism organization Politico, reporters who usually interview and report on the president's doings are extremely unsatisfied with their access to President Obama.

    2. However, the president claims to have an extremely transparent administration because his staff uses social media to disseminate information in a politically savvy way.

    3. The position Obama takes on this issue will most likely only become more common in the future.

    4. Pew Research Center reports that 92 percent of teens, between the ages of 13 and 17, are active on social media at least once a day. Imagine what role social media will play in politics when this generation grows up (Lenhart, 2015).

Transition

So we really can't deny the fact that online social networks have impacted and will continue to impact the political process today and in years to come. Let's take a few minutes now to examine some of the ways social networks are influencing news reporting today.

III. Thanks to online social networking, news reporting has forever changed in terms of access and immediacy.

A. Because technology now makes it possible for anyone to post news to social networking sites anywhere and anytime, viewers can see events occurring around the world as they happen. Consequently, the traditional news media can no longer set the agenda for what viewers do and do not have access to. (*Slide 7: Image of a young girl documenting the Unity Walk in Charleston, South Carolina with her camera phone, tweets and images of protests to gun violence shared via Twitter*)

B. When tragedies occur, the power of the online community is remarkably clear.

1. In June of 2015, a gunman shot and killed 9 black Americans in an historic African-American church in Charleston, South Carolina.

2. Vigils were organized across the country, from New York City to Atlanta, and were documented across social networks (Kuruvilla, 2015). Through social media, Americans who were separated by geographical space were able to "meet online" to support the families of victims, and to raise awareness about controversial issues, like gun control (Lee-Johnson, 2015).

3. Social media also allowed for activists to organize and spread the word about events like the Unity March, during which thousands of local and out-of-state residents walked the Cooper River Bridge in Charleston (Boughton, 2015).

4. Social media has become so interwoven into our society that even photos of the Unity Walk became documentation of our use of social media, as people captured in photos people doing the same thing: taking photos and videos, writing posts, and live-tweeting.

5. Because everyday citizens have the power to broadcast information from their pocket—whenever they want, we now can look to each other for information, and connect over many media platforms, instead of only looking to news syndicates for the facts.

C. As we know, social media is also more immediate than traditional news. The current format of a 24-hour news cycle means that major news channels are always broadcasting and can respond to events as they unfold. (*Slide 8: Picture of plane in the Hudson River*)

1. For example, when a plane had crashed in the Hudson River in 2013, the news story actually broke on Twitter. A twitterer on the scene commented about it, and that comment got retweeted many times before any news organization had wind of the story (Curtis, 2013).

2. Because of the immediacy and reach that social networks offer users, traditional news is feeling the pressure to keep up as an information supplier. The Pew Research Center notes that news organizations like CNN, ABC News, and Fox News are losing audience share and are trying to adapt to control the pressure from social media (2014). While we've not seen how this will play out in the long term, this emphasizes our main point: social media is forcing news reporting to change.

Conclusion

I. Whether for better or for worse, social media is a driving force of change in our culture.

II. In a matter of two decades, online social networks have dramatically impacted our political and news reporting processes.

III. I hope you now realize like I do that online social networks like Facebook and Twitter and YouTube are not just fun ways to interact with our friends. They are powerful communication phenomena impacting our cultural norms, our communication practices, and our society. I hope you think about that the next time you read or post a comment or tweet.

Thesis statement

Main point summary

Clincher

References

Andrews, N. (2015, February 17). On Twitter, candidates let the jabs fly. *Wall Street Journal*. Retrieved from http://www.wsj.com/articles/on-twitter-2016-rivals-let-the-jabs-fly-1424201759

Boughton, M. (2015, June 21). Thousands gather for Bridge to Peace event: "We will rise above the hate." *The Post and Courier*. Retrieved from http://www.postandcourier.com/article/20150621/PC16/150629842

Curtis, A. (2013). A brief history of social media. Retrieved from http://www.uncp.edu/home/acurtis/NewMedia/SocialMedia/SocialMediaHistory.html

Dewey, C. (2014, October 29). Almost as many people use Facebook as live in the entire country of China. *The Washington Post*. Retrieved from http://www.washingtonpost.com/news/the-intersect/wp/2014/10/29/almost-as-many-people-use-facebook-as-live-in-the-entire-country-of-china/

Dwyer, D. (2011, May 10). Rick Santorum's "Google problem" resurfaces with Jon Stewart plug. ABC News. Retrieved from http://abcnews.go.com/blogs/politics/2011/05/rick-santorums-google-problem-resurfaces-with-jon-stewart-plug/

Fletcher, D. (2009, November 9). Internet atrocity! GeoCities' demise erases Web history. Time. Retrieved from http://www.time.com/time/business/article/0,8599,1936645,00.html

Gray, O. (2013, March 8). A valediction: AOL Instant Messenger. *20 Something Magazine*. Retrieved from http://20somethingmagazine.com/2013/03/08/a-valediction-aol-instant-messenger/

Kuruvilla, C. (2015, June 18). AME church clergy gathering for prayer service in wake of shooting. *The Huffington Post*. Retrieved from http://www.huffingtonpost.com/2015/06/18/ame-church-prayer-shooting_n_7612386.html

Lee-Johnson, L. (2015, June 25). Help Charleston heal from church massacre. *CNN*. Retrieved from http://www.cnn.com/2015/06/18/us/iyw-help-charleston-heal/

Lee Kaid, L. (N.d). Political processes and television. The Museum of Broadcast Communications. Retrieved from http://www.museum.tv/eotv/politicalpro.htm.

Lenhart, A. (2015, (April 9). Teens, social media & technology overview 2015. Pew Research Center. Retrieved from: http://www.pewinternet.org/2015/04/09/teens-social-media-technology-2015/

Milian, M. (2009, December 29). The business and culture of our digital lives. *Los Angeles Times*. Retrieved from http://latimesblogs.latimes.com/technology/2009/12/top-10-social-media-events.html

O'Neill, M. (2012, March 7). How has social media impacted political fundraising? [infographic]. Retrieved from http://socialtimes.com/political-fundraising-infographic_b91001

Pew Research Center. (2014, January). Social networking fact sheet. Pew Research Center. Retrieved from http://www.pewinternet.org/fact-sheets/social-networking-fact-sheet/

Sasseen, J., Olmstead, K., & Mitchell A. (2013). Digital: As mobile grows rapidly, the pressures on news intensify. Pew Research Center. Retrieved online from http://stateofthemedia.org/2013/digital-as-mobile-grows-rapidly-the-pressures-on-news-intensify/

Schwartz, H. (2015, January 6). 2016 may yet be the first "Instagram election." *The Washington Post*. Retrieved from http://www.washingtonpost.com/blogs/post-politics/wp/2015/01/06/2016-may-yet-be-the-first-instagram-election/.

Vandehei, J. & Allen, M. (2013, February 18). Obama, the puppet master. *Politico*. Retrieved from http://www.politico.com/story/2013/02/obama-the-puppet-master-87764.html

Speech and Analysis

Speech

A man dies—cheery way to start out, right?—and ends up sitting there in front of heaven's pearly gates. St Peter asks, "What have you done with your life?" The man responds indignantly with, "You mean you haven't been reading my tweets!?"

All joking aside, I imagine most of us in this room use social media, whether it be Facebook, Twitter, LinkedIn, or even—dare I say it—Myspace—remember that one?—for nostalgia. (*Slide 1: Scattered logos of significant or previously significant social media Web sites. Facebook, Twitter, Myspace, Friendster, etc.*) To illustrate my point, go ahead and take out your smartphone, notebook, or laptop and log on to any one of them. This is a race: When you're "on," raise your hand (*time them*). Every hand went up in less than five seconds! But how many of us really understand the significant impact this modern online social network phenomenon is having our society? If we're being honest, I sincerely doubt that many of us have thought about it. We know not to post raunchy stuff on Facebook or Twitter before going to an important job interview and not to "friend" professional supervisors if we don't want them to see what we talk about online, but how much more?

After realizing I knew next to nothing about these complex social networks I use everyday, I decided to explore what the experts have to say about the nature

Analysis

▶ Notice how Logan uses a humorous anecdote to get the attention of his listeners.

▶ Here Logan does a great job of establishing relevance with his audience of young adults and appealing to the doing dimension of the learning cycle by asking them to check their social network sites.

▶ Logan admits not knowing much about the nature of online social networks, which make him seem trustworthy before also establishing credibility by stating that he did some homework to prepare this speech.

of online social networks and how they are shaping communication practices and society today.

So today, I'd like to share what I've discovered about the history and rapid growth of our modern online social networks and how they are impacting both politics and news reporting.

To really understand how online social networks, that is, Web sites that allow users to easily create content and interact with one another about that content, affect our lives and the world we live in today, we first need to understand a bit about their convoluted but significant history.

Historically speaking, online social media is rather young, dating back only about 20 years to 1994 when a Beverly Hills Internet company created a Web-hosting service called GeoCities.com. According to Dr. Anthony Curtis, professor of mass communication at the University of North Carolina at Pembroke, this marks the first time users could create customizable Web pages organized by interests with feedback sections and other features unavailable to non-corporate Web site creators at the time. According to a 2009 *LA Times* article, it wasn't in the sleek and attractive style we expect today. (*Slide 2: Example GeoCities site with its unorganized content*) Although it was rather unattractive, it was still the first of its kind in being a way for users to create their own content and respond to that of others.

Three short years later, blogging took off. People began creating personas for themselves and engaging in regular, frequent dialog through blog posts, responses to posts, and of course, responses to the responses of blog posts. For example, AOL Instant Messenger changed what users wanted from the Internet as a communication tool (*Slide 3: AIM, MSN Messenger icons*). We all remember our middle school days of being mystified at the thought of instantly sending and receiving messages from our friends, right? Well, this was the start of that. And what's more, this was the start of a demand for instant gratification when it came to online social interaction with friends, according to Oliver Gray in a *20 Something Magazine* article posted in March 2013.

In 2002 and 2003, two sites that would become outrageously popular began. Although neither is a most frequented site today, Friendster and Myspace took the Internet by storm. Users of Friendster, which was invented in 2002, catapulted to 3 million in just three short months, which was a fantastic feat. By 2004, however, just one year after it was created in 2003, Myspace overtook Friendster in terms of the number of accounts created. That same year, 2004, marks the point when a similar site was created by a group of students at Harvard. Dubbed the college version of Friendster, it didn't receive much attention at the time, but you may have heard of it: (*Slide 4: Cartoon of Facebook icon on top of Myspace and Friendster icons*) Facebook. It's pretty incredible to think that Facebook is not even a decade old, and according to an article in the *Wall Street Journal,* boasts of having more than a billion members worldwide.

Another dramatic shift occurred in 2005 when YouTube was founded. Thanks to YouTube, aspiring musicians had an outlet to post musical recordings without getting a recording studio to do so. Parents also began posting home videos of their kids. Corporations began posting recordings to promote their products and people began posting hilarious creative videos that previously could only be seen on programs such as *America's Funniest Home Videos*. Today, online social networks such as Facebook, YouTube, and Twitter are taken-for-granted communication outlets for most Americans, especially digital natives like those of us here in the room today.

If you are like I was before I did my research, you might be thinking "so what's the big deal? Online social networks are here to stay." But, let me tell you now how they have changed and will continue to change our cultural norms; norms ranging

Here Logan shares his goal in the form of a thesis statement with main point preview. Listeners have a macrostructural framework by which to listen to the body of the speech.

Notice how Logan states his first main point in a way that also provides listener relevance, piquing curiosity to keep paying attention.

Notice how Logan provides an oral footnote establishing the credentials of the source of his information, which ultimately boosts listeners' perceived credibility of Logan, as well.

Here Logan offers listener relevance that addresses the feeling dimension of the learning cycle, as well. Listeners are encouraged to reflect on their own personal memories of using AOL Instant Messenger.

Although Logan provides a good deal of interesting supporting material here, he only cites a source for one of the facts he presents. He could have improved the speech by citing the sources for more of the information shared in this paragraph.

Logan could have made this paragraph more compelling by offering some specific examples for each of the ways in which YouTube has broken through traditional gatekeeper barriers for the general public.

Again, Logan does a great job with this transition statement that reminds his audience about the point he is done talking about and introducing the next one in a way that also highlights listener relevance for it.

from how we make friends, find romantic partners, and pay our taxes to how we choose our president.

Online social networks have changed the way a generation examines politics. (*Slide 6: Arrangement of President Obama, Hillary Clinton, Ted Cruz, Marco Rubio, other noteworthy politicians*)

Consider for example how social media has fundamentally transformed the campaign trail. Dwight D. Eisenhower is known for introducing the first political TV ads when he ran for president in 1952. According to the Museum of Broadcast Communications, using that innovation gave him the winning edge: personality. Today, successful candidates often use social media for this same reason. If a politician posts a photo with their family—or makes fun of themselves on social media—they no longer seem like a figurehead but a real person. An article in the *The Wall Street Journal* had this to say about the ability of social media to showcase personality: "Twitter and other social-media outlets have become an extension of [candidate's] efforts to build a national following, and in many cases a way to mix personality with policy."

Creating a cult of personality is easier than ever before because social media reaches such a vast audience, and with unparalleled speed. Social media dwarfs all campaigning mechanisms that came before it. According to Pew Research, 74 percent of adults, or voters, use social media. What you may find interesting is that gender, education, and income are not significant factors in who chooses to use social networks. That fact is critical for politicians. In seconds, one post on Instagram or Facebook can reach huge portions of multiple voting demographics, from the young to even those over age 65.

When it comes to social media, the rapid pace of technology evolution also influences politics. Today, social media is no longer a new and untapped tool—but a top priority for all campaign managers. To show how quickly social media evolves, all we have to do is look at the difference between how Senator Obama used social media after the 2008 election and how President Obama used it after the 2012 election. *The Washington Post* reported that, in 2008, when Senator Obama tweeted that he won the presidential election, his post only received 157 retweets. Now, keep in mind that in 2008, the app Instagram, which now has more users than Twitter, hadn't even been invented. Jump forward to the 2012 election. After the 2012 election, 800,000 people retweeted Obama's announcement that he had won a second term. In addition, the President posted a photo on his Instagram account the next day. (I know, by today's standards, waiting a day to post a photo is incredibly slow.) That post received 301,000 likes. Although that may seem like a large number, it's actually rather small. When pop icon Taylor Swift posted a candid photo of herself laughing on the beach, she racked up 1,741,928 likes. Instagram now has 300 million users each month, and will surely be even more influential in the 2016 elections.

Social media is not used for campaigning alone. It is also used for governing. According to the American political journalism organization Politico, reporters who usually interview and report on the president's doings are extremely unsatisfied with their access to President Obama. The president, however, claims to have an extremely transparent administration because his staff uses social media to disseminate information in a politically savvy way. This position on social media usage will most likely only become more common in the future. Nearly 100 percent of teens are active on social media at least once a day. Imagine what role social media will play in politics when this generation grows up.

So we really can't deny the fact that online social networks have impacted and will continue to impact the political process today and in years to come. Let's take a few minutes now to examine some of the ways social networks are influencing news reporting today.

Thanks to online social networking, news reporting has forever changed in terms of access and immediacy. Technology now makes it possible for anyone to post

▶ Logan makes his facts compelling by providing a concrete example about President Obama's use of social media.

▶ Notice here how Logan uses personal pronouns and "we" language to create nonverbal immediacy and a sense of talking *with* rather than speaking *to* his audience.

▶ Logan's of presentation aids and images are very effective and increase the power of his example.

news to social networking sites anywhere and anytime, so viewers can see events occurring around the world as they happen. Consequently, the traditional news media can no longer set the agenda for what viewers do and do not have access to. (*Slide 7: Image of a young girl documenting the Unity Walk in Charleston, South Carolina with her camera phone, tweets and images of protests to gun violence shared via Twitter*) When tragedies occur, the power of the online community is remarkably clear. After a gunman shot and killed 9 black Americans in an historic African American church in Charleston, South Carolina in June 2015, Americans across the country organized vigils using social media. Americans who were separated by geographical space were able to "meet online" to support the families of victims, and to raise awareness about controversial issues. Social media has become so interwoven into our society that even photos of the Unity Walk over Cooper River Bridge became documentation of our use of social media. People captured in photos other people doing the same thing: taking photos and videos, writing posts, and live-tweeting.

Because everyday citizens have the power to broadcast information from their pocket, social media can also be more immediate than traditional news. The current format of a 24-hour news cycle means that major news channels are always broadcasting and can respond to events as they unfold on social media. (*Slide 8: Picture of plane in the Hudson River*) For example, when a plane had crashed in the Hudson River in 2013, the news story actually broke on Twitter. A twitterer on the scene commented about it, and that comment got retweeted many times before any news organization had wind of the story. Because of the immediacy and reach that social networks offer users, traditional news is feeling the pressure to keep up as an information supplier. The Pew Research Center notes that news organizations like CNN, ABC News, and Fox News are losing audience share and are trying to adapt to control the pressure from social media (2014). While we've not seen how this will play out in the long term, this emphasizes our main point: social media is forcing news reporting to change.

Whether for better or for worse, social media is a driving force of change in our culture. In a matter of two decades, online social networks have dramatically impacted our political and news reporting processes. I hope you now realize like I do that online social networks like Facebook and Twitter and YouTube are not just fun ways to interact with our friends. They are powerful communication phenomena impacting our cultural norms, our communication practices, and our society. I hope you think about that the next time you read or post a comment or tweet.

▶ *Here it would have been nice to include the actual tweet from the Hudson River example Logan describes.*

▶ *Notice how nicely Logan concludes the speech with a thesis restatement and main point summary, as well a clincher encouraging his audience to think twice from this point on every time they interact with an online social network. If he is successful, his speech will have lasting impact on his audience.*

STUDY TOOLS **12**

LOCATED IN TEXTBOOK

☐ Tear-out Chapter Review cards at the end of the book

☐ Review with the Quick Quiz below

LOCATED ON SPEAK3 ONLINE AT CENGAGEBRAIN.COM

☐ Review Key Term flashcards and create your own cards

☐ Track your knowledge and understanding of key concepts in speech communication

☐ Complete practice and graded quizzes to prepare for tests

☐ Complete interactive content within SPEAK3 Online

☐ View the chapter highlight boxes for SPEAK3 Online

Quick Quiz (answers in Solutions Appendix)

T   F   1. One of the goals of an informative speech is to present information in a way to help the audience remember it.

T   F   2. A synonym of "hot" is "spicy."

T   F   3. A speaker who is describing the effects of World War II on the European economy is giving a process speech.

T   F   4. In an effective speech, the speaker should not have to explain to the audience how the information is relevant to them.

T   F   5. Using presentational aids will help your speech be more memorable.

6. The method of informing that explains the meaning of something is:

   a. description
   b. definition
   c. comparison
   d. narration
   e. contrast

7. The primary goal of an informative speech is to:

   a. entertain
   b. incite
   c. educate
   d. encourage
   e. aggravate

8. According to the text, creativity comes from:

   a. traits
   b. personality
   c. heredity
   d. timing
   e. hard work

9. Information that is new to an audience and piques curiosity is:

   a. creative
   b. thought provoking
   c. challenging
   d. intellectually stimulating
   e. mind blowing

10. If you were giving a speech on how to make smoked salmon, you would be giving a(n):

   a. persuasive speech
   b. process speech
   c. ceremonial speech
   d. expository speech
   e. creative speech

Chapter Takeaways

List three key takeaways from this chapter:

-

-

-

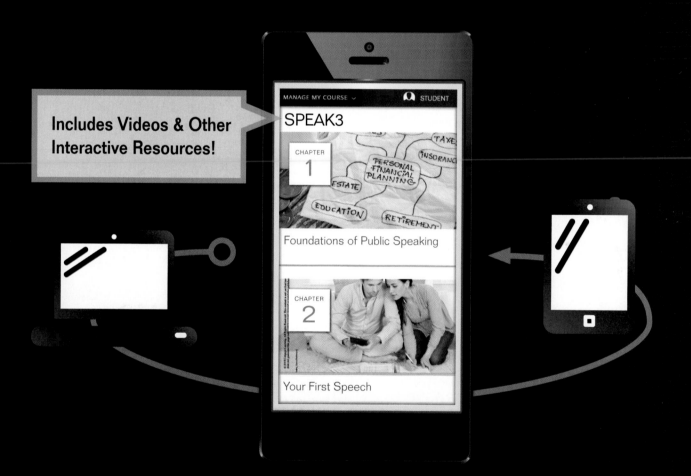

13 Persuasive Messages

LEARNING OUTCOMES

13-1 Describe the nature of persuasion.

13-2 Explain how people process persuasive messages.

13-3 Identify and apply logos in persuasive messages.

13-4 Identify and apply ethos in persuasive messages.

13-5 Identify and apply pathos in persuasive messages.

After finishing this chapter go to **PAGE 244** for **STUDY TOOLS.**

Sound Familiar?

Rick loves his golden retriever, Trini. He lives in an apartment downtown and enjoys taking Trini for walks twice a day, but he wishes there was a place nearby where he could let Trini off her leash to run. He decides to try to persuade the city council to fence off an area of a large inner-city park to turn it into a dog park where owners can let their dogs run free. He needs to circulate a petition about the idea, get at least 500 others to sign it, and collect $1,000 in donations to help pay for the fence. After a few weeks of knocking on doors, Rick has gathered more than enough signatures. However, he has managed to raise less than half of the $1,000 he needs. He wonders what he can do to persuade more people to actually donate money for the cause.

Does the above scenario sound familiar? As was the case with Rick and the downtown dog park, whenever we attempt to convince others to agree with our position or behave a certain way, we actually construct and present persuasive messages. How successful we are, however, depends on how effectively we employ persuasive strategies. **Persuasion** is the process of influencing people's attitudes, beliefs, values, or behaviors. **Persuasive speaking** is the process of doing so in a public speech.

Persuasive messages are pervasive. Whether we are attempting to convince others or others are attempting to influence us, we are constantly involved in influencing or being influenced. Friends persuade us to go to a particular movie or to eat at a certain restaurant, salespeople persuade us to buy a certain sweater or pair of shoes, and advertisements bombard us whenever we turn on the radio or television or surf the Internet. It is crucial for you to understand persuasion so you can critically examine and evaluate the persuasive messages you receive, and so you can create effective and ethical persuasive messages of your own.

We begin our two-chapter discussion of persuasive speaking by first describing the nature of persuasive messages and the rhetorical strategies used in them. Next, using the elaboration likelihood model (ELM), we explain how people process persuasive messages. Then we focus specifically on how to use the rhetorical strategies of logos, ethos, and pathos to develop your persuasive messages and offer guidelines for you to consider when evaluating and constructing them.

13-1 THE NATURE OF PERSUASION

Persuasive messages are fundamentally different from informative ones. Whereas the goal of an informative message is to teach, the goal of a persuasive message is to lead. So persuasive speakers are successful only when their audience members are convinced to agree, change their behavior, or take action. In the opening scenario, Rick was successful in convincing others to agree with him but unsuccessful in getting them to take action.

As a speaker, you can develop informative and persuasive speeches on the same topic depending on your ultimate goal. Last semester, Susan completed a term project on the fracking boom on North Dakota's Bakken formation, so she decided to use her expertise on this topic for her three required speeches. For her informative speech, her goal was to explain the process of hydraulic fracturing (fracking) and how it is being used to extract oil from the Bakken formation. The goal of her first persuasive speech was to convince her audience to agree with her position on the importance of fracking for U.S. energy independence, so she focused on persuading listeners that fracking is a safe method of oil extraction and one that will enable the United States to significantly reduce its petroleum imports. In her second persuasive speech, her goal was to motivate her classmates to take action, so she focused on persuading them to reduce their oil dependence by avoiding drinks packaged in plastic containers and limiting their use of plastic overall.

To further explain the nature of persuasion, we draw on the work of the ancient Greeks and Romans who described *persuasion* as logical and well-supported arguments developed through rhetorical appeals to logos,

persuasion the process of influencing people's attitudes, beliefs, values, or behaviors

persuasive speaking the process of influencing people's attitudes, beliefs, values, or behaviors in a public speech

ethos, and pathos. Argument, in this context, is not synonymous with "quarrel" as we sometimes define it today. Rather, **argument** means articulating a position with the support of logos, ethos, and pathos.[1] Recall from Chapter 1 that logos is a persuasive strategy of constructing logical arguments that support your point of view. Ethos is a persuasive strategy of highlighting your competence, credibility, and good character as means by which to convince others to accept your point of view. Pathos is a persuasive strategy of appealing to emotions in order to convince others to support your position.[2]

While all speakers are expected to behave ethically, persuasive speakers have an extra burden to demonstrate that what they are advocating is in the best interest of the audience. So persuasive speakers must evaluate their message strategies and eliminate those that even begin to violate the ethical principles of truthfulness, integrity, fairness, respect, and responsibility.

Now that we have a basic understanding of the nature of persuasion, let's look more closely at how people think about the persuasive messages they receive.

13-2 PROCESSING PERSUASIVE MESSAGES

What determines how closely we listen to and how carefully we evaluate the hundreds of persuasive messages we hear each day? Richard Petty and John Cacioppo developed the *elaboration likelihood model* (ELM) to explain how we evaluate information (such as the arguments that we hear in a speech) before making our decisions.[3]

The model suggests that we process information in one of two ways. As illustrated in Exhibit 13.1, sometimes we use the "central route" and listen carefully, reflect thoughtfully, and may even mentally elaborate on the message before making a decision. When we do this, we based our decision primarily on appeals to logic and reasoning (logos). The second way, called the "peripheral route," is a shortcut that relies on simple cues such as a quick evaluation of the speaker's competence, credibility,

argument articulating a position with the support of logos, ethos, and pathos

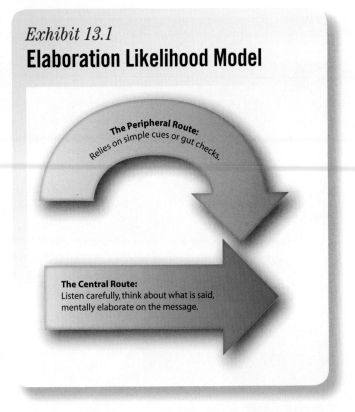

Exhibit 13.1
Elaboration Likelihood Model

The Peripheral Route: Relies on simple cues or gut checks.

The Central Route: Listen carefully, think about what is said, mentally elaborate on the message.

and character (ethos) or a gut check about what we feel (pathos) about the message.

We choose a route based on how important we perceive the issue to be for us. When we believe the issue is important, we will expend the energy necessary to process it using the central route. When we don't, we take the peripheral route. For example, if you have a serious chronic illness that is expensive to treat, you are more likely to pay attention to and evaluate carefully any proposals to change health care benefits. If you are healthy, you are more likely to quickly agree with suggestions from someone you perceive to be credible or with a proposal that seems compassionate. The ELM also suggests that when we form attitudes as a result of central processing, we are less likely to change our minds than when we base our decisions on peripheral cues.

When you prepare a persuasive speech, you will want to use strategies that address both the central and peripheral routes. To do so, be sure to integrate logos strategies that will be most influential for audience members who use the central processing route. And integrate ethos

www.BillionPhotos.com/Shutterstock.com

and pathos strategies to appeal to those in your audience who make their decision based on the peripheral route. Ultimately, the most compelling persuasive messages offer appeals to all three: logos, ethos, and pathos.

13-3 THE RHETORICAL STRATEGY OF LOGOS

Logos strategies are arguments built on logic and reasoning. Stephen Toulmin (1958) developed a three-part model to explain logos-based arguments that has stood the test of time.[4] A solid logos argument consists of a claim, the support, and the warrant.

The **claim** (C) is the conclusion the persuader wants others to agree with. For example, you might *claim*: "Jim's car needs a tune-up." The **support** (S) is the evidence offered as grounds for accepting/agreeing with the claim. You can support a claim with various types of evidence such as facts, opinions, experiences, and observations. In the car example, we might note as evidence that "the car is missing at slow speeds" and "stalling at stoplights." The **warrant** (W) is the reasoning process that connects the support to the claim. Sometimes the warrant is verbalized and sometimes it is implied. In the car example, you might offer a warrant such as "missing at slow speeds and stalling at stoplights are *common indications* that a car needs a tune-up." Or you might assume that others realize these are signs that a car needs a tune-up. Not knowing whether their audience members will make these connections, the most effective public speakers verbalize their reasoning warrants.

You can connect your supporting evidence to the claim using one of two different types of reasoning warrants. You can do so inductively or deductively. **Inductive reasoning** is arriving at a general conclusion based on several pieces of specific evidence. When we reason inductively, how much our audience agrees with our conclusion depends on the number, quality, and typicality of each piece of evidence we offer. For Jim's car, an inductive reasoning argument might look like this:

S: *Jim's car is missing at slow speeds.*

S: *Jim's car is stalling at stoplights.*

W: *These are common indicators that a car needs a tune-up.*

C: *Jim's car needs a tune-up.*

Deductive reasoning is arguing that if something is true for everything that belongs to a certain class (**major premise**) and a specific instance is part of that class

For over a century, deductive reasoning has been the hallmark of Sherlock Holmes, played most recently by Benedict Cumberbatch (above) in the BBC series *Sherlock*.

Robert Viglasky/BBC/Hartswood Filmas/Everett Collection

(**minor premise**), then we must conclude that what is true for all members of the class must be true in the specific instance (claim). This three-part form of deductive reasoning is called a **syllogism**. For Jim's car, a deductive syllogism might look like this:

Major premise: *Cars need a tune-up when the engine misses consistently at slow speeds.*

Minor premise: *Jim's car is missing at slow speeds.*

Logical conclusion/Claim: *Jim's car needs a tune-up.*

With this introduction in mind, let's look at some different types of logical arguments.

13-3a Types of Logical Arguments

Although an argument *always* includes a claim and support, different types of reasoning warrants can be used to illustrate the relationship between the claim and the support on which it is based. Four common types of logical arguments are sign, example, analogy, and causation.

claim the proposition or conclusion to be proven

support the reason or evidence the speaker offers as the grounds for accepting the conclusion

warrant the reasoning process that connects the support to the claim

inductive reasoning arriving at a general conclusion based on several pieces of specific evidence

deductive reasoning arriving at a conclusion based on a major premise and minor premise

major premise a general principle that most people agree upon

minor premise a specific point that fits within the major premise

syllogism the three-part form of deductive reasoning

Arguing from Sign

If certain events, characteristics, or situations usually or always accompany something, those events, characteristics, or situations are called *signs*. You **argue from sign** when you support a claim by providing evidence that the events that signal the claim have occurred. The general warrant for reasoning from sign is, "When phenomena that usually or always accompany a specific situation occur, then we can expect that the specific situation is occurring (or will occur)."

For example: "Hives and a slight fever are indicators (signs) of an allergic reaction. Since you have hives and a fever (sign), you must be having an allergic reaction (claim)." Signs should not be confused with causes; signs accompany a phenomenon but do not bring about, lead to, or create the claim. In fact, signs may actually be the effects of the phenomenon. A rash and fever don't cause an allergic reaction; they are indications, or effects, of a reaction.

Let's look at another example. Suppose you are supporting Juanita Martinez for president of the local neighborhood council. You believe that Juanita is electable (claim). If you notice that she has more campaign workers than all the other candidates combined (sign) and more community members are wearing "Juanita for President" buttons than any others (sign), you might reason that "Juanita's campaign has the key signs of a presidential victory" (warrant).

When arguing from sign, you can make sure that your reasoning is valid by answering the following questions.

1. Do these signs usually or always accompany the conclusion drawn? If the signs cited do not usually indicate the conclusion, then the argument might not be valid because the reasoning is flawed.

2. Are a sufficient number of signs present? Several signs often indicate events or situations. If enough signs are not present, then the conclusion may not follow. If there are insufficient signs, then the argument may not be valid because the reasoning is flawed.

3. Are contradictory signs in evidence? If many signs exist that indicate different conclusions, then the argument may not be valid because the reasoning is flawed.

Arguing from Example

You **argue from example** when the evidence you use as support are examples of the claim you are making. The warrant for reasoning from example is, "What is true in the examples provided is (or will be) true in general or in other instances."

Let's revisit the claim that "Juanita is electable" for neighborhood council president. In examining her résumé, you find several examples of previous victories. She was elected president of her high school senior class, treasurer of her church council, and president of her college Phi Beta Kappa honor society chapter.

When arguing from example, you can make sure your reasoning is solid by answering the following questions.

1. Are enough examples cited? Are three elections enough examples to convince others to agree with your claim? You must cite enough examples to satisfy others that the instances are not isolated or handpicked. Otherwise the argument may not be valid because the reasoning is flawed.

2. Are the examples typical? Are the three offices Juanita previously held similar to the one she is now running for? Typical means that the examples cited must be similar to or representative of most or all within the category. Otherwise the argument may not be valid because the reasoning is flawed.

3. Are negative examples accounted for? There may be one or more examples that contradict the argument. If the exceptions are minor or infrequent, then they won't invalidate the argument. For instance, perhaps Juanita ran for president of the Sociology Club in college and lost. That one failure does not necessarily invalidate the argument. If, however, Juanita had run for office twelve times and was successful on only the three occasions cited, then the argument may not be valid because the reasoning is flawed.

Arguing from Analogy

You **argue from analogy** when you support a claim with a single comparable example that is so significantly similar to the claim as to be strong proof. The general

argue from sign to support a claim by providing evidence that the events that signal the claim have occurred

argue from example to support a claim by providing one or more individual examples

argue from analogy to support a claim with a single comparable example that is significantly similar to the subject of the claim

razihusin/Shutterstock.com

warrant for reasoning from analogy is, "What is true for situation A will also be true in situation B, which is similar to situation A" or "What is true for situation A will be true in all similar situations."

Suppose you wanted to argue that the Cherry Fork volunteer fire department should conduct a raffle to raise money for three portable defibrillator units (claim). You could support the claim by analogy with a single example: Jefferson City Fire Department, which is very similar to that of Cherry Fork (warrant) conducted a raffle and raised enough money to purchase four units (support).

Let us return to the claim that Juanita is electable (claim). If you discover that Juanita has essentially the same characteristics as Paula Jefferson, who was elected president two years ago (both are very bright and have a great deal of drive), then you can use the single example of Paula to form a reasoning warrant: "Juanita has the same characteristics of being bright and driven that got Paula Jefferson elected two years ago."

When arguing from analogy, you can make sure that your reasoning is solid by answering the following questions.

1. Are the subjects being compared similar in every important way? Are intelligence and drive the most important characteristics for determining electability? If the characteristics are not the most important ones, then the argument may not be valid because the reasoning is flawed.

2. Are any of the ways in which the subjects are dissimilar important to the claim? If Paula is a native of the community, whereas Juanita has only been in the area for a year, is this dissimilarity important? When the dissimilarities outweigh the subjects' similarities, then the argument may be invalid because the reasoning is flawed.

Arguing from Causation

You **argue from causation** when you support a claim by citing events that always (or almost always) bring about or lead to a predictable effect or set of effects. The general warrant for arguments from cause is: "If A, which is known to bring about B, has been observed, then we can expect B to occur."

Let's return to Juanita's election campaign one more time. In researching Juanita's election campaign, you might discover that (1) she has campaigned intelligently (support) and (2) she has won the endorsement of key community leaders (support). In the past, these two events have usually been associated with victory (warrant), thus Juanita is electable (claim).

When arguing from causation, you can make sure your reasoning is solid by answering the following questions.

1. Are the events alone sufficient to cause the stated effect? Are intelligent campaigning and key endorsements alone important enough to result in winning elections? If the events are truly causes, then the effect would not occur if the event were eliminated. If the effect can occur without these two events occurring, then the argument may not be valid because the reasoning is flawed.

2. Do other events accompanying the cited events actually cause the effect? Are other factors (such as luck, drive, friends) more important in determining whether a person wins an election? If these other events are more important in causing the effect, then the argument may not be valid because the reasoning is flawed.

3. Is the relationship between the causal events and the effect consistent? Do intelligent campaigning and key endorsements always (or usually) yield electoral victories? If there are times when the effect has not followed the cause, then the argument may not be valid because the reasoning is flawed.

Combining Arguments in a Persuasive Speech

An effective persuasive speech usually uses several types of logical arguments. To convince voters that Juanita is electable, for instance, Juanita's campaign speakers might organize their speeches this way:

I. *Juanita has run successful campaigns in the past. (argument by example)*
   A. *Juanita was successful in her campaign for president of her high school class.*
   B. *Juanita was successful in her campaign for treasurer of her church council.*
   C. *Juanita was successful in her campaign for president of her college honor society.*

II. *Juanita has engaged in actions that result in campaign victory. (argued by cause)*
   A. *Juanita has campaigned intelligently.*
   B. *Juanita has secured key endorsements.*

III. *Juanita is a strong leader. (argued by sign)*
   A. *Juanita has more volunteer campaign workers than all other candidates combined.*
   B. *Most community members are wearing Juanita's campaign buttons.*

Exhibit 13.2 lists questions you can ask to validate arguments using all four bases.

argue from causation to support a claim by citing events that have occurred that result in the claim

Exhibit 13.2
Four Argument Bases

Signs
- Do the signs cited usually or always indicate the conclusion drawn?
- Are a sufficient number of signs present?
- Are contradictory signs in evidence?

Example
- Are enough examples cited?
- Are the examples typical?
- Are negative examples accounted for?

Analogy
- Are the subjects being compared similar in every important way?
- Are any of the ways in which the subjects are dissimilar important to the claim?

Causation
- Are the events alone sufficient to cause the stated effect?
- Do other events accompanying the cited events actually cause the effect?
- Is the relationship between the causal events and the effect consistent?

13-3b Reasoning Fallacies

As you test the validity of your arguments from sign, example, analogy, and causation, you should check to make sure that your reasoning is sound. We refer to errors in reasoning as **reasoning fallacies**. As shown in Exhibit 13.3, five common reasoning fallacies to avoid are hasty generalization, false cause, either/or, straw man, and ad hominem arguments.

1. A **hasty generalization** occurs when a claim is either not supported with evidence or is supported with only one weak example. Enough supporting material must be cited to satisfy the audience that the

reasoning fallacies errors in reasoning

hasty generalization a fallacy that presents a generalization that is either not supported with evidence or is supported with only one weak example

false cause a fallacy that occurs when the alleged cause fails to be related to, or to produce, the effect

either/or a fallacy that argues there are only two alternatives when, in fact, there are many

straw man a fallacy that occurs when a speaker weakens the opposing position by misrepresenting it and then attacks that weaker position

Exhibit 13.3
Five Fallacies

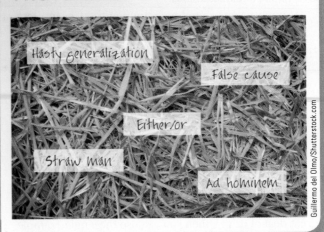

Guillermo del Olmo/Shutterstock.com

instances are not isolated or handpicked. For example, someone who argued, "All Akitas are vicious dogs," whose sole piece of evidence was, "My neighbor had an Akita and it bit my best friend's sister," would be guilty of a hasty generalization. It is hasty to generalize about the temperament of a whole breed of dogs based on a single action of one dog.

2. A **false cause** occurs when the alleged cause fails to produce the effect. The Latin term for this fallacy is *post hoc, ergo propter hoc,* meaning "after this, therefore because of this." Just because two things happen one after the other does not mean that the first necessarily caused the second. An example of a false cause fallacy is when people claim that school violence is caused by television violence, the Internet, a certain song or musical group, or lack of parental involvement. When one event follows another, there may be no connection between them at all. Or the first event might be just one of many that contribute to the second.

3. An **either/or** fallacy occurs by suggesting there are only two alternatives when, in fact, others exist. Many such cases are an oversimplification of a complex issue. For example, when Robert claimed "we'll either have to raise taxes or close the library," he committed an either/or fallacy. He reduced a complex issue to one oversimplified solution when many other possible solutions existed.

4. A **straw man** fallacy occurs when a speaker weakens the opposing position by misrepresenting it in some way and then attacks that weaker (straw man) position. For example, in her speech advocating a seven-day waiting period to purchase handguns, Colleen favored regulation, not prohibition, of gun ownership. Bob argued against that by claiming "it is our constitutional right to bear arms." However, Colleen did not propose abolishing the right to bear arms. Hence, Bob distorted Colleen's position, making it easier for him to refute.

5. An **ad hominem** fallacy attacks or praises the person making the argument rather than addressing the argument itself. *Ad hominem* literally means "to the man." For example, if Jamal claims that everyone should buy a Mac because Apple's founder, Steve Jobs, was a genius, he is making an ad hominem argument. Jobs's intelligence isn't really a reason to buy a particular brand of computer. Unfortunately, politicians sometimes resort to ad hominem arguments when they attack their opponent's character rather than their platforms while campaigning for office. Bullying in person, over the Internet, and via text messaging is another example of ad hominem attacks that can have dire consequences. TV commercials or advertisements that feature celebrities using a particular product are often guilty of ad hominem reasoning. For example, Robert De Niro and Jerry Seinfeld have both appeared in American Express commercials, and Gwyneth Paltrow has done ads for Estée Lauder. What makes any of these celebrities experts about the products they are endorsing?

13-3c Evaluating Evidence and Sources

As you research a topic, you are likely to find far more evidence than you will be able to use in the time allotted for your speech. So you will want to evaluate your evidence and the sources you found them in and select the best ones to use in your speech. You can use answers to the following questions to guide your decision.

1. Does the evidence come from a well-respected source? This question involves both the people who offered the opinions or compiled the facts and the book, journal, or Internet source where they were reported. Just as some people's opinions are more reliable than others, so are some printed and Internet sources more reliable than others. Eliminate evidence that comes from a questionable, unreliable, or overly biased source.

2. Is the evidence recent and, if not, is it still valid? Things change, so information that was accurate for a particular time period may or may not be valid today. Consider when the evidence was gathered. Something that was believed to be true five years ago may not be true today. A trend that was forecast a year ago may have been revised since then. And a statistic that was reported last week may be based on data that were collected three years ago.

For example, the evidence "The total cost of caring for individuals with Alzheimer's is at least $100 billion, according to the Alzheimer's Association and the National Institute on Aging"[5] was cited in a 2003 National Institutes of Health publication. Although the source is credible, the date of the publication suggests that the cost may no longer be accurate and, in fact, may be much higher today. Moreover, the report was actually based on information from a study conducted using 1991 data. In cases like this, you would want to find the most recent figures reported by a credible source.

3. Does the evidence really support the claim? Some of the evidence you find may be only indirectly related to the claim and should be eliminated in favor of evidence that provides more direct support.

4. Will this evidence be persuasive for this audience? Finally, you will want to choose evidence that your particular audience is likely to find persuasive. If, for example, you have two quotations from experts, you will want to use the one from the person your audience is likely to find more compelling.

13-4 THE RHETORICAL STRATEGY OF ETHOS

Not everyone will choose the central processing route to make a decision regarding a persuasive message. One important cue people use when they process information by the peripheral route is ethos. So you will want to demonstrate good character as well as say and do things to convey competence and credibility.

13-4a Conveying Good Character

We turn again to the ancient Greek philosopher Aristotle (384–322 B.C.E.) who first observed that a speaker's credibility depends on the audience's perception of the speaker's goodwill. Today, we define **goodwill** as a perception the audience forms of a speaker who they believe (1) understands them, (2) empathizes with them, and (3) is responsive to them.[6] When audience members believe in the speaker's goodwill, they are willing

> **ad hominem** a fallacy that occurs when a speaker attacks or praises a person making an argument rather than addressing the argument itself
>
> **goodwill** a perception the audience forms of a speaker who they believe understands them, empathizes with them, and is responsive to them

to believe what the speaker says. In our opening scenario, Rick was able to convey good character with other dog owners living downtown because he lived there too. So he could talk about sharing their concerns and empathizing with their frustrations.

One way to demonstrate that you understand your audience is by personalizing your information. Use examples that are directly related to them and their experiences.

Not only do you demonstrate goodwill by understanding your audience, but also by empathizing with them. **Empathy** is the ability to see the world through the eyes of someone else. Empathizing goes beyond understanding to also identify emotionally with your audience members' views. Empathizing with the views of the audience doesn't necessarily mean that you accept their views as your own. It does mean, however, that you acknowledge them as valid. For example, consider what spokespersons lead with when responding to a national emergency or crisis event. They begin with "our hearts go out to the victims and their loved ones." In short, they demonstrate empathy.

Finally, you can demonstrate goodwill by being responsive. Speakers who are **responsive** show that they care about the audience by acknowledging feedback, especially subtle negative cues. This feedback may occur during the presentation, but it also may have occurred prior to the speech.

13-4b Conveying Competence and Credibility

Not surprisingly, we are more likely to be persuaded when we perceive a speaker to be competent and credible, that is, when we perceive him or her to be well informed about the topic. We propose the following strategies so that your **terminal credibility**, the audience's perception of your expertise at the end of your speech, is greater than your **initial credibility**, their perception of your expertise at the beginning of your speech.

1. Explain your competence. Unless someone has formally introduced you and your qualifications to your audience, your initial credibility will be low; therefore, you will need to tell your audience about your expertise as you speak. Sending these types of messages during the speech results in your achieving a level of **derived credibility** with your audience. You can interweave comments about your expertise into introductory comments and at appropriate places within the body of the speech.[7] If you've done a good deal of research on the topic, say so. If you have personal experience, say so. It's important for the audience to know why they can trust what you are saying.

2. Use evidence from respected sources. You can also increase your derived credibility by using supporting material from well-recognized and respected sources. If you have a choice between using a statistic from a known partisan organization or from a dispassionate professional association, choose the professional association. Likewise, if you can quote a local expert who is well known and respected by your audience or an international scholar your audience may never have heard of, use the local expert's opinion.

3. Use nonverbal delivery to enhance your credibility. Your audience assesses your credibility not only from what it hears about you before you begin speaking but also from what it observes by looking at you. Although professional attire enhances credibility in any speaking situation, it is particularly important for persuasive speeches. Research shows that persuasive speakers dressed more formally are perceived as more credible than those dressed casually or sloppily.[8]

The audience will also notice how confident you appear as you prepare to address them. From the moment you rise to speak, you will want to convey through your nonverbal behavior that you are competent. Plant your feet firmly, glance at your notes, and then make eye contact or audience contact with one person or group before taking a breath and beginning to speak. Likewise, pause and establish eye contact upon finishing the speech. Just as pausing and establishing eye contact or audience contact before the speech enhances credibility, doing so upon delivering the closing lines of the speech has the same result.

4. Use vocal expression to enhance your credibility. Research shows that credibility is strongly influenced by how you sound. Speaking fluently, using a moderately fast rate, and expressing yourself with conviction makes you appear more intelligent and competent.[9]

empathy the ability to see the world through the eyes of someone else

responsive when speakers show that they care about the audience by acknowledging feedback, especially subtle negative cues

terminal credibility perception of a speaker's expertise at the end of the speech

initial credibility perception of a speaker's expertise at the beginning of the speech

derived credibility strategies employed throughout the speech that signal a speaker's expertise

From Papers to Twitter, Determining the Credibility of Your Sources

A strong claim supported by the right facts can make for a very persuasive message. Not every argument supporting a claim is factual, however. Misrepresentations, half-truths, and downright lies can all make for perfectly persuasive arguments—and even be logically sound.

When conducting research on a topic, a researcher must responsibly separate fact from fiction. As a researcher, you must consider whether each source employs rhetoric designed to persuade rather than inform.

Ideally, news publishers would present only the facts, allowing their readers to develop their own opinions on a story or issue. But historically, that hasn't been the case.

In the 1890s, magnates William Randolph Hearst and Joseph Pulitzer built their media empires by appealing to their readers' lust for dramatics and excitement and selling newspapers adorned with bold, sensationalist headlines.[10] This brand of reporting became known as yellow journalism and would prove to be a successful and persuasive marketing strategy. Historians often credit yellow papers with playing off rising anti-Spanish sentiments in the U.S. and building the political momentum that would lead to the Spanish-American war.[11]

In today's media, conflation of fact, persuasion, and selling can make it difficult to discern accurate information. In newspapers and magazines, advertorials, a combination of paid advertising and editorial content, are often formatted to look like regular news. The same is true of sponsored content. Public relations firms provide finished articles for free to magazines and papers to promote their clients or issues. And individual companies write, publish, and distribute white papers on a range of topics. Those types of content can be informative,

...credibility enhances your ability to persuade.

but there is no denying the companies' self-interest in publishing the material (or having it published).

It can be equally challenging to determine the credibility of information you collect from online sources, especially social media. Over the years, various researchers have developed tools to allow users to ascertain the credibility of tweets posted during catastrophic events (natural disasters, political upheaval, etc.). The now defunct Truthy.com allowed users to separate news information about a topic from other conversations in a Twitter feed.[12] Today, the TweetCred plug-in on Chrome assigns tweets a credibility score in real time.[13]

With traditional news sources and professional journalists now being joined by a proliferation of bloggers, microbloggers, and news aggregators, what passes as news may actually be fact, fiction, rumor, or propaganda.

As you craft your own persuasive message, think critically about your sources. Evidence needs to be credible, not merely convincing.

13-5 THE RHETORICAL STRATEGY OF PATHOS

We are more likely to be involved with a topic when we have an emotional stake in it. **Emotions** are the buildup of action-specific energy.[14] When we experience the tension associated with any emotion, we look for a way to release the energy. For example, consider how people's facial expressions change when they receive good or bad news. Smiling is one way to release built-up feelings of happiness. Crying is a way to release built-up feelings of sadness. You can increase audience involvement, then, by stimulating both negative and positive emotions in your speeches.[15]

13-5a Evoking Negative Emotions

Negative emotions are disquieting, so when people experience them, they look for ways to eliminate them. During your speech, if you can help your audience experience negative emotions, they will be more involved with what you are saying. As a result, they will be motivated to use their energy to listen carefully to you to see if you give them a way to reduce their feelings of discomfort. Although you can tap numerous negative emotions, we describe five of the most common and how you can use them in a persuasive speech.

> **emotions** the buildup of action-specific energy
>
> **negative emotions** disquieting feelings people experience

Fear

We experience **fear** when we perceive that we have no control over a situation that threatens us. We may fear physical harm or psychological harm. Fear is reduced when the threat is eliminated or when we escape. If you use examples, stories, and statistics that create fear in your audience, they will be more motivated to hear how your proposal can eliminate the source of their fear or allow them to escape. For example, in a speech whose goal was to convince the audience that they were at risk of developing high blood pressure, the speaker might use a fear appeal in this way:

One of every three Americans aged eighteen and older has high blood pressure. It is a primary cause of stroke, heart disease, heart failure, kidney disease, and blindness. It triples a person's chance of developing heart disease, boosts the chance of stroke seven times, and the chance of congestive heart failure six times. Look at the person on your right; look at the person your left. If they don't get it, chances are, you will. Today, I'd like to convince you that you are at risk for developing high blood pressure.

Guilt

We feel **guilt** when we personally violate a moral, ethical, or religious code that we hold dear. We experience guilt as a gnawing sensation that we have done something wrong. When we feel guilty, we are motivated to "make things right" or to atone for our transgression. For example, in a speech designed to motivate the audience to take their turn as designated drivers, a speaker might evoke guilt like this:

Have you ever promised your mom that you wouldn't ride in a car driven by someone who had been drinking? And then turned around and got in the car with your buddy even though you both had had a few? You know that wasn't right. Lying to your mother, putting yourself and your buddy at risk . . . (pause) but what can you do? Well, today I'm going to show you how you can avoid all that guilt, live up to your promises to mom, and keep both you and your buddy safe.

Shame

We feel **shame** when a moral code we have violated is revealed to

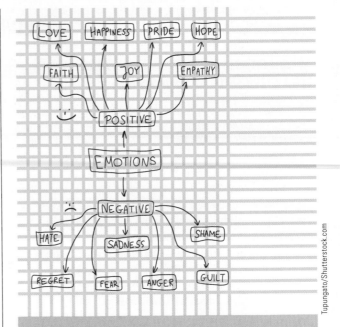

Guilt, shame and anger are among the negative emotions one can tap using the strategy of pathos.

someone we think highly of. The more egregious our behavior or the more we admire the person who finds out, the more shame we experience. When we feel shame, we are motivated to "redeem" ourselves in the eyes of that person. If in your speech you can evoke feelings of shame and then demonstrate how your proposal can either redeem someone after a violation has occurred or prevent feelings of shame, then you can motivate the audience to carefully consider your arguments. For example, in a speech advocating thankfulness, the speaker might use a shame-based approach by quoting the old saying, "I cried because I had no shoes until I met a man who had no feet."

Anger

When faced with an obstacle that stands in the way of something we want, we experience **anger**. We may also experience anger when someone demeans us or someone we love. As with all emotions, the intensity of what we feel may vary from mild annoyance to blind rage. Speakers who choose to evoke anger in their audience members must be careful that they don't incite so much anger that reasoning processes are short-circuited.

If you can rouse your audience's anger and then show how your proposal will help them to achieve their goals or stop the demeaning that has been occurring, you can motivate them to carefully consider your arguments. For example, suppose you want to convince the audience

fear feeling when we perceive no control over a situation that threatens us

guilt feeling when we personally violate a moral, ethical, or religious code that we hold dear

shame feeling when we have violated a moral code and it is revealed to someone we think highly of

anger feeling when we are faced with an obstacle in the way of something we want

to support a law requiring community notification when a convicted sex offender moves into the neighborhood. You might arouse the audience's anger to get their attention by personalizing the story of Megan Kanka.

She was your little girl, just seven years old, and the light of your world. She had a smile that could bring you to your knees. And she loved puppies. So when that nice man who had moved in down the street invited her in to see his new puppy, she didn't hesitate. But she didn't get to see the puppy, and you didn't ever see her alive again. He beat her, he raped her, and then he strangled her. He packaged her body in an old toy chest and dumped it in a park. Your seven-year-old princess would never dig in a toy chest again or slip down the slide in that park. And that hurts. But what makes you really angry is she wasn't his first. But you didn't know that. Because no one bothered to tell you that the guy down the street was likely to kill little girls. The cops knew it. But they couldn't tell you. You, the one who was supposed to keep her safe, didn't know. Angry? You bet. Yeah, he's behind bars again, but you still don't know who's living down the street from you. But you can. There is a law pending before Congress that will require active notification of the community when a known sex offender takes up residence, and today I'm going to tell how you can help to get this passed.[16]

Sadness

When we fail to achieve a goal or experience a loss or separation, we experience **sadness**. Unlike other negative emotions whose energy is projected outward, we tend to withdraw and become isolated when we feel sad. Because sadness is an unpleasant feeling, we look for ways to end it. When we are sad, we are already "looking for answers." So speeches that help us understand and find answers for what has happened can comfort us and help relieve this unpleasant feeling. For example, after 9/11, many Americans were sad. Yes, they were also afraid and angry, but overlaying it all was profound sadness for those who had been lost and what had been lost. The questions, "Why? Why did they do this? Why do they hate us so?" captured the national melancholy. So when politicians suggested that they understood the answers to these questions, Americans tended to perk up and listened to what they had to say.

13-5b Evoking Positive Emotions

Just as evoking negative emotions can cause audience members to internalize your arguments, so too can you tap **positive emotions**, which are feelings that people

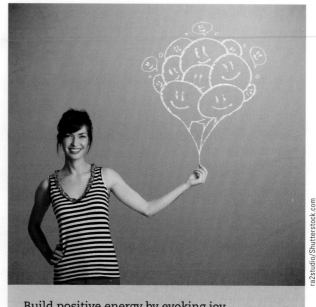

Build positive energy by evoking joy...

enjoy experiencing. With negative emotions, our goal is to show how our proposal will reduce or eliminate the feeling. With positive emotions, our goal is to help the audience maintain or enhance the feeling. We discuss five positive emotions here.

Happiness and Joy

Happiness or joy is the buildup of positive energy we experience when we accomplish something, when we have a satisfying interaction or relationship, or when we see or possess objects that appeal to us. As a speaker, if you can show how your proposal will lead your audience members to be happy or joyful, then they are likely to listen and to think carefully about your proposal. For example, suppose you want to motivate your audience to attend a couples encounter weekend where they will learn how to "rekindle" their relationship with a partner. If you can remind them about how they felt early in their relationship and then suggest how the weekend can reignite those feelings, they may be more motivated to listen.

Pride

When we experience satisfaction about something we or someone we care about accomplishes, we feel **pride**. "We're number one! We're number one!"

sadness feeling when we fail to achieve a goal or experience a loss or separation

positive emotions feelings that people enjoy experiencing

happiness or joy the buildup of positive energy when we accomplish something or have a satisfying interaction or relationship

pride feeling of self-satisfaction and increased self-esteem as the result of an accomplishment

is the chant of the crowd feeling pride in the accomplishment of "their" team. Whereas happiness is related to feelings of pleasure, pride is related to feelings of self-worth. If you can demonstrate how your proposal will help audience members feel good about themselves, they will be more motivated to consider your arguments. For example, suppose you want to persuade your audience to volunteer to work on the newest Habitat for Humanity house being constructed in your community. You might allude to the pride they will feel when they see people moving into the house they helped to build. As Rick revised his persuasive speech campaign to raise money for a dog park, he decided to appeal to his listeners' sense of pride about helping to build a park that would provide beautiful green space in the heart of the city and, at the same time, provide a welcome place for our family friends to run and play.

Relief

When a threatening situation has been alleviated, we feel the positive emotion of **relief**. We relax and put down our guard. As a speaker, you use relief to motivate audience members by combining it with the negative emotion of fear. For example, suppose your goal is to convince the audience that they are not at risk for high blood pressure. You might use the same personalization of statistics that was described in the example of fear appeals, but instead of stopping at convincing them that they are at risk, you could also promise relief if they hear you out and do what you advocate.

Hope

The emotional energy that stems from believing something desirable is likely to happen is called **hope**. Like relief, hope is a positive emotion that has its roots in a difficult situation. Whereas relief causes us to relax and let down our guard, hope energizes us to take action to overcome the situation. Hope empowers. As with relief, hope appeals are usually accompanied by fear appeals. You can motivate audience members to listen by showing them how your proposal provides a plan for overcoming a difficult situation. For

example, if you propose adopting a low-fat diet to reduce the risk of high blood pressure, you can use the same personalization of statistics that were cited in the example of fear but change the ending to state: "Today, I'm going to convince you to beat the odds by adopting a low-fat diet."

Compassion

When we feel selfless concern for the suffering of another person and that concern energizes us to try to relieve that suffering, we feel **compassion**. Speakers can evoke audience members' feelings of compassion by vividly describing the suffering endured by someone. The audience will then be motivated to listen to see how the speaker's proposal plans to end that suffering. For example, when a speaker who wants you donate to Project Peanut Butter displays a slide of an emaciated child, claims that 13 percent of all Malawi children die of malnutrition, and then states that for just $10 you can save a child, he or she is appealing to your compassion.

Javier Brosch/Shutterstock.com

13-5c Guidelines for Appealing to Emotions

You can evoke negative emotions, positive emotions, or both as a way to encourage listeners to internalize your message. In this section, we offer several guidelines for doing so effectively in your speech content, language, and delivery.

1. Tell vivid stories. Dramatize your arguments by using stories and testimonials that personalize the issue for listeners by appealing to specific emotions. In his speech on bone marrow donation, David Slater simply could have said, "By donating bone marrow—a simple procedure—you can save lives." Instead, he dramatized both the simplicity of the bone marrow donation procedure and the lifesaving impact with a short story designed to heighten audience members' feelings of compassion.

When Tricia Matthews decided to undergo a simple medical procedure, she had no idea what impact it could have on her life. But more than a year later, when she saw five-year-old Tommy and his younger brother Daniel walk across the stage of the Oprah Winfrey Show,

relief feeling when a threatening situation has been alleviated

hope emotional energy that stems from believing something desirable is likely to happen

compassion feeling of selfless concern for the suffering of another *she realized that the short amount of time it took her to donate her bone marrow was well worth it. Tricia is not related to the boys who suffered from a rare immune deficiency disorder treated by a transplant of her marrow. Tricia and the boys found each other through the National Marrow Donor Program, or NMDP, a national network which strives to bring willing donors and needy patients together. Though the efforts Tricia made were minimal, few Americans made the strides she did. Few of us would deny anyone the gift of life, but sadly, few know how easily we can help.*[17]

Notice how David used a compelling example to appeal to his listeners' emotions and personalize the information for them.

Similarly, Ryan Labor began his speech on shaken baby syndrome with the following vivid story designed to raise feelings of fear, anger, and sadness:

Last winter, two-year-old Cody Dannar refused to eat or play. He had a headache. Doctors said he just had the flu. After a couple weeks home with his mother, Cody felt better. Days later . . . Cody's headaches returned. Coming home from work the next afternoon, his parents found the babysitter frantically calling 911 and Cody lying rigid and unconscious on the floor. He didn't have the flu; in fact, he wasn't sick at all. The babysitter had caused his headaches. To quiet Cody down, she had shaken him, damaging the base of Cody's brain that now risked his life as he lay on the ground.[18]

2. Use startling statistics. Statistics don't have to be boring; instead, when used strategically, they can evoke strong emotions. To provoke emotions, statistics need to be startling. A statistic may surprise because of its sheer magnitude. For example, in a speech urging the audience to attend a local protest march organized by the Mobilization for Global Justice, Cory used the following statistic to shame and anger his audience about the global problem of wealth distribution: "Did you know that the USA has 25.4 percent of the world's wealth? And of that, the top 20 percent of Americans control 89 percent?"[19] Sometimes, by comparing two statistics, you can increase the emotional impact. For example, during his second main point, Cory used the following comparative statistic to highlight wealth disparity. "In the U.S., not only does the top 20 percent control 89 percent of the

wealth, but the bottom 40 percent of Americans control less than 1 percent!"[20] In Ryan's speech on shaken baby syndrome, he strengthened his emotional appeal by following his vivid story with these startling statistics:

Unfortunately, Cody isn't alone. Over one million infants and young children suffer from shaken baby syndrome annually while thousands die. . . . Only 15 percent survive without damage. The remaining children suffer from blindness, learning disabilities, deafness, cerebral palsy, or paralysis.

3. Incorporate listener-relevance links. You can also appeal to emotions by integrating listener-relevance links because emotions are stronger when listeners feel personally involved. At a later point in Ryan's shaken baby syndrome speech, he appealed to emotions through listener relevance. Notice how he brings the problem close to each listener by suggesting the universality of the problem.

Jacy Showers, director of the first National Conference on shaken baby syndrome, says "shaking occurs in families of all races, incomes, and education levels" and "81 percent of SBS offenders had no previous history of child abuse." The reason? The offenders were so young, either babysitters or new parents.

4. Choose striking presentational aids. Because "a picture is worth a thousand words," consider how you can reinforce your verbal message with dramatic

Veronique de Viguerie/Getty Images

Striking presentational aids contribute to the persuasiveness of a speech. The image of 11 children who were being trafficked to cocoa plantations in the Ivory Coast, above, is a compelling visual for a speech about child slave labor in the chocolate industry.

presentational aids. Still pictures and short video clips can at times create an emotional jolt that is difficult to achieve with words. Jonna used several before-and-after pictures of female celebrities Nicole Richie, LeAnn Rimes, and Mary-Kate Olsen to reinforce her point that emaciated celebrities were contributing to the eating disorder epidemic in teenage girls. Likewise, Anton used a 15-second clip from the documentary film *The Dark Side of Chocolate* to dramatize the problem of child labor and child trafficking in the global chocolate industry.[21] His goal was to shame his audience members into sending one postcard to the manufacturer of their favorite brand of chocolate asking about what they are doing to prevent buying cocoa beans from cooperatives that used child slave labor. Additionally, Rick solicited help from a graphic designer to provide an artist's rendering of what the currently empty space would look like once the dog park was finished.

5. Use descriptive and provocative language. When developing your speech, include persuasive punch words—words that evoke emotion—where you can. Here's how Ryan used persuasive punch words to strengthen his emotional appeal:

The worst of all epidemics is a silent one. With the majority of all victims either infants or young children, shaken baby syndrome can be classified as a stealthy plague. . . . When shaken, the brain is literally ricocheted inside the skull, bruising the brain and tearing blood vessels coming from the neck . . . cutting off oxygen and causing the eyes to bulge.

6. Use nonverbal delivery to reinforce your emotional appeal. Even the most eloquently phrased emotional appeal will lose its impact unless the nonverbal parts of delivery heighten and highlight the emotional content of the message. Practice using your voice to emphasize what you are saying with the use of pauses, volume, and pitch to heighten and highlight the emotional content of your message. A dramatic pause before a startling statistic can magnify its emotional effect. Similarly, lowering or raising the volume or pitch of your voice at strategic places can create an emotional response. If you experiment as you practice out loud, you will find a combination of vocal elements that can enhance emotional appeal when delivering your speech.

7. Use gestures and facial expressions that highlight the emotions you are conveying. Your message will lose its emotional impact if you deliver it with a deadpan expression or if your demeanor contradicts the emotional content of your message. So if you want your audience to feel angry, you should model this feeling by looking annoyed or livid or furious. You might clench your fists, furrow your brows, and frown. When you want to foster feelings of joy in your audience, you can smile, nod, and use other nonverbal gestures that are natural for you when you experience joy. Remember, as an ethical speaker, you are appealing to emotions that you yourself feel about the situation, so allow yourself to experience these emotions as you practice. Then, when you give your speech, you will be more comfortable displaying your feelings for your audience.

Quick Quiz (answers in Solutions Appendix)

T F 1. One way to make an argument in a persuasive speech is to support a claim by linking it to a comparable example.

T F 2. Listeners are more likely to use the central route of processing when they believe that the information in a speech is important to them.

T F 3. A person who is able to see the world through someone else's eyes has empathy.

T F 4. A speaker commits the straw man fallacy when he or she presents a generalization that is not supported with evidence.

T F 5. The two types of reasoning are inductive reasoning and conductive reasoning.

6. ELM stands for:
   a. estimated linkage model
   b. elaboration likelihood model
   c. exhibition landscape model
   d. elaborate listener model
   e. extended localization model

7. During his speech on Internet privacy, Alan argues that Mark Zuckerberg, the CEO of Facebook, should be ignored as an authority since he never graduated college. This is an example of which fallacy?
   a. hasty generalization
   b. ad hominem
   c. straw man
   d. either/or
   e. false cause

8. A speaker who is appealing to the audience's emotions is using which means of persuasion?
   a. ethos
   b. kairos
   c. pathos
   d. logos
   e. cosmos

9. The evidence that a speaker offers as the grounds for accepting the conclusion is called a(n):
   a. claim
   b. warrant
   c. support
   d. argument
   e. criteria

10. When a speaker is describing someone's suffering, he or she is trying to arouse the audience's:
   a. relief
   b. hope
   c. joy
   d. pride
   e. compassion

Chapter Takeaways

List three key takeaways from this chapter:

-

-

-

14 Persuasive Speaking

LEARNING OUTCOMES

14-1 Identify the initial attitude of your target audience.

14-2 Phrase your persuasive speech goal as a proposition.

14-3 Identify some dispositional and actuation persuasive speech patterns.

14-4 Follow ethical communication guidelines when preparing persuasive speeches.

After finishing this chapter go to **PAGE 275** for **STUDY TOOLS.**

Martin Barraud/Getty Images

Sound Familiar?

As Tomeka finished her speech on "Save our Schools: Get Out the Vote!" the audience rose to their feet, chanting, "Funds now! Funds now! Funds now! . . . " Not only had she convinced her audience, but some were visibly angry. Upon leaving the platform, she heard someone shout out, "There's no way families in our community can afford more taxes!" The room quickly divided into those for a tax levy and those opposed. People began pushing and shoving each other, and shouting filled the room. Tomeka's enthusiasm faded; all she could think was, "This wasn't what I intended."

In the previous chapter, we focused on how persuasive messages employ what Aristotle called the available means of persuasion (logos, ethos, and pathos) to seek agreement or to encourage action. In this chapter, we focus on how to organize those rhetorical appeals into persuasive speeches that are both effective and ethical.

So what are the steps you need to follow to create persuasive speeches that are both effective and ethical? First, you need to understand where your audience stands on your topic, and then phrase your goal as a proposition that is appropriate to the rhetorical situation. Next, you need to organize your speech using an appropriate persuasive speech pattern. Finally, you need to evaluate and, if necessary, revise your speech based on ethical guidelines for persuasive speeches.

14-1 AUDIENCE ATTITUDE

Because it is very difficult to convince people to change their minds, what you can hope to accomplish in one speech depends on where your audience stands on your topic. So you'll want to analyze your audience members' attitudes about your topic.

Audience members' attitudes can range from highly favorable to strongly opposed and can be

visualized as lying on a continuum like the one pictured in Exhibit 14.1. Even though an audience will include individuals whose opinions fall at nearly every point along the continuum, audience members' opinions generally tend to cluster in one area. For instance, the opinions of the audience represented in Exhibit 14.1 cluster around "mildly opposed," even though a few people are more hostile and a few have favorable opinions. This cluster point represents your **target audience**, the group of people you most want to persuade. Based on your target audience, you can classify your audience's initial attitude toward your topic as "in favor" (already supportive), "no opinion" (uninformed, neutral, or apathetic), or "opposed" (holding an opposite point of view).

14-1a Opposed

It is unrealistic to believe you will be able to change your target audience's attitude from "opposed" to "in favor" in only one short speech. Instead, seek **incremental change**, that is, attempt to move them only a small degree in your direction, hoping for additional movement later. For example, if your target audience is opposed to the goal "I want to convince my audience that same-sex marriage should be legal," you might rephrase your goal as "I want to convince my audience that committed

oleandra/Shutterstock.com

Exhibit 14.1
Sample Opinion Continuum

Highly opposed	Opposed	Mildly opposed	Neither in favor nor opposed	Mildly in favor	In favor	Highly in favor
2	2	11	1	2	2	0

target audience the group of people you most want to persuade

incremental change attempting to move your audience only a small degree in your direction

same-sex couples should be afforded the same legal protection as committed heterosexual couples through state-recognized civil unions." Then brainstorm potential objections, questions, and criticisms that might arise and shape your speech around them.

14-1b No Opinion

If your target audience has no opinion for or against your topic, consider whether they are uninformed, neutral, or apathetic. If they are **uninformed**—that is, they do not know enough about the topic to have formed an opinion—you will need to provide the basic arguments and information needed to become informed. For example, if your target audience is uninformed about same-sex marriage, you might begin by highlighting the legal benefits of marriage in general. If your target audience is **neutral**—that is, they know the basics about your topic but not enough to have formed an opinion—you will want to provide evidence and reasoning illustrating why your position is superior to others. Perhaps your target audience knows the legal benefits of marriage in general but needs to understand how committed same-sex couples who do not have these benefits are disadvantaged. When target audiences have no opinion because they are **apathetic**—that is, they are uninterested in or indifferent toward your topic—you will need to find ways to show how it relates to them or their needs. For the same-sex example, you will want to address possible questions such as, "I'm not gay, so why should I care?" You can do this by including strong listener-relevance links for each main point.

---

uninformed the audience doesn't know enough about a topic to have formed an opinion

neutral the audience has some information about a topic but does not really understand why one position is preferred and so still has no opinion

apathetic the audience is uninterested in, unconcerned about, or indifferent toward your topic

proposition the specific goal of a persuasive speech stated as a declarative sentence that clearly indicates the position the speaker will advocate

proposition of fact a statement designed to convince the audience that something did or did not exist or occur, is or is not true, or will or will not occur

14-1c In Favor

If your target audience is only mildly in favor of your proposal, your task is to reinforce and strengthen their beliefs. Audience members who favor your position may become further committed to it after hearing new reasons and more recent evidence supporting it. When your target audience strongly agrees with your position, then you can consider a goal that moves them to act on it. So, if your target audience strongly favors the idea of same-sex marriage, then your goal might be "I want my audience to e-mail or write letters to their state representatives urging them to support legislation extending the right to marry to same-sex couples." In the opening vignette, Tomeka's audience was already in favor of her proposition, so she focused on motivating them to act.

oleandra/Shutterstock.com

14-2 IDENTIFYING YOUR PROPOSITION

Persuasive speech goals are stated as propositions. A **proposition** is a declarative sentence that clearly indicates the position you advocate. For example, "I want to convince my audience that pirating (downloading from the Internet) copyrighted media without paying for it is wrong" is a proposition. Notice how a persuasive proposition differs from an informative speech goal on the same subject: "I want to inform my audience about the practice of pirating copyrighted media." In the informative speech, you will achieve your goal if the audience understands and remembers what you talk about. In the persuasive speech, however, they must not only understand and remember, but also agree with your position and possibly even take action. The three types of propositions are fact, value, or policy.

A **proposition of fact** is a statement designed to convince your audience that something: (1) did, probably did, probably did not, or did not exist or occur; (2) is, probably is, probably is not, or is not true; or (3) will, probably will, probably will not, or will not occur. Although propositions of fact may or may not be true—both positions are arguable—they are stated as though they are, without question, true. For example, whether or not Princess Diana's death was an unfortunate car accident or an assassination is debatable. So you could argue a proposition of fact in two ways: "Princess Diana's death was nothing more than a tragic car accident" or "Princess Diana's death was, in fact, a successful assassination attempt." Examples of propositions of fact concerning the present are "God exists" or "There is no such thing as God" and "Cell phone use causes brain cancer" or "Cell phone use does not cause brain cancer." Claims of fact concerning the future are predictions. For example, "Thanks to the Internet, paperbound books will eventually cease to exist" and "The New York Yankees will surely win the World Series next year" are both propositions of fact concerning the future.

A **proposition of value** is a statement designed to convince your audience that something is good, bad, desirable, undesirable, fair, unfair, moral, immoral, sound, unsound, beneficial, harmful, important, or unimportant.[1] You can attempt to convince your audience that something has more value than something else, or you can convince your audience that something meets valued standards. "Running is a better form of exercise than bicycling" is an example of the former and "The real value of a college education is that it creates an informed citizenry" is an example of the latter.

A **proposition of policy** is a statement designed to convince your audience that a particular rule, plan, or course of action should be taken. Propositions of policy will implore listeners using words such as "do it/don't do it," "should/shouldn't," or "must/must not." "All college students *should* be required to take a public speaking course," "The United States *must* stop deep-sea oil drilling," "*Don't* text while driving," and "Water packaged in plastic bottles *should* be taxed to pay for the cost associated with recycling empties" are propositions of policy. Tomeka's speech focused on a proposition of policy as well: "We must get out and vote." Exhibit 14.2 provides several examples of how propositions of fact, value, and policy can be developed from the same topic idea.

As you begin working on your persuasive speeches, you can use the Speech Planning Action Steps to help you organize and develop them, although some of the steps will be modified to provide you with guidance that is particular to persuasive speeches. You can use Activity 1Ep and the sample student response to help you develop a specific goal for a persuasive speech stated as a proposition.

proposition of value a statement designed to convince the audience that something is good, bad, desirable, undesirable, fair, unfair, moral, immoral, sound, unsound, beneficial, harmful, important, or unimportant

proposition of policy a statement designed to convince the audience that they should take a specific course of action

---

1Ep

ACTION STEP ACTIVITY

Writing a Specific Goal as a Persuasive Proposition

1. **Identify your topic and tentatively phrase your goal.**

2. **Check whether you believe that your target audience is opposed to, has no opinion of, or is in favor of your position. Why?**

3. **Rephrase your goal as a proposition of fact, value, or policy appropriately tailored to the attitude of your target audience.**

Student Response: Writing a Specific Goal as a Persuasive Proposition

1. **Identify your topic and tentatively phrase your goal.**
   I want to convince the audience not to download copyrighted music from the Internet without paying for it.

2. **Check whether you believe that your target audience is opposed to, has no opinion of, or is in favor of your position. Why?**
   Although some students may be opposed to or in favor of this proposition, I think the majority are undecided because it's easy to download free music and there don't seem to be any imminent penalties.

3. **Rephrase your goal as a proposition of fact, value, or policy appropriately tailored to the attitude of your target audience.**
   Because my audience is neutral, I will phrase my goal as a proposition of value: Downloading copyrighted music from the Internet without paying for it is wrong.

Exhibit 14.2
Examples of Persuasive Speech Propositions

Propositions of Fact	Propositions of Value	Propositions of Policy
Mahatma Gandhi was the father of passive resistance.	Mahatma Gandhi was a moral leader.	Mahatma Gandhi should be given a special award for his views on and practices of passive resistance.
Pharmaceutical advertising to consumers increases prescription drug prices.	Advertising of new prescription drugs on TV is better than marketing new drugs directly to doctors.	Pharmaceutical companies should be prohibited from advertising prescription drugs on TV.
Using paper ballots is a reliable method for voting in U.S. elections.	Paper ballots are better than electronic voting machines.	Using paper ballots should be required for U.S. elections.

MEDIA MOMENT

Forget Argument—Today, Persuasion Is About Influence

Whether written or spoken, marketing messages have always been driven by persuasion. In the early days of marketing, that persuasion was founded upon argument. Early twentieth-century advertisements were often dominated by text and contained lengthy descriptions of why the listed product was superior to the competition. As the field progressed, however, ads used fewer words and relied more heavily on pithy statements and spokespeople who lent their celebrity to marketing campaigns for all manner of products—most often for a fee. For example, when Taylor Swift appears in a Diet Coke commercial, or David Beckham appears in a Breitling ad, it is part of their paid endorsement contracts as brand spokespersons.

Today, marketers supplement those direct, paid attempts at persuasion with a more indirect approach that involves convincing influential people to become advocates for their products and services—often for no compensation. The goal is to generate support through word-of-mouth or social media.

Today's "influencers" can be neighbors, friends, or family members. Influence and word-of-mouth marketing is most persuasive, however, when highly influential (and well-known) people participate. After all, more people are likely to see Taylor Swift's tweets about her favorite clothing brands than your own—unless you happen to be Katy Perry, who has the most Twitter followers in the world (nearly 73 million in 2015).[2]

Influence marketing might look like a form of celebrity endorsement when it works, but it *feels* more genuine. Seeing public figures mention a brand on a personal social media account alongside the rest of their unsolicited opinions is more

Tinseltown/Shutterstock.com

persuasive than a TV commercial with the same person touting a product's benefits in front of a camera. In fact, psychological research suggests that word of mouth is 10 times more effective (i.e., persuasive) than traditional advertising.[3] For a persuasive message to be powerful, it seems that, these days, few arguments are more compelling than the influence of the person delivering it.

14-3 PERSUASIVE SPEECH PATTERNS

Persuasive speeches are organized as speeches to convince or speeches to actuate. **Speeches to convince** focus on reinforcing or changing your audience's belief or attitude. **Speeches to actuate** focus on persuading your audience to take action.

14-3a Speeches to Convince

Most speeches to convince follow one of four organizational patterns: statement of reasons, comparative advantages, criteria satisfaction, and refutative. The following paragraphs describe each pattern and show how it might be used to arrange Tomeka's speech to convince her audience to agree with her about how they should vote on a school tax proposition.

Statement of Reasons

A **statement of reasons** pattern is used to confirm propositions of fact by presenting the best-supported reasons in a meaningful order. For a speech with three reasons or more, place the strongest reason last because this is the reason you believe the audience will find most persuasive. Place the second strongest reason first because you want to start with a significant point. Place the other reasons in between.

Proposition of Fact: *The proposed school tax levy is necessary.*

I. *The income is needed to restore vital programs. (second strongest)*
II. *The income is needed to give teachers cost of living raises.*
III. *The income is needed to maintain local control. (strongest)*

Comparative Advantages

A **comparative advantages** pattern attempts to convince others that something has more value or is better than any of the alternatives.[4] A comparative advantages approach to the school tax proposition might look like this:

Proposition of Value: *Passing the school tax levy will be better than not passing it. (compares the value of change to the status quo)*

I. *With new income from a tax levy, schools can reintroduce important programs that have been cut. (advantage 1)*

II. *New income from a tax levy will provide salaries for teachers and prevent a strike. (advantage 2)*
III. *New income from a tax levy will make it possible to retain local control of our schools, which will be lost to the state if additional local funding is not provided. (advantage 3)*

Criteria Satisfaction

A **criteria satisfaction** pattern seeks agreement on criteria that should be considered when evaluating a particular proposition and then shows how the proposition satisfies those criteria. A criteria satisfaction pattern is especially useful when your audience is opposed to your proposition, because it approaches the proposition indirectly by first focusing on criteria that the audience will probably agree with before introducing the specific proposition. A criteria satisfaction organization for the school tax proposition might look like this:

Proposition of Value: *Passing a school tax levy is a good way to fund our schools.*

I. *We all agree that the funding method we select must meet three key criteria:*
   A. *The funding method must provide resources needed to reinstate important programs.*
   B. *The funding method must pay for teachers.*
   C. *The funding method must generate enough income to maintain local control.*

II. *Passing a local school tax levy will satisfy each of these criteria.*
   A. *A local levy will allow us to fund important programs again.*
   B. *A local levy will provide needed revenue to give teachers a raise.*
   C. *A local levy will generate enough income to maintain local control.*

Refutative

A **refutative** pattern arranges main points according to opposing arguments and then both challenges them and bolsters your own. This pattern is particularly useful

speech to convince a speech designed to refocus or change an audience's belief or attitude

speech to actuate a speech designed to persuade an audience to action

statement of reasons a straightforward organization in which you present your best-supported reasons in a meaningful order

comparative advantages an organization that shows that one alternative is better than any of the others

criteria satisfaction an indirect organization that seeks audience agreement on criteria that should be considered when evaluating a particular proposition and then shows how the proposition satisfies those criteria

refutative an organization that persuades by both challenging the opposing position and bolstering one's own when the target audience opposes your position. Begin by acknowledging the merit of opposing arguments and then showing their flaws. Once listeners understand the flaws, they will be more receptive to the arguments you present to support your proposition. A refutative pattern for the school tax proposition might look like this:

Proposition of Value: *A school tax levy is the best way to fund our schools.*

I. *Opponents of the tax levy argue that the tax increase will fall only on property owners.*
   A. *Landlords will recoup property taxes in the form of higher rents.*
   B. *Thus, all people will be affected.*

II. *Opponents of the tax levy argue that there are fewer students in the school district, so schools should be able to function on the same amount of revenue.*
   A. *Although there are fewer pupils, costs continue to rise.*
      1. *Salary costs are increasing.*
      2. *Energy costs are increasing.*
      3. *Maintenance costs are increasing.*
      4. *Costs from unfunded federal and state government mandates are increasing.*
   B. *Although there are fewer pupils, there are many aging school buildings that need replacing or renovating.*

III. *Opponents of the tax levy argue that parents should be responsible for the excessive cost of educating their children.*
   A. *Historically, our nation flourished under a publicly funded educational system.*
   B. *Parents today are already paying more than parents in previous generations did.*
      1. *Activity fees*
      2. *Lab fees*
      3. *Book fees*
      4. *Transportation fees*
   C. *Of school-age children today in this district, 42 percent live in families that are below the poverty line and have limited resources.*

Ollyy/Shutterstock.com

14-3b Speeches to Actuate

Implicit in speeches to actuate is the assumption that there is a problem

problem-solution a form of persuasive organization that reveals details about a problem and proposes solutions to it

that audience members can help solve by taking certain actions. As a result, most actuation persuasive speeches follow one of three organizational frameworks: problem-solution, problem-cause-solution, and the motivated sequence.

Problem-Solution

A **problem-solution** pattern explains the nature of a problem and proposes a solution. This pattern is particularly effective when the audience is neutral or agrees that there is a problem but has no opinion about a particular solution. A problem-solution speech usually has three main points. The first examines the problem, the second presents the solution(s), and the third suggests what action the listener should take.

To convince the audience that there is a problem, you will need to explore the breadth and depth of the issue, as well as provide listener-relevance links. You provide breadth by showing the scope or scale of the problem, for example, giving the number of people it affects and proving upward trends over time, including forecasted trends if the problem is not solved. You might provide depth by showing the gravity of the problem. Both breadth and depth may be described through stories and startling statistics. When you describe the solution, you should be detailed enough for the audience to understand how and why it will solve the problem. The call to action should provide your audience with specific steps that they ought to take to help implement the solution(s).

A problem-solution organization for Tomeka's speech about the school tax levy proposition might look like this:

Proposition of Policy: *We must solve the current fiscal crisis in the school district.*

I. *The current funding is insufficient. (statement of the problem)*
   A. *The schools have had to cut programs.*
   B. *Teachers have not had a cost of living raise in five years.*
   C. *The state could take over control.*

II. *The proposed tax levy will address these problems (proposed solution)*
   A. *The schools will be able to reinstate important programs.*
   B. *Teachers will be afforded raises.*
   C. *The district will be able to maintain control.*

III. We must do our part to make this happen. *(call to action)*
  A. Vote "yes."
  B. Encourage your friends and neighbors to vote "yes."

Problem-Cause-Solution

A **problem-cause-solution** pattern is similar to a problem-solution pattern but differs from it by adding a main point that reveals the causes of the problem and then proposes a solution designed to alleviate those causes. This pattern is particularly useful for addressing seemingly intractable problems that have been dealt with unsuccessfully in the past as a result of treating symptoms rather than underlying causes. A problem-cause-solution pattern for the school tax levy proposition might look like this:

Proposition of Policy: *We must solve the current fiscal crisis in the school district.*

I. *The current funding is insufficient. (statement of the problem)*
  A. *The schools have had to cut programs.*
  B. *Teachers have not had a cost of living raise in five years.*
  C. *The state could take over control.*

II. *We can trace these problems to several key things. (causes)*
  A. *Dwindling government support.*
  B. *Rising costs for operating expenses.*

III. *The proposed tax levy will address these issues (solutions)*
  A. *The levy will supplement inadequate government support.*
  B. *The levy will fill the gap in operating expense needs.*

IV. *We each have a responsibility to make sure the tax levy proposition passes. (call to action)*
  A. *Vote "yes."*
  B. *Encourage your friends and neighbors to vote "yes."*

Monroe's Motivated Sequence

The **motivated sequence** is an organizational pattern that combines a problem-solution pattern with explicit appeals designed to motivate the audience to act. Allan Monroe articulated the motivated sequence as a distinct speech pattern in the 1930s. In the motivated sequence, the normal introduction, body, and conclusion are unified into a five-step sequence described as follows:

1. **The attention step** is essentially the introduction. It should begin by piquing the audience's curiosity by

Visualizing a negative outcome can be very motivating.

referring to the knowledge and experiences you have that build your credibility. As in any introduction, you will want to clearly identify your goal stated as a proposition and preview the main points of your speech.

2. **The need step** explores the nature of the problem that gives rise to the need for change. In it, you will point out the conditions that are unsatisfactory using statistics, examples, and expert opinion to bolster your argument. Then you will describe the implications or ramifications of this problem. What is happening because the condition is allowed to continue? Finally, you will allude to how the audience might be instrumental in changing the situation.

3. **The satisfaction step** explains the proposed solution to the problem. In this step, you will show, point by point, how what you are proposing will satisfy each of the needs that you articulated in the previous step. If there are other places where your proposal has been tried successfully, you will want to mention these. In addition, you will want to present and refute any objections to the proposal that you can anticipate.

4. **The visualization step** asks the audience to imagine what will happen if your proposal is implemented and is successful. You might also ask the audience to visualize how things will be if your proposal is not adopted. This step draws heavily on rhetorical appeals to pathos.

5. **The action appeal step** is essentially the conclusion. In it, you will want to emphasize the specific action(s) you advocate. You will also state or restate your own commitment and action that you have taken. You also

> **problem-cause-solution** a form of persuasive organization that examines a problem, its cause(s), and solutions designed to eliminate or alleviate the underlying cause(s)
>
> **motivated sequence** a form of persuasive organization that combines a problem-solution pattern with explicit appeals designed to motivate the audience

offer a direct call to action indicating what your listeners are to do and how. Finally, you will want to conclude with a quote, story, or other element that is emotionally compelling.

A motivated sequence pattern for the school tax levy proposition might look like this:

Proposition of Policy: *We must solve the current fiscal crisis in the school district.*

I. **Attention step:** *Highlight the dismal rankings of U.S. schools*
   A. *Comparisons of worldwide test scores in math and science show the United States continues to lose ground.*
   B. *I've made an extensive study of this problem, and today I'm going to tell you how you can help stop this decline.*
   C. *I'll start by describing the problem; then, I will tell you what you should do and why it will help.*

II. **Need step:** *The local schools are underfunded.*
   A. *The current funding is insufficient and has resulted in program cuts.*
   B. *Qualified teachers leave because of stagnant wages.*
   C. *A threatened state takeover of local schools would lead to more bureaucracy and less learning.*

III. **Satisfaction step:** *The proposed local tax levy is large enough to solve these problems.*
   A. *Programs will be restored.*
   B. *Qualified teachers will be compensated so they will stay.*
   C. *We will retain local control.*
   D. *You'll once again have pride in your community.*

IV. **Visualization step:** *Imagine the best, and imagine the worst.*
   A. *What it will be like if we pass the levy. How will you feel?*
   B. *What it will be like if we don't. How will you feel?*

V. **Action appeal step:** *Vote "yes" for the levy in November.*
   A. *If you want to see schools improve and the United States catch up to the rest of the world, vote for the levy.*
   B. *Come join me. I'm registered, I'm ready, I'm voting for the levy.*

C. *It costs to be the best in the world. Where there is pain, there is gain.*
D. *They say it takes a village, so you can make a difference.*

 # 14-4 ETHICAL GUIDELINES FOR PERSUASIVE SPEECHES

Throughout this book, we have discussed the fundamental behaviors of ethical communicators. At this point, we want to look at five ethical guidelines speakers should follow when their specific goal is to convince the audience to agree with a proposition or to move the audience to action.

1. Ethical persuasive speeches advocate the genuine beliefs of the speaker. Sometimes people get excited about arguing for a belief or action just to stir up discussion. However, it is unethical to give a speech on a proposition that you do not genuinely endorse.

2. Ethical persuasive speeches provide choice. Ethical persuasive speeches let audiences evaluate what is said before making up their own minds.

3. Ethical persuasive speeches use representative supporting information. You can probably find a piece of "evidence" to support any claim, but ethical speakers make sure the evidence they cite is representative of all the evidence that could be used. It is unethical to misrepresent what a *body* of evidence (as opposed to a single item) would show if all of it were presented to the audience.

4. Ethical persuasive speeches use emotional appeals conscientiously. Emotional appeals are a legitimate strategy to get an audience involved in your persuasive speech. However, using excessive emotional appeals as the basis of persuasion, without strong evidence and reasoning, is unethical.

5. Ethical persuasive speeches honestly present the speaker's credibility. Ethical speakers present their expertise and trustworthiness honestly. It is unethical to act as if you know a great deal about a subject when you do not. Ethical speakers also disclose interests that may influence their stance on the issue. You might say, for example, "I work for the Literacy Project as a paid intern, so my experiences there do influence my position on what must be done regarding illiteracy in this country."

Speech to Convince
Evaluation Checklist

You can use this checklist to critique a speech to convince that you hear in class or a recording of your own. As you listen, outline the speech. Pay close attention to the reasoning process the speaker uses. Note the claims and supports used in the arguments, and identify the types of warrants used. Then, answer the following questions.

General Criteria

_____ **1.** Was the introduction effective in creating interest, involving the audience in the speech, and previewing the main points?

_____ **2.** Were section transitions used to help you follow the organization of the main points?

_____ **3.** Did the conclusion summarize the thesis and main points in a memorable way?

_____ **4.** Was the language appropriate, accurate, clear, and vivid?

_____ **5.** Was the speech delivered conversationally, intelligibly, expressively, and convincingly?

Specific Criteria

_____ **1.** Was the specific goal stated as a proposition?

_____ **2.** Was the speech organized into an appropriate pattern? _____ Statement of reasons? _____ Comparative advantages? _____ Criteria satisfaction? _____ Refutative?

_____ **3.** Did the speaker use logos effectively? _____ Use strong evidence? _____ Use reasoning to link evidence to claims? _____ Avoid reasoning fallacies?

_____ **4.** Did the speaker use ethos effectively? _____ Establish expertise? _____ Demonstrate trustworthiness? _____ Convey goodwill?

_____ **5.** Did the speaker use pathos effectively? _____ Appeal to negative emotions?

If so, check all that were tapped: _____ fear _____ guilt _____ anger _____ shame _____ sadness Appeal to positive emotions? If so, check all that were tapped: _____ happiness/joy _____ pride _____ relief _____ hope _____ compassion

Based on these criteria, evaluate the speech (check one):

■ **excellent**　■ **good**　■ **satisfactory**　■ **fair**　■ **poor**

Explain:

Sample Speech to Convince:

"Do You Doubt the Drought? The Pressing Importance of the California Drought"

This section presents a sample speech to convince given by a student, including an adaptation plan, an outline, and a transcript.

1. Read the speech adaptation plan, outline, and transcript of a speech about the California water shortage.

2. Access the Chapter 14 resources of *SPEAK3* Online to identify some of the strengths of Megan's speech by preparing an evaluation checklist and an analysis.

Adaptation Plan

1. **Audience attitude:** When I asked my classmates if they were concerned about the California drought, most of them replied that, although they did feel bad for the California farmers and citizens who are plagued by the drought, they did not feel very connected to the topic. From this, I concluded that the majority of my classmates are unfamiliar with issues related to water conservation and the wide scale effects of the drought—even though its impact is felt across the entire United States.

2. **Reasons:** California is experiencing one of the worst droughts in its history. Meanwhile, the state is using 80 percent of its freshwater to provide our nation with half of all our food needs. We must revise our agricultural system, or we will cause irreversible damage to our nation's water and food security.

3. **Organizational pattern:** My speech will use a comparative advantages pattern to convince the audience that national water conservation is the best possible solution for limiting the severe economic, environmental, and agricultural effects of the California drought.

Megan's Speech

"Do You Doubt the Drought? The Pressing Importance of the California Drought"

General Goal:
To persuade

Specific Goal:
I want to convince my audience that the California drought poses severe economic, environmental, and agricultural threats for the entire United States, and ultimately persuade them to be in favor of national water conservation.

Introduction

I. Who here likes science fiction? Have you ever dreamed aliens were real? Do you love reading or watching movies about unknown galaxies warring over a rare element with fantastical powers? What if I told you a similar war was brewing right at your own backdoor? How would you feel?

Attention getter

II. It might sound like make-believe, but freshwater shortages are rapidly going to change the face of our planet if we don't stop our nation's careless water usage.

Listener-relevance

III. Think of all the fresh produce stocked at your local supermarket: the barrels of limes and crates of blueberries and raspberries, the shelves of spinach and asparagus, and the varieties of fish and meat that are not sourced from where you live. Basically anything these days, if you look hard enough, can be found at a store near you.

Listener-relevance

IV. Now imagine waking up one day, and it's all missing. More than that, the water prices are so high no one can afford to buy fresh drinking water or food.

Listener-relevance

V. Today, we owe our plethora of foodstuffs, this cornucopia on steroids, in large part to California farmers, who grow nearly half of our nation's meats, vegetables, fruits, and nuts. (Parsons, *Los Angeles Times*)

VI. But turn to California, and the ground is scorched from drought. The snowpack in the mountains, which recharges water reservoirs, is only 6 percent of its usual amount. (Clark Howard, *National Geographic*)

VII. Growing up in California, I've experienced firsthand the severity of living in drought conditions. As an environmental studies major, I also interned at a desalination plant on my summer abroad in Israel. There I learned just how much water conservation is a global issue.

Establishing speaker credibility

VIII. I'm here to tell you today that the California drought is about more than just limiting a few showers. The clock is ticking. Our national demand for food diversity, and usage of precious groundwater to grow food, is at an all-time high. It's time we face up to the fact that the California drought is more than an inconvenience for local residents, but a severe economic, environmental, and agricultural threat affecting the future of the entire United States.

Thesis statement

Body

I. First, the problem: We, as a nation, rely on California to sustain an opulent agricultural food system. The state of California alone supplies our nation with a third of all vegetables and two-thirds of all fruits and nuts consumed, while 80 percent of California's freshwater supply is used for farming.

    A. Here's where you come into the picture: Every week, the average American consumes 300 gallons worth of California freshwater, through the purchasing of California grown food.

Listener-relevance link

        1. For example, if you eat three mandarins in a week, that alone requires 42.5 gallons of water to grow.

        2. Or if you eat a mere three-and-a-half walnuts, you also consume the seven gallons of water that were used in their production.

        3. If you think just because you don't cook very much, or because you don't waste your food, or even because you don't like vegetables, that you're excluded from this equation, you're not.

        4. In fact, meat and dairy are the real water killers.

            a. If you drink four glasses of milk from California, you've consumed 143 gallons of water.

            b. Or if you eat 1.75 ounces of California beef, a normal-sized portion of steak or hamburger, 86 gallons of water was required. This takes into account caring for the cow, properly cleaning and storing the meat, and delivering it to your local grocery store. (Buchanan, *New York Times*)

    B. It is crucial that we start making structural changes to our food industry, and update our methods for growing, distributing, and selling foods in the United States.

        1. We are an opulent food nation because we have grown accustomed to food looking unnaturally perfect. Why?

a. As a country, we spend 10 percent of our energy budget on transporting food to consumers, 50 percent of our land farming food, and 80 percent of our freshwater in the production of meat, dairies, grains, and produce.

b. But here's the kicker: we throw out 40 percent of our food due to superficial imperfections. (Aubrey, New England Public Radio)

c. Grocery stores do not sell blemished produce. If an apple is misshapen, it is garbage.

d. This means that 32 percent of our freshwater is wasted on food that never even has the opportunity to be eaten.

e. In other words, while a sixth, or nearly 17 percent, of Americans do not have food security, we throw away $165 billion dollars of edible food straight into the landfill every year. (Gunders, National Resources Defense Council)

    i. At the garbage dump, food waste accounts for the biggest single body of any material, releasing tremendous amounts of methane, a greenhouse gas, which heavily contributes to climate change.

    ii. To get an idea of how much damage it's causing, in the UK, if all food waste was eliminated from landfills, it would equal taking 20 percent of UK cars off the road.

    iii. When we know the average American consumer discards ten times as much as the average Southeast Asian, we know that it's possible to do better.

2. All of this is leading up to one thing: As Americans, we need to reimagine our food system—and fast, because a country which knowingly operates under the mindset of "waste more, want more" is a recipe for disaster.

Water conservation is about seeing the bigger picture, but in order to do that, we must first understand the root of the problem: the science of a drought.	**Transition**

II. Second, the consequences: Once we exhaust California of its natural water resources, there is no turning back.

Freshwater is rarer than you may think. Freshwater makes up only 3 percent of all the water on planet earth. The other 97 percent is salt water. (NOAA, n.d.)	**Listener Relevance Link**

A. It may seem like a simple fact. However, we can forget that freshwater is a precious commodity just like any other resource, such as petroleum oil or natural gas, which takes time and energy to produce.

1. The reason for all of the commotion in California? There just isn't enough freshwater to go around.

2. The drought is caused by decreased rainfall as well as snowfall in the mountains. When this happens, rivers are not replenished in the spring when the snow melts, and water reserves are not recharged. This leads to reduced surface water, and an increased usage of groundwater.

B. So what's the big difference between surface water and groundwater?

1. Surface water is the water you would find in a lake, river, or stream.

2. Surface water feeds the reservoirs where California gets its freshwater.

3. In a drought, surface water runs short and reservoirs drop (and, in this case, they are extremely low).

4. When reservoirs are low, we turn to groundwater, which is stored in aquifers deep underground.

5. But groundwater is different than surface water: It cannot be easily recharged. There are many different kinds of aquifers, and some took thousands or even millions of years to naturally build up water.

6. This makes groundwater a nonrenewable resource; once it is depleted, it is gone for good.

C. In the United States, we use groundwater for half of our freshwater needs.

1. This is highly problematic as it interrupts nature's attempt to replenish surface water, as well as frivolously consumes our irreplaceable water reserve.

2. When groundwater is pumped, it causes the water table, or "the depth which water is found below the surface," (Dimick, *National Geographic*) to fall dramatically. This is because we use water faster than the system can recharge itself.

3. This is not only expensive, but dangerous.

4. To find more water, we must then dig deeper into the ground, increasing the usual depth of wells to between 500 and 1,000 feet. This is not only a pricy operation, but increases the likelihood that abrupt sinkholes may appear, which can instantaneously swallow up homes and people.

D. Adding to this problem, California has outdated water rights that go back to the state's settlement, before 1903.

1. These rights have little to do with modern science, and do not take into account the exponential population growth that has occurred between the state's founding and now. (Stockton, *Wired*)

2. Only very recently has California suspended some of these antiquated water rights, now mandating that water be rationed for residents and farmers. (Audi, *The Wall Street Journal*)

3. And although a Groundwater Data Bill recently passed, California is still the only western state to not provide public access to data that details how much water is privately extracted by well owners.

4. This means the public cannot know how much water is actually left underground. (Walton, *Circle of Blue*)

E. However, it is estimated that groundwater usage now accounts for 60 percent of California's freshwater. (Dimick, *National Geographic*)

1. This is simply unsustainable.

2. If you were someone who answered yes to loving science fiction, then you're in luck. If we don't appropriately ration groundwater, our future will resemble something out of an apocalyptic blockbuster.

   a. Farmers will lose their farms and jobs, which is already happening now.

   b. Crops will be lost, and the economy will be sorely bruised, as billions of dollars of revenue will be lost.

   c. Grocery stores will be economically hit, and the industry will be forced to downsize dramatically.

   d. National food and water scarcity will occur.

   e. Drinking water and food will either be unaffordable or not available in many climates which now boast huge populations.

   f. Even today, this issue is spreading to other states beyond California, like Nebraska and Colorado, which are experiencing similar water shortages due to agricultural water use.

We're driving down a two-lane water highway, and we can either back up and turn around, or continue to drive ourselves straight into a wall.   **Transition**

III. Lastly, our future: The choice is ours. We are all factors when it comes to freshwater consumption.   **Listener Relevance Link**

A. Water conservation in the U.S. starts with reducing food waste and being more resourceful.

1. According to the Natural Resources Defense Council, the grocery chain Stop and Shop discovered that, when they decreased the number of perishable items they placed on their shelves, they saved $100 million in food that otherwise would have gone bad.

   a. Remember, 40 percent of food is thrown out before it reaches grocery stores, and 80 percent of freshwater is used in farming. Now that's a lot of water savings!

2. Additionally, The Farm to Family program in California recovers 120 million pounds of produce a year to distribute to foodbanks.

3. Although a successful program, the produce is still too expensive for many foodbanks to purchase the goods. However, there is a huge opportunity for grocery stores to sell these items at a discounted price, turn a profit, feed more people, and reduce waste.

B. However, water conservation is not only limited to the United States. It is a global issue, and looking to other countries can be helpful when assessing our current strategies and finding new solutions.

    1. For instance, the history and present day climate of the Aral Sea provides a strong example of what *not* to do.

    2. In the 1960s, the Soviet Union decided they wanted to plant large amounts of wheat. The snag: It didn't have enough water to do so.

        a. Its solution was to build a massive irrigation system that used water from the Aral Sea, which at the time was the fourth largest body of freshwater in the world. Although a lake, it was called a sea for a reason. It was huge.

        b. However, only half a century later, the lake is now completely dry.

        c. Additionally, agricultural runoff polluted the water with toxic pesticides. Now that the water has evaporated, the remaining dust that blows up from the dry land is now a biohazard, hurting nearby residents.

    4. What once was a fertile land is now wasteland.

    5. Although it seems impossible, this too could happen in the U.S. if we do not change our ways. (Clark Howard, *National Geographic*)

C. There are positive examples too, however, like Israel's treatment of their freshwater.

    1. The country has a very dry climate and is surrounded by the Mediterranean Sea and the incredibly salty Dead Sea.

    2. Despite this, the country was able to resolve its water shortages by utilizing desalination, a method which takes the salt out of seawater.

    3. By transforming seawater to freshwater, they have significantly made up for water they desperately needed.

    4. However, this doesn't simply fix all their problems. Israelis says they do not view desalination as the final solution. (Harris, NPR)

    5. Desalination is very costly, and costs double the amount of imported water.

    6. The process is also energy inefficient, and could have severe environmental impacts. (Cavanaugh, *Los Angeles Times*)

    7. So the first and most important step is to conserve natural freshwater. Desalinated water should only serve as plan B.

D. Today, the same Israeli technology is being brought to San Diego, California.

    1. This could have amazing benefits, but only if we treat desalinated water as a reserve for emergencies, not the solution. (Harris, NPR)

Conclusion

I. We've all heard that knowledge is power. Now that we have learned why the California drought is a significant economic, environmental, and agricultural threat, don't feel afraid—feel empowered!   **Thesis statement**

II. Water conservation is about protecting the future. If someone told you there was a forecast for rain, would you still go ahead and leave your car windows open? The problem is solvable: Stop wasting water when it is not needed. Tell grocery stores to stop rejecting 40 percent of our grown foods and sending them to landfills. Eat more foods that are grown and produced in your own region—not California. When buying food grown from California, remember to actually eat it before it spoils.   **Main point summary**

III.   I hope you each feel inspired by the positive outcome we can create together. Remember, knowledge is   **Clincher**
power. We have the power to stop water scarcity in its tracks!

References

Audi, T. (2015, June 13). California orders large water cuts by farmers. *The Wall Street Journal.* pp. A2.

Aubrey, A. (2015, June 17). To tackle food waste, big grocery chain will sell produce rejects. *New England Public Radio.* Retrieved online from: http://nepr.net/news/2015/06/17/to-tackle-food-waste-big-grocery-chain-will-sell-produce-rejects/

Buchanan, L., Keller, L.J., Park, H. (2015, May 21). Your contribution to the California drought. *The New York Times.* Retrieved online from: http://www.nytimes.com/interactive/2015/05/21/us/your-contribution-to-the-california-drought.html?_r=1

Cavanaugh, K. (2013, November 13). Desalination isn't the answer to California's water problem. *Los Angeles Times.* http://articles.latimes.com/2013/nov/13/news/la-ol-ocean-water-desalination-20131112.

Clark Howard, B. (2014, October 2). Aral Sea's eastern basin is for first time in 600 years. *National Geographic.* Retrieved online from: http://news.nationalgeographic.com/news/2014/10/141001-aral-sea-shrinking-drought-water-environment/

Clark Howard, B. (2015, April 2). Behind California's historic water restrictions: Low snowpack. *National Geographic.* Retrieved online from: http://news.nationalgeographic.com/2015/04/150402-california-snowpack-drought-water-science/

Dimick, D. (2014, August 21). If you think the water crisis can't get worse, wait until the aquifers are drained. *National Geographic.* Retrieved online from: http://news.nationalgeographic.com/news/2014/08/140819-groundwater-california-drought-aquifers-hidden-crisis/

Gunders, D. (2012, August). Wasted: How America is losing up to 40 percent of its food from farm to fork to landfill. *Natural Resources Defense Council.* Retrieved online from: http://www.nrdc.org/food/files/wasted-food-ip.pdf

Harris, E. (2015, June 14). Israel bringing its years of desalination experience to California. *NPR.* Retrieved online from: http://www.npr.org/sections/parallels/2015/06/14/413981435/israel-bringing-its-years-of-desalination-experience-to-california

Parsons, R. (2014, March 12). California farmers: How the state feeds a nation. *Los Angeles Times.* Retrieved online from: http://www.latimes.com/food/dailydish/la-dd-calcook-california-its-whats-for-dinner-20140312-story.html

Stockton, N. (2015, June 16). In epic drought, California's water cops get tough at last. *Wired.* http://www.wired.com/2015/06/california-finally-brings-water-kings-account/

Walton, B. (2015, June 4). Groundwater data bill passes California Senate. *Circle of Blue.* Retrieved online from: http://www.circleofblue.org/waternews/2015/world/groundwater-data-bill-passes-california-senate/

Where is all of the Earth's water? *NOAA.* Retrieved online from: http://oceanservice.noaa.gov/facts/wherewater.html

Speech and Analysis

Who here likes science fiction? Have you ever dreamed aliens were real? Do you love reading or watching movies about unknown galaxies warring over a rare element with fantastical powers? What if I told you a similar war was brewing right at your own backdoor? How would you feel?

It might sound like make-believe, but freshwater shortages are going to rapidly change the face of our planet if we don't stop our nation's careless water usage.

Think of all the fresh produce stocked at your local supermarket: The barrels of limes, crates of blueberries and raspberries, the shelves of spinach and asparagus, and the varieties of fish and meat that are not sourced from where you live. If you look hard enough, you can find basically anything at a store near you.

Now imagine waking up one day to find that it's all missing. More than that, the water prices are so high that no one can afford to buy fresh drinking water.

Today, we owe our plethora of foodstuffs, this cornucopia on steroids, in large part to California farmers, who grow nearly half of our nation's meats, vegetables, fruits, and nuts, according to Russ Parsons of the *Los Angeles Times.*

But California's agricultural productivity may not be guaranteed for long: Years of ongoing drought have scorched the ground. The snowpack in the mountains,

Analysis

Megan plays to her audience's literary and film tastes to grab their attention.

Here, Megan establishes listener relevance by asking a series of rhetorical questions, which engages her audience from the outset.

Megan further establishes listener relevance by describing a very familiar scenario and then subverting the audience's expectations about its outcome.

which recharges the state's water reservoirs, is only 6 percent of its usual amount, according to a National Geographic article by Brian Clark.

Growing up in California, I've experienced firsthand the severity of living in drought conditions. As an environmental studies major, I also interned at a desalination plant on my summer abroad in Israel. There, I learned just how much water conservation is a global issue.

> Megan establishes credibility by pointing out her personal experience with the topic as a Californian, an environmental studies major, and as an intern at a desalination plant.

I'm here today to tell you that the California drought is about more than just limiting a few showers. The clock is ticking. Our national demand for food diversity, and usage of precious groundwater to grow food, is at an all-time high. It's time we face the facts: The California drought is not just an inconvenience for local residents, but a severe economic, environmental, and agricultural threat affecting the future of the entire United States.

> Megan's thesis is clear, and we understand how she has organized her arguments to convince us to agree with her proposition.

First, the problem: We, as a nation, rely on California to sustain an opulent agricultural food system. *The New York Times* recently published an article by Larry Buchanan explaining that the state of California alone supplies our nation with a third of all vegetables and two-thirds of all fruits and nuts consumed. A full 80 percent of California's freshwater supply is used for farming.

Here's where you come into the picture: Every week, the average American consumes 300 gallons' worth of California freshwater. How? By purchasing and consuming California-grown food. For example, if you eat three mandarins in a week, those pieces of fruit required 42.5 gallons of water to grow. Or, if you eat as few as three-and-a-half walnuts, you also consume the seven gallons of water that were used in their production. If you think just because you don't cook very much, or don't waste your food, or you don't even like vegetables, that you're excluded from this equation, you're not.

> Megan quickly drives the point home that every American (and every audience member) is responsible for California's water loss.

In fact, Buchanan says meat and dairy are the real water killers. If you drink four glasses of milk from California over the course of a week, you've actually consumed 143 gallons of water. And 86 gallons of water was necessary for you to eat 1.75 ounces of California beef, a normal-sized portion of steak or hamburger. This takes into account caring for the cow, properly cleaning and storing the meat, and delivering it to your local grocery store.

> Megan provides a transition that effectively connects her previous point regarding produce production to her next point about meat and dairy production.

It is crucial that we start making structural changes to our food industry and update our methods for growing, distributing, and selling foods in the United States. We are an opulent food nation because we have grown accustomed to food looking unnaturally perfect. Why?

> Megan could improve her speech by better transitioning between these points.

As a country, we spend 10 percent of our energy budget on transporting food to consumers, 50 percent of our land farming food, and 80 percent of our freshwater in the production of meat, dairy products, grains, and produce, according to an article by Aubrey Allison.

> Using percent figures and an oral citation, Megan illustrates just how costly food production is.

But here's the kicker: We throw out 40 percent of our food supply because of superficial imperfections. Grocery stores do not sell blemished produce. If an apple is misshapen, it's garbage. This means that 32 percent of our freshwater is wasted on food that never even has the opportunity to be eaten. In other words, while a sixth—nearly 17 percent—of Americans do not have food security, we toss $165 billion of edible food straight into the landfill every year.

At the garbage dump, food waste accounts for the largest portion of refuse. As it decomposes, it releases tremendous amounts of methane, a greenhouse gas that heavily contributes to climate change. To get an idea of how much damage this waste is causing, consider the United Kingdom. An article by Dana Gunders suggests that, if all food waste was eliminated from landfills, it would equal taking 20 percent of UK cars off the road.

> While Megan offers another oral citation, she relies on her audience's knowledge of a foreign country's population to make her point. She could improve by making a point that better addresses her audience's knowledge.

When we realize that the average American consumer discards 10 times as much food as the average Southeast Asian, it becomes clear that it's possible to do better. All of this adds up to one thing: As Americans, we need to reimagine our food system—and fast, because a country that knowingly operates under the mindset of "waste more, want more" is headed for disaster.

Water conservation is about seeing the bigger picture, but in order to do that, we must first understand the root of the problem: the science of a drought. We must also understand the consequences of our actions: Once we exhaust California of its natural water resources, there is no turning back.

Freshwater is rarer than you may think. According to the National Oceanic and Atmospheric Administration, freshwater makes up only 3 percent of all the water on Earth. The other 97 percent, of course, is salt water. It may seem like a simple fact, however, we seem ready to forget that freshwater is a commodity no less precious than petroleum oil or natural gas and that it takes time and energy to produce.

The reason for all of the commotion in California? There simply isn't enough freshwater to go around. The drought is caused by decreased rainfall as well as reduced snowfall in the mountains. Without enough precipitation, rivers are not replenished in the spring by snowmelt, and water reserves are not recharged. The amount of surface water decreases, and usage of groundwater increases.

So what's the big difference between surface water and groundwater?

Surface water is the water that fills lakes, rivers, and streams. Surface water feeds the reservoirs where California gets its freshwater. In a drought, surface water runs short and reservoirs drop (and, in this case, they are extremely low). When reservoirs are low, we turn to groundwater, which is stored in aquifers deep underground.

But groundwater is different than surface water: It cannot be easily recharged. There are many different kinds of aquifers, and some take thousands or even millions of years to naturally collect water. This makes groundwater a nonrenewable resource; once it is depleted, it is gone for good.

In the United States, we use groundwater for half of our freshwater needs. This is highly problematic, as it interrupts nature's attempts to replenish surface water, as well as frivolously consumes our irreplaceable water reserve.

When groundwater is pumped, it causes the water table, or "the depth at which water is found below the surface," in the words of National Geographic's Dennis Dimick, to fall dramatically. This is because we use water faster than the system can recharge itself. This is not only expensive, but dangerous.

To find more water, we must then dig deeper into the ground, increasing the usual depth of wells to between 500 and 1,000 feet. This is not only a pricy operation, but increases the likelihood that abrupt sinkholes may appear, which can instantaneously swallow up homes and people.

Adding to this problem, California has outdated water rights that go back to the state's settlement, before 1903. These rights have little to do with modern science, and do not take into account the exponential population growth that has occurred between the state's founding and now, according to an article by Nick Stockton published in *Wired*.

A *Wall Street Journal* article by Tamara Audi points out that only very recently has California suspended some of these antiquated water rights, now mandating that water be rationed for residents and farmers. And although a Groundwater Data Bill was passed in the summer of 2015, California is still the only western state that doesn't provide public access to data detailing how much water is privately extracted by well owners. This means the public cannot know how much water is actually left underground. However, Dimick notes that groundwater usage now accounts for an estimated 60 percent of California's freshwater. This is simply unsustainable.

This is a good supporting fact, but again, Megan relies on her audience's knowledge of a foreign country to make her point.

Megan makes a strong argument in this transition and continues to use inclusive language to connect with the audience.

Here, the audience could infer that water is also no more important than other commodities, which could undermine Megan's argument. She could improve by clarifying this point.

Some of Megan's listeners might find this fact startling, which will keep their interest focused on learning more.

Megan employs another oral citation here, but the quote might come off as a little clunky to listeners. She could improve by paraphrasing the quote instead.

The vivid imagery of sinkholes "swallowing" homes and people will likely hold the audience's attention.

If you were someone who answered yes to loving science fiction, then you're in luck. If we don't appropriately ration groundwater, our future will resemble something out of an apocalyptic blockbuster.

Farmers are already losing their farms and jobs, and will continue to do so. Crop production will shrink, and the economy will be sorely bruised as billions of dollars of revenue will be lost.

Grocery stores will be economically damaged, and the industry will be forced to downsize dramatically. National food and water scarcity will occur as drinking water and food products will either be unaffordable or not available in many climates that now boast huge populations.

Even today, this issue is spreading to other states beyond California, such as Nebraska and Colorado, which are experiencing similar water shortages due to agricultural water use.

We're driving down a two-lane water highway, and we can either back up and turn around, or continue to drive ourselves straight into a wall. When it comes to our future, the choice is ours. We are all factors when it comes to freshwater consumption. Water conservation in the U.S. starts with reducing food waste and being more resourceful. According to the Natural Resources Defense Council, the grocery chain Stop and Shop discovered that when it decreased the number of perishable items it placed on their shelves, the company saved $100 million in food that otherwise would have gone bad.

Remember, 40 percent of food is thrown out before it reaches grocery stores, and 80 percent of freshwater is used in farming. Now that's a lot of water savings!

Additionally, the Farm to Family program in California recovers 120 million pounds of produce a year, and distributes it to foodbanks. Although it's a successful program, the produce is still too expensive for many foodbanks to purchase the goods. However, there is a huge opportunity for grocery stores to sell these items at a discounted price, turn a profit, feed more people, and reduce waste.

Furthermore, water conservation is not only limited to the United States. It is a global issue, and looking to other countries can be helpful when assessing our current strategies and finding new solutions. For instance, the history and present day climate of the Aral Sea provide a strong example of what *not* to do. In the 1960s, the Soviet Union decided it wanted to plant large amounts of wheat. The snag: It didn't have enough water to do so.

Its solution was to build a massive irrigation system that used water from the Aral Sea, which at the time was the fourth largest body of freshwater in the world. Although a lake, it was called a sea for a reason. It was huge. Now, only half a century later, the lake is now completely dry.

As if the irrigation drainage wasn't enough, agricultural runoff polluted the water with toxic pesticides. Now that the water has evaporated, the remaining dust that blows up from the dry land is a biohazard, harming nearby residents.

What once was a fertile land is now wasteland. Although it seems impossible, this too could happen in the U.S. if we do not change our ways.

There are, however, positive examples of water management we can look to, such as Israel's treatment of its freshwater. Israel has a very dry climate and is surrounded by the Mediterranean Sea and the incredibly salty Dead Sea. Despite this, the country was able to resolve its water shortages by utilizing desalination, a method that takes the salt out of seawater. By transforming seawater to freshwater, Israel has significantly made up for water its population needed.

Desalination has not, however, fixed all of Israel's problems. Israelis say they do not view desalination as the final solution. The desalination process is very costly—it

Megan refers back to her introduction with a listener relevance link.

Megan paints a vivid picture of a future under water scarcity, drawing her audience's attention.

Megan uses a strong analogy and inclusive language in this effective transition.

Megan refers back to an earlier part in her speech, and provides a positive outlook on a fact previously presented as negative.

Here, Megan broadens the scope of her speech's audience relevance by discussing water conservation on a global scale. She could capitalize on this further by referring to water conservation as a global issue earlier in the speech.

Megan provides a listener relevance link by providing a real-world example of what could happen to the U.S. if water waste continues.

costs up to double the amount of imported water. The process is also energy inefficient and could have severe environmental impacts. Nonetheless, it is an important part of a multi-pronged solution to Israeli water shortages.

Today, the same Israeli desalination technology is being brought to San Diego, California, according to an NPR article by Emily Harris. This could have amazing benefits, but only if we treat desalinated water as a reserve for emergencies, not the solution. The first and most important step is to conserve natural freshwater. Desalination should only serve as plan B.

We've all heard that knowledge is power. Now that we have learned why the California drought is a significant economic, environmental, and agricultural threat, don't feel afraid—feel empowered!

Water conservation is about protecting the future. If someone told you there was a forecast for rain, would you still go ahead and leave your car windows open? The problem is solvable: Stop wasting water when it is not needed. Tell grocery stores to stop rejecting 40 percent of our grown foods and sending them to landfills. Eat more foods that are grown and produced in your own region—not California. When buying food grown in California, remember to eat it before it spoils.

I hope you each feel inspired by a vision for a positive outcome that we can create together. Remember, knowledge is power. With it, we have the power to stop water scarcity in its tracks!

Megan uses plenty of oral citations, but her speech is heavy on journalistic sources. She could improve her credibility by citing more academic sources.

Megan does a nice job restating her proposition and providing a clincher that ties back nicely to previously mentioned facts.

Speech to Actuate
Evaluation Checklist

Use this checklist to evaluate a speech to actuate.

General Criteria

_____ **1.** Was the introduction effective in creating interest, involving the audience in the speech, and previewing the main points?

_____ **2.** Were section transitions used to help you follow the organization of the main points?

_____ **3.** Did the conclusion summarize the thesis and main points in a memorable way?

_____ **4.** Was the language appropriate, accurate, clear, and vivid?

_____ **5.** Was the speech delivered conversationally, intelligibly, expressively, and convincingly?

Specific Criteria

_____ **1.** Was the specific goal clear and phrased as a proposition of policy?

_____ **2.** Was the speech organized into an appropriate actuation persuasive speech framework?
_____ Problem solution _____ Problem-cause-solution _____ Motivated sequence

_____ **3.** Did the speaker use logos effectively?
_____ Use strong evidence? _____ Use reasoning to link evidence to claims? _____ Avoid fallacies?

(Continued)

_____ **4.** Did the speaker use ethos effectively?
_____ Establish expertise? _____ Demonstrate trustworthiness? _____ Convey goodwill?

_____ **5.** Did the speaker use pathos effectively? _____ Appeal to negative emotions?

If so, check all that were tapped: _____ fear _____ guilt _____ anger _____ shame _____ sadness

Appeal to positive emotions? If so, check all that were tapped: _____ happiness/joy _____ pride _____ relief _____ hope _____ compassion

_____ **6.** Did the speaker offer a compelling call to action?

Based on these criteria, evaluate the speech (check one):

☐ **excellent** ☐ **good** ☐ **satisfactory** ☐ **fair** ☐ **poor**

Explain:

Actuation Persuasive Speech:

Together, We Can Stop Cyber-Bullying[5]

By Adam Parrish

This section presents a sample speech to actuate given by a student, including an adaptation plan, an outline, and a transcript.

1. Read the speech adaptation plan, outline, and transcript of a speech given by Adam Parrish in an introductory speaking course.

2. Access a video clip of Adam's speech through the Chapter 14 resources in SPEAK 3 Online.

3. Use SPEAK 3 Online to identify some of the strengths of Adam's speech by preparing an evaluation checklist and an analysis.

4. Compare your answers with those of the authors.

Adaptation Plan

1. **Target audience initial attitude and background knowledge:** My audience is composed of traditional-aged college students with varying majors and classes. Most are from middle-class backgrounds. The initial attitude about bullying for most will be to agree with me already that it's a bad thing. So I will try to get them to take action. My perception is that my audience knows about cyber-bullying but not the nuances of it.

2. **Organizational pattern:** I will organize my speech using a problem-cause-solution framework because my audience already agrees that bullying is bad but may not know what they can and should do to help stop it.

3. **Arguments (logos):** I will demonstrate what widespread (breadth) and harmful (depth of effects) cyber-bullying is and why it persists (causes). Once I've convinced my audience, I will propose solutions that must be taken and cite specifically what we must do to help stop this horrible practice.

4. **Building competence, credibility, and good character (ethos):** I will use credible sources to support my claims and cite them using oral footnotes. I will also offer personal stories to create goodwill.

5. **Creating and maintaining interest (pathos):** I will involve my audience by appealing to several emotions, including guilt, sadness, relief, hope, and compassion.

Actuation Persuasive Speech Outline
Together, We Can Stop Cyber-Bullying

General Goal:
To persuade

Specific Goal:
To convince my audience to take action to help stop cyber-bullying.

Introduction

I. "I'll miss just being around her." "I didn't want to believe it." "It's such a sad thing." These quotes are from the friends and family of 15-year-old Phoebe Prince, who, on January 14, 2010, committed suicide by hanging herself. Why did this senseless act occur? The answer is simple: Phoebe Prince was bullied to death. — **Attention getter**

II. Many of us know someone who has been bullied in school. Perhaps they were teased in the parking lot or in the locker room. In the past, bullying occurred primarily in and around schools. However, with the advent of new communication technologies such as cell phones with text messaging capability, instant messaging, e-mails, blogs, and social networking sites, bullies can now follow their victims anywhere, even into their own bedrooms. Using electronic communications to tease, harass, threaten, and intimidate another person is called cyber-bullying. — **Listener-relevance link**

III. As a tutor and mentor to young students, I have witnessed cyber-bullying firsthand, and by examining current research, I believe I understand the problem, its causes, and how we can help end cyber-bullying. — **Speaker credibility**

IV. Cyber-bullying is a devastating form of abuse that must be confronted and stopped. — **Thesis statement (stated as proposition)**

V. Today, we will examine the widespread and harmful nature of cyber-bullying, discover how and why it persists, and propose some simple solutions that we must engage in to thwart cyber-bullies and comfort their victims. — **Preview**

Transition
Let's begin by tackling the problem head on.

Body

I. Cyber-bullying is a pervasive and dangerous behavior.

Many of us have read rude, insensitive, or nasty statements posted about us or someone we care about on social networking sites like Twitter and Facebook. Whether or not those comments were actually intended to hurt another person's feelings, they are perfect examples of cyber-bullying.

Problem

Listener-relevance link

A. Cyber-bullying takes place all over the world through a wide array of electronic media.

1. According to Statisticbrain.com, as of 2014, 52 percent of American middle-school students had experienced instances of cyber-bullying ranging from hurtful comments to threats of physical violence (Statisticbrain.com, 2014).

2. Females are just as likely as males to engage in cyber-bullying, although women are 10 percent more likely to be victimized (Li, 2007).

3. A 2011 study reported in the journal *Pediatrics* noted that instances of bullying via text messages have risen significantly since 2006 (Ybarra, Mitchell, & Korchmaros, 2011).

4. Quing Li (2007), a researcher of computer-mediated communication, noted that Internet and cell-phone technologies have been used by bullies to harass, torment, and threaten young people in North America, Europe, and Asia.

5. A particularly disturbing incident occurred in Dallas, Texas, where an overweight student with multiple sclerosis was targeted on a school's social networking page. One message read, "I guess I'll have to wait until you kill yourself, which I hope is not long from now, or I'll have to wait until your disease kills you" (Keith & Martin, 2005, p. 226).

Transition

Clearly, cyber-bullying is a widespread problem. What is most disturbing about cyber-bullying, however, is its effects upon victims, bystanders, and perhaps even upon the bullies themselves.

B. Cyber-bullying can lead to traumatic physical and psychological injuries upon its victims.

1. According to a 2007 article in the *Journal of Adolescent Health*, 36 percent of the victims of cyber-bullies are also harassed by their attackers in school (Ybarra, Diener-West, & Leaf, 2007).

2. For example, the Dallas student with MS had eggs thrown at her car and a bottle of acid thrown at her house (Keith & Martin, 2005).

3. Ybarra et al. (2007) reported that victims of cyber-bullying experience such severe emotional distress that they often exhibit behavioral problems such as poor grades, skipping school, and receiving detentions and suspensions.

4. Smith et al. (2008) suggested that even a few instances of cyber-bullying can have these long-lasting and heartbreaking results.

5. What is even more alarming is that victims of cyber-bullying are significantly more likely to carry weapons to school as a result of feeling threatened (Ybarra et al., 2007). Obviously, this could lead to violent, and perhaps even deadly, outcomes for bullies, victims, and even bystanders.

6. In fact, a string of nine suicides in 2013 were linked to cyber-bullying on the social network site Ask.fm (Pappas 2015).

Transition

Now that we realize the devastating nature, scope, and effects of cyber-bullying, let's look at its causes.

II. Cyber-bullying is perpetuated because victims and bystanders do not report their abusers to authorities.

Cause

Think back to a time when you may have seen a friend or loved one being harassed online. Did you report the bully to the network administrator or other authorities? Did you console the victim? I know I didn't. If you are like me, we may unknowingly be enabling future instances of cyber-bullying.

Listener-relevance link

A. Cyber-bullies are cowards who attack their victims anonymously.

1. Ybarra et al. (2007) discovered that 13 percent of cyber-bullying victims did not know who was tormenting them.

2. This is an important statistic because, as Keith and Martin (2005) point out, traditional bullying takes place face to face and often ends when students leave school. However, today students are subjected to bullying in their own homes.

3. Perhaps the anonymous nature of cyber-attacks partially explains why Li (2007) found that nearly 76 percent of victims of cyber-bullying and 75 percent of bystanders never reported instances of bullying to adults.

B. Victims and bystanders who do not report attacks from cyber-bullies can unintentionally enable bullies.

1. According to De Nies, Donaldson, and Netter of ABCNews.com (2010) several of Phoebe Prince's classmates were aware that she was being harassed but did not inform the school's administration.

2. Li (2007) suggested that victims and bystanders often do not believe that adults will actually intervene to stop cyber-bullying.

3. However, *ABCNews.com* (2010) reports that 41 states have laws against bullying in schools, and 23 of those states target cyber-bullying specifically.

Transition

Now that we realize that victims of cyber-bullies desperately need the help of witnesses and bystanders to report their attacks, we should arm ourselves with the information necessary to provide that assistance.

III. Cyber-bullying must be confronted on national, local, and personal levels.

Solution

Think about the next time you see a friend or loved one being tormented or harassed online. What would you be willing to do to help?

Listener-relevance link

A. There should be a comprehensive national law confronting cyber-bullying in schools. Certain statutes currently in state laws should be amalgamated to create the strongest protections for victims and the most effective punishments for bullies as possible.

1. On July 1, 2015, a Georgia law went into effect requiring students to provide social media passwords to school administrators so that bullying posts could removed when necessary (Rodriguez, 2015).

2. Furthermore, Connecticut law *requires* school employees to report bullying as part of their hiring contract (Limber & Small, 2003). Washington takes this a step further by protecting employees from any legal action if a reported bully is proven to be innocent (Limber & Small, 2003).

3. When it comes to protecting victims, West Virginia law demands that schools must ensure that a bullied student does not receive additional abuse at the hands of his or her bully (Limber & Small, 2003).

4. Legislating punishment for bullies is difficult. As Limber and Small (2003) noted, zero-tolerance polices often perpetuate violence because at-risk youth (bullies) are removed from all of the benefits of school, which might help make them less abusive.

5. A comprehensive anti-cyber-bullying law should incorporate the best aspects of these state laws and find a way to punish bullies that is both punitive and has the ability to rehabilitate abusers.

B. Local communities must organize and mobilize to attack the problem of cyber-bullying.

1. According to Greene (2006), communities need to support bullying prevention programs by conducting a school-based bullying survey for individual school districts. We can't know how to best protect victims in our community without knowing how they are affected by the problem.

2. It is critical to know this information. As Greene noted, only 3 percent of teachers in the United States perceive bullying to be a problem in their schools (Greene, 2006).

3. Local school districts should create a coordinating committee made up of "administrators, teachers, students, parents, school staff, and community partners" to gather bullying data and rally support to confront the problem (Greene, 2006, p. 73).

4. Even if your local school district is unable or unwilling to mobilize behind this dire cause, there are some important actions you can take personally to safeguard those you love against cyber-bullying.

C. Take note of these warning signs that might indicate a friend or loved one is a victim of a cyber-bully.

1. Victims of cyber-bullies often use electronic communication more frequently than do people who are not being bullied.

2. Victims of cyber-bullies have mood swings and difficulty sleeping (Keith & Martin, 2005).

3. Victims of cyber-bullies seem depressed and/or become anxious (Keith & Martin, 2005).

4. An analysis of ten studies found a connection between cyber-bullying and depression (Pappas, 2015).

5. Victims of cyber-bullies become withdrawn from social activities and fall behind in scholastic responsibilities (Keith & Martin, 2005).

D. If you see a friend or loved one exhibiting any of these signs, I implore you not to ignore them. Rather, take action. Get involved. Do something to stop it.

1. According to Raskauskas and Stoltz (2007), witnesses of cyber-bullying should inform victims to take the attacks seriously, especially if the bullies threaten violence.

2. Tell victims to report their attacks to police or other authority figures (Raskauskas & Stoltz, 2007).

3. Tell victims to block harmful messages by blocking e-mail accounts and cell phone numbers (Raskauskas & Stoltz, 2007).

4. Tell victims to save copies of attacks and provide them to authorities (Raskauskas & Stoltz, 2007).

5. If you personally know the bully and feel safe confronting him or her, do so! As Raskauskas and Stoltz (2007) noted, bullies will often back down when confronted by peers.

6. By being a good friend and by giving good advice, you can help a victim report his or her attacks from cyber-bullies and take a major step toward eliminating this horrendous problem.

Transition

So, you see, we are not helpless to stop the cyber-bulling problem as long as we make the choice NOT to ignore it.

Conclusion

I. Cyber-bullying is a devastating form of abuse that must be reported to authorities.

II. Cyber-bullying is a worldwide problem perpetuated by the silence of both victims and bystanders. By paying attention to certain warning signs, we can empower ourselves to console victims and report their abusers.

Thesis statement

Main point summary

III. Today, I implore you to do your part to help stop cyber-bullying. I know that you agree that stopping cyber-bullying must be a priority. First, although other states have cyber-bullying laws in place, ours does not. So I'm asking you to sign this petition that I will forward to our district's state legislators. We need to make our voices heard that we want specific laws passed to stop this horrific practice and to punish those caught doing it. Second, I'm also asking you to be vigilant in noticing signs of cyber-bullying and then taking action. Look for signs that your friend, brother, sister, cousin, boyfriend, girlfriend, or loved one might be a victim of cyber-bullying and then get involved to help stop it! Phoebe Prince showed the warning signs, and she did not deserve to die so senselessly. None of us would ever want to say, "I'll miss just being around her," "I didn't want to believe it," "It's such a sad thing" about our own friends or family members. We must work to ensure that victims are supported and bullies are confronted nationally, locally, and personally. I know that, if we stand together and refuse to be silent, we can and will stop cyber-bullying.

Call to action and clincher

References

Cyber Bullying Statistics (2014). Retrieved online from http://www.statisticbrain.com/cyber-bullying-statistics/

De Nies, Y., Donaldson, S., & Netter, S. (2010, January 28). Mean girls: Cyberbullying blamed for teen suicides. *ABCNews .com*. Retrieved online from http://abcnews.go.com/GMA/Parenting/girls-teen-suicide-calls-attention-cyberbullying /story?id=9685026

Greene, M. B. (2006). Bullying in schools: A plea for measure of human rights. *Journal of Social Issues, 62*(1), 63–79.

Keith, S., & Martin, M. (2005). Cyber-bullying: Creating a culture of respect in the cyber world. *Reclaiming Children and Youth, 13*(4), 224–228.

Li, Q. (2007). New bottle of old wine: A research of cyberbullying in schools. *Computers in Human Behavior, 23*, 1777–1791.

Limber, S. P., & Small, M. A. (2003). State laws and policies to address bullying in schools. *School Psychology Review, 32*(3), 445–455.

Pappas, S. (2015, June 22). Cyberbullying on social media linked to teen depression. Livescience.com. Retrieved online from http://www.livescience.com/51294-cyberbullying-social-media-teen-depression.html

Raskauskas, J., & Stoltz, A. D. (2007). Involvement in traditional and electronic bullying among adolescents. *Developmental Psychology, 43*(3), 564–575.

Smith, P. K., Mahdavi, J., Carvalho, M., Fisher, S. Russel, S., & Tippett, N. (2008). Cyberbullying: Its nature and impact in secondary school pupils. *Journal of Child Psychology and Psychiatry, 49*(4), 374–385.

Ybarra, M. L., Diener-West, M., & Leaf, P. J. (2007). Examining the overlap in Internet harassment and school bullying: Implications for school intervention. *Journal of Adolescent Health, 41*, S42–S50.

Ybarra, M. L., Mitchell, K. J., Wolak, J., & Finkelhor, D. (2006). Examining characteristics and associated distress related to Internet harassment: Findings from the second Youth Internet Safety Survey. *Pediatrics, 118*, 1169–1177.

Ybarra, M. L., Mitchell, K. M., & Korchmaros, J. D. (2011). National trends in exposure to and experiences of violence on the Internet among children. *Pediatrics*, Retrieved online from http://pediatrics.aappublications .org/content/early/2011/11/16/peds.2011-0118.full.pdf+html

Speech and Analysis

Speech

"I'll miss just being around her." "I didn't want to believe it." "It's such a sad thing." These quotes are from the friends and family of 15-year-old Phoebe Prince, who, on January 14, 2010, committed suicide by hanging herself. Why did this senseless act occur? The answer is simple . . . Phoebe Prince was bullied to death.

Many of us know someone who has been bullied in school. Perhaps they were teased in the parking lot or in the locker room. In the past, bullying occurred primarily in school. However, with the advent of new communication technologies such as cell phones, text messaging, instant messaging, blogs, and social networking sites, bullies can now follow and terrorize their victims anywhere, even into

Analysis

Adam uses quotes from family and friends of cyber-bullying victim Phoebe Prince to get attention and lead into his proposition.

Here Adam further entices his listeners to pay attention by offering listener relevance that we all can relate to.

Using the vivid term "terrorize," Adam appeals to negative emotions (pathos).

their own bedrooms. Using electronic communications to tease, harass, threaten, and intimidate another person is called cyber-bullying.

As a tutor and mentor to young students, I have witnessed cyber-bullying firsthand, and by examining current research, I believe I understand the problem, its causes, and how we can help end cyber-bullying. What I know for sure is that cyber-bullying is a devastating form of abuse that must be confronted on national, local, and personal levels.

Today, we will examine the widespread and harmful nature of cyber-bullying, uncover how and why it persists, and pinpoint some simple solutions we must begin to enact in order to thwart cyber-bullies and comfort their victims. Let's begin by tackling the problem head on.

Many of us have read rude, insensitive, or nasty statements posted about us or someone we care about on social networking sites like Twitter and Facebook. Well, whether or not those comments were actually intended to hurt another person's feelings, if they did hurt their feelings, then they are perfect examples of cyber-bullying.

Cyber-bullying is a pervasive and dangerous behavior. It takes place all over the world and through a wide array of electronic media. According to Statisticbrain.com, as of 2014, 52 percent of American middle-school students had experienced instances of cyber-bullying ranging from hurtful comments to threats of physical violence. Quing Li's article published in the journal *Computers in Human Behavior* noted that cyber-bullying is not gender biased. According to Li, females are just as likely as males to engage in cyber-bullying, although women are 10 percent more likely to be victimized.

A 2011 study reported in the journal *Pediatrics* noted that instances of bullying via text messages have risen significantly since 2006. The problem does not exist in the United States alone.

Li noted that Internet and cell-phone technologies have been used by bullies to harass, torment, and threaten young people in North America, Europe, and Asia. However, some of the most horrific attacks happen right here at home.

According to Keith and Martin, a particularly disturbing incident occurred in Dallas, Texas, where an overweight student with multiple sclerosis was targeted on a school's social networking page. One message read, "I guess I'll have to wait until you kill yourself which I hope is not long from now, or I'll have to wait until your disease kills you." Clearly, cyber-bullying is a worldwide and perverse phenomenon. What is most disturbing about cyber-bullying is its effects upon victims, bystanders, and perhaps even upon bullies themselves.

Cyber-bullying can lead to physical and psychological injuries upon its victims. According to a 2007 article in the *Journal of Adolescent Health*, Ybarra and colleagues noted that 36 percent of the victims of cyber-bullies are also harassed by their attackers in school. For example, the Dallas student with MS had eggs thrown at her car and a bottle of acid thrown at her house.

Ybarra et al. reported that victims of cyber-bullying experience such severe emotional distress that they often exhibit behavioral problems such as poor grades, skipping school, and receiving detentions and suspensions. Furthermore, Smith et al. suggested that even a few instances of cyber-bullying can have these long-lasting negative effects.

What is even more alarming is that, according to Ybarra and colleagues, victims of cyber-bullying are significantly more likely to carry weapons to school as a result of feeling threatened. Obviously, this could lead to violent outcomes for bullies, victims, and even bystanders. Some victims may even feel that death is the only way to

Adam begins to establish ethos by mentioning why he has credibility about this topic. Mentioning that he is a tutor and mentor also conveys goodwill. Listeners are likely to think he must have good character if he volunteers as a tutor and mentor.

Adam does a nice job of previewing his problem-cause-solution organizational framework, but his thesis statement phrased as a proposition is somewhat lost and could be made more overtly here.

Again, Adam's use of a listener-relevance link helps keep listeners tuned in and interested in hearing more.

Here Adam bolsters his ethos (and avoids plagiarism) by citing an oral footnote for his statistics.

Notice Adam's word choices (harass, torment, threaten, horrific) to enhance pathos.

This example provides an emotional appeal by offering a real example of a real victim in Dallas, Texas.

This vivid example enhances pathos.

Now that Adam has established the breadth of the problem as widespread, he moves into a discussion about the depth of the effects it can have on victims.

Here Adam helps pique listener interest by pointing out how bystanders could also be hurt if we don't do something to stop this form of terrorism.

escape their tormentors. In 2013, a string of nine teen suicides were linked to cyber-bullying on the social network site Ask.fm.

Now that we have heard about the nature, scope, and effects of cyber-bullying, let's see if we can discover its causes. Let's think back to a time when we may have seen a friend or loved one being harassed online. Did we report the bully to the network administrator or other authorities? Did we console the victim? I know I didn't. If you are like me, we may unknowingly be enabling future instances of cyber-bullying.

Cyber-bullying occurs because of the anonymity offered to bullies by cell phone and Internet technologies, as well as the failure of victims and bystanders to report incidents of cyber-bullying. You see, unlike schoolyard bullies, cyber-bullies can attack their victims anonymously.

Ybarra and colleagues discovered that 13 percent of cyber-bullying victims did not know who was tormenting them. This devastating statistic is important because, as Keith and Martin noted, traditional bullying takes place face to face and often ends when students leave school. However, today, students are subjected to nonstop bullying, even when they are alone in their own homes.

Perhaps the anonymous nature of cyber-attacks partially explains why Li found that nearly 76 percent of victims of cyber-bullying and 75 percent of bystanders never reported instances of bullying to adults. Victims and bystanders who do not report attacks from cyber-bullies can unintentionally enable bullies.

According to De Nies, Donaldson, and Netter of ABCNews.com (2010), several of Phoebe Prince's classmates were aware that she was being harassed but did not inform the school's administration. Li suggested that victims and bystanders often do not believe that adults will actually intervene to stop cyber-bullying. However, ABCNews.com reports that 41 states have laws against bullying in schools, and 23 of those states target cyber-bullying specifically.

Now that we know that victims of cyber-bullies desperately need the help of witnesses and bystanders to report their attacks, we should arm ourselves with the information necessary to provide that assistance. Think about the next time you see a friend or loved one being tormented or harassed online. What would you be willing to do to help?

Cyber-bullying must be confronted on national, local, and personal levels. There should be a comprehensive national law confronting cyber-bullying in schools. Certain statutes currently in state laws should be amalgamated to create the strongest protections for victims and the most effective punishments for bullies as possible.

On July 1, 2015, a Georgia law went into effect requiring students to provide their social media passwords to school administrators so bullying posts could be removed when necessary.

Furthermore, Connecticut law *requires* school employees to report bullying as part their hiring contract. Washington takes this a step further by protecting employees from any legal action if a reported bully is proven to be innocent. When it comes to protecting victims, West Virginia law demands that schools must ensure that a bullied student does not receive additional abuse at the hands of his or her bully.

Legislating punishment for bullies is difficult. As Limber and Small noted, zero-tolerance polices often perpetuate violence because at-risk youth, i.e., bullies, are removed from all of the benefits of school, which might help make them less abusive. A comprehensive anti-cyber-bullying law should incorporate the best aspects of these state laws and find a way to punish bullies that is both punitive and has the

---

Notice how Adam's transition verbally ties the point he is finishing (problem) to the next point (causes) clearly using inclusive "we" language. This, too, bolsters a sense of goodwill and uses a conversational style that keeps listeners engaged.

Again, Adam does a nice job with his transition.

Notice how Adam gets right to the point about needing to take action on a variety of levels to stop this practice.

Adam gives credence to his policy statement by pointing to several states that have already succeeded in creating such laws.

Here Adam points to the need for consequences for bullying behavior when it is caught.

ability to rehabilitate abusers. However, for national laws to be effective, local communities need to be supportive.

Local communities must organize and mobilize to attack the problem of cyber-bullying. According to Greene's 2006 article published in the *Journal of Social Issues*, communities need to support bullying prevention programs by conducting a school-based bullying survey for individual school districts. We can't know how to best protect victims in our community without knowing how they are affected by the problem. It is critical to know this information. As Greene noted, only 3 percent of teachers in the United States perceive bullying to be a problem in their schools.

Adam offers specific action steps that communities ought to do to help stop cyber-bullying.

Local school districts should create a coordinating committee made up of administrators, teachers, students, parents, school staff, and community partners to gather bullying data and rally support to confront the problem. Even if your local school district is unable or unwilling to mobilize behind this dire cause, there are some important actions you can take personally to safeguard those you love against cyber-bullying.

Here Adam gets personal when he points out that each person in the room has an ethical responsibility to help stop cyber-bullying.

There are several warning signs that might indicate a friend or loved one is a victim of a cyber-bully. If you see a friend or loved one exhibiting these signs, the decision to get involved can be the difference between life and death.

According to Keith and Martin's article "Cyber-Bullying: Creating a Culture of Respect in a Cyber World," victims of cyber-bullies often use electronic communication more frequently than do people who are not being bullied. Victims of cyber-bullies have mood swings and difficulty sleeping. They seem depressed and/or become anxious. Victims can also become withdrawn from social activities and fall behind in scholastic responsibilities. If you witness your friends or family members exhibiting these symptoms, there are several ways you can help.

According to Raskauskas and Stoltz's 2007 article in *Developmental Psychology*, witnesses of cyber-bullying should inform victims to take the attacks seriously, especially if the bullies threaten violence. You should tell victims to report their attacks to police or other authorities, to block harmful messages by blocking e-mail accounts and cell phone numbers, and to save copies of attacks and provide them to authorities.

Adam could make this statement more compelling by offering a specific example of what one might tell the police, as well as how to install blockers on e-mail and cell phones.

If you personally know the bully and feel safe confronting him or her, do so! As Raskauskas and Stoltz noted, bullies will often back down when confronted by peers. By being a good friend and by giving good advice, you can help a victim report his or her attacks from cyber-bullies and take a major step toward eliminating this horrendous problem. So, you see, we are not helpless to stop the cyber-bulling problem as long as we make the choice NOT to ignore it.

To conclude, cyber-bullying is a devastating form of abuse that must be reported to authorities. Cyber-bullying is a worldwide problem perpetuated by the silence of both victims and bystanders. By paying attention to certain warning signs, we can empower ourselves to console victims and report their abusers.

Here Adam restates his proposition, but it actually could be more comprehensive (beyond just our need to report bullying to authorities).

Today, I'm imploring you to do your part to help stop cyber-bullying. I know that you agree that stopping cyber-bullying must be a priority. First, although other states have cyber-bullying laws in place, ours does not. So I'm asking you to sign this petition that I will forward to our district's state legislators. We need to make our voices heard that we want specific laws passed to stop this horrific practice and to punish those caught doing it.

Second, I'm also asking you to be vigilant in noticing signs of cyber-bullying and then taking action. Look for signs that your friend, brother, sister, cousin, boyfriend,

Adam reminds us of his specific call to action and even asks listeners to sign a petition today. His approach encourages listeners to follow through with his goal, that is, to actuate.

girlfriend, or loved one might be a victim of cyber-bullying, and then get involved to help stop it! Phoebe Prince showed the warning signs, and she did not deserve to die so senselessly. None of us would ever want to say, "I'll miss just being around her," "I didn't want to believe it," or "It's such a sad thing" about our own friends or family members. We must work to ensure that victims are supported and bullies are confronted nationally, locally, and personally.

If we stand together and refuse to be silent, we can and will stop cyber-bullying.

Adam does a nice job with his clincher in terms of tying back to the Phoebe story in his attention getter. Doing so also appeals to emotions (pathos) in a way that should make his speech very memorable.

STUDY TOOLS 14

LOCATED IN TEXTBOOK

☐ Tear-out Chapter Review cards at the end of the book

☐ Review with the Quick Quiz below

LOCATED ON SPEAK3 ONLINE AT CENGAGEBRAIN.COM

☐ Review Key Term flashcards and create your own cards

☐ Track your knowledge and understanding of key concepts in speech communication

☐ Complete practice and graded quizzes to prepare for tests

☐ Complete interactive content within SPEAK3 Online

☐ View the chapter highlight boxes for SPEAK3 Online

Quick Quiz (answers in Solutions Appendix)

T F 1. The primary goal of a persuasive speech is to seek agreement or encourage action.

T F 2. An audience is neutral only because it does not understand why a speaker prefers a certain position on an issue.

T F 3. A speaker who is describing why young children should not watch more than 30 minutes of TV per day is using a proposition of value.

T F 4. One of the ways that people express their attitude is to give their opinions.

T F 5. The proposition of a persuasive speech should be framed as an exclamatory sentence.

6. "The goal of my speech is to convince you that the government should censor Web sites" is an example of a:
   a. proposition of policy
   b. proposition of intent
   c. proposition of fact
   d. proposition of value
   e. All propositions are reflected in this statement.

7. The term that refers to the group of people that a speaker most wants to persuade is:
   a. core audience
   b. key demographic
   c. target group
   d. target audience
   e. constituency

8. If you wanted to convince an audience that an increase in taxes will lead to job loss, you should use a:
   a. proposition of value
   b. proposition of fact
   c. proposition of policy
   d. proposition of legislation
   e. fiscal proposition

9. Dorothy wants to give a speech in which she explores the rise in violent crime and makes a proposal for how to address it. She should use the _____ framework.
   a. problem-solution
   b. statement of reasons
   c. problem-cause-solution
   d. motivated sequence
   e. statement of fact

10. The first step of the motivated sequence organizational pattern is the:
    a. satisfaction step
    b. visualization step
    c. attention step
    d. action appeal step
    e. resolution step

Chapter Takeaways

List three key takeaways from this chapter:

-

-

-

SPEAK ONLINE

STUDY YOUR WAY
WITH STUDYBITS!

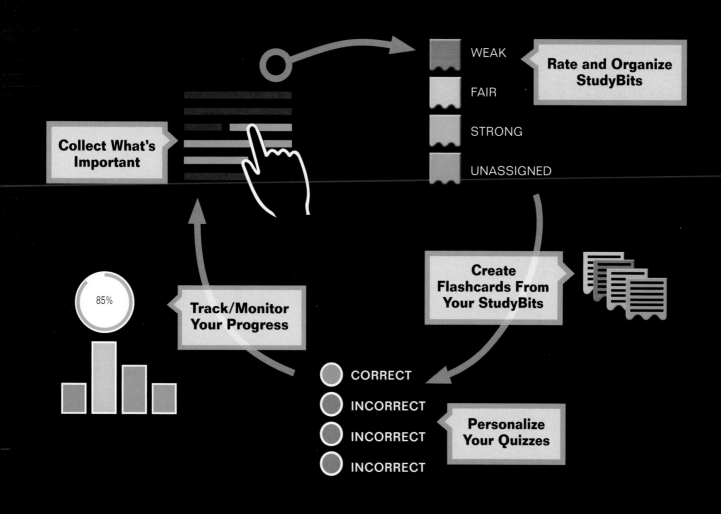

Rate and Organize StudyBits

WEAK

FAIR

STRONG

UNASSIGNED

Collect What's Important

Track/Monitor Your Progress

85%

Create Flashcards From Your StudyBits

CORRECT

INCORRECT

INCORRECT

INCORRECT

Personalize Your Quizzes

4LTR PRESS

Access SPEAK ONLINE at www.cengagebrain.com

15 Ceremonial Speaking

LEARNING OUTCOMES

15-1 Identify the elements of a speech of welcome.

15-2 Explain why a speech of introduction should be brief.

15-3 Identify the goal of a speech of nomination.

15-4 Discuss the context for a speech of recognition.

15-5 Describe the elements for a speech of acceptance.

15-6 List common types of speeches of tribute.

15-7 Identify and describe additional types of ceremonial speeches.

After finishing this chapter go to **PAGE 291** for **STUDY TOOLS.**

Sheer Photo. Inc/Getty Images

Sound Familiar?

Because Ben didn't know his biological father, his grandfather had been like a father to him. He and his grandfather used to spend hours playing ball, fishing, or simply watching television together. Although Ben's grandfather had lived a long and fruitful life, when he died Ben found it difficult to say goodbye. Still, he wanted to give the eulogy at the funeral. How could he find the right words to do justice to his grandfather's memory?

On special occasions, such as weddings and funerals, we may be called on to "say a few words." On these ceremonial occasions, your audience has distinct expectations for what they will hear. So, although the speech plan action steps you have learned will help you prepare your remarks, you also need to understand how the occasion affects the way you should shape your speech.

The goal of ceremonial speaking lies somewhere between informing and persuading. In ceremonial speeches, you invite listeners to agree with you about the value of the person, object, event, or place the special occasion revolves around. Another characteristic of most ceremonial speeches is brevity: They are generally—although not always—fewer than five minutes long. This chapter describes six common types of ceremonial speeches given on special occasions: speeches of welcome, introduction, nomination, recognition, acceptance, and tribute. For each speech type, we describe the typical expectations to keep in mind as you prepare.

15-1 SPEECHES OF WELCOME

A **speech of welcome** greets and expresses pleasure for the presence of a person, group, or organization. You can welcome someone on your own, but you will usually give a speech of welcome as the representative of a group. You must be familiar with the group that you are representing and the occasion. As you prepare your welcome, you may need to do some research so you can accurately describe the group, circumstances, and occasion to the person or people you are welcoming. A speech of welcome is generally not more than two to four minutes long.

A speech of welcome invites listeners to agree that the occasion is friendly and their attendance is appreciated. Do this by respectfully catching listeners' attention and, after expressing appreciation on behalf of your group for their presence, providing a brief description of the group and setting to which they are being welcomed. The conclusion should briefly express your hope for the outcome of the visit, event, or relationship. A typical speech of welcome might be as simple as this:

Today, I want to welcome John Sheldon, who is joining us from the North Thurston Club. John, as you are aware, we are a newer club, having been established in 2014. At that time, we had only ten members. But we had big hopes. Today, we are 127 members strong, and we raised more than $250,000 last year to support local children's organizations. We hope that our talks here today will lead to closer cooperation between the North Thurston Club and ours here in Yelm.

On some occasions, you may be asked to serve as **master of ceremonies**, an individual designated to welcome guests, set the mood for the program, introduce participants, and keep the program moving. (Either a woman or a man can be referred to as a master of ceremonies.) Year-end honorary banquets, corporate dinner meetings, and local charity events typically

> **speech of welcome** a brief, formal ceremonial address that greets and expresses pleasure for the presence of a person or an organization
>
> **master of ceremonies** an individual designated to set the mood of the program, introduce participants, and keep the program moving

use someone in this role. As master of ceremonies, you might actually be asked to give a speech that both welcomes and introduces a speaker. When this is the case, the speech can be a bit longer and should also include the type of information described in the next section.

15-2 SPEECHES OF INTRODUCTION

A **speech of introduction** introduces the main speaker by establishing a supportive climate, highlighting pertinent biographical information, and generating enthusiasm for listening to the speech. At times, you will be given a résumé or brief biography of the speaker; at other times, you may need to research the speaker's background yourself. Regardless of what you learn, you should also try to contact the speaker and ask what points in the biography the speaker would like you to emphasize. Generally, a speech of introduction is not more than three to five minutes long.

The beginning of a speech of introduction should quickly establish the nature of the occasion. The body of the speech should focus on three or four things the audience ought to know about the person being introduced. The conclusion should mention the speaker by name and briefly identify the topic and title of the speech. If the person is well known, you might simply say something like, "Ladies and gentlemen, the president of the United States." If the person is less well known, however, then mentioning his or her name specifically during the speech of introduction and especially at the end is imperative.

Speeches of introduction should honestly represent the person being introduced. Do not hype a speaker's credentials or over-praise the speaker. If you set the audience's expectations too high, even a good speaker may have trouble living up to them. For instance, an overzealous introducer can doom a competent speaker by saying, "This man [woman] is undoubtedly one of the greatest speakers of our time. I have no doubt that what you are about to hear will change your thinking." Although this introduction is meant to be complimentary, it does the speaker a grave disservice. A typical speech of introduction might look like the following:

antoniodiaz/Shutterstock.com

Today, it is my pleasure to introduce our speaker, Ms. Susan Wong, the new president of the finance club. I've worked with Susan for three years and have found her to have a gift for organization, insight into the financial markets, and an interest in aligning student organizations with leaders in our community. Susan, as you may not know, has spent the past two summers working as an intern at Morgan Stanley and has now laid the groundwork for more college internships for students from our university. She is a finance major, with a minor in international business. Today, she is going to talk with us about the benefits of summer internships. Let's give a warm welcome to Susan Wong!

15-3 SPEECHES OF NOMINATION

A **speech of nomination** proposes a nominee for an elected office, honor, position, or award. Every four years, the Democratic and Republican parties have speeches of nomination at their national conventions. Those speeches are rather long, but most speeches of nomination are brief, lasting only about two to four minutes.

The goal of a speech of nomination is to highlight the qualities that make this person the most credible candidate. To do so, first clarify the importance of the position, honor, or award by describing the responsibilities involved, related challenges or issues, and the characteristics needed to fulfill it. Second, list the candidate's personal and professional qualifications that meet those criteria. Doing so links the candidate with the position, honor, or award in ways that make him or her appear to be a natural choice. Finally, formally place the candidate's name in nomination, creating a dramatic climax to clinch your speech. A speech of nomination could be as simple and brief as this:

I am very proud to place in nomination for president of our association the name of one of our most active members, Ms. Adrienne Lamb.

speech of introduction a brief ceremonial speech that establishes a supportive climate for the main speaker, highlights the speaker's credibility by familiarizing the audience with pertinent biographical information, and generates enthusiasm for listening to the speaker and topic

speech of nomination a ceremonial presentation that proposes a nominee for an elected office, honor, position, or award

We all realize the demands of this particular post. It requires leadership. It requires vision. It requires enthusiasm and motivation. And, most of all, it requires a sincere love for our group and its mission.

Adrienne Lamb meets and exceeds each one of these demands. It was Adrienne Lamb who chaired our visioning task force. She led us to articulate the mission statement we abide by today. It was Adrienne Lamb who chaired the fund-raising committee last year when we enjoyed a record drive. And it was Adrienne Lamb who acted as mentor to so many of us, myself included, when we were trying to find our place in this association and this community. This association and its members have reaped the benefits of Adrienne Lamb's love and leadership so many times and in so many ways. We now have the opportunity to benefit in even greater ways.

It is truly an honor and a privilege to place in nomination for president of our association Ms. Adrienne Lamb!

 ## 15-4 SPEECHES OF RECOGNITION

At the Lifetime Achievement Awards in 2013, Mel Brooks spoofed the speech he planned to deliver in 2014.

A **speech of recognition** acknowledges someone and usually presents an award, a prize, or a gift to the individual or a representative of a group. You have probably watched speeches of recognition given as lifetime achievement awards on the Academy Awards or the Grammy Awards. Speeches of recognition may be a bit longer depending on the prestigious nature of the award, but are more commonly quite brief (fewer than three minutes long).

Because the audience wants to know why the recipient is being recognized, you must recount the nature and history of the award, as well as the recognition criteria and how the recipient met them. If the recognition is based on a competition, this might include the number of contestants and the way the contest was judged. If the person earned the award through years of achievement, you will want to describe the specific milestones that the person passed. Every year the American Film Institute awards its Lifetime Achievement Award to a person who has had a successful and important career in the movie industry. Each recipient is called upon the year after winning to return to the banquet to announce the next winner. In 2013, Martin Scorsese presented the award to Mel Brooks who then delivered an acceptance speech that included a spoof of the speech of recognition he planned to deliver in 2014 when introducing the next winner. Although Brooks's speech was certainly

comedic, it provides a good reminder of the importance of being sincere when delivering speech of recognition. (To see Mel Brooks' speech, visit https://www.youtube.com/watch?v=70kYzWx2TNs)

Ordinarily, the speech begins by describing what the recognition is for, then states the criteria for winning or achieving the recognition, and finally describes how the person being recognized won or achieved the award. In some cases, the recognition is meant to be a surprise, so you will deliberately omit the name of the recipient in what you say, building to a climax when the name is announced.

Keep two special considerations in mind when preparing a speech of recognition. First, refrain from over-praising; do not explain everything in superlatives that make the presentation seem to lack sincerity and honesty. Second, in the United States, it is traditional to shake hands with recipients as awards are received. So, if you have a certificate or other tangible award that you are going to hand to the recipient, be careful to hold it in your left hand and present it to the recipient's left hand. That way, you will be able to shake the right

> **speech of recognition** a ceremonial presentation that acknowledges someone and usually presents an award, a prize, or a gift to the individual or a representative of a group

hand in congratulations. A typical speech of recognition may look like this:

I'm honored to present this year's Idea of the Year Award to Ryan Goldbloom from the installation department. As you may remember, this is an award that we have been giving since 1985 to the employee who has submitted an idea that resulted in the largest first-year cost savings for the company. Ryan's idea to equip all installation trucks with prepackaged kits for each type of job has resulted in a $10,458 savings in the first twelve months. And in recognition of this contribution to our bottom line, I am pleased to share our savings with Ryan in the form of a check for $2,091.60, one fifth of what he has saved us. Good work, Ryan.

15-5 SPEECHES OF ACCEPTANCE

A **speech of acceptance** acknowledges receipt of an honor or award. The goal is to sincerely convey your appreciation for the honor. You should briefly thank the person or group bestowing the honor, acknowledge the competition, express gratitude about receiving the award, and thank those who contributed to your success. To be effective, the speech should be brief, humble, and gracious. Remember that your goal is to convey appreciation in a way that makes the audience feel good about you receiving the award. Rarely, as in the case of a politician accepting a nomination, a professional accepting the presidency of a national organization, or a person receiving a prestigious award that is the focus of the gathering, an audience will expect a longer speech. Generally, however, acceptance speeches are no longer than one to two minutes.

Acceptance speeches that don't adhere to expectations often have disastrous results. If you have ever watched award programs such as the Academy Awards, MTV Music Awards, the People's Choice Awards, or the Grammys, you no doubt have observed an award winner who gave an overly long or otherwise inappropriate acceptance speech. In 2015, dozens of Oscar recipients at the Academy Awards ceremony used their acceptance speeches as platforms to promote political or charitable causes. Instead of graciously thanking the Academy of Motion Picture Arts and Sciences for honoring them, Patricia Arquette used her acceptance speech to advocate

Helga Esteb/Shutterstock.com

In her 2015 Oscar speech, Best Actress winner Julianne Moore said that "people with Alzheimer's deserve to be seen, so that we can find a cure."

for equal pay for women; Julianne Moore used her time to promote research efforts for Alzheimer's disease; Dana Perry used her time to advocate for suicide prevention; John Legend spoke out against racial injustice; and Alejandro González Iñárritu argued for immigration reform in the United States and political reform in Mexico.[1] The volume of acceptance speeches that tilted toward advocacy and argument was so pronounced that, in the days following the ceremony, journalists of every media type and bias were criticizing, and even lampooning, the celebrities who had made them.

So when you have the opportunity to give an acceptance speech, practice it so that you are confident you can accomplish your purpose quickly. It is also important to focus your remarks on the recognition you have been given or on the position you are accepting. It is inappropriate to use an acceptance speech to advocate for an unrelated cause. The following is an example of an appropriate speech of acceptance:

I would like to thank the hospital for hosting this beautiful luncheon today. It is absolutely lovely! Thank you, too, to the chef, cooks, and wait staff. You have really

speech of acceptance a ceremonial speech given to acknowledge receipt of an honor or award

made this event memorable in so many ways. In all honesty, I must admit I am a bit stunned and also truly honored to be recognized today as this year's Volunteer of the Year. As I look out at all of you here today, I am humbled to think of the countless hours you all spend giving freely of your time, and your love for the hurting children in our community. I am grateful to count myself among such amazing, selfless servant leaders. Each one of you deserves this trophy. I want to also thank my husband, Terry, for encouraging me to join Big Hearts, Big Hands and for supporting me when I became involved as a volunteer. You are my rock and I love you! Thank you, again, for this award. I will treasure it forever.

15-6 SPEECHES OF TRIBUTE

A **speech of tribute** praises or celebrates a person, a group, or an event. You might be asked to pay tribute to a person or persons on the occasion of their birthday, wedding, anniversary, oath of office, retirement, or funeral. There are many special types of speeches of tribute based on the specific special occasion they are meant for. The goal in any of them, however, is to invite listeners to truly appreciate the person, group, or event by arousing their sentiments. This is achieved by focusing on the most notable characteristics or achievements of the person, group, or event with vivid stories, examples, and language that arouses sentiments. Speeches of tribute can vary from brief to lengthy depending on the nature of the occasion. Let's take a closer look at three types of tribute that you are likely to be asked to give at some point in your life.

15-6a Toasts

A **toast**, usually offered at the start of a reception or meal, pays tribute to the occasion or to a person. On most occasions, a toast is expected to be very brief (lasting less than a minute), consisting of only a few sentences, and focusing on a single characteristic of the person or occasion. Usually, a short example is used to support or illustrate the characteristic. Wedding toasts, given at a rehearsal dinner or reception by a family member or member of the wedding party, are generally longer speeches (three to four minutes) that may use humor but should not embarrass the persons at whom they are directed.

A toast should be sincere and express a sentiment that is likely to be widely shared by those in attendance. Generally, the person giving the toast and all other attendees

have a drink in hand, which they raise and sip from at the conclusion of the toast. So, before offering a toast, it is customary to make sure that drinks are refreshed so that all can participate. If particular people are being toasted, the toast is drunk in their honor, so they do not drink. The following is a typical toast by a daughter given to honor her mother's college graduation:

Tonight, I'd like to offer a toast to a woman I admire and respect. My mom has always supported my brother and me. So when she told me that she wanted to go back and finish college, I was worried about how we'd all manage. But I shouldn't have worried. Mom not only finished her degree in less than two years, but she also continued to work full time and, what's more, she's even had time to coach my brother's Little League team. Here's to you, Mom—you're amazing!

15-6b Roasts

One unique type of tribute speech is given as part of a **roast**, which is an event where family and friends share short speeches in honor of one person. In these short speeches, guests might offer good-natured insults or anecdotes, heartwarming or outlandish personal stories, or uplifting accolades. Roasts became mainstream in popular culture when singer and actor Dean Martin hosted a series of celebrity roasts on television during the 1970s. Some of the most famous celebrity roasts have been of William Shatner, Pamela Anderson, Frank Sinatra, Hugh Hefner, Johnny Carson, and Muhammad Ali. The key when offering a speech of tribute during a roast is to demonstrate the ethical communication principles of respect and integrity by offering only jokes, stories, and anecdotes that do not offend the featured guest by sharing stories that are too private or too vulgar for a general audience. The point, after all, is to honor and laud the guest.

15-6c Eulogies

A **eulogy** is a ceremonial speech of tribute presented at a funeral or memorial service that praises someone's life and accomplishments. You might recall from our opening scenario that Ben was preparing a eulogy for

speech of tribute a ceremonial speech that praises or celebrates a person, a group, or an event

toast a ceremonial speech offered at the start of a reception or meal that pays tribute to the occasion or to a person

roast an event where guests provide short speeches of tribute about the featured guests that are developed with humorous stories and anecdotes

eulogy a ceremonial speech of tribute during a funeral or memorial service that praises someone's life and accomplishments

© iStockPhoto.com/FLOORTJE

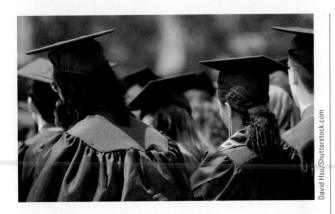
David Hsu/Shutterstock.com

his grandfather. Your goal with a eulogy is to comfort the mourners by focusing on positive memories of the deceased person. Based on what you know about the person, select three or four positive personal characteristics of the person to use as the main points, and then use personal stories you have collected about the person to provide support. Your audience will enjoy hearing new stories that exemplify the characteristics as well as revisiting widely shared stories. Incidents that reveal how a personal characteristic helped the person overcome adversity will be especially powerful.

15-7 OTHER CEREMONIAL SPEECHES

Other occasions that call for ceremonial speeches include graduations, holidays, anniversaries of major events, and special events. A **commencement address**, for example, is a speech of tribute praising graduating students and inspiring them to reach for their goals. A **commemorative address** is a ceremonial speech of tribute that celebrates national holidays or anniversaries of important events. This chapter concludes with a sample commemorative address given in tribute at a Remembrance Day celebration. A **keynote address** is a ceremonial speech that both sets the

tone and generates enthusiasm for the topic of a conference or convention. A **dedication** is a speech of tribute that honors a worthy person or group by naming a structure such as a building, monument, or park after the honoree. A **farewell** is a ceremonial speech of tribute honoring someone who is leaving an organization. A **speech to entertain** is a humorous speech that makes a serious point.

commencement address
a speech of tribute praising graduating students and inspiring them to reach for their goals

commemorative address
a speech of tribute that celebrates national holidays or anniversaries of important events

keynote address a ceremonial speech that both sets the tone and generates enthusiasm for the topic of a conference or convention

dedication a speech of tribute that honors a worthy person or group by naming a structure, monument, or park after them

farewell a speech of tribute honoring someone who is leaving an organization

speech to entertain a humorous speech that makes a serious point

TECH TALK

Teleprompters—To Use or Not to Use?

If anything can be considered a common theme across the many types of formal, ceremonial speeches and the diversity of occasions where they are delivered, that common element may be the teleprompter.

Developed in the 1950s by the TelePrompTer Company, the modern teleprompter uses glass panes, mirrors, and a personal computer to feed text to a speaker, allowing the speaker to reference their remarks without looking down at a set of notes.[2] When used by an experienced speaker, teleprompters can make a speech seem more fluid and polished. But when the technology fails, it can have disastrous and embarrassing results.

Nonetheless, many public speakers rely on teleprompters simply because they're required to speak often, and it can be next to impossible to memorize a different ceremonial speech day after day. The opposite holds true as well: Inexperienced speakers may use the devices to avoid succumbing to nerves. Actors Margot Robbie and Jonah Hill,[3] director Michael Bay,[4] and Fox News anchor Megyn Kelly[5] are among those who have leaned—perhaps too heavily—on this technology, only to trip up publicly when it fails.

Even when all goes well, however, teleprompters can still pose a challenge to camera operators, who can struggle to keep a speaker in frame without shooting through the glass panes. Additionally, teleprompters can make a speech seem *too* polished and scripted, which might be off-putting during commemorative speeches or other instances where unrehearsed emotion is expected.

The teleprompter isn't going anywhere anytime soon, and for many people, its benefits outweigh the challenges it presents. If you're ever in a position to use one yourself, you may find that the device is a godsend—or perhaps just another technological crutch.

Commemorative Address Speech
Evaluation Checklist

You can use this checklist to critique a speech of tribute that you hear in class or a recording of your own. As you listen, outline the speech. Pay close attention to the celebratory language the speaker uses. Note the descriptions and anecdotes used to describe the person's character, personality, achievements, and demeanor. Then, answer the following questions.

General Criteria

_____ **1.** Did the speech provide all the basic elements of an effective speech: introduction, body, conclusion, and transitions?

_____ **2.** Did the introduction

_____   catch the audience's interest?

_____   identify the speech topic/goal?

_____   preview the main points?

_____ **3.** Were transitions provided between each main point?

_____ **4.** Did the conclusion

_____   remind the audience of the main points?

_____   motivate the audience to remember the main ideas of the speech?

_____ **5.** Did the speaker use words that were

_____   appropriate and inclusive?

_____   accurate and clear?

_____   vivid and expressive?

Specific Criteria

_____ **1.** Did the speech effectively invite the audience to appreciate the person, group, or event?

_____ **2.** Did the speech arouse your sentiments in favor of the person, group, or event?

_____ **3.** Was the length of the speech appropriate for the occasion?

_____ **4.** Was the tone of the speech appropriate for the occasion?

Based on these criteria, evaluate the speech (check one):

    ☐ **excellent**   ☐ **good**   ☐ **satisfactory**   ☐ **fair**   ☐ **poor**

Explain:

Sample Commemorative Address Speech:

Little-Known Heroes: A Tribute to the Girl Guides in the World Wars

This chapter concludes with an outline and transcript of a sample commemorative address given as a tribute speech honoring the contribution of Girl Guides during the World Wars. As you read the outline, consider how you might address the rhetorical situation effectively if you were to present the speech yourself. Then, read the transcript, noting any similarities and differences between your version and the transcript.

Speech Outline

Little-Known Heroes: A Tribute to the Girl Guides in the World Wars

General Goal: To pay tribute

Specific Goal: I would like to pay tribute to the courageous women, young and old, who gallantly worked for the Girl Guides during the First and Second World Wars.

Introduction

I.	Imagine this: It's World War II, and members of the Nazi resistance are sneaking across enemy lines. It's 5am, and they're on a mission to rescue prisoners of war. If caught—they face death.	**Attention getter**
II.	Who are you imagining in your mind's eye? What if I told you this story is about a troop of Girl Guides, England's version of the Girl Scouts?	**Listener-relevance link**
III.	I am an international student from the United Kingdom—I know, you may have already guessed from my accent—and across the pond, I grew up being a Girl Guide. However, unlike what you might be thinking, I wasn't very good at selling cookies or starting fires. It wasn't until I was older, when I learned my grandmother was a leader for the Girl Guides during the war, that I understood just how incredibly important the Girl Guides are in world history.	**Speaker credibility**
IV.	This week the UK will celebrate Remembrance Day, which is similar to your Veteran's Day. In honor of the holiday, I'd like to pay tribute to the Girl Guides who served in World War I and World War II, and so bravely helped British and American soldiers alike, with sheer optimism and resourcefulness.	**Listener-relevance link** **Thesis statement**

Body

I. It might sound old fashioned—but one of the ways the Girl Guides fought the war was through song and cheer. The first story I'd like to share with you is about a concentration camp in Chefoo, China.

    1. In 1941, Japan attacked Hawaii's Pearl Harbor. Japan had already occupied China, and the following day, after attacking the U.S., closed down all of China's British and American schools. They rounded up all of the American and British citizens—adults and children, and placed them into concentration camps, separating children from their parents (*This American Life*, 2015).

2. Among these prisoners were Girl Guides and their leaders.

    A. The Girl Guides were about to spend four years at the concentration camp in Chefoo.

        1. There at the camp they were deprived of food and heat, and had to eat crushed egg shells to receive calcium—many were starving.

        2. Although this sounds impossibly grim, the silver lining to the monstrous situation was that the Girl Guides had their leaders with them—the Brown Owls (*This American Life*, 2015).

    B. What happened then was truly remarkable and showed just how strong the human spirit can be. The Brown Owls made a single decision early on—one that Mary Previte, a surviving Girl Guide, says allowed them to "live a miracle where grownups preserved our childhood" (*This American Life*, 2015).

        1. The Brown Owls required the girls to uphold the same manners, respectfulness, and gratitude that they were normally required to show in civilian life.

        2. In the direst of situations, the leaders made up new awards and badges to give to the girls that tremendously benefited their survival.

        3. Now they were winning contests for who could build a fire out of scraps of coal and keep it going the longest. It may sound odd, but it truly motivated everyone around them.

    C. Janie Hampton, author of *How the Girl Guides Won the War*, says their attitude was infectious. She remarks, "It made a difference to all the adults in this camp and kept them going. The whole atmosphere was better because they had this very strong promise that they wouldn't stop smiling" (*This American Life*, 2015).

        1. The adults in this camp were brought out of their grimmest moments when these small girls came through singing, and created a semblance of the daily routine they had before internment.

        2. Survivor Mary Previte, at age 82, still sings songs like it was yesterday!

This exemplifies the spirit of the Girl Guides—to never quit! The effects of the Girl Guide's resilience and dedication were seen not only in Chefoo, but all over the world. **Thesis statement**

II. Girl Guides served as secret agents, army aids, and medical attendants, taking on remarkable responsibility for their age.

    A. In World War I, 90 Girl Guides ages 14-16 served as spies for M15, England's security agency. They were given perilous tasks, like carrying top-secret messages. Originally, M15 used Boy Scouts and Girl Guides, but they discontinued their relationship with the Scouts, who proved over time to be less reliable—or to put it simply—they acted like the kids that they were (*The Courier Mail*, 2010). But the Girl Guides showed maturity and wisdom beyond their years.

    B. In 1942, during the Second World War, the British Girl Guides created the Guide Emergency Committee.

        1. The Guide International Service (GIS) worked with the Red Cross, Salvation Army, and the Quakers, to help men, women, and children civilians who were hurt by the conflict (Heathcote, 2010).

        2. GIS were on call 24/7. And in 18 months, the guides were able to raise £120,000 (Heathcote, 2010), which by today's standards is an incredibly large sum of money—roughly £4,750,000 (Bank of England, 2014)—or $7,300,000. How many groups have you known capable of doing that? **Listener Relevance**

        3. They traveled to Yugoslavia and Greece (Heathcote, 2010), as well as Germany and the Netherlands (World Scouting Museum, 2007), taking care of thousands who suffered from bombings, starvation, and disease.

        4. Hampton's research indicates they also assisted civilians by doing anything from using DDT powder to ward off tick-typhus, mediating arguments and disputes, helping suicidal victims, treating hemorrhages, and getting rid of snakes in the water supply (Daily Express, 2011).

        5. In 1945, the GIS even went to the Bergen-Belsen concentration camp where Anne Frank was once held (World Scouting Museum, 2007) to rescue prisoners.

6. A Girl Guide reported, "When we got to Belsen the people were cold, hungry and unhoused. They were lying about on the floor with no clothes, just scraps of bone" (Heathcote, 2010). But the guides helped escort them to safety at last.

C. The Girl Guides were internationally known and beloved. In Greece, at a refugee camp, when the GIS arrived, a Greek woman cried out, "The Guides from England! You've come! You've come" (Heathcote, 2010)!

1. Hampton states, "They became the embodiment of the homefront spirit, digging shelters, and pushing trek-carts around to collect jam jars for recycling and feeding bombed-out families" (Daily Express, 2011).

Girl Guides of other nationalities had profound effects on the war as well.	**Transition**

III. Polish Girl Guides and American Girl Scouts made incredible sacrifices and contributions to the war effort.

A. Nazi law prohibited young women from being Girl Guides, but Polish girls continued the fight in secret (Heathcote, 2010).

1. Polish Girl Guides actually saved Jewish children from genocide by illegally removing them from the Warsaw Ghetto, and other areas of German-occupied Poland (Heathcote, 2010).

2. They achieved amazing feats. They helped British prisoners of war escape from the Nazis—and sometimes even planned the escapes themselves (Hampton, 2011).

   i. Tragically, many Polish Girl Guides died for their efforts. Some guides were sent to Auschwitz, a concentration camp, where they perished for their noble and fearless deeds, like those who wrote anti-Nazi news pamphlets (Heathcote, 2010).

   ii. Yet all of this was relatively unknown to the general public until recently—because no one recorded the Girl Guide's history. Hampton was able to find this information by digging deep into historical archives (Hampton, 2011).

B. Girl Scouts in the United States were also active during WWII.

1. Girl Scouts collected large amounts of scrap metal to be used for creating munitions.

2. Girl Scouts organized a clothing drive and were able to distribute 1.5 million clothing items.

3. Girl Scouts also worked in hospitals, trained civilian women in survival skills, organized bike couriers, and planted vegetable gardens, called Victory Gardens, when food was limited (Girl Scouts, n.d).

Conclusion

I. History isn't only confined to the past—it is connected to the present day and our future. It is fundamentally important that we remember and honor the courageous actions of these young women—who went above and beyond in their fight for good.

Listener relevance

II. It is clear that these girls were anything but ordinary. They demonstrated the kind of valor that we usually only attribute to the bravest heroes in the military. During one of the darkest moments in human history, Girl Guides served as a light and symbolized hope for innocent children, civilians, and soldiers. On this Remembrance Day, I salute my grandmother—and all the other Guides who made such great sacrifices during the war.

Thesis restatement

Main point summary

III. The next time you see a young Girl Scout, or if you travel abroad and see a Girl Guide, remember this: Girl Guides and Scouts are more than crafters and cookie sellers. They are heirs to a tradition of courage, confidence, and character that played an important role in the freedoms you enjoy today.

References

Kroonenberg, Piet J. (November, 2007). Guide International Service & Scout International Relief Service. *World Scouting Museum*. Retrieved from http://www.worldscoutingmuseum.org/files/GIS-SIRS.pdf

Girl Scouts Timeline, (n.d). *Girl Scouts*. Retrieved from http://girlscouts.org/who_we_are/history/timeline/

Heathcote, C. (2010, August 1). The Girl Guides who won the war. *Daily Express*. Retrieved from http://www.express.co.uk/expressyourself/190435/The-Girl-Guides-who-won-the-war

Glass, I. (Executive Producer). (2015, June 26). *This American life* [Radio broadcast]. Chicago: WBEZ. Retrieved from http://www.thisamericanlife.org/radio-archives/episode/559/transcript

Girl Guides used as spies in World War I. (2010, February 27). *The Courier Mail*. Retrieved online from: http://www.couriermail.com.au/news/girl-guides-used-as-spies-in-world-war-i/story-e6frep26-1225835112172.

Hampton, J. (2011, July 18). How the Girl Guides helped beat Hitler. *Daily Express*. Retrieved from http://www.express.co.uk/expressyourself/259504/How-the-Girl-Guides-helped-beat-Hitler

Inflation Calculator. *Bank of England*. Retrieved from http://www.bankofengland.co.uk/education/Pages/resources/inflationtools/calculator/index1.aspx

Speech and Analysis

Speech

Imagine this: It's World War II, and members of the Nazi resistance are sneaking across enemy lines at five in the morning on a mission to rescue prisoners of war. If caught—they face certain death.

Who are you imagining in your mind's eye? What if I told you this story is about a troop of Girl Guides, England's version of the Girl Scouts?

I am an international student from the United Kingdom. (I know, it's a shocker—as if you couldn't already tell from my accent. Across the pond, I grew up being a Girl Guide. However, contrary to what you might be thinking, I wasn't very good at selling cookies or starting fires. It wasn't until I was older, when I learned my grandmother was a leader for the Girl Guides during the war, that I understood just how incredibly important the Girl Guides are in world history.

This week the UK will celebrate Remembrance Day, which is similar to your Veteran's Day. In honor of the holiday, I'd like to pay tribute to the Girl Guides who served in World War I and World War II, and so bravely helped British and American soldiers alike, with sheer optimism and resourcefulness.

It might sound old fashioned—but one of the ways the Girl Guides fought the war was through song and cheer. The first story I'd like to share with you is about a concentration camp in Chefoo, China.

When Japan entered World War II, it immediately set about rounding up British and American citizens living and studying in China, which Japanese troops had been occupying during the ongoing Second Sino-Japanese War. The day after the attack on Pearl Harbor, Hawaii, all British and American schools in China were closed, and teachers and students were interned in concentration camps. According to Janie Hampton, an accidental Girl Guide historian and author of *How Girl Guides Won the War*, teachers grabbed as much as they could before leaving the building. They took paper, pencils and musical instruments—and they also grabbed Brownie uniforms, Girl Guide uniforms, and materials for making badges.

The teachers knew that, wherever they were going, they would need to keep the children occupied. Little did they know, however, that they were about to spend four years at the Chefoo concentration camp. At the camp, prisoners were deprived of food and heat. One survivor, Mary Previte, recalls that monks used to smuggle eggs into the camp for the children, who also had to eat the crushed egg shells for calcium. And even though children and parents had been separated, a group of Girl Guide leaders, called Brown Owls, actually stayed with their Girl Guides.

Analysis

Jane presents a gripping scenario to grab the audience's attention.

Here, Jane directly addresses the audience to establish listener relevance.

By explaining her own experience with the Girl Guides, Jane contributes to her own credibility.

Jane is presumably speaking to an American audience, and references American soldiers to better connect with her listeners.

Jane clearly states the purpose of her speech so the audience knows what to expect.

By recounting the story of the Girl Guides of Chefoo, Jane creates a captivating introduction to her address.

What happened was truly remarkable and showed just how strong the human spirit can be. The Brown Owls made a single decision early on—that they were going to run the Girl Guide troop at Chefoo as if it were a regular Girl Guide troop. The Brown Owls required the girls to uphold the same manners, respectfulness, and gratitude that they were normally required to show in civilian life.

Merit badges are part of the normal Girl Guide experience, so leaders at Chefoo made up new awards and badges to give to the girls. The difference at Chefoo was that the badges and awards helped the girls survive. Girls won contests for building a fire out of scraps of coal and keeping it going the longest. It may sound odd, but it truly motivated everyone around them.

Janie Hampton says the Girl Guides' attitude was infectious. In an interview for *This American Life* on American Public Media, Ms. Hampton remarked, "It made a difference to all the adults in this camp and kept them going. The whole atmosphere was better because they had this very strong promise that they wouldn't stop smiling."

▶ *By using an oral citation, Jane increases the credibility of her tribute by showing that is it has merit.*

The adults in this camp were brought out of their grimmest moments when these small girls came through singing, and created a semblance of the daily routine they had before internment. How powerful was that commitment to smiling and singing under the gravest of circumstances? At age 82, Chefoo survivor Mary Previte still sings songs like it was yesterday! Indeed, Ms. Previte exemplifies the spirit of the Girl Guides—to never quit!

The effects of the Girl Guide's resilience and dedication were seen not only in Chefoo, but all over the world and multiple theaters of war. Girl Guides served as secret agents, army aids, and medical attendants, taking on remarkable responsibility for their age.

▶ *Transition*

In World War I, 90 Girl Guides ages 14 to 16 years old served as spies for MI5, England's security agency. They were given perilous tasks, like carrying top-secret messages. Originally, MI5 used Boy Scouts *and* Girl Guides. MI5 ultimately discontinued its relationship with the Boy Scouts, but it kept working with the Girl Guides, who were more reliable and showed maturity and wisdom beyond their years.

In 1942, during the Second World War, the British Girl Guides created the Guide Emergency Committee and the Guide International Service, or GIS. The GIS worked with the Red Cross, Salvation Army, and the Quakers, to help men, women, and children who had been hurt in the war. The service was on call around the clock, seven days a week. Within 18 months of starting, the GIS guides were able to raise £120,000 to support their relief efforts. Even by today's standards, that is an incredibly large sum of money. But in 1942 currency, it's even more astounding. Plugging £120,000 into the Bank of England's currency converter shows that £120,000 in 1942 equals roughly £4,750,000 today. That's roughly $7,300,000! How many groups have you known capable of doing that?

▶ *Jane connects with her audience by communicating the value of the fundraising in today's terms.*

Girl Guides traveled around Europe conducting relief efforts. They traveled to Yugoslavia, Greece, Germany, and the Netherlands, taking care of thousands who suffered from bombings, starvation, and disease. Ms. Hampton's research also found that Girl Guides assisted civilians by doing anything from using DDT powder to ward off tick-typhus, to mediating arguments and disputes, helping with suicide prevention, treating hemorrhages, getting rid of snakes in the water supply, and setting up hospitals to contain a typhoid outbreak.

Files at the World Scouting Museum show that, in 1945, the GIS even rescued prisoners from the Nazi concentration camp at Bergen-Belsen. A Girl Guide on the rescue team reported, "When we got to Belsen the people were cold, hungry and unhoused. They were lying about on the floor with no clothes, just scraps of bone."

▶ *This personal testimonial from a Girl Guide who rescued prisoners at Bergen-Belsen strengthens portion of Jane's speech.*

The Girl Guides were internationally known and beloved. When the GIS Guides arrived at a refugee camp, a Greek woman cried out, "The Guides from England! You've come! You've come!" Ms. Hampton sums up feelings about the Girl Guides when she writes, "They became the embodiment of the homefront spirit, digging shelters, and pushing trek-carts around to collect jam jars for recycling and feeding bombed-out families."

Girl Guides of other nationalities had profound effects on the war as well. Polish Girl Guides and American Girl Scouts made incredible sacrifices and contributions to the war effort. Even though Nazi law prohibited young women from being Girl Guides, Polish girls continued the fight in secret. In fact, Polish Girl Guides actually saved Jewish children from genocide by illegally removing them from the Warsaw Ghetto, and other areas of German-occupied Poland. Not only did they help British prisoners of war escape from the Nazis, Girl Guides sometimes even planned the escapes themselves. Tragically, many Polish Girl Guides died for their efforts. Some guides were sent to the Auschwitz concentration camp, where they perished for their noble and fearless deeds, like those who wrote anti-Nazi news pamphlets.

Girl Scouts in the United States were also active during World War II. Girl Scouts collected large amounts of scrap metal to be used for creating munitions. They organized a clothing drive and distributed 1.5 million garments. Girl Scouts also worked in hospitals, trained civilian women in survival skills, organized bike couriers, and planted vegetable gardens, called Victory Gardens, when food was limited.

▶ By including the U.S. Girl Scouts in her address, Jane adapts to the audience and makes a connection to their experience.

All of this amazing history has been relatively unknown to the general public until recently because no one had recorded the history of the Girl Guides. Thanks largely to Ms. Hampton, information that had been deeply buried in disparate historical archives is now available.

The inspirational history of the Girl Guides reminds us that history isn't only confined to the past—it is connected to the present day and our future. It is fundamentally important that we remember and honor the courageous actions of these young women—who went above and beyond in their fight for good.

▶ Jane brings her tribute back to the listener by connecting history to the present moment.

Clearly, these girls were anything but ordinary. They demonstrated the kind of valor that we usually only attribute to the bravest heroes in the military. During one of the darkest moments in human history, Girl Guides served as a light and symbolized hope for innocent children, civilians, and soldiers. On this Remembrance Day, I salute my grandmother—and all the other Guides who made such great sacrifices during the war.

▶ Jane does a nice job of restating her reason for commemorating Girl Guides and tying her conclusion back to her opening remarks.

The next time you see a young Girl Scout, or if you travel abroad and see a Girl Guide, remember this: Girl Guides and Scouts are more than crafters and cookie sellers. They are heirs to a tradition of courage, confidence, and character that played an important role in the freedoms you enjoy today.

▶ Jane's clincher reinforces the point of her address—that Girl Guides are strong women of character and worthy of tribute.

STUDY TOOLS

LOCATED IN TEXTBOOK

☐ Tear-out Chapter Review cards at the end of the book

☐ Review with the Quick Quiz below

LOCATED ON SPEAK3 ONLINE AT CENGAGEBRAIN.COM

☐ Review Key Term flashcards and create your own cards

☐ Track your knowledge and understanding of key concepts in speech communication

☐ Complete practice and graded quizzes to prepare for tests

☐ Complete interactive content within SPEAK3 Online

☐ View the chapter highlight boxes for SPEAK3 Online

Quick Quiz (answers in Solutions Appendix)

T F 1. The goal of a speech to entertain is just to be humorous.

T F 2. Before giving a speech of welcome, you should do some research to become familiar with the group you are representing.

T F 3. During a speech of introduction, it is not very important to mention the main speaker by name.

T F 4. The goal of a ceremonial speech is a hybrid of the goals for informative speeches and persuasive speeches.

T F 5. It is inappropriate to use a speech of acceptance to advocate for an unrelated cause.

6. A _____ is a speech given at the start of a reception or meal that pays tribute to the occasion.

a. roast
b. dedication
c. eulogy
d. toast
e. keynote address

7. In general, ceremonial speeches should be fewer than _____ minutes long.

a. ten
b. twenty
c. fifteen
d. five
e. forty-five

8. Adam is assigned to give a speech in which he will present Sam Jones as a candidate for mayor. He should be giving a speech of:

a. nomination
b. tribute
c. introduction
d. welcome
e. recognition

9. The main goal of a speech of introduction is to:

a. make the audience laugh
b. establish the credibility of the speaker
c. give a preview of the speech
d. get familiar with the audience's expectations
e. set the mood of the program

10. During a ceremony, the _____ is responsible for welcoming guests, introducing participants, and keeping the program moving.

a. sponsor
b. lead
c. entertainer
d. greeter
e. master of ceremonies

Chapter Takeaways

List three key takeaways from this chapter:

-

-

-

16 Group Communication and Presentations

LEARNING OUTCOMES

16-1 Share leadership responsibilities when working in groups.

16-2 Manage conflict effectively among group members.

16-3 Engage in the steps of the systematic problem-solving process.

16-4 Communicate more effectively in virtual groups.

16-5 Use collaboration tools to prepare your group presentation.

16-6 Present your group findings effectively in different formats.

16-7 Evaluate group dynamics and presentations.

After finishing this chapter go to **PAGE 307** for **STUDY TOOLS.**

Sound Familiar?

WORK SESSION 1: Julio, Kristi, Luke, Bryn, and Nick have been asked to work as a small group on a project that will count for one third of their course grade. The other group members consider Nick a troublemaker. He regularly contradicts the instructor, is often absent, and doesn't care about his grades. The others worry that Nick will negatively affect the group grade.

WORK SESSION 2: Resigned, the team restricts Nick's participation by not asking him for substantive help. When he offers an insightful—but opposing—viewpoint, Kristi and Luke become disgruntled because they disagree. Bryn, however, asks Nick to share more. His highly relevant information ultimately strengthens the group's speech, and the group realizes they judged Nick too quickly.

Perhaps you have already been part of a group whose task was to prepare a joint presentation. If so, the opening scenario might sound familiar. In fact, when asked to work in small groups on a class or work project, many people respond—as Julio, Kristi, Luke, and Bryn did—with resistance. Their reasons usually focus on concerns that a few members will end up doing most of the work, that the group process will slow them down, that they'll earn a lower grade than if they worked alone, or that they will be forced to work on a topic that they aren't interested in or take a position they don't agree with.

Although working in a group to develop and deliver a presentation has its disadvantages, it is the preferred approach in business and industry.[1] These **problem-solving groups** (usually composed of four to seven people) are formed to carry out a specific task or solve a particular problem. Whether you want to or not, you can expect to work in a problem-solving group or team in your professional life, sometimes in face-to-face settings and often in virtual settings through e-mail, chat rooms, discussion boards, and video conferences.[2] Leaders in business and industry have come to realize that the advantages of problem-solving groups (e.g., deeper analysis of problems, greater breadth of ideas and of potential solutions, improved group morale, increased productivity) far outweigh the disadvantages.

We include a chapter on problem-solving groups in this book because these groups typically present their findings in formal presentations, for example, as progress reports, sales presentations, proposals, or staff reports.[3] So it makes sense to learn how to work effectively in groups and then how to present your group findings. In this chapter, we begin by talking about effective leadership and the responsibilities of group members in achieving it, as well as managing conflict among members. Then we explain an effective problem-solving method first described by educational philosopher John Dewey. From there, we turn our attention to particular strategies for effective communication in virtual groups. Finally, we describe several formats for communicating your findings publicly and evaluating group effectiveness both in terms of group dynamics and presentations.

16-1 LEADERSHIP

Leadership is a process "whereby an individual influences a group of individuals to achieve a common goal."[4] When we think of leadership, we often think of a person who is *in charge*.[5] In fact, scholars once thought leaders were "born"—that some people inherited traits that made them naturally

> **problem-solving group**
> four to seven people who work together to complete a specific task or solve a particular problem
>
> **leadership** a process whereby an individual influences a group of individuals to achieve a common goal

suited to be leaders. This trait theory approach was called "The Great Man Theory of Leadership."[6] Later, scholars believed that different leadership styles were more or less effective based on the goal and situation. These classic theories suggested that *leadership* is enacted by just one person. Today, however, we understand leadership as a set of communication functions performed by different group members at various times based on each person's unique strengths and expertise.[7] So, although a group may have a **formal leader** (a person designated or elected to oversee the group process), a series of **informal leaders** (members who help lead the group to achieve different leadership functions) make for the most effective leadership in groups.

16-1a Shared Leadership Roles

Shared leadership functions are the sets of roles you and other members perform to facilitate the work of the group and to help maintain harmonious relations among members. A **role** is a specific communication behavior group members perform to address the needs of the group at any given point in time. When these roles are performed effectively, the group functions smoothly. Shared leadership functions may be categorized as task, procedural, and maintenance roles.

1. Task leadership roles help the group acquire, process, or apply information that contributes directly to completing a task or goal. Task leaders are good at finding pertinent research related to the goal and sharing it with the group. They may also be good at summarizing group discussions in ways that pull them together toward the group goal.

2. Procedural leadership roles provide logistical support and record

the group's decisions and accomplishments. Procedural leaders are usually good at arranging a time and place for face-to-face meetings or setting up links for access to teleconferences or videoconferences. They may also be good at taking notes and keeping track of group decisions.

3. Maintenance leadership roles help the group to develop and maintain cohesion, commitment, and positive working relationships. Maintenance leaders are good at encouraging others to share ideas and praising them for sharing, as well as intervening when conflict is threatening to harm the group process.

16-1b Shared Leadership Responsibilities

When problem-solving groups work well, the product is better than what any one member could have accomplished alone. This is known as **synergy**. We believe small groups usually fail when members do not engage in shared leadership in ways that adhere to the ethical responsibilities shown in Exhibit 16.1. When met by all members, these five responsibilities result in shared leadership where every member and his or her contributions are valued and synergy can occur.

1. Be committed to the group goal. Being committed to the group goal means finding a way to align your expertise with the agreed-upon goal of the group. In addition to demonstrating responsibility, commitment also conveys both integrity and respect. So, for a class project, this might mean working together on a topic that wasn't your first choice. Once the decision has been agreed upon, however, it is no longer appropriate to dredge up old issues that have already been settled.

2. Keep discussions on track. It is every member's responsibility to keep the discussion on track by offering only comments that are relevant and by gently reminding others to stay focused if the discussion starts to get off track. It is unproductive to talk about personal issues

formal leader a person designated or elected to oversee the group process

informal leader group members who help lead the group to achieve different leadership functions

shared leadership functions the sets of roles you and other members perform to facilitate the work of the group and to help maintain harmonious relations among members

role a specific communication behavior group members perform to address the needs of the group at any given point in time

task leadership role a role that helps the group acquire, process, or apply information that contributes directly to completing a task or goal

procedural leadership role a role that provides logistical support and records the group's decisions and accomplishments

maintenance leadership role a role that helps the group to develop and maintain cohesion, commitment, and positive working relationships

synergy when the result of group work is better than what one member could achieve alone

> ### Exhibit 16.1
> ## Responsibilities of Group Members
>
> 1. Be committed to the group goal
> 2. Keep the discussion on track
> 3. Complete individual assignments
> 4. Encourage input from all members
> 5. Manage interpersonal conflicts

during the team's work time. Moreover, it is unethical to try to get the discussion off track because you disagree with what is being said.

3. **Complete individual assignments on time.** One potential advantage of group work is that tasks can be divided among members. However, each member is responsible for completing his or her tasks thoroughly and on time.

4. **Encourage input from all members.** All too often, extroverts overshadow quiet group members. Sometimes, outspoken members interpret this silence as having nothing to contribute or not wanting to contribute. On the contrary, all members have valuable perspectives. If you are an extrovert, you have a special responsibility to refrain from dominating the discussion and to ask others for their opinions. Likewise, if you tend to be an introvert, make a conscious effort to express yourself. You might write down what you want to share or even raise your hand to get the attention of other members in an unobtrusive way.

5. **Manage conflict among members.** All small groups experience some **conflict**—disagreement or clash among ideas, principles, or people. If managed appropriately, however, conflict can actually be beneficial to the group goal by stimulating thinking, fostering open communication, encouraging diverse opinions, and enlarging members' understanding of the issues.[8] Doing your part to manage conflict demonstrates the ethical principles of responsibility and respect for others. Because managing conflict effectively is so essential to successful group work, we focus specifically on conflict management and resolution in the next section.

baki/Shutterstock.com

16-2 CONFLICT IN GROUPS

As we have already mentioned, all small groups experience some conflict. When managed effectively, conflict enhances synergy. In fact, groups that *don't* experience some conflict risk the problem of **groupthink**—when group members accept information and ideas without subjecting them to critical analysis.[9] Behaviors that signal groupthink include:

- Avoiding conflict to prevent hurting someone's feelings.
- Pressuring members who do not agree with the majority of the group to conform.
- Reaching "consensus" without the support of all members.
- Discouraging or ignoring disagreements.
- Rationalizing a decision without testing it.

So we know that, when groups don't experience any conflict, they run the risk of engaging in groupthink. But if effective groups actually experience conflict, then how do they manage it successfully? Effective groups do so when all members understand their personal conflict management styles and follow certain guidelines when addressing potentially conflict-arousing situations. Let's begin by discussing several potential sources of conflict and then five of the most common conflict management styles as they function in groups.

16-2a Sources of Conflict

1. **Pseudo-conflict** occurs when group members who actually agree about something believe they disagree due to poor communication. Since *pseudo* means *fake*, the perceived conflict is actually a misperception.

2. **Issue-related conflict** occurs when two or more group members' goals, ideas, or opinions about the topic are incompatible. Issue-related conflict can be a good thing when handled effectively because, without it, groupthink is far more likely to occur.

3. **Personality-related conflict** occurs when two or more group members become defensive because they feel as though they are being attacked.

conflict disagreement or clash among ideas, principles, or people

groupthink when group members accept information and ideas without subjecting them to critical analysis

pseudo-conflict conflict that occurs when group members who actually agree about something believe they disagree due to poor communication

issue-related conflict conflict that occurs when two or more group members' goals, ideas, or opinions about the topic are incompatible

personality-related conflict conflict that occurs when two or more group members become defensive because they feel as though they are being attacked

Typically, personality-related conflicts are rooted in a power struggle.[10]

4. Culture-related conflict occurs when the communication norms of group members are incongruent. For example, people who identify with individualistic cultural norms tend to use direct communication to manage conflict, whereas those who identify with collectivist norms tend to manage conflict through indirect, nonverbal means.[11]

5. Virtual group-related conflict arises as a result of meeting through this technology-enhanced channel. For example, most technology channels reduce our ability to send and receive subtle nonverbal messages, particularly those related to emotions and relational issues. Most of us use emoticons and emoji to represent missing nonverbal cues when we communicate electronically; however, a smiley face can be offered sincerely or sarcastically and it can be difficult for the receiver to distinguish the difference. Unfortunately, conflict often goes unresolved in virtual groups because we cannot see the nonverbal reactions of frustration that are visible when interacting in person.[12] When communication is effective, however, the bonds among members of virtual groups can be even stronger than those in face-to-face groups.[13] Effective members of virtual groups make a conscious effort to communicate both what they *think* and how they *feel* about a topic.

We can deal with these sorts of conflict in several ways. We can manage disagreements by separating the issues from the people involved, keeping our emotions in check, and phrasing our comments descriptively, not judgmentally. Rather than calling a particular idea stupid, for example, ask for clarification about why people think or feel the way they do. Seek first to understand.

We can also employ perception checking or paraphrasing, using "I language" that phrases our interpretations and opinions as our own rather than as defense-arousing "you language."[14] In other words, our language needs to reflect the fact that we are responsible for our feelings.[15] Exhibit 16.2 shows some examples of how to change a "you" statement into an "I" statement.

Perception checking is a verbal statement that reflects your understanding of another's behavior. It is a process of describing what you have seen and heard and then asking for feedback. A perception check statement consists of three parts: (1) In a non-evaluative way, describe what you observed or sensed from someone's behavior; (2) offer two possible interpretations; (3) ask

culture-related conflict conflict that occurs when the communication norms of group members are incongruent

virtual group-related conflict conflict that arises as a result of missed nonverbal cues when meeting through technology

perception checking a verbal statement that reflects your understanding of another's behavior

Exhibit 16.2
Reframing "You" Statements into "I" Statements

"You hurt my feelings."

"You're so irresponsible."

"Don't be so critical."

"I can't believe you said that!"

"I feel hurt when you don't acknowledge what I say."

"I feel my efforts don't matter when you come to the meeting unprepared."

"I feel disrespected when you say my opinion is stupid."

"I feel humiliated when you mention my problems in front of others."

© Petr Vaclavek/Shutterstock.Com

Exhibit 16.3
Perception Checking and Paraphrasing

Situation	Perception Check	Paraphrase
As you are offering your idea about whom the group might interview to get more information on your topic, you notice that Tomika, who you see as uncommitted to the group, says, "Whatever…" and begins reading a message on her cell phone.	Tomika, when you give a dismissive response to my ideas and then start checking your messages, I sense that you don't like my suggestion. Is that an accurate read, or are you just expecting an important message, or is it something else?	From your "whatever" response, I sense that either you don't really agree with my suggestion, you aren't really committed to the project, or you just don't respect me. Or is it something else?
Over the term, Jose has been quick to volunteer for the easiest assignments and has never taken on a difficult piece of work. Today the group was finalizing who would deliver which part of the group presentation and Jose quickly volunteered, saying: "I'll be the master of ceremonies and introduce our topic and each speaker."	Jose, I have been noticing that you have been quick to volunteer and you usually choose the least time-consuming and simplest tasks. Now you're offering to take a role in the presentation that will again require little effort. Are you really overextended in your other classes, or trying to take the easy way out, or is there some other explanation?	Jose, it seems to me like you are again volunteering to do the part of the presentation that will be the least amount of work. Are you really overextended with other courses or not committed to doing your share? Or is there some other reason that you want to be the master of ceremonies?
Today is the day that Madison is supposed to lead the group's discussion, as she was responsible for the research on this part of the group's project. As the group waits for her to begin, she avoids eye contact and rummages through her backpack, finally looking up and saying, "Well, I guess that you all are going to be kind of mad at me."	Madison, I'm noticing that you don't seem to want to get the meeting started, are avoiding eye contact, and have been rummaging around in your bag. I get the sense that you haven't done your homework or lost it. Am I on target, or is it something else?	Madison, from what you said, I understand that you are not prepared to lead the meeting. I'm wondering if you did your homework and lost it. Or is there something else?

for clarification. Recall from Chapter 3 that paraphrasing is putting your understanding of another person's verbal message into words. It is a four-step process: (1) Listen carefully to the message; (2) notice what images, ideas, and feelings you experience from the message; (3) determine what the message means to you; (4) share your interpretation and ask for confirmation that you did so correctly. Exhibit 16.3 provides examples of perception checking and paraphrasing as they may be applied to avoid personality conflict.

16-2b Conflict Management Styles

Perception checking and paraphrasing are useful strategies for resolving conflict. Members also can be effective at resolving conflicts when they understand conflict management styles and employ the most effective ones when working in groups. Research has revealed five common conflict management styles: avoiding, accommodating, competing, compromising, and collaborating.[16]

Avoiding involves physically or psychologically removing yourself from the conflict. For instance, in our opening scenario, if Nick decided to leave the first group session and then not show up at others because he perceived other members didn't agree with him, he would be managing conflict by avoiding. Similarly, if he attended the work sessions but did not share his input, he would also be avoiding. When a group member engages in avoiding as a conflict management style, the whole group suffers because everyone is not committed to the group goal and all members' input is not being considered. Researchers describe this as a lose-lose conflict management style.

avoiding a conflict management style that involves physically or psychologically removing yourself from the conflict

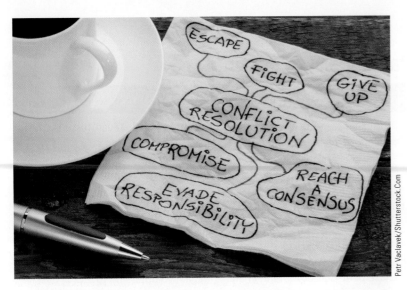

Petr Vaclavek/Shutterstock.Com

interpersonal conflicts are not being managed, and the arguments may even impede the completion of individual assignments. If Nick and Luke engage in competing behavior over the gun control issue, other input is squelched and the group process comes to a halt. Researchers describe this as a win-lose conflict management style.

Compromising occurs when individuals give up part of what they want to provide at least some satisfaction to other opinions. If the group members can't find an ideal time to meet outside of class because they all have busy schedules, they might compromise on a time to meet that isn't particularly ideal for any of them. In terms of coming to a solution, one drawback of this style is that the quality of the decision is probably affected when someone "trades away" a better solution to reach a compromise. Researchers describe this as a partial lose-lose conflict management style.

Collaborating occurs when people work through the problem together to discover a mutually acceptable solution. Researchers describe this as a win-win conflict management style. A win-win solution occurs when input from all members is heard, valued, and evaluated honestly and fairly until the group reaches consensus about how to proceed. Consider the tips in Exhibit 16.4 to achieve effective collaborative conflict management.

Accommodating is accepting others' ideas and opinions while neglecting our own, even when we disagree with their views. If we continue with the example of Nick and his group members, we could say that Nick is engaging in accommodation if he goes along with Kristi and Luke, who want to support increased gun control, even though he personally opposes that view. When a group member engages in accommodation as a conflict management style, the whole group suffers because not all potential ideas are being weighed in the discussion. Researchers describe this as a lose-win conflict management style.

Competing is satisfying our own needs with no concern for the needs of the others and no concern for the harm it does to the group dynamics or problem-solving process. When one member dominates the group discussion by forcing his or her opinions without considering other views or even allowing them to be expressed, the whole group suffers because input from all group members is not being heard. If two or more members engage in competing conflict styles, the whole group suffers, not only because all ideas are not being heard, but also because the discussion gets off track,

 16-3 # SYSTEMATIC PROBLEM SOLVING

When you meet to work on a project with your classmates, coworkers, or community members, you will be trying to solve a problem. To be effective, your group will need to follow a concrete process for analyzing the problem and coming up with a productive solution in a short amount of time. One effective means for doing this is the **systematic problem-solving method**.[17] This six-step process, first described by John Dewey in 1933 and since revised by others, remains a tried and true method for individual and group problem solving.[18]

1. Identify and define the problem. The first step is to identify the problem and define it in a way all group members understand and agree with. Groups might begin by coming up with a number of problems and then narrowing them to a particular one. So your class project group might identify the problems as developing an effective group presentation, identifying a topic for the presentation,

Exhibit 16.4
Collaborative Conflict Management

Initiating Collaboration

- Identify the problem as your own using "I language."
  - ▲ *"I could really use your help here."*
- Describe the behavior in terms of behavior, consequences, and feelings.
  - ▲ *"When I see you checking your e-mail, I feel we're missing out on your ideas for the project, and I get frustrated."*
- Refrain from blaming or accusing.
- Find common ground.
  - ▲ *"Figuring this out is really tough. I know I feel overwhelmed about it sometimes."*
- Mentally rehearse so you can state your request briefly.

Responding Collaboratively

- Disengage to avoid a defensive response.
- Respond empathically with genuine interest and concern by first describing the behavior you observe.
  - ▲ *"I see you checking your e-mail, and I wonder if you're angry or frustrated with something."*
- Paraphrase your understanding of the problem.
- Ask questions to clarify issues.
  - ▲ *"Is there something bothering you or something we're overlooking?"*
- Seek common ground.
  - ▲ *"I know that trying to come to one goal and solution seems impossible at times."*
- Ask the other person to suggest alternative solutions.
  - ▲ *"What other ideas do you have that we might consider?"*

fairly sharing the workload, etc. By posing questions, you can also identify and define a problem: What is the problem? What is its history? Who is affected by it, and how does it affect them? How many people are affected, in what ways, and to what degree? These questions help a group realize what kinds of information must be gathered to help define the problem. To ensure that your group is focusing on the problem itself and not just the symptoms of the problem, don't rush through this step.

2. **Analyze the problem.** To analyze the problem, you must find out as much as possible about it. Most groups begin with each member sharing information he or she already knows about the problem. Then the group needs to determine what additional questions they need to answer and search for additional information to answer them.

3. **Determine criteria for judging solutions. Criteria** are standards used for judging the merits of proposed solutions—a blueprint for evaluating them. Research suggests that when groups develop criteria before they think about specific solutions, they are more likely to come to a decision that all members can accept[19] Without clear criteria, group members may argue for their preferred solution without thoughtfully considering whether it will adequately address the problem or whether it is truly feasible.

4. **Generate a host of solutions.** Arriving at a good solution depends on having a wide variety of possible solutions to choose from. Many groups fail to generate a variety of possible solutions because they criticize the first ideas expressed, which discourages members from taking the risk to put their ideas out there for the group to consider. One way to encourage input is to use the brainstorming technique. Brainstorming, you'll recall, is an uncritical, non-evaluative process of generating alternatives by being creative, suspending judgment, and combining or adapting the ideas of others. It involves verbalizing your ideas as they come to mind without stopping to evaluate their merits. At least one member should record all solutions as they are suggested. To ensure that creativity is not stifled, no solution should be ignored, and members should build on the ideas presented by others. You might come up with twenty or more solutions. As a minimum, try to come up with eight to ten solutions before moving to the next step.

5. **Evaluate solutions based on the criteria and select one.** Here you need to evaluate the merits of each potential solution based on the criteria established by the group. Consider each solution as it meets the criteria, and eliminate solutions that do not meet them adequately. In addition to applying the criteria, the group might also ask questions such as the following: How will the solution solve the problem? How difficult will it be to implement? What problems might be caused as a result of implementing the solution? Once each potential solution has been thoroughly evaluated based on the criteria, the group must select the best one(s).

criteria standards used for judging the merits of proposed solutions

6. Implement the agreed-upon solution and assess it. Finally, the group implements the agreed-upon solution or, if the group is presenting the solution to others for implementation, makes recommendations for how the solution should be implemented. The group has already considered implementation in terms of selecting a solution but now must fill in the details. What tasks are required by the solution(s)? Who will carry out these tasks? What is a reasonable time frame for implementation generally and for each of the tasks specifically? Because the agreed-upon solution may or may not prove effective, the group should determine a point at which they will revisit and assess its success. Doing so builds in an opportunity to revise or replace the solution if warranted.

Andrey_Popov/Shutterstock.com

16-4 COMMUNICATING EFFECTIVELY IN VIRTUAL GROUPS

Virtual groups that convene using telephone or computer technology are becoming increasingly popular for many reasons. First, members need not be physically present. Before these technologies became available, groups had to meet face-to-face to exchange information, solve problems, and make decisions. But today, group members can interact while in different cities, states, and countries. Second, **asynchronous virtual groups**—those whose members can post and respond to messages at any time, although usually within a few days—allow people to participate across time. Busy people often struggle to find a meeting time that works with everyone's schedule. So a group can "meet" via a threaded discussion instead. Third, virtual meetings can save money. Before these technologies, people often had to travel to a meeting site. That often also meant paying for travel, accommodations, meals, parking, and even meeting space rental. Because virtual meetings can be conducted over the phone or Internet, meeting costs can be reduced for both participants and hosts.

virtual groups groups that convene using telephone or computer technology

asynchronous virtual groups groups whose members can post and respond to messages at any time, although usually within a few days

netiquette etiquette rules users should follow when communicating over computer networks

However, these benefits can also come with potential costs. For example, research has found that communication problems can impact both task and relational outcomes.[20] Face-to-face groups are often more dedicated to completing the task, fostering positive relationships among members, and building cohesion than virtual groups.[21] Thus, we offer a few guidelines to follow for effective communication when working in a virtual group.

1. Use the richest form of technology available. While e-mails and threaded discussions allow people the freedom to communicate at their own convenience, these technologies also convey the fewest social nonverbal cues. When possible, try to meet via videoconference to both see and hear the other group members.

2. Make sure all members are both equipped and trained to use the technology. Don't assume that all members know how to use the technology or are aware of all of its capabilities. Although this is crucial for virtual work groups and teams, it is equally important for any group that chooses to meet online.

3. Create opportunities for group members to become acquainted, develop and maintain social bonds, and build trust. Just as members of face-to-face groups take time to socialize and get to know one another, so is doing so important when meeting virtually.

4. Develop ground rules. Because misunderstandings can abound when communicating via technology, virtual groups will operate most effectively when rules for communicating are set up at the outset. These rules are often referred to as **netiquette**. They may include, for example, being courteous and respectful, being attentive and focused (e.g., not checking e-mail during the meeting), using emoticons and imogees, keeping messages short, and being patient with new users.[22]

5. Create regular opportunities to evaluate the technology and use of it. Regularly scheduled surveys of group members can identify emerging problems some members may be experiencing in order to correct them before they undermine the group's goals.

Obviously, group communication in virtual settings poses an additional set of challenges to ensure an effective outcome. As more and more people opt to engage in virtual groups, it is critical to continue developing and engaging in communication strategies that will promote effective outcomes.

GROUP COLLABORATION TOOLS

Whether part of a virtual or an in-person group, your group can benefit from using collaboration tools to develop your presentation. **Collaboration tools** are digital tools that allow groups of people to work together, coordinate activities, and share information regardless of their location. For some people, public speaking and working in a group are equally stressful. Add in a little geographic distance, and you've got a recipe for a meltdown. Luckily, there are plenty of digital tools that can make collaboration at any distance relatively simple.

Whether you're separated from one or more of your teammates temporarily or for the duration of your project, the biggest problem with working at a distance is often communication. Minor misunderstandings and disagreements can quickly escalate in the absence of in-person communication.

Free video chat services such as Skype and Google Hangouts enable group members to speak face-to-face, whether across campus or from separate time zones. Many of these services also permit text chat, file transmission, and screen sharing, which can be useful to show off work in progress.

Google and Microsoft both offer collaborative productivity suites with software you're already used to—word processors and slideshow presentation tools, namely—in familiar, simple packaging. Multiple users can log in simultaneously to work together, leave comments, suggest edits, and chat using built-in services in real time. Both of these suites also utilize cloud storage with various sharing and access options, allowing group members to keep their work in a common, secure environment.

Although Evernote and Microsoft's OneNote focus primarily on note-taking, both applications can also

function as all-in-one collaborative productivity tools. They feature many of the same capabilities as the software suites mentioned above, but in a more streamlined (albeit slightly less functional) environment. One major advantage of these tools is their ability to set timed reminders—especially useful when planning deadlines or working with forgetful teammates.

Social media can also be beneficial for small teams looking to collaborate. Services such as Facebook and Google Hangouts enable users to form small, private groups. Group members can communicate with one another with the same conveniences that these services provide on a larger scale, including video and text chat, calendars and event scheduling, file sharing, and voice-over-IP calling.

Other types of collaboration tools are available as well. Exhibit 16.5 provides some examples of collaboration tools groups can use to increase their effectiveness when creating collective presentations.

GROUP PRESENTATION FORMATS

Once a group has completed its deliberations, it is usually expected to communicate its results. **Deliverables** are tangible or intangible products of your work that must be provided to someone else. Although some deliverables are objects, the deliverables from problem-solving groups typically come in the form of communicating the information, analyses, and recommendations of the group. These deliverables can be communicated in written formats, oral formats, or virtual formats.

16-6a Written Formats

Written formats include a written brief and a comprehensive report. A **written brief** is a very short document that describes the problem, background, process, decision, and rationale so that the reader can quickly understand and evaluate the group's product. Most briefs are one or two pages long. When preparing a brief, begin by describing your group's task. What problem were you attempting to solve and why? Then briefly provide the background

collaboration tools digital tools that allow groups of people to work together, coordinate activities, and share information regardless of their location

deliverables tangible or intangible products of your work that must be provided to someone else

written brief a very short document that describes the problem, background, process, decision, and rationale so that the reader can quickly understand and evaluate the group's product

Exhibit 16.5
Examples of Digital Collaboration Tools

Tool	Description
Dropbox	Cloud-based file sharing that allows users to invite others to share folders and edit files.
Box	Cloud-based file sharing that allows users to invite others to share folders and edit files. Content can also be encrypted for protection.
Slack	A messaging app for teams that integrates e-mail, chat, file sharing, and allows deep contextual search across all of those conversations. It also can integrate over 80 plug-ins.
Mango	A collaborative communication platform that integrates intranet, collaboration, messaging, and social media.
Wrike	A real-time workspace that combines collaboration, discussion, document sharing, and progress analytics.
Trello	Cross-platform project management board that uses a card-type system to help teams organize the tasks and work they need to do, what they have done, and who is responsible for what.
Asana	A project-management platform that allows collaboration without e-mail. Teams can organize tasks by priority, track progress to completion, and communicate about projects inside the app.
Podio	A project-management platform that allows collaboration without e-mail. Teams can organize task by priority, track progress to completion, and communicate about projects inside the app.
Smartsheet	Project management software based on spreadsheets that all users can edit.

information the reader will need to evaluate whether the group has adequately studied the problem. Present solution steps and timelines for implementation as bullet points so that the reader can quickly understand what is being proposed. Close with a sentence or very short paragraph that describes how the recommendation will solve the problem, as well as any potential side effects.

A **comprehensive report** is a written document that provides a detailed review of the problem-solving process used to arrive at the recommendation. A comprehensive report is usually organized into sections that parallel the problem-solving process.

Because comprehensive reports can be very long, they usually include an executive summary. An **executive summary** is a one-page synopsis of the report. This summary contains enough information to acquaint readers with the highlights of the full document without reading it. Usually, it contains a statement of the problem, some background information, a description of any alternatives, and the major conclusions.

16-6b Oral Formats

There are four main oral formats: an oral brief, an oral report, a panel discussion, and a symposium. An **oral brief** is essentially a summary of a written brief delivered to an audience by a group member. Typically, an oral brief can be delivered in less than 10 minutes. An **oral report** is similar to a comprehensive report. It provides a more detailed review of a group's problem-solving process. Oral reports can range from 30 to 60 minutes.

A **panel discussion** is a structured problem-solving discussion held by a group in front of an audience. One member serves as moderator, introducing the topic and providing structure by asking a series of planned questions that panelists answer. Their answers and the interaction among them provide the supporting evidence. A well-planned panel discussion seems spontaneous and interactive but requires careful planning and rehearsal to ensure that all relevant information is presented and that all speakers are afforded equal speaking time. After the formal discussion, the audience is often encouraged to question the participants. Perhaps you've seen or heard a panel of experts discuss a topic on a radio or television talk show like *SportsCenter, Meet the Press,* or *The Doctors.*

comprehensive report a written document that provides a detailed review of the problem-solving process used to arrive at the recommendation

executive summary a one-page synopsis of a comprehensive report

oral brief an oral summary of a written brief delivered to an audience by a group member

oral report an oral version of a comprehensive report, which provides a detailed review of a group's problem-solving process

panel discussion a structured problem-solving discussion held by a group in front of an audience

One popular format for group presentations is a panel discussion. Here, Sarah Wayne Callies, Andrew Lincoln, and Frank Darabont speak about *The Walking Dead* TV series at Comic-Con.

A **symposium** is a set of prepared oral reports delivered sequentially by group members before a gathering of people who are interested in the work of the group. A symposium may be organized so that each person's speech focuses on one step of the problem-solving process, or it may be organized so that each speaker covers all of the steps in the problem-solving process as they relate to one of several issues or recommendations that the group worked on or made. In a symposium, the speakers usually sit together at the front of the room. One member acts as moderator, offering the introductory and concluding remarks and providing transitions between speakers. When introduced by the moderator, each speaker may stand and walk to a central spot, usually a lectern. Speakers who use a computerized slideshow should coordinate their slides so that there are seamless transitions between speakers. Symposiums often conclude with a question-and-answer session facilitated by the moderator, who directs one or more of the members to answer based on their expertise. Questions can be directed to individuals or to the group as a whole.

16-6c Virtual Formats

In addition to written and oral formats for group communication, technology makes virtual formats available as well. A **remote access report (RAR)** is a computer-mediated audiovisual presentation of the group's process and outcome that others can receive through e-mail, Web posting, and so forth. Prepared by one or more members of the group, the RAR is prepared using PowerPoint, Keynote, Prezi, or other slideshow software and provides a visual overview of the group's process, decisions, and recommendations. Effective RARs typically consist of no more than 15 to 20 slides. Slides are titled and content is presented in outline or bullet-point phrases or keywords (rather than complete sentences or paragraphs), as well through visual representations of important information. For example, a budget task force might have a slide with a pie chart depicting the portions of the proposed budget that are allocated to operating expenses, salaries, fundraising, and travel. RARs may be self-running so that the slides automatically forward after a certain number of seconds, but it is better to let the viewer choose the pace and control when the next slide appears. RARs can be silent or narrated. When narrated, a voice-over accompanies each slide, providing additional or explanatory information.

A **streaming video** is a recording that is sent in compressed form over the Internet. You are probably familiar with streaming video from popular Web sites such as YouTube. Streaming videos are a great way to distribute oral briefs, but they also can be used to distribute recordings of oral reports, symposiums, or panel presentations. Streaming videos are useful when it is inconvenient for some or all the people who need to know the results of the group's work to meet at one time or in one place. Read the Tech Talk box for examples of live streaming platforms and what extra preparation you'll need to live stream a presentation.

 16-7 # EVALUATING GROUP EFFECTIVENESS

Just as preparing and presenting are a bit different for group speeches than for individual speeches, so is the process of evaluating effectiveness. Evaluations should focus on group dynamics during the preparation process as well as on the effectiveness of the actual presentation.

16-7a Group Dynamics

To be effective, groups must work together as they define and analyze a problem, generate solutions, and select a course of action. They also need to work together as they prepare their written report, as well as prepare and practice

symposium a set of prepared oral reports delivered sequentially by group members before a gathering of people who are interested in the work of the group

remote access report (RAR) a computer-mediated audiovisual presentation of a group's process and outcome that others can receive electronically

streaming video a pre-recording that is sent in compressed form over the Internet

TECH TALK

Want to Reach a Bigger Audience? Consider Live Streaming Your Panel Discussion

No longer is live streaming confined to concerts and sporting events. A quick Internet search for "live streaming panel discussions" produces results on topics ranging from *Star Wars* to equity for children to women in tech.

Several live streaming platforms can help groups amplify their presentations. Platforms such as Ustream, JustinTV, and Livestream allow presenters not only to become broadcasters but to engage with the audience in real time through social media plug-ins. Meerkat and Periscope are two newer platforms that are more tightly integrated with Twitter. At the right moment, a broadcaster can send out a tweet that its event is ready to go live. Then, during the discussion, the virtual audience can use Twitter to ask questions and make comments as easily as members of the physical audience can.

As exciting as it is to go live, doing so requires three extra steps during the preparation.[23] First, you need to rehearse. Even though practice is part of the preparation for any public speaking event, when the event is being broadcast, both the speaker and the cameraperson will need to rehearse to ensure the highest quality of video is streaming. Second, if you plan on using music or other video as part of your discussion—or even in the background—make sure that you secure appropriate rights to use that material. Streaming platforms are obligated to take down or mute videos that pose copyright concerns, so if you can't secure the rights, remove the material from the presentation. And finally, get a signed release from every person who appears on camera. Having photo and video releases keeps you in legal compliance, which will be particularly useful should your panel discussion go viral or become a source of revenue.

their oral presentation if warranted. These communication interactions among members to achieve a goal are known as **group dynamics**.

You can evaluate group dynamics by judging the merit of each member's efforts in terms of the five group member responsibilities discussed earlier in this chapter. In addition, each group member could prepare a "reflective thinking process paper," which details in paragraph form what each member did well and could improve upon in terms of the five member responsibilities. In the final paragraph of the paper, each member should provide a self-evaluation of what he or she did and what he or she could do to improve the group process in future sessions.

Like the evaluations business managers make of employees, these evaluations document the efforts of group members. They can be submitted to the instructor, just as they would be submitted to a supervisor. In business, these evaluations provide a basis for determining

Monkey Business Images/Shutterstock.com

It pays to evaluate group dynamics. Take time to judge the individual merits of each member's efforts and overall contribution.

group dynamics how individuals work together as a team toward a common goal

promotions, merit pay, and salary adjustments. In the classroom, they can provide a basis for determining one portion of each member's grade.

16-6b Group Presentations

Effective group presentations depend on quality individual presentations as well as quality overall group performance. So evaluations of group presentations should consist of both an individual and a group component. Exhibit 16.6 shows a form you can use to evaluate the effectiveness of a group presentation.

Effective group presentations also depend on the combined efforts of individuals. So it's also a good idea to conduct a self-evaluation to determine whether you could be doing something better during the group problem-solving process, while preparing the group presentation, and when giving your portion of the group speech. Exhibit 16.6 also includes an example of a self-critique form used to evaluate your own efforts.

Exhibit 16.6

Sample Evaluation Form for Group Presentations

Group Member Name: _____

Critic (your name): _____

Directions: Evaluate the effectiveness of each group member according to each of the following criteria for effective presentations individually and as a group. Then, provide a rationale for the rating you gave in each category.

Rating Scale:

1	2	3	4	5	6	7
(poor)						(excellent)

INDIVIDUAL PERFORMANCE CRITIQUE

_____ **Content** (*Breadth and depth and listener relevance*)

Critique:

_____ **Structure** (*Macrostructure and microstructure/ language*)

Critique:

_____ **Delivery** (*Use of body and voice*)

Critique:

GROUP PERFORMANCE CRITIQUE

_____ **Content** (*Thematic? Focused? Thorough? Construction of presentational aids?*)

Critique:

_____ **Structure** (*Balanced? Transitions? Flow? Attention/ Clincher?*)

Critique:

_____ **Content** (*Teamwork? Cooperation? Fluency? Use of aids?*)

Critique:

Overall Comments:

SELF-CRITIQUE

Directions: Complete the items below with regard to your presentation in the group symposium.

1. If I could do my portion of the oral presentation over again, I would do the following things differently:
   a. _____
   b. _____

2. In terms of content, I did the following things well in my oral presentation:
   a. _____
   b. _____

3. In terms of structure, I did the following things well in my oral presentation:
   a. _____
   b. _____

4. In terms of delivery, I did the following things well in my oral presentation:
   a. _____
   b. _____
   c. _____

5. In terms of my role as a group member, I am most proud of how I:
   _____
   _____

6. In terms of my role as a group member, I am least proud of how I:
   _____
   _____

7. Overall, I would give myself a grade of _____ for the group speech because:
   _____
   _____

STUDY TOOLS 16

LOCATED IN TEXTBOOK

☐ Tear-out Chapter Review cards at the end of the book

☐ Review with the Quick Quiz below

LOCATED ON SPEAK3 ONLINE AT CENGAGEBRAIN.COM

☐ Review Key Term flashcards and create your own cards

☐ Track your knowledge and understanding of key concepts in speech communication

☐ Complete practice and graded quizzes to prepare for tests

☐ Complete interactive content within SPEAK3 Online

☐ View the chapter highlight boxes for SPEAK3 Online

Quick Quiz (answers in Solutions Appendix)

T F 1. The conflict management style in which you accept others' ideas and neglect your own is known as *forcing*.

T F 2. One of the advantages of working in a group is that groups can present a greater breadth of ideas and potential solutions.

T F 3. The first step in preparing a group presentation is to draft an outline of the topic area.

T F 4. Synergy occurs when the most talented people in the group do the work that less-talented people can't do.

T F 5. The most effective way to achieve a win-win result in conflict is to collaborate.

6. _____ occurs when group members accept ideas without critically analyzing them.

   a. Conformity
   b. Blindness
   c. Acquiescence
   d. Groupthink
   e. Acceptance

7. A problem-solving discussion that occurs in front of an audience is a:

   a. panel discussion
   b. town hall meeting
   c. symposium
   d. conference
   e. streaming video

8. A problem-solving group typically has _____ members.

   a. two to four
   b. five to ten
   c. ten to fifteen
   d. four to seven
   e. more than twenty

9. The first step in the systematic problem-solving method is to:

   a. analyze the problem
   b. determine criteria for judging solutions
   c. identify and define the problem
   d. generate a host of solutions
   e. evaluate solutions

10. Which of the following is NOT a responsibility of a group member?

    a. Keep discussion on track.
    b. Ignore unproductive members.
    c. Be committed to the group goal.
    d. Complete individual assignments on time.
    e. Manage conflict among members.

Chapter Takeaways

List three key takeaways from this chapter:

-

-

-

Quick Quiz Solutions

Chapter 1
1. F
2. F
3. T
4. F
5. T
6. a
7. e
8. d
9. b
10. c

Chapter 2
1. T
2. T
3. T
4. F
5. F
6. b
7. b
8. c
9. d
10. e

Chapter 3
1. T
2. F
3. F
4. F
5. T
6. b
7. d
8. e
9. a
10. a

Chapter 4
1. F
2. T

3. T
4. T
5. F
6. e
7. b
8. d
9. c
10. a

Chapter 5
1. T
2. T
3. T
4. F
5. T
6. b
7. c
8. d
9. a
10. e

Chapter 6
1. F
2. T
3. F
4. F
5. T
6. d
7. d
8. b
9. c
10. a

Chapter 7
1. F
2. T
3. T
4. T
5. T
6. c

7. b
8. e
9. e
10. a

Chapter 8
1. T
2. F
3. T
4. F
5. F
6. d
7. c
8. e
9. d
10. b

Chapter 9
1. F
2. F
3. T
4. F
5. T
6. b
7. a
8. d
9. c
10. e

Chapter 10
1. F
2. F
3. T
4. F
5. T
6. e
7. b
8. d
9. a
10. a

Chapter 11
1. F
2. T
3. T
4. T
5. F
6. d
7. b
8. b
9. c
10. a

Chapter 12
1. T
2. T
3. F
4. F
5. T
6. b
7. c
8. c
9. d
10. b

Chapter 13
1. T
2. T
3. T
4. F
5. F
6. b
7. b
8. c
9. c
10. e

Chapter 14
1. T
2. F
3. T

4. T
5. F
6. a
7. d
8. b
9. a
10. c

Chapter 15
1. F
2. T
3. F
4. T
5. T
6. d
7. d
8. a
9. b
10. e

Chapter 16
1. F
2. T
3. F
4. F
5. T
6. d
7. a
8. d
9. c
10. b

SPEAK
ONLINE

REVIEW FLASHCARDS ANYTIME, ANYWHERE!

Create Flashcards from Your StudyBits

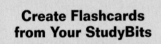

Review Key Term Flashcards Already Loaded on the StudyBoard

4LTR PRESS

Access SPEAK ONLINE at www.cengagebrain.com

ENDNOTES

Chapter 1

1. Morreale, S., Hugenberg, L., & Worley, D. (2006). The basic communication course at U.S. colleges and universities in the 21st century: Study VII. *Communication Education*, 55(4), 415–437.

2. Ankita. (2012). 9 most essential civic rights enjoyed by a citizen. Preserve Articles. Retrieved online from http://www.preservearticles.com /201106248527/9-most-essential-civic-rights -enjoyed-by-a-citizen.html

3. Aristotle. (1960). *On rhetoric* (p. 16, L. Cooper, Trans.). New York, NY: Appleton-Century-Crofts.

4. A brief history of speakers' corner. Speakers' Corner Trust, no date, accessed June 3, 2015, http:// www.speakerscornertrust.org/library/about-free -speech/a-brief-history-of-londons-speakers-corner/.

5. Adams, S. (2014, November 12). The 10 skills employers most want in 2015 graduates. *Forbes*. Retrieved online from http://www.forbes.com/sites /susanadams/2014/11/12/the-10-skills-employers -most-want-in-2015-graduates/.

6. Groysberg, B. (2014, March). The seven skills you need to thrive in the C-suite. *Harvard Business Review*. Retrieved online from https: //hbr.org/2014/03/the-seven-skills-you-need-to -thrive-in-the-c-suite/.

7. Schworm, P. (2014, July 14). Newton schools chief fined for use of Patrick's words. *Boston Globe*. Retrieved online from https://www.bostonglobe .com/metro/2014/07/24/newton-superintendent -accused-plagiarizing-passages-from-patrick-speech /se0KbCtFbDwzj3fKJAdacN/story.html

8. Taylor, P., Parker, K., Lenhart, A., & Patten, E. (2011, August 28). The digital revolution and higher education: College presidents, public differ on value of online learning. Washington, D.C.: Pew Research Center.

9. ASBPE Staff (2014, May 6). Even at graduate school level plagiarism reaches new heights. American Society of Business Publication. Retrieved online from http://www.asbpe.org /blog/2014/05/06/even-at-graduate-school-level -plagiarism-reaches-new-heights/.

10. Weimer, M. (2015, January 13). Plagiarism: An interesting disconnect between students' thoughts and actions. *Faculty Focus*. Retrieved online from http://www.facultyfocus.com/articles/teaching-and -learning/plagiarism-interesting-disconnect-students -thoughts-actions/.

11. Article based on Risquez, A., O'Dwyer, M., & Ledwith, A. (2013). "Thou shalt not plagiarize": From self-reported views to recognition and avoidance of plagiarism. *Assessment & Evaluation in Higher Education*, 38 (1), 34–43.

12. McCullen, C. (2003). Tactics and resources to help students avoid plagiarism. *Multimedia Schools*, 10(6), 40–43.

13. Wall, B. (2015, February 13). Ruth Bader Ginsburg had too much wine and fell asleep during the State of the Union. *Chicago Sun Times*. Retrieved online from http://chicago.suntimes.com /politics/7/71/367340/ruth-bader-ginsburg-much -wine-fell-asleep-state-union.

14. Cragen, J. F., & Shields, D. C. (1998). *Understanding communication theory: The communicative forces for human action*. Boston, MA: Allyn & Bacon; Frey, L. R., Otan, C. H., & Kreps, G. L. (2000). *Investigating communication: An introduction to research methods*. (2nd ed.). Needham Heights, MA: Allyn & Bacon.

15. Littlejohn, S. W., & Foss, K. A. (2011). *Theories of human communication* (10th ed.). Longrove, IL: Waveland.

16. Kellerman, K. (1992). Communication: Inherently strategic and primarily automatic. *Communication Monographs*, 59, 288–300.

17. Ibid; Knapp, M., & Daly, J. (2002). *Handbook of interpersonal communication*. Thousand Oaks, CA: Sage.

18. Beebe, S., & Masterson, J. (2006). *Communicating in groups: Principles and practice* (8th ed.). Boston, MA: Pearson; Hirokawa, R., Cathcart, R., Samovar, I., & Henman, I. (Eds.). (2003). *Small group communication theory and practice* (8th ed.). Los Angeles, CA: Roxbury.

19. Devine, D. J., Clayton, L. D., Phillips, J. L., Dunford, B. B., & Melner, S. B. (1999). Teams in organizations: Prevalence, characteristics, and effectiveness. *Small Group Research*, 30, 678–711.

20. Shepherd, G.A. (1986). When the president spoke at Balboa Stadium. *Journal of San Diego History*, 32 (2). Retrieved online from https://www .sandiegohistory.org/journal/86spring/president.htm.

21. Coules, A. (2014, 9 December). The history of PA, part 1. ProSoundWeb. Retrieved online from http://www.prosoundweb.com/article/print/the _history_of_pa_part_1.

22. Ibid.

23. Krebber, J.F., et al. (2008). PA systems for indoor and outdoor. *Handbook of signal processig in acoustics*. New York, NY: Springer Science & Business Media, 668. Digital book retrieved online from https:// books.google.com/books?id=YaNCAAAAQBAJ&lpg =PA668&ots=LiGWe3_7zZ&dq=yaxleys%20 sound%20system&pg=PA668#v=onepage&q&f=false.

24. Imagining the Internet: A history and forecast. Elon University School of Communications. Retrieved online from http://www.elon.edu/e-web /predictions/150/1930.xhtml.

25. Significant achievements in space communications and navigation, 1958–1964. (1966). *NASA -SP-93*. National Aeronautics and Space Administration, 30–32.

26. Forsythe, D. R., & Burnette, J. L. (2005). The history of group research. In S. A. Wheelen (Ed.). *The handbook of group research and practice*. Thousand Oaks, CA: Sage; Knapp, M. L., & Daly, J. A. (Eds.). (2011). *The SAGE handbook of interpersonal communication* (4th ed.). Thousand Oaks, CA: Sage; Watzlawick, P., Bavelas, J., & Jackson, D. (1967). *Pragmatics of human communication: A study of interactional patterns, pathologies, and paradoxes*. New York, NY: Norton.

27. Aristotle. *On rhetoric* (p. 16).

28. Bitzer, L. F. (1995). The rhetorical situation. In W. A. Covino, D. A. Jolliffe (Eds.), *Rhetoric: Concepts, definitions, boundaries*. Boston, MA: Allyn & Bacon.

29. Ibid.

30. Exigence. (2009). In *Microsoft Encarta world English dictionary* (North American edition). Retrieved online from http://encarta.msn.com /dictionary_1861609760/exigency.html

31. T. Schleifer. (2015, April. 28). Baltimore mayor struggles in response to riots. CNN Politics. Retrieved online from http://www.cnn .com/2015/04/23/politics/stephanie-rawlings -blake-freddie-gray-baltimore/.

32. Greenberg, J. (2015, April 28). In context: What Baltimore's mayor said about space for rioters. *Politifact.com*. Retrieved online from http:// www.politifact.com/truth-o-meter/article/2015 /apr/28/context-baltimores-mayor-space-rioters/.

33. Ibid.

34. Mosby, M. (2015, May 1). Transcript of Marliyn J. Mosby's statement on Freddie Gray. *Time*. Retrieved online from http://time.com/3843870 /marilyn-mosby-transcript-freddie-gray/.

35. Hirschield Davis, J., & Appuzo, M. (2015, April 29). President Obama condemns both the Baltimore riots and the nation's "slow-rolling crisis." *New York Times*, A15.

36. Sanchez, L. (2015, April 28). Baltimore gang members speak out against the violence. KLAQ. Retrieved online from http://klaq.com/baltimore -gang-members-speak-out-against-the-violence/.

37. McCauley, M.C. (2015, April 29). 1,000 show for BSO performance in response to protests. *Baltimore Sun*. Retrieved online from http://www .baltimoresun.com/entertainment/arts/bs-ae -freddie-gray-arts-20150428-story.html#page=1.

38. Roenigk, A. (214, November 2). An unforgettable Sunday afternoon for Lauren Hill. *ABC News* [online]. Retrieved online from http://abcnews .go.com/Sports/unforgettable-sunday-afternoon -lauren-hill/story?id=26644432.

39. Aristotle. *On rhetoric* (p. 16).

40. Jensen, V. (1985). Teaching ethics in speech communication. *Communication Education*, 34, 324–330.

41. Decker, B. (1992). *You've got to be believed to be heard*. New York, NY: St. Martin's Press.

42. Gallo, C. (2014, March 17). The one habit that brilliant TED speakers practice up to 200 times. *Forbes*. Retrieved online from http://www.forbes .com/sites/carminegallo/2014/03/17/the-one -habit-that-brilliant-ted-speakers-practice-up -to-200-times/.

Chapter 2

1. Hahner, J. C., Sokoloff, M. A., & Salisch, S. L. (2001). *Speaking clearly: Improving voice and diction* (6th ed.). New York, NY: McGraw-Hill.

2. BBC. (2014, December 1). World aids day: Prince Harry reveals fear of public speaking. *BBC News*. Retrieved online from http://www.bbc.com /news/uk-30272563.

3. Gallo, C. (2013, May 16). How Warren Buffett and Joel Osteen conquered their terrifying fear of public speaking. *Forbes*. Retrieved online from http://www.forbes.com/sites/carminegallo /2013/05/16/how-warren-buffett-and-joel -osteen-conquered-their-terrifying-fear-of-public -speaking/.

4. Ibid.

5. Gmoser, J. (2014, September). Richard Branson hates public speaking—here's how he gets over it. *Business Insider*. Retrieved online from http://www.businessinsider.com/richard-branson-hates-public-speaking-2014-9.

6. Social Reality Index, Wave 1. (2014). Chapman University. Retrieved online from http://www.chapman.edu/wilkinson/_files/new%20research%20centers/babbie%20pics/social-reality-index.pdf.

7. Ingraham, C. (2014, October 30). America's top fears: Public speaking, heights, and bugs. *Washington Post*. Retrieved online from http://www.washingtonpost.com/blogs/wonkblog/wp/2014/10/30/clowns-are-twice-as-scary-to-democrats-as-they-are-to-republicans/.

8. Phillips, G. M. (1977). Rhetoritherapy versus the medical model: Dealing with reticence. *Communication Education*, 26, 37.

9. Motley, M. (1997). COM therapy. In J. A. Daly, J. C. McCroskey, J. Ayres, T. Hopf, & D. M. Ayres (Eds.), *Avoiding communication: Shyness, reticence, and communication apprehension* (2nd ed., p. 382). Cresskill, NJ: Hampton Press.

10. Phillips, Rhetoritherapy versus the medical model, 37.

11. Richmond, V. P., & McCroskey, J. C. (2000). *Communication apprehension, avoidance, and effectiveness* (5th ed.). Scottsdale, AZ: Gorsuch Scarisbrick.

12. Behnke, R. R., & Carlile, L. W. (1971). Heart rate as an index of speech anxiety. *Speech Monographs*, 38, 66.

13. Beatty, M. J., & Behnke, R. R. (1991). Effects of public speaking trait anxiety and intensity of speaking task on heart rate during performance. *Human Communication Research*, 18, 147–176.

14. Richmond & McCroskey, Communication.

15. Beatty, M. J., McCroskey, J. C., & Heisner, A. D. (1998). Communication apprehension as temperamental expression: A communibiological paradigm. *Communication Monographs*, 65, 200.

16. Richmond & McCroskey, Communication.

17. Bandura, A. (1973). *Social learning theory*. Englewood Cliffs, NJ: Prentice Hall.

18. Daly, J. A., Caughlin, J. P., & Stafford, L. (1997). Correlates and consequences of social-communicative anxiety. In J. A. Daly, J. C. McCroskey, J. Ayres, T. Hopf, & D. M. Ayres (Eds.), *Avoiding communication: Shyness, reticence, and communication apprehension* (2nd ed., p. 27). Cresskill, NJ: Hampton Press.

19. Dunn, J. (2008, April). Tina Fey: Funny girl. *Reader's Digest Magazine* [online]. Retrieved online from http://www.rd.com/advice/tina-fey-interview/

20. Grant, A. (2015, February 20.) How you can finally conquer your fear of public speaking. *Fast Company*. Retrieved online from http://www.fastcompany.com/3042570/how-you-can-finally-conquer-your-fear-of-public-speaking.

21. Motley, *COM therapy*, 382.

22. Ibid., 380.

23. Gmoser, J. (2014, September). Richard Branson hates public speaking—here's how he gets over it. *Business Insider*. Retrieved online from http://www.businessinsider.com/richard-branson-hates-public-speaking-2014-9.

24. Ayres, J., & Hopf, T. S. (1990). The long-term effect of visualization in the classroom: A brief research report. *Communication Education*, 39, 77.

25. Ayres, J., Hopf, T., & Ayres, D. M. (1994). An examination of whether imaging ability enhances the effectiveness of an intervention designed to reduce speech anxiety. *Communication Education*, 43, 256.

26. Bourne, E. J. (1990). The anxiety and *phobia workbook*. Oakland, CA: New Harbinger Publications.

27. Friedrich, G., & Goss, B. (1984). Systematic desensitization. In J. A. Daly & J. C. McCroskey (Eds.), *Avoiding communication*. Beverly Hills, CA: Sage.

28. Davis, M., Echelon, E. & McKay, M. (1988). *The relaxation and stress workbook*. Oakland, CA: New Harbinger Publications.

29. Richmond & McCroskey, *Communication*.

30. Ibid.

31. Griffin, K. (1995). Beating performance anxiety. *Working Woman*, 62–65, 76.

32. Burson, A. (2013). Self-distancing before an acute stressor buffers against maladaptive psychological and behavioral consequences: Implications for distancing theory and social anxiety treatment. University of Michigan Deep Blue Library. Retrieved online from http://deepblue.lib.umich.edu/handle/2027.42/99929?show=full

33. Kross, E. et al. (2014). Self-talk as a regulatory mechanism: How you do it matters. *Journal of Personality and Social Psychology*, 106, 304–324.

34. Burson, A. (2013).

35. Starecheski, L. (2014, Cotober 7). Why saying is believing—the science of self-talk. *National Public Radio*. Retrieved online from http://www.npr.org/sections/health-shots/2014/10/07/353292408/why-saying-is-believing-the-science-of-self-talk.

36. Ibid.

37. Dwyer, K. K. (2000). The multidimensional model: Teaching students to self-manage high communication apprehension by self-selecting treatments. *Communication Education*, 49, 79.

38. Richmond & McCroskey, *Communication*.

39. Study shows how sleep improves memory. (2005, 29 June). *Science Daily*. Retrieved online from http://www.sciencedaily.com/releases/2005/06/050629070337.htm

40. *Rhetorica ad herennium*. (1954, H. Caplan, Trans.). Cambridge, MA: Harvard University Press.

41. Bitzer, L. (1968). The rhetorical situation. *Philosophy and Rhetoric*, 1(1), 1–14. 30. Aristotle. (1960). *On rhetoric*. (L. Cooper, Trans.). New York, NY: Appleton-Century-Crofts.

Chapter 3

1. Donaghue, P. J., & Seigal, M. E. (2005). *Are you really listening? Keys to successful communication*. Notre Dame, IN: Sorin Books.

2. Hansen, R. S., & Hansen, K. (2013, July 15). Quintessential careers: What do employers really want? Top skills and values employers seek from job-seekers. EmpoweringSites.com. Retrieved online from http://www.quint careers.com/job_skills_values.html

3. Forgetting curve—it's up to you. Festo Didactic. Retrieved online from http://www.festo-didactic.co.uk/gb-en/news/forgetting-curve-its-up-to-you.htm?fbid=Z2IuZW4uNTUwLjE3LjE2LjM0Mzc; Thalheimer, W. (2010). How much do people forget. Work-Learning Research, Inc, Retrieved online from http://willthalheimer.typepad.com/files/how-much-do-people-forget-v12-14-2010.pdf. Note that, although the figures cited in the text conform to the Ebbinghaus curve, Thalheimer's own meta-analysis discovered that retention rates vary widely instead of being clustered tightly around the points on Ebbinghaus's curve, making the Ebbinghaus curve an average more than a discrete measurement.

4. International Listening Association. (1996). Retrieved online from http://www.listen.org/

5. Janusik, L. A., & Wolvin, A. D. (2006). 24 hours in a day: A listening update to the time studies. Paper presented at the meeting of the International Listening Association, Salem, OR.

6. DeWine, S., & Daniels, T. (1993). Beyond the snapshot: Setting a research agenda in organizational communication. In S. A. Deetz (Ed.), *Communication yearbook 16* (pp. 252–230). Thousand Oaks, CA: Sage.

7. Salopek, J. J. (1999). Is anyone listening? *Training and Development*, 53(9), 58–60.

8. Larcker, D. F., Miles S., Tayan, B., & Gutman, M. E. (2013) 2013 CEO performance evaluation survey. *Stanford Graduate School of Business*, 9. Retrieved online from http://www.gsb.stanford.edu/cldr/research/surveys/performance.html.

9. Ibid.

10. Lloyd, K.J., Boer, D., Keller, J.W., Voelpel, S. (2014). Is my boss really listening to me? The impact of perceived supervisor listening on emotional exhaustion, turnover intention, and organizational citizenship behavior. *Journal of Business Ethics*, 130(3), 509–524.

11. Wolvin, A., & Coakley, C. G. (1996). *Listening* (5th ed.). New York, NY: McGraw-Hill.

12. Watson, K. W., Barker, L. L., & Weaver, J. B. III. (1995). The listening styles profile (LSP-16): Development and validation of an instrument to assess four listening styles. *International Journal of Listening*, 9, 1–13.

13. Greenwald, A. G., McGhee, D. E., & Schwartz, J. L. K. (1998). Measuring individual differences in implicit cognition: The Implicit Association Test. *Journal of Personality and Social Psychology*, 74, 1464–1480.

14. Y. Yi, H., Smiljanic, R., & Chandrasekaran, B. (2014). The neural processing of foreign-accented speech and its relationship to listener bias. *Frontiers in Human Neuroscience*, 8, 768.

15. Weaver, J. B. III, & Kirtley, M. D. (1995). Listening styles and empathy. *The Southern Communication Journal*, 60(2), 131–140.

16. O'Shaughnessy, B. (2003). Active attending or a theory of mental action. *Consciousness and the World*, 29, 379–407.

17. Wolvin, A., & Coakley, C. G. (1996). *Listening* (5th ed.). New York, NY: McGraw-Hill.

18. Harding, S., Cooke, M., König, P. (2007) Auditory gist perception: An alternative to attentional selection of auditory streams? In L. Paletta, E. Rome (Eds.), *Attention in cognitive systems*: (pp. 399–416). Berlin: Springer-Verlag.

19. Dukette, D., & Cornish, D. (2009). *The essential 20: Twenty components of an excellent health care team* (pp. 72–73). RoseDog Books.

20. Turning into digital goldfish (22 February 2002). BBC News. Retrieved online from http://news.bbc.co.uk/2/hi/science/nature/1834682.stm

21. *Sharpening your listening skills*. (2002). Teller Vision, 0895-1039, 7.

22. Estes, W. K. (1989). Learning theory. In A. Lesgold & R. Glaser (Eds.). *Foundations for a psychology of education* (pp. 1–49). Hillsdale, NJ: Erlbaum.

23. Lukits, A. (2014, November 24). The secret to resisting temptation: People who excel at resisting temptation deliberately avoid tempting situations, says a study. *Wall Street Journal*. Retrieved online from http://www.wsj.com/articles/the-secret-to-resisting-temptation-1416852990.

24. Dunkel, P., & Pialorsi, F. (2005). *Advanced listening comprehension: Developing aural and notetaking skills*. Boston, MA: Thomson Heinle; Wolvin & Coakley.

25. Levitin, D. J. (2015, January 15). Why the modern world is bad for your brain. *The Guardian*.

Retrieved online from http://www.theguardian.com /science/2015/jan/18/modern-world-bad-for-brain -daniel-j-levitin-organized-mind-information -overload.

26. Chow, D. (2013, June 13). Why humans are bad at multitasking. *Live Science*. Retrieved online from http://www.livescience.com/37420-multitasking -brain-psychology.html.

27. Mueller, P.A., & Oppenheimer, D.M. (2014, April 23). The pen is mightier than the keyboard: Advantages of longhand over laptop note taking. *Psychological Science, 6*, 1159–1168.

28. Bernstein, E. (2015, January 12). How 'active listening' makes both participants in a conversation feel better. *Wall Street Journal*. Retrieved online from http://www.wsj.com/articles/how-active -listening-makes-both-sides-of-a-conversation -feel-better-1421082684.

Chapter 4

1. Berger, C. R. (1988). Uncertainty reduction and information exchange in developing relation-ships. In S. Duck, D. Hay, S. Hobfoll, W.Ickes, & B. Montgomery (Eds.), *Handbook of interpersonal relationships: Theory, research, and interventions* (pp. 239–255). New York, NY: Wiley.

2. TBD

3. Callison, D. (2001). Concept mapping. *School Library Media Activities Monthly, 17*(10), 30–32.

4. Walters D. & Siders, D. (2015, June 8). Politi-cal polling pioneer Mervin Fields dies. *Sacramento Bee*. Retrieved online from http://www.sacbee .com/news/politics-government/capitol-alert /article23517094.html.

5. Google apps for work. (2015). Google. Re-trieved online from https://www.google.com/work /apps/business/products/forms//

6. Callahan, G. (2015, March 16). Personalizing social emotional learning with Google forms. *EdSurge*. Retrieved online from https://www .edsurge.com/n/2015-03-16-personalizing-social -emotional-learning-with-google-forms; Stirling, S. (2015, June 5). N.J. NHL fan map: Battle lines have been drawn between Devils, Rangers, Flyers fans. Retrieved online from http://www.nj.com /sports/njsports/index.ssf/2015/06/nj_nhl_fan_map _battle_lines_have_been_drawn_betwee.html.

7. Edwards, A. (2012, July 25). Once blocked, boy's appeal for gays to wed gets Council audience. *New York Times*. Retrieved online from http://www .nytimes.com/2012/07/26/nyregion/kameron-slades -appeal-for-gay-marriage-once-blocked-at-school -gets-councilaudience.html?_r=0

Chapter 5

1. Littleton, C. (2014, January 21). Warner Bros.'s deal with Sohu Video marks a first for a daily U.S. talkshow in the market. *Variety*. Retrieved online from http://variety.com/2014/tv/news/the-ellen -degeneres-show-to-air-in-china-1201065996/.

2. What makes a story newsworthy? MediaCol-lege.com. *Wavelength Media*. Retrieved online from http://www.mediacollege.com/journalism /news/newsworthy.html.

3. Curtis, A. (2013). What are the seven news val-ues? Mass Communication Department. The Uni-versity of North Carolina at Pembroke. Retrieved online from http://www2.uncp.edu/home/acurtis /Courses/ResourcesForCourses/NewsValues.html.

4. Blackburn, E. (2015). Blackburn Lab, University of California San Francisco. Retrieved online from http://biochemistry2.ucsf.edu/labs

/blackburn/index.php?option=com_content&view =article&id=1&Itemid=3.

5. Cha, A. E. (2013, December 2). Jack Andraka, Maryland's boy wonder, on mean scientists, home-coming and tricorders. *Washington Post*. Retrieved online from http://www.washingtonpost.com /national/health-science/jack-andraka-marylands -boy-wonder-on-mean-scientists-homecoming-and -tricorders/2013/12/02/e15606be-4173-11e3-a624 -41d661b0bb78_story.html.

6. Blumer, H. (1969). *Symbolic interactionism*. Englewood Cliffs, NJ: Prentice Hall.

7. Barbe, W., & Swassing, R. H. (1979). *The Swassing-Barbe modality index*. Columbus, OH: Zaner-Bloser; Canfield, A. A. (1980). *Learning styles inventory manual*. Ann Arbor, MI: Humanics Inc.; Dunn, R., Dunn, K., & Price, G. E. (1975). *Learn-ing styles inventory*. Lawrence, KS: Price Systems; Gardner, H. (1983). *Frames of mind: The theory of multiple intelligences*. New York, NY: Basic Books; Kolb, D. (1984). *Experiential learning: Experience as the source of learning and development*. Engle-wood Cliffs, NJ: Prentice Hall.

8. Kolb, *Experiential learning*.

9. Dewey, J. (1938/1997). *Experience and educa-tion*. New York, NY: Macmillan.

10. Ibid.

11. *The CIA world factbook*. (2014). Washington, D.C.: Central Intelligence Agency. Retrieved online from https://www.cia.gov/library/publications /resources/the-world-factbook/.

Chapter 6

1. Raya, A.L. (2014, November 17). A true role calling. *Deadline*. Retrieved online from http:// deadline.com/2014/11/selma-star-david-oyelowo -talks-about-the-long-path-to-becoming-martin -luther-king-jr-1201286465/; Lee, B. (2015). David Oyelowo: Spielberg asked me to reprise Martin Luther King role. *The Guardian*. Retrieved online from http://www.theguardian.com/film/2015/jun/01 /david-oyelowo-steven-spielberg-asked-him-play -martin-luther-king-again.

2. Munger, D., Anderson, D., Benjamin, B., Busiel, C., & Pardes-Holt, B. (2000). *Researching online* (3rd ed.). New York, NY: Longman.

3. Tengler, C., & Jablin, F. M. (1983). Effects of question type, orientation, and sequencing in the employment screening interview. *Communication Monographs, 50*, 261.

4. Biagi, S. *Interviews that work: A practical guide for journalists* (2nd ed., p. 94). Belmont, CA: Wadsworth.

5. Frances, P. (1994). Lies, damned lies. *American Demographics, 16*, 2.

6. Ahladas, J. (1989, April 1). Global warming. *Vital Speeches*, 382.

7. Shalala, D. (1994, May 15). Domestic terror-ism: An unacknowledged epidemic. *Vital Speeches*, 451.

8. van Uhm, P. (2011). Why I choose a gun. TEDxAmsterdam. Retrieved online from https:// www.ted.com/talks/peter_van_uhm_why_i _chose_a_gun/transcript?language=en#t-279000.

9. Howard, J. A. (2000, August 1). Principles in default: Rediscovered and reapplied. *Vital Speeches*, 618.

10. Nelson, J. C. (2006). Leadership. Utah School Boards Association 83rd Annual Conference, Salt Lake City, Utah. Retrieved online from http://www .ama-assn.org/ama/pub/category /15860.html

11. Trachtenberg, S. (1986, August 15). Five ways in which thinking is dangerous. *Vital Speeches*, 653.

12. Durst, G. M. (1989, March 1). The manager as a developer. *Vital Speeches*, 309–310.

13. Becherer, H. (2000, September 15). Enduring values for a secular age: Faith, hope and love. *Vital Speeches*, 732.

Chapter 7

1. Fisher, W. (1987). *Human communication as narration: Toward a philosophy of reason, value, and action*. Columbia: University of South Carolina Press.

2. May, M. E. (2014, Mar 17). Talk like TED: The world's best public speakers reveal their secrets. *OPEN Forum*. N.p. Retrieved online from https://www.americanexpress.com/us/small -business/openforum/articles/talk-like-ted-the -worlds-best-public-speakers-reveal-their-secrets/.

3. Gallo, C. (2014, March 13). The science behind TED's 18-minute rule. *Linkedin*. N.p. Retrieved online from https%3A%2F%2Fwww.linkedin .com%2Fpulse%2F20140313205730-5711504-the -science-behind-ted-s-18-minute-rule.

4. Are you with me? Measuring student attention in the classroom. (2014, May 23). *The Teaching Center Journal*. Washington University in St. Louis. Retrieved online from http://teachingcenter.wustl .edu/Journal/Reviews/Pages/student-attention.aspx.

5. Gallo. The science behind TED's 18-minute rule.

6. Kinder, L. (2013, September 23). The very short speeches that have become famous. *The Telegraph*. Telegraph Media Group. Retrieved online from http://www.telegraph.co.uk/culture /film/10328058/The-very-short-speeches-that -have-become-famous.html.

Chapter 8

1. Trenholm, S. (1989). *Persuasion and social influence*. Englewood Cliffs, NJ: Prentice-Hall; Crano, W. D. (1977). Primacy versus recency in retention of information and opinion change. *The Journal of Social Psychology, 101*, 87–96.

2. Mackay, H. (2009, July). Changing the world: Your future is a work in progress. *Vital Speeches*, 319–323.

3. Reckford, J.T.M. (2012, January). Three myths about affordable housing: Affordable housing is everyone's problem—and everyone's opportunity. *Vital Speeches*, 23.

4. Humes, J. C. (1988). *Standing ovation: How to be an effective speaker and communicator*. New York, NY: Harper & Row.

5. Olsteen, J. (2012). Best jokes of Joel Olsteen. Better Days TV. Retrieved online from http:// www .betterdaystv.net/play.php?vid=247

6. Bitzer, L. F. (1995). The rhetorical situation. In W. A. Covino & D.A. Jolliffe (Eds.), *Rhetoric: concepts, definitions, bounadries*. Boston, MA: Allyn and Bacon.

7. Aristotle. (1954). *The rhetoric*. (W. Rhys Roberts, Trans.). New York, NY: Modern Library.

8. Mariano, C. (2010, January). Unity, quality, responsibility: The real meaning of the words. *Vital Speeches*, 20–22.

9. Kutcher, A. (2013). Teen Choice Awards, Ash-ton Kutcher speech. Original speech and transcript posted to Genius.com. Retrieved online from http:// genius.com/Ashton-kutcher-teen-choice-awards -2013-speech-annotated.

10. The inverted pyramid structure [Web blog post]. *Purdue OWL: Journalism and Journalistic Writing*. Purdue University, n.d. Retrieved from

https://owl.english.purdue.edu/owl/resource/735/04/.

11. Scanlan, C. (2014, November 25). Writing from the top down: Pros and cons of the inverted pyramid. *Poynter*. The Poynter Institute. Retrieved from http://www.poynter.org/news/media-innovation/12754/writing-from-the-top-down-pros-and-cons-of-the-inverted-pyramid/.

12. Purdue Owl, The inverted pyramid structure.

13. Scanlan, Writing from the top down.

14. Cossolotto, M. (2009, December). An urgent call to action for study abroad alumni to help reduce our global awareness deficit. *Vital Speeches*, 564–568.

15. Kutcher. Teen Choice Awards.

Chapter 9

1. Rantz, J. (2014). Fact check everything. Presentation at Ignite Seattle 25. Retrieved from https://www.youtube.com/watch?v=v-vl3mcJCng

2. Tversky, B. (1997). Memory for pictures, maps, environments, and graphs. In D. G. Payne & F. G. Conrad (Eds.), *Intersections in basic and applied memory research* (pp. 257– 277). Hillsdale, NJ: Erlbaum.

3. Gallo, C. (2006, December 5). "Presentations with something for everyone." *Bloomberg Businessweek*. Retrieved online from http:// www.businessweek.com/smallbiz/content /dec2006/sb20061205_454055.htm; Kolb, D. (1984). *Experiential learning: Experience as the source of learning and development*. Englewood Cliffs, NJ: Prentice Hall.

4. Hanke, J. (1998). The psychology of presentation visuals. *Presentations*, *12*(5), 42–47.

5. Ayers, J. (1991). Using visual aids to reduce speech anxiety. *Communication Research Reports*, *8*, 73–79; Dwyer, K. (1991). *Conquer your speech fright*. Orlando, FL: Harcourt Brace.

6. Booher, D. D. (2003). *Speak with confidence [electronic resources]: Powerful presentations that inform, inspire, and persuade*. New York, NY: McGraw-Hill.

7. Kolb, *Experiential learning*; Long, K. (1997). *Visual-Aids and Learning, University of Portsmouth*. Retrieved online from http:// www.mech.port.ac.uk/av/AVInfo.htm

8. Union Metrics. (n.d.). 16 ways to use Twitter to improve your next conference. Retrieved from https://unionmetrics.com/resources/16-ways-use-twitter-improve-next-conference/

9. Williams, E. (n.d.). How to use social media while public speaking. *Houston Chronicle* by Demand Media. Retrieved from http://work.chron.com/use-social-media-public-speaking-7111.html

10. Union Metrics. (n.d.). 16 ways to use Twitter to improve your next conference.

11. Williams, E. How to use social media while public speaking.

Chapter 10

1. Witt, P. L., Wheeless, L. R., & Allen, M. (2007, May). A meta-analytical review of the relationship between teacher immediacy and student learning. Paper presented at the annual meeting of the International Communication Association, San Diego, CA. Retrieved online from http://www.allacademic.com/meta/ p112238_index.html

2. Edwards, C. C. (2002). Verbal immediacy and androgyny: An examination of student perceptions of college instructors. *Academic Exchange Quarterly*, *6*, 180–185; Gorham, J. (1998). The relationship between teacher verbal immediacy behaviors and student learning. *Communication Education*, *37*, 40–53; Powell R. G., & Harville, B. (1990). The effects of teacher immediacy and clarity on instructional outcomes: An intercultural assessment. *Communication Education*, *39*, 369–379.

3. Braithwaite D., & Braithwaite, C. (1997). Viewing persons with disabilities as a culture. In L. Samovar & R. Porter (Eds.), *Intercultural communication: A reader* (8th ed., pp. 154– 164). Belmont, CA: Wadsworth; Treinen, K., & Warren, J. (2001). Antiracist pedagogy in the basic course: Teaching cultural communication as if whiteness matters. *Basic Communication Course Annual*, *13*, 46–75.

4. Stewart, L. P., Cooper, P. J., Stewart, A. D., & Friedley, S. A. (2003). *Communication and gender* (4th ed., p. 63). Boston, MA: Allyn & Bacon.

5. Gastil, J. (1990). Generic pronouns and sexist language: The oxymoronic character of masculine generics. *Sex Roles*, *23*, 629–643; Hamilton, M. C. (1991). Masculine bias in the attribution of personhood: People = male, male = people. *Psychology of Women Quarterly*, *15*, 393–402; Switzer, J. W. (1990). The impact of generic word choices: An empirical investigation of age- and sex-related differences. *Sex Roles*, *22*, 69–82.

6. Treinen & Warren, Antiracist pedagogy in the basic course, 13.

7. O'Connor, J. V. (2000). "FAQs #1." Cuss Control Academy. Retrieved online from http://www.cusscontrol.com/faqs.html

8. Duck, S. W. (1994). *Meaningful relationships*. Thousand Oaks, CA: Sage. See also Shotter, J. (1993). *Conversational realities: The construction of life through language*. Newbury Park, CA: Sage.

9. Schmidt, A. (2014). The 10 trials of Jim Gaffigan. *Paste*. Retrieved from http://www.pastemagazine.com/blogs/lists/2014/04/the-10-trials-of-jim-gaffigan.html

10. Hofstede, G., Hofstede, G. J., & Minkov, M. (2010). *Cultures and Organizations: Software of the Mind* (3rd ed., pp. 89–134). New York, NY: McGraw-Hill.

11. Levine, D. (1985). *The flight from ambiguity* (p. 28). Chicago, IL: University of Chicago Press.

12. Richards, I. A., & Ogden, C. K. (1923). *The meaning of meaning: A study of the influence of language upon thought and the science of symbolism*. Orlando, FL: Harcourt.

13. Ibid.

14. Ibid.

15. O'Grady, W., Archibald, J., Aronoff, M., & Rees-Miller, J. (2001). *Contemporary linguistics* (4th ed.). Boston: Bedford/St. Martin's.

16. Fought, C. (2003). *Chicano English in context* (pp. 64–78). New York, NY: Pallgrave MacMillan.

17. Glenn, C., & Gray, L. (2013). *Hodges Harbrace handbook* (18th ed.). Belmont, CA: Cengage Learning.

18. Princeton Review (2012). *Word smart: How to build a more educated vocabulary* (5th ed.) Princeton, NJ: Princeton Review, Inc.; Sadlier-Oxford regularly revises and publishes the *Vocabulary Workshop* series in levels A–H.

19. Lamb, J. (2014, October 29). To get your hands on a seabird, you have to go "grubbing." *All Things Considered*. NPR.org. http://www.npr.org/2014/10/29/359892907/to-get-your-hands-on-a-seabird-you-have-to-go-grubbing

20. Friedman, H. (2014, September 23). Trade lingo: "Aunt Minnie" lives in your x-rays. *All Things Considered*. NPR.org. http://www.npr.org/2014/09/23/350946921/trade-lingo-aunt-minnie-lives-in-your-x-rays

21. Prady, B. (2014, November 5). In comedy writing, fear the "Bono's" and "Nakamura." *All Things Considered*. NPR.org. http://www.npr.org/2014/11/05/361820803/in-comedy-writing-fear-the-bonos-and-nakamura

22. Ibid.

23. Rader, W. (2007). The online slang dictionary. Retrieved online from http://onlineslangdictionary.com/

24. Macris, A. (2010, May 10). What grade is your content comprehension? *The Escapist*. N.p. Web. Retrieved from http://www.escapistmagazine.com/articles/view/video-games/columns/publishers-note/7536-What-Grade-is-Your-Content-Comprehension

25. Macris, What grade is your content comprehension?

26. Readability Formulas. (n.d.). The Gunning's Fog Index (or FOG) Readability Formula. Retrieved from http://www.readabilityformulas.com/gunning-fog-readability-formula.php

27. Readability Formulas. (n.d.). The Flesch Reading Ease Readability Formula. Retrieved from http://www.readabilityformulas.com/flesch-reading-ease-readability-formula.php

28. Van Zuylen-Wood, S. (2012, December 21). Terry Gross: The queen of "like." *Philly Mag*. Retrieved from http://www.phillymag.com/news/2012/12/21/npr-terry-gross-queen-like/

29. Saul, M. (2008, December 29). Caroline Kennedy no whiz with words. *New York Daily News*. Retrieved from http://www.nydailynews.com/news/politics/caroline-kennedy-no-whiz-words-article-1.355586

30. Siemaszko, C. (2009, January 23). Why Caroline Kennedy's Senate bid flamed out. *U.S. News & World Report*. Retrieved from http://www.usnews.com/news/articles/2009/01/23/why-caroline-kennedys-senate-bid-flamed-out

31. Saul, Caroline Kennedy no whiz with words.

32. Lyttle, N. (2015, May 20). Study: Recent no. 1 hits are written at third grade reading level. *WYMT*. Gray Digital Media. Retrieved from http://www.wkyt.com/wymt/home/headlines/Study-Recent-No-1-hits-are-written-at-third-grade-reading-level-304414621.html

33. Hensley, C. W. (1995, September 1). Speak with style and watch the impact. *Vital Speeches of the Day*, 703.

34. Schertz, R. H. (1977, November 1). Deregulation: After the airlines, is trucking next? *Vital Speeches of the Day*, 40.

35. Reagan, R. (1987, June 12). *Address at the Brandenburg Gate*. Retrieved from http://www.reagan.utexas.edu/archives/speeches/1987/061287d.htm

Chapter 11

1. Decker, B. (1992). *You've got to be believed to be heard*. New York, NY: St. Martin's Press.

2. Watzlawick, P., Bavelas, J. B., & Jackson, D. D. (1967). *Pragmatics of human communication*. New York, NY: Norton.

3. Eidell, L. (2015, April 21). The Only Public Speaking Advice You'll Ever Need, Plus More Professional and Personal Tips from *The Five's* Dana Perino. *Glamour*. Retrieved from http://www.glamour.com/inspired/blogs/the-conversation/2015/04/dana-perino-interview

4. Kzan, O. (2014, May 29). Vocal fry may hurt women's job prospects. *The Atlantic*. Retrieved from http://www.theatlantic.com/business/archive/2014/05/employers-look-down-on-women-with-vocal-fry/371811/

5. Ibid.

6. Lachance Shandrow, K. (2014, November 3). 7 Power public speaking tips from one of the most-watch TED Talks speakers. *Entrepreneur*. Retrieved from http://www.entrepreneur.com/article/239308

7. Bates, B. (1992). *Communication and the sexes*. Prospect Heights, IL: Waveland Press; Cherulnik, P. D. (1989). Physical attractiveness and judged suitability for leadership, Report No. CG 021 893. Paper presented at the annual meeting of the Midwestern Psychological Association, Chicago, IL (ERIC Document Services No. ED 310 317); Lawrence S. G., & Watson, M. (1991). Getting others to help: The effectiveness of professional uniforms in charitable fund raising. *Journal of Applied Communication Research*, 19, 170–185; Malloy, J. T. (1975). Dress for success. New York, NY: Warner; Temple, L. E., & Loewen, K. R. (1993). Perceptions of power: First impressions of a woman wearing a jacket. *Perceptual and Motor Skills*, 76, 339–348.

8. Phillips P. A., & Smith, L. R. (1992). The effects of teacher dress on student perceptions, Report No. SP 033 944. (ERIC Document Services No. ED 347 151).

9. Morris, T. L., Gorham, J., Cohen, S. H., & Huffman, D. (1996). Fashion in the classroom: Effects of attire on student perceptions of instructors in college classes. *Communication Education*, 45, 135–148.

10. Burgoon, J. K., Coker, D. A., & Coker, R. A. (1986). Communicative effects of gaze behavior: A test of two contrasting explanations. *Human Communication Research*, 12, 495–524.

11. Hironori, A. et al. (2013). Attention to eye contact in the West and East: Autonomic responses and evaluative ratings. Ed. A. Mesoudi. *PLoS One* 8(3). Retrieved from http://www.ncbi.nlm.nih.gov/pmc/articles/PMC3596353/

12. Shipman, S. (2015). 5 public speaking lessons from Lady Gaga's 2015 Oscar performance [Web blog post]. Retrieved from http://www.staceyshipman.com/2015/02/24/5-public-speaking-lessons-lady-gagas-oscar-performance/

13. Vanmetre, E. (2015, February 24). Lady Gaga's *The Sound of Music* tribute at Oscars took 6 months of daily vocal rehearsals. *New York Daily News*. Retrieved from http://www.nydailynews.com/entertainment/music/lady-gaga-works-vocal-coach-6-months-oscars-article-1.2126965

14. Menzel, K. E., & Carrell, L. J. (1994). The relationship between preparation and performance in public speaking. *Communication Education*, 43, 23.

15. Boardman, M. (2013, February 26). Anne Hathaway acceptance speech: Best supporting actress winner practiced a lot. *Huffington Post*. Retrieved online from http://www.huffingtonpost.com/2013/02/26/anne-hathaway-acceptance-speech-best-supporting-actress_n_2767270.html; Exclusive: Anne Hathaway practiced her Oscar speech a lot to be more likable. (2013, February 26). *UsWeekly*. Retrieved online from http://www.usmagazine.com/celebrity-news/news/anne-hathaway-practiced-her-oscar-speech-a-lot-to-be-more-likable-2013262

16. Mankowski, D., & Jose, R. (2012). MBC flashback: The 70th anniversary of FDR's fireside chats. The Museum of Broadcast Communications. Retrieved online from http://www.museum.tv/exhibitionssection.php?page=79

17. Obama, B. (n.d.). Your weekly address. The White House. Retrieved online from http://www.whitehouse.gov/briefing-room/weekly-address/

18. Thomas, W. G. (2004). Television news and the civil rights struggle: The views in Virginia and Mississippi. *Southern Spaces*. Retrieved online from http://southernspaces.org/2004/television-news-and-civil-rights-struggle-views-virginia-and-mississippi

19. Moran, L. (2015, May 18). California congresswoman puts foot in mouth with hand-to-mouth Native American stereotypical gesture. *New York Daily News*. Retrieved online http://www.nydailynews.com/news/politics/calif-pol-puts-foot-mouth-hand-to-mouth-gesture-article-1.2226314; Brumfield, B. (2015, May 18). Congresswoman makes ethnically touchy gesture. *CNN*. Retrieved http://www.cnn.com/videos/us/2015/05/17/dnt-ca-sanchez-gaffe-native-american.kcra; Bobic, I. (2015, May 17). Senate Candidate Loretta Sanchez makes disparaging gesture about Native Americans. *Huffington Post*. Retrieved from http://www.huffingtonpost.com/2015/05/17/loretta-sanchez-whooping-native-americans_n_7300466.html; Bienick, D. (2015, May 17). Did Rep. Loretta Sanchez make a questionable gesture about Native Americans? KRCA. Retrieved from http://www.kcra.com/news/did-rep-loretta-sanchez-make-a-questionable-comment-about-native-americans/33065344

20. Mitchell, O. (2010, September 30). 18 tips on how to conduct an engaging webinar. *Speaking about Presenting*. Retrieved from http://www.speakingaboutpresenting.com/presentation-skills/how-to-conduct-engaging-webinar/; Persson, D. (2009 February 19). How to give a webinar (and not look like an idiot). *CIO*. Retrieved from http://www.cio.com/article/2430651/careers-staffing/how-to-give-a-webinar--and-not-look-like-an-idiot-.html; Andersen, MM. (2010, January). Elearn magazine: Tips for effective webinars. *ELearn Magazine, an ACM Publication*. Association for Computing Machinery, Inc. Retrieved from http://elearnmag.acm.org/featured.cfm?aid=1710034

21. Used with permission of Alyssa Grace Millner.

Chapter 12

1. Otzi, the ice man. (n.d.). Dig: The archaeology magazine for kids. Retrieved from http://www.digonsite.com/drdig/mummy/22.html

2. Michalko, M. (1998). Thinking like a genius: Eight strategies used by the supercreative, from Aristotle and Leonardo to Einstein and Edison. *Futurist* 32(4). Retrieved from http://www.questia.com/library/1G1-20925508/thinking-like-a-genius-eight-strategies-used-by-the

3. Vegan Society website. Retrieved from http://www.vegansociety.com

4. Based on Baerwald, D., & Northshore School District. Narrative. Retrieved from http://ccweb.norshore.wednet.edu/writingcorner/narrative.html

5. Used with permission of Anna Rankin.

6. Thier, D. (2012, July 18). How this guy lied his way into MSNBC, ABC News, *The New York Times* and more. *Forbes*. Retrieved from http://www.forbes.com/sites/davidthier/2012/07/18/how-this-guy-lied-his-way-into-msnbc-abc-news-the-new-york-times-and-more

7. Ibid.

8. Ibid.

9. Holiday, R. (2012, July 16). What is media manipulation? A definition and explanation. *Forbes*. Retrieved from http://www.forbes.com/sites/ryanholiday/2012/07/16/what-is-media-manipulation-a-definition-and-explanation/

10. Farsetta, D. (2006, March 16). Fake TV news: Widespread and undisclosed. *PR Watch*. The Center for Media and Democracy. Retrieved from http://www.prwatch.org/fakenews/execsummary

11. Holiday. What is media manipulation?

12. Used with permission of Logan Hurley.

Chapter 13

1. Perloff, R. M. (1993). *The dynamics of persuasion*. Hillsdale, NJ: Erlbaum.

2. Kennedy, G. A. (1980). *Classical rhetoric and its Christian and secular tradition from ancient to modern times*. Chapel Hill, NC: University of North Carolina Press.

3. Petty, R. E., & Cacioppo, J. (1996). *Attitudes and persuasion: Classic and contemporary approaches* (p. 7). Boulder, CO: Westview.

4. Toulmin, S. (1958). *The uses of rhetoric*. Cambridge, England: Cambridge University Press.

5. National Institute on Aging. Alzheimer's disease: A looming national crisis. Retrieved online from http://www.nia.nih.gov/Alzheimers/Publications/ADProgress2005_2006/Part1/looming.htm

6. McCroskey, J. C., & Teven, J. J. (1999, March). Goodwill: A reexamination of the construct and its measurement. *Communication Monographs* 66, 22.

7. Stewart, R. (1994). Perceptions of a speaker's initial credibility as a function of religious involvement and religious disclosiveness. *Communication Research Reports*, 11, 169–176.

8. Lightstone, K., Francis, R., & Kocum, L. (2011). University faculty style of dress and students' perception of instructor credibility. *International Journal of Business and Social Science* (2)15. Retrieved from http://www.ijbssnet.com/journals/Vol_2_No_15_August_2011/3.pdf

9. U.S. diplomacy and yellow journalism, 1895–1898 - 1866–1898 - Milestones - Office of the Historian, U.S. Department of State. Retrieved from https://history.state.gov/milestones/1866-1898/yellow-journalism

10. Yellow journalism. (1999). *PBS*. Great Projects Film Company, Inc. Retrieved from http://www.pbs.org/crucible/frames/_journalism.html

11. Castillo, C., Mendoza, M. & Poblete, B. (2011, March 28–April 1). Information credibility on Twitter. Proceedings of the 20th International Conference on World Wide Web. ACM, pp. 675–684.

12. Gupta, A. et al. (2014, May 21). TweetCred: A real-time web-based system for assessing credibility of content on Twitter. Proceedings of the 1st Workshop on Privacy and Security in Online Social Media. Retrieved online http://cm.1-s.es/Cryptome-update-14-0602/2014/05/tweetcred.pdf

13. Perloff, *The dynamics of persuasion*.

14. Petri, H. L., & Govern, J. M. (2004). *Motivation: Theory, research, and application* (5th ed., p. 376). Belmont, CA: Wadsworth.

15. Nabi, R. L. (2002). Discrete emotions and persuasion. In J. P. Dillard & M. Pfau (Eds.), *The persuasion handbook: Developments in theory and practice* (pp. 291–299). Thousand Oaks, CA: Sage.

16. Megan's law passes, mom promises to fight any judicial appeals. Retrieved online from http://www.accessmylibrary.com/coms2/summary_0286-6368573_ITM

17. Slator, D. (1998). Sharing life. In *Winning orations* (pp. 63–66). Mankato, MN: Interstate Oratorical Association.

18. Labor, R. (1998). Shaken baby syndrome: The silent epidemic. In *Winning orations* (pp. 70–72). Mankato, MN: Interstate Oratorical Association.

19. Domhoff, G. W. (2013, February). Wealth, income, and power. *Who rules America?* Retrieved from http://www2.ucsc.edu/whorulesamerica/power/wealth.html

20. Ibid.

21. Mistrati, M. & Romano, U.R. (2010). *The dark side of chocolate* [Video file]. Retrieved from http://topdocumentaryfilms.com/dark-side-chocolate/

Chapter 14

1. Van Eemeren, F. H., Garssen, B., Krabbe, E. C. W., Henkemans, A. F. S., Verheij, B., & Wagemans, J. H. M. (2014). *Handbook of argumentation theory*. New York: Springer.

2. Twitter top 100 most followed. (2015, June). *Twitter Counter*. Retrieved online http://twittercounter.com/pages/100

3. Carter, Nicole. (2014, March 8). The fascinating psychology behind word-of-mouth marketing. *Inc.* Retrieved online http://www.inc.com/nicole-carter/jonah-berger-marketing-word-of-mouth.html

4. Ziegelmueller, G. W., Kay, J., & Dause, C. A. (1990). *Argumentation: Inquiry and advocacy* (2nd ed., p. 186). Englewood Cliffs, NJ: Prentice Hall.

5. Used with permission of Adam Parrish.

Chapter 15

1. Moylan, B. (2015, February 23). Celebrity activism flames out at the Oscars. *Time.* Retrieved online http://time.com/3718993/celebrity-oscars-activism-common-john-legend-patricia-arquette/

2. Stromberg, J. (2012, October 22). A brief history of the teleprompter. *Smithsonian.* Smithsonian Institution.

3. Corriston, M. (2014, January 12). Oops! See how Jonah Hill and Margot Robbie handled their globes gaffe. *People.* Time Inc.

4. Wigler, J. (2014, January 7). Michael Bay explains 'embarrassing' teleprompter fail. *MTV News.* MTV.

5. Shapiro, R. (2012, June 27). Megyn Kelly teleprompter fail: Fox News host tripped up by missing words (VIDEO). *The Huffington Post.* TheHuffingtonPost.com.

Chapter 16

1. Levi, D. (2014). *Group dynamics for teams* (4th ed.). Thousand Oaks, CA: Sage; Northouse, P. G. (2013). *Leadership: Theory and practice* (6th ed.). Thousand Oaks, CA: Sage; Williams, C. (2013).

Management (7th ed.). Mason, OH: South-Western/Cengage Learning.

2. Tullar, W., & Kaiser, P. (2000). The effect of process training on process and outcomes in virtual groups. *Journal of Business Communication, 37,* 408–427.

3. Lesikar, R., Pettit J. Jr., & Flately, M. (1999). *Basic business communication* (8th ed.). New York, NY: McGraw-Hill.

4. Northouse, P. G. (2013). *Leadership: Theory and practice* (6th ed.). Thousand Oaks, CA: Sage.

5. Gardner, H. (2011). *Leading minds: An anatomy of leadership.* New York, NY: Basic Books.

6. Kippenberger, T. (2002). *Leadership styles.* New York, NY: John Wiley and Sons.

7. Fairhurst, G. T. (2011). *The power of framing: Creating the language of leadership.* San Francisco, CA: John Wiley and Sons.

8. Rahim, M. A. (2001). *Managing conflict in organizations* (3rd ed.). Westport, CT: Greenwood Press.

9. Janis, I. L. (1982). *Groupthink: Psychological studies of policy decision and fiascos* (2nd ed.). Boston, MA: Houghton Mifflin.

10. Sell, J., Lovaglia, M. J., Mannix, E. A., Samuelson, C. D., & Wilson, R. K. (2004). Investigating conflict, power, and status within and among groups. *Small Group Research, 35,* 44–72.

11. Ting-Toomey, S., & Chung, L.C. (2012). *Understanding Intercultural Communication,* (2nd Ed.). New York: Oxford University Press.

12. Bordia, P., DiFonzo, N., & Change, A. (1999). Rumor as group problem-solving: Development patterns in informal computer-mediated groups. *Small Group Research, 30,* 8–28.

13. Jiang, L., Bazarova, N. N., & Hancock, J. T. (2011). The disclosure-intimacy link in computer-mediated communication: An attributional extension of the hyperpersonal model. *Human Communication Research, 37,* 58–77; Wang, Z., Walther, J. B., & Hancock, J. T. (2009). Social identification

and interpersonal communication in computer mediated communication: What you do versus who you are in virtual groups. *Human Communication Research, 35,* 59–85.

14. Godamer, H. (1989). *Truth and method* (2nd ed., J. Weinsheimer & D. G. Marshall, Trans.). New York, NY: Crossroad.

15. Braithwaite, D. O., & Eckstein, N. (2003). Reconceptualizing supportive interactions: How persons with disabilities communicatively manages assistance. *Journal of Applied Communication Research, 31,* 1–26.

16. Conrad, C. (1997). *Strategic organizational communication: Toward the 21st century.* Orlando, FL: Harcourt Brace.

17. Dewey, J. (1933). *How we think.* Boston, MA: Heath.

18. Duch, B. J., Groh, S. E., & Allen, D. E. (Eds.). (2001). *The power of problem-based learning.* Sterling, VA: Stylus; Edens, K. M. (2000). Preparing problem solvers for the 21st century through problem-based learning. *College Teaching, 48*(2), 55–60; Levin, B. B. (Ed.). (2001). *Energizing teacher education and professional development with problem-based learning.* Alexandria, MN: Association for Supervision and Curriculum Development.

19. Young, Wood, Phillips, & Pedersen. (2007).

20. Andres, H. P. (2002). A comparison of face-to-face and virtual software development teams. *Team Performance Management: An International Journal, 8,* 39-48.

21. Huang, W. W., Wei, K. K., Watson, R. T., & Tan, B. C. Y. (2003). Supporting virtual team-building with a GSS: An empirical investigation. *Decision Support Systems, 34,* 359–367.

22. Shoemaker-Galloway, J. (2007, August 6). Top 10 netiquette guidelines. Suite 101, Retrieved online from http://suite101.com/article /netiquette-guidelines-a26615

23. Washenko, A. (2015, April 9). Broadcast your brand with Meerkat or Periscope. SproutSocial.com. Retrieved from http:/sproutsocial.com/insights/live-streaming-apps/

INDEX

Key terms are **boldface**.

I

ideas, unfamiliar/familiar, 78–79
identify speech topics, 54–55, 58
"I" language, 47, 298
imogees, 303
impression formation and management, 76
impressions, first, 76
impromptu speeches, 178–179
Improving Sports Performance in Middle
   and Long-Distance Running, 87
Iñárritu, Alejandro González, 282
incremental change, 247
indications, 234
individualistic cultures, norms, 298
inductive reasoning, 233
inductive reasoning, 233
ineffective listening behaviors, 42
inferences, 45
informal leaders, 296
informal observation, 60
information
   comprehension and retention, 76–79
   gather and evaluate, 30–31
   irrelevant, 90
   recent, 90
   record, 99
   selecting relevant, 94–99
information processing, central and peripheral
      routes, 232
information sources, 85–94
   gathering and evaluating, 95
   locate and evaluate, 85–94
informative expository speeches, 214–224
informative goal, 66, 68, 126
informative process speeches, 205–214
informative speaking, 198–227
   characteristics of, 199–202
informative speech, 199
   techniques, 201
informing, methods of, 202–205
initial audience disposition, 71
initial credibility, 238
Instagram, 87
integrity, 5, 93, 232
intellectually stimulating, 199–200
intelligible, 15, 31, 48, 160
   delivery, 172
interest, audience, 56
interference/noise, 7
International Listening Association, 39
The International Thesaurus of Quotations, 88
International Who's Who, 88
Internet, 64
   as information source, 86
   speaking apprehension and, 23
Internet identity theft speech, 207–214
Internet sources, 86
   source citations, 102
interpersonal communication, 8
interview, 90
   conducting, 92–93
   processing, 93
   recording, 93
   sample interview question, 92
   selecting the best person, 90–91
   source citations, 101
interview protocol, 90
   preparing, 91–92
intrapersonal communication, 7–8
introductions, 13, 31, 104
   action, 123
   action step activity, 126
   attention, creating, 121–124
   creating suspense, 8–9
   credibility, 124
   joke, 123
   personal reference, 123
   primacy-recency effect, 120

questions, 122
quotation, 123
relevance, establishing, 124
selecting the best, 125
speech of, 280
story, 122–123
thesis, stating, 124
introvert, 22, 297
invention, 29
inverted pyramid, 125
iPads, 160
irrelevant association, 158
irrelevant information, 90
Isocrates, 8
Issue-related conflict, 297

J

jargon, 78, 163, 164
Jensen, Edwin, 9
Johnson, Hiram, 9
joke, 123
journals, 87
   source citations, 101
joy or happiness, 241
JustinTV, 306

K

Kaling, Mindy, 164
Kardashian, Kim, 174
Kelly, Clinton, 204
Kelly, Megyn, 284
Kennedy, Caroline, 164
Keynote, 305
keynote address, 284
kindergarten, 160
King, Martin Luther, Jr., 113, 186–187
knowledge, audience, 55–56
knowledge and expertise, 75
Kolb's cycle of learning, 76–77
Kross, Ethan, 28
Kutcher, Ashton, 124, 128

L

Lady Gaga, 179
language, 57
   abstract, 160
   arbitrary, 159
   changes over time, 160
   and cultural differences, 79
   descriptive and provocative, 244
   "I," 47, 298
   oral style and, 155–167
   reframing "you" into "I" statements, 298
   sensory, 165
   specific, 78, 162
   vivid, 164
   "you," 47, 298
laptops, 160
Latino Encyclopedia, 87
LCD projector, 142, 150
leaders, 296
   formal, 296
   informal, 296
leadership, 295–297
   functions, shared, 296
   maintenance, 296
   procedural, 296
   task, 296
leading questions, 91
learning style, 76
   appeal to diverse, 76–77, 202
   models for understanding, 76–77
Legend, John, 282
length, speech, 63

Les Misérables, 184
Less I Forget: A Collection of Quotations by People
   of Color, 88
LexisNexis, 86
liberal art, 2, 3
   public speaking as, 2–4
libraries, 87
Library of Congress, 89
line graph, 144, 145
linguistic sensitivity, 157–158
LinkedIn, 87
listener relevance link(s), 13, 200, 243
listener(s)
   action-oriented, 41
   active, 41
   content-oriented, 41
   passive, 41
   people-oriented, 41
   time-oriented, 41
listening, 39
   active, 41
   behaviors, 42
   burnout, 46
   challenges, 40–41
   comprehensive, 40
   critical, 40
   discriminative, 40
   empathic, 40
   improvement strategies, 42–46
   interview and, 93
   passive, 41
   recording and, 45
   technology on, 45
   what is, 39–40
listening apprehension, 40
listening style, 41
listing, ideas, 105
live streaming panel discussions, 306
location, 63
logic, 233
logical arguments, types of, 233–237
logical conclusion/claim, 233
logical reasons order, 110
logos, 232
   rhetorical strategy of, 233–236
logos, 13, 124
Los Angeles Times, 88
lose-lose conflict management style, 299
lose-win conflict management style, 300
loudspeaker, public speaking and, 9
Lynch, Drew, 13

M

Mackay, Harvey, 122
macrostructure, 13, 47–48, 205
magazine(s), 87
   articles, source citations, 101
Maher, Bill, 85
main point
   action steps, 108, 111
   analysis and synthesis, 107
   conclusion, 126
   developing, 112
   identifying, 105–106
   parallel in structure, 108–109
   pattern selection, 109–110
   wording, 106–109
maintenance leadership role, 296
major premise, 233
management styles, 299–300
   lose-lose conflict, 299
   lose-win conflict, 300
   partial lose-lose conflict, 300
   win-lose conflict, 300
   win-win conflict, 300
mankle, 160
mapping, concept, 55, 200

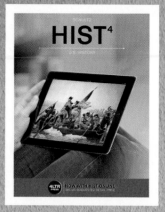

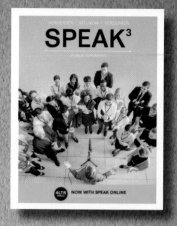

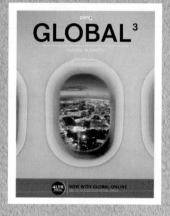

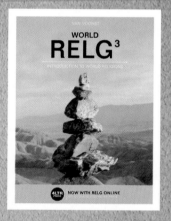

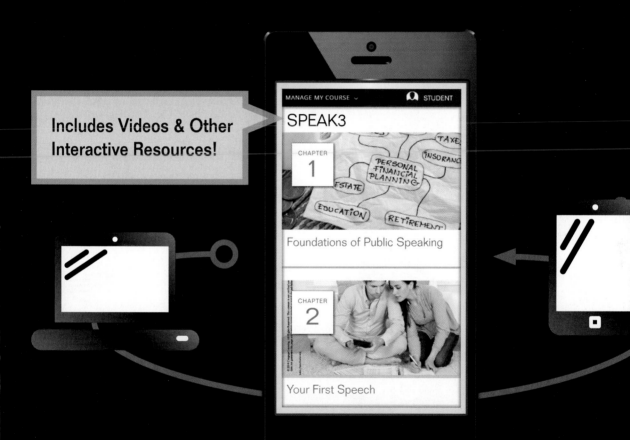

SPEAK
ONLINE

STUDY YOUR WAY
WITH STUDYBITS!

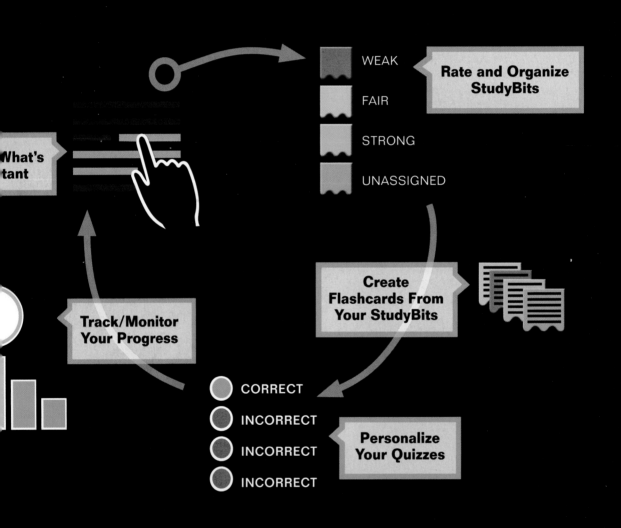

WEAK

FAIR

STRONG

UNASSIGNED

Rate and Organize StudyBits

What's tant

Create Flashcards From Your StudyBits

Track/Monitor Your Progress

CORRECT

INCORRECT

INCORRECT

INCORRECT

Personalize Your Quizzes

4LTR PRESS

SECTION SUMMARIES

1-1 Public Speaking as a Liberal Art Effective public speaking is a liberal art that make it possible for us to enact our civic responsibility to participate actively as members of a democratic society. The study of public speaking teaches us not what to think but how to think, and in so doing equips us to critically evaluate the arguments of others—a central skill for a responsible citizen living in a democracy.

1-2 Ethical Responsibilities of Public Speakers Ethical communicators adhere to five essential ethical principles: honesty, integrity, fairness, respect, and responsibility. Public speaking challenges us to behave ethically.

1-3 Public Speaking as Communication Public speaking is a specialized type of communication, so it is part of the process of creating shared meaning. Like other forms of communication, public speaking involves a sender (the speaker), a receiver (the audience), a message (the speech), channels (both traditional and technological), encoding, decoding, noise, and feedback. The context of communication is determined by the number of participants and the balance of their roles. Contexts can be intrapersonal, interpersonal, small group, or public.

1-4 Audience-Centered Speaking and the Rhetorical Situation Public speaking is an audience-centered process that occurs within a rhetorical situation that consists of speaker, audience, and occasion and is guided by exigence.

1-5 Effective Speaking Components Speakers create and achieve shared meaning with their audiences by using the rhetorical appeals of ethos, pathos, and logos and by applying those appeals to the content, structure, and delivery of the speech. Effective speakers include listener-relevance links in their content, and they use a clear structure for their material to help listeners follow what they are saying. Effective speakers are conversational, intelligible, poised, and expressive in their delivery.

Do you have to give a speech for this chapter? Use the deck of perforated speech note cards to get ready!

SPEECH NOTE CARDS

KEY TERMS

public speaking a sustained formal presentation by a speaker to an audience

liberal art a body of general knowledge needed to effectively participate in a democratic society

civic rights the essential conditions for individuals to live happy and successful lives

ethics moral principles that a society, group, or individual hold that differentiate right from wrong and good behavior from bad behavior

plagiarism passing off the ideas, words, or created works of another as one's own by failing to credit the source

communication the process of creating shared meaning

participants the individuals who assume the roles of senders and receivers during an interaction

senders participants who form and transmit messages using verbal symbols and nonverbal behaviors

receivers participants who interpret the messages sent by others

messages the verbal utterances, visual images, and nonverbal behaviors to which meaning is attributed during communication

encoding the process of putting our thoughts and feelings into words and nonverbal behaviors

decoding the process of interpreting the verbal and nonverbal messages sent by others

feedback the reactions and responses to messages that indicate to the sender whether and how a message was heard, seen, and interpreted

channels both the route traveled by a message and the means of transportation

mediated channels channels enhanced by audiovisual technology

virtual presence simulated presence made possible through the use of digital technology

interference/noise any stimulus that interferes with the process of achieving shared meaning

CHAPTER REVIEW 1

communication context the environment in which communication occurs

intrapersonal communication communicating with yourself (i.e., self-talk)

interpersonal communication communication between two people

small group communication the interaction that occurs in a group of approximately three to ten people

public communication communication that occurs among more than ten people where one message is presented to the participants who function as receivers whose own messages are limited to feedback

mass communication communication produced and transmitted via media to large audiences

rhetorical situation the composite of the occasion, speaker, and the audience that influences the speech that is given

exigence some real or perceived need that a speech might help address

speaker the source or originator of the speech

audience the specific group of people to whom your speech is directed

audience analysis the process of learning about the diverse characteristics of audience members and then, based on these characteristics, to predict how audience members are apt to listen to, understand, and be motivated to act on your speech

audience adaptation the process of tailoring your message to address exigence in terms of their unique interests, needs, and expectations

occasion the expected purpose for a speech and the setting, or location, in which the speech is given

ethos everything you say and do to convey competence and good character

pathos everything you say and do to appeal to emotions

REFLECTION

Public speaking is important to achieving success in nearly every walk of life. Effective public speaking makes it possible to enact our civic engagement responsibility actively and ethically. To assess how well you've learned what we addressed in these pages, answer the following questions. If you have trouble answering any of them, go back and review that material before reading the next chapter. Check off the questions you can answer completely.

1. _____ What is the nature and purpose of public speaking as a liberal art?

2. _____ What are five ethical responsibilities of public speakers?

3. _____ How does public speaking fit into the realm of communication?

4. _____ What is the rhetorical situation and how can it help you determine an appropriate speech goal?

5. _____ What are the components of an effective audience-centered public speech?

logos everything you say and do to appeal to logic and sound reasoning

content the information and ideas presented in the speech

listener-relevance links statements informing listeners of how and why they should be interested in or care about an idea

structure the framework that organizes the speech content

macrostructure the overall organizational framework you use to present your speech content

transitions statements that verbally summarize one main point in a speech and introduce the next one

microstructure the specific language and style you use within the sentences of your speech

delivery how you use your voice and body to present your message

SECTION SUMMARIES

2-1 Understanding the Nature of Public Speaking Apprehension Public speaking apprehension is the level of fear a person experiences when speaking. Symptoms include cognitive, physical, and emotional reactions that vary from person to person. The level of apprehension varies over the course of speaking. The most common cause of speaking apprehension is negative self-talk, which has three sources: biologically based temperament, previous experience, and level of skill. Speaking apprehension also produces recognizable behaviors during the speech: using distracting expressions, babbling, and mechanical speech.

2-2 Managing Public Speaking Apprehension Several methods are available for managing public speaking apprehension. General methods include communication orientation motivation (COM) techniques, visualization, relaxation, systematic desensitization, cognitive restructuring, self-distancing self-talk, and public speaking skills training. Specific techniques include allowing sufficient time to prepare, using presentational aids, practicing the speech aloud, dressing up, choosing an appropriate time to speak, using positive self-talk, facing the audience with confidence, and focusing on sharing your message.

2-3 Developing an Effective Speech Plan Gaining confidence through effective speech planning reduces public speaking apprehension and increases speaking effectiveness. An effective speech plan is the product of six action steps. The first step is to select a speech goal that is appropriate to the rhetorical situation. The second step is to understand your audience and adapt to it. The third step is to gather and evaluate information to use in the speech. The fourth step is to organize and develop ideas into a well-structured outline. The fifth step is to choose appropriate presentational aids. And the sixth step is to practice oral language and delivery style of the speech until you sound confident and fluent.

Do you have to give a speech for this chapter? Use the deck of perforated speech note cards to get ready!

SPEECH NOTE CARDS

KEY TERMS

public speaking apprehension the level of fear a person experiences when anticipating or actually speaking to an audience

anticipation phase the anxiety you experience prior to giving the speech, including the nervousness you feel while preparing and waiting to speak

confrontation phase the surge of anxiety you feel as you begin delivering your speech

adaptation phase the period during which your anxiety level gradually decreases

self-talk intrapersonal communication regarding success or failure in a particular situation

modeling learning by observing and then imitating those you admire or are close to

reinforcement learning from personal experiences so that past responses to our behavior shape expectations about how our future behavior will be received

communication orientation motivation (COM) methods techniques designed to reduce anxiety by helping the speaker adopt a "communication" rather than a "performance" orientation toward the speech

performance orientation viewing public speaking as a situation demanding special delivery techniques to impress an audience aesthetically or viewing audience members as hypercritical judges who will not forgive even minor mistakes

communication orientation viewing a speech as just an opportunity to talk with a number of people about an important topic

visualization a method that reduces apprehension by helping speakers develop a mental picture of themselves giving a masterful speech

relaxation exercises breathing techniques and progressive muscle relaxation exercises that help reduce anxiety

systematic desensitization a method that reduces apprehension by gradually visualizing oneself in and performing increasingly more frightening events while remaining in a relaxed state

CHAPTER REVIEW 2

cognitive restructuring the systematic process of replacing anxiety-arousing negative self-talk with anxiety-reducing positive self-talk

self-distancing self-talk a general method for minimizing the effect of public speaking anxiety on performance by talking to oneself in the second or third person

speech plan a strategy for achieving your speech goal

canons of rhetoric five general rules for effective public speeches

speech goal a specific statement of what you want your audience to know, believe, or do

chronological following an order that moves from first to last

topical following an order of interest

REFLECTION

This chapter focused on public speaking apprehension and how to manage it in ways that will help you become a confident and effective public speaker. To assess how well you've learned what we addressed in these pages, answer the following questions. If you have trouble answering any of them, go back and review that material before reading the next chapter. Check off the questions you can answer completely.

1. _____ What is public speaking apprehension? Describe its symptoms and its causes.

2. _____ Why is the goal of effective public speakers to manage rather than eliminate apprehension?

3. _____ What are some methods and techniques you can use to manage public speaking apprehension effectively?

4. _____ What are the six steps in an effective speech action plan? List and describe them below.

Step 1:

Step 2:

Step 3:

Step 4:

Step 5:

Step 6:

SECTION SUMMARIES

3-1 What Is Listening? Listening is an intentional and important component of communicating. We use many types of listening depending on the situation: appreciative listening (for enjoyment), discriminative listening (to infer additional information), comprehensive listening (to learn and understand), empathic listening (provide emotional support), or critical listening (to evaluate the worth of the message).

3-2 Listening Challenges Four challenges impede our ability to be effective listeners. First, we experience listening apprehension, or anxiety related to listening. Second, our individual biases can minimize our effectiveness as listeners. Third, our preferred listening style may not match the rhetorical situation or the speaker. And finally, our approach to processing—either active or passive listening—may not be appropriate for the rhetorical situation.

3-3 Active Listening Improvement Strategies Effective listening is an active process that requires the skills of attending, understanding, remembering, evaluating, and responding. The process of attending to a message is sharpened by getting ready to listen, resisting mental distractions while you listen, hearing the speaker out regardless of your thoughts or feelings, and identifying benefits of attending to the speaker. Understanding and remembering are enhanced by determining the speaker's organization, asking questions, silently paraphrasing, paying attention to nonverbal cues, and taking good notes. Evaluating involves critically analyzing a message to determine how truthful, useful, and trustworthy it is. To do this, you need to distinguish between facts and inferences. Responding involves providing feedback, either verbal or nonverbal, in a constructive manner.

3-4 Constructive Critiques In public speaking situations, effective listeners respond nonverbally in the form of smiles, head nods, and applause, as well as verbally by critiquing the speeches. Constructive critique statements are specific, based on observations, provide clear explanations of observations, and use nonthreatening "I" language.

Do you have to give a speech for this chapter? Use the deck of perforated speech note cards to get ready!

SPEECH NOTE CARDS

KEY TERMS

hearing the physiological process that occurs when the brain detects sound waves

listening the process of receiving, attending to, constructing meaning from, and responding to spoken or nonverbal messages

listening apprehension the anxiety we feel about listening

listening style our favored and usually unconscious approach to listening

content-oriented listeners listeners who focus on and evaluate the facts and evidence

people-oriented listeners listeners who focus on the feelings their conversational partners may have about what they are saying

action-oriented listeners listeners who focus on the ultimate point the speaker is trying to make

time-oriented listeners listeners who prefer brief and hurried conversations and often use nonverbal and verbal cues to signal that their partner needs to be more concise

passive listening the habitual and unconscious process of receiving messages

active listening the deliberate and conscious process of attending to, understanding, remembering, evaluating, and responding to messages

attending the process of intentionally perceiving and focusing on a message

understanding accurately interpreting a message

question a statement designed to clarify information or get additional details

paraphrasing putting a message into your own words

mnemonic device a memory technique in which you associate a special word or very short statement with new and longer information

evaluating critically analyzing a message to determine its truthfulness, utility, and trustworthiness

facts statements whose accuracy can be verified as true

inferences assertions based on the facts presented

responding providing feedback to the speaker; can be verbal or nonverbal

constructive critique an evaluative response that identifies what was effective and what could be improved in a message

CHAPTER REVIEW 3

REFLECTION

Effective active listening takes conscious effort and is crucial to the communication process of creating shared meaning. To assess how well you've learned what we've discussed in this chapter, answer the following questions. If you have trouble answering any of them, go back and review that material before reading the next chapter. Check off the questions you can answer completely.

1. _____ What is listening and why should you study it in a public speaking course?

2. _____ Why is effective listening challenging and what makes it most challenging for you?

3. _____ What are some specific strategies you will employ to improve your listening skills?

4. _____ What makes an effective and ethical constructive critique statement?

5. _____ What elements should be addressed in an effective constructive speech critique?

SECTION SUMMARIES

4-1 Identify Potential Speech Topics To identify a speech topic, select a subject that is important to you and that you know something about, such as a job, hobby, or social issue. Then brainstorm a list of roughly related words under each subject. Identify the two or three specific topics under each heading that are most meaningful to you and develop a concept map to flesh out smaller topic areas and related ideas.

4-2 Analyze the Audience Audience analysis is the study of the intended audience for your speech. Gather both demographic and subject-related data. Survey audience members beforehand using two-sided, multiple-response, scaled, or open-ended questions, or gather data through informal observation, by questioning the person who invited you to speak, and by making educated guesses about audience demographics and attitudes.

4-3 Ethical Uses of Audience Data Use information you collect about your audience ethically by demonstrating respect for the demographic diversity represented in your audience. You act ethically by not marginalizing or stereotyping your listeners.

4-4 Analyze the Occasion Analyze the occasion, which will affect your overall speech plan, by asking such questions as: What is the intended purpose for the speech? What is the expected length? Where will the speech be given? When will the speech be given? What equipment is necessary and available?

4-5 Select a Topic Select a topic that is appropriate for the rhetorical situation by considering complexity, interest, audience fit, and the occasion.

4-6 Write a Speech Goal Statement There are two types of speech goals. The general goal of a speech (the overarching purpose) is to entertain, to inform, or to persuade. The specific goal is a single statement that identifies the exact response the speaker wants from the audience. When writing your speech goal, make sure it contains only one goal statement phrased in a complete sentence. Revise your goal until it reflects the focus of your speech and the reaction you intend to generate.

Do you have to give a speech for this chapter? Use the deck of perforated speech note cards to get ready!

SPEECH NOTE CARDS

KEY TERMS

subject a broad area of expertise, such as movies, renewable energy, computer technology, or the Middle East

topic a narrower aspect of a subject

brainstorming an uncritical, nonevaluative process of generating associated ideas

concept mapping a visual means of exploring connections between a subject and related ideas

credibility the perception that you are knowledgeable, trustworthy, and personable

survey a direct examination of people to gather information about their ideas and opinions

two-sided items survey items that force respondents to choose between two answers, such as yes/no, for/against, or pro/con

multiple-response items survey items that give the respondents several alternative answers from which to choose

scaled items survey items that measure the direction and/or intensity of audience members' feelings or attitudes toward something

open-ended items survey items that encourage respondents to elaborate on their opinions without forcing them to answer in a predetermined way

marginalizing ignoring the values, needs, and interests of certain audience members, leaving them feeling excluded from the speaking situation

stereotyping assuming all members of a group have similar knowledge, behaviors, or beliefs simply because they belong to the group

audience diversity the range of demographic and subject-related differences represented in an audience

general goal the overall intent of the speech

specific goal a single statement that identifies the exact response a speaker wants from the audience

CHAPTER REVIEW 4

REFLECTION

To assess how well you've learned what we've discussed in this chapter, answer the following questions. If you have trouble answering any of them, go back and review the material before reading the next chapter. Check off the questions you can answer completely.

1. _____ How do you go about brainstorming potential speech topics?

2. _____ What are some kinds of demographic and subject-related audience data you should collect?

3. _____ What methods might you employ to collect audience data?

4. _____ What do we mean by using audience data ethically?

5. _____ What questions might you need to ask (and answer) to fully analyze and understand the speech occasion?

6. _____ What are the characteristics of an effective specific speech goal statement?

SECTION SUMMARIES

5-1 Initial Audience Disposition Acknowledge the audience's initial disposition by framing the speech in a way that takes into account how much audience members know about your topic and what their attitudes about it are.

5-2 Common Ground Develop common ground by using personal pronouns, asking rhetorical questions, and drawing from common experiences.

5-3 Relevance Help the audience see the relevance of your material by demonstrating timeliness (showing how the information is useful now or in the near future), demonstrating proximity (showing relevance to personal life space), and demonstrating personal impact.

5-4 Speaker Credibility Build your credibility by demonstrating knowledge and expertise, good character, and a friendly, courteous, professional disposition.

5-5 Information Comprehension and Retention Increase audience comprehension and retention of information by creating material that appeals to diverse learning styles, orienting listeners, choosing specific and familiar language, using vivid language and examples, personalizing information, and comparing unknown ideas with familiar ones.

5-6 Language and Cultural Differences Adapting to cultural differences involves demonstrating respect and working to make yourself understood, especially in a second language.

5-7 Forming a Specific Audience Adaptation Plan Develop a specific plan that ensures your speech addresses the previous six topics.

Do you have to give a speech for this chapter? Use the deck of perforated speech note cards below to get ready!

SPEECH NOTE CARDS

KEY TERMS

initial audience disposition the knowledge of and opinions about your topic that your listeners have before they hear you speak

common ground the background, knowledge, attitudes, experiences, and philosophies audience members and the speaker share

personal pronouns "we," "us," and "our"—pronouns that directly link the speaker to members of the audience

rhetorical questions questions phrased to stimulate a mental response rather than an actual spoken response from the audience

relevance adapting the information in a speech so that audience members view it as important to them

timeliness showing how information is useful now or in the near future

proximity the relevance of information to personal life space

credibility the perception that you are knowledgeable, trustworthy, and personable

knowledge and expertise how well you convince your audience that you are qualified to speak on the topic

trustworthiness the extent to which the audience can believe that what you say is accurate, true, and in their best interests

personableness the extent to which you project an agreeable or pleasing personality

learning style a person's preferred way of receiving information

transition a sentence or two that summarizes one main point and introduces the next one

CHAPTER REVIEW 5

REFLECTION

Audience adaptation is the process of tailoring your speech to the needs, interests, and expectations of your specific audience. To assess how well you've learned what we've discussed in this chapter, answer the following questions. If you have trouble answering any of them, go back and review that material before reading the next chapter. Check off the questions you can answer completely.

1. _____ How can you find out about and then address initial audience disposition toward your topic?

2. _____ What techniques can you use to emphasize aspects of common ground you share with your audience?

3. _____ What are some ways you can point to the relevance of your speech to your audience?

4. _____ How can you establish yourself as a credible speaker?

5. _____ In what ways might you promote audience comprehension and retention?

6. _____ What might you do to overcome potential language and cultural differences?

7. _____ What is involved in drafting an audience adaptation plan? Describe the elements of the plan and questions you can ask yourself to ensure your speech reaches your audience.

SECTION SUMMARIES

6-1 Locate and Evaluate Information Sources

Information for your speech can come from primary research or secondary research. Primary research is the process of collecting data about your topic directly from the real world, while secondary research is the process of locating information that has been discovered by other people. Sources for secondary research include encyclopedias, books, articles, newspapers, statistical sources, biographies, quotation books and Web sites, and government documents. Primary sources include fieldwork observations, surveys, interviews, original artifacts, and experiments.

Skim secondary sources to determine whether or not to read them in full. Skimming is a method of rapidly going through a work to determine what is covered and how. Evaluate each source for its authority, objectivity, currency, and relevance.

6-2 Select Relevant Information
The information that you collect from primary and secondary research comes in many different forms—factual statements, expert opinions, and elaborations that are presented in a variety of written, aural, or visual forms. When selecting information be sure to include a variety of cultural perspectives.

6-3 Record Information
As you find the facts, opinions, and elaborations that you want to use in your speech, record the information accurately and keep a careful account of your sources so that they can be cited appropriately during your speech. A proven method for organizing your information is to use research cards.

6-4 Cite Sources
In your speeches, as in any communication in which you use ideas that are not your own, you need to acknowledge the sources of your ideas and statements. Specifically mentioning your sources not only helps the audience evaluate the content but also adds to your credibility. In addition, citing sources will provide concrete evidence of the depth of your research. Failure to cite sources, especially when you are presenting information that is meant to substantiate a controversial point, is unethical. So, just as you would provide footnotes in a written document, you must provide oral footnotes during your speech.

Do you have to give a speech for this chapter? Use the deck of perforated speech note cards to get ready!

SPEECH NOTE CARDS

KEY TERMS

evidence any information that clarifies, explains, or otherwise adds depth or breadth to a topic

secondary research the process of locating information that has been discovered by other people

primary research the process of conducting your own study to acquire the information you need

credentials your experience or education that qualifies you to speak with authority on a specific subject

hits links to all sorts of Web pages, images, videos, articles and other sources that include material about the keywords entered into a search engine

blogs Web sites that provide personal viewpoints of their author

online social networks Web sites where communities of people interact with one another over the Internet

periodicals magazines and journals published at regular intervals

skimming a method of rapidly going through a work to determine what is covered and how

abstract a short paragraph summarizing the research findings

valid sources information sources that report factual information that can be counted on to be true

accurate sources information sources that attempt to present unbiased information and often include a balanced discussion of controversial topics

reliable sources information sources that have a history of presenting valid and accurate information

stance an attitude, perspective, or viewpoint on a topic

fieldwork observations (ethnography) a form of primary research based on fieldwork observations

interview a planned, structured conversation where one person asks questions and another answers them

interview protocol the list of questions you plan to ask

rapport-building questions non-threatening questions designed to put the interviewee at ease

primary questions introductory questions about each major interview topic

secondary questions follow-up questions designed to probe the answers given to primary questions

CHAPTER REVIEW 6

open questions broad-based questions that ask the interviewee to provide perspective, ideas, information, or opinions

closed questions narrowly focused questions that require only very brief answers

neutral questions questions phrased in ways that do not direct a person's answers

leading questions questions phrased in a way that suggests the interviewer has a preferred answer

transcribe to translate interview responses word for word into written form

hypothesis an educated guess about a cause-and-effect relationship between two or more things

factual statements information that can be verified

statistics numerical facts

examples specific instances that illustrate or explain a general factual statement

hypothetical examples specific illustrations based on reflections about future events

definition a statement that clarifies the meaning of a word or phrase

expert opinions interpretations and judgments made by authorities in a particular subject area

expert a person recognized as having mastered a specific subject, usually through long-term study

anecdotes brief, often amusing stories

narratives accounts, personal experiences, tales, or lengthier stories

comparison illuminating a point by showing similarities

contrast illuminating a point by highlighting differences

plagiarism the unethical act of representing another person's work as your own

annotated bibliography a preliminary record of the relevant sources you find pertaining to your topic

research cards individual index cards that identify information speakers might cite during a speech

oral footnote reference to an original source, made at the point in the speech where information from that source is presented

REFLECTION

Effective speeches are developed by doing good research. To do good research, you need to know where to locate different types of information and sources, as well as how to evaluate them. You also need to know how to integrate the information into your speech effectively and ethically. To assess how well you've learned what we've discussed in this chapter, answer the following questions. If you have trouble answering any of them, go back and review that material before reading the next chapter. Check off all the questions you can answer completely.

1. _____ How do you locate and evaluate information sources to develop your topic?

2. _____ What information types might you use as relevant evidence to support your topic?

3. _____ How can you go about recording information accurately?

4. _____ How do you cite sources appropriately? Use the space below to practice writing a citation for a television program, Internet source, interview, or magazine article.

SECTION SUMMARIES

7-1 Organize Main Points The first step in organizing your speech is to identify two to four main points that you want to make in your speech. You can identify main points by listing ideas that are related to the specific goal of the speech, eliminating ideas that you think the audience already knows, eliminating ideas that might be too complicated or broad, grouping some of the ideas together, and choosing two to four from those that remain. The main points can be organized in one of several patterns: time order, narrative order, topical order, or logical reasons order.

7-2 Construct a Clear Thesis Statement Your thesis statement provides a blueprint from which you will organize the body of your speech.

7-3 Develop Main Points Subpoints are statements that elaborate on the main point, while the supporting material provides the evidence that backs up a subpoint.

7-4 Create Transitions Section transitions bridge major parts of the speech and occur between the introduction and the body, between main points within the body, and between the body and the conclusion. Section transitions should be planned and placed in the outline as parenthetical statements where they are to occur. Whereas section transitions serve as the glue that holds together the macrostructural elements of your speech, signposts serve as the glue that holds together the subpoints and supporting material within each main point. Together, these types of transitions serve as a roadmap for listeners to follow as you present your speech.

7-5 Outline the Speech Body A formal speech outline is a diagram of your speech material that presents how your ideas are related to one another. Creating a detailed outline will help you confirm that your arguments are strong and that they flow in logical order. The result will be a more effective speech.

Do you have to give a speech for this chapter? Use the deck of perforated speech note cards to get ready!

SPEECH NOTE CARDS

KEY TERMS

organizing the process of arranging your speech material

preparation outline a first-draft speech outline that identifies main points but does not specify clearly how each is related to the speech goal

parallel wording that follows the same structural pattern, often using the same introductory words

time order organizing the main points of the speech in a chronological sequence or by steps in a process

narrative order organizing the main points of the speech as a story or series of stories

topical order organizing the main points of the speech using some logical relationship among them

logical reasons order organizing the main points of a persuasive speech by the reasons that support the speech goal

thesis statement a one- or two-sentence summary of the speech that incorporates the general and specific goals and previews the main points

subpoints statements that elaborate on a main point

supporting material evidence you gathered through secondary and primary research along with the logical reasoning you use to link it to the main point it supports

transitions words, phrases, or sentences that show the relationship between two ideas

section transitions complete sentences that show the relationship between major parts of a speech

signposts words or phrases that connect pieces of supporting material to the main point or subpoint they address

formal speech outline a sentence representation of the hierarchical and sequential relationships among the ideas presented in the speech

CHAPTER REVIEW 7

REFLECTION

Effective public speeches are well organized. The body of the speech includes main points and subpoints that should be written in complete sentences and checked to make sure that they are clear, parallel in structure, meaningful, and limited in number to four or fewer. To assess how well you've learned what we've discussed in this chapter, answer the following questions. If you have trouble answering any of them, go back and review that material before reading the next chapter. Check off the questions you can answer completely.

1. _____ Why should you organize your speech body into two to four main points using an appropriate main point pattern?

2. _____ How do you construct a clear thesis statement?

3. _____ How do you go about developing main points?

4. _____ How are effective section transitions constructed and why are they important in public speeches?

5. _____ What is a formal speech outline? Use the space below to practice creating a formal speech outline.

SECTION SUMMARIES

8-1 The Introduction A speech's introduction and conclusion are important because we are more likely to remember the first and last items conveyed orally in a series than the items in between. Listeners are more likely to remember the beginning and ending of your speech than what you say in the body. The introduction and conclusion are also important because of the need for listeners to quickly grasp your goal and main points as they listen to your speech and to remember them after you've finished.

8-2 Selecting the Best Introduction The introduction to the speech establishes the relationships the speaker will have with the audience. When preparing an introduction, you should create several options, and then choose the one that best fits the specific audience and speech goals you have.

8-3 The Conclusion An effective conclusion heightens the impact of a good speech by summarizing the main points and providing a sense of closure. If running out of space, start deleting from the last sentence up. Two effective strategies for providing that closure, or clinching, are using vivid imagery or articulating an appeal to action. Techniques for getting attention are useful for creating vivid imagery. Appealing to action is common for persuasive speeches.

8-4 The Complete Formal Outline with Reference List Regardless of the type and length of a speech, preparation should include creation of a formal outline. This includes sources, title, and detailed outline. Sources should be formatted using a formal bibliographical style. The title can be a statement of the speech subject, a question, or a creative title. In the formal outline, all major points and subpoints should each express only a single idea and are all written in complete sentences. Each subpoint supports the major point to which it relates.

Do you have to give a speech for this chapter? Use the deck of perforated speech note cards to get ready!

SPEECH NOTE CARDS

KEY TERMS

primacy-recency effect the tendency to remember the first and last items conveyed orally in a series rather than the items in between

startling statement an expression or example that grabs your listeners' attention by shocking them in some way

questions requests for information that encourage your audience to think about something related to your topic

direct question a question that demands an overt response from the audience, usually by a show of hands

story an account of something that has happened (actual) or could happen (hypothetical)

joke an anecdote or a piece of wordplay designed to be funny and make people laugh

personal reference a brief story about something that happened to you or a hypothetical situation that listeners can imagine themselves in

quotation a comment made by and attributed to someone other than the speaker

action an attention-getting act designed to highlight and arouse interest in your topic or purpose

creating suspense wording an attention getter so that what is described generates initial uncertainty or mystery and excites the audience

clincher a one- or two-sentence statement in a conclusion that provides a sense of closure by driving home the importance of your speech in a memorable way

appeal to action a statement in a conclusion that describes the behavior you want your listeners to follow after they have heard your arguments

formal outline A full sentence outline of your speech that includes internal references and a reference list

CHAPTER REVIEW 8

REFLECTION

You finish organizing your speech by preparing an introduction and a conclusion, as well as listing the sources used, writing a title (if required), and reviewing the formal outline. To assess how well you've learned what we've discussed in this chapter, answer the following questions. If you have any trouble answering any of them, go back and review the material before reading the next chapter. Check off the questions you can answer completely.

1. _____ What are the goals of an effective speech introduction?

2. _____ What are the ways that you can get an audience's attention at the beginning of your speech? List those ways and write an example of one as a practice.

3. _____ What are the goals of an effective speech conclusion?

4. _____ What techniques can you use to successfully clinch your speech? List some methods, and then write an example of one as a practice.

5. _____ How do you go about completing the outline and reference list?

SECTION SUMMARIES

9-1 Benefits of Presentational Aids Presentational aids are useful when they help audience members understand and remember important information.

9-2 Types of Presentational Aids The most common types of visual aids are objects, models, photographs, simple drawings and diagrams, maps, charts, and graphs. Audio aids include recordings of music, speeches, and environmental sounds. Audiovisual aids include clips from movies, television programs, commercials, and YouTube. Other sensory aids enhance the verbal message by focusing on taste, smell, or touch. Methods that speakers can use to present presentational aids include posters, flipcharts, whiteboards and chalkboards, handouts, and computerized slide shows using a computer, projector, and screen.

9-3 Choosing Presentational Aids Choose presentational aids for the most important ideas you want your audience to understand and remember; ideas that are complex or difficult to explain verbally but would be easier to explain (audio)visually. Determine the number of presentational aids you'll need; size of the audience; availability of the necessary equipment; and whether making or getting the visual aid or equipment is cost-effective and a good use of time.

9-4 Preparing Presentational Aids Design your visual aids with the following principles in mind: Use a print or font size that can be seen easily by your entire audience. Use a font that is easy to read and pleasing to the eye. Use upper- and lowercase type. Try to limit the lines of type to six or fewer. Include only information that you will emphasize in your speech. Lay out information in an aesthetically pleasing manner. Add clip art where appropriate. Use color strategically.

9-5 Displaying Presentational Aids Display your aids in a professional manner so that it enhances your credibility and the speech as a whole.

9-6 Using Presentational Aids Practice using presentational aids as you rehearse. Carefully plan when to use each aid. Position aids and equipment before starting your speech. Show presentational aids only when talking about them; introduce video and audio clips to give your audience a context for them. Display items so the entire audience can see them. Talk to your audience, not to your presentational aid. Avoid passing objects around the audience. Keep your audience focused on *you* as the speaker as well as your presentational aids.

Do you have to give a speech for this chapter? Use the deck of perforated speech note cards to get ready!

SPEECH NOTE CARDS

KEY TERMS

presentational aid any visual, audio, audiovisual, or other sensory material used in a speech

visual aid a presentational aid that enhances a speech by allowing the audience to see what the speaker is describing or explaining

audio aid a presentational aid that enhances the speaker's verbal message with additional sound

audiovisual aid a presentational aid that enhances the speech using a combination of sight and sound

actual object an inanimate or animate sample of the idea you are communicating

model a three-dimensional scaled-down or scaled-up version of an actual object

diagram a type of drawing that shows how the whole relates to its parts

chart a graphic representation that distills a lot of information into an easily interpreted visual format

flowchart a chart that diagrams a sequence of steps through a complicated process

organizational chart a chart that shows the structure of an organization in terms of rank and chain of command

pie chart a chart that shows the relationships among parts of a single unit

graph a diagram that presents numerical information in visual form

bar graph a graph that uses vertical or horizontal bars to show relationships between or among two or more variables

line graph a graph that indicates changes in one or more variables over time

flipchart a large pad of paper mounted on an easel

handout material printed on sheets of paper and distributed to the audience

CHAPTER REVIEW 9

REFLECTION

Presentational aids are useful when they help audience members understand and remember important information. To assess how well you've learned what we've discussed in this chapter, answer the following questions. If you have trouble answering any of them, go back and review that material before reading the next chapter. Check off the questions you can answer completely.

1. _____ What are the benefits of using presentational aids in your speech?

2. _____ Identify the different types of presentational aids, including a list of visual aids. If you are a visual learner, make thumbnail sketches of each type of visual aid.

3. _____ What are some criteria for choosing appropriate presentational aids?

4. _____ What are some guidelines you can follow when preparing presentational aids?

5. _____ How might you display presentational aids in a speech?

6. _____ What should you consider when using presentational aids during your speech?

SECTION SUMMARIES

10-1 Oral Style Oral style refers to the manner in which one conveys messages through the spoken word. An effective oral style tends toward short sentences and familiar language; features plural personal pronouns; features descriptive words and phrases that appeal to the ear and are designed to sustain listener interest and promote retention; incorporates clear section transitions and signposts.

10-2 Speaking Appropriately Being appropriate means using language that adapts to the audience's needs, interests, knowledge, and attitudes and avoids alienating or offending listeners. Appropriate language demonstrates respect for all audience members. Hallmarks of appropriate language include using "we" language and bias-free language; adapting to cultural diversity; and avoiding offensive humor, profanity, vulgarity, and hate speech.

10-3 Speaking Accurately Being accurate begins with a realization that words are only representations of ideas, objects, and feelings. Meaning is a product of both denotation (dictionary meaning) and connotation (positive, neutral, and negative feelings and evaluations that words evoke). To ensure that your ideas are interpreted accurately, consider denotation, connotation, and dialect.

10-4 Speaking Clearly Clear language is specific and precise. Specific language clarifies meaning. Precise words narrow down a broad idea. It helps to have a large vocabulary when looking for exact words. Study vocabulary-building books, look up meanings of words you don't understand, and use a thesaurus to identify synonyms. Clarity can also be achieved by providing details and examples.

10-5 Speaking Vividly Vivid language is full of life—vigorous, bright, and intense. Increase the vividness of your language by using sensory language as well as rhetorical figures and structures of speech.

Do you have to give a speech for this chapter? Use the deck of perforated speech note cards to get ready!

SPEECH NOTE CARDS

KEY TERMS

oral style the manner in which one conveys messages through the spoken word

speaking appropriately using language that adapts to the needs, interests, knowledge, and attitudes of the listener and avoiding language that alienates audience members

verbal immediacy when the language you use reduces the psychological distance between you and your audience

generic language language that uses words that apply only to one sex, race, or other group as though they represent everyone

nonparallelism denotes when terms are changed because of the sex, race, or other group characteristics of the individual

marking the addition of sex, race, age, or other group designations to a description

irrelevant association emphasizing one person's relationship to another when that relationship is irrelevant to the point

accurate language language that conveys your meaning precisely

intelligible capable of being understood

denotation the explicit meaning a language community formally gives a word; a word's "dictionary meaning"

context the position of a word in a sentence and its relationship to other words around it

connotation the positive, neutral, or negative feelings or evaluations we associate with a word

dialect a unique form of a more general language spoken by a specific cultural or co-cultural group

speech communities smaller groups that speak a common dialect

Standard English the form of English taught in American schools and detailed in grammar handbooks

specific language language that uses precise words to narrow what is understood from a general category to a particular item or group within that category

jargon unique technical terminology of a trade or profession that is not generally understood by outsiders

slang informal, nonstandard vocabulary and nonstandard definitions assigned to words by a social group or subculture

vocalized pauses unnecessary words interjected into sentences to fill moments of silence

vivid language language that is full of life—vigorous, bright, and intense

CHAPTER REVIEW 10

sensory language language that appeals to the senses of seeing, hearing, tasting, smelling, and feeling

rhetorical figures of speech phrases that make striking comparisons between things that are not obviously alike

rhetorical structures of speech phrases that combine ideas in a particular way

simile a direct comparison of dissimilar things using *like* or *as*

metaphor an implied comparison between two unlike things without using *like* or *as*

analogy an extended metaphor

alliteration repetition of consonant sounds at the beginning of words that are near one another

assonance repetition of vowel sounds in a phrase or phrases

onomatopoeia words that sound like the things they stand for

personification attributing human qualities to a concept or an inanimate object

repetition restating words, phrases, or sentences for emphasis

antithesis combining contrasting ideas in the same sentence

REFLECTION

Your overall goal with regard to language and oral style is to be appropriate, accurate, clear, and vivid. If you have trouble answering any of the following questions, go back and review that material before reading the next chapter. Check off the questions you can answer completely.

1. _____ In what ways does oral style differ from written style?

2. _____ What are some guidelines to determine appropriate words for the audience and occasion?

3. _____ How do you choose the most accurate words to convey your ideas?

4. _____ What does it mean to use clear language?

5. _____ What are some examples of vivid words that appeal to the senses?

6. _____ List and give examples of rhetorical figures and structures of speech you can use to enliven a speech.

SECTION SUMMARIES

11-1 Characteristics of Effective Delivery Delivery refers to the use of voice and body to communicate the message of the speech; it is what the audience sees and hears. Effective delivery is conversational and animated.

11-2 Use of Voice One physical element of delivery is the use of voice. By varying the four characteristics of voice (pitch, volume, rate, and quality) and using strategically placed pauses, you can ensure that your speech is intelligible to your audience and is vocally expressive.

11-3 Use of Body During a speech, you can use your body (eye contact, facial expressions, gestures, movement, posture, poise, and appearance) to convey ethos, reinforce the emotional tone of your ideas, and clarify structure.

11-4 Delivery Methods Impromptu speeches are delivered on the spot without notes or much advanced preparation. Scripted speeches are prepared in advance and delivered by reading from or memorizing the written copy. Extemporaneous speeches are researched ahead of time but delivered without a script.

11-5 Rehearsal Effective speakers rehearse in a series of sessions consisting of a practice, an analysis, and another practice. During these sessions, it is important to use a keyword outline of the speaking notes; you should also practice using presentational aids and an effective oral language and delivery style.

11-6 Adapting while Delivering the Speech Speakers need to adapt their speeches to the audience. To do this, be aware of audience feedback, be prepared with additional material, correct yourself when you misspeak, adapt to unexpected events and audience reactions with poise, and handle questions respectfully.

11-7 Adapting Your Speech for Virtual Audiences Today, speakers must adapt their speeches for multiple audiences, including unintended ones on the Internet. Choose presentational aids that work in an online environment, become proficient with technology, and follow the strategies of effective speaking.

Do you have to give a speech for this chapter? Use the deck of perforated speech note cards to get ready!

SPEECH NOTE CARDS

KEY TERMS

delivery how a message is communicated orally and visually through the use of voice and body

nonverbal communication all speech elements other than the words themselves

conversational style delivery that seems spontaneous, relaxed, and informal and allows the speaker to talk *with*, not *at*, an audience

spontaneity a naturalness of speech where what is said sounds as if the speaker is really thinking about the ideas *and* the audience as he or she speaks

animated delivery delivery that is lively, energetic, enthusiastic, and dynamic

voice the sound you produce using your vocal organs

pitch the highness or lowness of the sounds you produce

volume how loudly or softly you speak

rate the speed at which you talk

quality the tone, timbre, or sound of your voice

intelligible capable of being understood

articulation using the tongue, palate, teeth, jaw movement, and lips to shape vocalized sounds that combine to produce a word

pronunciation the form and accent of various syllables of a word

accent the inflection, tone, and speech habits typical of native speakers of a language

vocal expression variety you create in your voice through changing pitch, volume, and rate, as well as stressing certain words and using pauses

monotone a voice in which the pitch, volume, and rate remain constant, with no word, idea, or sentence differing significantly in sound from any other

up-talk the tendency to end every sentence with a rising intonation

vocal fry a creaky vocal effect produced by slowly fluttering the vocal cords, resulting in a popping or creaking sound at the bottom of the vocal register

stress emphasis placed on certain words by speaking them more loudly than the rest of the sentence

pauses moments of silence strategically placed to enhance meaning

appearance the way you look to others

posture the position or bearing of the body

poise the graceful and controlled use of the body that gives the impression of self-assurance, calm, and dignity.

eye contact looking directly at the people to whom you are speaking

CHAPTER REVIEW 11

audience contact creating a sense of looking listeners in the eye when speaking to large audiences

facial expression eye and mouth movements that convey emotions

nonverbal immediacy facial expressions that communicate that you are personable and likeable

gestures the movements of your hands, arms, and fingers

movement changing the position or location of the entire body

motivated movement movement with a specific purpose

impromptu speech a speech that is delivered with only seconds or minutes of advance notice for preparation and is usually presented without referring to notes of any kind

scripted speech a speech that is prepared by creating a complete written manuscript and delivered by reading a written copy or from memory

extemporaneous speech a speech that is researched and planned ahead of time, but the exact wording is not scripted and will vary from presentation to presentation

rehearsing practicing the presentation of your speech aloud

speaking notes a keyword or phrase outline of your speech, plus hard-to-remember information such as quotations and statistics, as well as delivery cues designed to trigger memory

REFLECTION

Delivery refers to the use of voice and body in presenting speeches. Effective delivery is conversational and animated. If you have trouble answering any of the following questions, go back and review that material before reading the next chapter. Check off the questions you can answer completely.

1. _____ What are the characteristics of effective delivery?

2. _____ How do you use your voice and body effectively to deliver a speech? Are there any areas of vocal expression or body language that you find difficult to implement when giving a speech? Which ones? How will you help yourself overcome those delivery challenges?

3. _____ What are the different speech delivery methods? Describe them here.

4. _____ How do you go about rehearsing your speech? Is there a speech type you feel more comfortable and confident delivering? If so, what can you do to bring your confidence level for the other types of delivery up to the same level?

5. _____ What can you do to adapt delivery while giving your speech?

6. _____ What special adaptation guidelines should you consider when delivering your speech to virtual audiences?

SECTION SUMMARIES

12-1 Characteristics of Effective Informative Speaking Effective informative speeches are intellectually stimulating (they pique curiosity and interest), relevant (audience cares about the topic), creative (they result from productive thinking), memorable (audience has a clear takeaway), and address diverse learning styles (they connect more deeply with more listeners).

12-2 Methods of Informing We can inform by describing something, defining it, comparing and contrasting it with other things, narrating stories about it, or demonstrating it. Descriptions address the who, what, where, when, why, and how of the topic. You can define something by classifying it, explaining its derivations and history, explaining its use or function, or by using antonym or synonym.

12-3 Informative Process Speeches Effective process speeches require you to carefully delineate the steps and the order in which they occur. The steps typically become the main points, and concrete explanations of each step become the subpoints.

12-4 Informative Expository Speeches Expository speeches are well-researched explanations of complex ideas. Types of expository speeches include those that explain political, economic, social, religious, or ethical issues; those that explain events or forces of history; those that explain a theory, principle, or law; and those that explain a creative work.

Do you have to give a speech for this chapter? Use the deck of perforated speech note cards to get ready!

SPEECH NOTE CARDS

KEY TERMS

informative speech a speech whose goal is to explain or describe facts, truths, and principles in a way that stimulates interest, facilitates understanding, and increases the likelihood of remembering

intellectually stimulating information that is new to audience members and is explained in a way that piques their curiosity

creative information that produces original, innovative ideas

productive thinking to contemplate something from a variety of perspectives

description a method of informing used to create an accurate, vivid, verbal picture of an object, geographic feature, setting, or image

definition a method of informing that explains something by identifying its meaning

synonym a word that has the same or a similar meaning

antonym a word that is directly opposite in meaning

comparison and contrast a method of informing that focuses on how something is similar to and different from other things

narration a method of informing that explains something by recounting events

demonstration a method of informing that shows how something is done, displays the stages of a process, or depicts how something works

process speech a speech that explains and shows how something is done, is made, or works

expository speech an informative presentation that provides carefully researched in-depth knowledge about a complex topic

CHAPTER REVIEW 12

REFLECTION

An informative speech is one whose goal is to explain or describe facts, truths, and principles in a way that stimulates interest, facilitates understanding, and increases the likelihood that audiences will remember. In short, informative speeches are designed to educate an audience. If you have trouble answering any of the following questions, go back and review that material before reading the next chapter. Check off the questions you can answer completely.

1. _____ What are the characteristics of informative speeches?

2. _____ What are the major methods of informing? Describe each here.

3. _____ What are the three main categories of process speeches? Give examples of topics for each.

4. _____ How do you prepare an informative process speech?

5. _____ List common categories of expository speech topics and give an example of each.

6. _____ How do you prepare an informative expository speech?

SECTION SUMMARIES

13-1 The Nature of Persuasion Persuasion is the process of influencing people's attitudes, beliefs, values, or behaviors, and persuasive speaking is doing so in a public speech. Persuasive messages differ from informative messages in that the primary goal is to seek agreement and sometimes to incite action. Both senders and receivers must pay special attention to the ethical principles of communication when creating and interpreting persuasive messages.

13-2 Processing Persuasive Messages The elaboration likelihood model (ELM) describes how audiences process persuasive messages. Understanding this model helps us focus on how to use logos, ethos, and pathos appeals as we construct and deliver persuasive speeches, as well as when we evaluate the worth of the persuasive messages we encounter in our daily lives.

13-3 The Rhetorical Strategy of Logos Logos is the means of persuasion devoted to appeals to logic and reasoning. You reason with your audience by making an argument that draws inferences from factual information to support a conclusion. You can reason inductively or deductively by addressing three basic elements of an argument: the claim, the support, and the warrant. Four common types of arguments used in persuasive messages are sign, example, analogy, and causation. When creating persuasive messages, it is important to avoid reasoning fallacies; when interpreting persuasive messages, it is important to discern them. Because you will rely on evidence to support your reasons, you must make sure it comes from a well-respected source, is still valid, is relevant to the argument, and is likely to persuade your audience.

13-4 The Rhetorical Strategy of Ethos Ethos is the means of persuasion devoted to conveying good character, competence, and credibility. You convey good character by demonstrating goodwill. Your goal is to encourage your audience to believe you understand them, empathize with them, and are responsive to them. You convey competence and credibility by explaining your competence, establishing common ground, using evidence from respected sources, and being nonverbally and vocally expressive in your delivery.

13-5 The Rhetorical Strategy of Pathos Pathos is the means of persuasion devoted to emotional appeals. You can appeal to negative emotions such as fear, guilt, shame, anger, and sadness. Or you can appeal to positive emotions such as happiness and joy, pride, relief, hope, and compassion. To appeal to emotions, tell vivid stories, use startling statistics, incorporate listener relevance links, use striking presentational aids and provocative language, and be vocally and visually expressive when delivering your message.

Do you have to give a speech for this chapter? Use the deck of perforated speech note cards to get ready!

SPEECH NOTE CARDS

KEY TERMS

persuasion the process of influencing people's attitudes, beliefs, values, or behaviors

persuasive speaking the process of influencing people's attitudes, beliefs, values, or behaviors in a public speech

argument articulating a position with the support of logos, ethos, and pathos

claim the proposition or conclusion to be proven

support the reason or evidence the speaker offers as the grounds for accepting the conclusion

warrant the reasoning process that connects the support to the claim

inductive reasoning arriving at a general conclusion based on several pieces of specific evidence

deductive reasoning arriving at a conclusion based on a major premise and minor premise

major premise a general principle that most people agree upon

minor premise a specific point that fits within the major premise

syllogism the three-part form of deductive reasoning

argue from sign to support a claim by providing evidence that the events that signal the claim have occurred

argue from example to support a claim by providing one or more individual examples

argue from analogy to support a claim with a single comparable example that is significantly similar to the subject of the claim

argue from causation to support a claim by citing events that have occurred that result in the claim

reasoning fallacies errors in reasoning

hasty generalization a fallacy that presents a generalization that is either not supported with evidence or is supported with only one weak example

false cause a fallacy that occurs when the alleged cause fails to be related to, or to produce, the effect

either/or a fallacy that argues there are only two alternatives when, in fact, there are many

straw man a fallacy that occurs when a speaker weakens the opposing position by misrepresenting it and then attacks that weaker position

ad hominem a fallacy that occurs when a speaker attacks or praises a person making an argument rather than addressing the argument itself

CHAPTER REVIEW 13

goodwill a perception the audience forms of a speaker who they believe understands them, empathizes with them, and is responsive to them

empathy the ability to see the world through the eyes of someone else

responsive when speakers show that they care about the audience by acknowledging feedback, especially subtle negative cues

terminal credibility perception of a speaker's expertise at the end of the speech

initial credibility perception of a speaker's expertise at the beginning of the speech

derived credibility strategies employed throughout the speech that signal a speaker's expertise

emotions the buildup of action-specific energy

negative emotions disquieting feelings people experience

fear feeling when we perceive no control over a situation that threatens us

guilt feeling when we personally violate a moral, ethical, or religious code that we hold dear

shame feeling when we have violated a moral code and it is revealed to someone we think highly of

anger feeling when we are faced with an obstacle in the way of something we want

sadness feeling when we fail to achieve a goal or experience a loss or separation

positive emotions feelings that people enjoy experiencing

happiness or joy the buildup of positive energy when we accomplish something or have a satisfying interaction or relationship

pride feeling of self-satisfaction and increased self-esteem as the result of an accomplishment

relief feeling when a threatening situation has been alleviated

hope emotional energy that stems from believing something desirable is likely to happen

compassion feeling of selfless concern for the suffering of another

REFLECTION

Persuasion is the process of influencing people's attitudes, beliefs, values, or behaviors, and persuasive speaking is doing so in a public speech. To assess how well you've learned the concepts in this chapter, answer the following questions. If you have trouble answering any of them, go back and review that material before reading the next chapter. Check off the questions you can answer completely.

1. _____ What is the nature of persuasive messages compared to informative ones?

2. _____ How do people process persuasive messages?

3. _____ What is the role of logos in persuasive messages?

4. _____ What are three types of logical arguments?

5. _____ What unique pitfalls do you need to be aware of when using the rhetorical strategy of logos?

6. _____ What is the role of ethos in persuasive messages?

7. _____ What is the role of pathos in persuasive messages?

8. _____ What are the advantages and disadvantages of appealing to negative emotions? To positive emotions?

SECTION SUMMARIES

14-1 Audience Attitude Persuasive speeches are designed to influence the attitudes, beliefs, values, or behaviors of audience members. This chapter focused on creating effective and ethical persuasive speeches. The first step in preparing an effective and ethical persuasive speech is to analyze your target audience to determine where they stand with regard to your topic so you can decide whether a speech to convince or a speech to actuate is most appropriate.

14-2 Identifying Your Proposition You can construct a persuasive speech goal phrased as a proposition that is based on your audience's initial attitude toward your topic. An audience may be opposed to the proposition, have no opinion (because they are uninformed, impartial, or apathetic), or be in favor. Generally, if the target audience is opposed to your proposition, seek incremental change. If they have no opinion, seek agreement. If they are in favor, seek action.

14-3 Persuasive Speech Patterns After formulating a proposition, you will choose an organizational framework. If you seek agreement through a speech to convince, you will likely select from among four frameworks: comparative advantages, criteria satisfaction, refutative, or statement of reasons. If you seek action, you will likely select from among three common frameworks—problem-solution, problem-cause-solution, or motivated sequence—to organize your arguments. One important element in an effective actuation persuasive speech is a call to action.

14-4 Ethical Guidelines for Persuasive Speeches Persuasive speakers must evaluate their speech plan based on the ethical guidelines you have learned as well as some additional ones that are specific to persuasive speeches. These include advocating the honest belief of the speaker, providing choice for the audience, using supporting information that is representative, using emotional appeal to engage audiences, and honestly presenting speaker credibility. Persuasive speaking is challenging but can also be extremely rewarding for those who do so effectively and ethically.

Do you have to give a speech for this chapter? Use the deck of perforated speech note cards to get ready!

SPEECH NOTE CARDS

KEY TERMS

target audience the group of people you most want to persuade

incremental change attempting to move your audience only a small degree in your direction

uninformed the audience doesn't know enough about a topic to have formed an opinion

neutral the audience has some information about a topic but does not really understand why one position is preferred and so still has no opinion

apathetic the audience is uninterested in, unconcerned about, or indifferent toward your topic

proposition the specific goal of a persuasive speech stated as a declarative sentence that clearly indicates the position the speaker will advocate

proposition of fact a statement designed to convince the audience that something did or did not exist or occur, is or is not true, or will or will not occur

proposition of value a statement designed to convince the audience that something is good, bad, desirable, undesirable, fair, unfair, moral, immoral, sound, unsound, beneficial, harmful, important, or unimportant

proposition of policy a statement designed to convince the audience that they should take a specific course of action

speech to convince a speech designed to refocus or change an audience's belief or attitude

speech to actuate a speech designed to persuade an audience to action

statement of reasons a straightforward organization in which you present your best-supported reasons in a meaningful order

comparative advantages an organization that shows that one alternative is better than any of the others

criteria satisfaction an indirect organization that seeks audience agreement on criteria that should be considered when evaluating a particular proposition and then shows how the proposition satisfies those criteria

refutative an organization that persuades by both challenging the opposing position and bolstering one's own

problem-solution a form of persuasive organization that reveals details about a problem and proposes solutions to it

problem-cause-solution a form of persuasive organization that examines a problem, its cause(s), and solutions designed to eliminate or alleviate the underlying cause(s)

motivated sequence a form of persuasive organization that combines a problem-solution pattern with explicit appeals designed to motivate the audience

CHAPTER REVIEW 14

REFLECTION

Persuasive speeches are designed to influence the attitudes, beliefs, values, or behaviors of audience members. This chapter focused on creating effective and ethical persuasive speeches. To assess how well you've learned what we've discussed in this chapter, answer the following questions. If you have trouble answering any of them, go back and review that material before reading the next chapter. Check off the questions you can answer completely.

1. _____ Why is it important to consider the initial audience attitude when constructing your persuasive speech goal?

2. _____ How do you phrase a persuasive speech goal as a proposition? Explain using examples.

3. _____ What are some dispositional persuasive speech frameworks?

4. _____ What are some actuation persuasive speech frameworks?

5. _____ Which persuasive speech framework do you feel more confident or comfortable delivering? What techniques can you use to bring your confidence with the other framework up to the same level?

6. _____ What ethical communication guidelines should you follow as a persuasive speaker?

SECTION SUMMARIES

15-1 Speeches of Welcome A speech of welcome is usually a very brief, formal ceremonial address that greets and expresses pleasure for the presence of a person or an organization. You must be familiar with the group that you are representing and the occasion. A speech of welcome invites listeners to agree that the occasion is friendly and their attendance is appreciated. The conclusion of the speech should briefly express your hope for the outcome of the visit, event, or relationship.

15-2 Speeches of Introduction Speeches of introduction should honestly represent the person being introduced. Do not hype a speaker's credentials or over-praise the speaker. If you set the audience's expectations too high, even a good speaker may have trouble living up to them.

15-3 Speeches of Nomination The goal of a speech of nomination is to highlight the qualities that make this person the most credible candidate. To do so, first clarify the importance of the position, honor, or award by describing the responsibilities involved, related challenges or issues, and the characteristics needed to fulfill it. Second, list the candidate's personal and professional qualifications that meet those criteria. Finally, formally place the candidate's name in nomination, creating a dramatic climax to clinch your speech.

15-4 Speeches of Recognition A speech of recognition is a ceremonial presentation that acknowledges someone and usually presents an award, a prize, or a gift to the individual or a representative of a group.

15-5 Speeches of Acceptance The goal of an acceptance speech is to convey a sincere appreciation for the honor or recognition being bestowed. Audiences expect award and honor recipients to give an acceptance speech and to keep it short—one to two minutes maximum.

15-6 Speeches of Tribute Common types of speeches of tribute include toasts, roasts, and eulogies. A toast pays tribute to an occasion or a person and is usually offered at the start of a meal. A roast is a unique tribute characterized by good-natured insults and teasing, funny anecdotes, and outlandish personal stories. A eulogy is a speech that praises someone's life accomplishments and memorializes the person after death.

15-7 Other Ceremonial Speeches Graduations, holidays, anniversaries of major events, and special events also call for ceremonial speeches. Commencement, commemorative, and keynote addresses fall into this category, as do speeches of dedication, farewell, and entertainment.

Do you have to give a speech for this chapter? Use the deck of perforated speech note cards to get ready!

SPEECH NOTE CARDS

KEY TERMS

speech of welcome a brief, formal ceremonial address that greets and expresses pleasure for the presence of a person or an organization

master of ceremonies an individual designated to set the mood of the program, introduce participants, and keep the program moving

speech of introduction a brief ceremonial speech that establishes a supportive climate for the main speaker, highlights the speaker's credibility by familiarizing the audience with pertinent biographical information, and generates enthusiasm for listening to the speaker and topic

speech of nomination a ceremonial presentation that proposes a nominee for an elected office, honor, position, or award

speech of recognition a ceremonial presentation that acknowledges someone and usually presents an award, a prize, or a gift to the individual or a representative of a group

speech of acceptance a ceremonial speech given to acknowledge receipt of an honor or award

speech of tribute a ceremonial speech that praises or celebrates a person, a group, or an event

toast a ceremonial speech offered at the start of a reception or meal that pays tribute to the occasion or to a person

roast an event where guests provide short speeches of tribute about the featured guests that are developed with humorous stories and anecdotes

eulogy a ceremonial speech of tribute during a funeral or memorial service that praises someone's life and accomplishments

commencement address a speech of tribute praising graduating students and inspiring them to reach for their goals

commemorative address a speech of tribute that celebrates national holidays or anniversaries of important events

keynote address a ceremonial speech that both sets the tone and generates enthusiasm for the topic of a conference or convention

dedication a speech of tribute that honors a worthy person or group by naming a structure, monument, or park after them

farewell a speech of tribute honoring someone who is leaving an organization

speech to entertain a humorous speech that makes a serious point

CHAPTER REVIEW 15

REFLECTION

You'll likely have occasion to give speeches to welcome, introduce, nominate, recognize, accept, and tribute. If you have trouble answering any of the questions below, go back and review that material before reading the next chapter. Check off the questions you can answer completely.

1. _____ What should you include in a speech of welcome?

2. _____ Why should a speech of introduction be brief?

3. _____ What is your goal in a speech of nomination?

4. _____ When might you be expected to give a speech of recognition?

5. _____ What are the key elements of an effective acceptance speech?

6. _____ What are some common types of speeches of tribute?

7. _____ What are some other types of ceremonial speeches?

8. _____ Which types of ceremonial speeches do you anticipate being asked to deliver in the future? List some ways you can prepare now for delivering a variety of ceremonial speeches in the future.

SECTION SUMMARIES

16-1 Leadership Leadership is about influence; in group situations, it is shared. To facilitate the work of the group, each member needs a defined and specific leadership role: task leadership, procedural leadership, or maintenance leadership. Each group member is responsible for maintaining commitment to the group goal, keeping discussions on track, completing individual assignments, encouraging input from fellow members, and managing interpersonal conflicts.

16-2 Conflict in Groups Conflict is part of group work. Lack of conflict could signal groupthink. Groups can experience conflict related to issues, personalities, culture, technology, and even to misunderstanding that members actually agree (pseudo-conflict). Using "I" statements, perception checking, and paraphrasing help minimize conflict. Of the five conflict-management styles—avoiding, accommodating, competing, compromising, and collaborating—the most effective is collaborating.

16-3 Systematic Problem Solving One effective process for solving problems in groups is systematic problem solving. Members work together to identify and define a problem, analyze the problem, determine criteria for judging solutions, generate many solutions, evaluate solutions and select the best one based on the criteria, and implement and assess the agreed-upon solution.

16-4 Communicating Effectively in Virtual Groups Technology is a cost-effective way for groups to meet. To communicate effectively in virtual groups, members must know how to use the technology, create team-building activities, develop ground rules, provide clear structure, use synchronous technology when possible, create opportunities to meet in real life, proactively assess how the group is working, and make adjustments as needed.

16-5 Group Collaboration Tools Collaboration tools simplify working together at any distance. Common collaboration tools include video chat services, collaborative productivity suites, collective note-taking tools, collaborative project management tools, and social media.

16-6 Group Presentation Formats Groups can present their findings in a variety of written, oral, and virtual formats.

16-7 Evaluating Group Effectiveness Evaluations of group effectiveness should focus on group dynamics during the preparation process as well as on the effectiveness of the actual presentation.

Do you have to give a speech for this chapter? Use the deck of perforated speech note cards to get ready!

SPEECH NOTE CARDS

KEY TERMS

problem-solving group four to seven people who work together to complete a specific task or solve a particular problem

leadership a process whereby an individual influences a group of individuals to achieve a common goal

formal leader a person designated or elected to oversee the group process

informal leader group members who help lead the group to achieve different leadership functions

shared leadership functions the sets of roles you and other members perform to facilitate the work of the group and to help maintain harmonious relations among members

role a specific communication behavior group members perform to address the needs of the group at any given point in time

task leadership role a role that helps the group acquire, process, or apply information that contributes directly to completing a task or goal

procedural leadership role a role that provides logistical support and records the group's decisions and accomplishments

maintenance leadership role a role that helps the group to develop and maintain cohesion, commitment, and positive working relationships

synergy when the result of group work is better than what one member could achieve alone

conflict disagreement or clash among ideas, principles, or people

groupthink when group members accept information and ideas without subjecting them to critical analysis

pseudo-conflict conflict that occurs when group members who actually agree about something believe they disagree due to poor communication

issue-related conflict conflict that occurs when two or more group members' goals, ideas, or opinions about the topic are incompatible

personality-related conflict conflict that occurs when two or more group members become defensive because they feel as though they are being attacked

culture-related conflict conflict that occurs when the communication norms of group members are incongruent

virtual group-related conflict conflict that arises as a result of missed nonverbal cues when meeting through technology

perception checking a verbal statement that reflects your understanding of another's behavior

avoiding a conflict management style that involves physically or psychologically removing yourself from the conflict

CHAPTER REVIEW 16

accommodating a conflict management style that involves accepting others' ideas while neglecting your own, even when you disagree with their views

competing a conflict management style that involves satisfying your own needs with no concern for the needs of the others and no concern for the harm it does to the group dynamics or problem-solution process of reaching the best solution

compromising a conflict management style that involves individuals giving up part of what they want in order to provide at least some satisfaction to other opinions

collaborating a conflict management style that involves discussing the issues, describing feelings, and identifying the characteristics of an effective solution before deciding what the ultimate solution will be

systematic problem-solving method an efficient six-step method for finding an effective solution to a problem

criteria standards used for judging the merits of proposed solutions

virtual groups groups that convene using telephone or computer technology

asynchronous virtual groups groups whose members can post and respond to messages at any time, although usually within a few days

netiquette etiquette rules users should follow when communicating over computer networks

collaboration tools digital tools that allow groups of people to work together, coordinate activities, and share information regardless of their location

deliverables tangible or intangible products of your work that must be provided to someone else

written brief a very short document that describes the problem, background, process, decision, and rationale so that the reader can quickly understand and evaluate the group's product

comprehensive report a written document that provides a detailed review of the problem-solving process used to arrive at the recommendation

executive summary a one-page synopsis of a comprehensive report

oral brief an oral summary of a written brief delivered to an audience by a group member

oral report an oral version of a comprehensive report, which provides a detailed review of a group's problem-solving process

panel discussion a structured problem-solving discussion held by a group in front of an audience

symposium a set of prepared oral reports delivered sequentially by group members before a gathering of people who are interested in the work of the group

remote access report (RAR) a computer-mediated audiovisual presentation of a group's process and outcome that others can receive electronically

streaming video a pre-recording that is sent in compressed form over the Internet

group dynamics how individuals work together as a team toward a common goal

REFLECTION

Today, working and speaking in groups are popular not only in the classroom but also in business and industry. To assess how well you understand the chapter concepts, check off the questions you can answer completely. If you have trouble answering any of them, go back and review that material.

1. _____ Why is shared leadership so critical when working in groups?

2. _____ What can you do to manage conflict effectively in groups?

3. _____ What are the steps in the systematic problem-solving method?

4. _____ What are some special guidelines to follow when communicating in virtual groups?

5. _____ What are some formats for group presentations?

6. _____ How can you evaluate group dynamics and presentations?